Little Lulu®

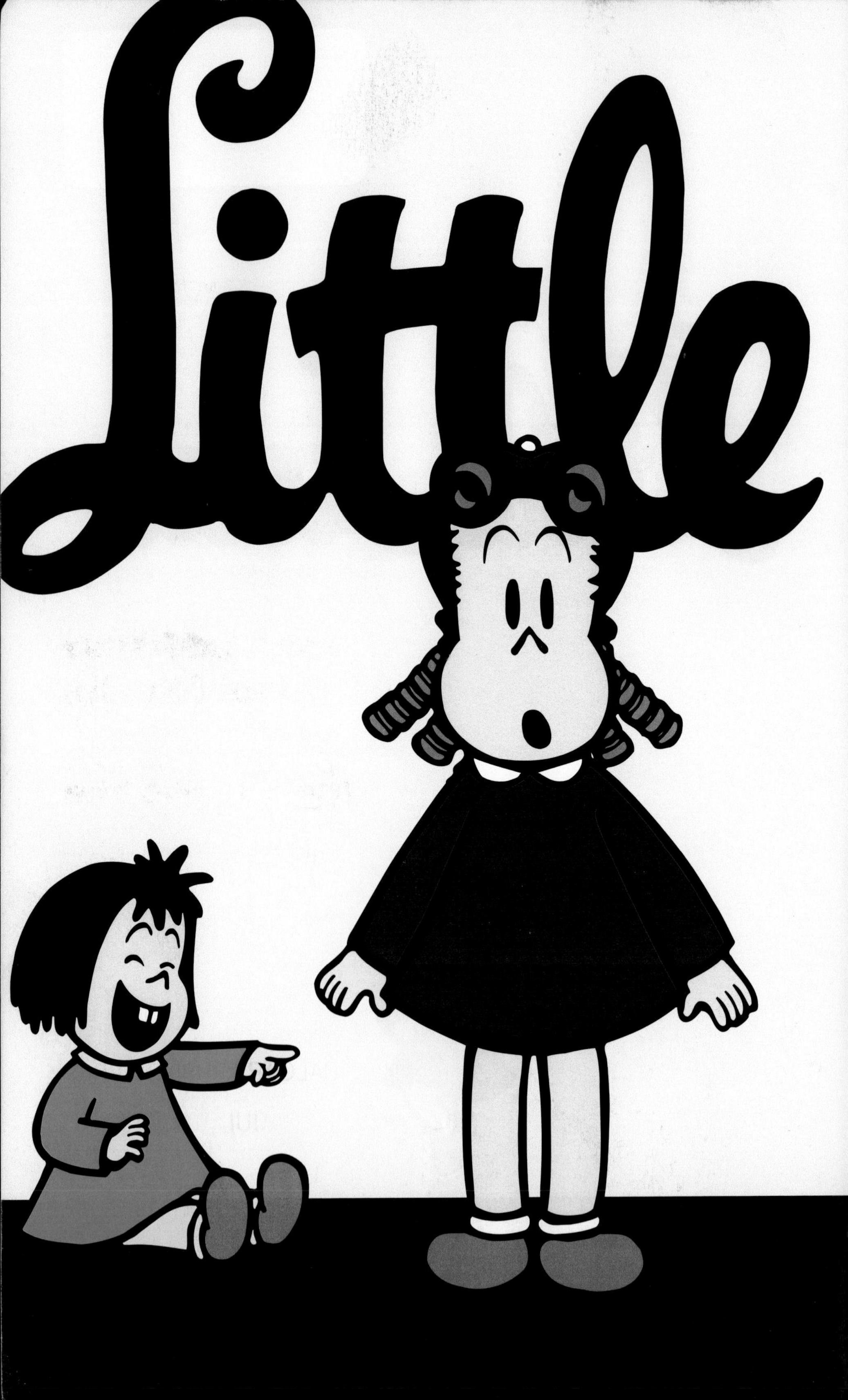
Little

Lulu®

The Burglar-Proof Clubhouse
and Other Stories

Story and Art
John Stanley & Irving Tripp

Based on the character created by
Marge Buell

Dark Horse Books®

Publisher **Mike Richardson**

Editor **Dave Marshall**

Assistant Editor **Brendan Wright**

Collection Designer **Krystal Hennes**

Published by Dark Horse Books

A division of Dark Horse Comics, Inc.

10956 SE Main Street

Milwaukie, Oregon 97222

First edition: November 2010

ISBN 978-1-59582-539-1

Little Lulu® Volume 25: The Burglar-Proof Clubhouse and Other Stories

This volume contains every comic from issues #124 through #129 of *Marge's Little Lulu*, originally published by Dell Comics between October 1958 and March 1959.

Mike Richardson, President and Publisher • Neil Hankerson, Executive Vice President • Tom Weddle, Chief Financial Officer • Randy Stradley, Vice President of Publishing • Michael Martens, Vice President of Business Development • Anita Nelson, Vice President of Business Affairs • Micha Hershman, Vice President of Marketing • David Scroggy, Vice President of Product Development • Dale LaFountain, Vice President of Information Technology • Darlene Vogel, Director of Purchasing • Ken Lizzi, General Counsel • Cara Niece, Director of Scheduling • Scott Allie, Senior Managing Editor • Chris Warner, Senior Books Editor • Diana Schutz, Executive Editor • Cary Grazzini, Director of Design and Production • Lia Ribacchi, Art Director • Davey Estrada, Editorial Director

DELL

OCTOBER Still 10¢

Marge's Little Lulu

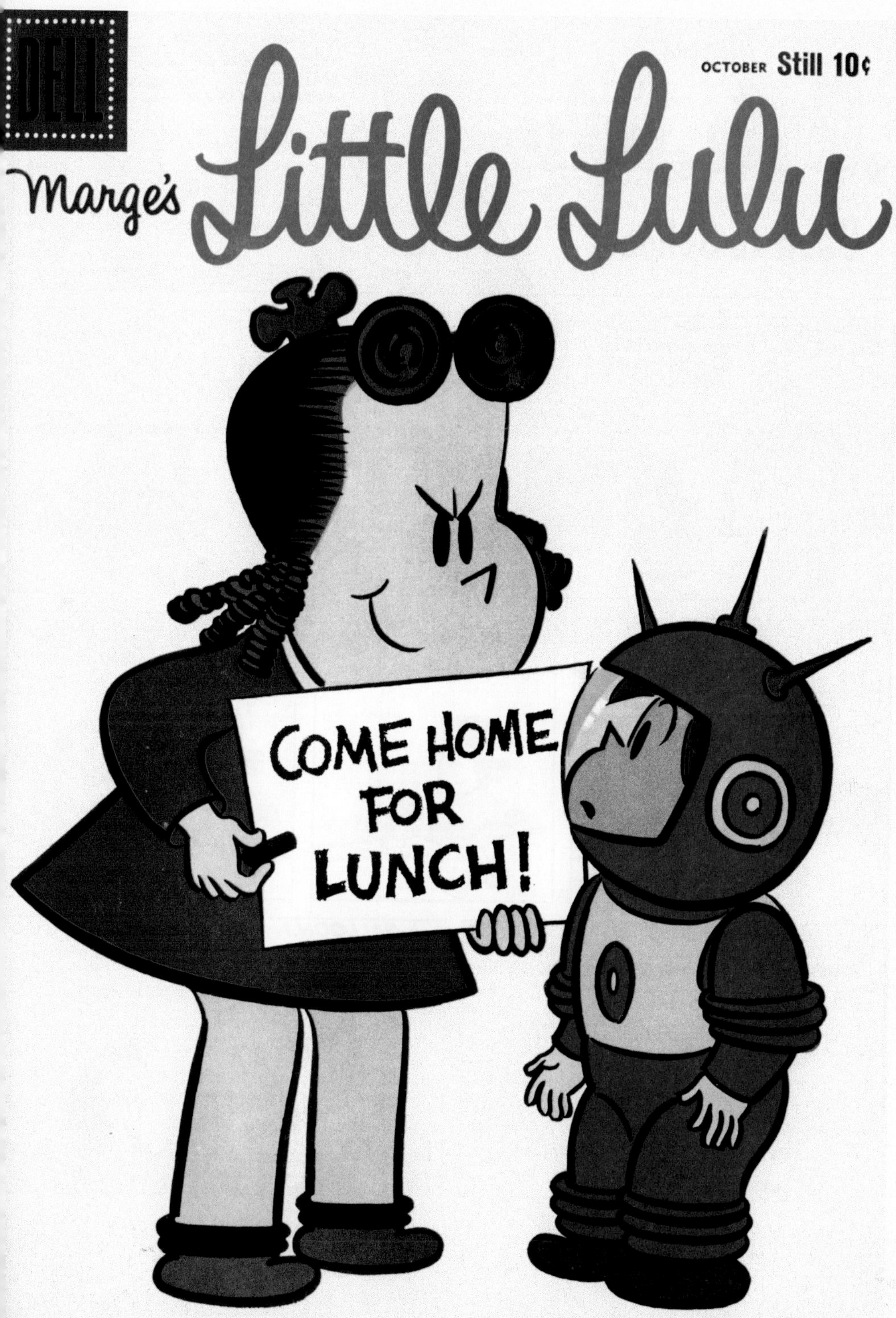
COME HOME FOR LUNCH!

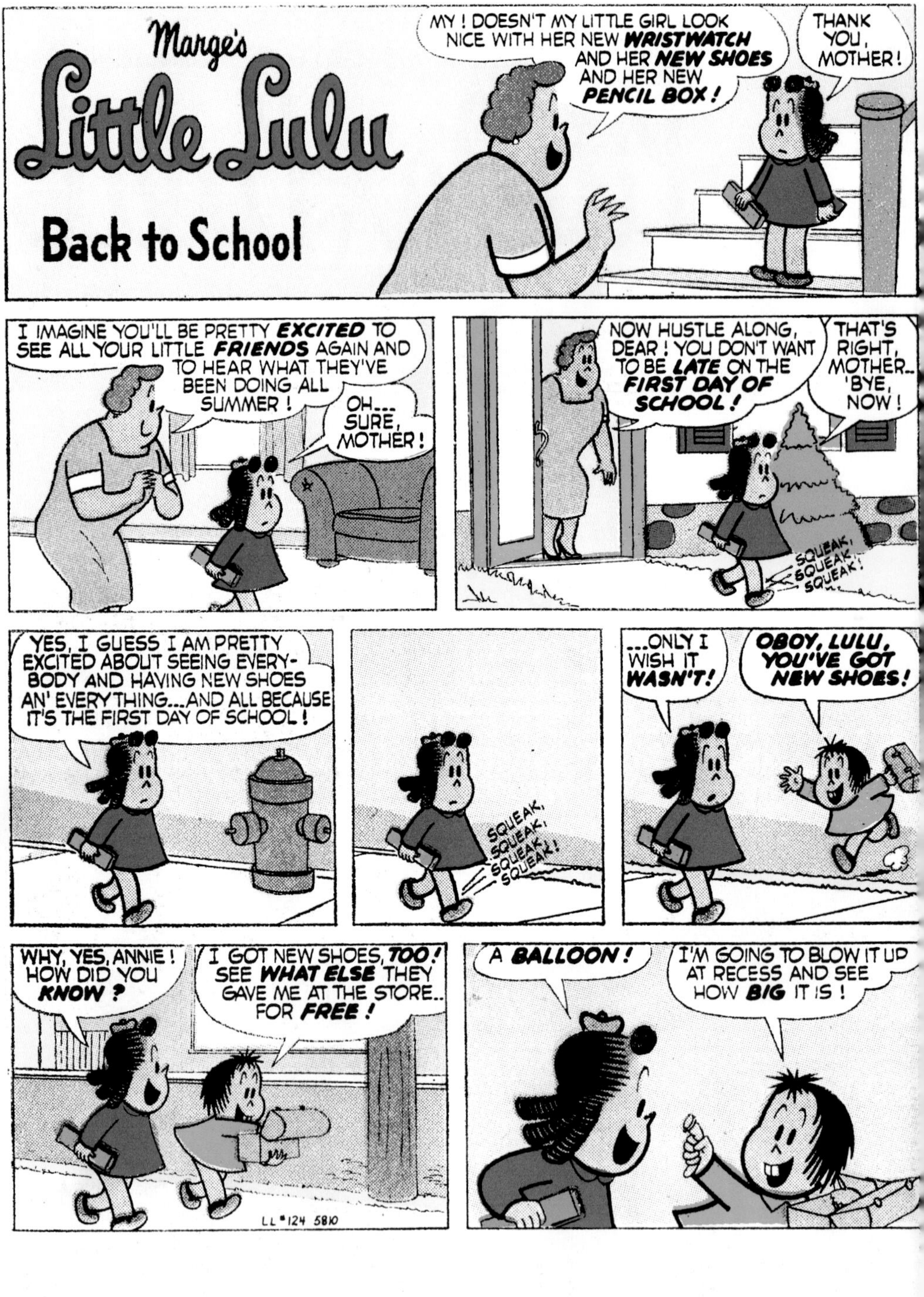
Marge's
Little Lulu
Back to School
MY! DOESN'T MY LITTLE GIRL LOOK NICE WITH HER NEW WRISTWATCH AND HER NEW SHOES AND HER NEW PENCIL BOX!
THANK YOU, MOTHER!
I IMAGINE YOU'LL BE PRETTY EXCITED TO SEE ALL YOUR LITTLE FRIENDS AGAIN AND TO HEAR WHAT THEY'VE BEEN DOING ALL SUMMER!
OH... SURE, MOTHER!
NOW HUSTLE ALONG, DEAR! YOU DON'T WANT TO BE LATE ON THE FIRST DAY OF SCHOOL!
THAT'S RIGHT, MOTHER... 'BYE, NOW!
SQUEAK, SQUEAK, SQUEAK!
YES, I GUESS I AM PRETTY EXCITED ABOUT SEEING EVERY-BODY AND HAVING NEW SHOES AN' EVERYTHING...AND ALL BECAUSE IT'S THE FIRST DAY OF SCHOOL!
SQUEAK, SQUEAK, SQUEAK, SQUEAK!
...ONLY I WISH IT WASN'T!
OBOY, LULU, YOU'VE GOT NEW SHOES!
WHY, YES, ANNIE! HOW DID YOU KNOW?
I GOT NEW SHOES, TOO! SEE WHAT ELSE THEY GAVE ME AT THE STORE.. FOR FREE!
LL#124 5810
A BALLOON!
I'M GOING TO BLOW IT UP AT RECESS AND SEE HOW BIG IT IS!

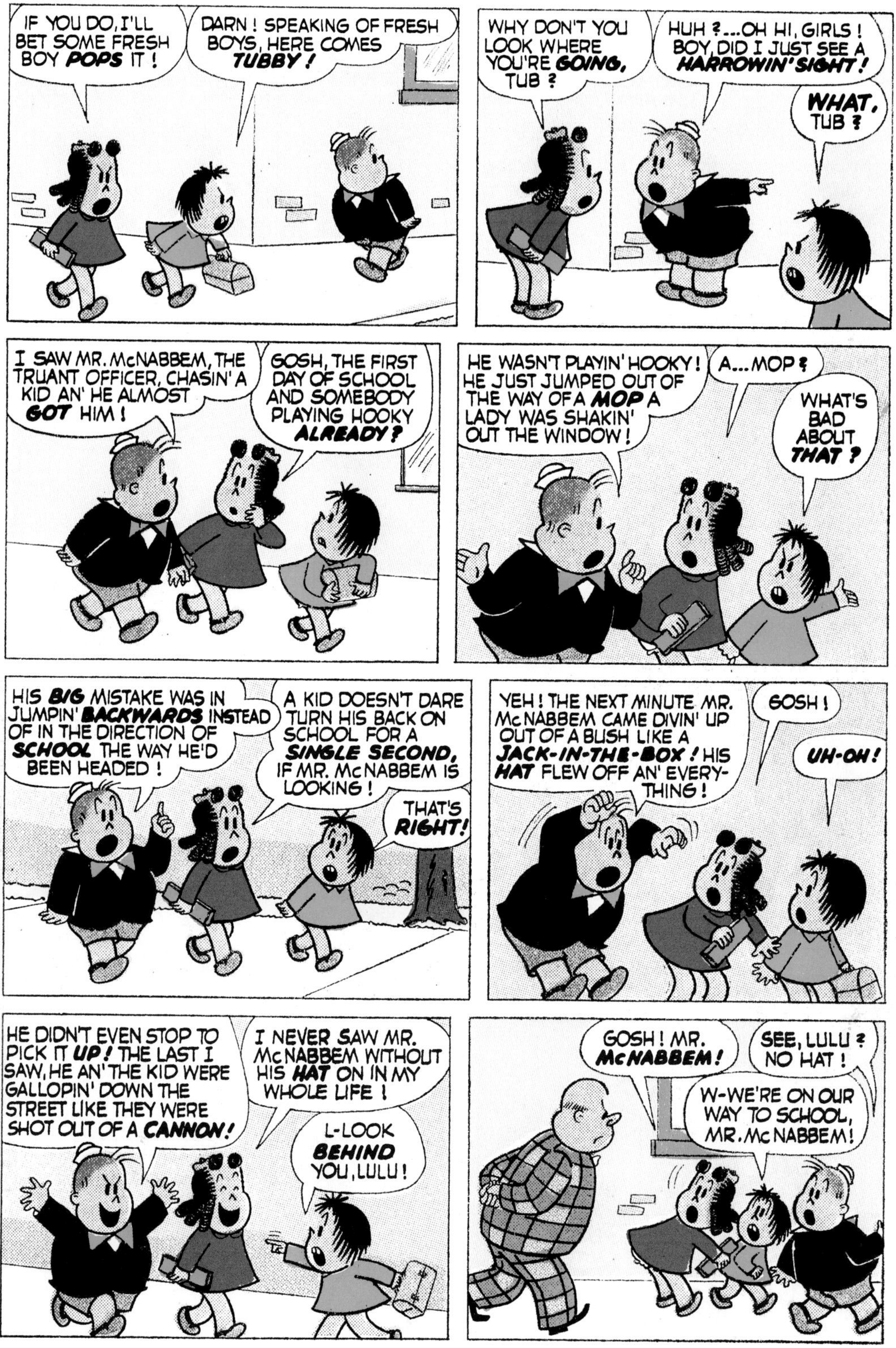
IF YOU DO, I'LL BET SOME FRESH BOY POPS IT !
DARN ! SPEAKING OF FRESH BOYS, HERE COMES TUBBY !
WHY DON'T YOU LOOK WHERE YOU'RE GOING, TUB ?
HUH ?...OH HI, GIRLS ! BOY, DID I JUST SEE A HARROWIN' SIGHT !
WHAT, TUB ?
I SAW MR. McNABBEM, THE TRUANT OFFICER, CHASIN' A KID AN' HE ALMOST GOT HIM !
GOSH, THE FIRST DAY OF SCHOOL AND SOMEBODY PLAYING HOOKY ALREADY ?
HE WASN'T PLAYIN' HOOKY ! HE JUST JUMPED OUT OF THE WAY OF A MOP A LADY WAS SHAKIN' OUT THE WINDOW !
A...MOP ?
WHAT'S BAD ABOUT THAT ?
HIS BIG MISTAKE WAS IN JUMPIN' BACKWARDS INSTEAD OF IN THE DIRECTION OF SCHOOL THE WAY HE'D BEEN HEADED !
A KID DOESN'T DARE TURN HIS BACK ON SCHOOL FOR A SINGLE SECOND, IF MR. McNABBEM IS LOOKING !
THAT'S RIGHT!
YEH ! THE NEXT MINUTE MR. McNABBEM CAME DIVIN' UP OUT OF A BUSH LIKE A JACK-IN-THE-BOX ! HIS HAT FLEW OFF AN' EVERYTHING !
GOSH !
UH-OH !
HE DIDN'T EVEN STOP TO PICK IT UP ! THE LAST I SAW, HE AN' THE KID WERE GALLOPIN' DOWN THE STREET LIKE THEY WERE SHOT OUT OF A CANNON !
I NEVER SAW MR. McNABBEM WITHOUT HIS HAT ON IN MY WHOLE LIFE !
L-LOOK BEHIND YOU, LULU !
GOSH ! MR. McNABBEM !
SEE, LULU ? NO HAT !
W-WE'RE ON OUR WAY TO SCHOOL, MR. McNABBEM !

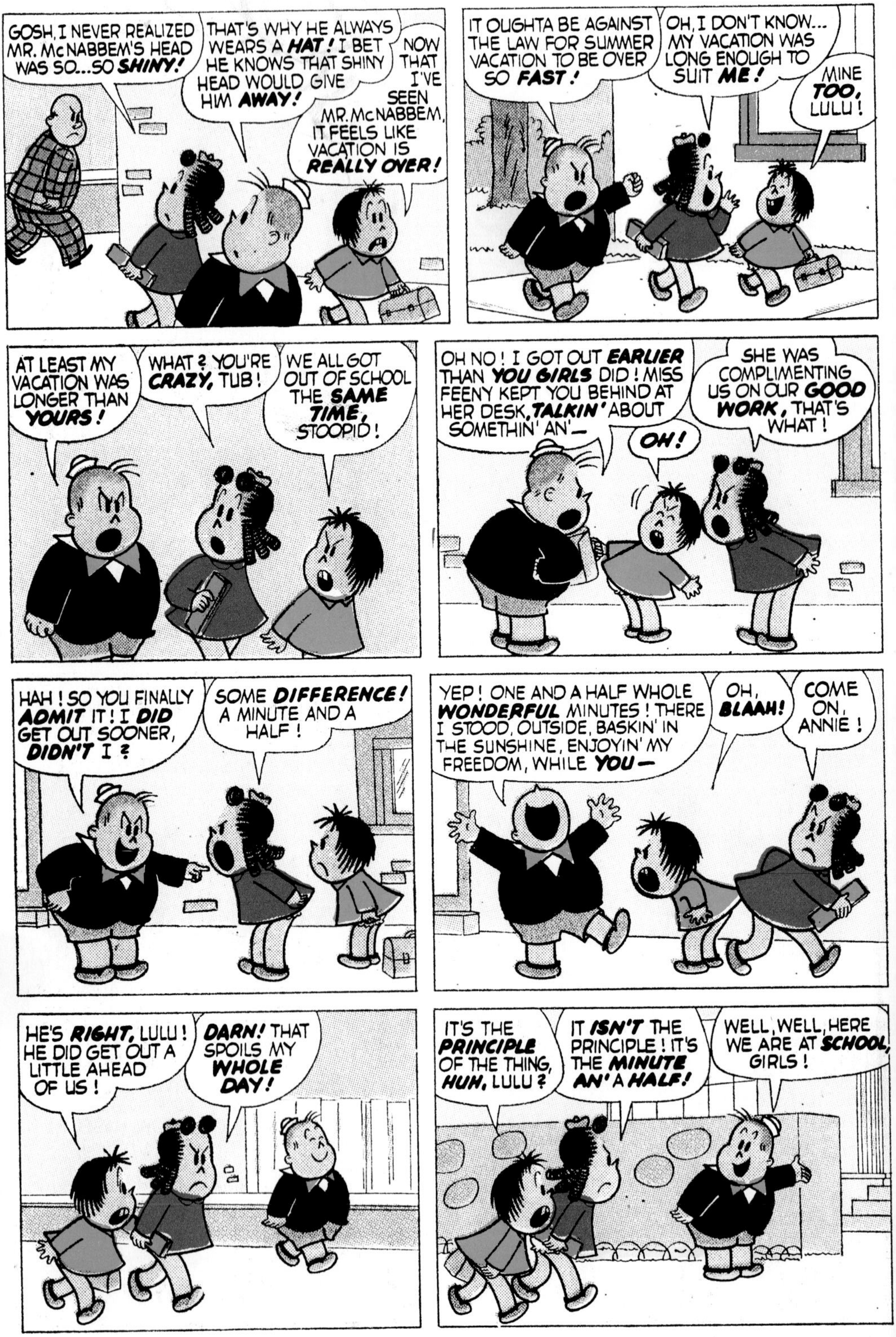
GOSH, I NEVER REALIZED MR. McNABBEM'S HEAD WAS SO... SO SHINY!
THAT'S WHY HE ALWAYS WEARS A HAT! I BET HE KNOWS THAT SHINY HEAD WOULD GIVE HIM AWAY!
NOW THAT I'VE SEEN MR. McNABBEM, IT FEELS LIKE VACATION IS REALLY OVER!
IT OUGHTA BE AGAINST THE LAW FOR SUMMER VACATION TO BE OVER SO FAST!
OH, I DON'T KNOW... MY VACATION WAS LONG ENOUGH TO SUIT ME!
MINE TOO, LULU!
AT LEAST MY VACATION WAS LONGER THAN YOURS!
WHAT? YOU'RE CRAZY, TUB!
WE ALL GOT OUT OF SCHOOL THE SAME TIME, STOOPID!
OH NO! I GOT OUT EARLIER THAN YOU GIRLS DID! MISS FEENY KEPT YOU BEHIND AT HER DESK, TALKIN' ABOUT SOMETHIN' AN'—
OH!
SHE WAS COMPLIMENTING US ON OUR GOOD WORK, THAT'S WHAT!
HAH! SO YOU FINALLY ADMIT IT! I DID GET OUT SOONER, DIDN'T I?
SOME DIFFERENCE! A MINUTE AND A HALF!
YEP! ONE AND A HALF WHOLE WONDERFUL MINUTES! THERE I STOOD, OUTSIDE, BASKIN' IN THE SUNSHINE, ENJOYIN' MY FREEDOM, WHILE YOU—
OH, BLAAH!
COME ON, ANNIE!
HE'S RIGHT, LULU! HE DID GET OUT A LITTLE AHEAD OF US!
DARN! THAT SPOILS MY WHOLE DAY!
IT'S THE PRINCIPLE OF THE THING, HUH, LULU?
IT ISN'T THE PRINCIPLE! IT'S THE MINUTE AN' A HALF!
WELL, WELL, HERE WE ARE AT SCHOOL, GIRLS!

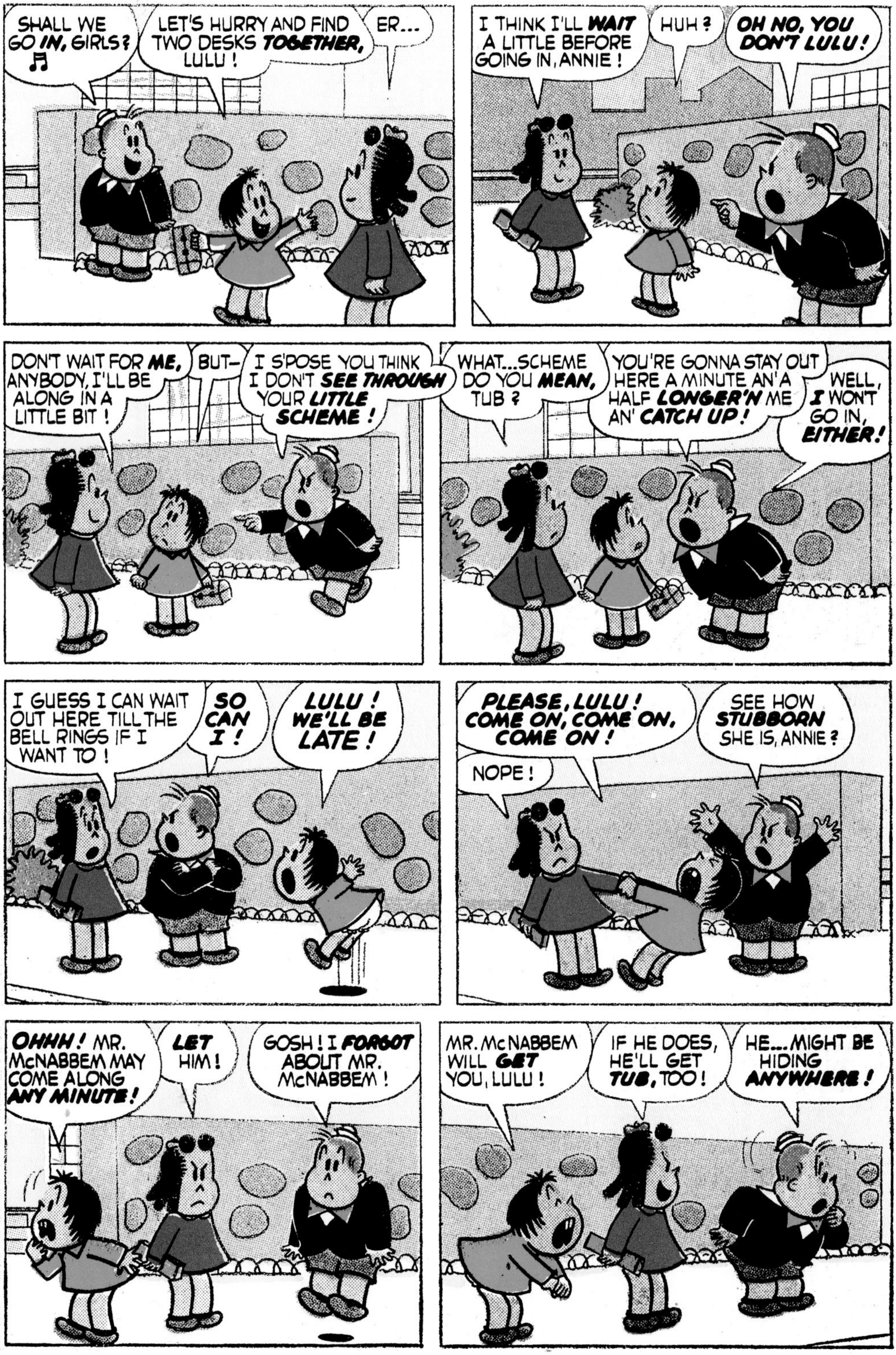
SHALL WE GO IN, GIRLS? ♫
LET'S HURRY AND FIND TWO DESKS TOGETHER, LULU!
ER...
I THINK I'LL WAIT A LITTLE BEFORE GOING IN, ANNIE!
HUH?
OH NO, YOU DON'T LULU!
DON'T WAIT FOR ME, ANYBODY, I'LL BE ALONG IN A LITTLE BIT!
BUT–
I S'POSE YOU THINK I DON'T SEE THROUGH YOUR LITTLE SCHEME!
WHAT...SCHEME DO YOU MEAN, TUB?
YOU'RE GONNA STAY OUT HERE A MINUTE AN' A HALF LONGER'N ME AN' CATCH UP!
WELL, I WON'T GO IN, EITHER!
I GUESS I CAN WAIT OUT HERE TILL THE BELL RINGS IF I WANT TO!
SO CAN I!
LULU! WE'LL BE LATE!
PLEASE, LULU! COME ON, COME ON, COME ON!
NOPE!
SEE HOW STUBBORN SHE IS, ANNIE?
OHHH! MR. McNABBEM MAY COME ALONG ANY MINUTE!
LET HIM!
GOSH! I FORGOT ABOUT MR. McNABBEM!
MR. McNABBEM WILL GET YOU, LULU!
IF HE DOES, HE'LL GET TUB, TOO!
HE...MIGHT BE HIDING ANYWHERE!

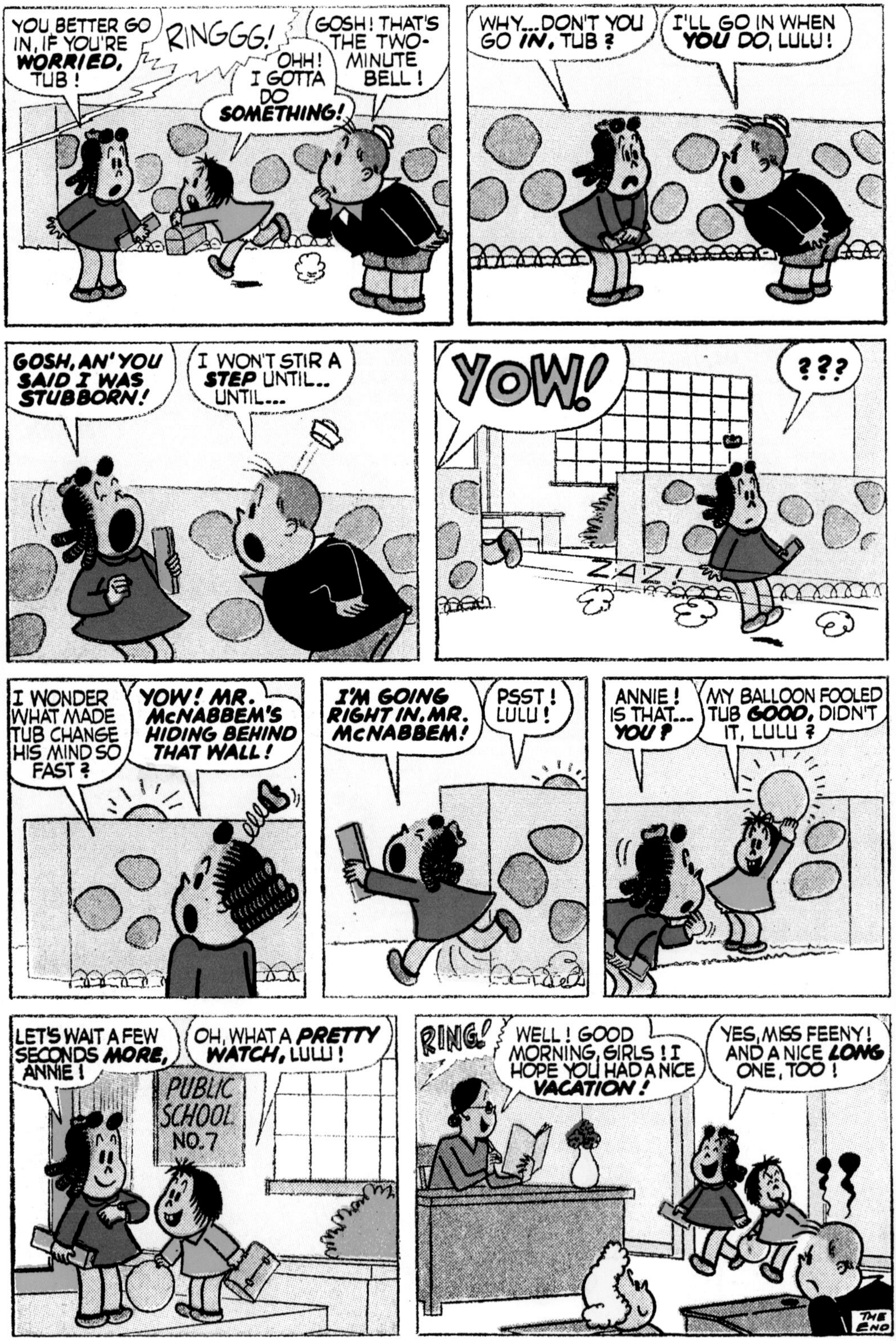
YOU BETTER GO IN, IF YOU'RE WORRIED, TUB!
RINGGG!
OHH! I GOTTA DO SOMETHING!
GOSH! THAT'S THE TWO-MINUTE BELL!
WHY...DON'T YOU GO IN, TUB?
I'LL GO IN WHEN YOU DO, LULU!
GOSH, AN' YOU SAID I WAS STUBBORN!
I WON'T STIR A STEP UNTIL.. UNTIL...
YOW!
???
ZAZ!
I WONDER WHAT MADE TUB CHANGE HIS MIND SO FAST?
YOW! MR. McNABBEM'S HIDING BEHIND THAT WALL!
I'M GOING RIGHT IN, MR. McNABBEM!
PSST! LULU!
ANNIE! IS THAT... YOU?
MY BALLOON FOOLED TUB GOOD, DIDN'T IT, LULU?
LET'S WAIT A FEW SECONDS MORE, ANNIE!
OH, WHAT A PRETTY WATCH, LULU!
PUBLIC SCHOOL NO. 7
RING!
WELL! GOOD MORNING, GIRLS! I HOPE YOU HAD A NICE VACATION!
YES, MISS FEENY! AND A NICE LONG ONE, TOO!
THE END

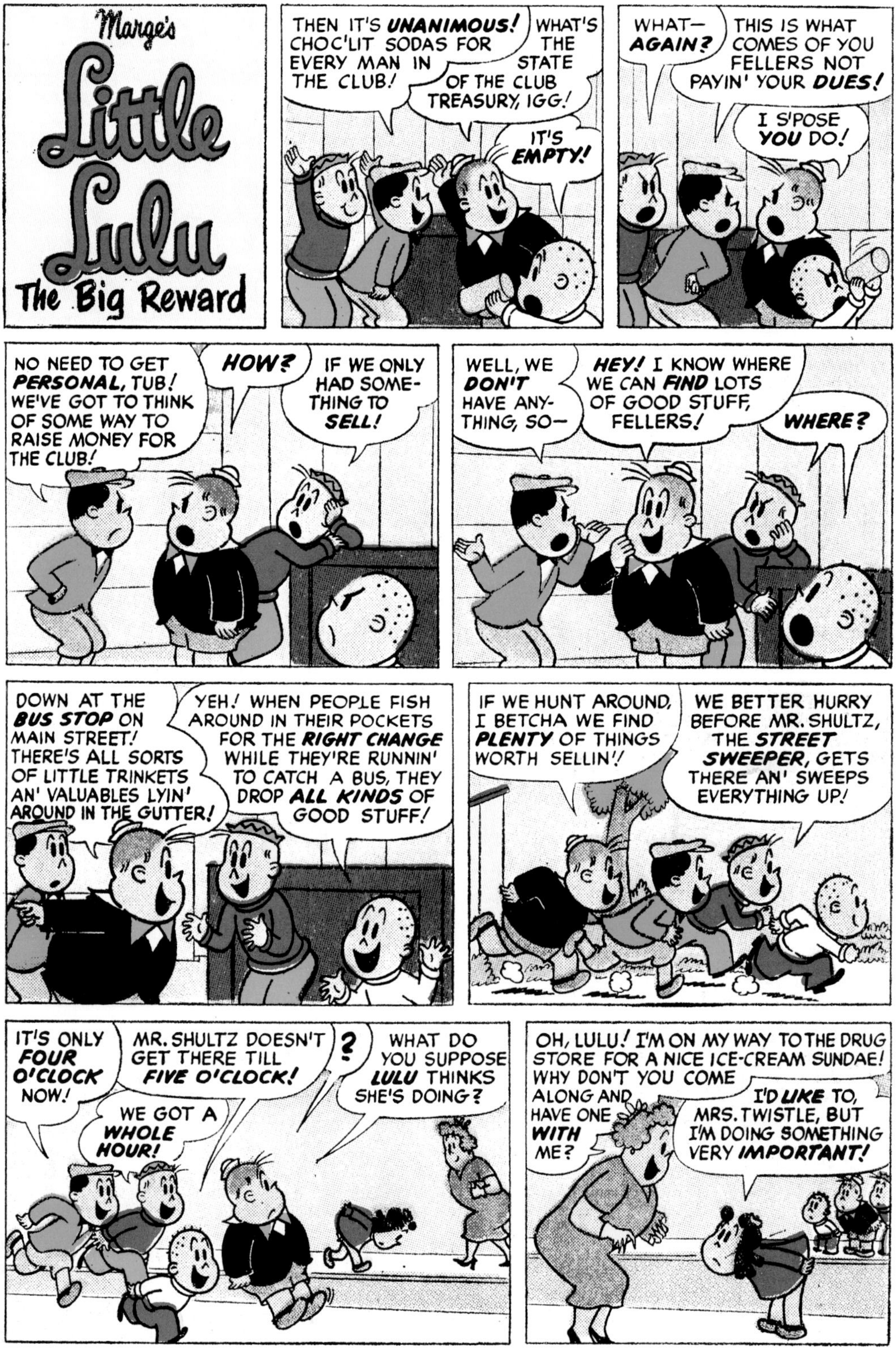
Marge's Little Lulu
The Big Reward
THEN IT'S UNANIMOUS! CHOC'LIT SODAS FOR EVERY MAN IN THE CLUB!
WHAT'S THE STATE OF THE CLUB TREASURY, IGG!
IT'S EMPTY!
WHAT— AGAIN?
THIS IS WHAT COMES OF YOU FELLERS NOT PAYIN' YOUR DUES!
I S'POSE YOU DO!
NO NEED TO GET PERSONAL, TUB! WE'VE GOT TO THINK OF SOME WAY TO RAISE MONEY FOR THE CLUB!
HOW?
IF WE ONLY HAD SOMETHING TO SELL!
WELL, WE DON'T HAVE ANYTHING, SO—
HEY! I KNOW WHERE WE CAN FIND LOTS OF GOOD STUFF, FELLERS!
WHERE?
DOWN AT THE BUS STOP ON MAIN STREET! THERE'S ALL SORTS OF LITTLE TRINKETS AN' VALUABLES LYIN' AROUND IN THE GUTTER!
YEH! WHEN PEOPLE FISH AROUND IN THEIR POCKETS FOR THE RIGHT CHANGE WHILE THEY'RE RUNNIN' TO CATCH A BUS, THEY DROP ALL KINDS OF GOOD STUFF!
IF WE HUNT AROUND, I BETCHA WE FIND PLENTY OF THINGS WORTH SELLIN'!
WE BETTER HURRY BEFORE MR. SHULTZ, THE STREET SWEEPER, GETS THERE AN' SWEEPS EVERYTHING UP!
IT'S ONLY FOUR O'CLOCK NOW!
MR. SHULTZ DOESN'T GET THERE TILL FIVE O'CLOCK!
WE GOT A WHOLE HOUR!
?
WHAT DO YOU SUPPOSE LULU THINKS SHE'S DOING?
OH, LULU! I'M ON MY WAY TO THE DRUG STORE FOR A NICE ICE-CREAM SUNDAE! WHY DON'T YOU COME ALONG AND HAVE ONE WITH ME?
I'D LIKE TO, MRS. TWISTLE, BUT I'M DOING SOMETHING VERY IMPORTANT!

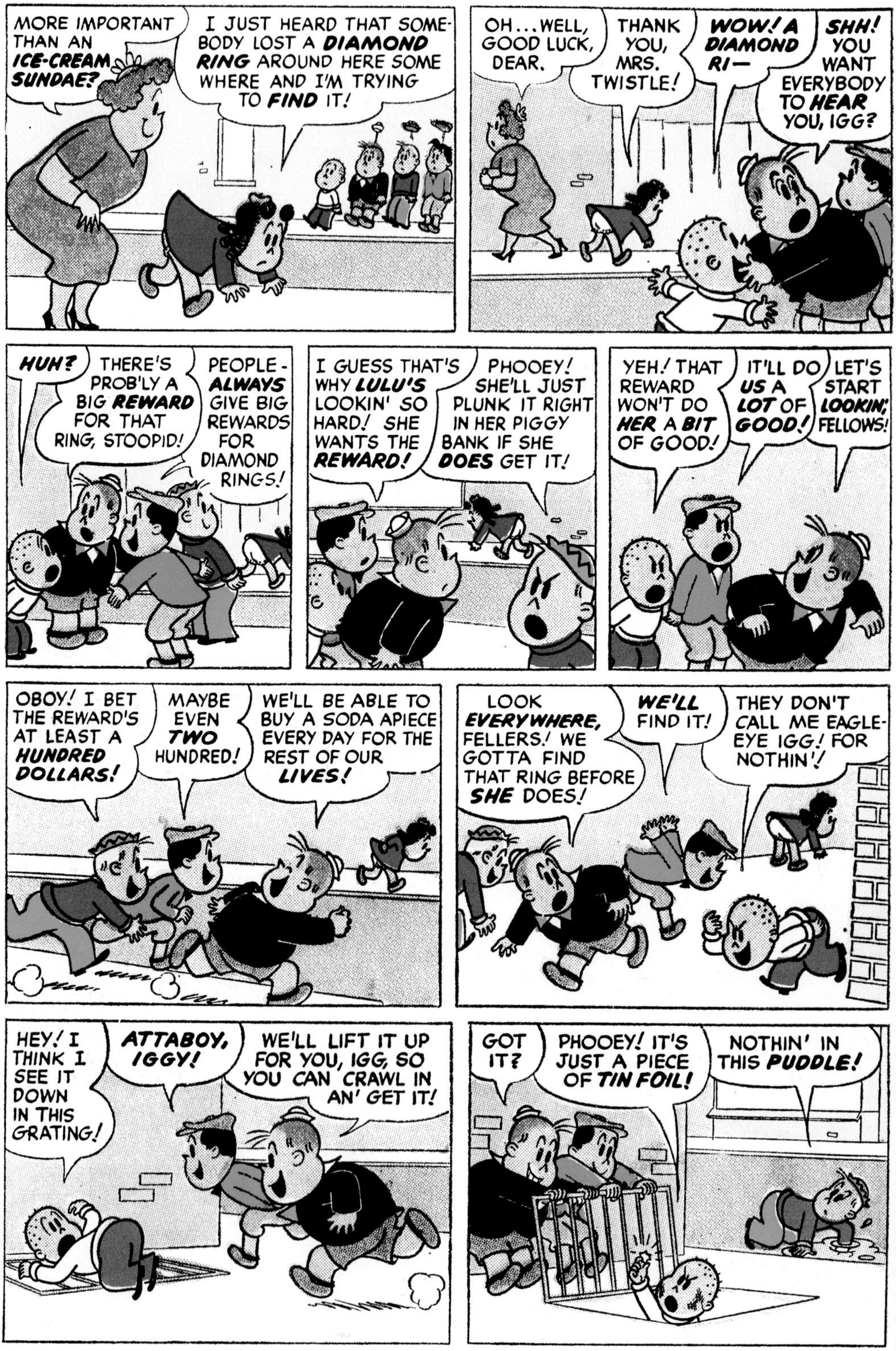
MORE IMPORTANT THAN AN ICE-CREAM SUNDAE?
I JUST HEARD THAT SOMEBODY LOST A DIAMOND RING AROUND HERE SOME WHERE AND I'M TRYING TO FIND IT!
OH...WELL, GOOD LUCK, DEAR.
THANK YOU, MRS. TWISTLE!
WOW! A DIAMOND RI—
SHH! YOU WANT EVERYBODY TO HEAR YOU, IGG?
HUH?
THERE'S PROB'LY A BIG REWARD FOR THAT RING, STOOPID!
PEOPLE - ALWAYS GIVE BIG REWARDS FOR DIAMOND RINGS!
I GUESS THAT'S WHY LULU'S LOOKIN' SO HARD! SHE WANTS THE REWARD!
PHOOEY! SHE'LL JUST PLUNK IT RIGHT IN HER PIGGY BANK IF SHE DOES GET IT!
YEH! THAT REWARD WON'T DO HER A BIT OF GOOD!
IT'LL DO US A LOT OF GOOD!
LET'S START LOOKIN', FELLOWS!
OBOY! I BET THE REWARD'S AT LEAST A HUNDRED DOLLARS!
MAYBE EVEN TWO HUNDRED!
WE'LL BE ABLE TO BUY A SODA APIECE EVERY DAY FOR THE REST OF OUR LIVES!
LOOK EVERYWHERE, FELLERS! WE GOTTA FIND THAT RING BEFORE SHE DOES!
WE'LL FIND IT!
THEY DON'T CALL ME EAGLE-EYE IGG! FOR NOTHIN'!
HEY! I THINK I SEE IT DOWN IN THIS GRATING!
ATTABOY, IGGY!
WE'LL LIFT IT UP FOR YOU, IGG, SO YOU CAN CRAWL IN AN' GET IT!
GOT IT?
PHOOEY! IT'S JUST A PIECE OF TIN FOIL!
NOTHIN' IN THIS PUDDLE!

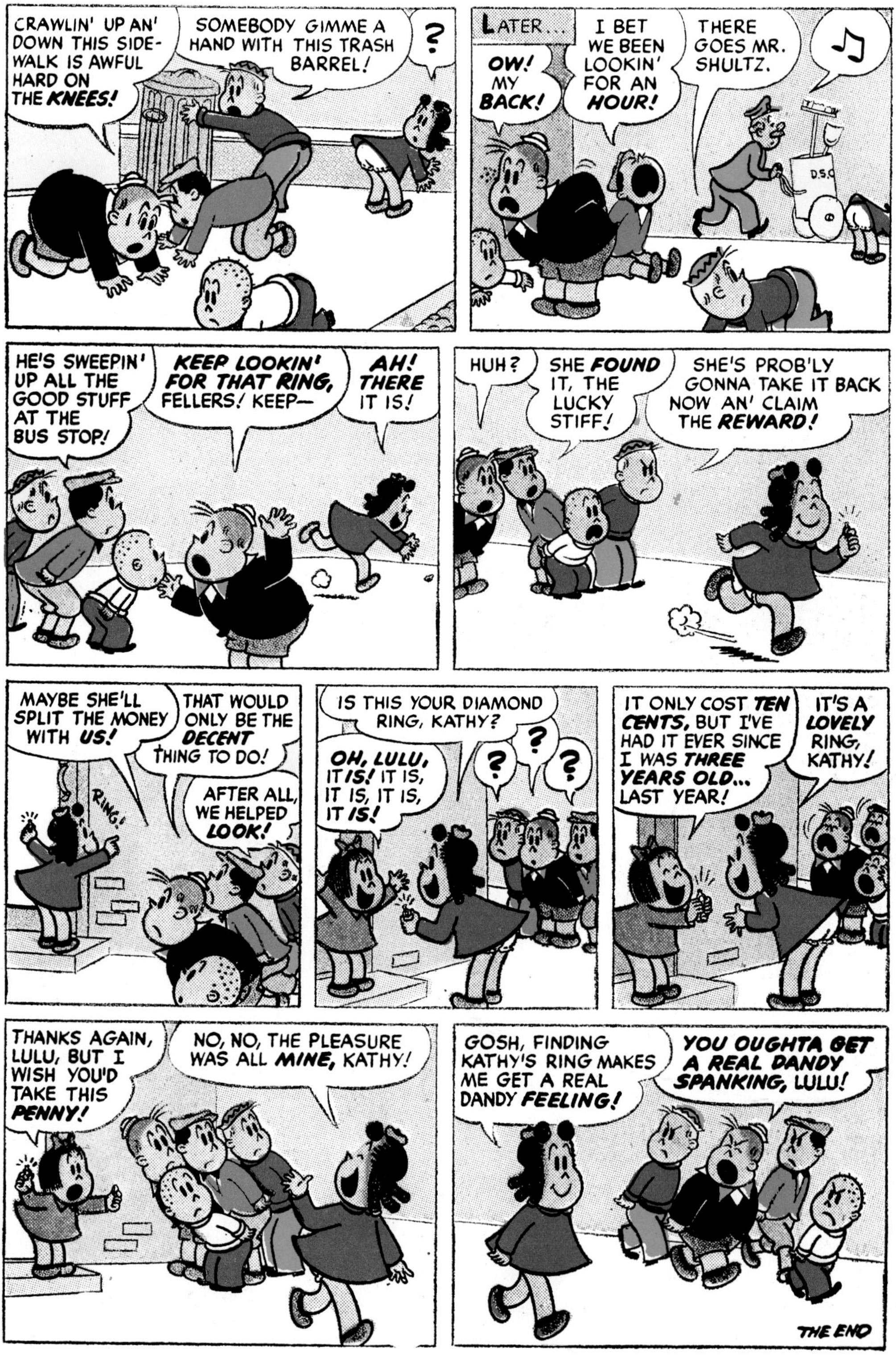
CRAWLIN' UP AN' DOWN THIS SIDE-WALK IS AWFUL HARD ON THE KNEES!
SOMEBODY GIMME A HAND WITH THIS TRASH BARREL!
?
LATER...
OW! MY BACK!
I BET WE BEEN LOOKIN' FOR AN HOUR!
THERE GOES MR. SHULTZ.
♫
D.S.C.
HE'S SWEEPIN' UP ALL THE GOOD STUFF AT THE BUS STOP!
KEEP LOOKIN' FOR THAT RING, FELLERS! KEEP—
AH! THERE IT IS!
HUH?
SHE FOUND IT, THE LUCKY STIFF!
SHE'S PROB'LY GONNA TAKE IT BACK NOW AN' CLAIM THE REWARD!
MAYBE SHE'LL SPLIT THE MONEY WITH US!
THAT WOULD ONLY BE THE DECENT THING TO DO!
AFTER ALL, WE HELPED LOOK!
RING!
IS THIS YOUR DIAMOND RING, KATHY?
OH, LULU, IT IS! IT IS, IT IS, IT IS, IT IS!
?
?
?
IT ONLY COST TEN CENTS, BUT I'VE HAD IT EVER SINCE I WAS THREE YEARS OLD... LAST YEAR!
IT'S A LOVELY RING, KATHY!
THANKS AGAIN, LULU, BUT I WISH YOU'D TAKE THIS PENNY!
NO, NO, THE PLEASURE WAS ALL MINE, KATHY!
GOSH, FINDING KATHY'S RING MAKES ME GET A REAL DANDY FEELING!
YOU OUGHTA GET A REAL DANDY SPANKING, LULU!
THE END

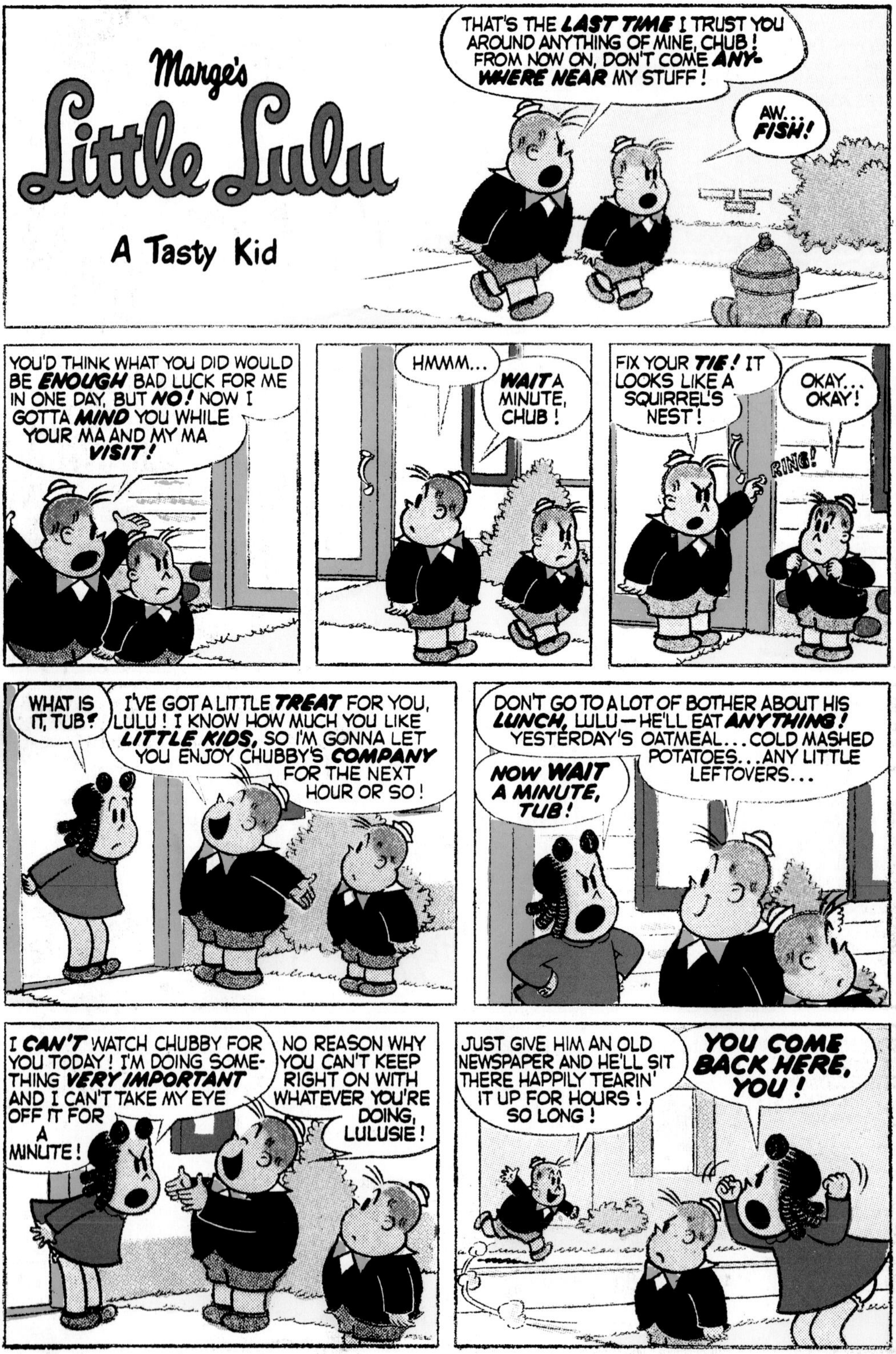
Marge's
Little Lulu
A Tasty Kid
THAT'S THE LAST TIME I TRUST YOU AROUND ANYTHING OF MINE, CHUB! FROM NOW ON, DON'T COME ANY-WHERE NEAR MY STUFF!
AW... FISH!
YOU'D THINK WHAT YOU DID WOULD BE ENOUGH BAD LUCK FOR ME IN ONE DAY, BUT NO! NOW I GOTTA MIND YOU WHILE YOUR MA AND MY MA VISIT!
HMMM...
WAIT A MINUTE, CHUB!
FIX YOUR TIE! IT LOOKS LIKE A SQUIRREL'S NEST!
OKAY... OKAY!
RING!
WHAT IS IT, TUB?
I'VE GOT A LITTLE TREAT FOR YOU, LULU! I KNOW HOW MUCH YOU LIKE LITTLE KIDS, SO I'M GONNA LET YOU ENJOY CHUBBY'S COMPANY FOR THE NEXT HOUR OR SO!
DON'T GO TO A LOT OF BOTHER ABOUT HIS LUNCH, LULU — HE'LL EAT ANYTHING! YESTERDAY'S OATMEAL... COLD MASHED POTATOES... ANY LITTLE LEFTOVERS...
NOW WAIT A MINUTE, TUB!
I CAN'T WATCH CHUBBY FOR YOU TODAY! I'M DOING SOME-THING VERY IMPORTANT AND I CAN'T TAKE MY EYE OFF IT FOR A MINUTE!
NO REASON WHY YOU CAN'T KEEP RIGHT ON WITH WHATEVER YOU'RE DOING, LULUSIE!
JUST GIVE HIM AN OLD NEWSPAPER AND HE'LL SIT THERE HAPPILY TEARIN' IT UP FOR HOURS! SO LONG!
YOU COME BACK HERE, YOU!

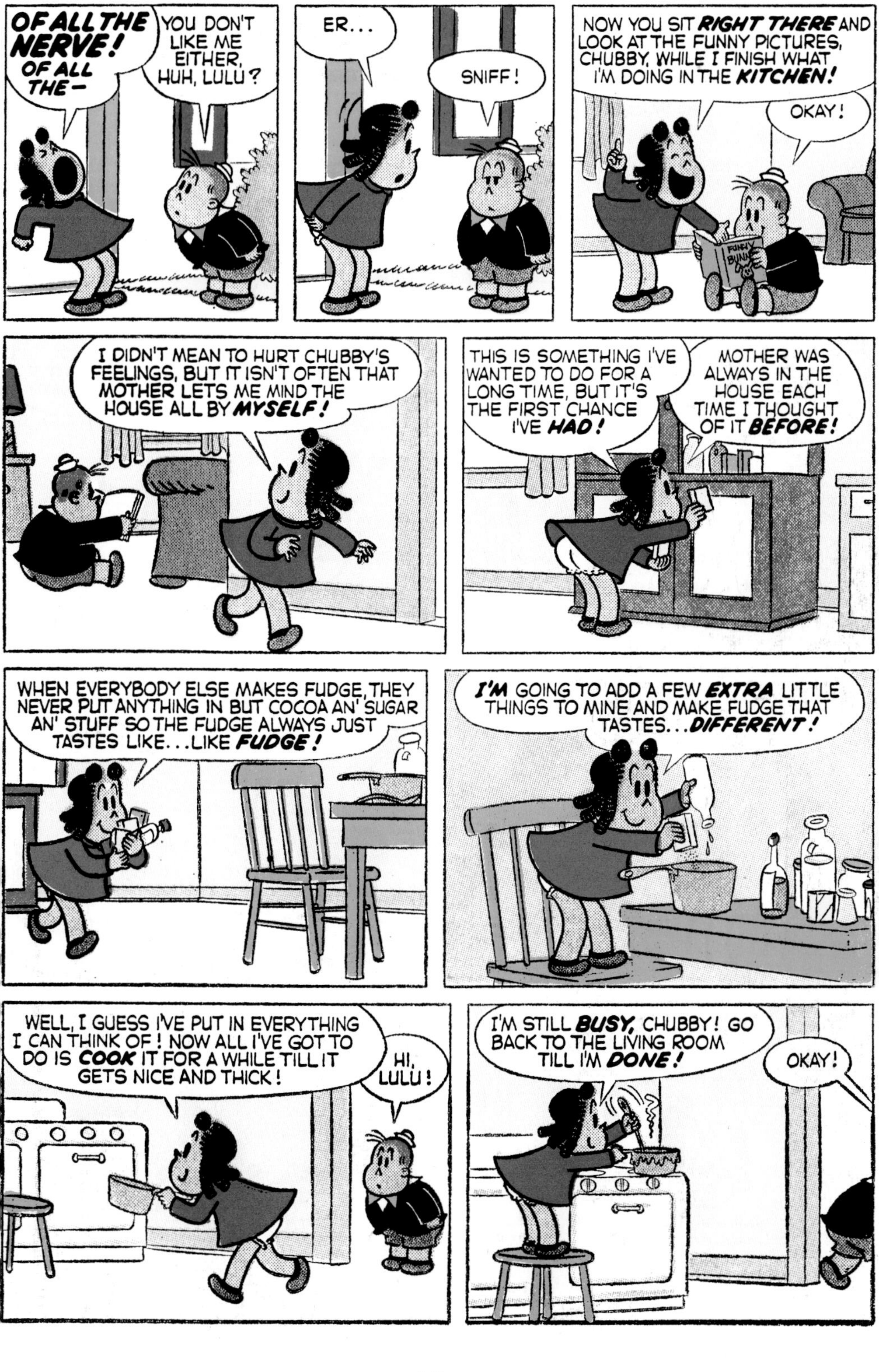
OF ALL THE NERVE! OF ALL THE—
YOU DON'T LIKE ME EITHER, HUH, LULU?
ER...
SNIFF!
NOW YOU SIT RIGHT THERE AND LOOK AT THE FUNNY PICTURES, CHUBBY, WHILE I FINISH WHAT I'M DOING IN THE KITCHEN!
OKAY!
I DIDN'T MEAN TO HURT CHUBBY'S FEELINGS, BUT IT ISN'T OFTEN THAT MOTHER LETS ME MIND THE HOUSE ALL BY MYSELF!
THIS IS SOMETHING I'VE WANTED TO DO FOR A LONG TIME, BUT IT'S THE FIRST CHANCE I'VE HAD!
MOTHER WAS ALWAYS IN THE HOUSE EACH TIME I THOUGHT OF IT BEFORE!
WHEN EVERYBODY ELSE MAKES FUDGE, THEY NEVER PUT ANYTHING IN BUT COCOA AN' SUGAR AN' STUFF SO THE FUDGE ALWAYS JUST TASTES LIKE...LIKE FUDGE!
I'M GOING TO ADD A FEW EXTRA LITTLE THINGS TO MINE AND MAKE FUDGE THAT TASTES...DIFFERENT!
WELL, I GUESS I'VE PUT IN EVERYTHING I CAN THINK OF! NOW ALL I'VE GOT TO DO IS COOK IT FOR A WHILE TILL IT GETS NICE AND THICK!
HI, LULU!
I'M STILL BUSY, CHUBBY! GO BACK TO THE LIVING ROOM TILL I'M DONE!
OKAY!

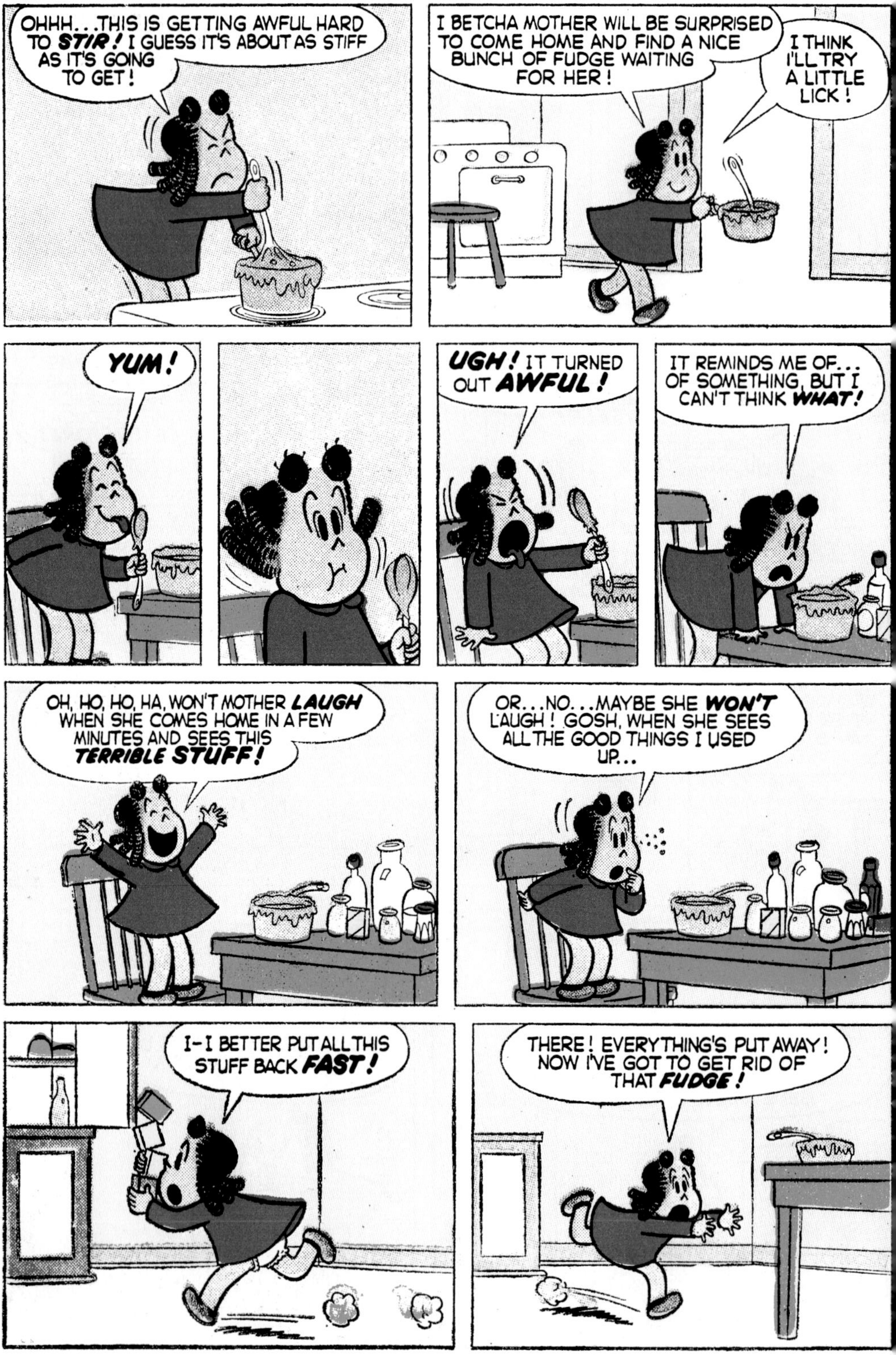
OHHH...THIS IS GETTING AWFUL HARD TO STIR! I GUESS IT'S ABOUT AS STIFF AS IT'S GOING TO GET!
I BETCHA MOTHER WILL BE SURPRISED TO COME HOME AND FIND A NICE BUNCH OF FUDGE WAITING FOR HER!
I THINK I'LL TRY A LITTLE LICK!
YUM!
UGH! IT TURNED OUT AWFUL!
IT REMINDS ME OF... OF SOMETHING, BUT I CAN'T THINK WHAT!
OH, HO, HO, HA, WON'T MOTHER LAUGH WHEN SHE COMES HOME IN A FEW MINUTES AND SEES THIS TERRIBLE STUFF!
OR...NO...MAYBE SHE WON'T LAUGH! GOSH, WHEN SHE SEES ALL THE GOOD THINGS I USED UP...
I-I BETTER PUT ALL THIS STUFF BACK FAST!
THERE! EVERYTHING'S PUT AWAY! NOW I'VE GOT TO GET RID OF THAT FUDGE!

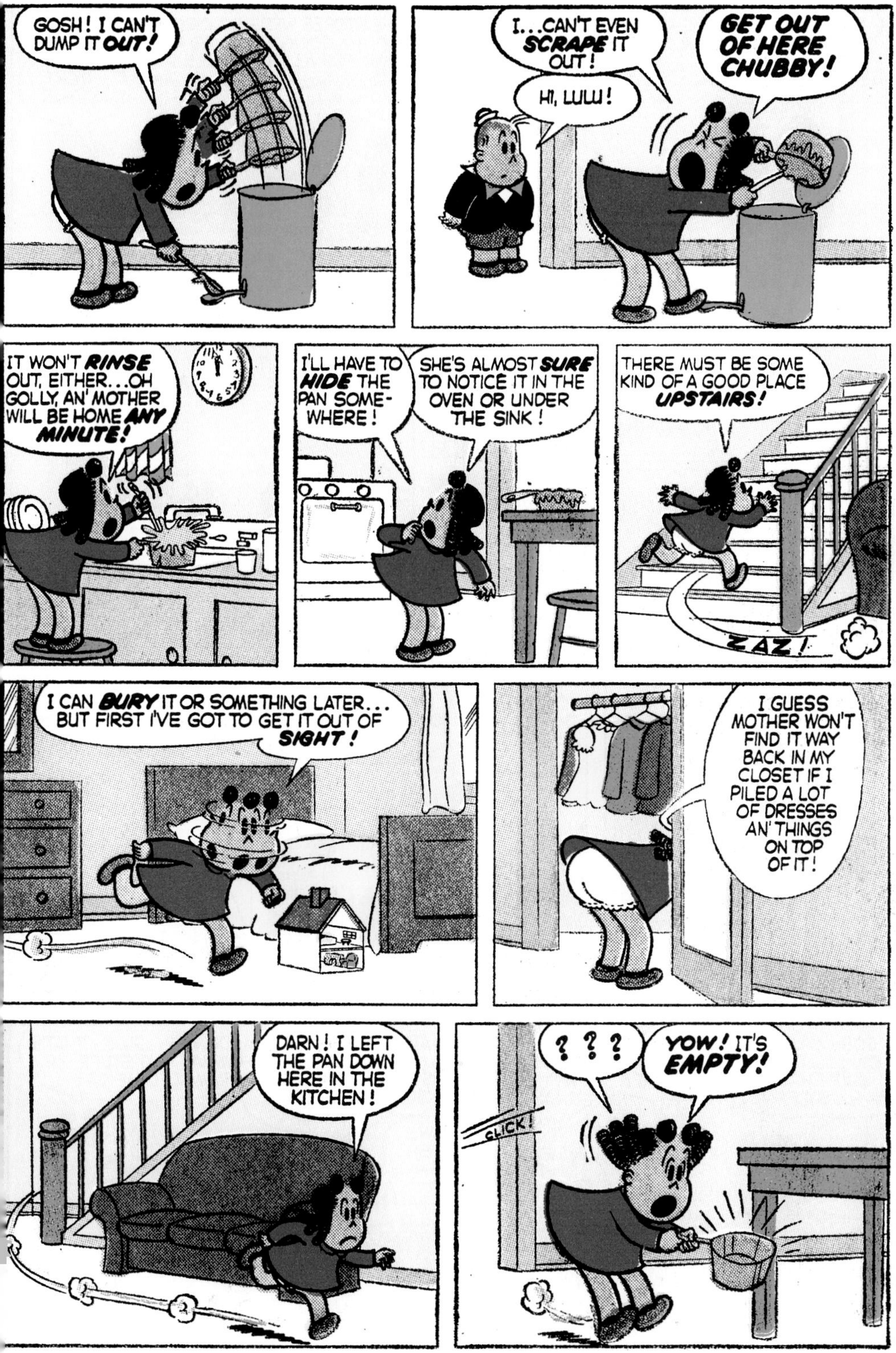
GOSH! I CAN'T DUMP IT OUT!
I...CAN'T EVEN SCRAPE IT OUT!
GET OUT OF HERE CHUBBY!
HI, LULU!
IT WON'T RINSE OUT, EITHER...OH GOLLY, AN' MOTHER WILL BE HOME ANY MINUTE!
I'LL HAVE TO HIDE THE PAN SOME-WHERE!
SHE'S ALMOST SURE TO NOTICE IT IN THE OVEN OR UNDER THE SINK!
THERE MUST BE SOME KIND OF A GOOD PLACE UPSTAIRS!
ZAZ!
I CAN BURY IT OR SOMETHING LATER... BUT FIRST I'VE GOT TO GET IT OUT OF SIGHT!
I GUESS MOTHER WON'T FIND IT WAY BACK IN MY CLOSET IF I PILED A LOT OF DRESSES AN' THINGS ON TOP OF IT!
DARN! I LEFT THE PAN DOWN HERE IN THE KITCHEN!
CLICK!
? ? ?
YOW! IT'S EMPTY!

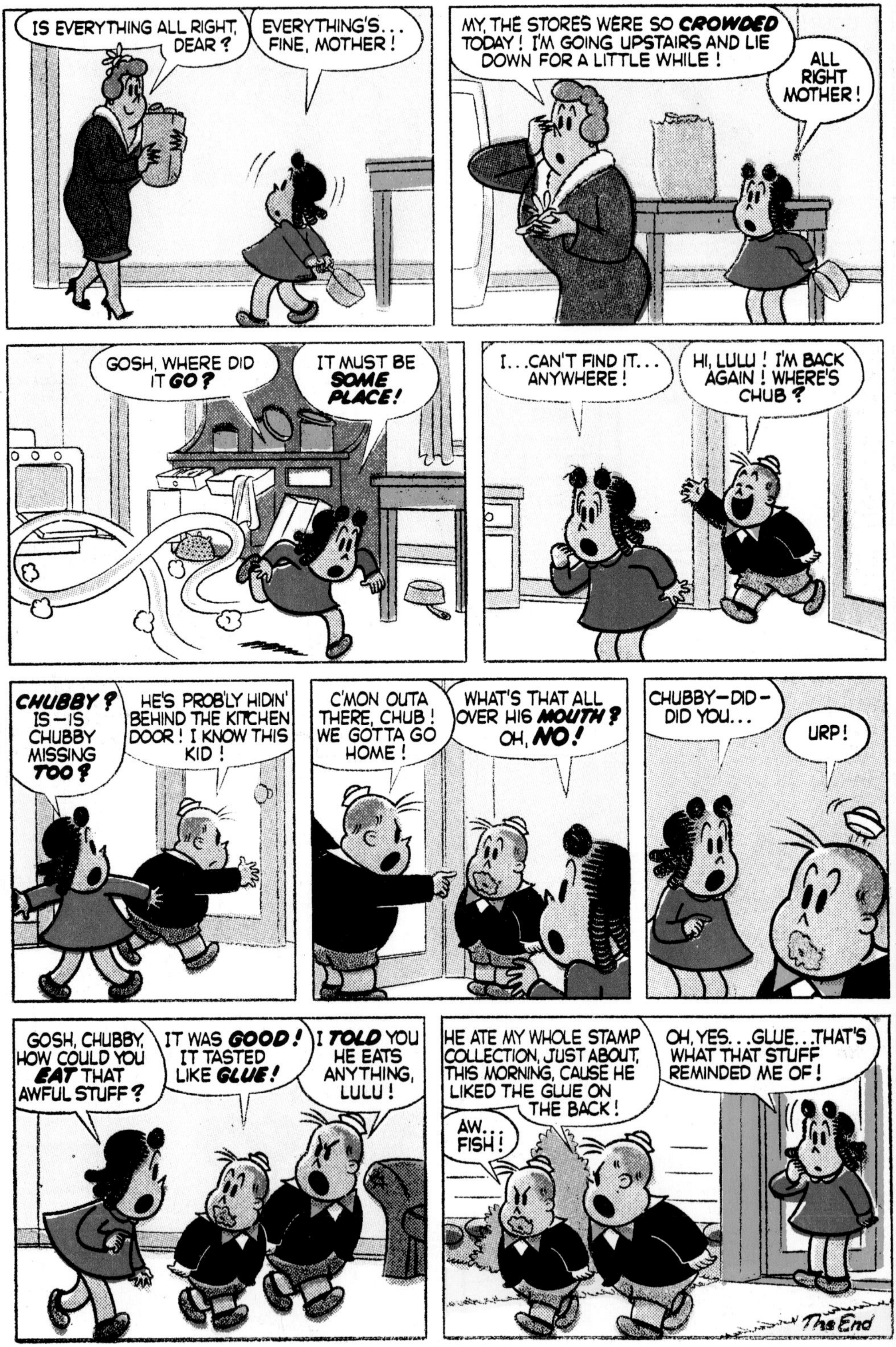
IS EVERYTHING ALL RIGHT, DEAR?
EVERYTHING'S... FINE, MOTHER!
MY, THE STORES WERE SO CROWDED TODAY! I'M GOING UPSTAIRS AND LIE DOWN FOR A LITTLE WHILE!
ALL RIGHT MOTHER!
GOSH, WHERE DID IT GO?
IT MUST BE SOME PLACE!
I...CAN'T FIND IT... ANYWHERE!
HI, LULU! I'M BACK AGAIN! WHERE'S CHUB?
CHUBBY? IS—IS CHUBBY MISSING TOO?
HE'S PROB'LY HIDIN' BEHIND THE KITCHEN DOOR! I KNOW THIS KID!
C'MON OUTA THERE, CHUB! WE GOTTA GO HOME!
WHAT'S THAT ALL OVER HIS MOUTH? OH, NO!
CHUBBY—DID-DID YOU...
URP!
GOSH, CHUBBY, HOW COULD YOU EAT THAT AWFUL STUFF?
IT WAS GOOD! IT TASTED LIKE GLUE!
I TOLD YOU HE EATS ANYTHING, LULU!
HE ATE MY WHOLE STAMP COLLECTION, JUST ABOUT, THIS MORNING, CAUSE HE LIKED THE GLUE ON THE BACK!
OH, YES...GLUE...THAT'S WHAT THAT STUFF REMINDED ME OF!
AW... FISH!
The End

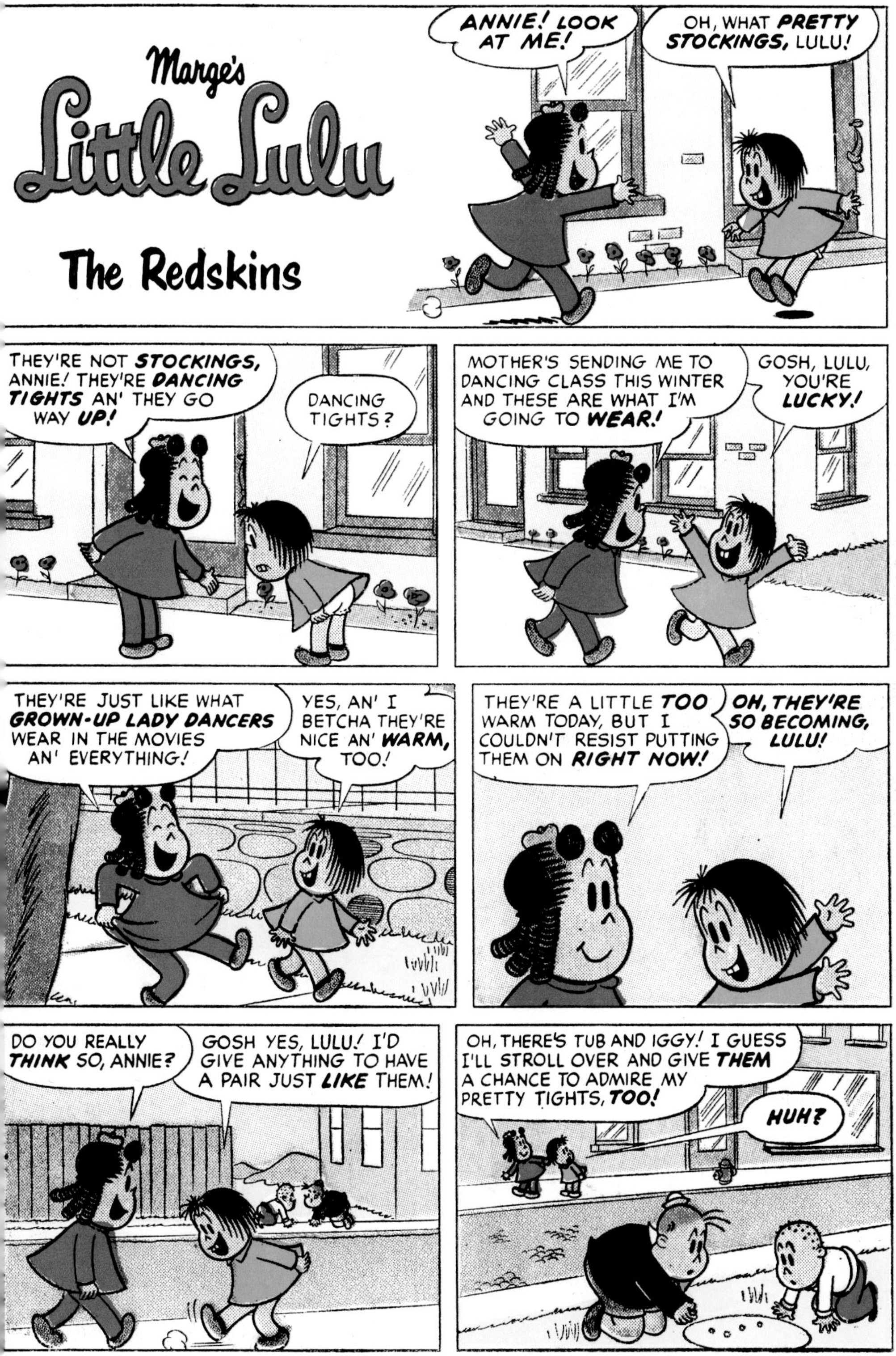

Marge's Little Lulu
The Redskins
ANNIE! LOOK AT ME!
OH, WHAT PRETTY STOCKINGS, LULU!
THEY'RE NOT STOCKINGS, ANNIE! THEY'RE DANCING TIGHTS AN' THEY GO WAY UP!
DANCING TIGHTS?
MOTHER'S SENDING ME TO DANCING CLASS THIS WINTER AND THESE ARE WHAT I'M GOING TO WEAR!
GOSH, LULU, YOU'RE LUCKY!
THEY'RE JUST LIKE WHAT GROWN-UP LADY DANCERS WEAR IN THE MOVIES AN' EVERYTHING!
YES, AN' I BETCHA THEY'RE NICE AN' WARM, TOO!
THEY'RE A LITTLE TOO WARM TODAY, BUT I COULDN'T RESIST PUTTING THEM ON RIGHT NOW!
OH, THEY'RE SO BECOMING, LULU!
DO YOU REALLY THINK SO, ANNIE?
GOSH YES, LULU! I'D GIVE ANYTHING TO HAVE A PAIR JUST LIKE THEM!
OH, THERE'S TUB AND IGGY! I GUESS I'LL STROLL OVER AND GIVE THEM A CHANCE TO ADMIRE MY PRETTY TIGHTS, TOO!
HUH?

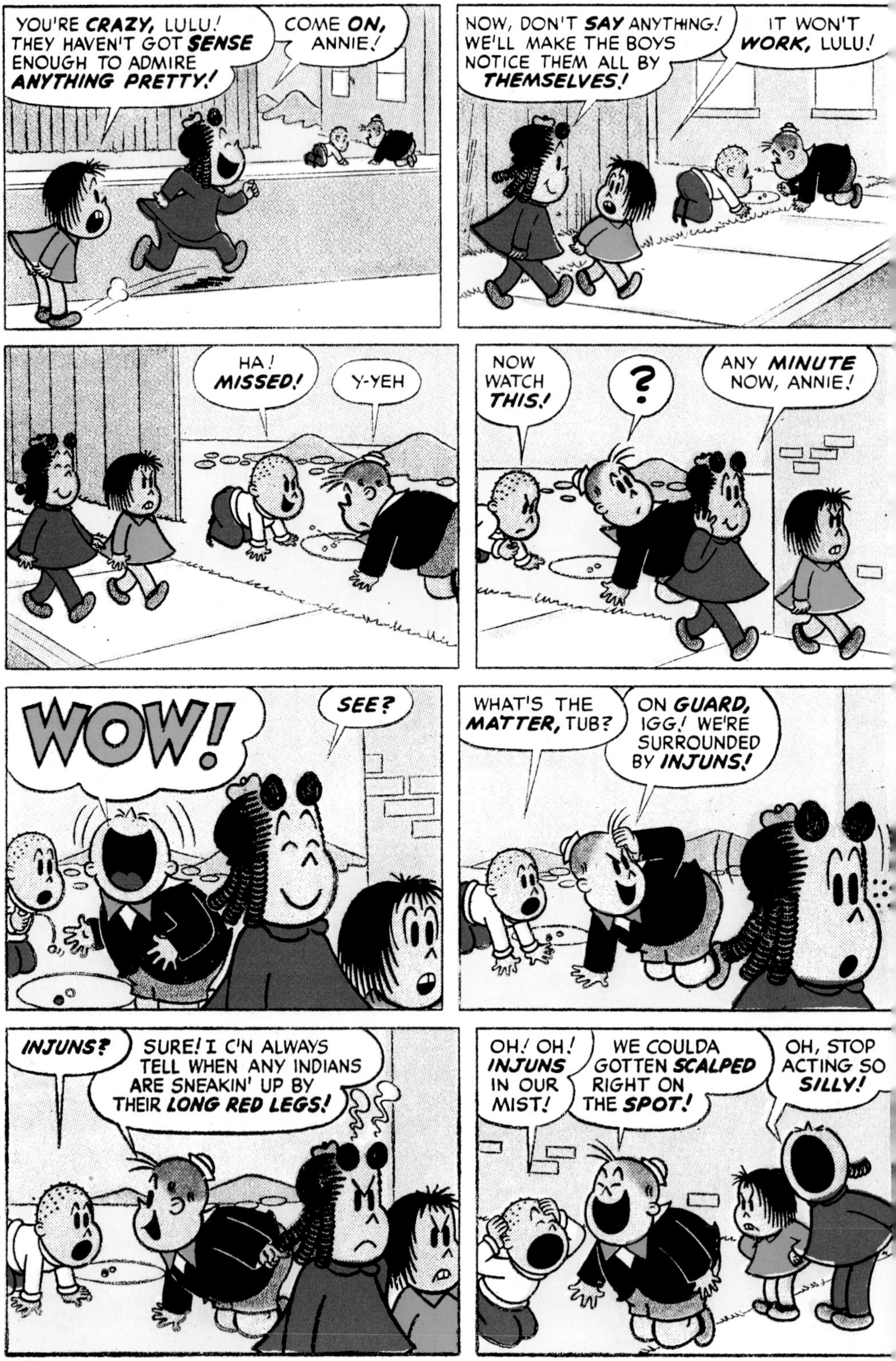
YOU'RE **CRAZY,** LULU! THEY HAVEN'T GOT **SENSE** ENOUGH TO ADMIRE **ANYTHING PRETTY!**
COME **ON,** ANNIE!
NOW, DON'T **SAY** ANYTHING! WE'LL MAKE THE BOYS NOTICE THEM ALL BY **THEMSELVES!**
IT WON'T **WORK,** LULU!
HA! **MISSED!**
Y-YEH
NOW WATCH **THIS!**
?
ANY **MINUTE** NOW, ANNIE!
WOW!
SEE?
WHAT'S THE **MATTER,** TUB?
ON **GUARD,** IGG! WE'RE SURROUNDED BY **INJUNS!**
INJUNS?
SURE! I C'N ALWAYS TELL WHEN ANY INDIANS ARE SNEAKIN' UP BY THEIR **LONG RED LEGS!**
OH! OH! **INJUNS** IN OUR MIST!
WE COULDA GOTTEN **SCALPED** RIGHT ON THE **SPOT!**
OH, STOP ACTING SO **SILLY!**

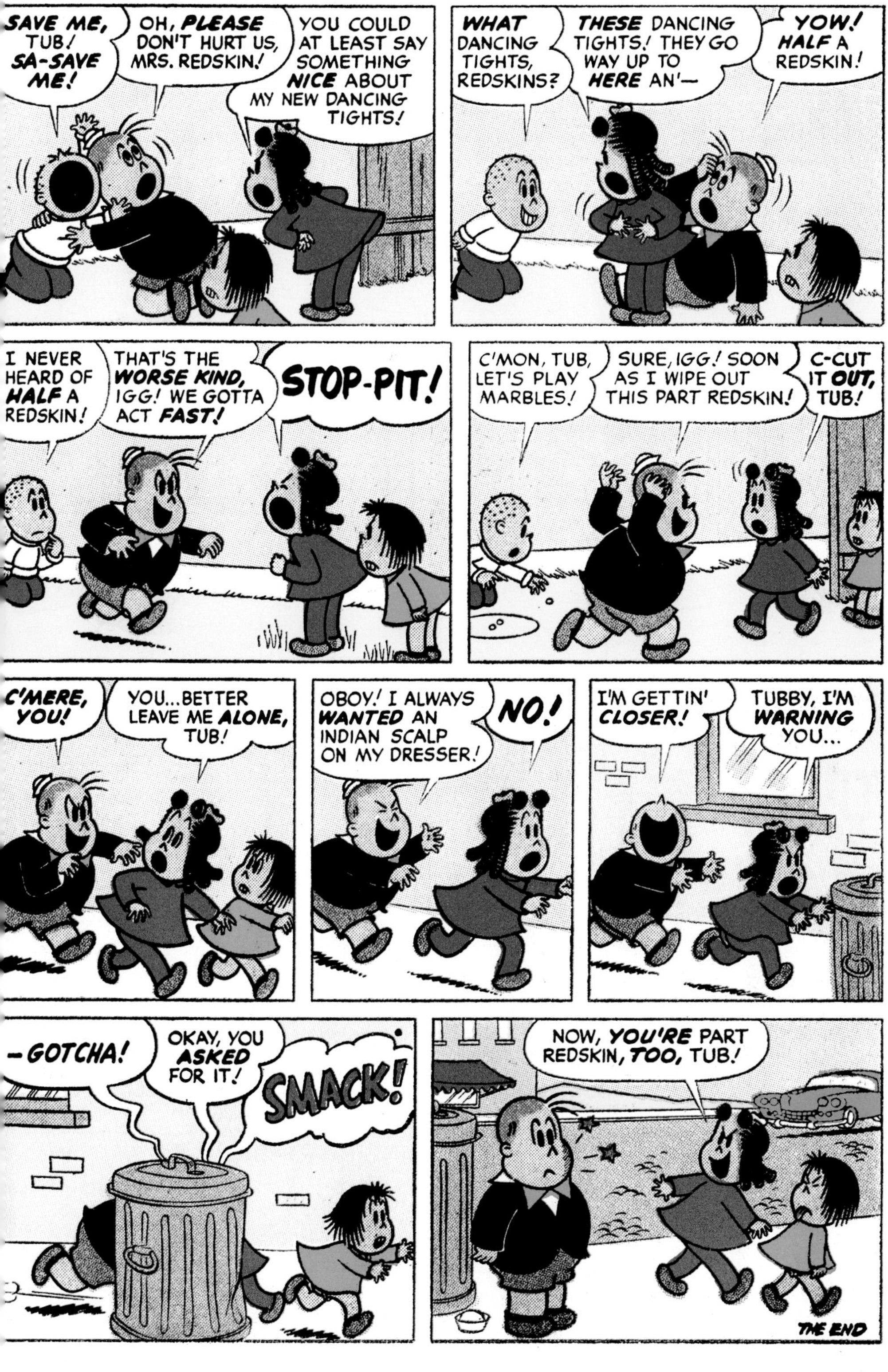
SAVE ME, TUB! SA-SAVE ME!
OH, PLEASE DON'T HURT US, MRS. REDSKIN!
YOU COULD AT LEAST SAY SOMETHING NICE ABOUT MY NEW DANCING TIGHTS!
WHAT DANCING TIGHTS, REDSKINS?
THESE DANCING TIGHTS! THEY GO WAY UP TO HERE AN'—
YOW! HALF A REDSKIN!
I NEVER HEARD OF HALF A REDSKIN!
THAT'S THE WORSE KIND, IGG! WE GOTTA ACT FAST!
STOP-PIT!
C'MON, TUB, LET'S PLAY MARBLES!
SURE, IGG! SOON AS I WIPE OUT THIS PART REDSKIN!
C-CUT IT OUT, TUB!
C'MERE, YOU!
YOU...BETTER LEAVE ME ALONE, TUB!
OBOY! I ALWAYS WANTED AN INDIAN SCALP ON MY DRESSER!
NO!
I'M GETTIN' CLOSER!
TUBBY, I'M WARNING YOU...
-GOTCHA!
OKAY, YOU ASKED FOR IT!
SMACK!
NOW, YOU'RE PART REDSKIN, TOO, TUB!
THE END

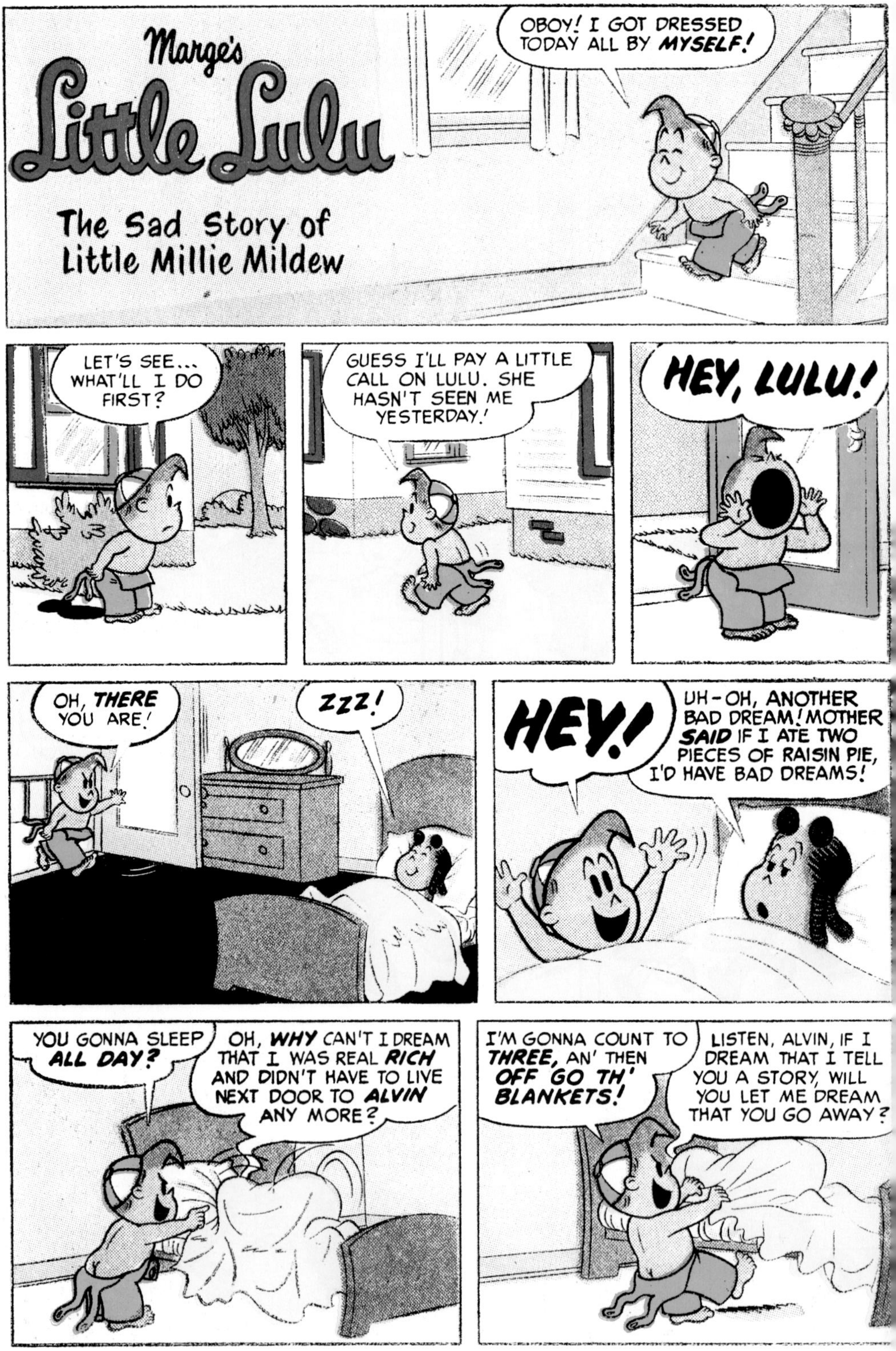

Marge's Little Lulu
The Sad Story of Little Millie Mildew
OBOY! I GOT DRESSED TODAY ALL BY MYSELF!
LET'S SEE... WHAT'LL I DO FIRST?
GUESS I'LL PAY A LITTLE CALL ON LULU. SHE HASN'T SEEN ME YESTERDAY!
HEY, LULU!
OH, THERE YOU ARE!
ZZZ!
HEY!!
UH-OH, ANOTHER BAD DREAM! MOTHER SAID IF I ATE TWO PIECES OF RAISIN PIE, I'D HAVE BAD DREAMS!
YOU GONNA SLEEP ALL DAY?
OH, WHY CAN'T I DREAM THAT I WAS REAL RICH AND DIDN'T HAVE TO LIVE NEXT DOOR TO ALVIN ANY MORE?
I'M GONNA COUNT TO THREE, AN' THEN OFF GO TH' BLANKETS!
LISTEN, ALVIN, IF I DREAM THAT I TELL YOU A STORY, WILL YOU LET ME DREAM THAT YOU GO AWAY?

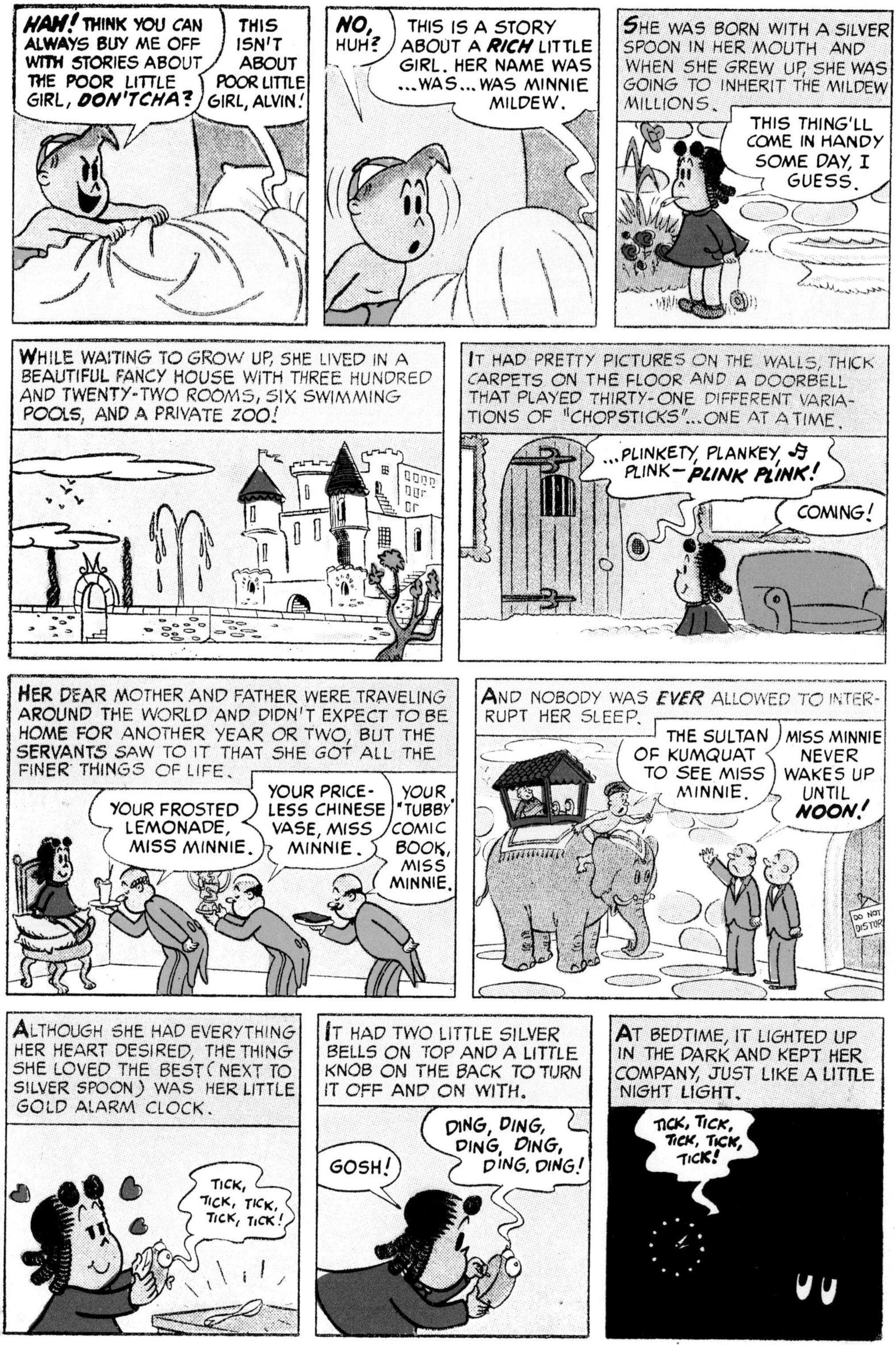
HAH! THINK YOU CAN ALWAYS BUY ME OFF WITH STORIES ABOUT THE POOR LITTLE GIRL, DON'TCHA?
THIS ISN'T ABOUT POOR LITTLE GIRL, ALVIN!
NO, HUH?
THIS IS A STORY ABOUT A RICH LITTLE GIRL. HER NAME WAS ...WAS... WAS MINNIE MILDEW.
SHE WAS BORN WITH A SILVER SPOON IN HER MOUTH AND WHEN SHE GREW UP, SHE WAS GOING TO INHERIT THE MILDEW MILLIONS.
THIS THING'LL COME IN HANDY SOME DAY, I GUESS.
WHILE WAITING TO GROW UP, SHE LIVED IN A BEAUTIFUL FANCY HOUSE WITH THREE HUNDRED AND TWENTY-TWO ROOMS, SIX SWIMMING POOLS, AND A PRIVATE ZOO!
IT HAD PRETTY PICTURES ON THE WALLS, THICK CARPETS ON THE FLOOR AND A DOORBELL THAT PLAYED THIRTY-ONE DIFFERENT VARIATIONS OF "CHOPSTICKS"...ONE AT A TIME.
...PLINKETY, PLANKEY, PLINK—PLINK PLINK!
COMING!
HER DEAR MOTHER AND FATHER WERE TRAVELING AROUND THE WORLD AND DIDN'T EXPECT TO BE HOME FOR ANOTHER YEAR OR TWO, BUT THE SERVANTS SAW TO IT THAT SHE GOT ALL THE FINER THINGS OF LIFE.
YOUR FROSTED LEMONADE, MISS MINNIE.
YOUR PRICELESS CHINESE VASE, MISS MINNIE.
YOUR "TUBBY" COMIC BOOK, MISS MINNIE.
AND NOBODY WAS EVER ALLOWED TO INTERRUPT HER SLEEP.
THE SULTAN OF KUMQUAT TO SEE MISS MINNIE.
MISS MINNIE NEVER WAKES UP UNTIL NOON!
DO NOT DISTUR
ALTHOUGH SHE HAD EVERYTHING HER HEART DESIRED, THE THING SHE LOVED THE BEST (NEXT TO SILVER SPOON) WAS HER LITTLE GOLD ALARM CLOCK.
TICK, TICK, TICK, TICK, TICK!
IT HAD TWO LITTLE SILVER BELLS ON TOP AND A LITTLE KNOB ON THE BACK TO TURN IT OFF AND ON WITH.
DING, DING, DING, DING, DING, DING!
GOSH!
AT BEDTIME, IT LIGHTED UP IN THE DARK AND KEPT HER COMPANY, JUST LIKE A LITTLE NIGHT LIGHT.
TICK, TICK, TICK, TICK, TICK!

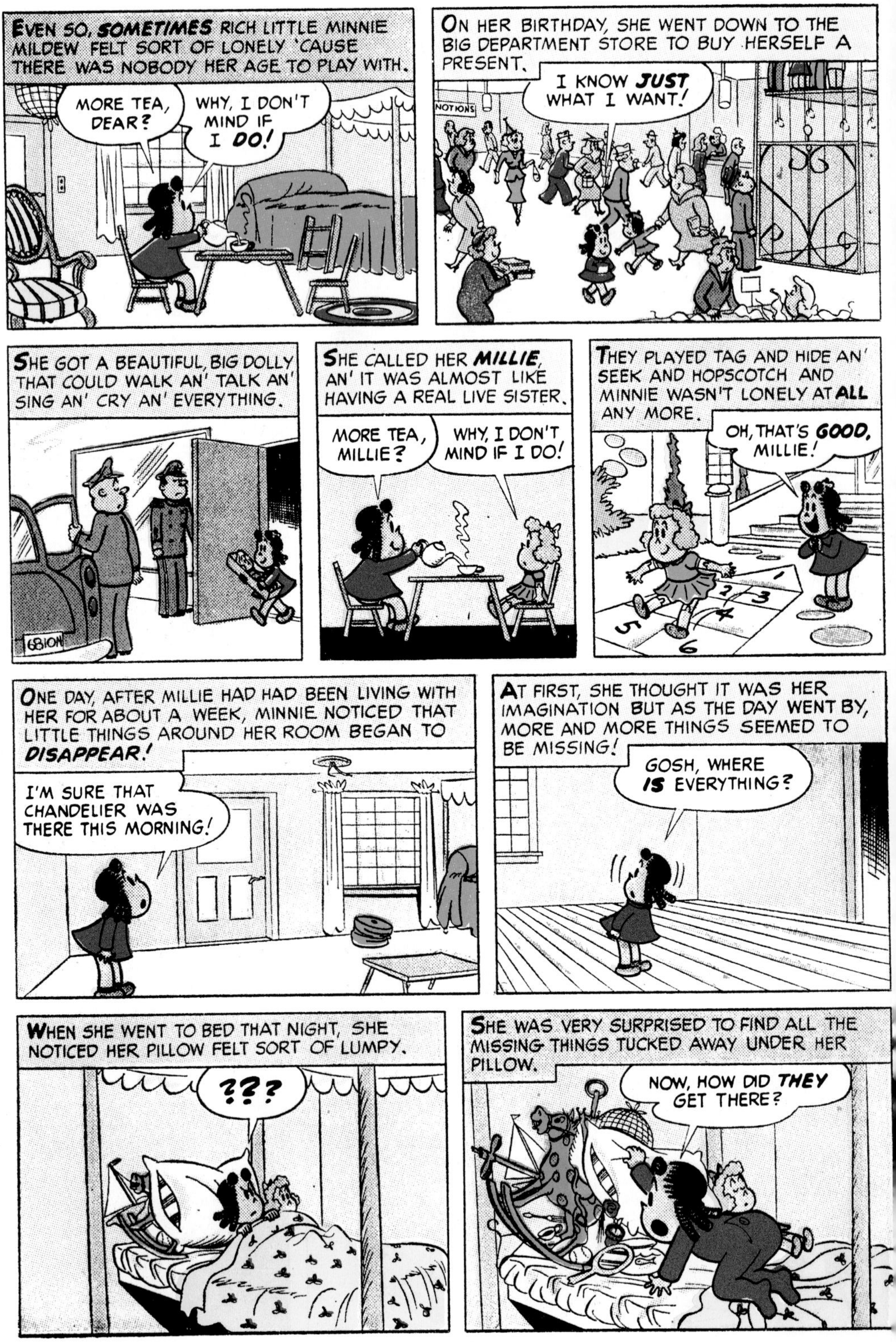
EVEN SO, SOMETIMES RICH LITTLE MINNIE MILDEW FELT SORT OF LONELY 'CAUSE THERE WAS NOBODY HER AGE TO PLAY WITH.
MORE TEA, DEAR?
WHY, I DON'T MIND IF I DO!
ON HER BIRTHDAY, SHE WENT DOWN TO THE BIG DEPARTMENT STORE TO BUY HERSELF A PRESENT.
I KNOW JUST WHAT I WANT!
NOTIONS
SHE GOT A BEAUTIFUL, BIG DOLLY THAT COULD WALK AN' TALK AN' SING AN' CRY AN' EVERYTHING.
6810W
SHE CALLED HER MILLIE, AN' IT WAS ALMOST LIKE HAVING A REAL LIVE SISTER.
MORE TEA, MILLIE?
WHY, I DON'T MIND IF I DO!
THEY PLAYED TAG AND HIDE AN' SEEK AND HOPSCOTCH AND MINNIE WASN'T LONELY AT ALL ANY MORE.
OH, THAT'S GOOD, MILLIE!
ONE DAY, AFTER MILLIE HAD HAD BEEN LIVING WITH HER FOR ABOUT A WEEK, MINNIE NOTICED THAT LITTLE THINGS AROUND HER ROOM BEGAN TO DISAPPEAR!
I'M SURE THAT CHANDELIER WAS THERE THIS MORNING!
AT FIRST, SHE THOUGHT IT WAS HER IMAGINATION BUT AS THE DAY WENT BY, MORE AND MORE THINGS SEEMED TO BE MISSING!
GOSH, WHERE IS EVERYTHING?
WHEN SHE WENT TO BED THAT NIGHT, SHE NOTICED HER PILLOW FELT SORT OF LUMPY.
???
SHE WAS VERY SURPRISED TO FIND ALL THE MISSING THINGS TUCKED AWAY UNDER HER PILLOW.
NOW, HOW DID THEY GET THERE?

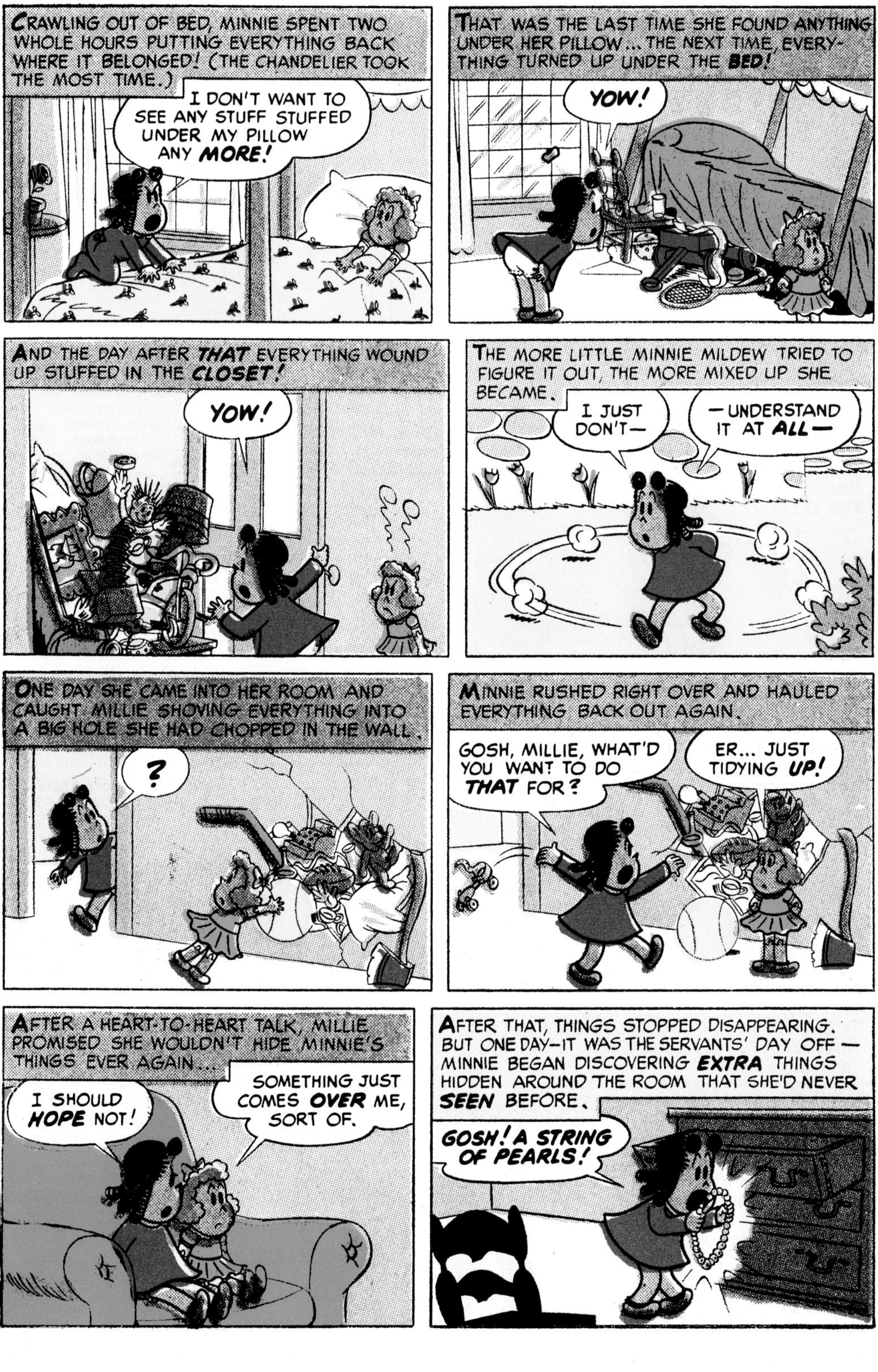
CRAWLING OUT OF BED, MINNIE SPENT TWO WHOLE HOURS PUTTING EVERYTHING BACK WHERE IT BELONGED! (THE CHANDELIER TOOK THE MOST TIME.)
I DON'T WANT TO SEE ANY STUFF STUFFED UNDER MY PILLOW ANY MORE!
THAT WAS THE LAST TIME SHE FOUND ANYTHING UNDER HER PILLOW... THE NEXT TIME, EVERYTHING TURNED UP UNDER THE BED!
YOW!
AND THE DAY AFTER THAT EVERYTHING WOUND UP STUFFED IN THE CLOSET!
YOW!
THE MORE LITTLE MINNIE MILDEW TRIED TO FIGURE IT OUT, THE MORE MIXED UP SHE BECAME.
I JUST DON'T—
—UNDERSTAND IT AT ALL—
ONE DAY SHE CAME INTO HER ROOM AND CAUGHT MILLIE SHOVING EVERYTHING INTO A BIG HOLE SHE HAD CHOPPED IN THE WALL.
?
MINNIE RUSHED RIGHT OVER AND HAULED EVERYTHING BACK OUT AGAIN.
GOSH, MILLIE, WHAT'D YOU WANT TO DO THAT FOR?
ER... JUST TIDYING UP!
AFTER A HEART-TO-HEART TALK, MILLIE PROMISED SHE WOULDN'T HIDE MINNIE'S THINGS EVER AGAIN...
I SHOULD HOPE NOT!
SOMETHING JUST COMES OVER ME, SORT OF.
AFTER THAT, THINGS STOPPED DISAPPEARING. BUT ONE DAY—IT WAS THE SERVANTS' DAY OFF—MINNIE BEGAN DISCOVERING EXTRA THINGS HIDDEN AROUND THE ROOM THAT SHE'D NEVER SEEN BEFORE.
GOSH! A STRING OF PEARLS!

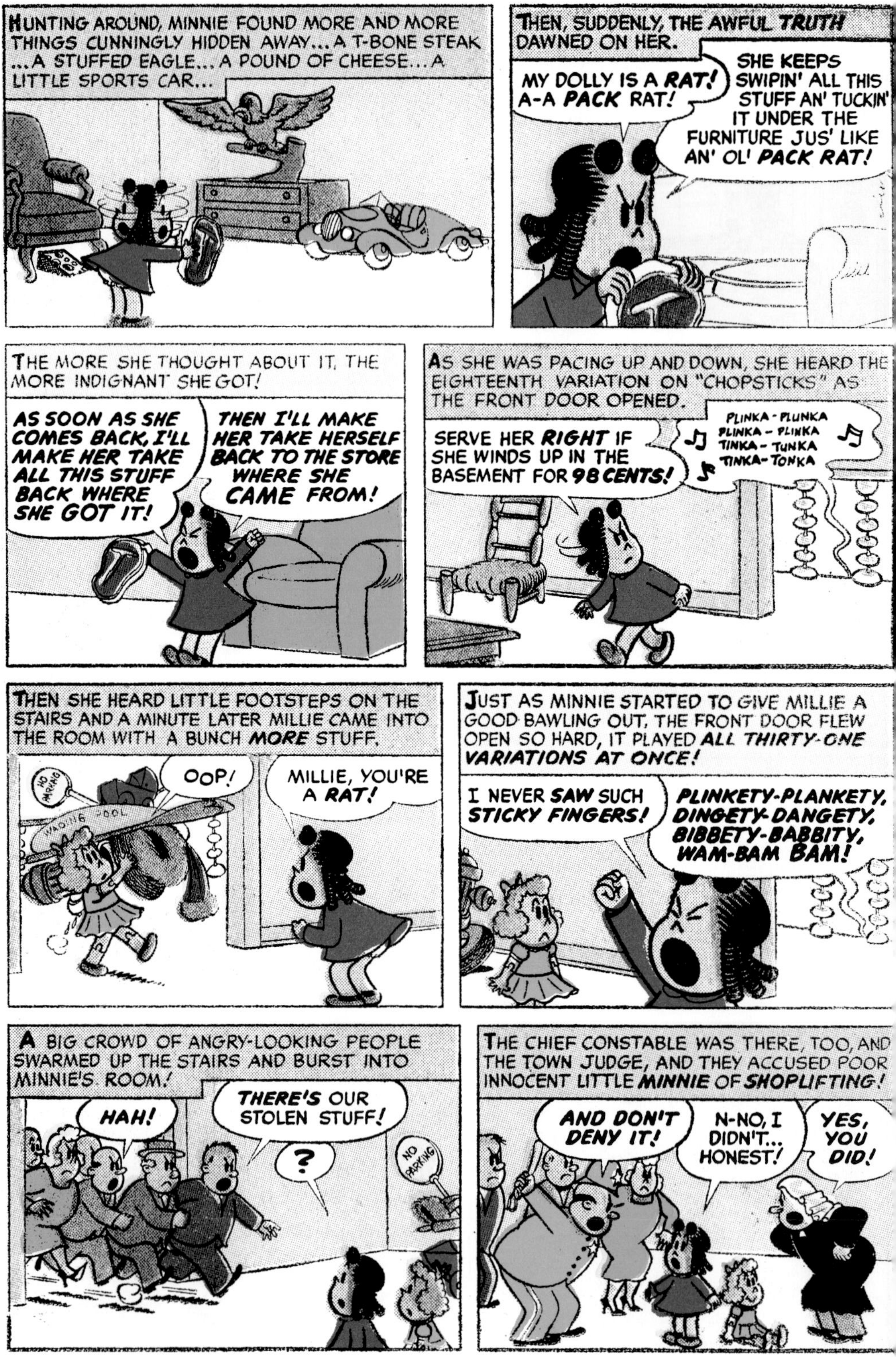
HUNTING AROUND, MINNIE FOUND MORE AND MORE THINGS CUNNINGLY HIDDEN AWAY... A T-BONE STEAK ...A STUFFED EAGLE... A POUND OF CHEESE... A LITTLE SPORTS CAR...
THEN, SUDDENLY, THE AWFUL TRUTH DAWNED ON HER.
MY DOLLY IS A RAT! A-A PACK RAT!
SHE KEEPS SWIPIN' ALL THIS STUFF AN' TUCKIN' IT UNDER THE FURNITURE JUS' LIKE AN' OL' PACK RAT!
THE MORE SHE THOUGHT ABOUT IT, THE MORE INDIGNANT SHE GOT!
AS SOON AS SHE COMES BACK, I'LL MAKE HER TAKE ALL THIS STUFF BACK WHERE SHE GOT IT!
THEN I'LL MAKE HER TAKE HERSELF BACK TO THE STORE WHERE SHE CAME FROM!
AS SHE WAS PACING UP AND DOWN, SHE HEARD THE EIGHTEENTH VARIATION ON "CHOPSTICKS" AS THE FRONT DOOR OPENED.
SERVE HER RIGHT IF SHE WINDS UP IN THE BASEMENT FOR 98 CENTS!
PLINKA-PLUNKA PLINKA-PLINKA TINKA-TUNKA TINKA-TONKA
THEN SHE HEARD LITTLE FOOTSTEPS ON THE STAIRS AND A MINUTE LATER MILLIE CAME INTO THE ROOM WITH A BUNCH MORE STUFF.
NO PARKING
WADING POOL
OOP!
MILLIE, YOU'RE A RAT!
JUST AS MINNIE STARTED TO GIVE MILLIE A GOOD BAWLING OUT, THE FRONT DOOR FLEW OPEN SO HARD, IT PLAYED ALL THIRTY-ONE VARIATIONS AT ONCE!
I NEVER SAW SUCH STICKY FINGERS!
PLINKETY-PLANKETY, DINGETY-DANGETY, BIBBETY-BABBITY, WAM-BAM BAM!
A BIG CROWD OF ANGRY-LOOKING PEOPLE SWARMED UP THE STAIRS AND BURST INTO MINNIE'S ROOM!
HAH!
THERE'S OUR STOLEN STUFF!
?
NO PARKING
THE CHIEF CONSTABLE WAS THERE, TOO, AND THE TOWN JUDGE, AND THEY ACCUSED POOR INNOCENT LITTLE MINNIE OF SHOPLIFTING!
AND DON'T DENY IT!
N-NO, I DIDN'T... HONEST!
YES, YOU DID!

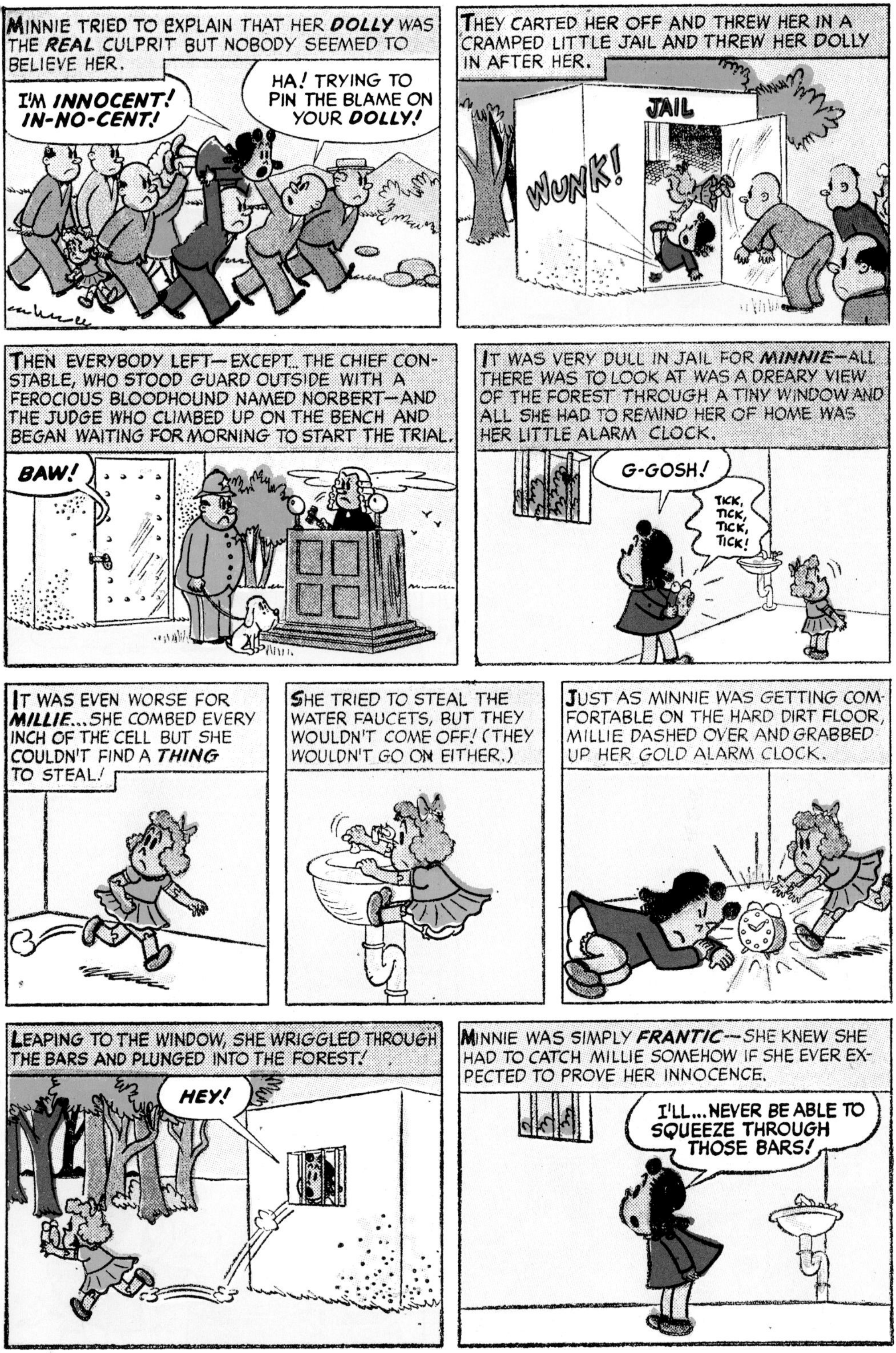

MINNIE TRIED TO EXPLAIN THAT HER DOLLY WAS THE REAL CULPRIT BUT NOBODY SEEMED TO BELIEVE HER.
I'M INNOCENT! IN-NO-CENT!
HA! TRYING TO PIN THE BLAME ON YOUR DOLLY!
THEY CARTED HER OFF AND THREW HER IN A CRAMPED LITTLE JAIL AND THREW HER DOLLY IN AFTER HER.
JAIL
WUNK!
THEN EVERYBODY LEFT—EXCEPT.. THE CHIEF CONSTABLE, WHO STOOD GUARD OUTSIDE WITH A FEROCIOUS BLOODHOUND NAMED NORBERT—AND THE JUDGE WHO CLIMBED UP ON THE BENCH AND BEGAN WAITING FOR MORNING TO START THE TRIAL.
BAW!
IT WAS VERY DULL IN JAIL FOR MINNIE—ALL THERE WAS TO LOOK AT WAS A DREARY VIEW OF THE FOREST THROUGH A TINY WINDOW AND ALL SHE HAD TO REMIND HER OF HOME WAS HER LITTLE ALARM CLOCK.
G-GOSH!
TICK, TICK, TICK, TICK!
IT WAS EVEN WORSE FOR MILLIE...SHE COMBED EVERY INCH OF THE CELL BUT SHE COULDN'T FIND A THING TO STEAL!
SHE TRIED TO STEAL THE WATER FAUCETS, BUT THEY WOULDN'T COME OFF! (THEY WOULDN'T GO ON EITHER.)
JUST AS MINNIE WAS GETTING COMFORTABLE ON THE HARD DIRT FLOOR, MILLIE DASHED OVER AND GRABBED UP HER GOLD ALARM CLOCK.
LEAPING TO THE WINDOW, SHE WRIGGLED THROUGH THE BARS AND PLUNGED INTO THE FOREST!
HEY!
MINNIE WAS SIMPLY FRANTIC—SHE KNEW SHE HAD TO CATCH MILLIE SOMEHOW IF SHE EVER EXPECTED TO PROVE HER INNOCENCE.
I'LL...NEVER BE ABLE TO SQUEEZE THROUGH THOSE BARS!

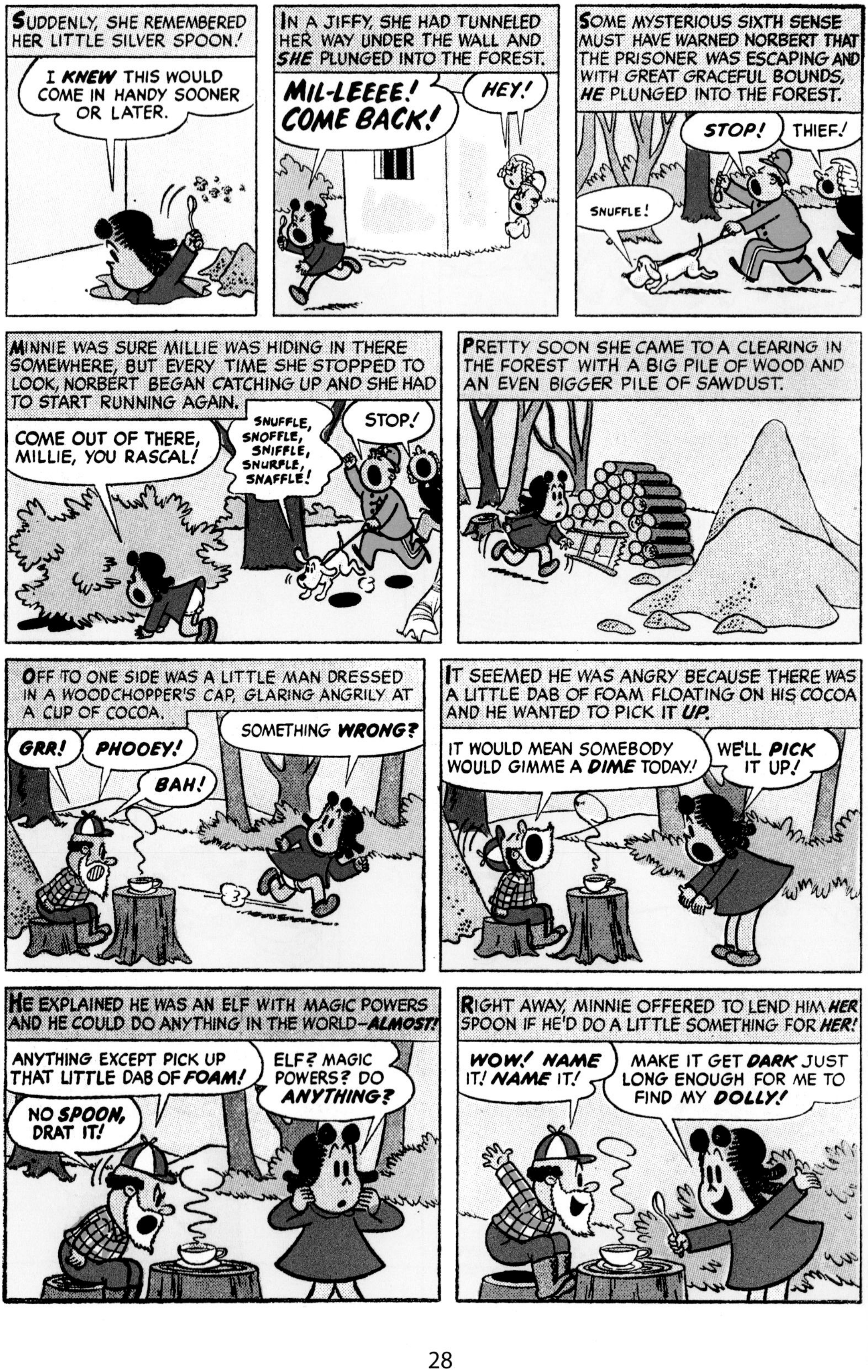
SUDDENLY, SHE REMEMBERED HER LITTLE SILVER SPOON!
I KNEW THIS WOULD COME IN HANDY SOONER OR LATER.
IN A JIFFY, SHE HAD TUNNELED HER WAY UNDER THE WALL AND SHE PLUNGED INTO THE FOREST.
MIL-LEEEE! COME BACK!
HEY!
SOME MYSTERIOUS SIXTH SENSE MUST HAVE WARNED NORBERT THAT THE PRISONER WAS ESCAPING AND WITH GREAT GRACEFUL BOUNDS, HE PLUNGED INTO THE FOREST.
STOP!
THIEF!
SNUFFLE!
MINNIE WAS SURE MILLIE WAS HIDING IN THERE SOMEWHERE, BUT EVERY TIME SHE STOPPED TO LOOK, NORBERT BEGAN CATCHING UP AND SHE HAD TO START RUNNING AGAIN.
COME OUT OF THERE, MILLIE, YOU RASCAL!
SNUFFLE, SNOFFLE, SNIFFLE, SNURFLE, SNAFFLE!
STOP!
PRETTY SOON SHE CAME TO A CLEARING IN THE FOREST WITH A BIG PILE OF WOOD AND AN EVEN BIGGER PILE OF SAWDUST.
OFF TO ONE SIDE WAS A LITTLE MAN DRESSED IN A WOODCHOPPER'S CAP, GLARING ANGRILY AT A CUP OF COCOA.
GRR!
PHOOEY!
BAH!
SOMETHING WRONG?
IT SEEMED HE WAS ANGRY BECAUSE THERE WAS A LITTLE DAB OF FOAM FLOATING ON HIS COCOA AND HE WANTED TO PICK IT UP.
IT WOULD MEAN SOMEBODY WOULD GIMME A DIME TODAY!
WE'LL PICK IT UP!
HE EXPLAINED HE WAS AN ELF WITH MAGIC POWERS AND HE COULD DO ANYTHING IN THE WORLD—ALMOST!
ANYTHING EXCEPT PICK UP THAT LITTLE DAB OF FOAM!
NO SPOON, DRAT IT!
ELF? MAGIC POWERS? DO ANYTHING?
RIGHT AWAY, MINNIE OFFERED TO LEND HIM HER SPOON IF HE'D DO A LITTLE SOMETHING FOR HER!
WOW! NAME IT! NAME IT!
MAKE IT GET DARK JUST LONG ENOUGH FOR ME TO FIND MY DOLLY!

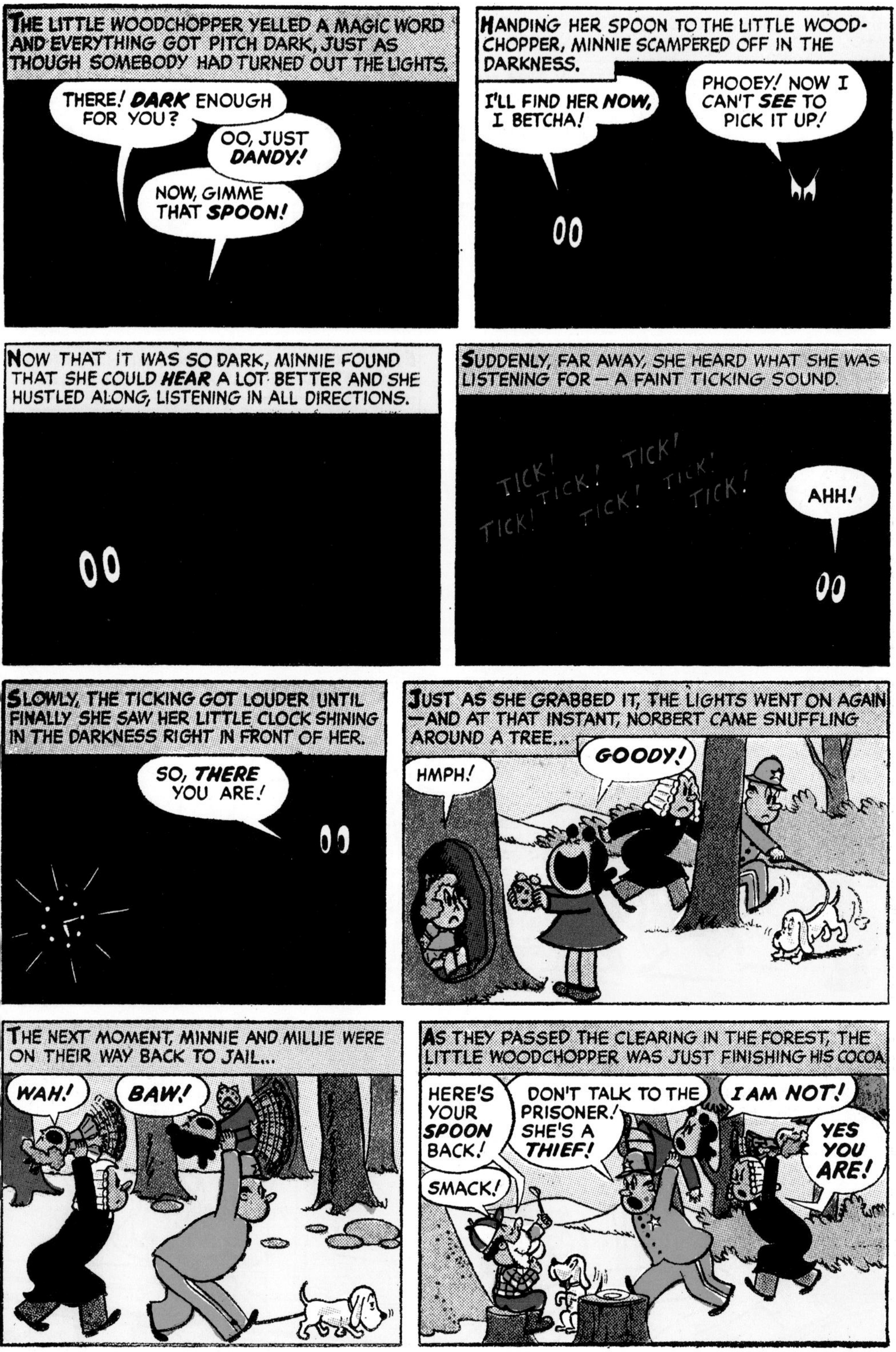
THE LITTLE WOODCHOPPER YELLED A MAGIC WORD AND EVERYTHING GOT PITCH DARK, JUST AS THOUGH SOMEBODY HAD TURNED OUT THE LIGHTS.
THERE! DARK ENOUGH FOR YOU?
OO, JUST DANDY!
NOW, GIMME THAT SPOON!
HANDING HER SPOON TO THE LITTLE WOOD-CHOPPER, MINNIE SCAMPERED OFF IN THE DARKNESS.
I'LL FIND HER NOW, I BETCHA!
PHOOEY! NOW I CAN'T SEE TO PICK IT UP!
NOW THAT IT WAS SO DARK, MINNIE FOUND THAT SHE COULD HEAR A LOT BETTER AND SHE HUSTLED ALONG, LISTENING IN ALL DIRECTIONS.
SUDDENLY, FAR AWAY, SHE HEARD WHAT SHE WAS LISTENING FOR — A FAINT TICKING SOUND.
TICK! TICK! TICK! TICK! TICK! TICK! TICK!
AHH!
SLOWLY, THE TICKING GOT LOUDER UNTIL FINALLY SHE SAW HER LITTLE CLOCK SHINING IN THE DARKNESS RIGHT IN FRONT OF HER.
SO, THERE YOU ARE!
JUST AS SHE GRABBED IT, THE LIGHTS WENT ON AGAIN —AND AT THAT INSTANT, NORBERT CAME SNUFFLING AROUND A TREE...
HMPH!
GOODY!
THE NEXT MOMENT, MINNIE AND MILLIE WERE ON THEIR WAY BACK TO JAIL...
WAH!
BAW!
AS THEY PASSED THE CLEARING IN THE FOREST, THE LITTLE WOODCHOPPER WAS JUST FINISHING HIS COCOA.
HERE'S YOUR SPOON BACK!
SMACK!
DON'T TALK TO THE PRISONER! SHE'S A THIEF!
I AM NOT!
YES YOU ARE!

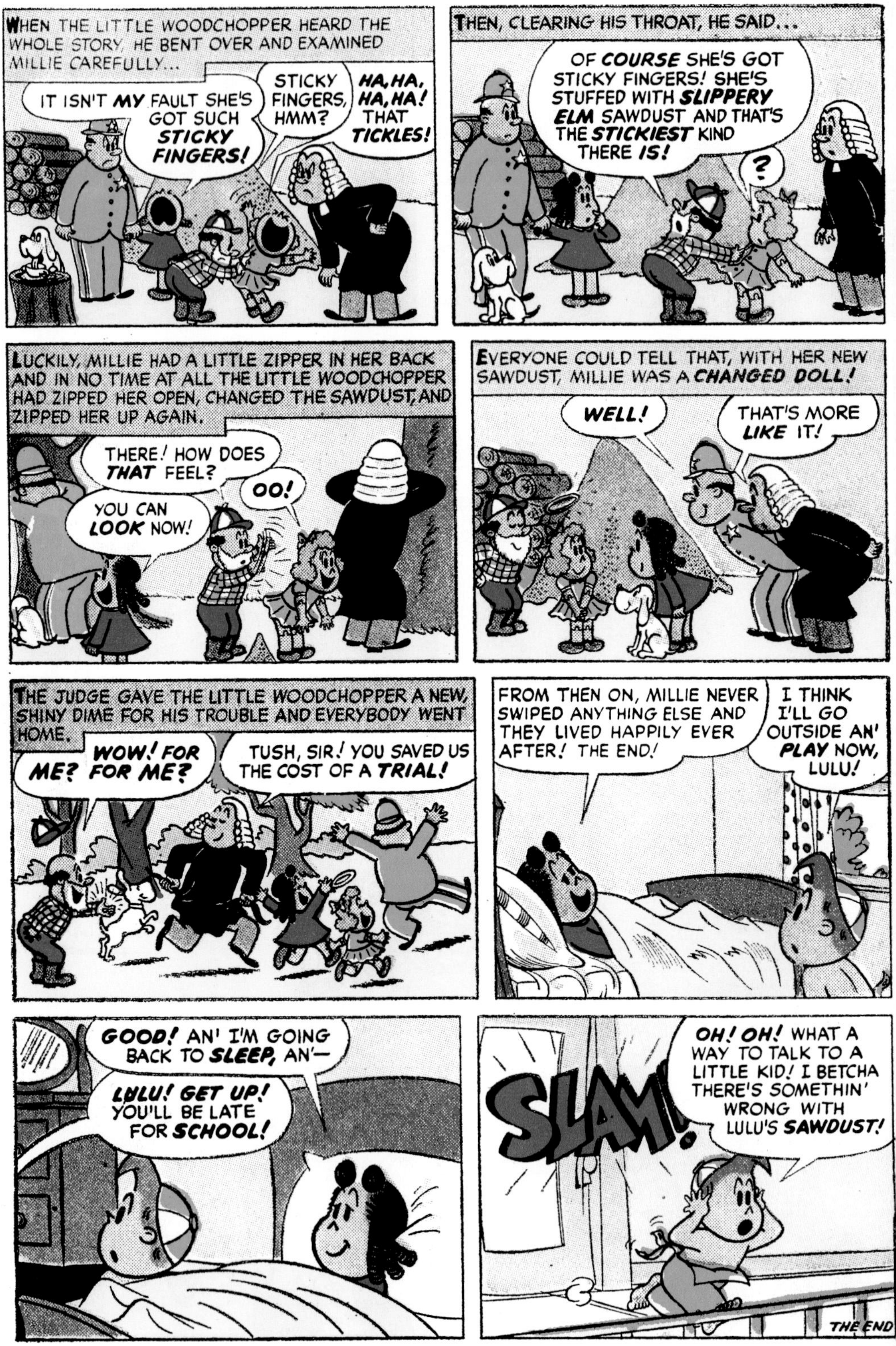
WHEN THE LITTLE WOODCHOPPER HEARD THE WHOLE STORY, HE BENT OVER AND EXAMINED MILLIE CAREFULLY...
IT ISN'T MY FAULT SHE'S GOT SUCH STICKY FINGERS!
STICKY FINGERS, HMM?
HA, HA, HA, HA! THAT TICKLES!
THEN, CLEARING HIS THROAT, HE SAID...
OF COURSE SHE'S GOT STICKY FINGERS! SHE'S STUFFED WITH SLIPPERY ELM SAWDUST AND THAT'S THE STICKIEST KIND THERE IS!
?
LUCKILY, MILLIE HAD A LITTLE ZIPPER IN HER BACK AND IN NO TIME AT ALL THE LITTLE WOODCHOPPER HAD ZIPPED HER OPEN, CHANGED THE SAWDUST, AND ZIPPED HER UP AGAIN.
THERE! HOW DOES THAT FEEL?
OO!
YOU CAN LOOK NOW!
EVERYONE COULD TELL THAT, WITH HER NEW SAWDUST, MILLIE WAS A CHANGED DOLL!
WELL!
THAT'S MORE LIKE IT!
THE JUDGE GAVE THE LITTLE WOODCHOPPER A NEW, SHINY DIME FOR HIS TROUBLE AND EVERYBODY WENT HOME.
WOW! FOR ME? FOR ME?
TUSH, SIR! YOU SAVED US THE COST OF A TRIAL!
FROM THEN ON, MILLIE NEVER SWIPED ANYTHING ELSE AND THEY LIVED HAPPILY EVER AFTER! THE END!
I THINK I'LL GO OUTSIDE AN' PLAY NOW, LULU!
GOOD! AN' I'M GOING BACK TO SLEEP, AN'—
LULU! GET UP! YOU'LL BE LATE FOR SCHOOL!
SLAM!
OH! OH! WHAT A WAY TO TALK TO A LITTLE KID! I BETCHA THERE'S SOMETHIN' WRONG WITH LULU'S SAWDUST!
THE END

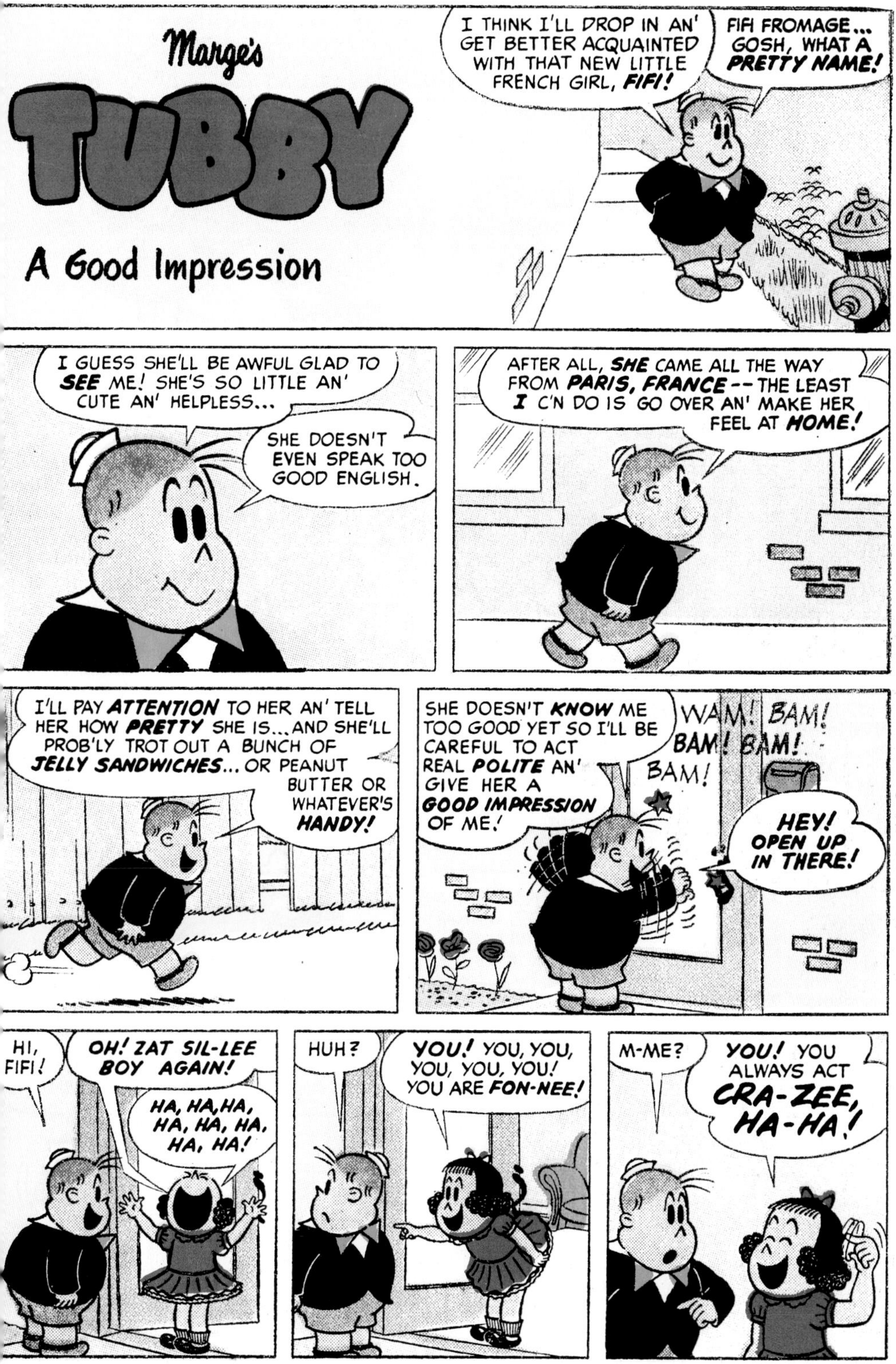

Marge's
TUBBY
A Good Impression
I THINK I'LL DROP IN AN' GET BETTER ACQUAINTED WITH THAT NEW LITTLE FRENCH GIRL, FIFI!
FIFI FROMAGE... GOSH, WHAT A PRETTY NAME!
I GUESS SHE'LL BE AWFUL GLAD TO SEE ME! SHE'S SO LITTLE AN' CUTE AN' HELPLESS...
SHE DOESN'T EVEN SPEAK TOO GOOD ENGLISH.
AFTER ALL, SHE CAME ALL THE WAY FROM PARIS, FRANCE -- THE LEAST I C'N DO IS GO OVER AN' MAKE HER FEEL AT HOME!
I'LL PAY ATTENTION TO HER AN' TELL HER HOW PRETTY SHE IS... AND SHE'LL PROB'LY TROT OUT A BUNCH OF JELLY SANDWICHES... OR PEANUT BUTTER OR WHATEVER'S HANDY!
SHE DOESN'T KNOW ME TOO GOOD YET SO I'LL BE CAREFUL TO ACT REAL POLITE AN' GIVE HER A GOOD IMPRESSION OF ME!
WAM! BAM! BAM! BAM! BAM!
HEY! OPEN UP IN THERE!
HI, FIFI!
OH! ZAT SIL-LEE BOY AGAIN!
HA, HA, HA, HA, HA, HA, HA, HA!
HUH?
YOU! YOU, YOU, YOU, YOU, YOU! YOU ARE FON-NEE!
M-ME?
YOU! YOU ALWAYS ACT CRA-ZEE, HA-HA!

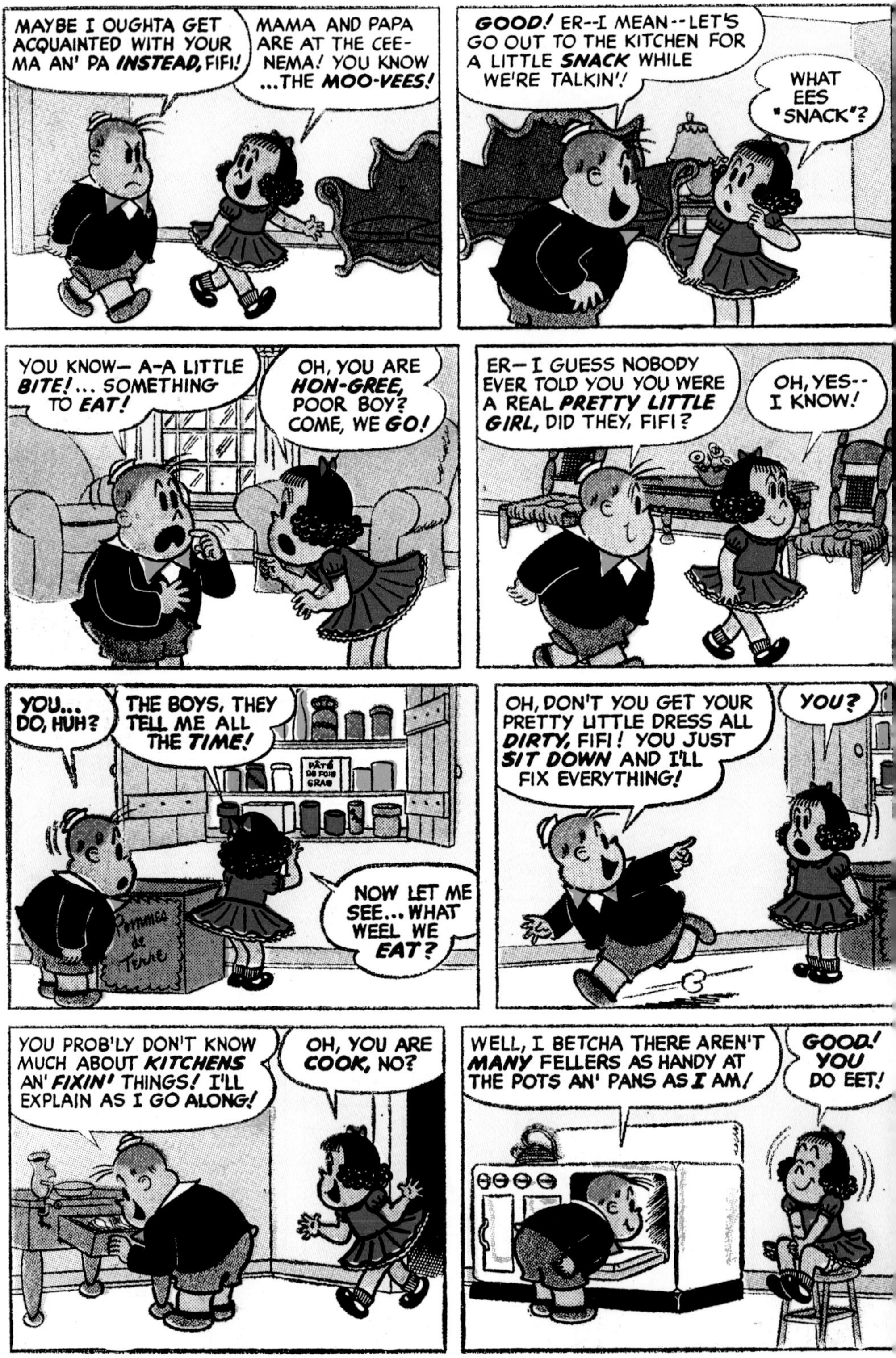
MAYBE I OUGHTA GET ACQUAINTED WITH YOUR MA AN' PA *INSTEAD,* FIFI!
MAMA AND PAPA ARE AT THE CEE-NEMA! YOU KNOW ...THE *MOO-VEES!*
GOOD! ER--I MEAN--LET'S GO OUT TO THE KITCHEN FOR A LITTLE *SNACK* WHILE WE'RE TALKIN'!
WHAT EES "SNACK"?
YOU KNOW— A-A LITTLE *BITE!*... SOMETHING TO *EAT!*
OH, YOU ARE *HON-GREE,* POOR BOY? COME, WE *GO!*
ER— I GUESS NOBODY EVER TOLD YOU YOU WERE A REAL *PRETTY LITTLE GIRL,* DID THEY, FIFI?
OH, YES-- I KNOW!
YOU... DO, HUH?
THE BOYS, THEY TELL ME ALL THE *TIME!*
NOW LET ME SEE... WHAT WEEL WE *EAT?*
Pommes de Terre
OH, DON'T YOU GET YOUR PRETTY LITTLE DRESS ALL *DIRTY,* FIFI! YOU JUST *SIT DOWN* AND I'LL FIX EVERYTHING!
YOU?
YOU PROB'LY DON'T KNOW MUCH ABOUT *KITCHENS* AN' *FIXIN'* THINGS! I'LL EXPLAIN AS I GO ALONG!
OH, YOU ARE *COOK,* NO?
WELL, I BETCHA THERE AREN'T *MANY* FELLERS AS HANDY AT THE POTS AN' PANS AS *I* AM!
GOOD! YOU DO EET!

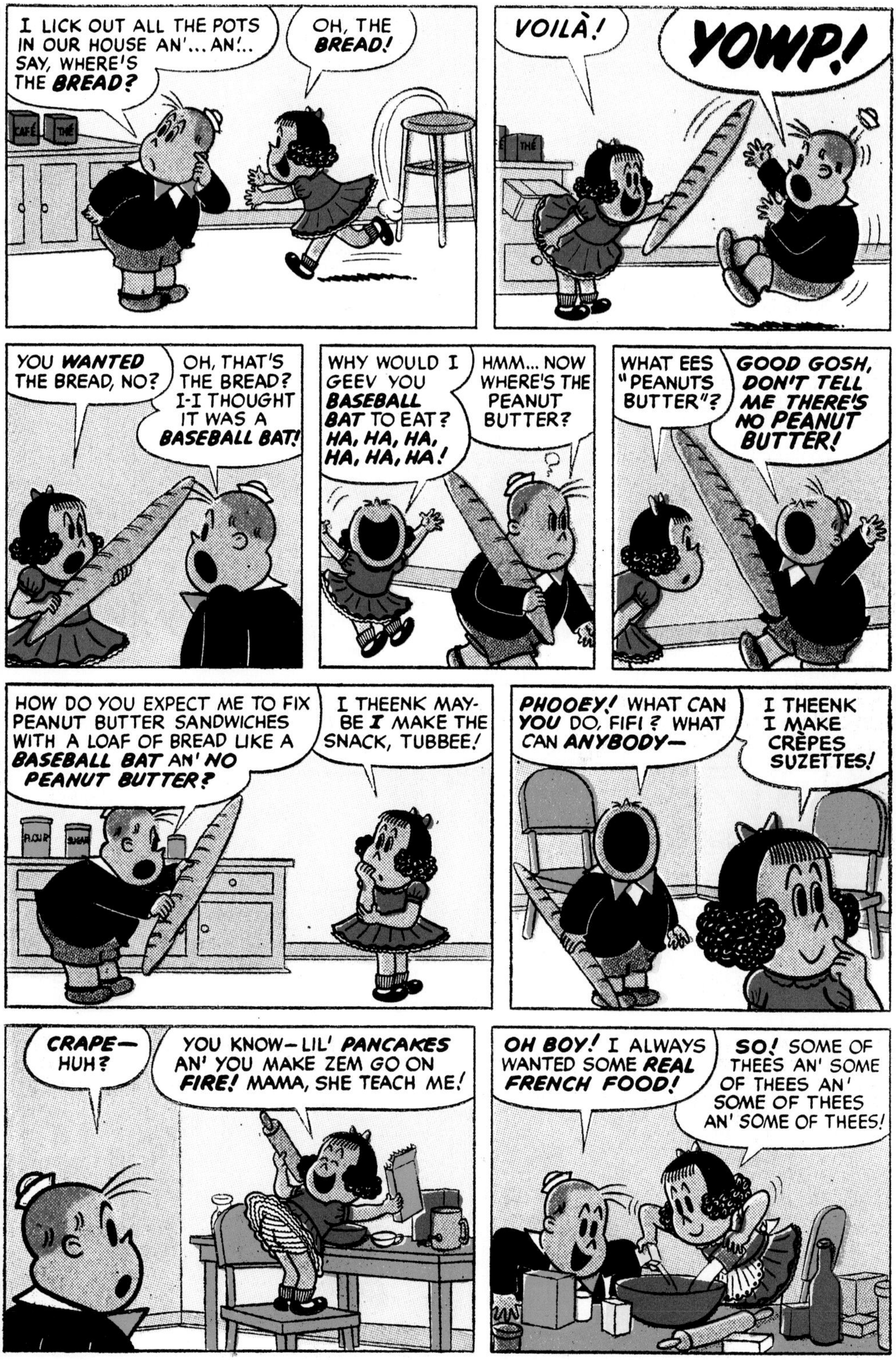
I LICK OUT ALL THE POTS IN OUR HOUSE AN'... AN'... SAY, WHERE'S THE BREAD?
OH, THE BREAD!
CAFÉ
THÉ
VOILÀ!
YOWP!
THÉ
YOU WANTED THE BREAD, NO?
OH, THAT'S THE BREAD? I-I THOUGHT IT WAS A BASEBALL BAT!
WHY WOULD I GEEV YOU BASEBALL BAT TO EAT? HA, HA, HA, HA, HA, HA!
HMM... NOW WHERE'S THE PEANUT BUTTER?
WHAT EES "PEANUTS BUTTER"?
GOOD GOSH, DON'T TELL ME THERE'S NO PEANUT BUTTER!
HOW DO YOU EXPECT ME TO FIX PEANUT BUTTER SANDWICHES WITH A LOAF OF BREAD LIKE A BASEBALL BAT AN' NO PEANUT BUTTER?
FLOUR
SUGAR
I THEENK MAY-BE I MAKE THE SNACK, TUBBEE!
PHOOEY! WHAT CAN YOU DO, FIFI? WHAT CAN ANYBODY—
I THEENK I MAKE CRÈPES SUZETTES!
CRAPE— HUH?
YOU KNOW—LIL' PANCAKES AN' YOU MAKE ZEM GO ON FIRE! MAMA, SHE TEACH ME!
OH BOY! I ALWAYS WANTED SOME REAL FRENCH FOOD!
SO! SOME OF THEES AN' SOME OF THEES AN' SOME OF THEES AN' SOME OF THEES!

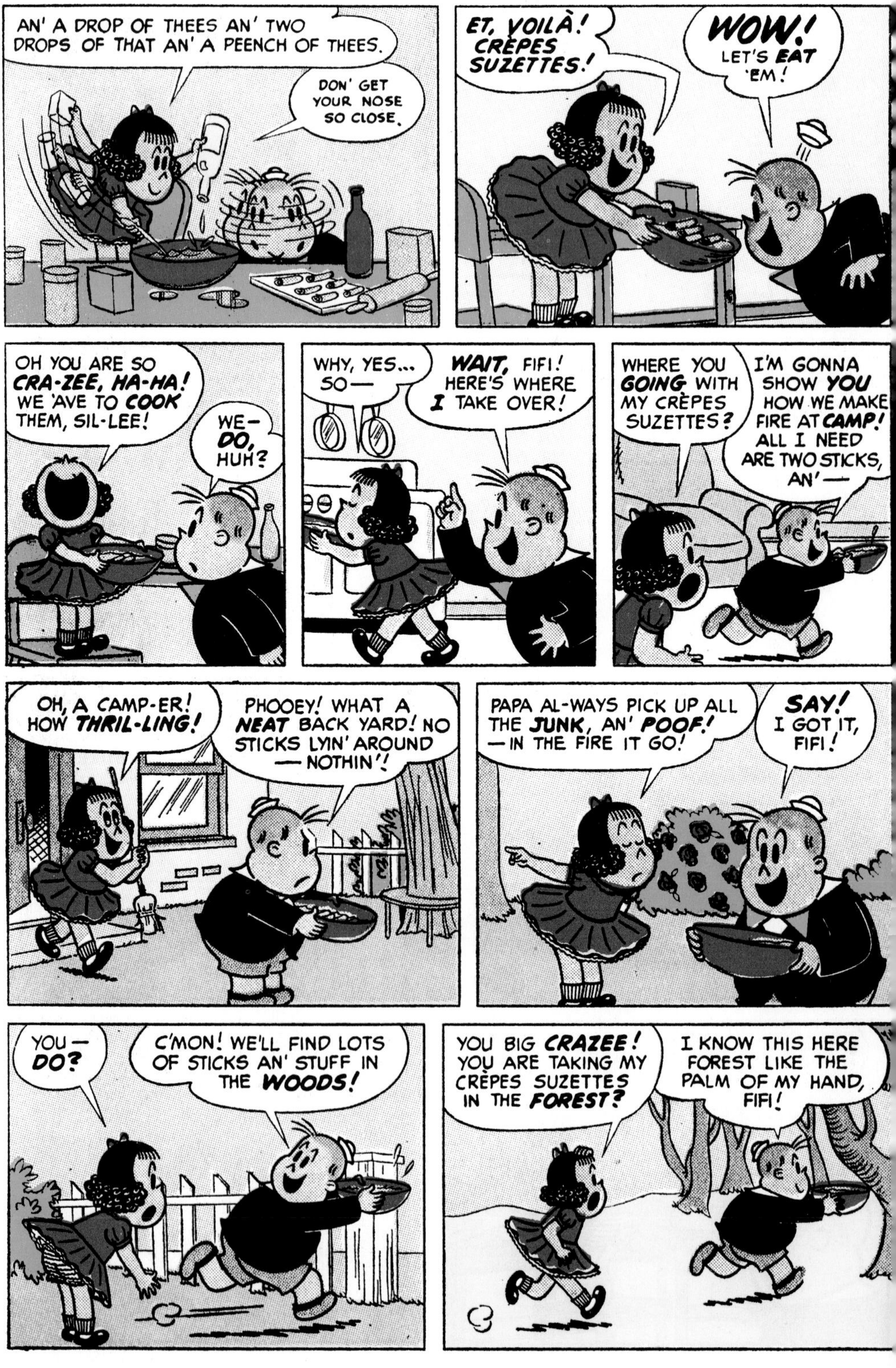
AN' A DROP OF THEES AN' TWO DROPS OF THAT AN' A PEENCH OF THEES.
DON' GET YOUR NOSE SO CLOSE.
ET, VOILÀ! CRÈPES SUZETTES!
WOW! LET'S EAT 'EM!
OH YOU ARE SO CRA-ZEE, HA-HA! WE 'AVE TO COOK THEM, SIL-LEE!
WE—DO, HUH?
WHY, YES... SO—
WAIT, FIFI! HERE'S WHERE I TAKE OVER!
WHERE YOU GOING WITH MY CRÈPES SUZETTES?
I'M GONNA SHOW YOU HOW WE MAKE FIRE AT CAMP! ALL I NEED ARE TWO STICKS, AN'—
OH, A CAMP-ER! HOW THRIL-LING!
PHOOEY! WHAT A NEAT BACK YARD! NO STICKS LYIN' AROUND —NOTHIN'!
PAPA AL-WAYS PICK UP ALL THE JUNK, AN' POOF! —IN THE FIRE IT GO!
SAY! I GOT IT, FIFI!
YOU—DO?
C'MON! WE'LL FIND LOTS OF STICKS AN' STUFF IN THE WOODS!
YOU BIG CRAZEE! YOU ARE TAKING MY CRÈPES SUZETTES IN THE FOREST?
I KNOW THIS HERE FOREST LIKE THE PALM OF MY HAND, FIFI!

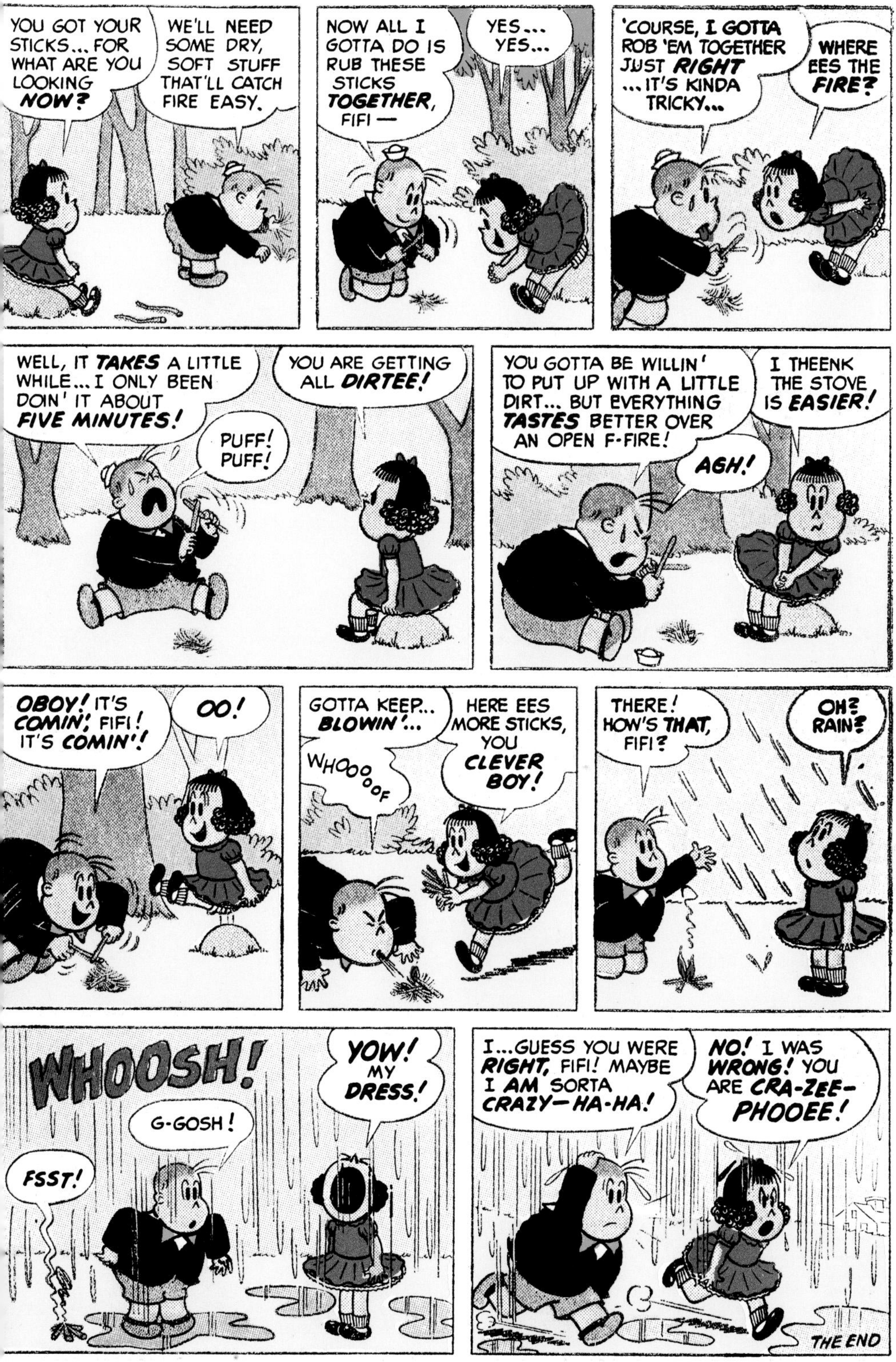

YOU GOT YOUR STICKS... FOR WHAT ARE YOU LOOKING NOW?
WE'LL NEED SOME DRY, SOFT STUFF THAT'LL CATCH FIRE EASY.
NOW ALL I GOTTA DO IS RUB THESE STICKS TOGETHER, FIFI —
YES... YES...
'COURSE, I GOTTA ROB 'EM TOGETHER JUST RIGHT ...IT'S KINDA TRICKY...
WHERE EES THE FIRE?
WELL, IT TAKES A LITTLE WHILE... I ONLY BEEN DOIN' IT ABOUT FIVE MINUTES!
PUFF! PUFF!
YOU ARE GETTING ALL DIRTEE!
YOU GOTTA BE WILLIN' TO PUT UP WITH A LITTLE DIRT... BUT EVERYTHING TASTES BETTER OVER AN OPEN F-FIRE!
AGH!
I THEENK THE STOVE IS EASIER!
OBOY! IT'S COMIN'; FIFI! IT'S COMIN'!
OO!
GOTTA KEEP... BLOWIN'...
WHOOOOOF
HERE EES MORE STICKS, YOU CLEVER BOY!
THERE! HOW'S THAT, FIFI?
OH? RAIN?
WHOOSH!
G-GOSH!
FSST!
YOW! MY DRESS!
I...GUESS YOU WERE RIGHT, FIFI! MAYBE I AM SORTA CRAZY—HA-HA!
NO! I WAS WRONG! YOU ARE CRA-ZEE-PHOOEE!
THE END

Little Lulu Littl
lu Little Lulu Li
Little Lulu Littl
lu Little Lulu Li
Little Lulu Littl
lu Little Lulu Li
Little Lulu Littl

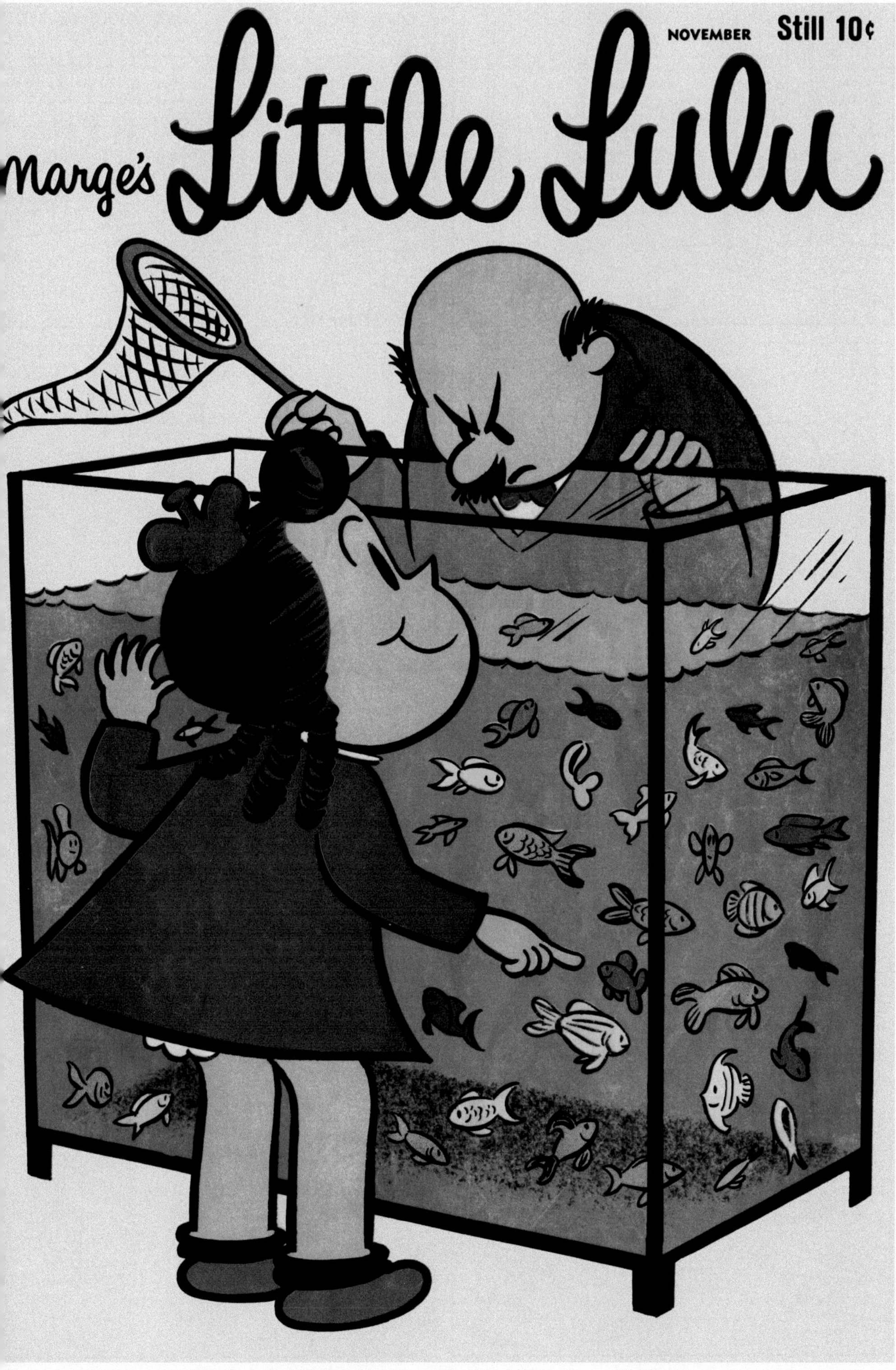
NOVEMBER
Still 10¢
Marge's
Little Lulu

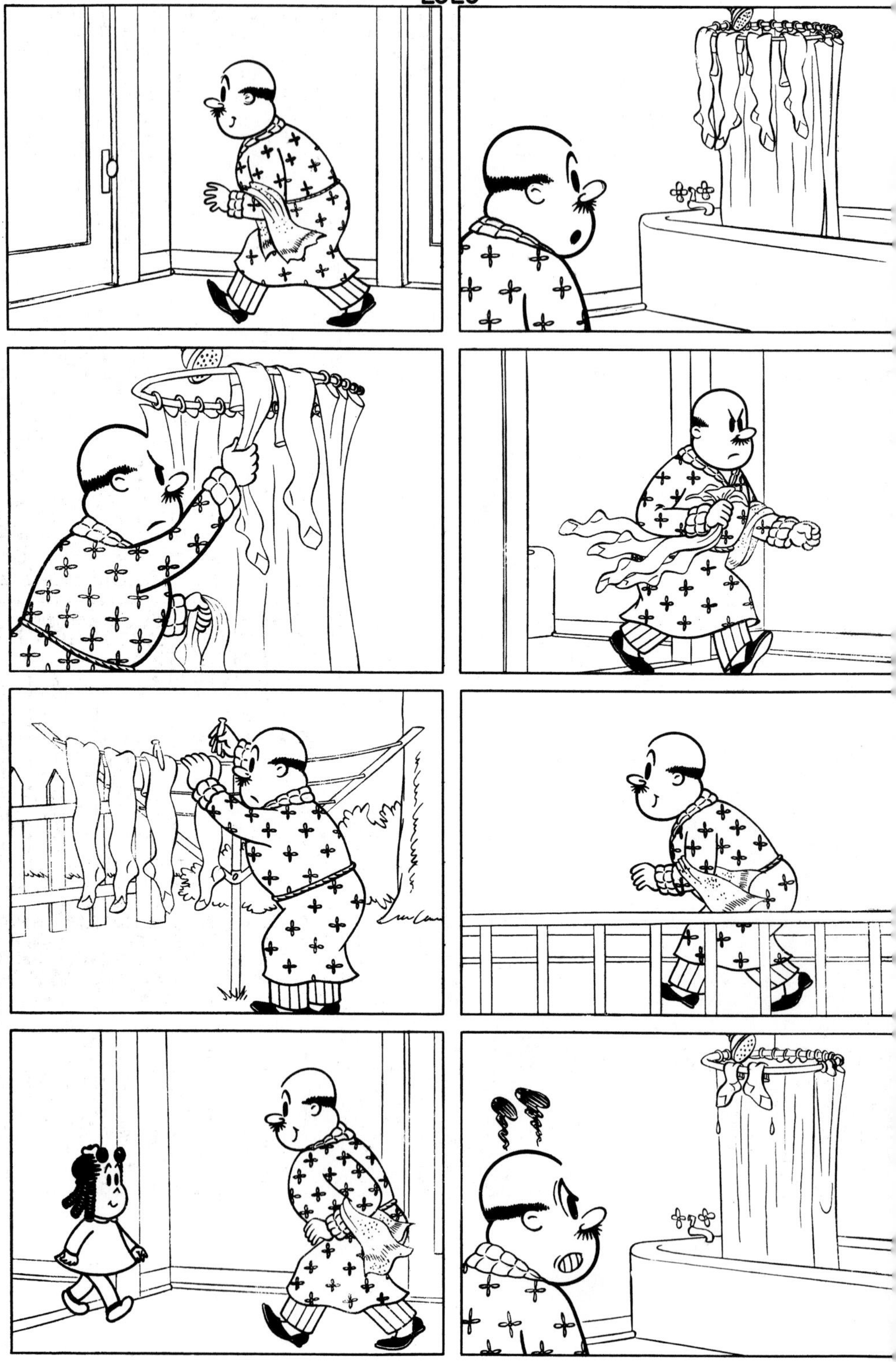

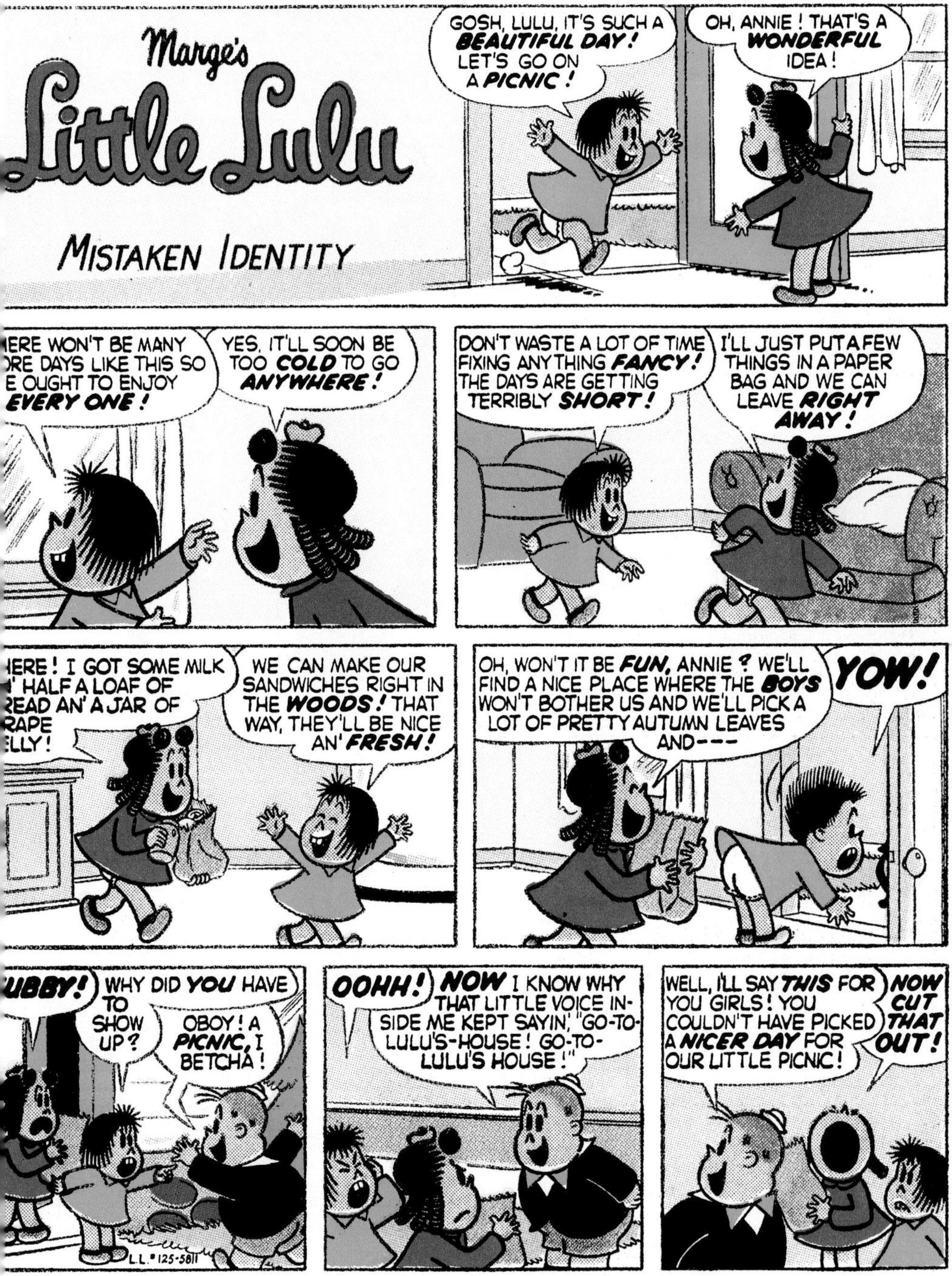
Marge's Little Lulu
MISTAKEN IDENTITY
GOSH, LULU, IT'S SUCH A BEAUTIFUL DAY! LET'S GO ON A PICNIC!
OH, ANNIE! THAT'S A WONDERFUL IDEA!
HERE WON'T BE MANY ORE DAYS LIKE THIS SO E OUGHT TO ENJOY EVERY ONE!
YES, IT'LL SOON BE TOO COLD TO GO ANYWHERE!
DON'T WASTE A LOT OF TIME FIXING ANYTHING FANCY! THE DAYS ARE GETTING TERRIBLY SHORT!
I'LL JUST PUT A FEW THINGS IN A PAPER BAG AND WE CAN LEAVE RIGHT AWAY!
HERE! I GOT SOME MILK ' HALF A LOAF OF READ AN' A JAR OF RAPE ELLY!
WE CAN MAKE OUR SANDWICHES RIGHT IN THE WOODS! THAT WAY, THEY'LL BE NICE AN' FRESH!
OH, WON'T IT BE FUN, ANNIE? WE'LL FIND A NICE PLACE WHERE THE BOYS WON'T BOTHER US AND WE'LL PICK A LOT OF PRETTY AUTUMN LEAVES AND---
YOW!
UBBY!
WHY DID YOU HAVE TO SHOW UP?
OBOY! A PICNIC, I BETCHA!
L.L.#125-5811
OOHH!
NOW I KNOW WHY THAT LITTLE VOICE INSIDE ME KEPT SAYIN', "GO-TO-LULU'S-HOUSE! GO-TO-LULU'S HOUSE!"
WELL, I'LL SAY THIS FOR YOU GIRLS! YOU COULDN'T HAVE PICKED A NICER DAY FOR OUR LITTLE PICNIC!
NOW CUT THAT OUT!

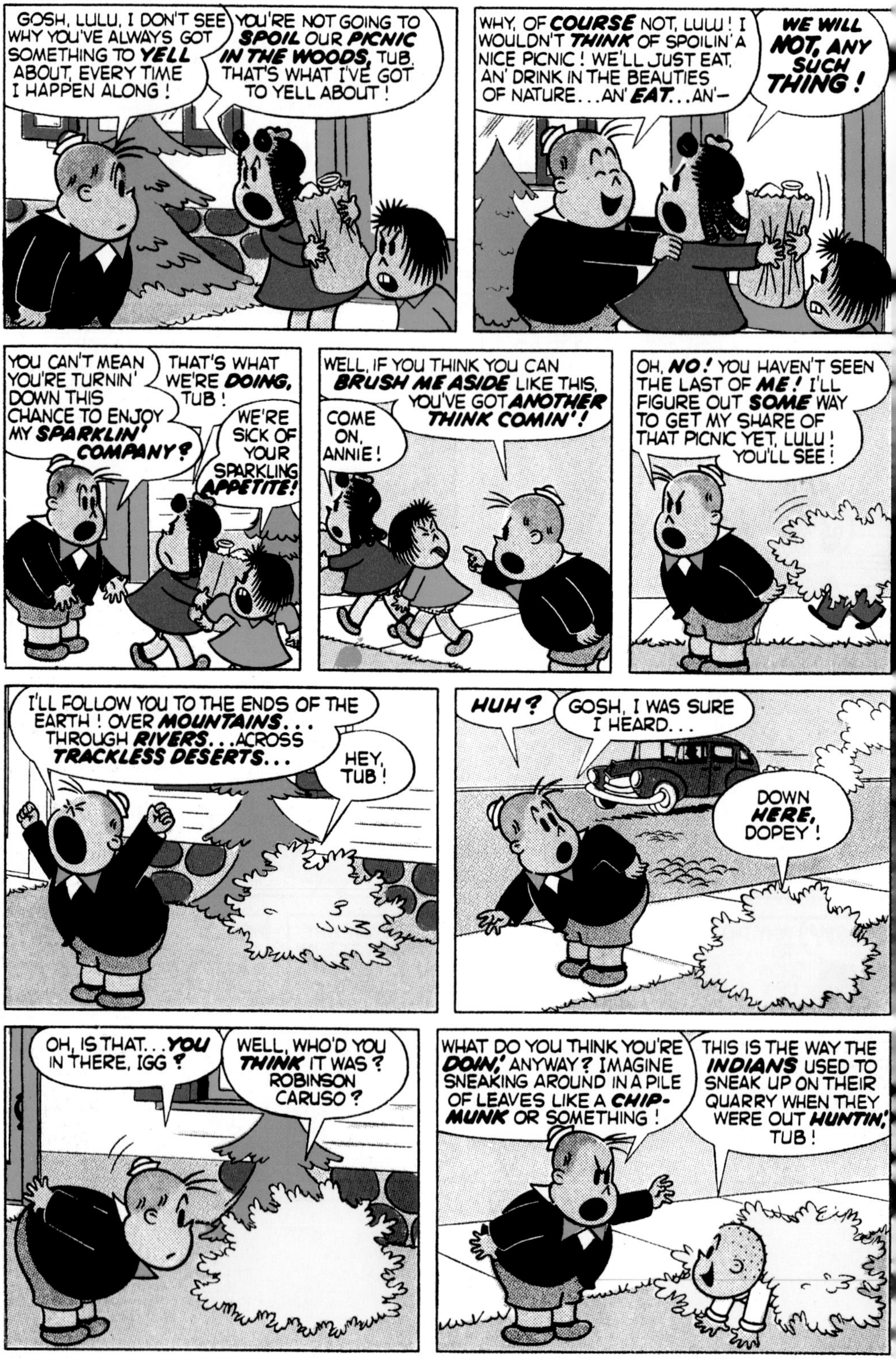

GOSH, LULU, I DON'T SEE WHY YOU'VE ALWAYS GOT SOMETHING TO YELL ABOUT, EVERY TIME I HAPPEN ALONG!
YOU'RE NOT GOING TO SPOIL OUR PICNIC IN THE WOODS, TUB. THAT'S WHAT I'VE GOT TO YELL ABOUT!
WHY, OF COURSE NOT, LULU! I WOULDN'T THINK OF SPOILIN' A NICE PICNIC! WE'LL JUST EAT, AN' DRINK IN THE BEAUTIES OF NATURE...AN' EAT...AN'—
WE WILL NOT, ANY SUCH THING!
YOU CAN'T MEAN YOU'RE TURNIN' DOWN THIS CHANCE TO ENJOY MY SPARKLIN' COMPANY?
THAT'S WHAT WE'RE DOING, TUB!
WE'RE SICK OF YOUR SPARKLING APPETITE!
WELL, IF YOU THINK YOU CAN BRUSH ME ASIDE LIKE THIS, YOU'VE GOT ANOTHER THINK COMIN'!
COME ON, ANNIE!
OH, NO! YOU HAVEN'T SEEN THE LAST OF ME! I'LL FIGURE OUT SOME WAY TO GET MY SHARE OF THAT PICNIC YET, LULU! YOU'LL SEE!
I'LL FOLLOW YOU TO THE ENDS OF THE EARTH! OVER MOUNTAINS... THROUGH RIVERS...ACROSS TRACKLESS DESERTS...
HEY, TUB!
HUH?
GOSH, I WAS SURE I HEARD...
DOWN HERE, DOPEY!
OH, IS THAT...YOU IN THERE, IGG?
WELL, WHO'D YOU THINK IT WAS? ROBINSON CARUSO?
WHAT DO YOU THINK YOU'RE DOIN,' ANYWAY? IMAGINE SNEAKING AROUND IN A PILE OF LEAVES LIKE A CHIP-MUNK OR SOMETHING!
THIS IS THE WAY THE INDIANS USED TO SNEAK UP ON THEIR QUARRY WHEN THEY WERE OUT HUNTIN,' TUB!

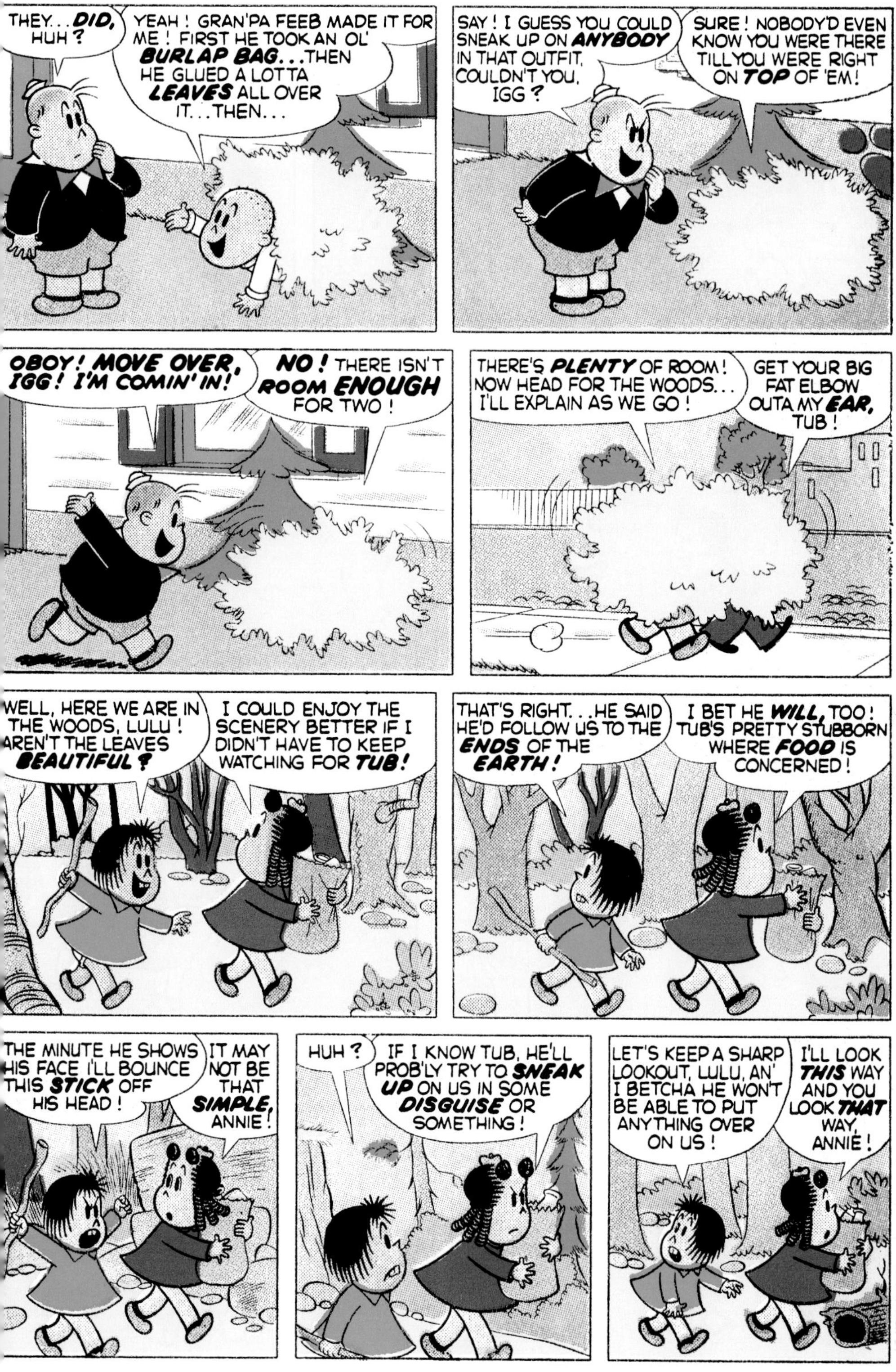
THEY...DID, HUH?
YEAH! GRAN'PA FEEB MADE IT FOR ME! FIRST HE TOOK AN OL' BURLAP BAG...THEN HE GLUED A LOTTA LEAVES ALL OVER IT...THEN...
SAY! I GUESS YOU COULD SNEAK UP ON ANYBODY IN THAT OUTFIT, COULDN'T YOU, IGG?
SURE! NOBODY'D EVEN KNOW YOU WERE THERE TILL YOU WERE RIGHT ON TOP OF 'EM!
OBOY! MOVE OVER, IGG! I'M COMIN' IN!
NO! THERE ISN'T ROOM ENOUGH FOR TWO!
THERE'S PLENTY OF ROOM! NOW HEAD FOR THE WOODS... I'LL EXPLAIN AS WE GO!
GET YOUR BIG FAT ELBOW OUTA MY EAR, TUB!
WELL, HERE WE ARE IN THE WOODS, LULU! AREN'T THE LEAVES BEAUTIFUL?
I COULD ENJOY THE SCENERY BETTER IF I DIDN'T HAVE TO KEEP WATCHING FOR TUB!
THAT'S RIGHT...HE SAID HE'D FOLLOW US TO THE ENDS OF THE EARTH!
I BET HE WILL, TOO! TUB'S PRETTY STUBBORN WHERE FOOD IS CONCERNED!
THE MINUTE HE SHOWS HIS FACE I'LL BOUNCE THIS STICK OFF HIS HEAD!
IT MAY NOT BE THAT SIMPLE, ANNIE!
HUH?
IF I KNOW TUB, HE'LL PROB'LY TRY TO SNEAK UP ON US IN SOME DISGUISE OR SOMETHING!
LET'S KEEP A SHARP LOOKOUT, LULU, AN' I BETCHA HE WON'T BE ABLE TO PUT ANYTHING OVER ON US!
I'LL LOOK THIS WAY AND YOU LOOK THAT WAY, ANNIE!

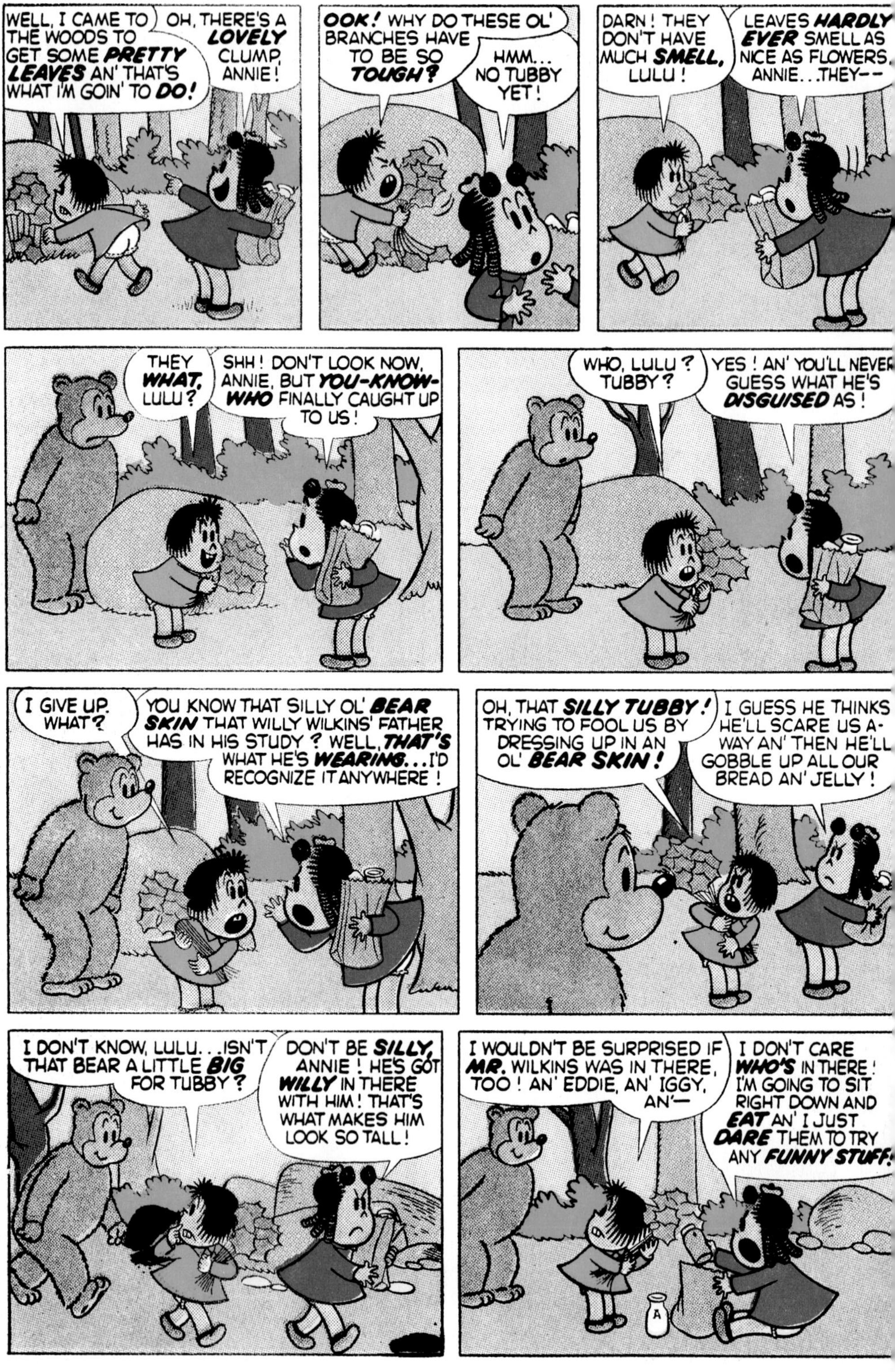
WELL, I CAME TO THE WOODS TO GET SOME PRETTY LEAVES AN' THAT'S WHAT I'M GOIN' TO DO!
OH, THERE'S A LOVELY CLUMP, ANNIE!
OOK! WHY DO THESE OL' BRANCHES HAVE TO BE SO TOUGH?
HMM... NO TUBBY YET!
DARN! THEY DON'T HAVE MUCH SMELL, LULU!
LEAVES HARDLY EVER SMELL AS NICE AS FLOWERS, ANNIE...THEY--
THEY WHAT, LULU?
SHH! DON'T LOOK NOW, ANNIE, BUT YOU-KNOW-WHO FINALLY CAUGHT UP TO US!
WHO, LULU? TUBBY?
YES! AN' YOU'LL NEVER GUESS WHAT HE'S DISGUISED AS!
I GIVE UP. WHAT?
YOU KNOW THAT SILLY OL' BEAR SKIN THAT WILLY WILKINS' FATHER HAS IN HIS STUDY? WELL, THAT'S WHAT HE'S WEARING...I'D RECOGNIZE IT ANYWHERE!
OH, THAT SILLY TUBBY! TRYING TO FOOL US BY DRESSING UP IN AN OL' BEAR SKIN!
I GUESS HE THINKS HE'LL SCARE US AWAY AN' THEN HE'LL GOBBLE UP ALL OUR BREAD AN' JELLY!
I DON'T KNOW, LULU...ISN'T THAT BEAR A LITTLE BIG FOR TUBBY?
DON'T BE SILLY, ANNIE! HE'S GOT WILLY IN THERE WITH HIM! THAT'S WHAT MAKES HIM LOOK SO TALL!
I WOULDN'T BE SURPRISED IF MR. WILKINS WAS IN THERE, TOO! AN' EDDIE, AN' IGGY, AN'—
I DON'T CARE WHO'S IN THERE! I'M GOING TO SIT RIGHT DOWN AND EAT AN' I JUST DARE THEM TO TRY ANY FUNNY STUFF!

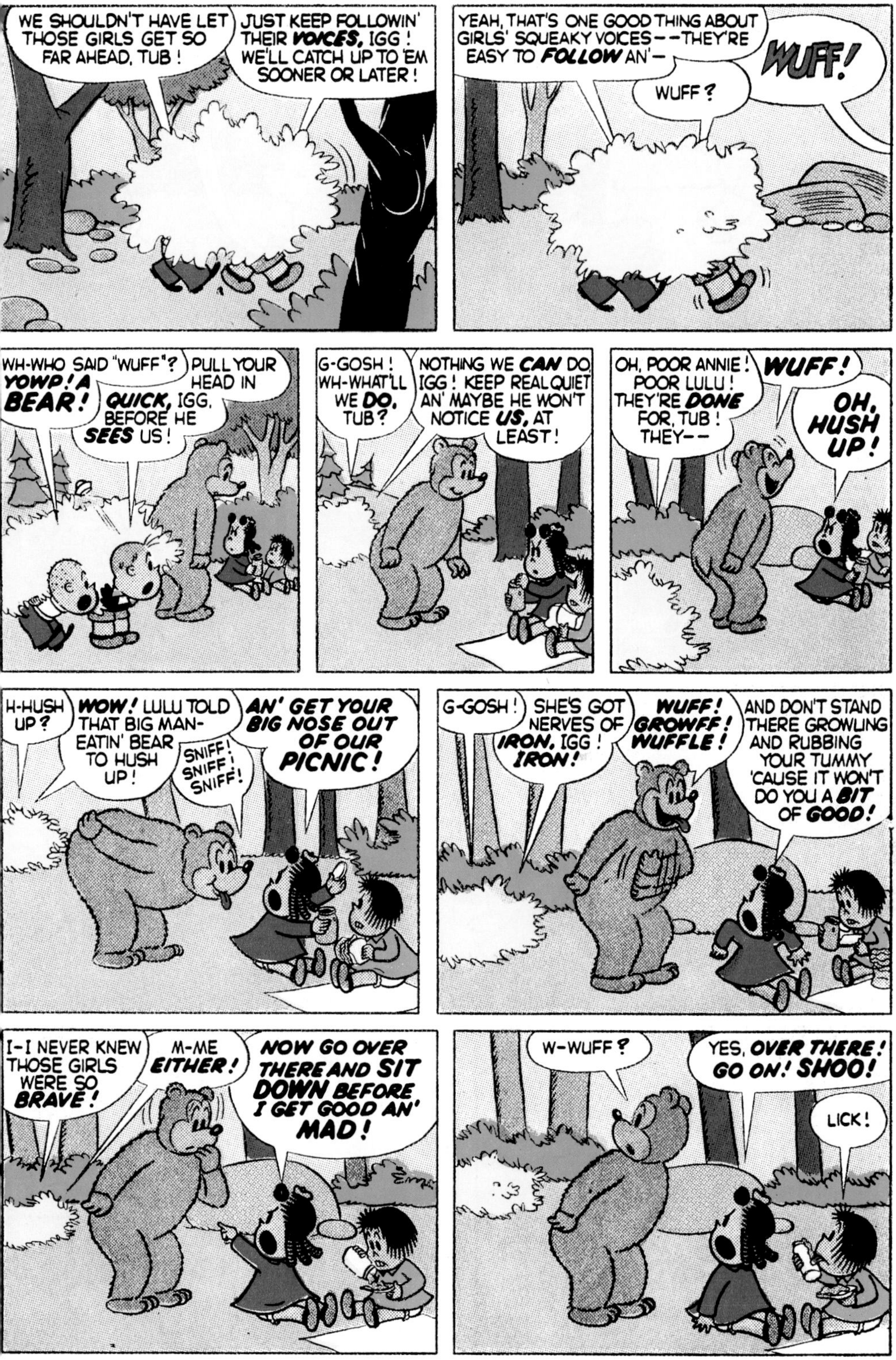
WE SHOULDN'T HAVE LET THOSE GIRLS GET SO FAR AHEAD, TUB!
JUST KEEP FOLLOWIN' THEIR VOICES, IGG! WE'LL CATCH UP TO 'EM SOONER OR LATER!
YEAH, THAT'S ONE GOOD THING ABOUT GIRLS' SQUEAKY VOICES--THEY'RE EASY TO FOLLOW AN'-
WUFF?
WUFF!
WH-WHO SAID "WUFF"? YOWP! A BEAR!
PULL YOUR HEAD IN QUICK, IGG, BEFORE HE SEES US!
G-GOSH! WH-WHAT'LL WE DO, TUB?
NOTHING WE CAN DO, IGG! KEEP REAL QUIET AN' MAYBE HE WON'T NOTICE US, AT LEAST!
OH, POOR ANNIE! POOR LULU! THEY'RE DONE FOR, TUB! THEY--
WUFF!
OH, HUSH UP!
H-HUSH UP?
WOW! LULU TOLD THAT BIG MAN-EATIN' BEAR TO HUSH UP!
SNIFF! SNIFF! SNIFF!
AN' GET YOUR BIG NOSE OUT OF OUR PICNIC!
G-GOSH!
SHE'S GOT NERVES OF IRON, IGG! IRON!
WUFF! GROWFF! WUFFLE!
AND DON'T STAND THERE GROWLING AND RUBBING YOUR TUMMY 'CAUSE IT WON'T DO YOU A BIT OF GOOD!
I-I NEVER KNEW THOSE GIRLS WERE SO BRAVE!
M-ME EITHER!
NOW GO OVER THERE AND SIT DOWN BEFORE I GET GOOD AN' MAD!
W-WUFF?
YES, OVER THERE! GO ON! SHOO!
LICK!

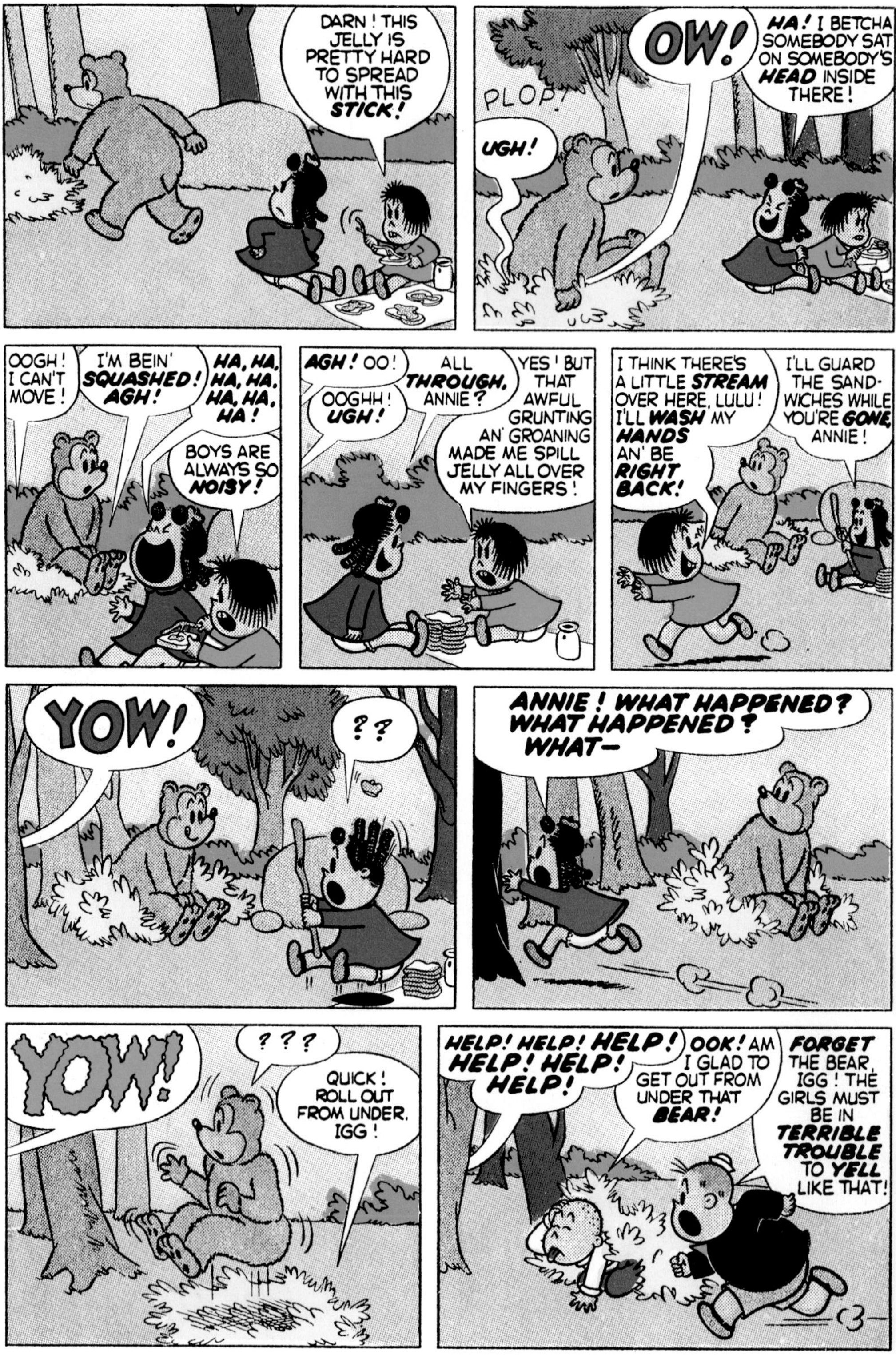
DARN ! THIS JELLY IS PRETTY HARD TO SPREAD WITH THIS STICK !
OW!
PLOP!
UGH!
HA! I BETCHA SOMEBODY SAT ON SOMEBODY'S HEAD INSIDE THERE !
OOGH ! I CAN'T MOVE !
I'M BEIN' SQUASHED ! AGH !
HA, HA, HA, HA, HA, HA, HA !
BOYS ARE ALWAYS SO NOISY !
AGH ! OO !
OOGHH ! UGH !
ALL THROUGH, ANNIE ?
YES ! BUT THAT AWFUL GRUNTING AN' GROANING MADE ME SPILL JELLY ALL OVER MY FINGERS !
I THINK THERE'S A LITTLE STREAM OVER HERE, LULU ! I'LL WASH MY HANDS AN' BE RIGHT BACK!
I'LL GUARD THE SAND-WICHES WHILE YOU'RE GONE, ANNIE !
YOW!
? ?
ANNIE ! WHAT HAPPENED ? WHAT HAPPENED ? WHAT—
YOW!
? ? ?
QUICK ! ROLL OUT FROM UNDER, IGG !
HELP! HELP! HELP! HELP! HELP! HELP!
OOK! AM I GLAD TO GET OUT FROM UNDER THAT BEAR !
FORGET THE BEAR, IGG ! THE GIRLS MUST BE IN TERRIBLE TROUBLE TO YELL LIKE THAT!

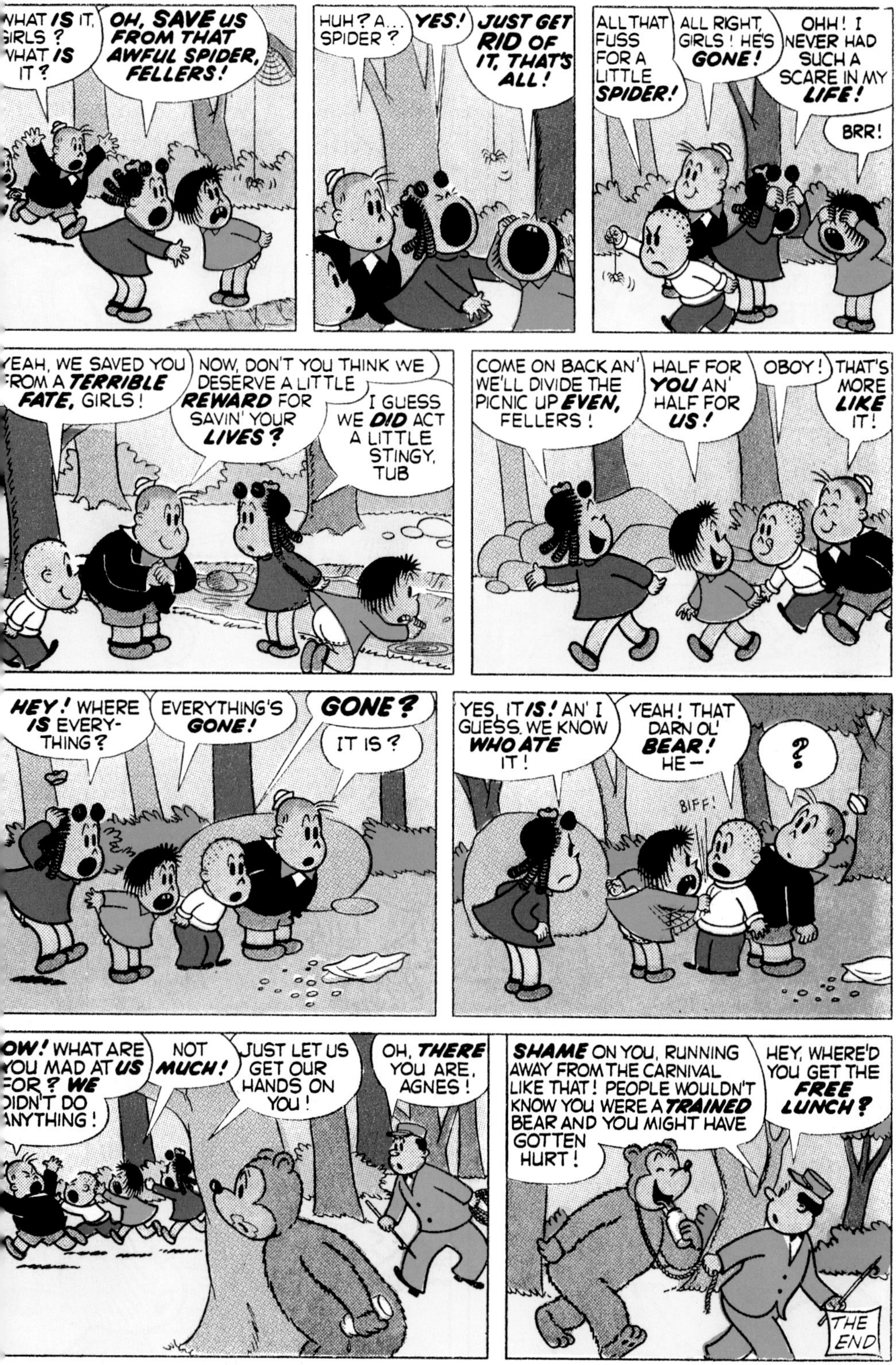

WHAT IS IT, GIRLS? WHAT IS IT?
OH, SAVE US FROM THAT AWFUL SPIDER, FELLERS!
HUH? A... SPIDER?
YES!
JUST GET RID OF IT, THAT'S ALL!
ALL THAT FUSS FOR A LITTLE SPIDER!
ALL RIGHT, GIRLS! HE'S GONE!
OHH! I NEVER HAD SUCH A SCARE IN MY LIFE!
BRR!
YEAH, WE SAVED YOU FROM A TERRIBLE FATE, GIRLS!
NOW, DON'T YOU THINK WE DESERVE A LITTLE REWARD FOR SAVIN' YOUR LIVES?
I GUESS WE DID ACT A LITTLE STINGY, TUB
COME ON BACK AN' WE'LL DIVIDE THE PICNIC UP EVEN, FELLERS!
HALF FOR YOU AN' HALF FOR US!
OBOY!
THAT'S MORE LIKE IT!
HEY! WHERE IS EVERYTHING?
EVERYTHING'S GONE!
GONE?
IT IS?
YES, IT IS! AN' I GUESS WE KNOW WHO ATE IT!
YEAH! THAT DARN OL' BEAR! HE--
BIFF!
?
OW! WHAT ARE YOU MAD AT US FOR? WE DIDN'T DO ANYTHING!
NOT MUCH!
JUST LET US GET OUR HANDS ON YOU!
OH, THERE YOU ARE, AGNES!
SHAME ON YOU, RUNNING AWAY FROM THE CARNIVAL LIKE THAT! PEOPLE WOULDN'T KNOW YOU WERE A TRAINED BEAR AND YOU MIGHT HAVE GOTTEN HURT!
HEY, WHERE'D YOU GET THE FREE LUNCH?
THE END

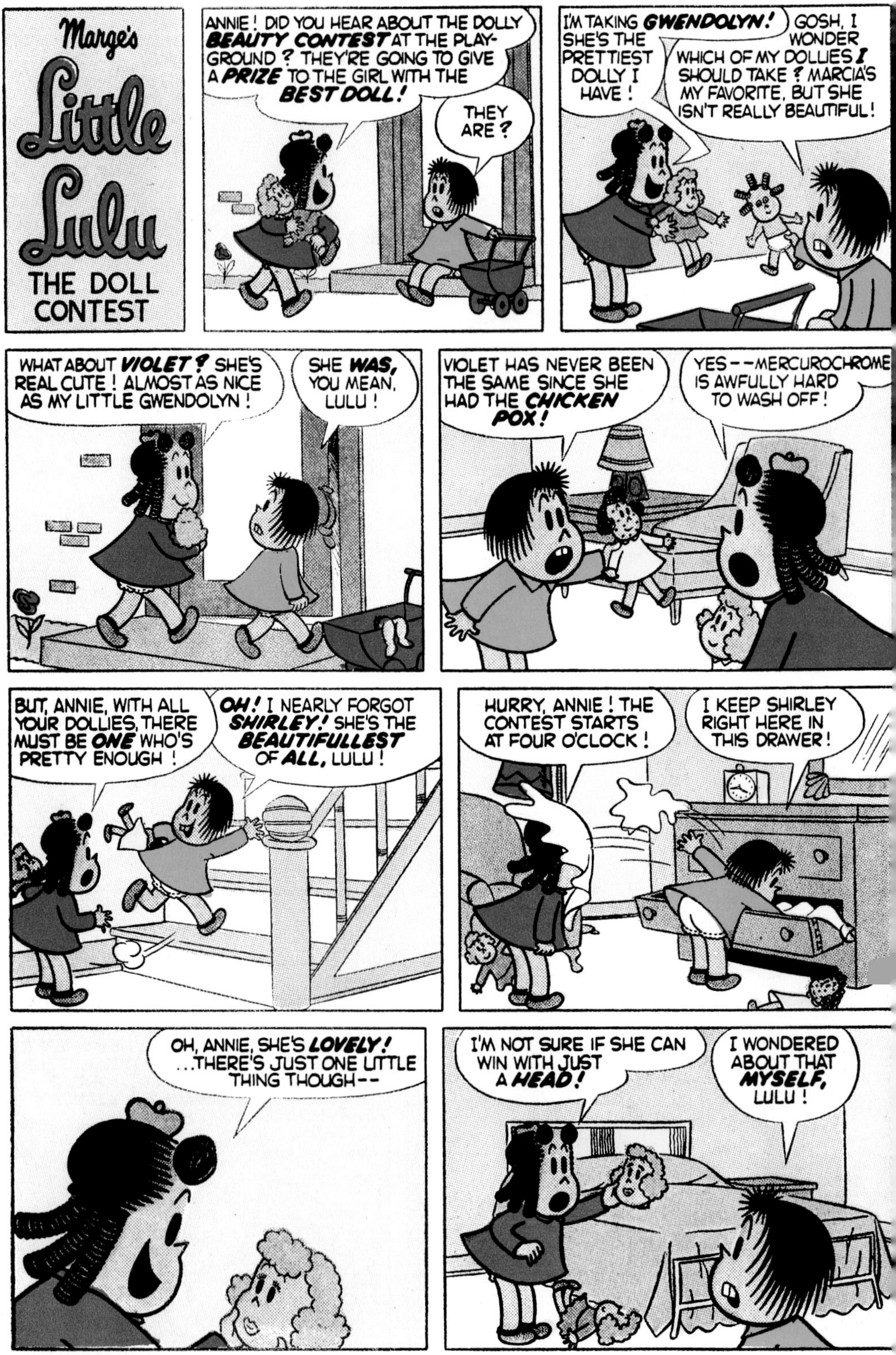
Marge's
Little Lulu
THE DOLL CONTEST
ANNIE! DID YOU HEAR ABOUT THE DOLLY BEAUTY CONTEST AT THE PLAYGROUND? THEY'RE GOING TO GIVE A PRIZE TO THE GIRL WITH THE BEST DOLL!
THEY ARE?
I'M TAKING GWENDOLYN! SHE'S THE PRETTIEST DOLLY I HAVE!
GOSH, I WONDER WHICH OF MY DOLLIES I SHOULD TAKE? MARCIA'S MY FAVORITE, BUT SHE ISN'T REALLY BEAUTIFUL!
WHAT ABOUT VIOLET? SHE'S REAL CUTE! ALMOST AS NICE AS MY LITTLE GWENDOLYN!
SHE WAS, YOU MEAN, LULU!
VIOLET HAS NEVER BEEN THE SAME SINCE SHE HAD THE CHICKEN POX!
YES--MERCUROCHROME IS AWFULLY HARD TO WASH OFF!
BUT, ANNIE, WITH ALL YOUR DOLLIES, THERE MUST BE ONE WHO'S PRETTY ENOUGH!
OH! I NEARLY FORGOT SHIRLEY! SHE'S THE BEAUTIFULLEST OF ALL, LULU!
HURRY, ANNIE! THE CONTEST STARTS AT FOUR O'CLOCK!
I KEEP SHIRLEY RIGHT HERE IN THIS DRAWER!
OH, ANNIE, SHE'S LOVELY! ...THERE'S JUST ONE LITTLE THING THOUGH--
I'M NOT SURE IF SHE CAN WIN WITH JUST A HEAD!
I WONDERED ABOUT THAT MYSELF, LULU!

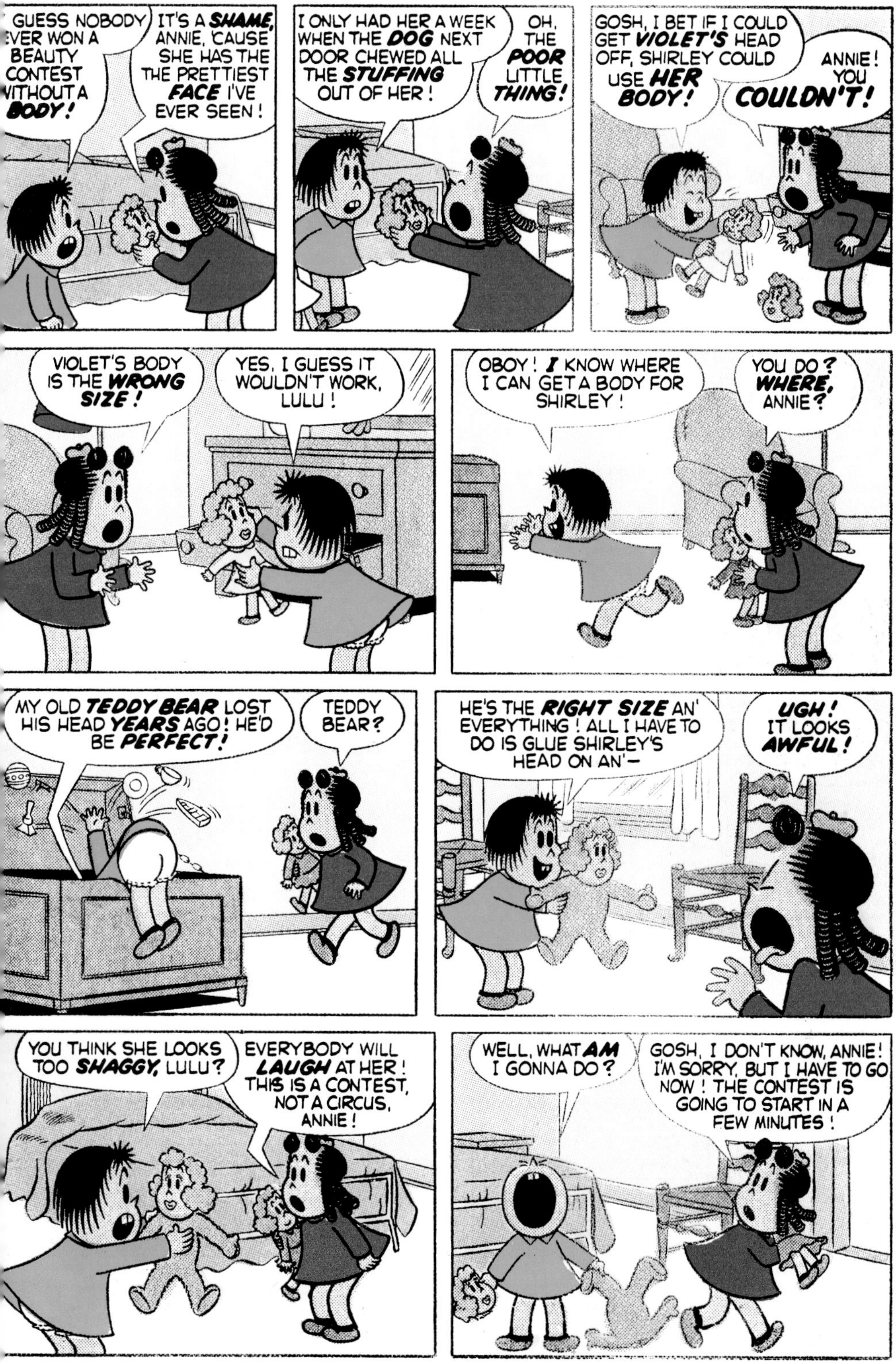
GUESS NOBODY VER WON A BEAUTY CONTEST VITHOUT A BODY!
IT'S A SHAME, ANNIE, 'CAUSE SHE HAS THE THE PRETTIEST FACE I'VE EVER SEEN!
I ONLY HAD HER A WEEK WHEN THE DOG NEXT DOOR CHEWED ALL THE STUFFING OUT OF HER!
OH, THE POOR LITTLE THING!
GOSH, I BET IF I COULD GET VIOLET'S HEAD OFF, SHIRLEY COULD USE HER BODY!
ANNIE! YOU COULDN'T!
VIOLET'S BODY IS THE WRONG SIZE!
YES, I GUESS IT WOULDN'T WORK, LULU!
OBOY! I KNOW WHERE I CAN GET A BODY FOR SHIRLEY!
YOU DO? WHERE, ANNIE?
MY OLD TEDDY BEAR LOST HIS HEAD YEARS AGO! HE'D BE PERFECT!
TEDDY BEAR?
HE'S THE RIGHT SIZE AN' EVERYTHING! ALL I HAVE TO DO IS GLUE SHIRLEY'S HEAD ON AN'—
UGH! IT LOOKS AWFUL!
YOU THINK SHE LOOKS TOO SHAGGY, LULU?
EVERYBODY WILL LAUGH AT HER! THIS IS A CONTEST, NOT A CIRCUS, ANNIE!
WELL, WHAT AM I GONNA DO?
GOSH, I DON'T KNOW, ANNIE! I'M SORRY, BUT I HAVE TO GO NOW! THE CONTEST IS GOING TO START IN A FEW MINUTES!

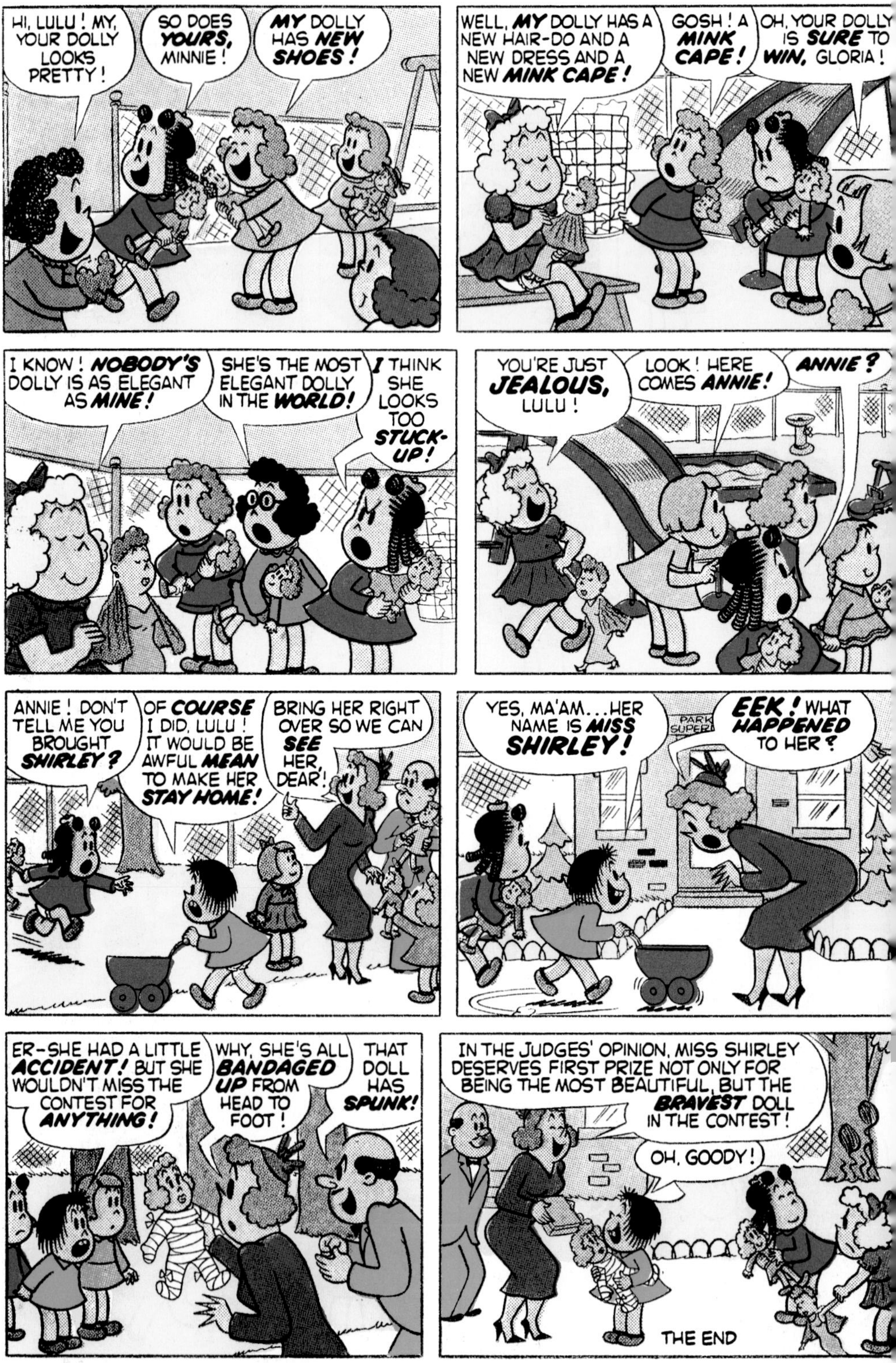
HI, LULU! MY, YOUR DOLLY LOOKS PRETTY!
SO DOES YOURS, MINNIE!
MY DOLLY HAS NEW SHOES!
WELL, MY DOLLY HAS A NEW HAIR-DO AND A NEW DRESS AND A NEW MINK CAPE!
GOSH! A MINK CAPE!
OH, YOUR DOLLY IS SURE TO WIN, GLORIA!
I KNOW! NOBODY'S DOLLY IS AS ELEGANT AS MINE!
SHE'S THE MOST ELEGANT DOLLY IN THE WORLD!
I THINK SHE LOOKS TOO STUCK-UP!
YOU'RE JUST JEALOUS, LULU!
LOOK! HERE COMES ANNIE!
ANNIE?
ANNIE! DON'T TELL ME YOU BROUGHT SHIRLEY?
OF COURSE I DID, LULU! IT WOULD BE AWFUL MEAN TO MAKE HER STAY HOME!
BRING HER RIGHT OVER SO WE CAN SEE HER, DEAR!
YES, MA'AM...HER NAME IS MISS SHIRLEY!
EEK! WHAT HAPPENED TO HER?
ER–SHE HAD A LITTLE ACCIDENT! BUT SHE WOULDN'T MISS THE CONTEST FOR ANYTHING!
WHY, SHE'S ALL BANDAGED UP FROM HEAD TO FOOT!
THAT DOLL HAS SPUNK!
IN THE JUDGES' OPINION, MISS SHIRLEY DESERVES FIRST PRIZE NOT ONLY FOR BEING THE MOST BEAUTIFUL, BUT THE BRAVEST DOLL IN THE CONTEST!
OH, GOODY!
THE END

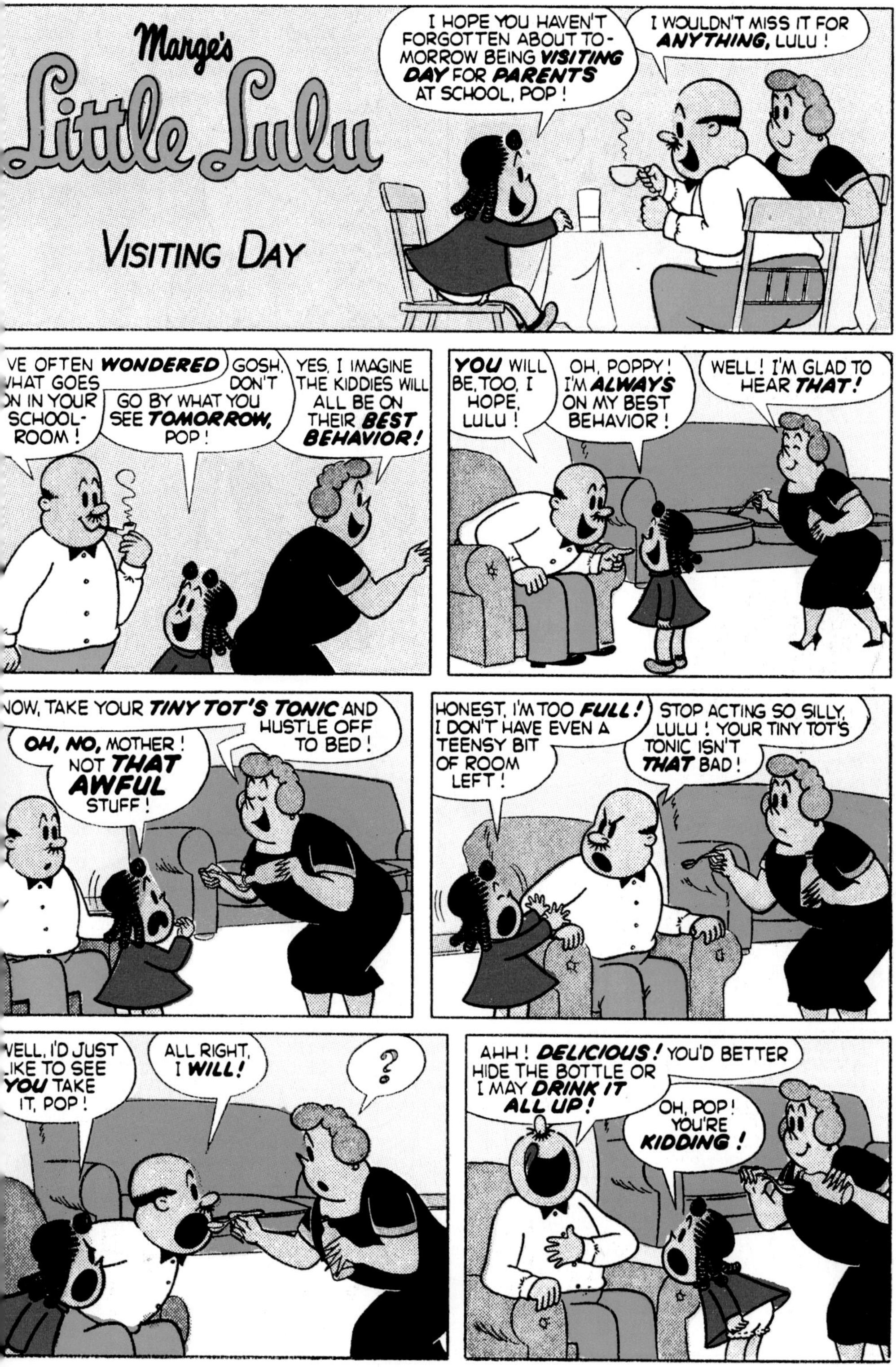
Marge's
Little Lulu
VISITING DAY
I HOPE YOU HAVEN'T FORGOTTEN ABOUT TO-MORROW BEING VISITING DAY FOR PARENTS AT SCHOOL, POP!
I WOULDN'T MISS IT FOR ANYTHING, LULU!
VE OFTEN WONDERED VHAT GOES ON IN YOUR SCHOOL-ROOM!
GOSH, DON'T GO BY WHAT YOU SEE TOMORROW, POP!
YES, I IMAGINE THE KIDDIES WILL ALL BE ON THEIR BEST BEHAVIOR!
YOU WILL BE, TOO, I HOPE, LULU!
OH, POPPY! I'M ALWAYS ON MY BEST BEHAVIOR!
WELL! I'M GLAD TO HEAR THAT!
OW, TAKE YOUR TINY TOT'S TONIC AND HUSTLE OFF TO BED!
OH, NO, MOTHER! NOT THAT AWFUL STUFF!
HONEST, I'M TOO FULL! I DON'T HAVE EVEN A TEENSY BIT OF ROOM LEFT!
STOP ACTING SO SILLY, LULU! YOUR TINY TOT'S TONIC ISN'T THAT BAD!
VELL, I'D JUST IKE TO SEE YOU TAKE IT, POP!
ALL RIGHT, I WILL!
?
AHH! DELICIOUS! YOU'D BETTER HIDE THE BOTTLE OR I MAY DRINK IT ALL UP!
OH, POP! YOU'RE KIDDING!

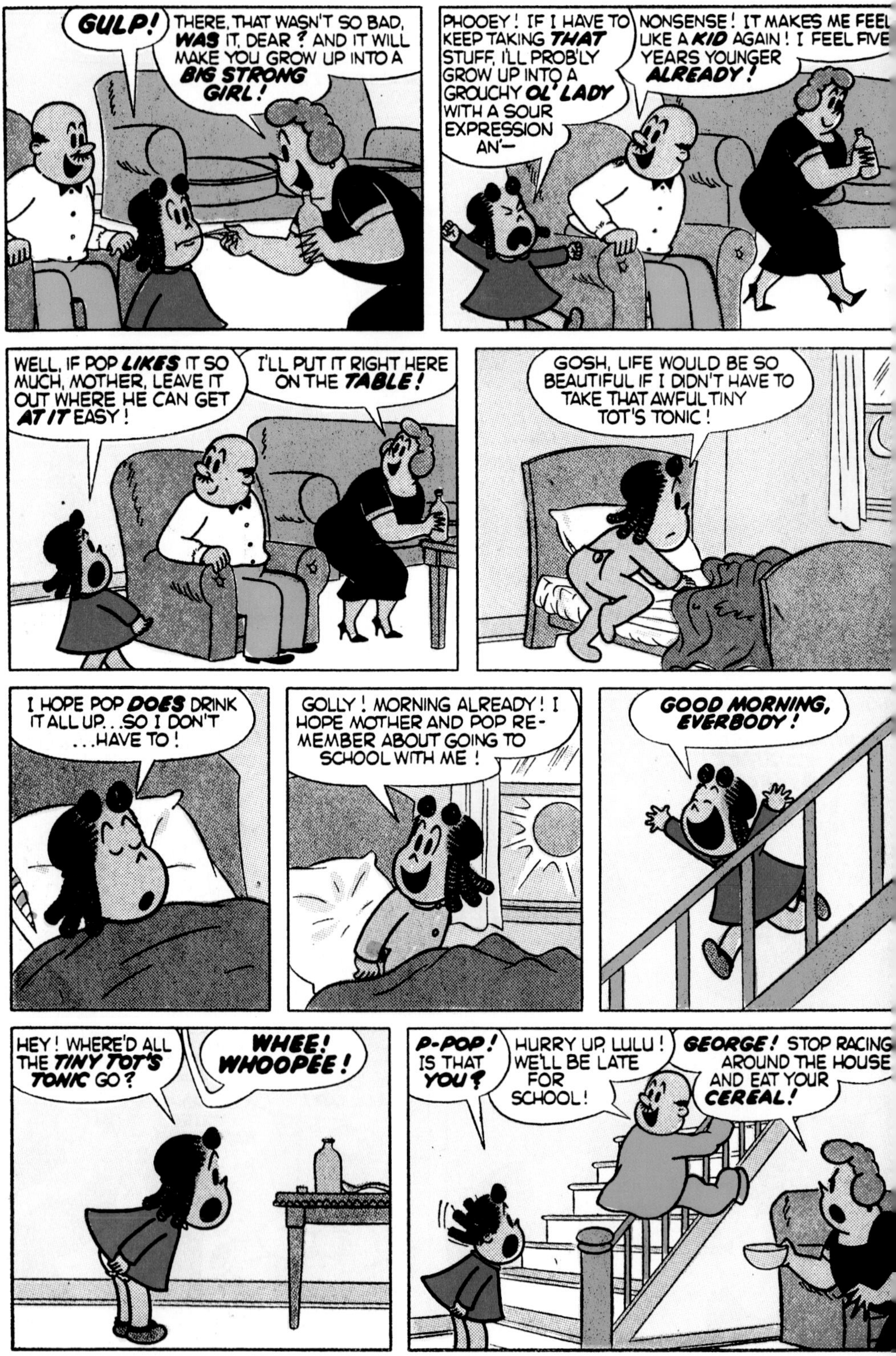
GULP!
THERE, THAT WASN'T SO BAD, WAS IT, DEAR? AND IT WILL MAKE YOU GROW UP INTO A BIG STRONG GIRL!
PHOOEY! IF I HAVE TO KEEP TAKING THAT STUFF, I'LL PROB'LY GROW UP INTO A GROUCHY OL' LADY WITH A SOUR EXPRESSION AN'—
NONSENSE! IT MAKES ME FEEL LIKE A KID AGAIN! I FEEL FIVE YEARS YOUNGER ALREADY!
WELL, IF POP LIKES IT SO MUCH, MOTHER, LEAVE IT OUT WHERE HE CAN GET AT IT EASY!
I'LL PUT IT RIGHT HERE ON THE TABLE!
GOSH, LIFE WOULD BE SO BEAUTIFUL IF I DIDN'T HAVE TO TAKE THAT AWFUL TINY TOT'S TONIC!
I HOPE POP DOES DRINK IT ALL UP...SO I DON'T ...HAVE TO!
GOLLY! MORNING ALREADY! I HOPE MOTHER AND POP RE-MEMBER ABOUT GOING TO SCHOOL WITH ME!
GOOD MORNING, EVERBODY!
HEY! WHERE'D ALL THE TINY TOT'S TONIC GO?
WHEE! WHOOPEE!
P-POP! IS THAT YOU?
HURRY UP, LULU! WE'LL BE LATE FOR SCHOOL!
GEORGE! STOP RACING AROUND THE HOUSE AND EAT YOUR CEREAL!

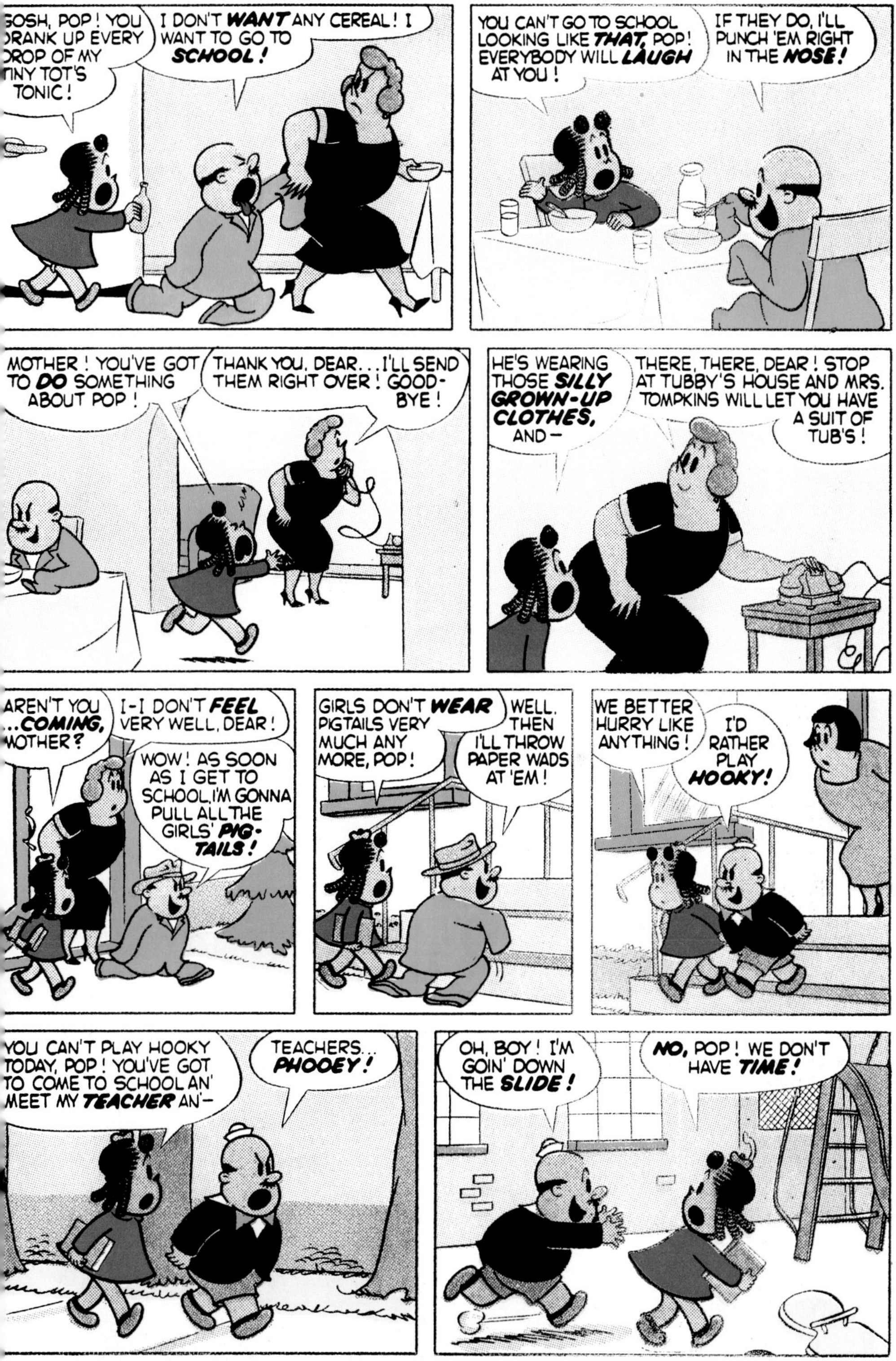
GOSH, POP! YOU DRANK UP EVERY DROP OF MY TINY TOT'S TONIC!
I DON'T WANT ANY CEREAL! I WANT TO GO TO SCHOOL!
YOU CAN'T GO TO SCHOOL LOOKING LIKE THAT, POP! EVERYBODY WILL LAUGH AT YOU!
IF THEY DO, I'LL PUNCH 'EM RIGHT IN THE NOSE!
MOTHER! YOU'VE GOT TO DO SOMETHING ABOUT POP!
THANK YOU, DEAR... I'LL SEND THEM RIGHT OVER! GOOD-BYE!
HE'S WEARING THOSE SILLY GROWN-UP CLOTHES, AND—
THERE, THERE, DEAR! STOP AT TUBBY'S HOUSE AND MRS. TOMPKINS WILL LET YOU HAVE A SUIT OF TUB'S!
AREN'T YOU ...COMING, MOTHER?
I-I DON'T FEEL VERY WELL, DEAR!
WOW! AS SOON AS I GET TO SCHOOL, I'M GONNA PULL ALL THE GIRLS' PIG-TAILS!
GIRLS DON'T WEAR PIGTAILS VERY MUCH ANY MORE, POP!
WELL, THEN I'LL THROW PAPER WADS AT 'EM!
WE BETTER HURRY LIKE ANYTHING!
I'D RATHER PLAY HOOKY!
YOU CAN'T PLAY HOOKY TODAY, POP! YOU'VE GOT TO COME TO SCHOOL AN' MEET MY TEACHER AN'—
TEACHERS... PHOOEY!
OH, BOY! I'M GOIN' DOWN THE SLIDE!
NO, POP! WE DON'T HAVE TIME!

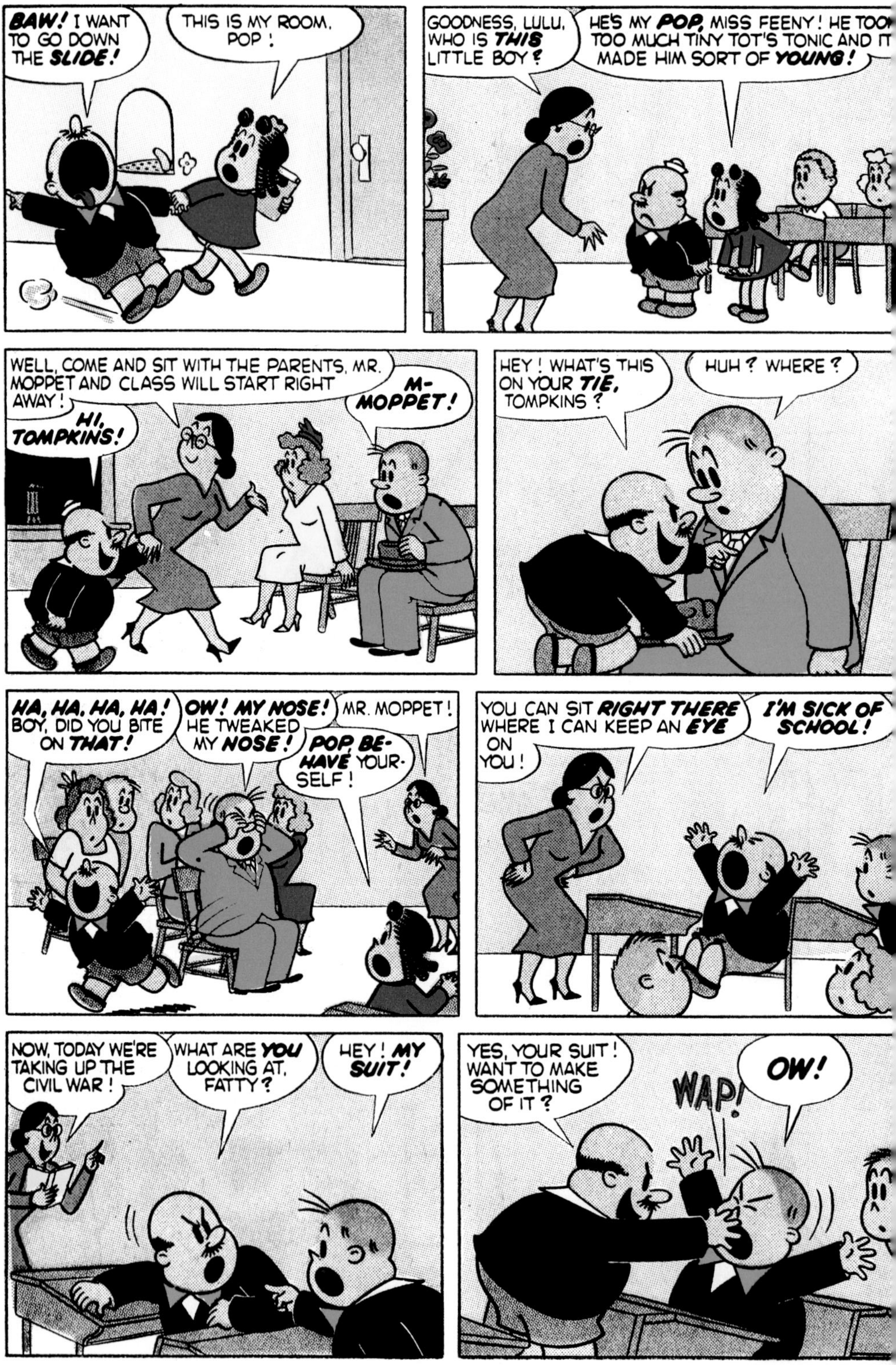

BAW! I WANT TO GO DOWN THE SLIDE!
THIS IS MY ROOM, POP!
GOODNESS, LULU, WHO IS THIS LITTLE BOY?
HE'S MY POP, MISS FEENY! HE TOOK TOO MUCH TINY TOT'S TONIC AND IT MADE HIM SORT OF YOUNG!
WELL, COME AND SIT WITH THE PARENTS, MR. MOPPET AND CLASS WILL START RIGHT AWAY!
HI, TOMPKINS!
M-MOPPET!
HEY! WHAT'S THIS ON YOUR TIE, TOMPKINS?
HUH? WHERE?
HA, HA, HA, HA! BOY, DID YOU BITE ON THAT!
OW! MY NOSE! HE TWEAKED MY NOSE!
MR. MOPPET!
POP, BE-HAVE YOUR-SELF!
YOU CAN SIT RIGHT THERE WHERE I CAN KEEP AN EYE ON YOU!
I'M SICK OF SCHOOL!
NOW, TODAY WE'RE TAKING UP THE CIVIL WAR!
WHAT ARE YOU LOOKING AT, FATTY?
HEY! MY SUIT!
YES, YOUR SUIT! WAN'T TO MAKE SOMETHING OF IT?
WAP!
OW!

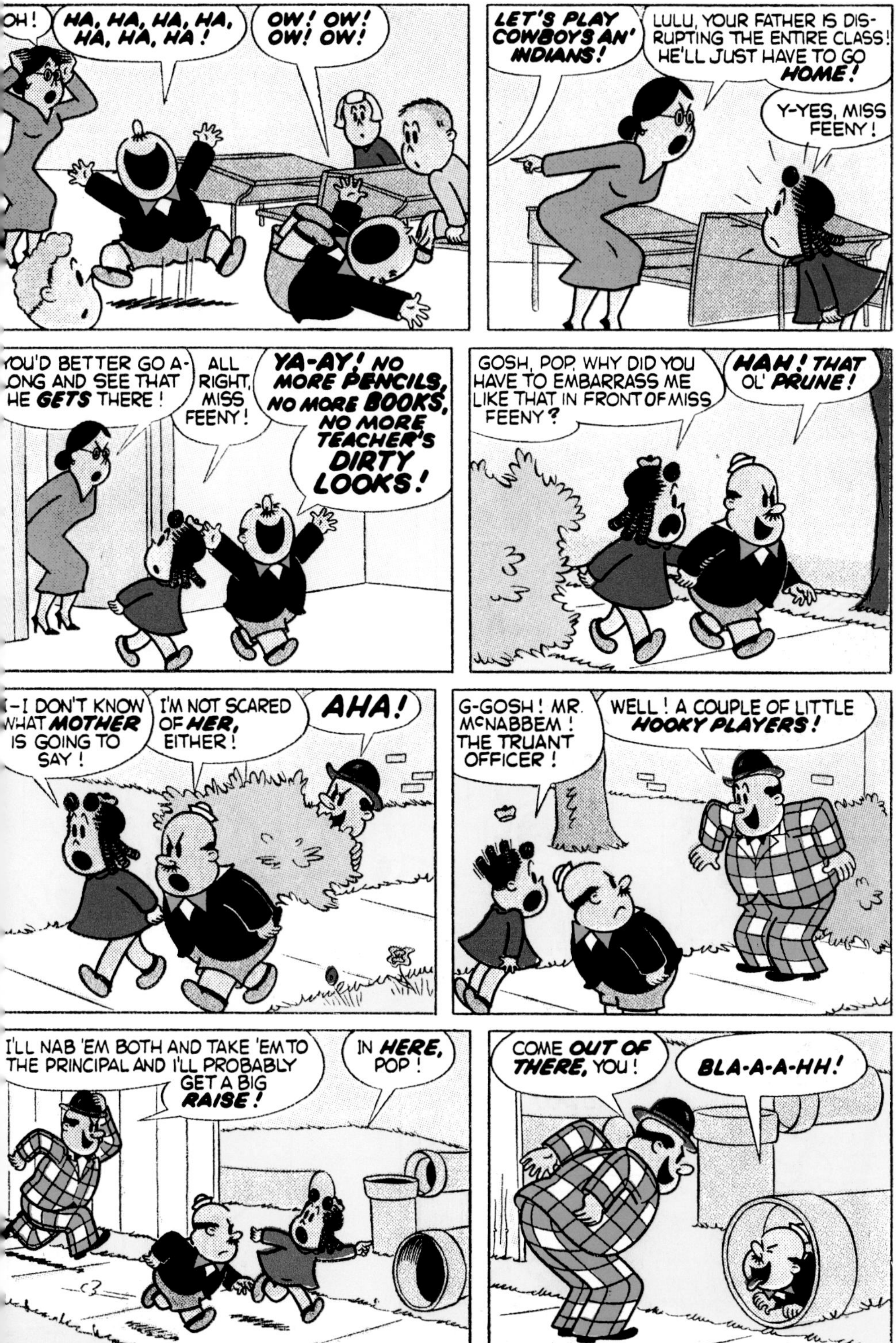
OH!
HA, HA, HA, HA, HA, HA, HA!
OW! OW! OW! OW!
LET'S PLAY COWBOYS AN' INDIANS!
LULU, YOUR FATHER IS DIS-RUPTING THE ENTIRE CLASS! HE'LL JUST HAVE TO GO HOME!
Y-YES, MISS FEENY!
YOU'D BETTER GO A-LONG AND SEE THAT HE GETS THERE!
ALL RIGHT, MISS FEENY!
YA-AY! NO MORE PENCILS, NO MORE BOOKS, NO MORE TEACHER'S DIRTY LOOKS!
GOSH, POP, WHY DID YOU HAVE TO EMBARRASS ME LIKE THAT IN FRONT OF MISS FEENY?
HAH! THAT OL' PRUNE!
I DON'T KNOW WHAT MOTHER IS GOING TO SAY!
I'M NOT SCARED OF HER, EITHER!
AHA!
G-GOSH! MR. McNABBEM! THE TRUANT OFFICER!
WELL! A COUPLE OF LITTLE HOOKY PLAYERS!
I'LL NAB 'EM BOTH AND TAKE 'EM TO THE PRINCIPAL AND I'LL PROBABLY GET A BIG RAISE!
IN HERE, POP!
COME OUT OF THERE, YOU!
BLA-A-A-HH!

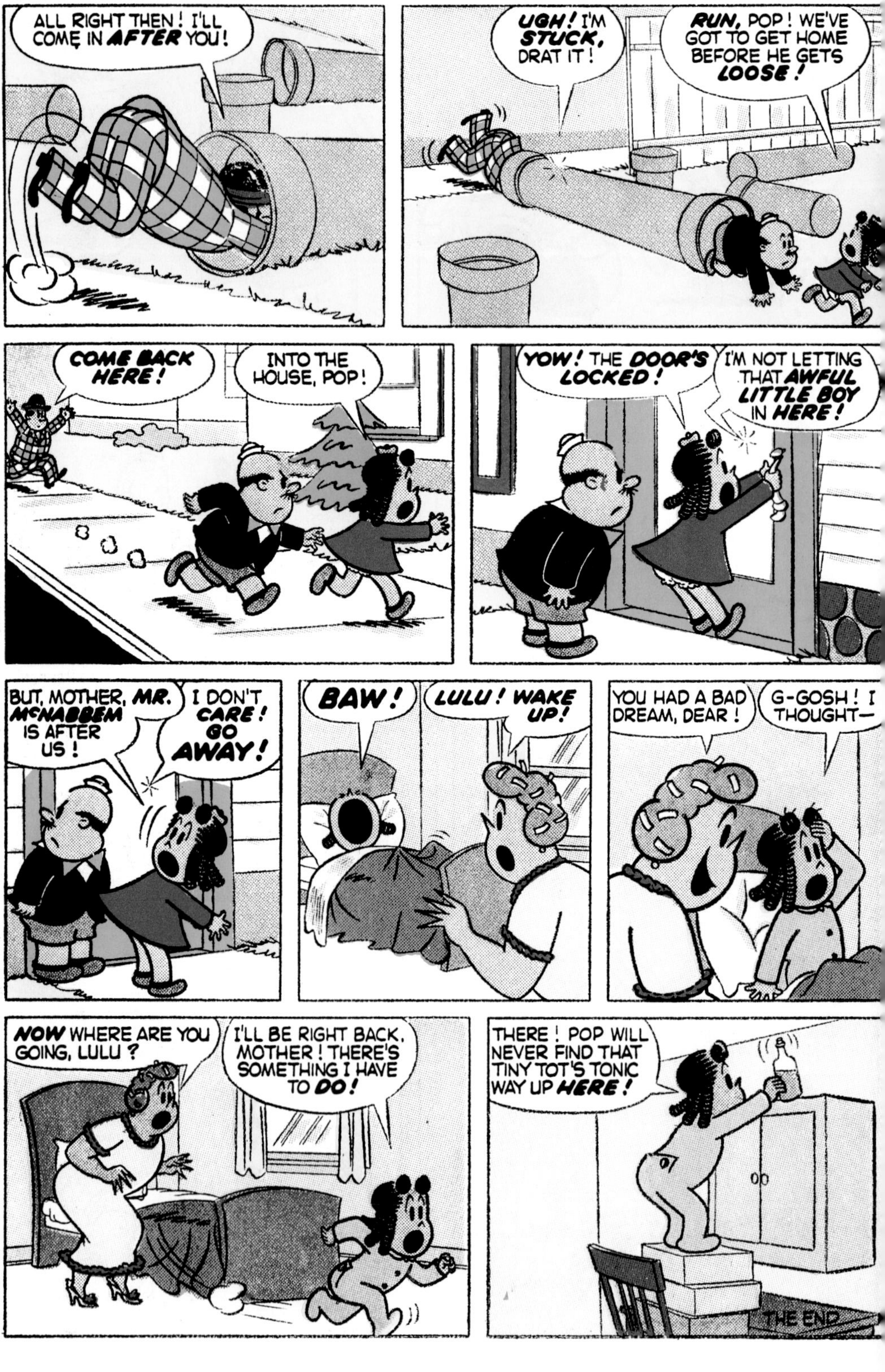
ALL RIGHT THEN! I'LL COME IN AFTER YOU!
UGH! I'M STUCK, DRAT IT!
RUN, POP! WE'VE GOT TO GET HOME BEFORE HE GETS LOOSE!
COME BACK HERE!
INTO THE HOUSE, POP!
YOW! THE DOOR'S LOCKED!
I'M NOT LETTING THAT AWFUL LITTLE BOY IN HERE!
BUT, MOTHER, MR. McNABBEM IS AFTER US!
I DON'T CARE! GO AWAY!
BAW!
LULU! WAKE UP!
YOU HAD A BAD DREAM, DEAR!
G-GOSH! I THOUGHT—
NOW WHERE ARE YOU GOING, LULU?
I'LL BE RIGHT BACK, MOTHER! THERE'S SOMETHING I HAVE TO DO!
THERE! POP WILL NEVER FIND THAT TINY TOT'S TONIC WAY UP HERE!
THE END

LULU

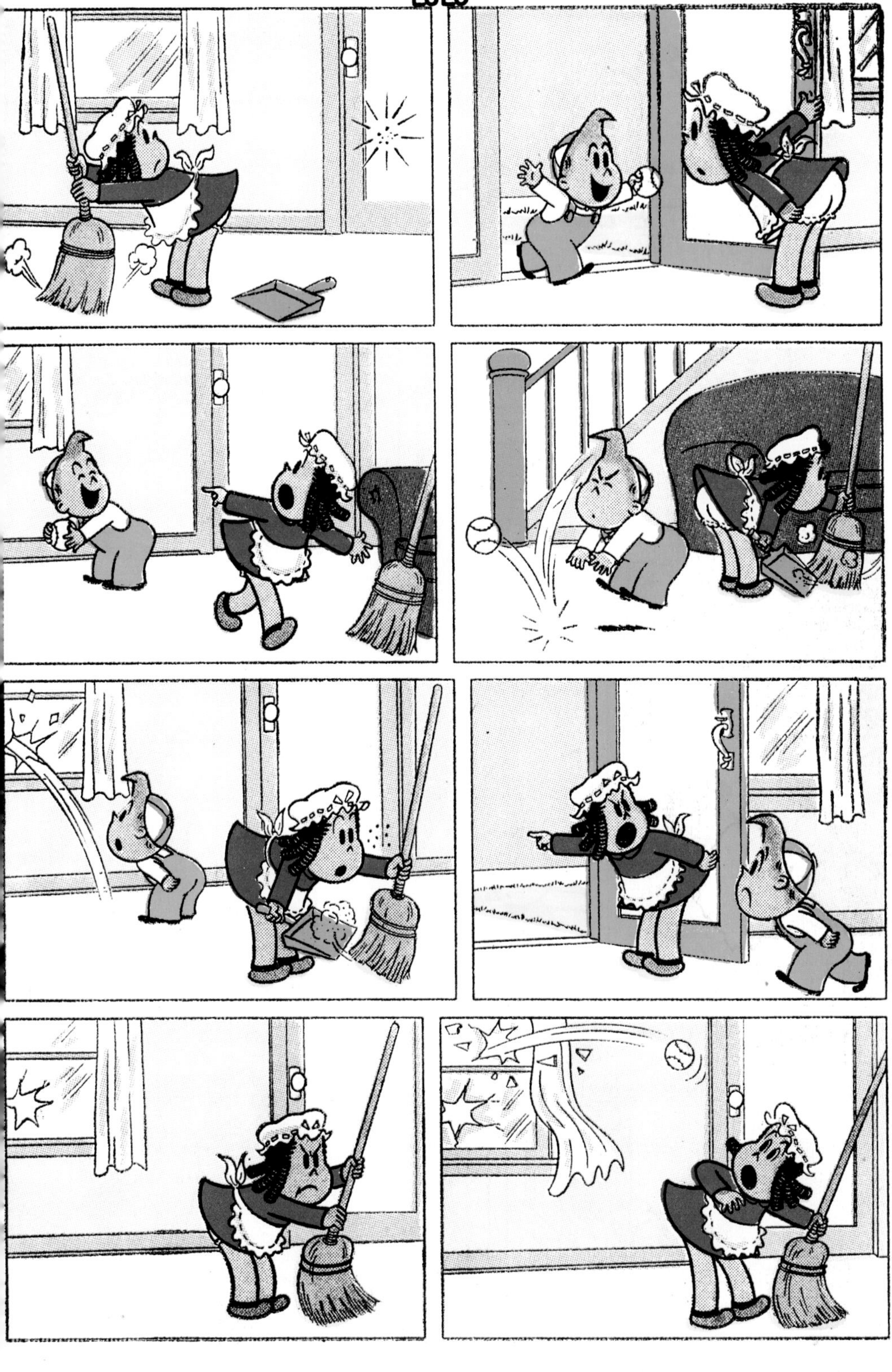

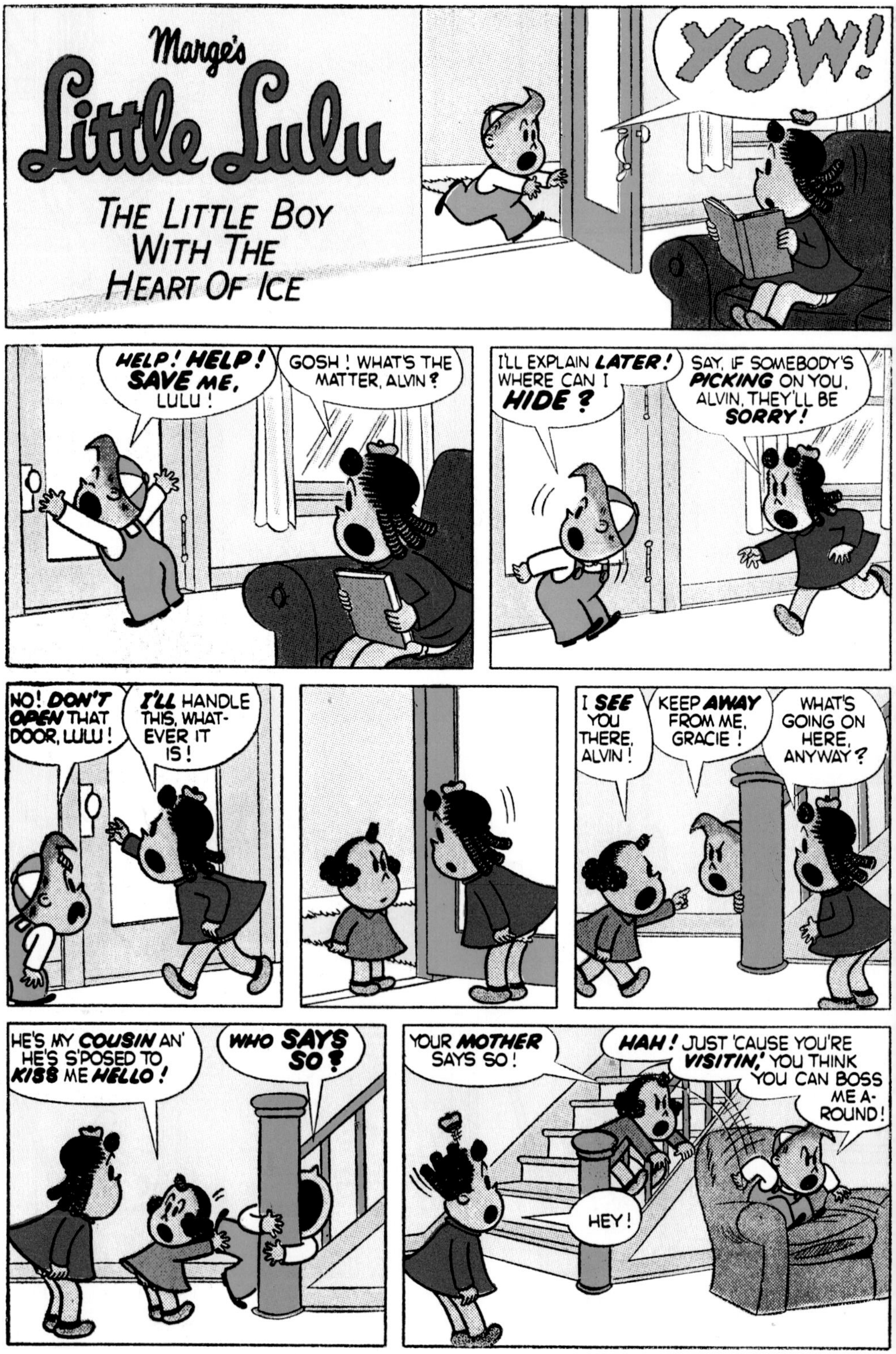

Marge's
Little Lulu
THE LITTLE BOY WITH THE HEART OF ICE
YOW!
HELP! HELP! SAVE ME, LULU!
GOSH! WHAT'S THE MATTER, ALVIN?
I'LL EXPLAIN LATER! WHERE CAN I HIDE?
SAY, IF SOMEBODY'S PICKING ON YOU, ALVIN, THEY'LL BE SORRY!
NO! DON'T OPEN THAT DOOR, LULU!
I'LL HANDLE THIS, WHATEVER IT IS!
I SEE YOU THERE, ALVIN!
KEEP AWAY FROM ME, GRACIE!
WHAT'S GOING ON HERE, ANYWAY?
HE'S MY COUSIN AN' HE'S S'POSED TO KISS ME HELLO!
WHO SAYS SO?
YOUR MOTHER SAYS SO!
HAH! JUST 'CAUSE YOU'RE VISITIN,' YOU THINK YOU CAN BOSS ME AROUND!
HEY!

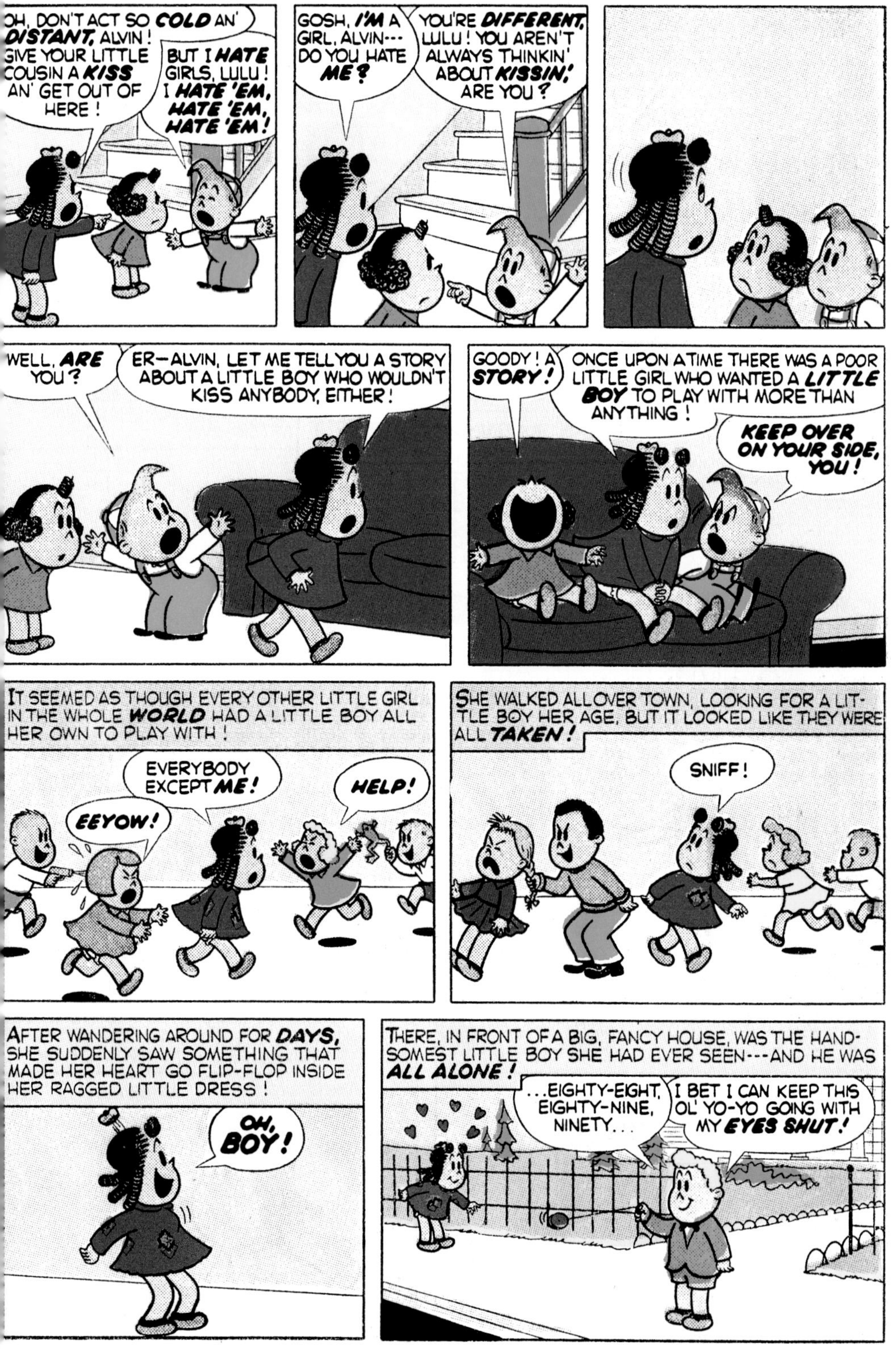
OH, DON'T ACT SO COLD AN' DISTANT, ALVIN! GIVE YOUR LITTLE COUSIN A KISS AN' GET OUT OF HERE!
BUT I HATE GIRLS, LULU! I HATE 'EM, HATE 'EM, HATE 'EM!
GOSH, I'M A GIRL, ALVIN--- DO YOU HATE ME?
YOU'RE DIFFERENT, LULU! YOU AREN'T ALWAYS THINKIN' ABOUT KISSIN,' ARE YOU?
WELL, ARE YOU?
ER—ALVIN, LET ME TELL YOU A STORY ABOUT A LITTLE BOY WHO WOULDN'T KISS ANYBODY, EITHER!
GOODY! A STORY!
ONCE UPON A TIME THERE WAS A POOR LITTLE GIRL WHO WANTED A LITTLE BOY TO PLAY WITH MORE THAN ANYTHING!
KEEP OVER ON YOUR SIDE, YOU!
IT SEEMED AS THOUGH EVERY OTHER LITTLE GIRL IN THE WHOLE WORLD HAD A LITTLE BOY ALL HER OWN TO PLAY WITH!
EVERYBODY EXCEPT ME!
EEYOW!
HELP!
SHE WALKED ALL OVER TOWN, LOOKING FOR A LITTLE BOY HER AGE, BUT IT LOOKED LIKE THEY WERE ALL TAKEN!
SNIFF!
AFTER WANDERING AROUND FOR DAYS, SHE SUDDENLY SAW SOMETHING THAT MADE HER HEART GO FLIP-FLOP INSIDE HER RAGGED LITTLE DRESS!
OH, BOY!
THERE, IN FRONT OF A BIG, FANCY HOUSE, WAS THE HANDSOMEST LITTLE BOY SHE HAD EVER SEEN---AND HE WAS ALL ALONE!
...EIGHTY-EIGHT, EIGHTY-NINE, NINETY...
I BET I CAN KEEP THIS OL' YO-YO GOING WITH MY EYES SHUT!

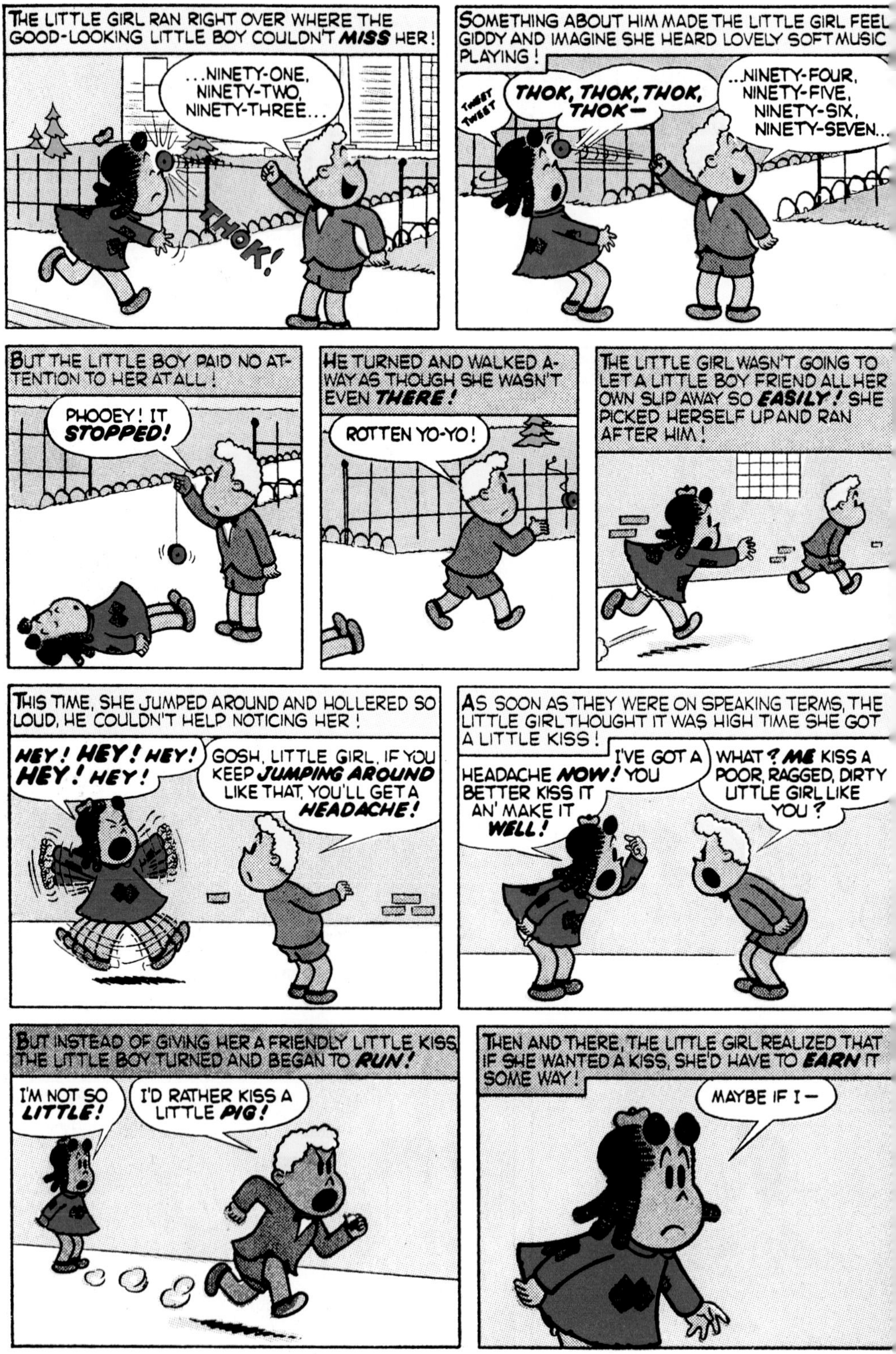
THE LITTLE GIRL RAN RIGHT OVER WHERE THE GOOD-LOOKING LITTLE BOY COULDN'T MISS HER!
...NINETY-ONE, NINETY-TWO, NINETY-THREE...
THOK!
SOMETHING ABOUT HIM MADE THE LITTLE GIRL FEEL GIDDY AND IMAGINE SHE HEARD LOVELY SOFT MUSIC PLAYING!
TWEET TWEET
THOK, THOK, THOK, THOK—
...NINETY-FOUR, NINETY-FIVE, NINETY-SIX, NINETY-SEVEN...
BUT THE LITTLE BOY PAID NO ATTENTION TO HER AT ALL!
PHOOEY! IT STOPPED!
HE TURNED AND WALKED AWAY AS THOUGH SHE WASN'T EVEN THERE!
ROTTEN YO-YO!
THE LITTLE GIRL WASN'T GOING TO LET A LITTLE BOY FRIEND ALL HER OWN SLIP AWAY SO EASILY! SHE PICKED HERSELF UP AND RAN AFTER HIM!
THIS TIME, SHE JUMPED AROUND AND HOLLERED SO LOUD, HE COULDN'T HELP NOTICING HER!
HEY! HEY! HEY! HEY! HEY!
GOSH, LITTLE GIRL, IF YOU KEEP JUMPING AROUND LIKE THAT, YOU'LL GET A HEADACHE!
AS SOON AS THEY WERE ON SPEAKING TERMS, THE LITTLE GIRL THOUGHT IT WAS HIGH TIME SHE GOT A LITTLE KISS!
I'VE GOT A HEADACHE NOW! YOU BETTER KISS IT AN' MAKE IT WELL!
WHAT? ME KISS A POOR, RAGGED, DIRTY LITTLE GIRL LIKE YOU?
BUT INSTEAD OF GIVING HER A FRIENDLY LITTLE KISS THE LITTLE BOY TURNED AND BEGAN TO RUN!
I'M NOT SO LITTLE!
I'D RATHER KISS A LITTLE PIG!
THEN AND THERE, THE LITTLE GIRL REALIZED THAT IF SHE WANTED A KISS, SHE'D HAVE TO EARN IT SOME WAY!
MAYBE IF I—

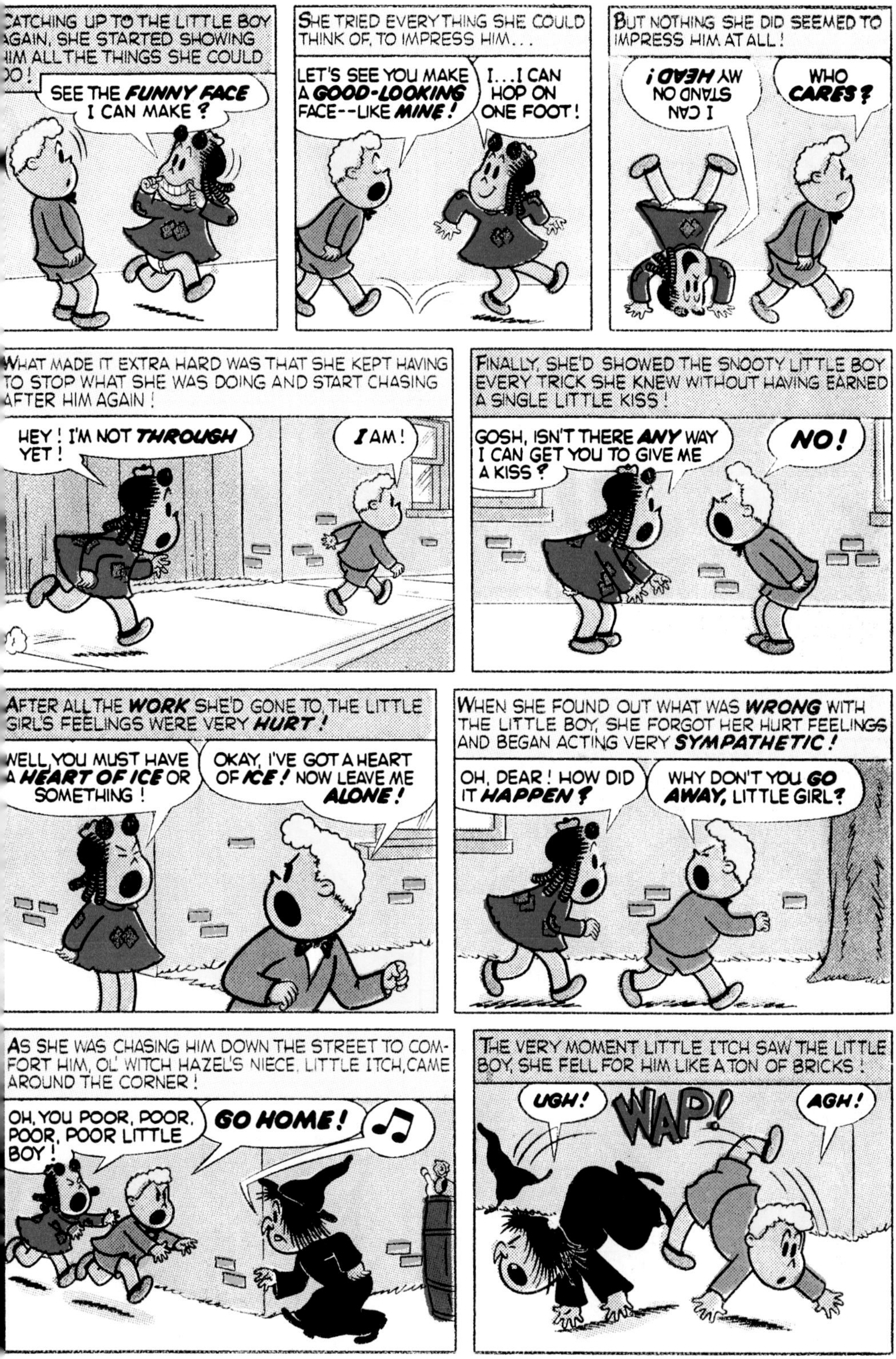

CATCHING UP TO THE LITTLE BOY AGAIN, SHE STARTED SHOWING HIM ALL THE THINGS SHE COULD DO!
SEE THE FUNNY FACE I CAN MAKE?
SHE TRIED EVERYTHING SHE COULD THINK OF, TO IMPRESS HIM...
LET'S SEE YOU MAKE A GOOD-LOOKING FACE--LIKE MINE!
I...I CAN HOP ON ONE FOOT!
BUT NOTHING SHE DID SEEMED TO IMPRESS HIM AT ALL!
I CAN STAND ON MY HEAD!
WHO CARES?
WHAT MADE IT EXTRA HARD WAS THAT SHE KEPT HAVING TO STOP WHAT SHE WAS DOING AND START CHASING AFTER HIM AGAIN!
HEY! I'M NOT THROUGH YET!
I AM!
FINALLY, SHE'D SHOWED THE SNOOTY LITTLE BOY EVERY TRICK SHE KNEW WITHOUT HAVING EARNED A SINGLE LITTLE KISS!
GOSH, ISN'T THERE ANY WAY I CAN GET YOU TO GIVE ME A KISS?
NO!
AFTER ALL THE WORK SHE'D GONE TO, THE LITTLE GIRL'S FEELINGS WERE VERY HURT!
WELL, YOU MUST HAVE A HEART OF ICE OR SOMETHING!
OKAY, I'VE GOT A HEART OF ICE! NOW LEAVE ME ALONE!
WHEN SHE FOUND OUT WHAT WAS WRONG WITH THE LITTLE BOY, SHE FORGOT HER HURT FEELINGS AND BEGAN ACTING VERY SYMPATHETIC!
OH, DEAR! HOW DID IT HAPPEN?
WHY DON'T YOU GO AWAY, LITTLE GIRL?
AS SHE WAS CHASING HIM DOWN THE STREET TO COMFORT HIM, OL' WITCH HAZEL'S NIECE, LITTLE ITCH, CAME AROUND THE CORNER!
OH, YOU POOR, POOR, POOR, POOR LITTLE BOY!
GO HOME!
♫
THE VERY MOMENT LITTLE ITCH SAW THE LITTLE BOY, SHE FELL FOR HIM LIKE A TON OF BRICKS!
UGH!
WAP!
AGH!

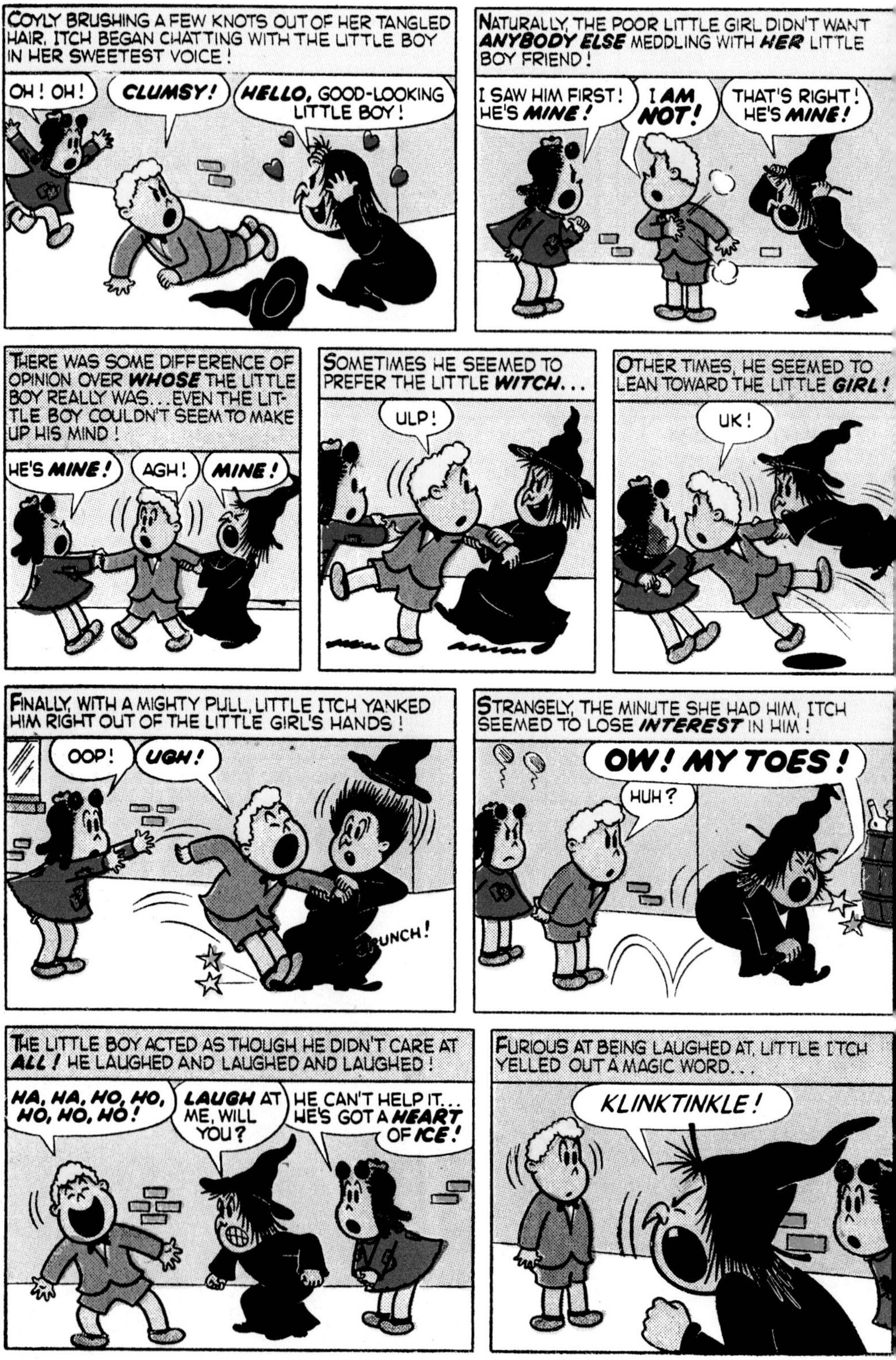
COYLY BRUSHING A FEW KNOTS OUT OF HER TANGLED HAIR, ITCH BEGAN CHATTING WITH THE LITTLE BOY IN HER SWEETEST VOICE!
OH! OH!
CLUMSY!
HELLO, GOOD-LOOKING LITTLE BOY!
NATURALLY, THE POOR LITTLE GIRL DIDN'T WANT ANYBODY ELSE MEDDLING WITH HER LITTLE BOY FRIEND!
I SAW HIM FIRST! HE'S MINE!
I AM NOT!
THAT'S RIGHT! HE'S MINE!
THERE WAS SOME DIFFERENCE OF OPINION OVER WHOSE THE LITTLE BOY REALLY WAS... EVEN THE LITTLE BOY COULDN'T SEEM TO MAKE UP HIS MIND!
HE'S MINE!
AGH!
MINE!
SOMETIMES HE SEEMED TO PREFER THE LITTLE WITCH...
ULP!
OTHER TIMES, HE SEEMED TO LEAN TOWARD THE LITTLE GIRL!
UK!
FINALLY, WITH A MIGHTY PULL, LITTLE ITCH YANKED HIM RIGHT OUT OF THE LITTLE GIRL'S HANDS!
OOP!
UGH!
CRUNCH!
STRANGELY, THE MINUTE SHE HAD HIM, ITCH SEEMED TO LOSE INTEREST IN HIM!
OW! MY TOES!
HUH?
THE LITTLE BOY ACTED AS THOUGH HE DIDN'T CARE AT ALL! HE LAUGHED AND LAUGHED AND LAUGHED!
HA, HA, HO, HO, HO, HO, HO!
LAUGH AT ME, WILL YOU?
HE CAN'T HELP IT... HE'S GOT A HEART OF ICE!
FURIOUS AT BEING LAUGHED AT, LITTLE ITCH YELLED OUT A MAGIC WORD...
KLINKTINKLE!

THEN SHE TURNED AND LIMPED AWAY, MUTTERING TO HERSELF!

LET'S SEE HOW HE LIKES BEING MADE OF ICE **ALL OVER**!

GOODY! SHE'S LEAVING!

THE LITTLE GIRL WAS SO HAPPY AT BEING LEFT ALONE WITH THE LITTLE BOY, SHE DIDN'T NOTICE THAT HE HAD TURNED INTO A SOLID CHUNK OF ICE, GLEAMING IN THE SUN!

WE'LL HAVE **LOADS** OF **FUN** TOGETHER!

PHOOEY!

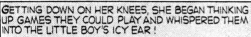
GETTING DOWN ON HER KNEES, SHE BEGAN THINKING UP GAMES THEY COULD PLAY AND WHISPERED THEM INTO THE LITTLE BOY'S ICY EAR!

WE'LL PLAY **HOUSE**, AN' **HOPSCOTCH**, AN'–

PHOOEY!

SUDDENLY, SHE NOTICED A STRANGE THING ..THE LITTLE BOY HAD MELTED RIGHT DOWN TO A LITTLE POOL OF ICE WATER...GLEAMING IN THE SUN!

YOW!

FOR A WHILE, SHE FELT JUST **AWFUL** ABOUT IT!

YOW! YOW! YOW! YOW! YOW!

THEN SHE MOPPED HIM UP CAREFULLY WITH HER HANKY AND SQUEEZED HIM INTO AN OLD JELLY GLASS THAT WAS LYING NEARBY!

SNIFF!

...AND THEY WENT OFF AND BLEW SOAP BUBBLES TOGETHER TILL SUPPERTIME!

I'LL ASK MOTHER FOR A CAKE OF **SOAP**!

NOW, YOU WOULDN'T WANT ANYTHING LIKE THAT TO HAPPEN TO **YOU**, WOULD YOU, ALVIN?

GOSH. **NO**, LULU!

GOOD! I GUESS YOU CAN COLLECT YOUR **KISS** NOW, GRACIE!

IF IT'S ALL THE **SAME**, I'D RATHER HAVE A **GLASS** OF **WATER**, LULU!

THE END

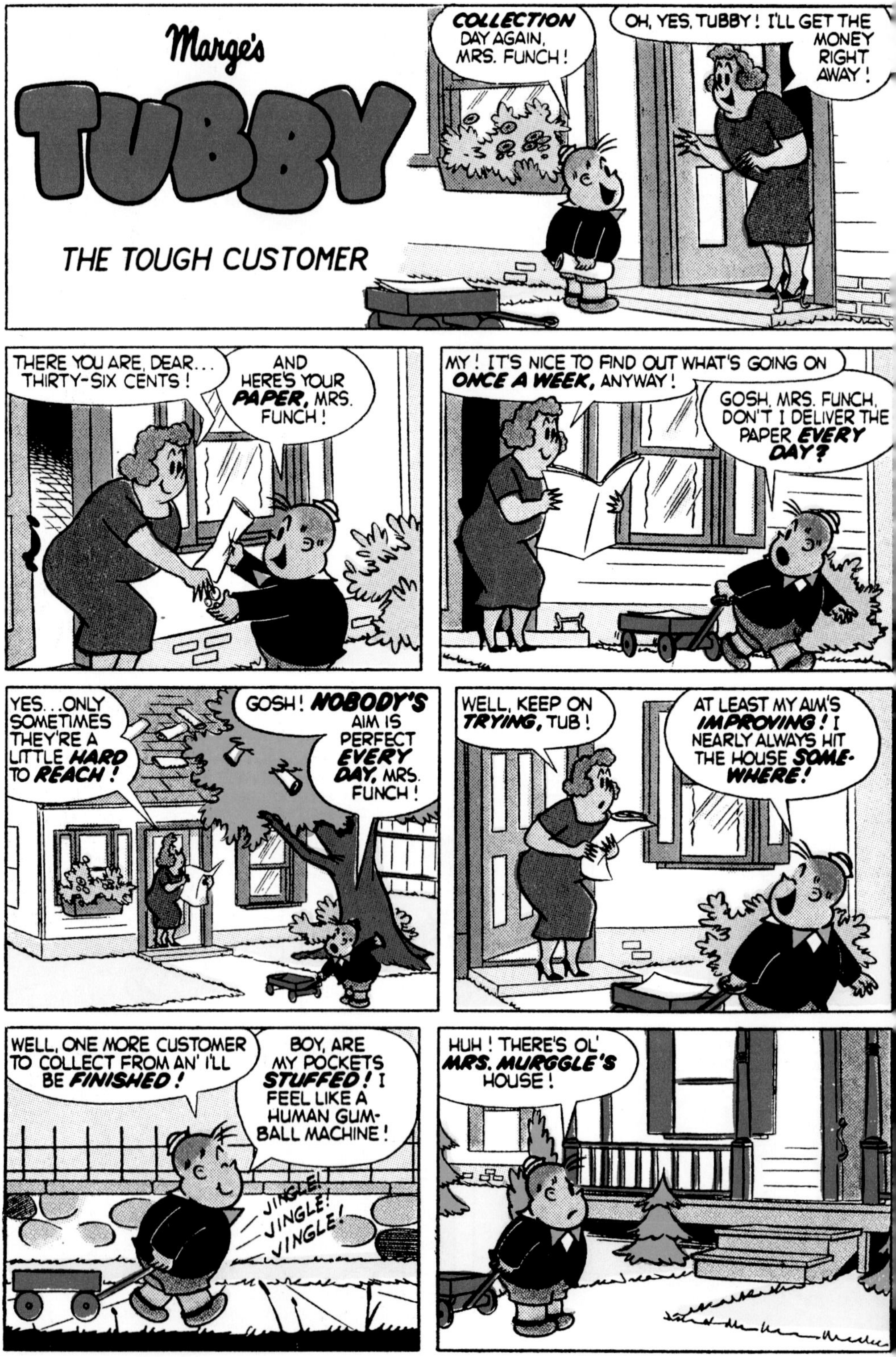
Marge's
TUBBY
THE TOUGH CUSTOMER
COLLECTION DAY AGAIN, MRS. FUNCH!
OH, YES, TUBBY! I'LL GET THE MONEY RIGHT AWAY!
THERE YOU ARE, DEAR... THIRTY-SIX CENTS!
AND HERE'S YOUR PAPER, MRS. FUNCH!
MY! IT'S NICE TO FIND OUT WHAT'S GOING ON ONCE A WEEK, ANYWAY!
GOSH, MRS. FUNCH, DON'T I DELIVER THE PAPER EVERY DAY?
YES...ONLY SOMETIMES THEY'RE A LITTLE HARD TO REACH!
GOSH! NOBODY'S AIM IS PERFECT EVERY DAY, MRS. FUNCH!
WELL, KEEP ON TRYING, TUB!
AT LEAST MY AIM'S IMPROVING! I NEARLY ALWAYS HIT THE HOUSE SOME-WHERE!
WELL, ONE MORE CUSTOMER TO COLLECT FROM AN' I'LL BE FINISHED!
BOY, ARE MY POCKETS STUFFED! I FEEL LIKE A HUMAN GUM-BALL MACHINE!
JINGLE! JINGLE! JINGLE!
HUH! THERE'S OL' MRS. MURGGLE'S HOUSE!

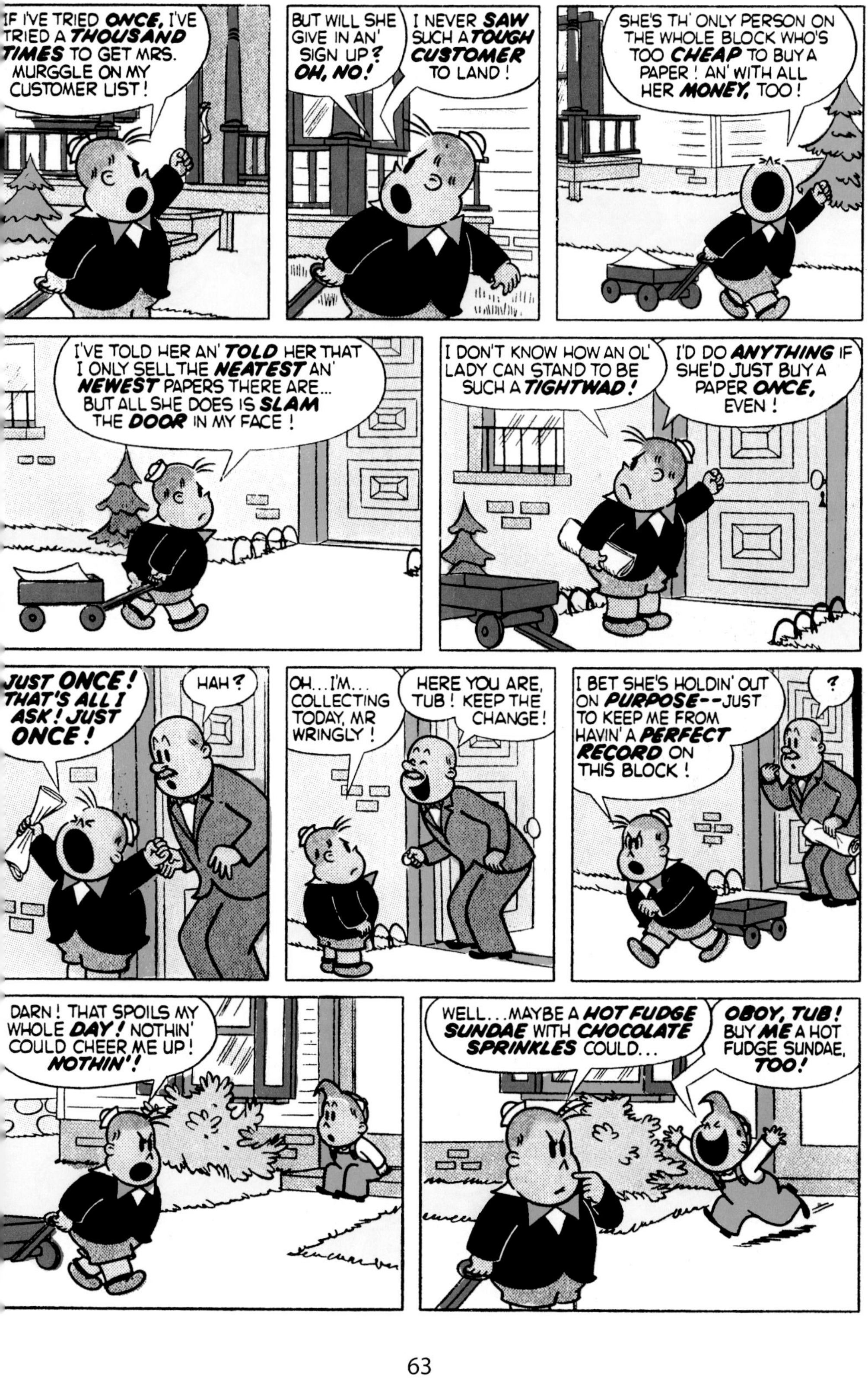
IF I'VE TRIED ONCE, I'VE TRIED A THOUSAND TIMES TO GET MRS. MURGGLE ON MY CUSTOMER LIST!
BUT WILL SHE GIVE IN AN' SIGN UP? OH, NO!
I NEVER SAW SUCH A TOUGH CUSTOMER TO LAND!
SHE'S TH' ONLY PERSON ON THE WHOLE BLOCK WHO'S TOO CHEAP TO BUY A PAPER! AN' WITH ALL HER MONEY, TOO!
I'VE TOLD HER AN' TOLD HER THAT I ONLY SELL THE NEATEST AN' NEWEST PAPERS THERE ARE... BUT ALL SHE DOES IS SLAM THE DOOR IN MY FACE!
I DON'T KNOW HOW AN OL' LADY CAN STAND TO BE SUCH A TIGHTWAD!
I'D DO ANYTHING IF SHE'D JUST BUY A PAPER ONCE, EVEN!
JUST ONCE! THAT'S ALL I ASK! JUST ONCE!
HAH?
OH... I'M... COLLECTING TODAY, MR WRINGLY!
HERE YOU ARE, TUB! KEEP THE CHANGE!
I BET SHE'S HOLDIN' OUT ON PURPOSE--JUST TO KEEP ME FROM HAVIN' A PERFECT RECORD ON THIS BLOCK!
?
DARN! THAT SPOILS MY WHOLE DAY! NOTHIN' COULD CHEER ME UP! NOTHIN'!
WELL... MAYBE A HOT FUDGE SUNDAE WITH CHOCOLATE SPRINKLES COULD...
OBOY, TUB! BUY ME A HOT FUDGE SUNDAE, TOO!

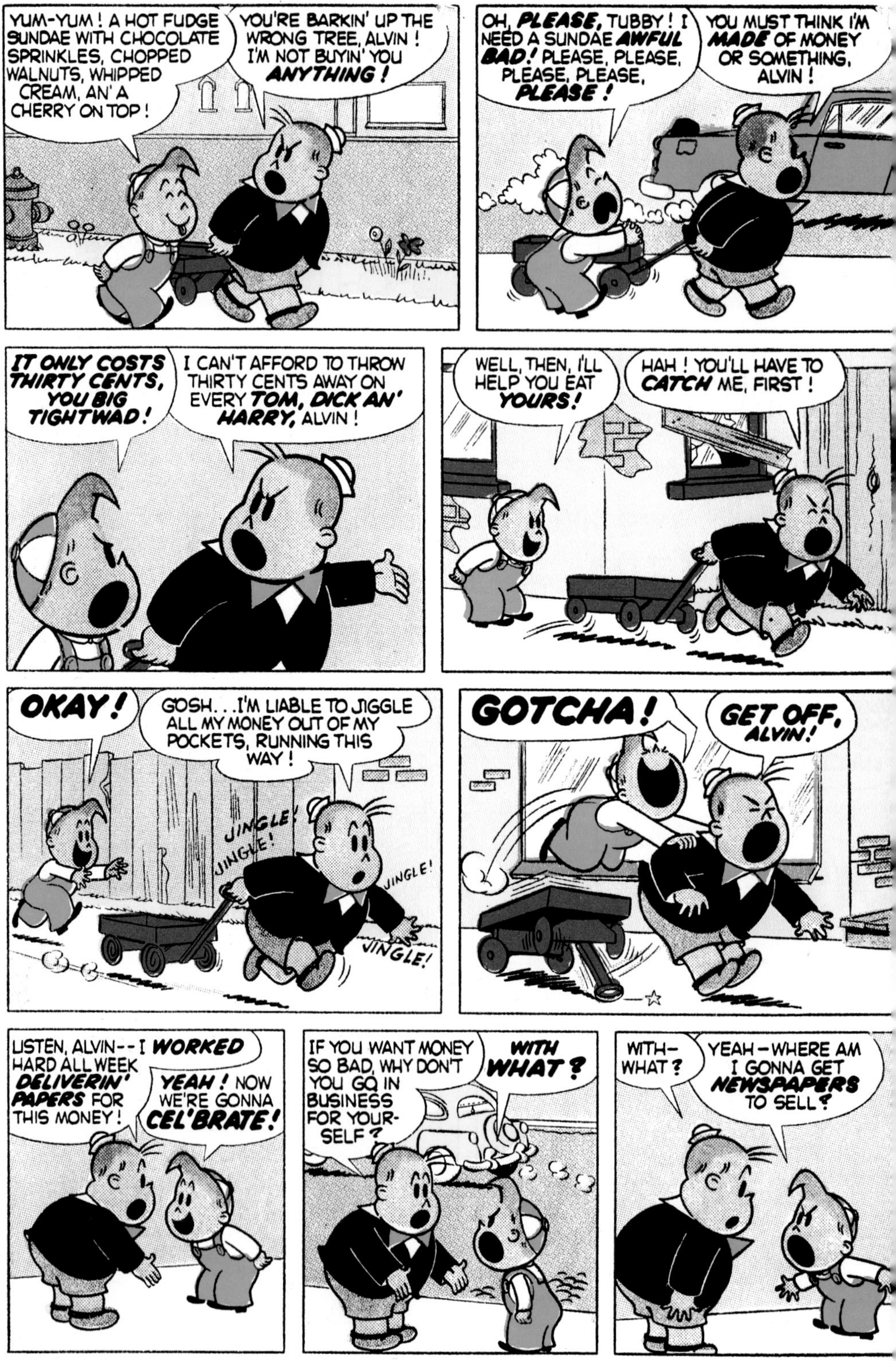
YUM-YUM! A HOT FUDGE SUNDAE WITH CHOCOLATE SPRINKLES, CHOPPED WALNUTS, WHIPPED CREAM, AN' A CHERRY ON TOP!
YOU'RE BARKIN' UP THE WRONG TREE, ALVIN! I'M NOT BUYIN' YOU ANYTHING!
OH, PLEASE, TUBBY! I NEED A SUNDAE AWFUL BAD! PLEASE, PLEASE, PLEASE, PLEASE, PLEASE!
YOU MUST THINK I'M MADE OF MONEY OR SOMETHING, ALVIN!
IT ONLY COSTS THIRTY CENTS, YOU BIG TIGHTWAD!
I CAN'T AFFORD TO THROW THIRTY CENTS AWAY ON EVERY TOM, DICK AN' HARRY, ALVIN!
WELL, THEN, I'LL HELP YOU EAT YOURS!
HAH! YOU'LL HAVE TO CATCH ME, FIRST!
OKAY!
GOSH...I'M LIABLE TO JIGGLE ALL MY MONEY OUT OF MY POCKETS, RUNNING THIS WAY!
JINGLE! JINGLE! JINGLE! JINGLE!
GOTCHA!
GET OFF, ALVIN!
LISTEN, ALVIN--I WORKED HARD ALL WEEK DELIVERIN' PAPERS FOR THIS MONEY!
YEAH! NOW WE'RE GONNA CEL'BRATE!
IF YOU WANT MONEY SO BAD, WHY DON'T YOU GO IN BUSINESS FOR YOURSELF?
WITH WHAT?
WITH-WHAT?
YEAH-WHERE AM I GONNA GET NEWSPAPERS TO SELL?

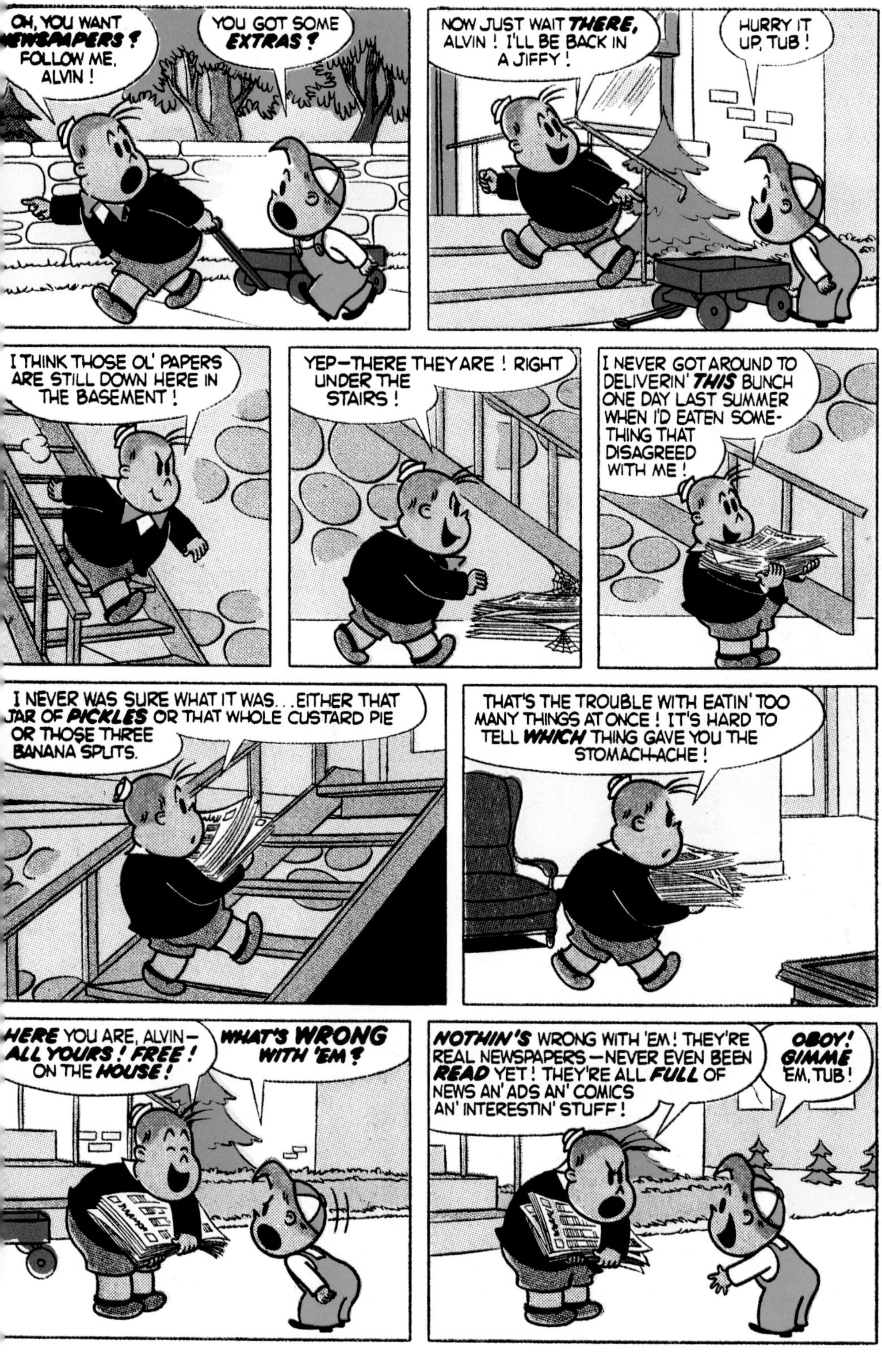

OH, YOU WANT NEWSPAPERS? FOLLOW ME, ALVIN!
YOU GOT SOME EXTRAS?
NOW JUST WAIT THERE, ALVIN! I'LL BE BACK IN A JIFFY!
HURRY IT UP, TUB!
I THINK THOSE OL' PAPERS ARE STILL DOWN HERE IN THE BASEMENT!
YEP—THERE THEY ARE! RIGHT UNDER THE STAIRS!
I NEVER GOT AROUND TO DELIVERIN' THIS BUNCH ONE DAY LAST SUMMER WHEN I'D EATEN SOME-THING THAT DISAGREED WITH ME!
I NEVER WAS SURE WHAT IT WAS... EITHER THAT JAR OF PICKLES OR THAT WHOLE CUSTARD PIE OR THOSE THREE BANANA SPLITS.
THAT'S THE TROUBLE WITH EATIN' TOO MANY THINGS AT ONCE! IT'S HARD TO TELL WHICH THING GAVE YOU THE STOMACH-ACHE!
HERE YOU ARE, ALVIN—ALL YOURS! FREE! ON THE HOUSE!
WHAT'S WRONG WITH 'EM?
NOTHIN'S WRONG WITH 'EM! THEY'RE REAL NEWSPAPERS—NEVER EVEN BEEN READ YET! THEY'RE ALL FULL OF NEWS AN' ADS AN' COMICS AN' INTERESTIN' STUFF!
OBOY! GIMME 'EM, TUB!

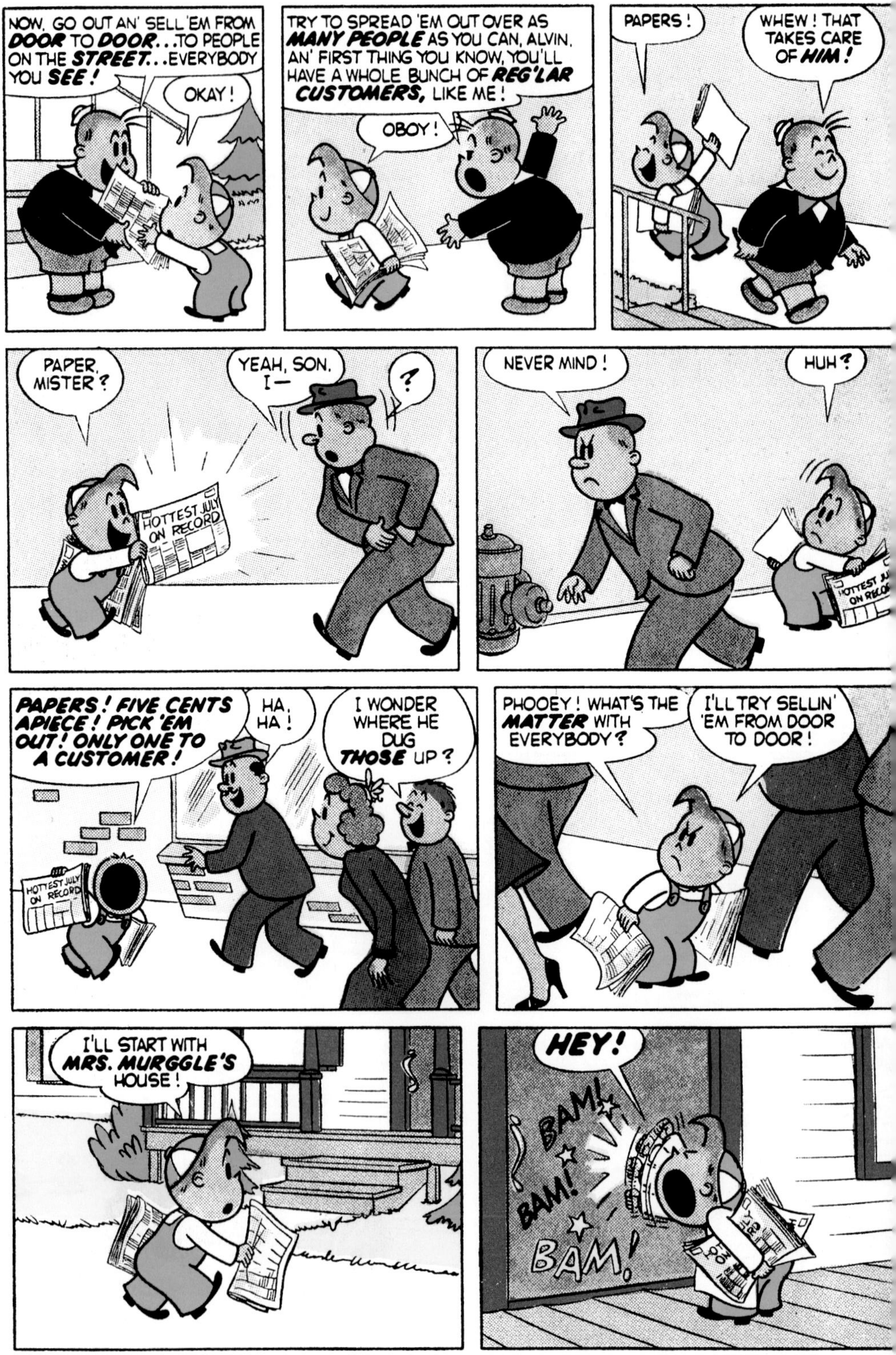
NOW, GO OUT AN' SELL 'EM FROM DOOR TO DOOR... TO PEOPLE ON THE STREET... EVERYBODY YOU SEE!
OKAY!
TRY TO SPREAD 'EM OUT OVER AS MANY PEOPLE AS YOU CAN, ALVIN. AN' FIRST THING YOU KNOW, YOU'LL HAVE A WHOLE BUNCH OF REG'LAR CUSTOMERS, LIKE ME!
OBOY!
PAPERS!
WHEW! THAT TAKES CARE OF HIM!
PAPER, MISTER?
YEAH, SON, I—
?
HOTTEST JULY ON RECORD
NEVER MIND!
HUH?
HOTTEST JULY ON RECORD
PAPERS! FIVE CENTS APIECE! PICK 'EM OUT! ONLY ONE TO A CUSTOMER!
HA, HA!
I WONDER WHERE HE DUG THOSE UP?
HOTTEST JULY ON RECORD
PHOOEY! WHAT'S THE MATTER WITH EVERYBODY?
I'LL TRY SELLIN' 'EM FROM DOOR TO DOOR!
I'LL START WITH MRS. MURGGLE'S HOUSE!
HEY!
BAM!
BAM!
BAM!

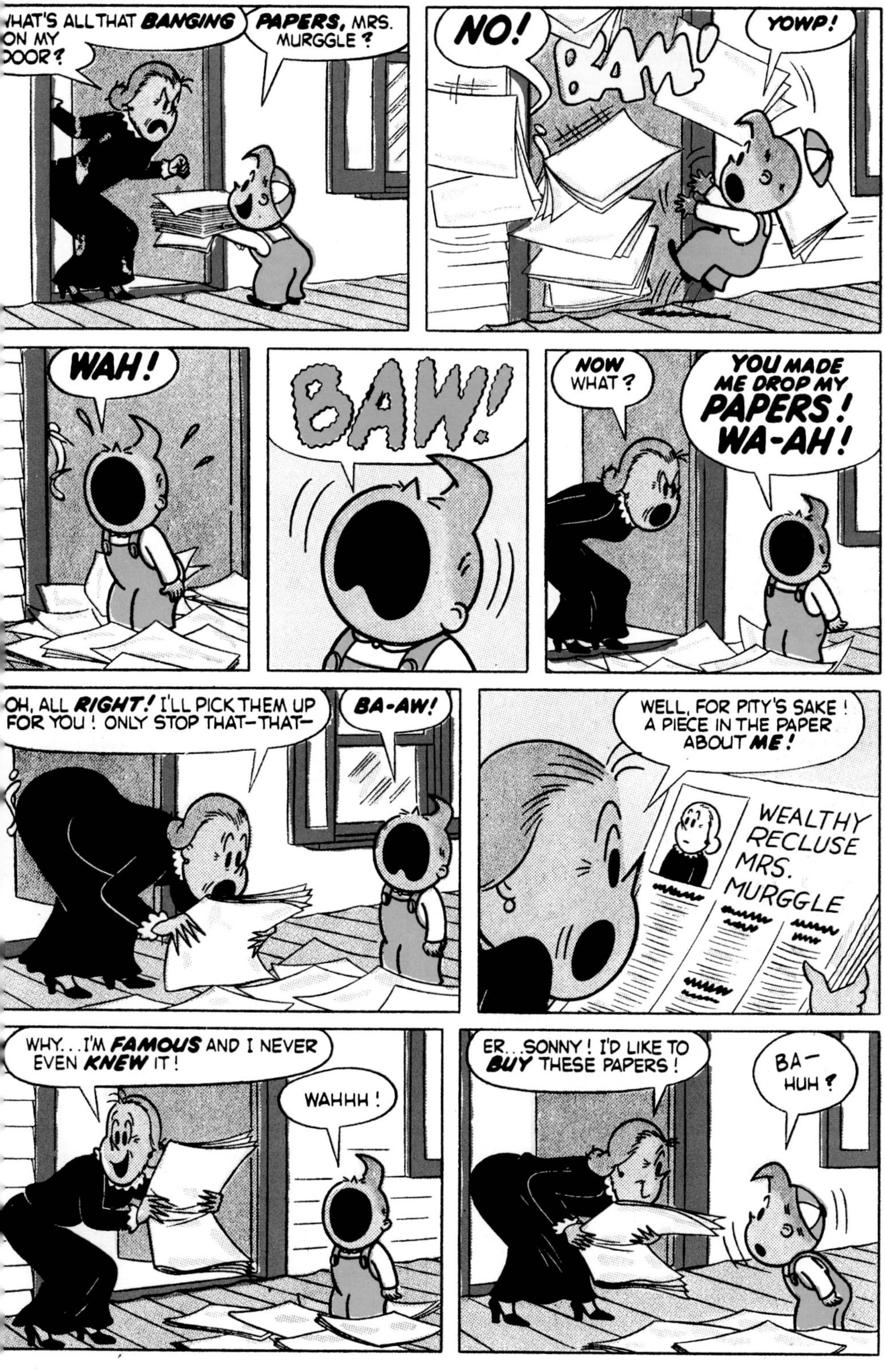

WHAT'S ALL THAT BANGING ON MY DOOR?
PAPERS, MRS. MURGGLE?
NO!
BAM!
YOWP!
WAH!
BAW!
NOW WHAT?
YOU MADE ME DROP MY PAPERS! WA-AH!
OH, ALL RIGHT! I'LL PICK THEM UP FOR YOU! ONLY STOP THAT—THAT—
BA-AW!
WELL, FOR PITY'S SAKE! A PIECE IN THE PAPER ABOUT ME!
WEALTHY RECLUSE MRS. MURGGLE
WHY... I'M FAMOUS AND I NEVER EVEN KNEW IT!
WAHHH!
ER... SONNY! I'D LIKE TO BUY THESE PAPERS!
BA— HUH?

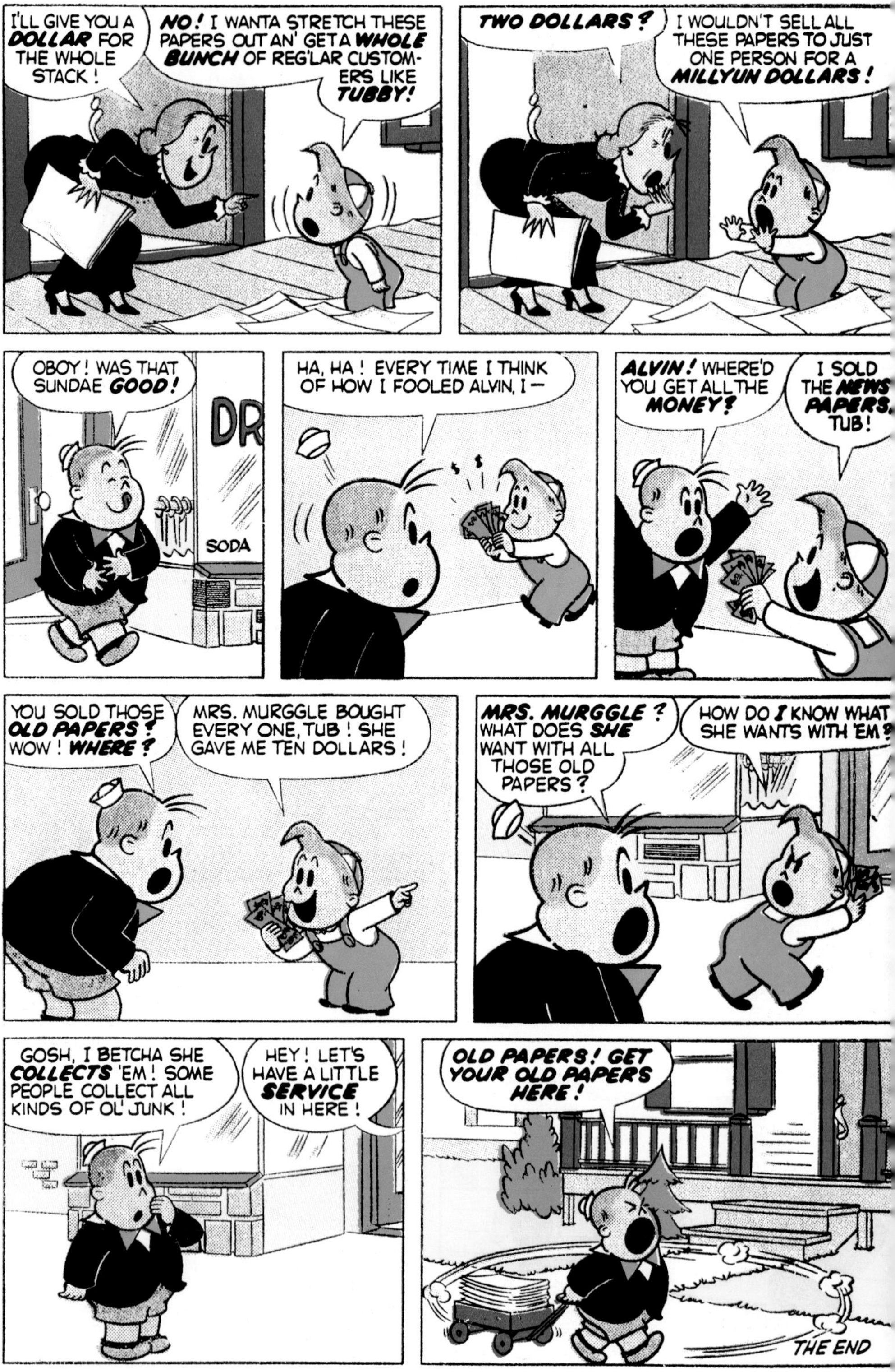
I'LL GIVE YOU A DOLLAR FOR THE WHOLE STACK!
NO! I WANTA STRETCH THESE PAPERS OUT AN' GET A WHOLE BUNCH OF REG'LAR CUSTOMERS LIKE TUBBY!
TWO DOLLARS?
I WOULDN'T SELL ALL THESE PAPERS TO JUST ONE PERSON FOR A MILLYUN DOLLARS!
OBOY! WAS THAT SUNDAE GOOD!
DR
SODA
HA, HA! EVERY TIME I THINK OF HOW I FOOLED ALVIN, I—
ALVIN! WHERE'D YOU GET ALL THE MONEY?
I SOLD THE NEWS PAPERS, TUB!
YOU SOLD THOSE OLD PAPERS? WOW! WHERE?
MRS. MURGGLE BOUGHT EVERY ONE, TUB! SHE GAVE ME TEN DOLLARS!
MRS. MURGGLE? WHAT DOES SHE WANT WITH ALL THOSE OLD PAPERS?
HOW DO I KNOW WHAT SHE WANTS WITH 'EM?
GOSH, I BETCHA SHE COLLECTS 'EM! SOME PEOPLE COLLECT ALL KINDS OF OL' JUNK!
HEY! LET'S HAVE A LITTLE SERVICE IN HERE!
OLD PAPERS! GET YOUR OLD PAPERS HERE!
THE END

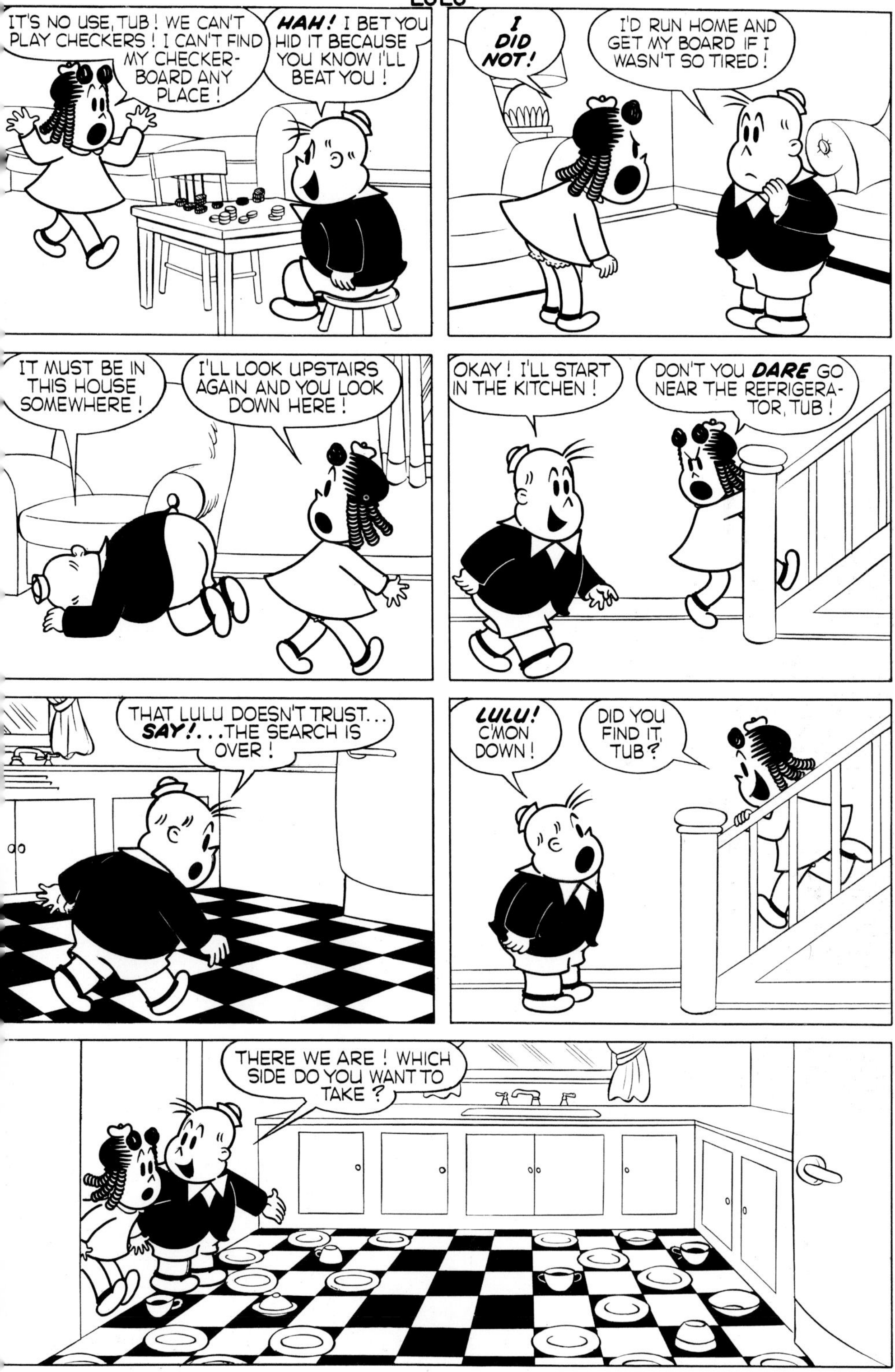
IT'S NO USE, TUB! WE CAN'T PLAY CHECKERS! I CAN'T FIND MY CHECKER-BOARD ANY PLACE!
HAH! I BET YOU HID IT BECAUSE YOU KNOW I'LL BEAT YOU!
I DID NOT!
I'D RUN HOME AND GET MY BOARD IF I WASN'T SO TIRED!
IT MUST BE IN THIS HOUSE SOMEWHERE!
I'LL LOOK UPSTAIRS AGAIN AND YOU LOOK DOWN HERE!
OKAY! I'LL START IN THE KITCHEN!
DON'T YOU DARE GO NEAR THE REFRIGERA-TOR, TUB!
THAT LULU DOESN'T TRUST... SAY!...THE SEARCH IS OVER!
LULU! C'MON DOWN!
DID YOU FIND IT, TUB?
THERE WE ARE! WHICH SIDE DO YOU WANT TO TAKE?

Little Lulu Little
Lulu Little Lulu Little
Little Lulu Little
Lulu Little Lulu Little
Little Lulu Little
Lulu Little Lulu Little
Little Lulu Little
Lulu Little Lulu Little
Little Lulu Little
Lulu Little Lulu

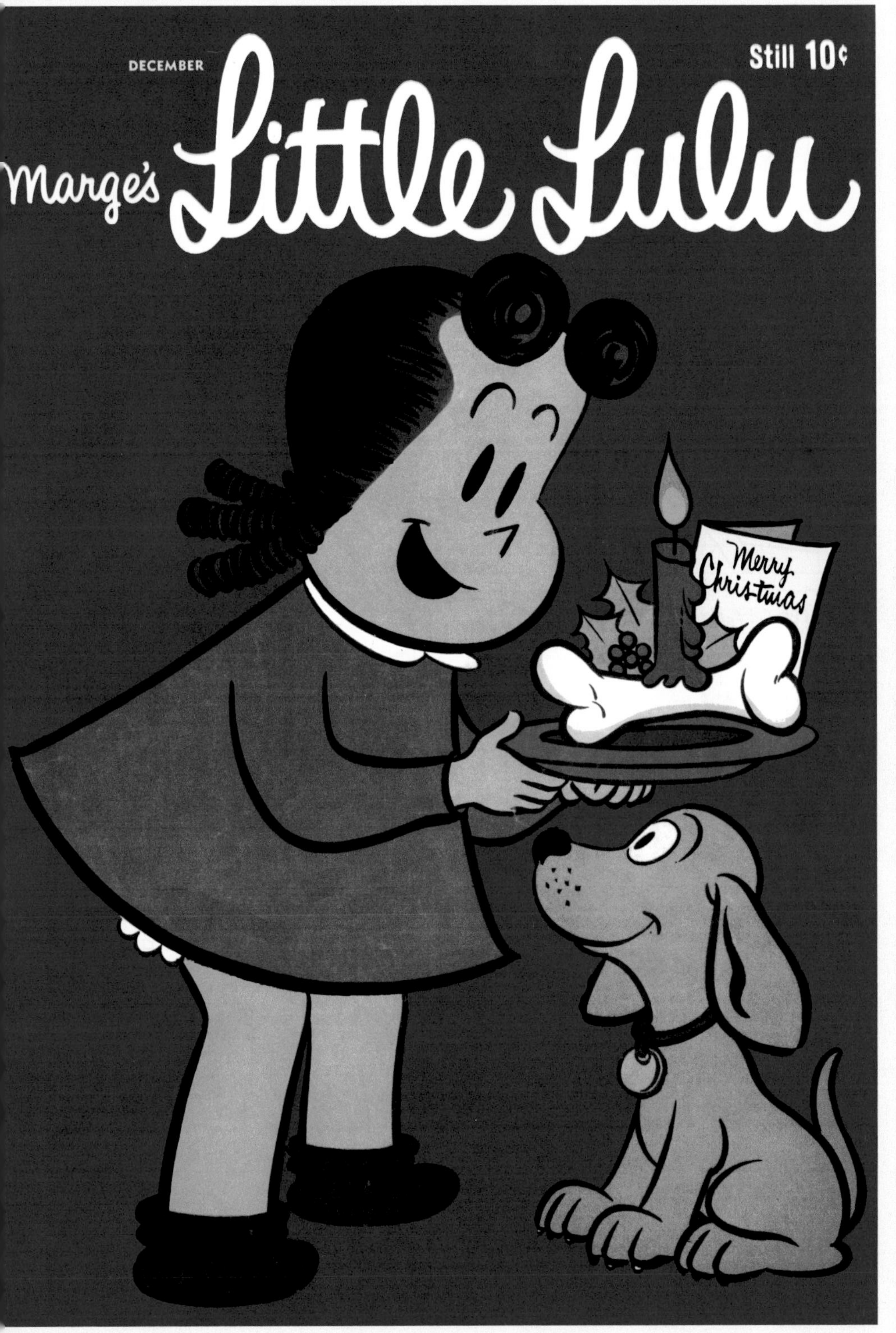
DECEMBER
Marge's Little Lulu
Still 10¢
Merry Christmas

Marge's Little Lulu

The Good Catcher

OBOY! THAT WAS AN *EXTRA BIG* BUBBLE! THIS PIECE OF BUBBLE GUM MUST BE EXTRA *STICKY!*

I BETCHA *THIS* TIME I'LL BLOW ONE THAT'S EVEN *BIGGER!*

PFFFFFFFFFFFFF...

PTOO!

?

DARN! NOW I GOT THAT STICKY OL' *BUBBLE GUM* ALL OVER MY *HAND!*

IT WON'T COME *OFF*, EITHER!

PHOOEY!

CATCH THIS PASS, WILLY!

?

UGGH! TOO *HIGH*, TUB!

IT'S GOIN' OUT IN THE STREET! IT'LL GET *RUN OVER!*

STOP THA BALL, SOMEBODY

L.L. #126-5812

72

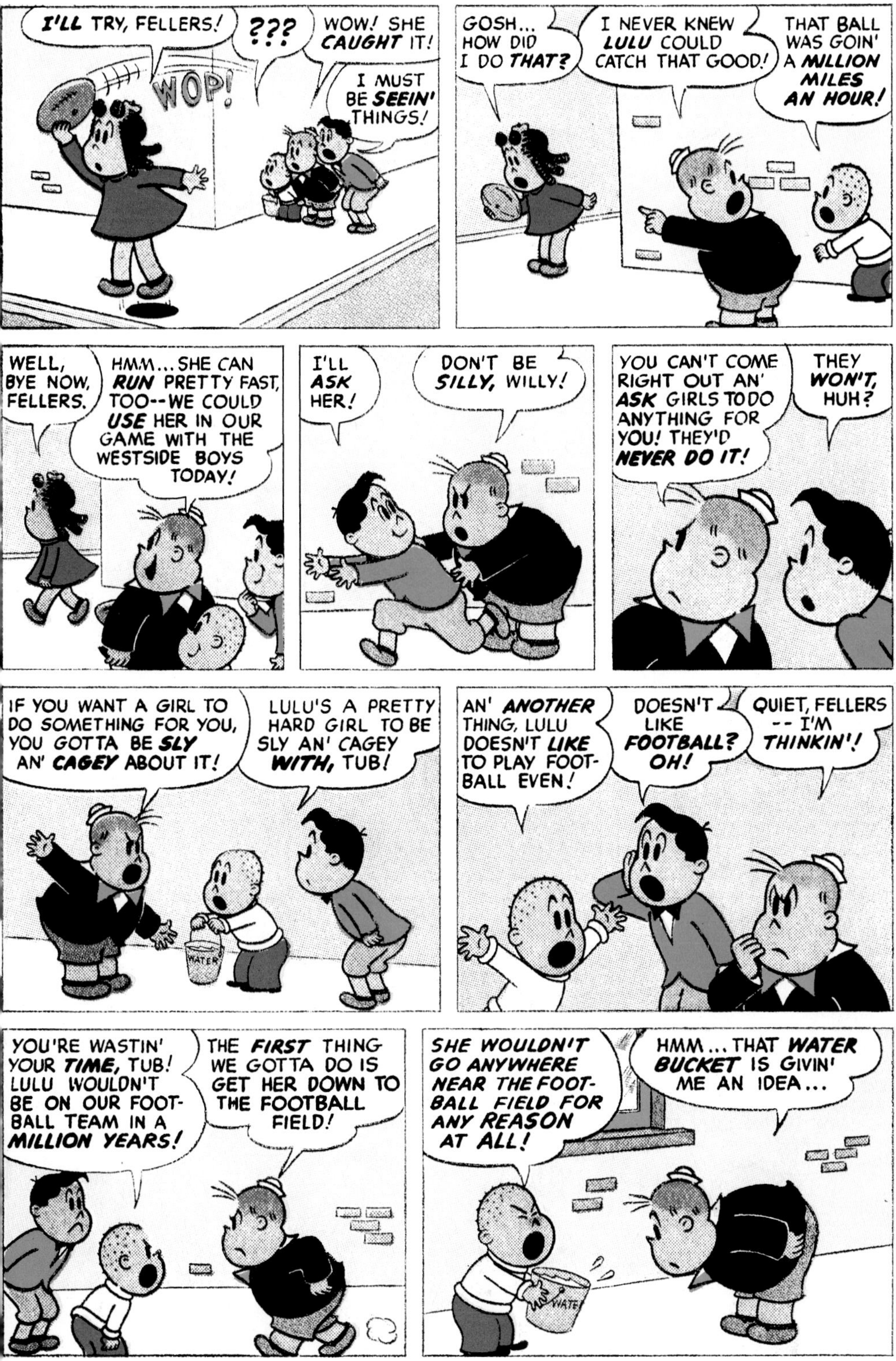
I'LL TRY, FELLERS!
WOP!
???
WOW! SHE CAUGHT IT!
I MUST BE SEEIN' THINGS!
GOSH... HOW DID I DO THAT?
I NEVER KNEW LULU COULD CATCH THAT GOOD!
THAT BALL WAS GOIN' A MILLION MILES AN HOUR!
WELL, BYE NOW, FELLERS.
HMM... SHE CAN RUN PRETTY FAST, TOO--WE COULD USE HER IN OUR GAME WITH THE WESTSIDE BOYS TODAY!
I'LL ASK HER!
DON'T BE SILLY, WILLY!
YOU CAN'T COME RIGHT OUT AN' ASK GIRLS TO DO ANYTHING FOR YOU! THEY'D NEVER DO IT!
THEY WON'T, HUH?
IF YOU WANT A GIRL TO DO SOMETHING FOR YOU, YOU GOTTA BE SLY AN' CAGEY ABOUT IT!
LULU'S A PRETTY HARD GIRL TO BE SLY AN' CAGEY WITH, TUB!
WATER
AN' ANOTHER THING, LULU DOESN'T LIKE TO PLAY FOOTBALL EVEN!
DOESN'T LIKE FOOTBALL? OH!
QUIET, FELLERS -- I'M THINKIN'!
YOU'RE WASTIN' YOUR TIME, TUB! LULU WOULDN'T BE ON OUR FOOTBALL TEAM IN A MILLION YEARS!
THE FIRST THING WE GOTTA DO IS GET HER DOWN TO THE FOOTBALL FIELD!
SHE WOULDN'T GO ANYWHERE NEAR THE FOOTBALL FIELD FOR ANY REASON AT ALL!
HMM... THAT WATER BUCKET IS GIVIN' ME AN IDEA...
WATER

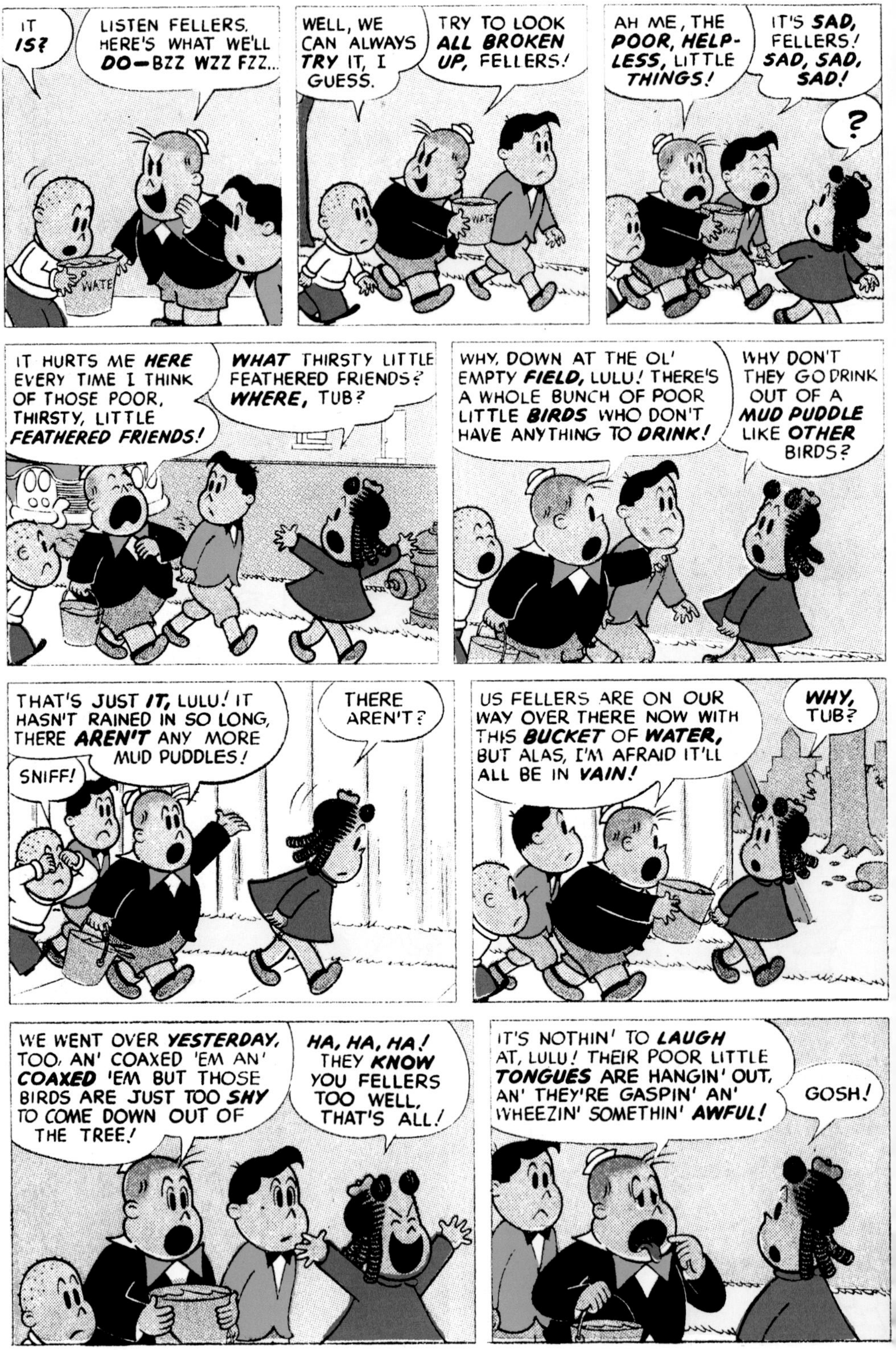

IT IS?
LISTEN FELLERS. HERE'S WHAT WE'LL DO—BZZ WZZ FZZ...
WATE
WELL, WE CAN ALWAYS TRY IT, I GUESS.
TRY TO LOOK ALL BROKEN UP, FELLERS!
WATE
AH ME, THE POOR, HELP-LESS, LITTLE THINGS!
IT'S SAD, FELLERS! SAD, SAD, SAD!
?
IT HURTS ME HERE EVERY TIME I THINK OF THOSE POOR, THIRSTY, LITTLE FEATHERED FRIENDS!
WHAT THIRSTY LITTLE FEATHERED FRIENDS? WHERE, TUB?
WHY, DOWN AT THE OL' EMPTY FIELD, LULU! THERE'S A WHOLE BUNCH OF POOR LITTLE BIRDS WHO DON'T HAVE ANYTHING TO DRINK!
WHY DON'T THEY GO DRINK OUT OF A MUD PUDDLE LIKE OTHER BIRDS?
THAT'S JUST IT, LULU! IT HASN'T RAINED IN SO LONG, THERE AREN'T ANY MORE MUD PUDDLES!
SNIFF!
THERE AREN'T?
US FELLERS ARE ON OUR WAY OVER THERE NOW WITH THIS BUCKET OF WATER, BUT ALAS, I'M AFRAID IT'LL ALL BE IN VAIN!
WHY, TUB?
WE WENT OVER YESTERDAY, TOO, AN' COAXED 'EM AN' COAXED 'EM BUT THOSE BIRDS ARE JUST TOO SHY TO COME DOWN OUT OF THE TREE!
HA, HA, HA! THEY KNOW YOU FELLERS TOO WELL, THAT'S ALL!
IT'S NOTHIN' TO LAUGH AT, LULU! THEIR POOR LITTLE TONGUES ARE HANGIN' OUT, AN' THEY'RE GASPIN' AN' WHEEZIN' SOMETHIN' AWFUL!
GOSH!

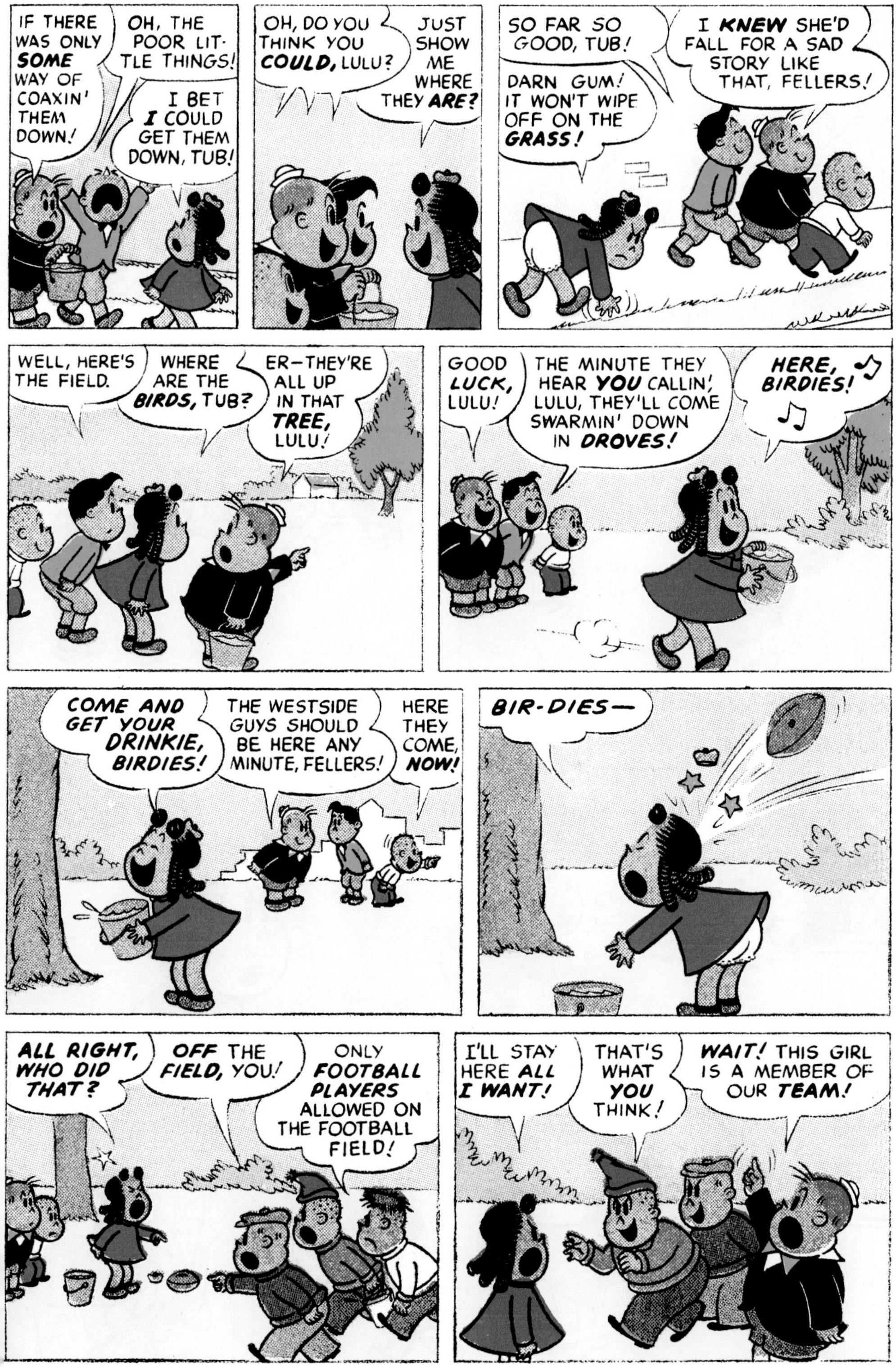
IF THERE WAS ONLY SOME WAY OF COAXIN' THEM DOWN!
OH, THE POOR LITTLE THINGS!
I BET I COULD GET THEM DOWN, TUB!
OH, DO YOU THINK YOU COULD, LULU?
JUST SHOW ME WHERE THEY ARE?
SO FAR SO GOOD, TUB!
DARN GUM! IT WON'T WIPE OFF ON THE GRASS!
I KNEW SHE'D FALL FOR A SAD STORY LIKE THAT, FELLERS!
WELL, HERE'S THE FIELD.
WHERE ARE THE BIRDS, TUB?
ER—THEY'RE ALL UP IN THAT TREE, LULU!
GOOD LUCK, LULU!
THE MINUTE THEY HEAR YOU CALLIN', LULU, THEY'LL COME SWARMIN' DOWN IN DROVES!
HERE, BIRDIES!
COME AND GET YOUR DRINKIE, BIRDIES!
THE WESTSIDE GUYS SHOULD BE HERE ANY MINUTE, FELLERS!
HERE THEY COME, NOW!
BIR-DIES—
ALL RIGHT, WHO DID THAT?
OFF THE FIELD, YOU!
ONLY FOOTBALL PLAYERS ALLOWED ON THE FOOTBALL FIELD!
I'LL STAY HERE ALL I WANT!
THAT'S WHAT YOU THINK!
WAIT! THIS GIRL IS A MEMBER OF OUR TEAM!

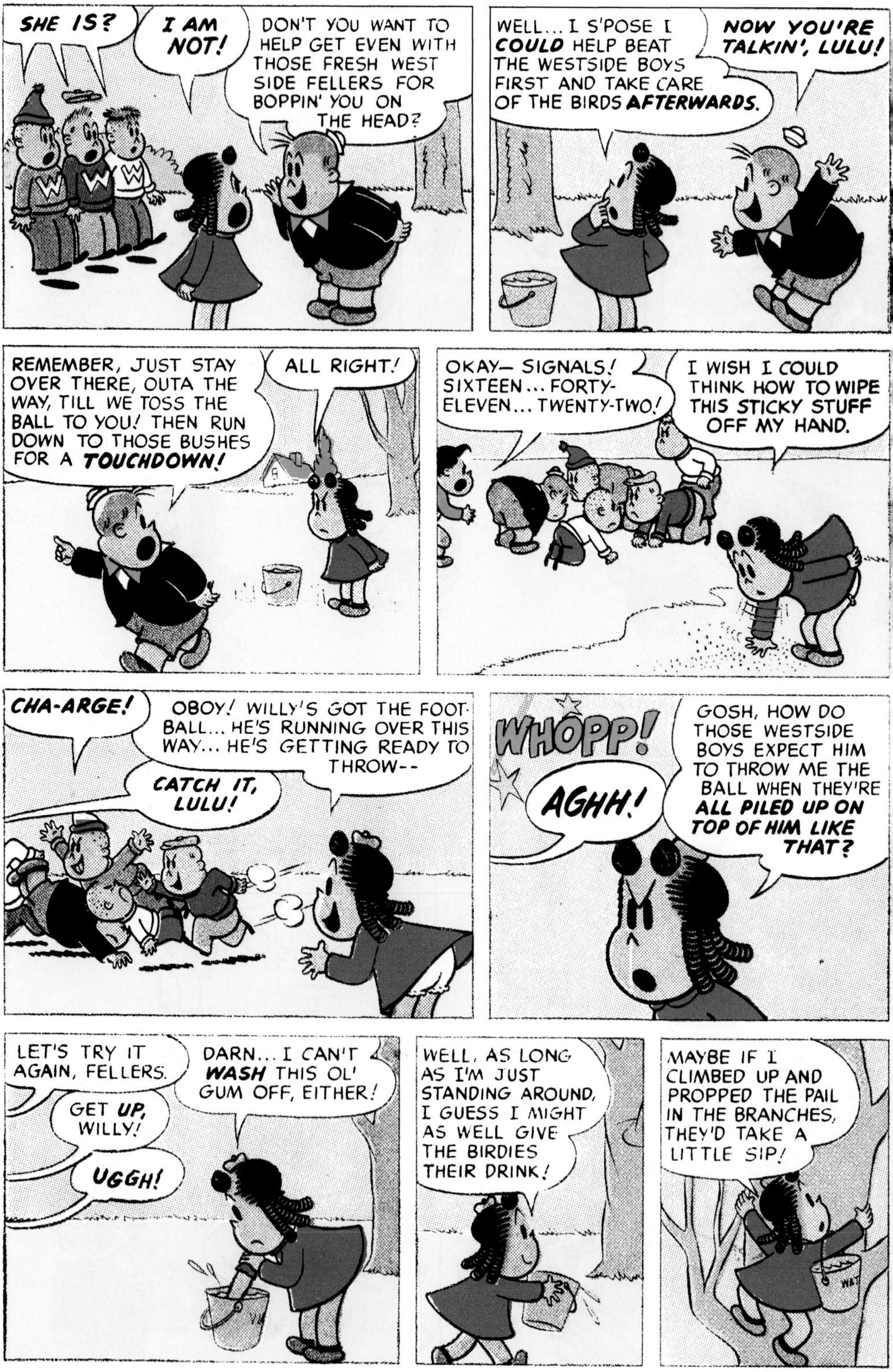
SHE IS?
I AM NOT!
DON'T YOU WANT TO HELP GET EVEN WITH THOSE FRESH WEST SIDE FELLERS FOR BOPPIN' YOU ON THE HEAD?
WELL... I S'POSE I COULD HELP BEAT THE WESTSIDE BOYS FIRST AND TAKE CARE OF THE BIRDS AFTERWARDS.
NOW YOU'RE TALKIN', LULU!
REMEMBER, JUST STAY OVER THERE, OUTA THE WAY, TILL WE TOSS THE BALL TO YOU! THEN RUN DOWN TO THOSE BUSHES FOR A TOUCHDOWN!
ALL RIGHT!
OKAY— SIGNALS! SIXTEEN... FORTY-ELEVEN... TWENTY-TWO!
I WISH I COULD THINK HOW TO WIPE THIS STICKY STUFF OFF MY HAND.
CHA-ARGE!
OBOY! WILLY'S GOT THE FOOTBALL... HE'S RUNNING OVER THIS WAY... HE'S GETTING READY TO THROW--
CATCH IT, LULU!
WHOPP!
AGHH!
GOSH, HOW DO THOSE WESTSIDE BOYS EXPECT HIM TO THROW ME THE BALL WHEN THEY'RE ALL PILED UP ON TOP OF HIM LIKE THAT?
LET'S TRY IT AGAIN, FELLERS.
GET UP, WILLY!
UGGH!
DARN... I CAN'T WASH THIS OL' GUM OFF, EITHER!
WELL, AS LONG AS I'M JUST STANDING AROUND, I GUESS I MIGHT AS WELL GIVE THE BIRDIES THEIR DRINK!
MAYBE IF I CLIMBED UP AND PROPPED THE PAIL IN THE BRANCHES, THEY'D TAKE A LITTLE SIP!

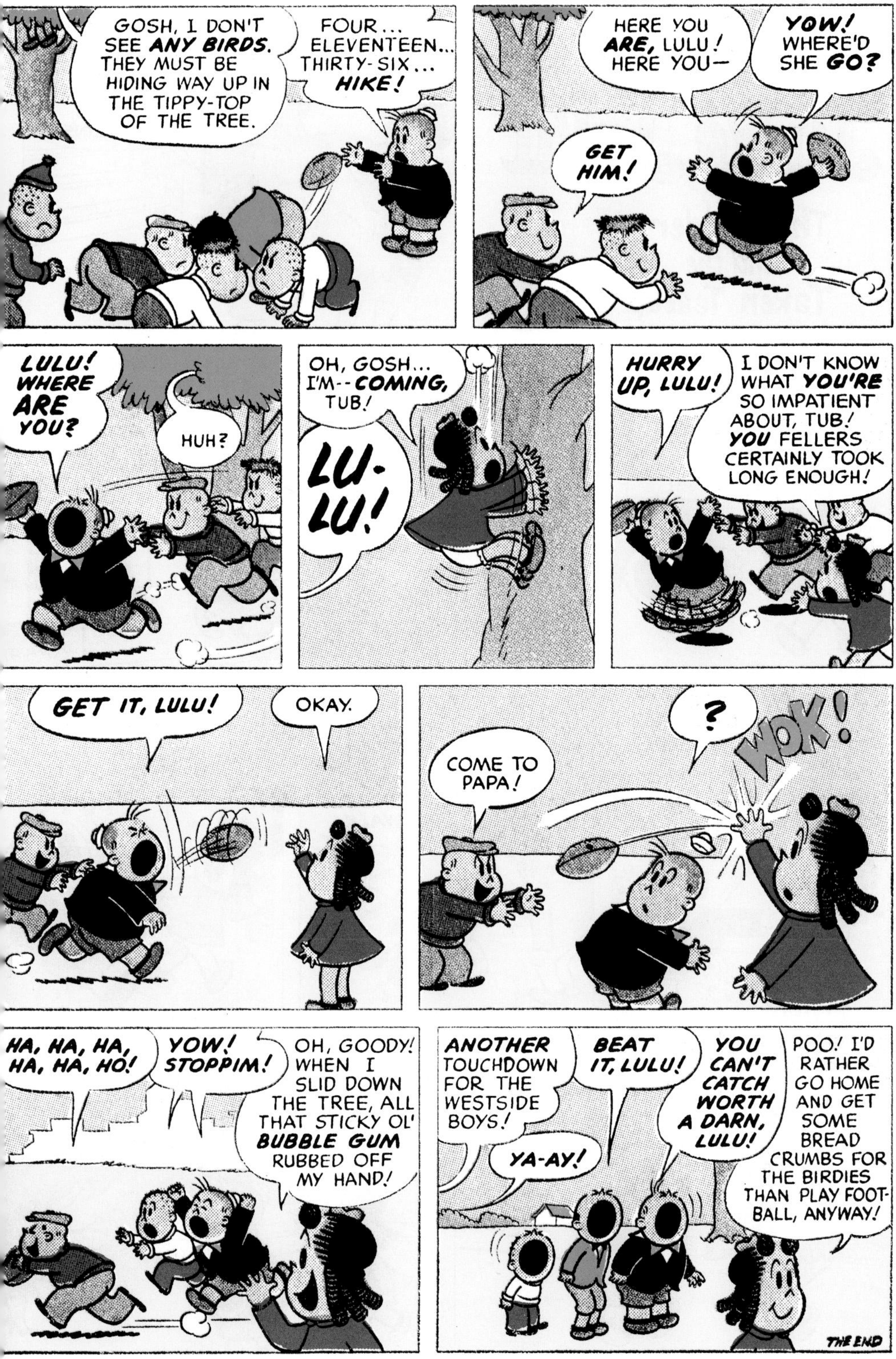

GOSH, I DON'T SEE ANY BIRDS. THEY MUST BE HIDING WAY UP IN THE TIPPY-TOP OF THE TREE.
FOUR... ELEVENTEEN... THIRTY-SIX... HIKE!
HERE YOU ARE, LULU! HERE YOU—
YOW! WHERE'D SHE GO?
GET HIM!
LULU! WHERE ARE YOU?
HUH?
OH, GOSH... I'M--COMING, TUB!
LU-LU!
HURRY UP, LULU!
I DON'T KNOW WHAT YOU'RE SO IMPATIENT ABOUT, TUB! YOU FELLERS CERTAINLY TOOK LONG ENOUGH!
GET IT, LULU!
OKAY.
COME TO PAPA!
?
WOK!
HA, HA, HA, HA, HA, HO!
YOW! STOPPIM!
OH, GOODY! WHEN I SLID DOWN THE TREE, ALL THAT STICKY OL' BUBBLE GUM RUBBED OFF MY HAND!
ANOTHER TOUCHDOWN FOR THE WESTSIDE BOYS!
YA-AY!
BEAT IT, LULU!
YOU CAN'T CATCH WORTH A DARN, LULU!
POO! I'D RATHER GO HOME AND GET SOME BREAD CRUMBS FOR THE BIRDIES THAN PLAY FOOTBALL, ANYWAY!
THE END

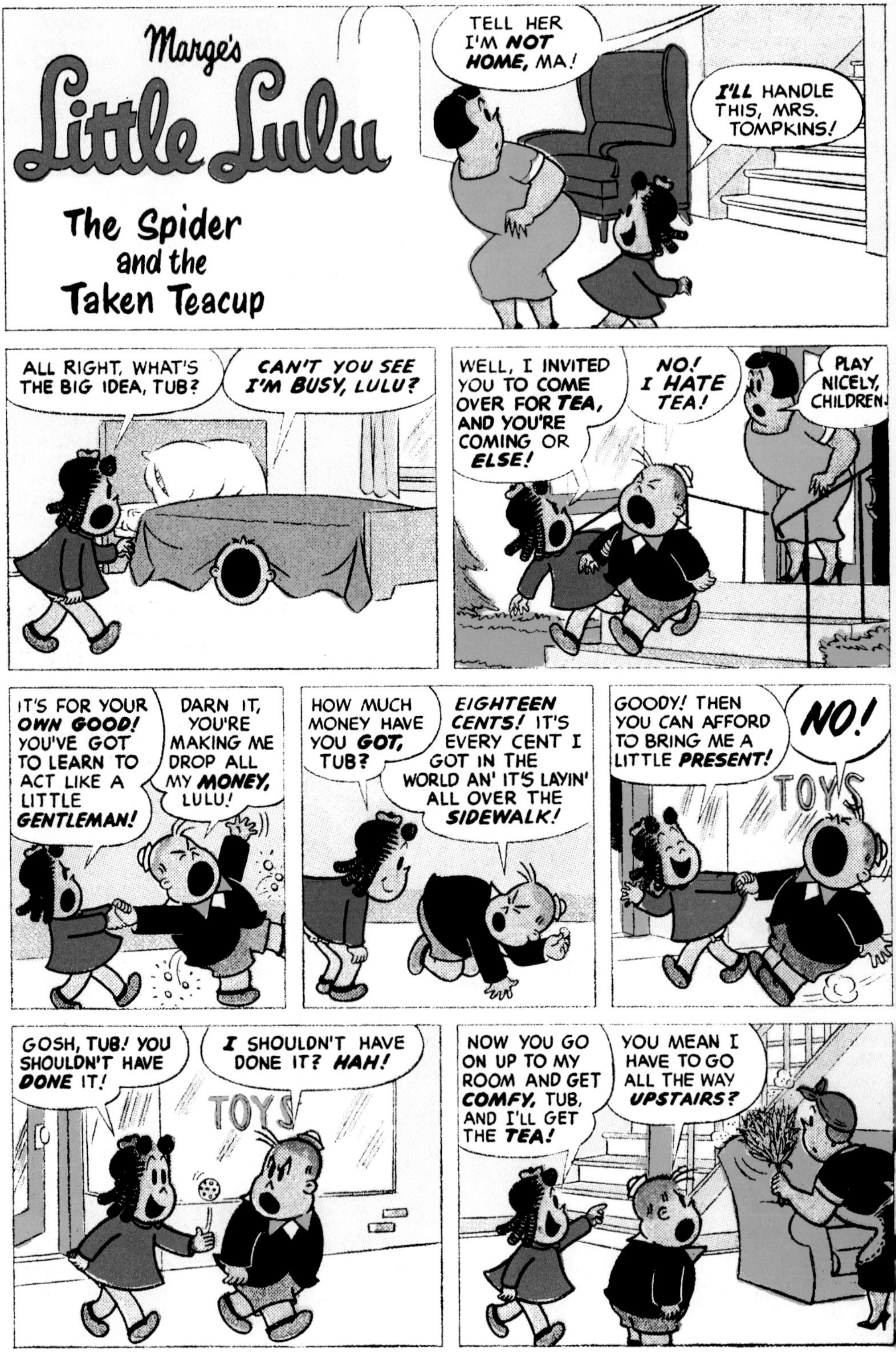

Marge's Little Lulu
The Spider and the Taken Teacup
TELL HER I'M NOT HOME, MA!
I'LL HANDLE THIS, MRS. TOMPKINS!
ALL RIGHT, WHAT'S THE BIG IDEA, TUB?
CAN'T YOU SEE I'M BUSY, LULU?
WELL, I INVITED YOU TO COME OVER FOR TEA, AND YOU'RE COMING OR ELSE!
NO! I HATE TEA!
PLAY NICELY, CHILDREN!
IT'S FOR YOUR OWN GOOD! YOU'VE GOT TO LEARN TO ACT LIKE A LITTLE GENTLEMAN!
DARN IT, YOU'RE MAKING ME DROP ALL MY MONEY, LULU!
HOW MUCH MONEY HAVE YOU GOT, TUB?
EIGHTEEN CENTS! IT'S EVERY CENT I GOT IN THE WORLD AN' IT'S LAYIN' ALL OVER THE SIDEWALK!
GOODY! THEN YOU CAN AFFORD TO BRING ME A LITTLE PRESENT!
NO!
TOYS
GOSH, TUB! YOU SHOULDN'T HAVE DONE IT!
I SHOULDN'T HAVE DONE IT? HAH!
TOYS
NOW YOU GO ON UP TO MY ROOM AND GET COMFY, TUB, AND I'LL GET THE TEA!
YOU MEAN I HAVE TO GO ALL THE WAY UPSTAIRS?

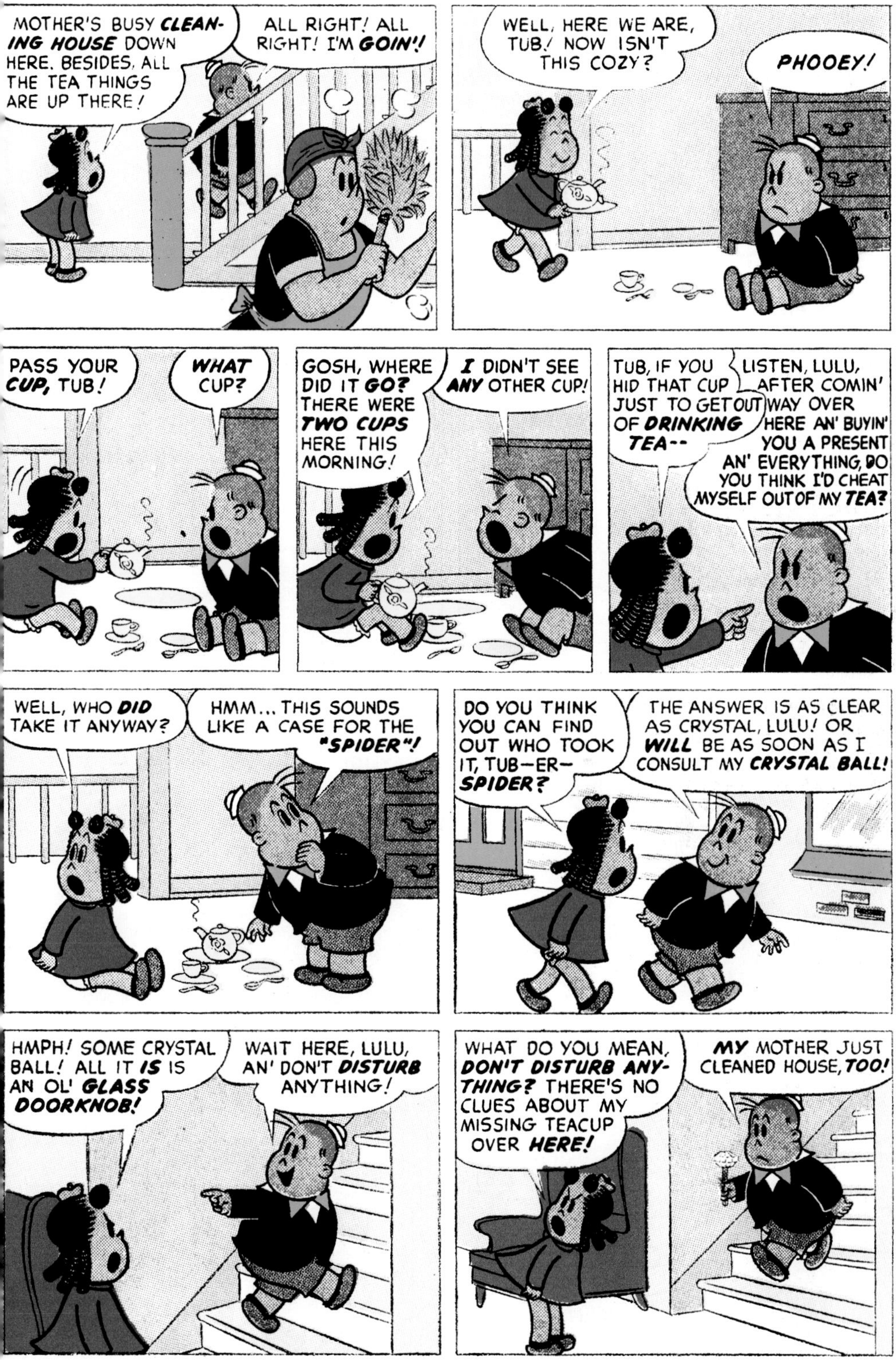
MOTHER'S BUSY CLEANING HOUSE DOWN HERE. BESIDES, ALL THE TEA THINGS ARE UP THERE!
ALL RIGHT! ALL RIGHT! I'M GOIN'!
WELL, HERE WE ARE, TUB! NOW ISN'T THIS COZY?
PHOOEY!
PASS YOUR CUP, TUB!
WHAT CUP?
GOSH, WHERE DID IT GO? THERE WERE TWO CUPS HERE THIS MORNING!
I DIDN'T SEE ANY OTHER CUP!
TUB, IF YOU HID THAT CUP JUST TO GET OUT OF DRINKING TEA--
LISTEN, LULU, AFTER COMIN' WAY OVER HERE AN' BUYIN' YOU A PRESENT AN' EVERYTHING, DO YOU THINK I'D CHEAT MYSELF OUT OF MY TEA?
WELL, WHO DID TAKE IT ANYWAY?
HMM... THIS SOUNDS LIKE A CASE FOR THE "SPIDER"!
DO YOU THINK YOU CAN FIND OUT WHO TOOK IT, TUB--ER--SPIDER?
THE ANSWER IS AS CLEAR AS CRYSTAL, LULU! OR WILL BE AS SOON AS I CONSULT MY CRYSTAL BALL!
HMPH! SOME CRYSTAL BALL! ALL IT IS IS AN OL' GLASS DOORKNOB!
WAIT HERE, LULU, AN' DON'T DISTURB ANYTHING!
WHAT DO YOU MEAN, DON'T DISTURB ANYTHING? THERE'S NO CLUES ABOUT MY MISSING TEACUP OVER HERE!
MY MOTHER JUST CLEANED HOUSE, TOO!

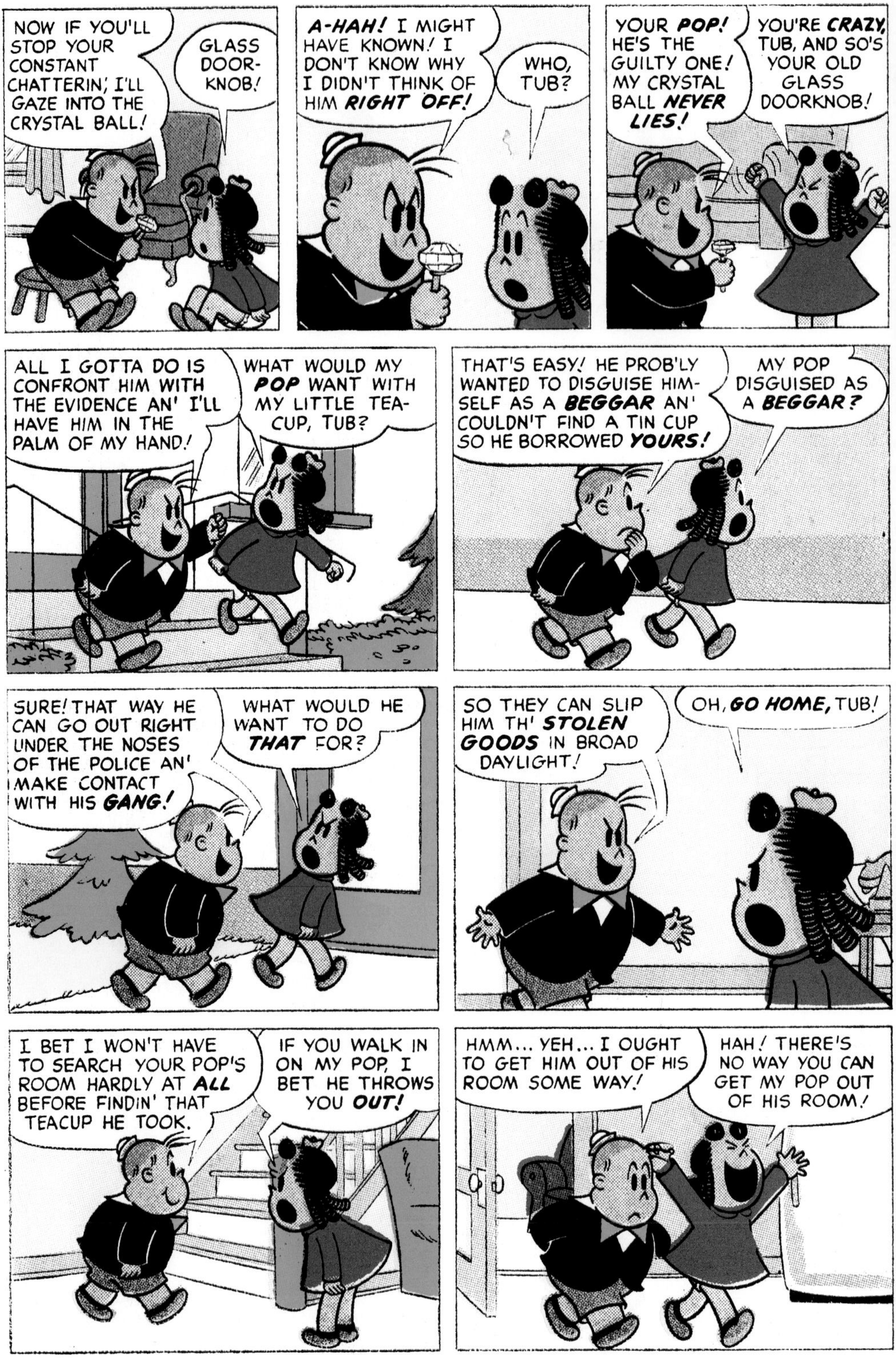
NOW IF YOU'LL STOP YOUR CONSTANT CHATTERIN', I'LL GAZE INTO THE CRYSTAL BALL!
GLASS DOOR-KNOB!
A-HAH! I MIGHT HAVE KNOWN! I DON'T KNOW WHY I DIDN'T THINK OF HIM RIGHT OFF!
WHO, TUB?
YOUR POP! HE'S THE GUILTY ONE! MY CRYSTAL BALL NEVER LIES!
YOU'RE CRAZY, TUB, AND SO'S YOUR OLD GLASS DOORKNOB!
ALL I GOTTA DO IS CONFRONT HIM WITH THE EVIDENCE AN' I'LL HAVE HIM IN THE PALM OF MY HAND!
WHAT WOULD MY POP WANT WITH MY LITTLE TEA-CUP, TUB?
THAT'S EASY! HE PROB'LY WANTED TO DISGUISE HIM-SELF AS A BEGGAR AN' COULDN'T FIND A TIN CUP SO HE BORROWED YOURS!
MY POP DISGUISED AS A BEGGAR?
SURE! THAT WAY HE CAN GO OUT RIGHT UNDER THE NOSES OF THE POLICE AN' MAKE CONTACT WITH HIS GANG!
WHAT WOULD HE WANT TO DO THAT FOR?
SO THEY CAN SLIP HIM TH' STOLEN GOODS IN BROAD DAYLIGHT!
OH, GO HOME, TUB!
I BET I WON'T HAVE TO SEARCH YOUR POP'S ROOM HARDLY AT ALL BEFORE FINDIN' THAT TEACUP HE TOOK.
IF YOU WALK IN ON MY POP, I BET HE THROWS YOU OUT!
HMM... YEH... I OUGHT TO GET HIM OUT OF HIS ROOM SOME WAY!
HAH! THERE'S NO WAY YOU CAN GET MY POP OUT OF HIS ROOM!

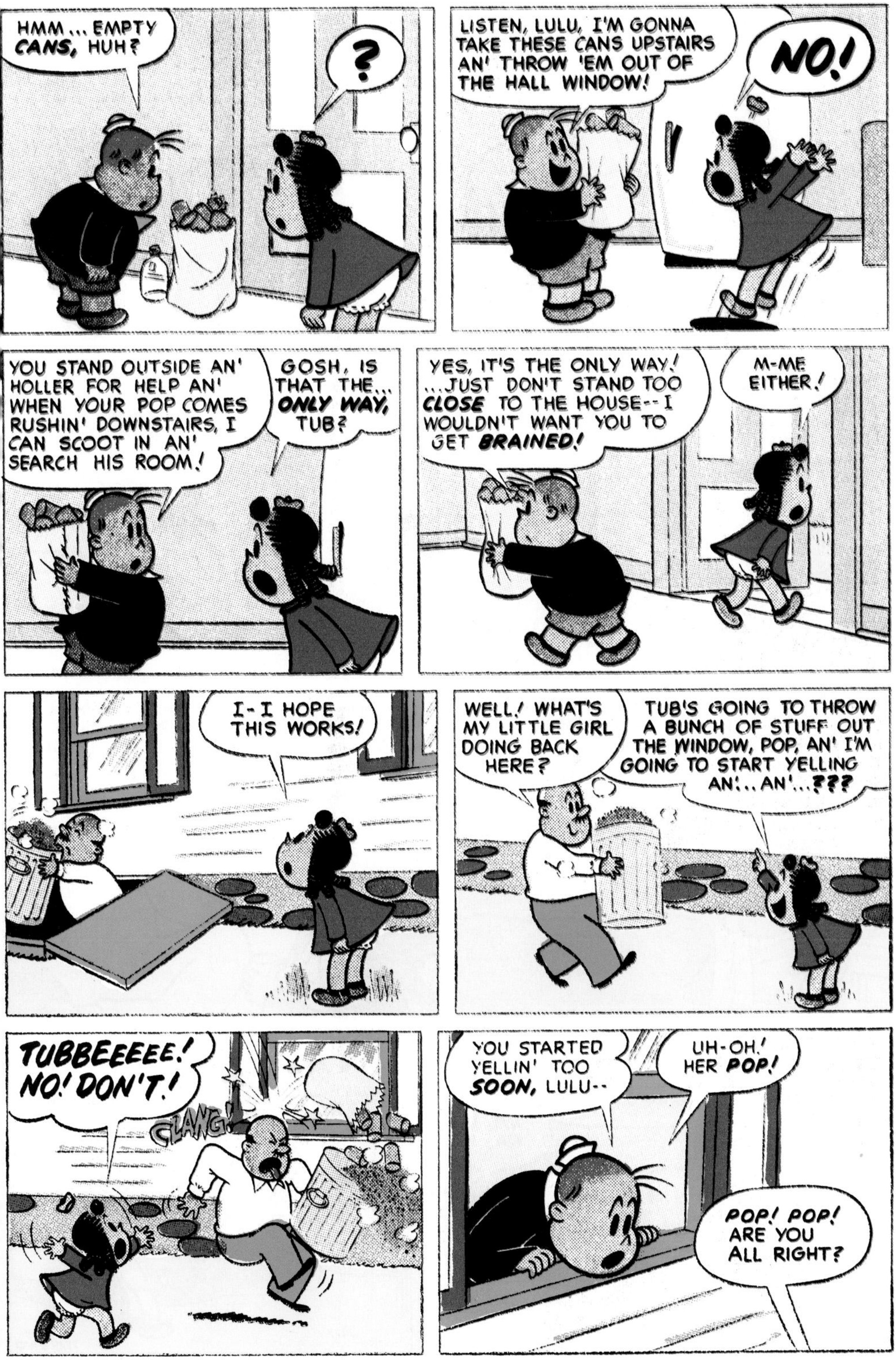
HMM... EMPTY CANS, HUH?
?
LISTEN, LULU, I'M GONNA TAKE THESE CANS UPSTAIRS AN' THROW 'EM OUT OF THE HALL WINDOW!
NO!
YOU STAND OUTSIDE AN' HOLLER FOR HELP AN' WHEN YOUR POP COMES RUSHIN' DOWNSTAIRS, I CAN SCOOT IN AN' SEARCH HIS ROOM!
GOSH, IS THAT THE... ONLY WAY, TUB?
YES, IT'S THE ONLY WAY! ...JUST DON'T STAND TOO CLOSE TO THE HOUSE--I WOULDN'T WANT YOU TO GET BRAINED!
M-ME EITHER!
I-I HOPE THIS WORKS!
WELL! WHAT'S MY LITTLE GIRL DOING BACK HERE?
TUB'S GOING TO THROW A BUNCH OF STUFF OUT THE WINDOW, POP, AN' I'M GOING TO START YELLING AN'... AN'...???
TUBBEEEEE! NO! DON'T!
CLANG!
YOU STARTED YELLIN' TOO SOON, LULU--
UH-OH! HER POP!
POP! POP! ARE YOU ALL RIGHT?

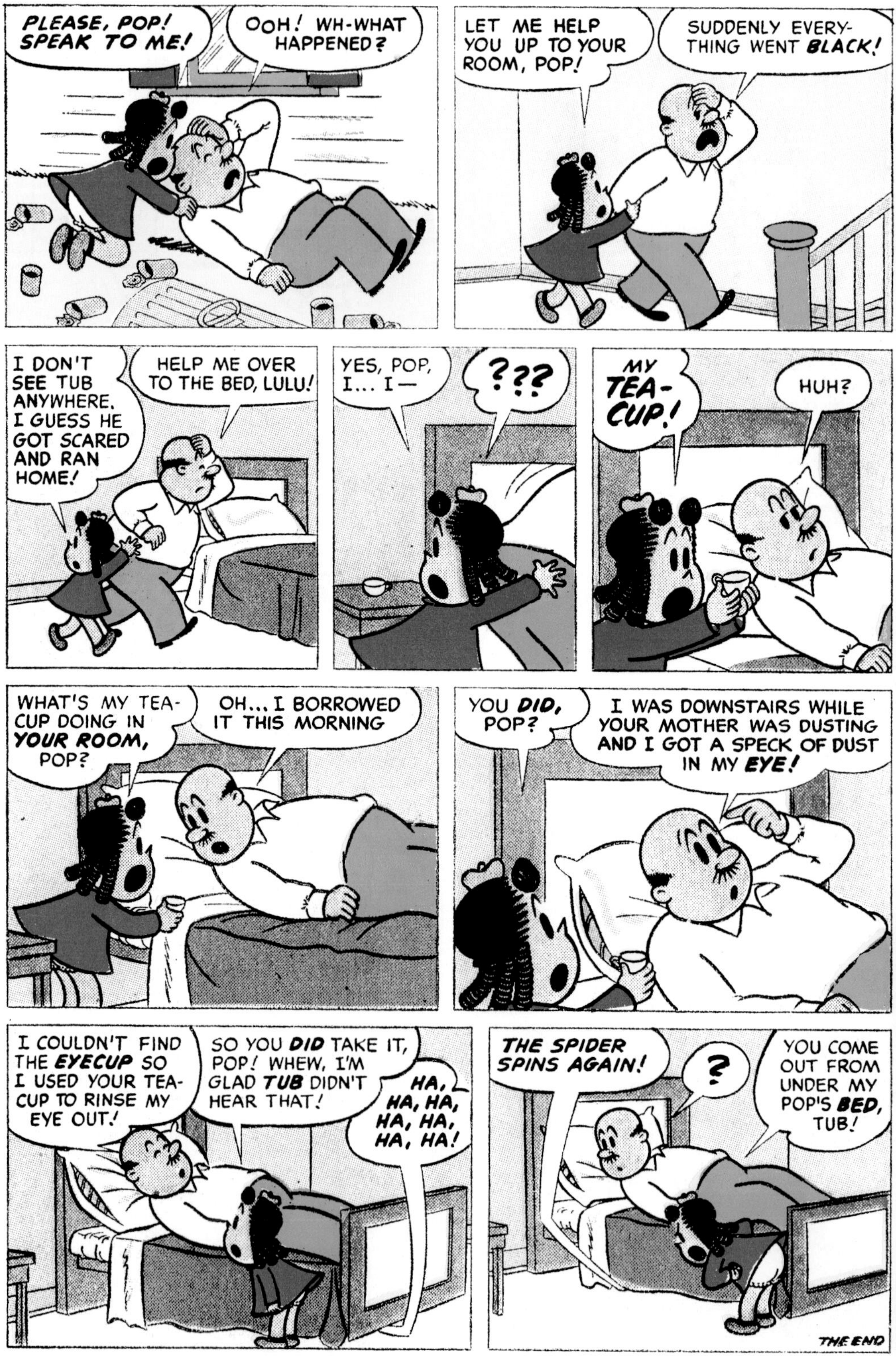
PLEASE, POP! SPEAK TO ME!
OOH! WH-WHAT HAPPENED?
LET ME HELP YOU UP TO YOUR ROOM, POP!
SUDDENLY EVERY-THING WENT BLACK!
I DON'T SEE TUB ANYWHERE. I GUESS HE GOT SCARED AND RAN HOME!
HELP ME OVER TO THE BED, LULU!
YES, POP, I... I—
???
MY TEA-CUP!
HUH?
WHAT'S MY TEA-CUP DOING IN YOUR ROOM, POP?
OH... I BORROWED IT THIS MORNING
YOU DID, POP?
I WAS DOWNSTAIRS WHILE YOUR MOTHER WAS DUSTING AND I GOT A SPECK OF DUST IN MY EYE!
I COULDN'T FIND THE EYECUP SO I USED YOUR TEA-CUP TO RINSE MY EYE OUT!
SO YOU DID TAKE IT, POP! WHEW, I'M GLAD TUB DIDN'T HEAR THAT!
HA, HA, HA, HA, HA, HA, HA!
THE SPIDER SPINS AGAIN!
?
YOU COME OUT FROM UNDER MY POP'S BED, TUB!
THE END

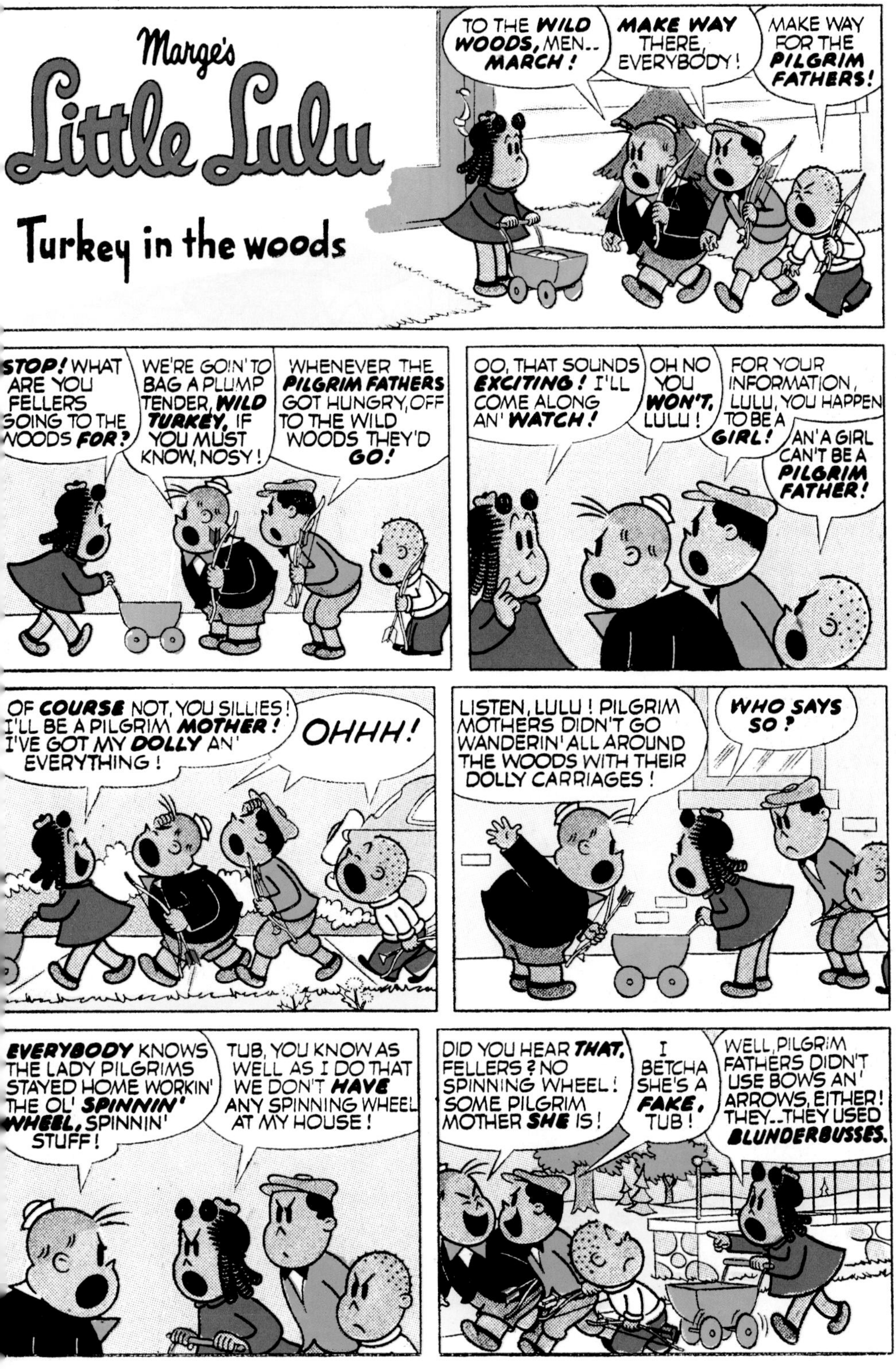

Marge's Little Lulu
Turkey in the woods
TO THE WILD WOODS, MEN.. MARCH!
MAKE WAY THERE, EVERYBODY!
MAKE WAY FOR THE PILGRIM FATHERS!
STOP! WHAT ARE YOU FELLERS GOING TO THE WOODS FOR?
WE'RE GOIN' TO BAG A PLUMP TENDER, WILD TURKEY, IF YOU MUST KNOW, NOSY!
WHENEVER THE PILGRIM FATHERS GOT HUNGRY, OFF TO THE WILD WOODS THEY'D GO!
OO, THAT SOUNDS EXCITING! I'LL COME ALONG AN' WATCH!
OH NO YOU WON'T, LULU!
FOR YOUR INFORMATION, LULU, YOU HAPPEN TO BE A GIRL!
AN' A GIRL CAN'T BE A PILGRIM FATHER!
OF COURSE NOT, YOU SILLIES! I'LL BE A PILGRIM MOTHER! I'VE GOT MY DOLLY AN' EVERYTHING!
OHHH!
LISTEN, LULU! PILGRIM MOTHERS DIDN'T GO WANDERIN' ALL AROUND THE WOODS WITH THEIR DOLLY CARRIAGES!
WHO SAYS SO?
EVERYBODY KNOWS THE LADY PILGRIMS STAYED HOME WORKIN' THE OL' SPINNIN' WHEEL, SPINNIN' STUFF!
TUB, YOU KNOW AS WELL AS I DO THAT WE DON'T HAVE ANY SPINNING WHEEL AT MY HOUSE!
DID YOU HEAR THAT, FELLERS? NO SPINNING WHEEL! SOME PILGRIM MOTHER SHE IS!
I BETCHA SHE'S A FAKE, TUB!
WELL, PILGRIM FATHERS DIDN'T USE BOWS AN' ARROWS, EITHER! THEY..THEY USED BLUNDERBUSSES.

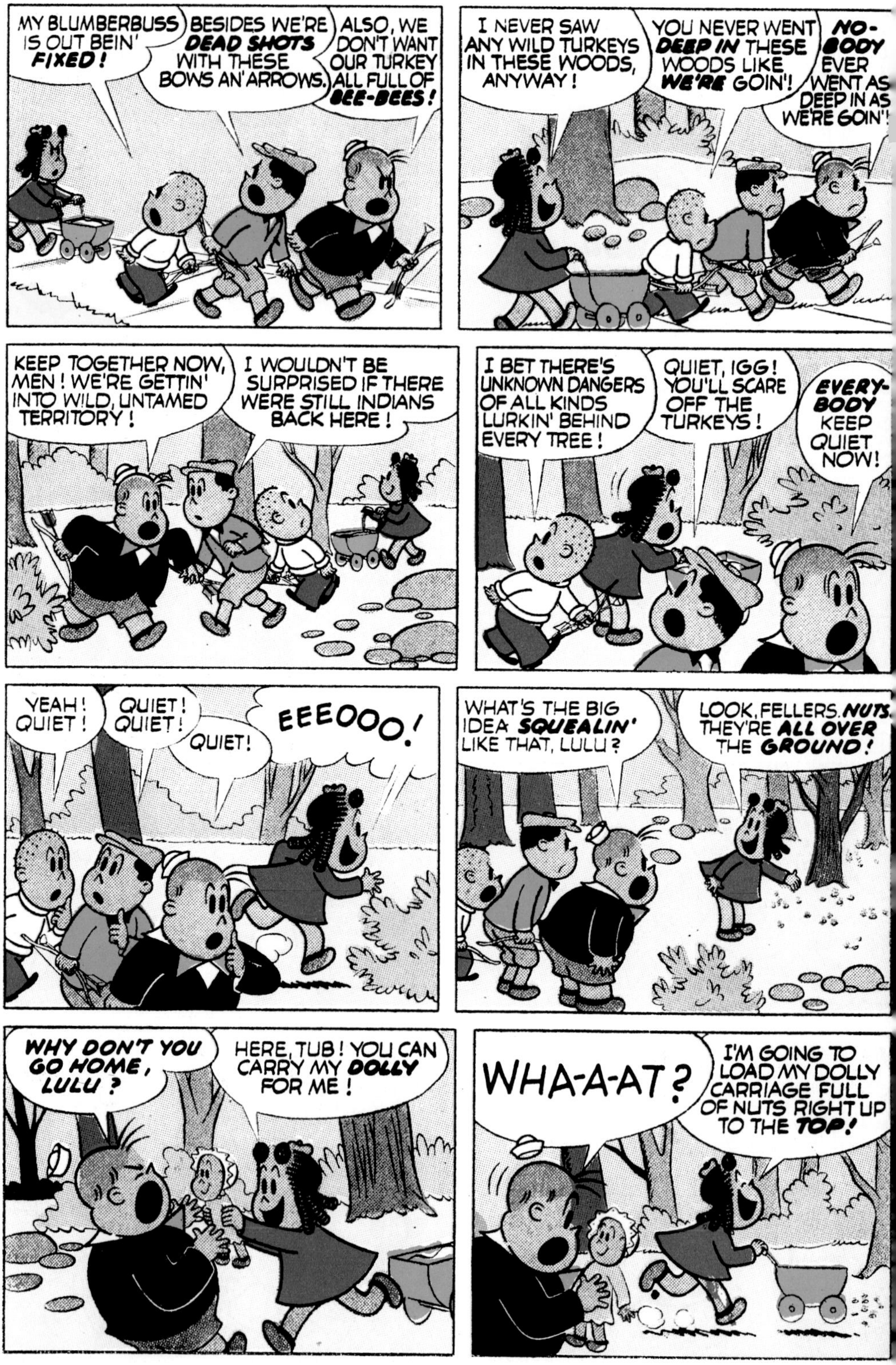
MY BLUMBERBUSS IS OUT BEIN' FIXED!
BESIDES WE'RE DEAD SHOTS WITH THESE BOWS AN' ARROWS.
ALSO, WE DON'T WANT OUR TURKEY ALL FULL OF BEE-BEES!
I NEVER SAW ANY WILD TURKEYS IN THESE WOODS, ANYWAY!
YOU NEVER WENT DEEP IN THESE WOODS LIKE WE'RE GOIN'!
NO-BODY EVER WENT AS DEEP IN AS WE'RE GOIN'!
KEEP TOGETHER NOW, MEN! WE'RE GETTIN' INTO WILD, UNTAMED TERRITORY!
I WOULDN'T BE SURPRISED IF THERE WERE STILL INDIANS BACK HERE!
I BET THERE'S UNKNOWN DANGERS OF ALL KINDS LURKIN' BEHIND EVERY TREE!
QUIET, IGG! YOU'LL SCARE OFF THE TURKEYS!
EVERY-BODY KEEP QUIET NOW!
YEAH! QUIET!
QUIET! QUIET!
QUIET!
EEEOOO!
WHAT'S THE BIG IDEA SQUEALIN' LIKE THAT, LULU?
LOOK, FELLERS. NUTS. THEY'RE ALL OVER THE GROUND!
WHY DON'T YOU GO HOME, LULU?
HERE, TUB! YOU CAN CARRY MY DOLLY FOR ME!
WHA-A-AT?
I'M GOING TO LOAD MY DOLLY CARRIAGE FULL OF NUTS RIGHT UP TO THE TOP!

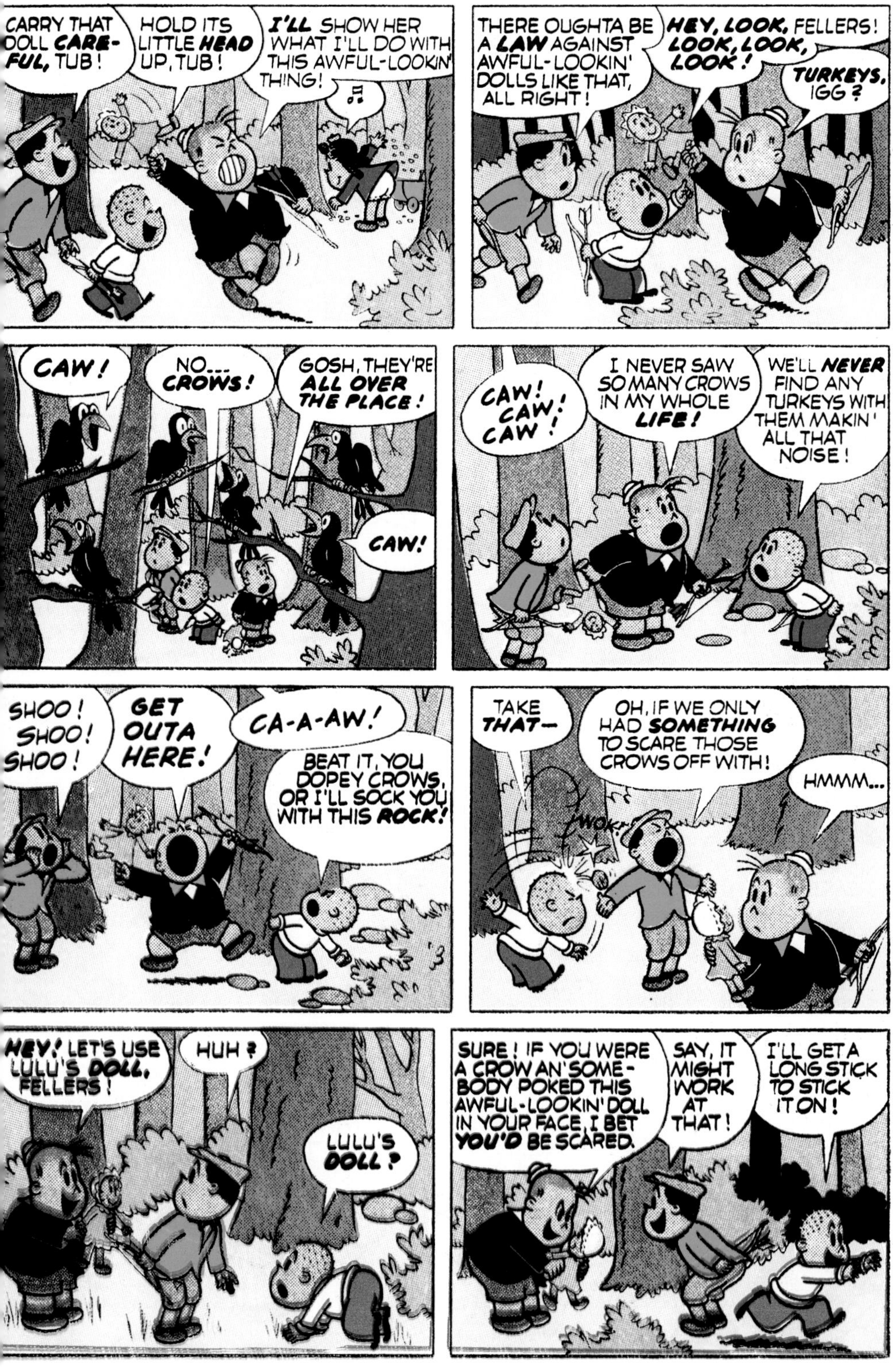
CARRY THAT DOLL CAREFUL, TUB!
HOLD ITS LITTLE HEAD UP, TUB!
I'LL SHOW HER WHAT I'LL DO WITH THIS AWFUL-LOOKIN' THING!
THERE OUGHTA BE A LAW AGAINST AWFUL-LOOKIN' DOLLS LIKE THAT, ALL RIGHT!
HEY, LOOK, FELLERS! LOOK, LOOK, LOOK!
TURKEYS, IGG?
CAW!
NO.... CROWS!
GOSH, THEY'RE ALL OVER THE PLACE!
CAW!
CAW! CAW! CAW!
I NEVER SAW SO MANY CROWS IN MY WHOLE LIFE!
WE'LL NEVER FIND ANY TURKEYS WITH THEM MAKIN' ALL THAT NOISE!
SHOO! SHOO! SHOO!
GET OUTA HERE!
CA-A-AW!
BEAT IT, YOU DOPEY CROWS, OR I'LL SOCK YOU WITH THIS ROCK!
TAKE THAT—
OH, IF WE ONLY HAD SOMETHING TO SCARE THOSE CROWS OFF WITH!
HMMM...
WOK!
HEY! LET'S USE LULU'S DOLL, FELLERS!
HUH?
LULU'S DOLL?
SURE! IF YOU WERE A CROW AN' SOMEBODY POKED THIS AWFUL-LOOKIN' DOLL IN YOUR FACE, I BET YOU'D BE SCARED.
SAY, IT MIGHT WORK AT THAT!
I'LL GET A LONG STICK TO STICK IT ON!

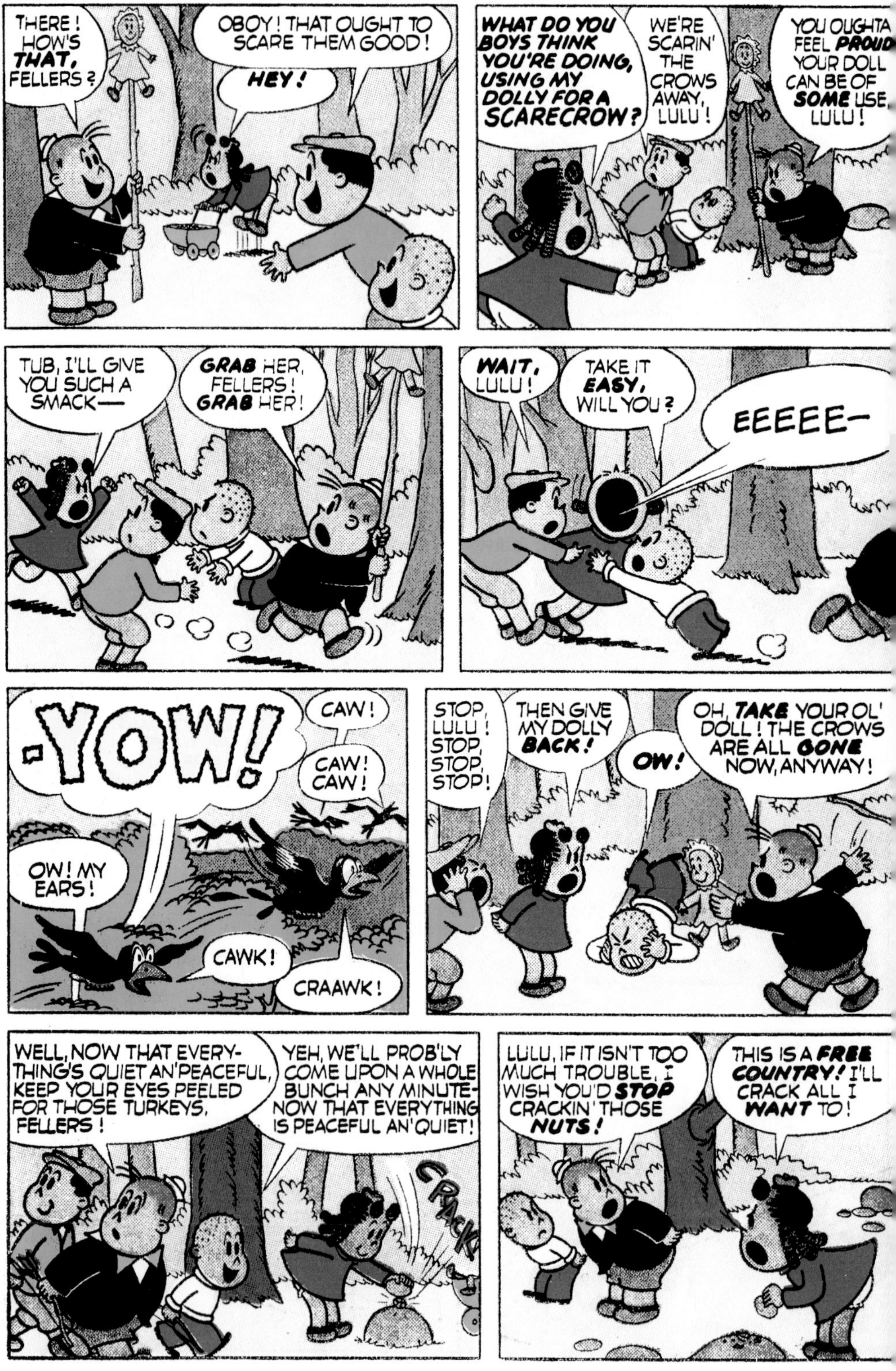

THERE! HOW'S **THAT,** FELLERS?
OBOY! THAT OUGHT TO SCARE THEM GOOD!
HEY!
WHAT DO YOU BOYS THINK YOU'RE DOING, USING MY DOLLY FOR A SCARECROW?
WE'RE SCARIN' THE CROWS AWAY, LULU!
YOU OUGHTA FEEL **PROUD** YOUR DOLL CAN BE OF **SOME** USE, LULU!
TUB, I'LL GIVE YOU SUCH A SMACK—
GRAB HER, FELLERS! **GRAB** HER!
WAIT, LULU!
TAKE IT **EASY,** WILL YOU?
EEEEE-
-YOW!
CAW!
CAW! CAW!
OW! MY EARS!
CAWK!
CRAAWK!
STOP, LULU! STOP, STOP, STOP!
THEN GIVE MY DOLLY **BACK!**
OW!
OH, **TAKE** YOUR OL' DOLL! THE CROWS ARE ALL **GONE** NOW, ANYWAY!
WELL, NOW THAT EVERY-THING'S QUIET AN' PEACEFUL, KEEP YOUR EYES PEELED FOR THOSE TURKEYS, FELLERS!
YEH, WE'LL PROB'LY COME UPON A WHOLE BUNCH ANY MINUTE- NOW THAT EVERYTHING IS PEACEFUL AN' QUIET!
CRACK!
LULU, IF IT ISN'T TOO MUCH TROUBLE, I WISH YOU'D **STOP** CRACKIN' THOSE **NUTS!**
THIS IS A **FREE COUNTRY!** I'LL CRACK ALL I **WANT** TO!

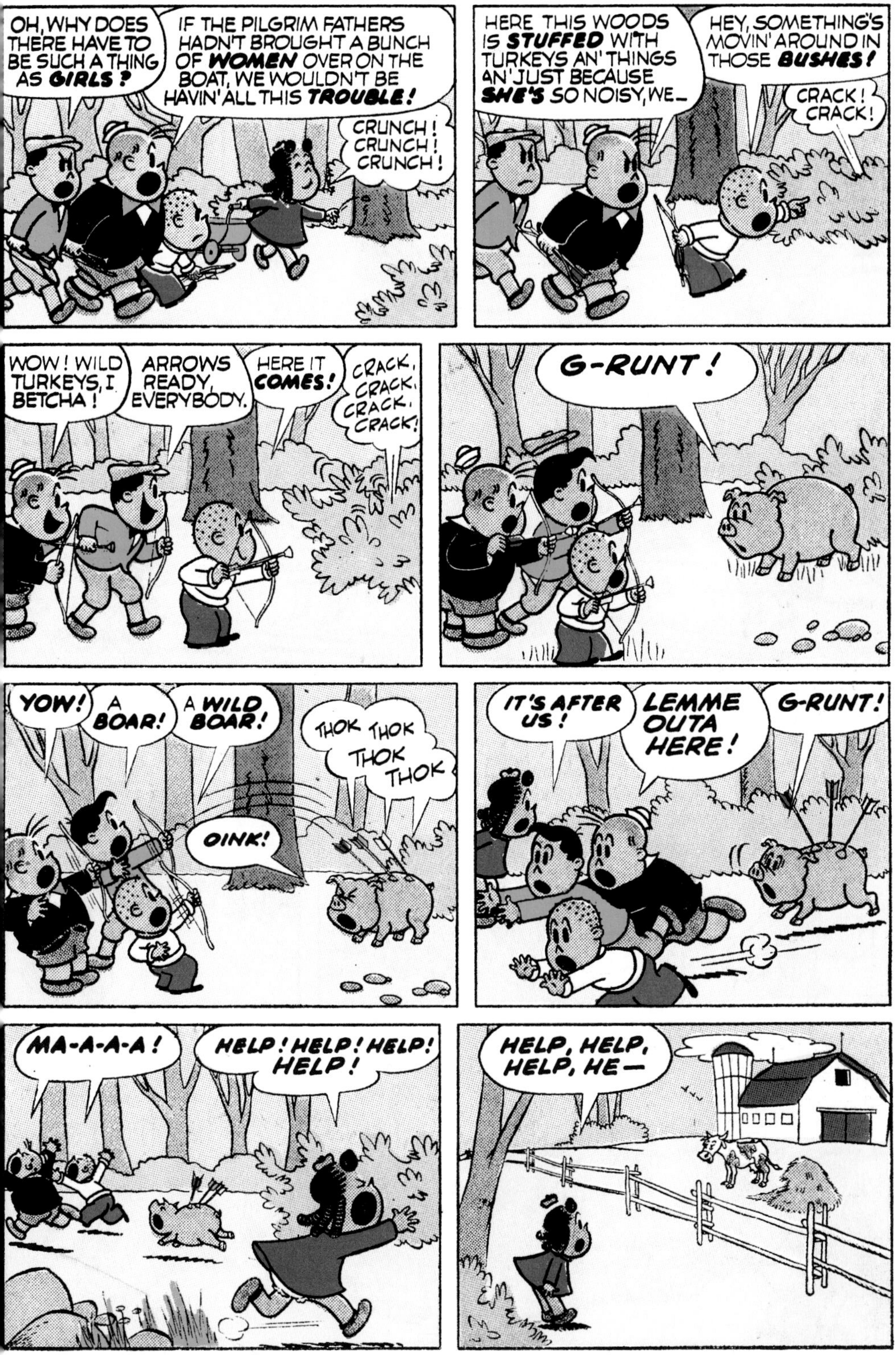
OH, WHY DOES THERE HAVE TO BE SUCH A THING AS GIRLS?
IF THE PILGRIM FATHERS HADN'T BROUGHT A BUNCH OF WOMEN OVER ON THE BOAT, WE WOULDN'T BE HAVIN' ALL THIS TROUBLE!
CRUNCH! CRUNCH! CRUNCH!
HERE THIS WOODS IS STUFFED WITH TURKEYS AN' THINGS AN' JUST BECAUSE SHE'S SO NOISY, WE_
HEY, SOMETHING'S MOVIN' AROUND IN THOSE BUSHES!
CRACK! CRACK!
WOW! WILD TURKEYS, I BETCHA!
ARROWS READY, EVERYBODY.
HERE IT COMES!
CRACK, CRACK, CRACK, CRACK!
G-RUNT!
YOW!
A BOAR!
A WILD BOAR!
THOK THOK THOK THOK
OINK!
IT'S AFTER US!
LEMME OUTA HERE!
G-RUNT!
MA-A-A-A!
HELP! HELP! HELP! HELP!
HELP, HELP, HELP, HE—

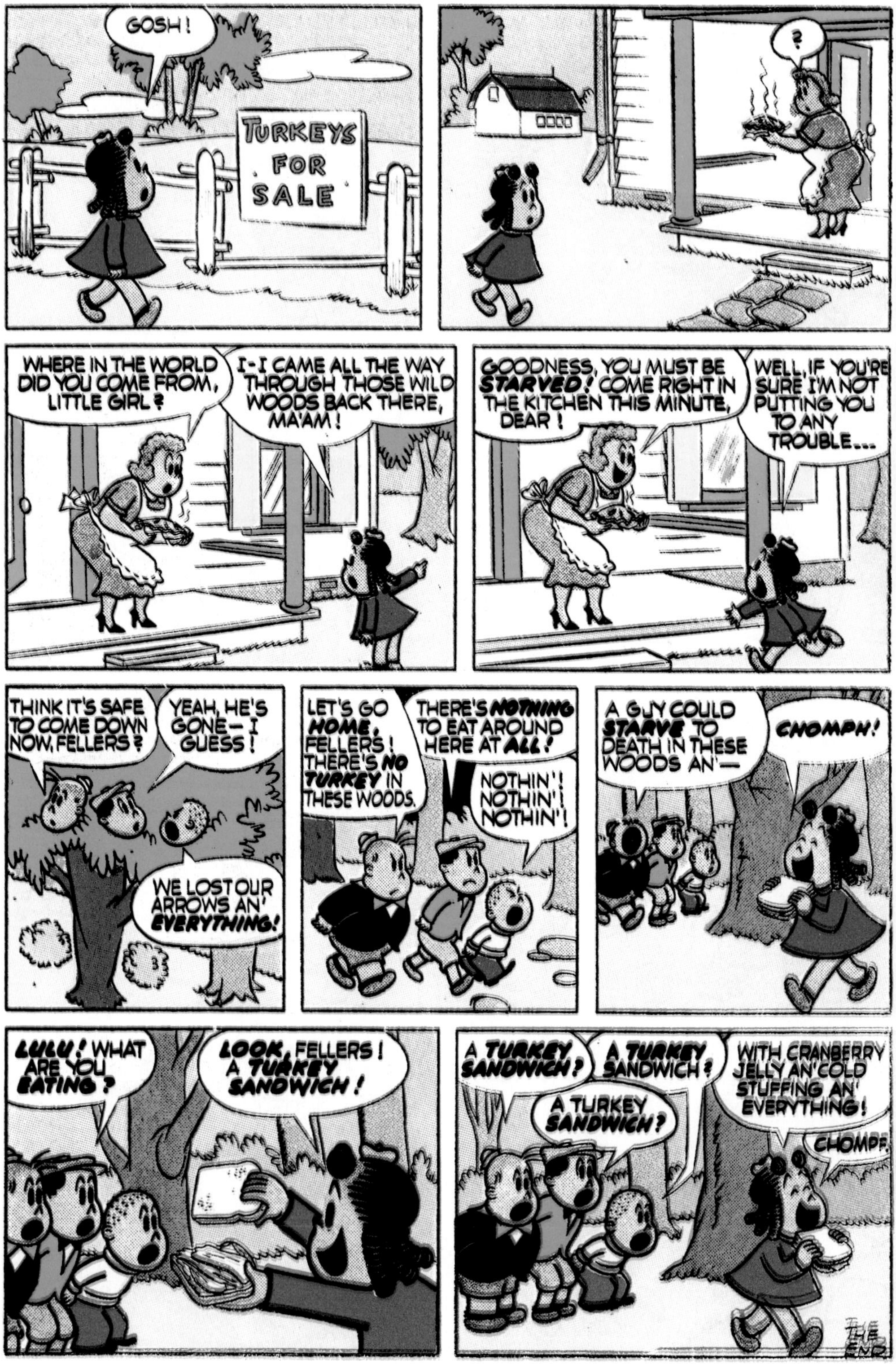
GOSH!
TURKEYS FOR SALE
?
WHERE IN THE WORLD DID YOU COME FROM, LITTLE GIRL?
I-I CAME ALL THE WAY THROUGH THOSE WILD WOODS BACK THERE, MA'AM!
GOODNESS, YOU MUST BE STARVED! COME RIGHT IN THE KITCHEN THIS MINUTE, DEAR!
WELL, IF YOU'RE SURE I'M NOT PUTTING YOU TO ANY TROUBLE...
THINK IT'S SAFE TO COME DOWN NOW, FELLERS?
YEAH, HE'S GONE—I GUESS!
WE LOST OUR ARROWS AN' EVERYTHING!
LET'S GO HOME, FELLERS! THERE'S NO TURKEY IN THESE WOODS.
THERE'S NOTHING TO EAT AROUND HERE AT ALL!
NOTHIN'! NOTHIN'! NOTHIN'!
A GUY COULD STARVE TO DEATH IN THESE WOODS AN'—
CHOMPH!
LULU! WHAT ARE YOU EATING?
LOOK, FELLERS! A TURKEY SANDWICH!
A TURKEY SANDWICH?
A TURKEY SANDWICH?
A TURKEY SANDWICH?
WITH CRANBERRY JELLY AN' COLD STUFFING AN' EVERYTHING!
CHOMPF!
THE END

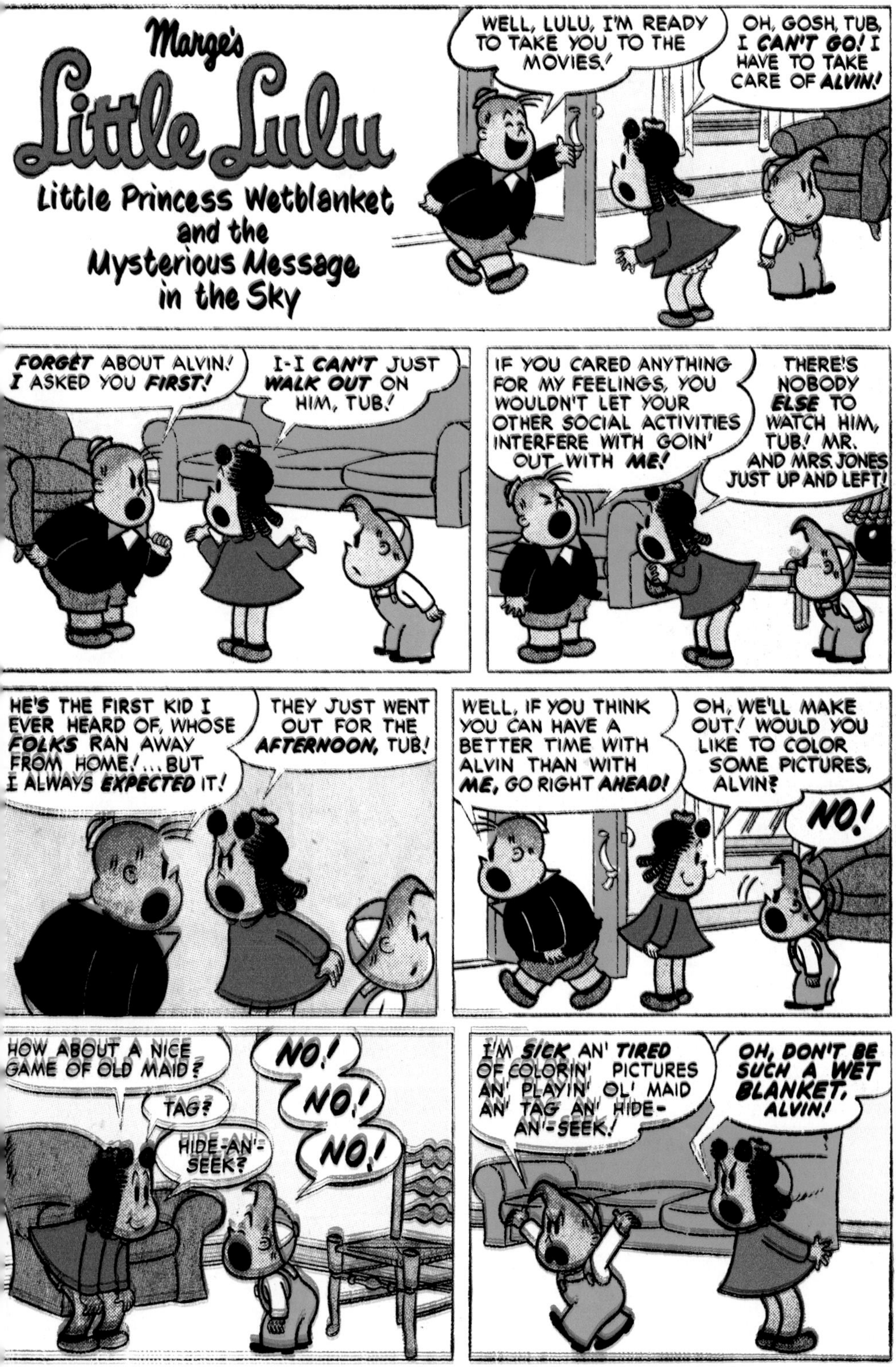
Marge's
Little Lulu
Little Princess Wetblanket and the Mysterious Message in the Sky
WELL, LULU, I'M READY TO TAKE YOU TO THE MOVIES!
OH, GOSH, TUB, I CAN'T GO! I HAVE TO TAKE CARE OF ALVIN!
FORGET ABOUT ALVIN! I ASKED YOU FIRST!
I-I CAN'T JUST WALK OUT ON HIM, TUB!
IF YOU CARED ANYTHING FOR MY FEELINGS, YOU WOULDN'T LET YOUR OTHER SOCIAL ACTIVITIES INTERFERE WITH GOIN' OUT WITH ME!
THERE'S NOBODY ELSE TO WATCH HIM, TUB! MR. AND MRS. JONES JUST UP AND LEFT!
HE'S THE FIRST KID I EVER HEARD OF, WHOSE FOLKS RAN AWAY FROM HOME!... BUT I ALWAYS EXPECTED IT!
THEY JUST WENT OUT FOR THE AFTERNOON, TUB!
WELL, IF YOU THINK YOU CAN HAVE A BETTER TIME WITH ALVIN THAN WITH ME, GO RIGHT AHEAD!
OH, WE'LL MAKE OUT! WOULD YOU LIKE TO COLOR SOME PICTURES, ALVIN?
NO!
HOW ABOUT A NICE GAME OF OLD MAID?
NO!
TAG?
NO!
HIDE-AN'-SEEK?
NO!
I'M SICK AN' TIRED OF COLORIN' PICTURES AN' PLAYIN' OL' MAID AN' TAG AN' HIDE-AN'-SEEK!
OH, DON'T BE SUCH A WET BLANKET, ALVIN!

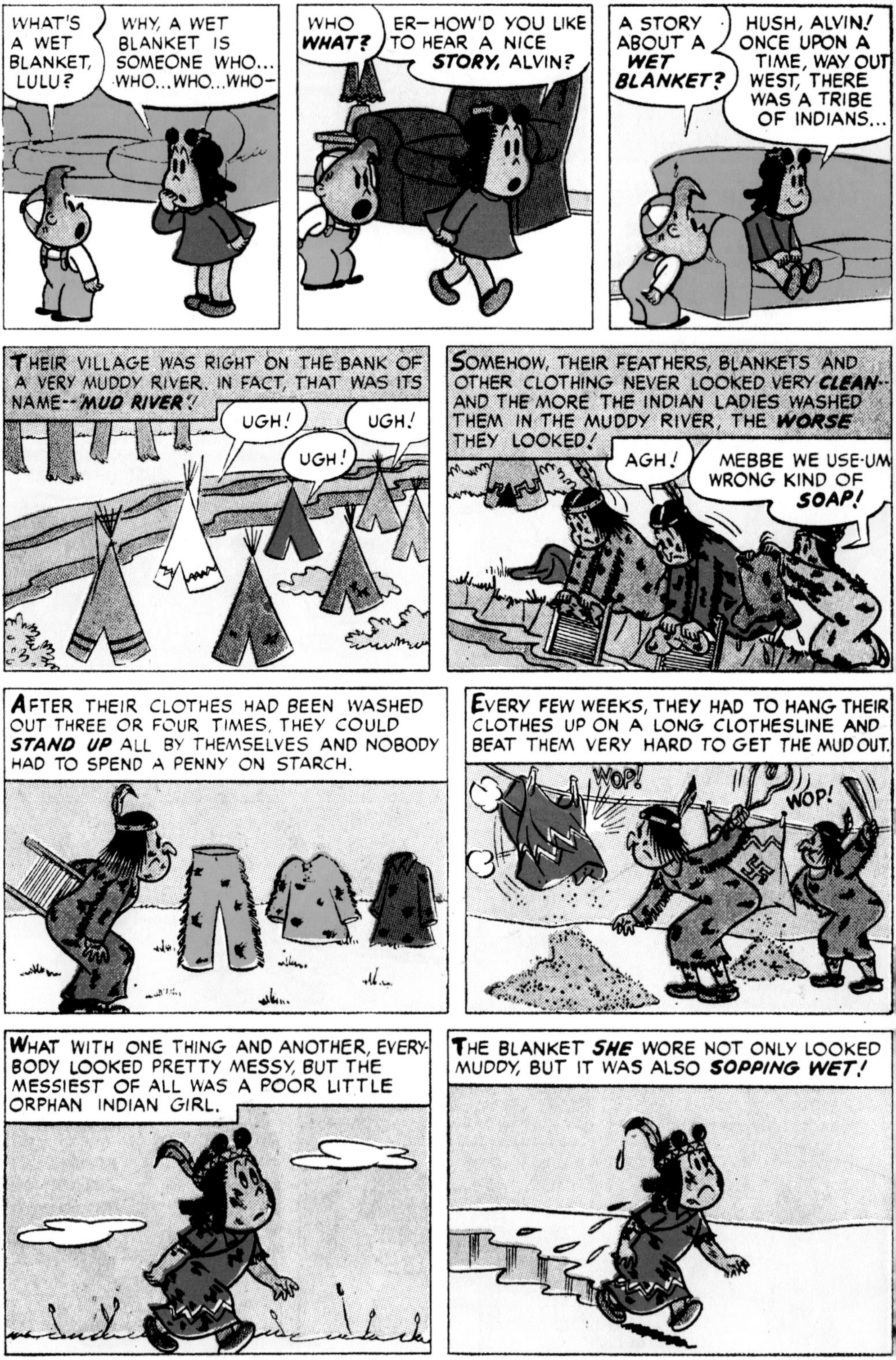

WHAT'S A WET BLANKET, LULU?
WHY, A WET BLANKET IS SOMEONE WHO... WHO...WHO...WHO-
WHO WHAT?
ER—HOW'D YOU LIKE TO HEAR A NICE STORY, ALVIN?
A STORY ABOUT A WET BLANKET?
HUSH, ALVIN! ONCE UPON A TIME, WAY OUT WEST, THERE WAS A TRIBE OF INDIANS...
THEIR VILLAGE WAS RIGHT ON THE BANK OF A VERY MUDDY RIVER. IN FACT, THAT WAS ITS NAME--"MUD RIVER"!
UGH!
UGH!
UGH!
SOMEHOW, THEIR FEATHERS, BLANKETS AND OTHER CLOTHING NEVER LOOKED VERY CLEAN--AND THE MORE THE INDIAN LADIES WASHED THEM IN THE MUDDY RIVER, THE WORSE THEY LOOKED!
AGH!
MEBBE WE USE-UM WRONG KIND OF SOAP!
AFTER THEIR CLOTHES HAD BEEN WASHED OUT THREE OR FOUR TIMES, THEY COULD STAND UP ALL BY THEMSELVES AND NOBODY HAD TO SPEND A PENNY ON STARCH.
EVERY FEW WEEKS, THEY HAD TO HANG THEIR CLOTHES UP ON A LONG CLOTHESLINE AND BEAT THEM VERY HARD TO GET THE MUD OUT.
WOP!
WOP!
WHAT WITH ONE THING AND ANOTHER, EVERYBODY LOOKED PRETTY MESSY, BUT THE MESSIEST OF ALL WAS A POOR LITTLE ORPHAN INDIAN GIRL.
THE BLANKET SHE WORE NOT ONLY LOOKED MUDDY, BUT IT WAS ALSO SOPPING WET!

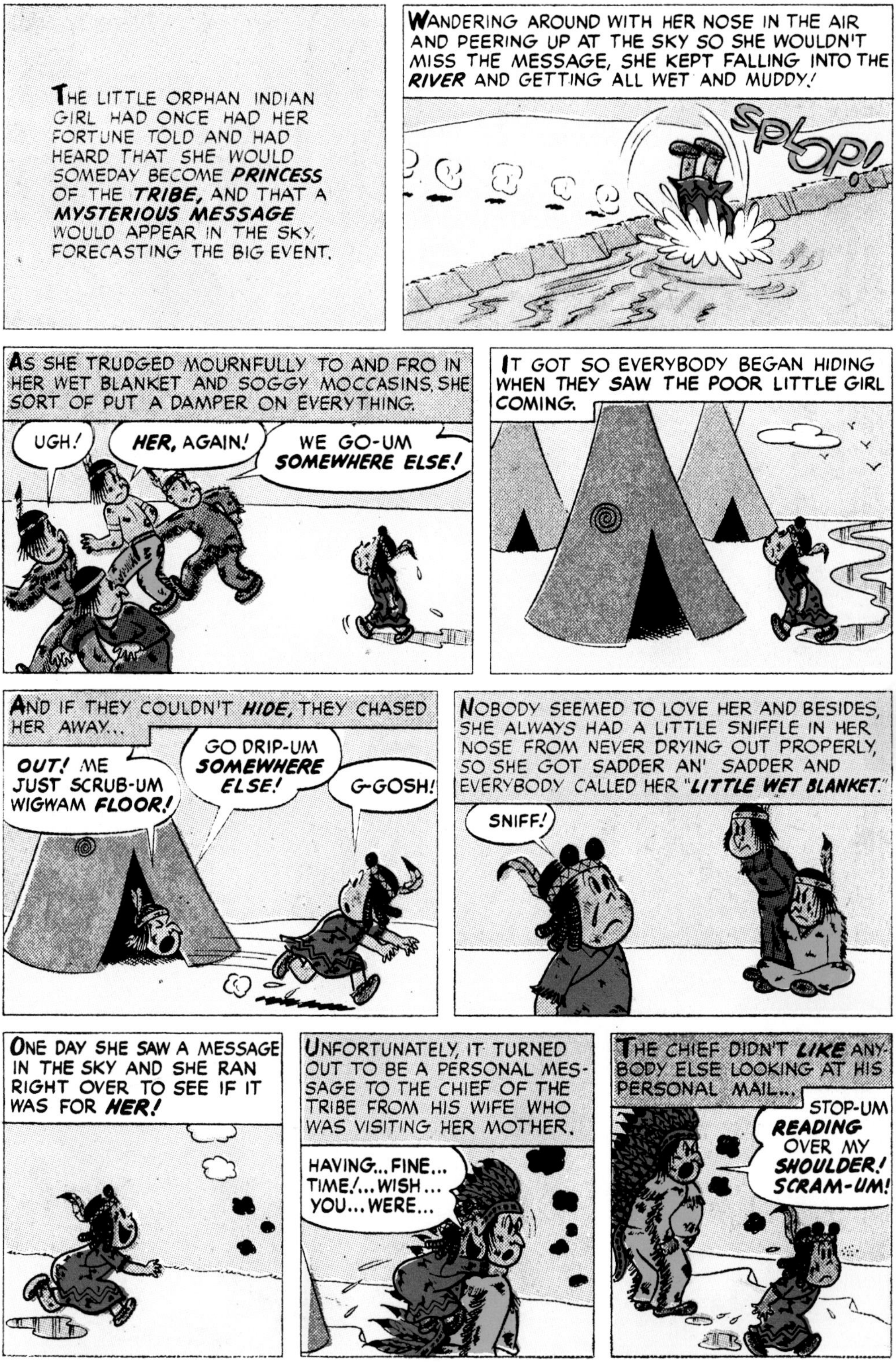
THE LITTLE ORPHAN INDIAN GIRL HAD ONCE HAD HER FORTUNE TOLD AND HAD HEARD THAT SHE WOULD SOMEDAY BECOME PRINCESS OF THE TRIBE, AND THAT A MYSTERIOUS MESSAGE WOULD APPEAR IN THE SKY, FORECASTING THE BIG EVENT.
WANDERING AROUND WITH HER NOSE IN THE AIR AND PEERING UP AT THE SKY SO SHE WOULDN'T MISS THE MESSAGE, SHE KEPT FALLING INTO THE RIVER AND GETTING ALL WET AND MUDDY!
SPLOP!
AS SHE TRUDGED MOURNFULLY TO AND FRO IN HER WET BLANKET AND SOGGY MOCCASINS, SHE SORT OF PUT A DAMPER ON EVERYTHING.
UGH!
HER, AGAIN!
WE GO-UM SOMEWHERE ELSE!
IT GOT SO EVERYBODY BEGAN HIDING WHEN THEY SAW THE POOR LITTLE GIRL COMING.
AND IF THEY COULDN'T HIDE, THEY CHASED HER AWAY...
OUT! ME JUST SCRUB-UM WIGWAM FLOOR!
GO DRIP-UM SOMEWHERE ELSE!
G-GOSH!
NOBODY SEEMED TO LOVE HER AND BESIDES, SHE ALWAYS HAD A LITTLE SNIFFLE IN HER NOSE FROM NEVER DRYING OUT PROPERLY, SO SHE GOT SADDER AN' SADDER AND EVERYBODY CALLED HER "LITTLE WET BLANKET."
SNIFF!
ONE DAY SHE SAW A MESSAGE IN THE SKY AND SHE RAN RIGHT OVER TO SEE IF IT WAS FOR HER!
UNFORTUNATELY, IT TURNED OUT TO BE A PERSONAL MESSAGE TO THE CHIEF OF THE TRIBE FROM HIS WIFE WHO WAS VISITING HER MOTHER.
HAVING... FINE... TIME!... WISH... YOU... WERE...
THE CHIEF DIDN'T LIKE ANYBODY ELSE LOOKING AT HIS PERSONAL MAIL...
STOP-UM READING OVER MY SHOULDER! SCRAM-UM!

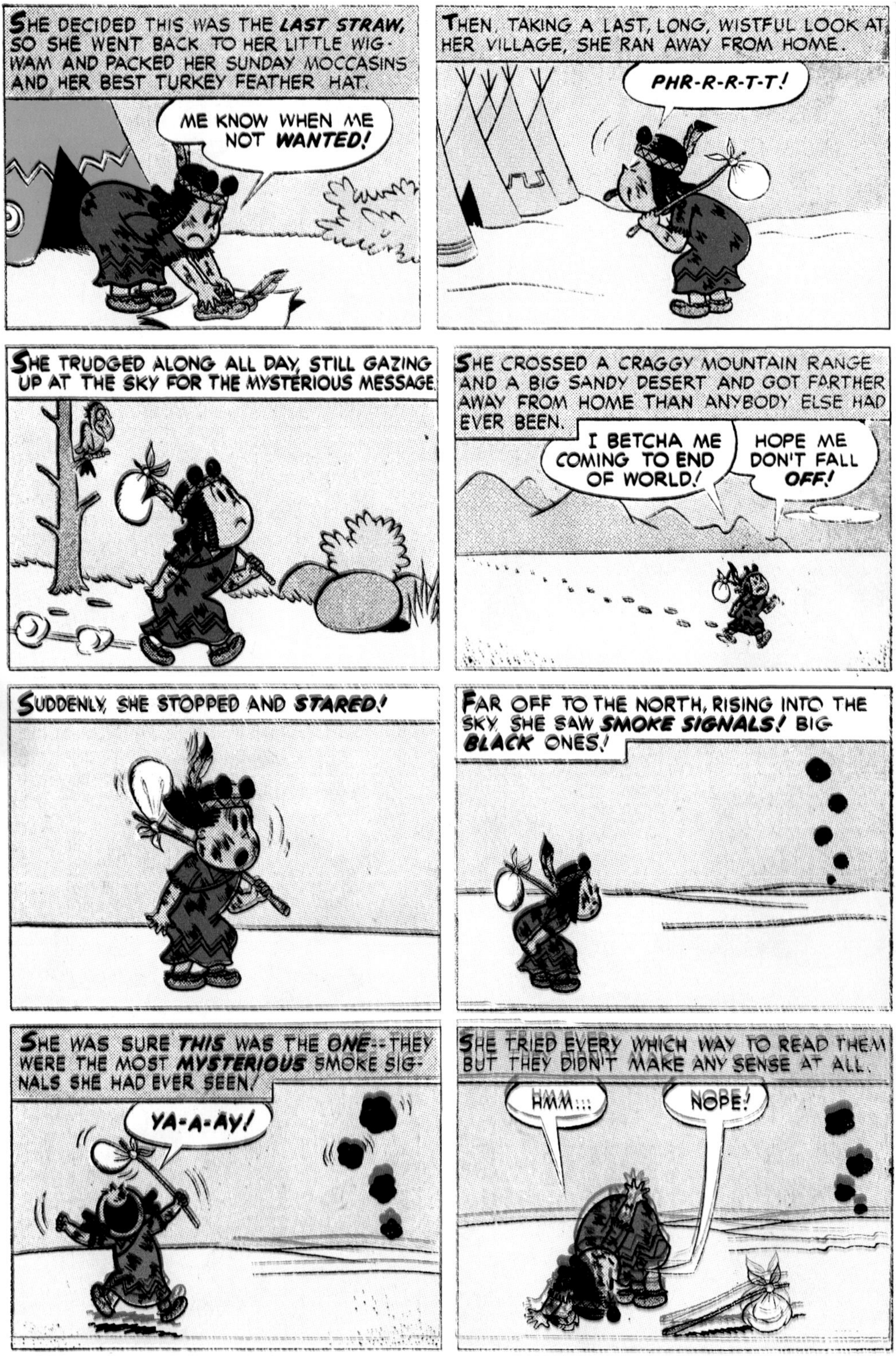
SHE DECIDED THIS WAS THE LAST STRAW, SO SHE WENT BACK TO HER LITTLE WIG-WAM AND PACKED HER SUNDAY MOCCASINS AND HER BEST TURKEY FEATHER HAT.
ME KNOW WHEN ME NOT WANTED!
THEN, TAKING A LAST, LONG, WISTFUL LOOK AT HER VILLAGE, SHE RAN AWAY FROM HOME.
PHR-R-R-T-T!
SHE TRUDGED ALONG ALL DAY, STILL GAZING UP AT THE SKY FOR THE MYSTERIOUS MESSAGE.
SHE CROSSED A CRAGGY MOUNTAIN RANGE AND A BIG SANDY DESERT AND GOT FARTHER AWAY FROM HOME THAN ANYBODY ELSE HAD EVER BEEN.
I BETCHA ME COMING TO END OF WORLD!
HOPE ME DON'T FALL OFF!
SUDDENLY, SHE STOPPED AND STARED!
FAR OFF TO THE NORTH, RISING INTO THE SKY, SHE SAW SMOKE SIGNALS! BIG BLACK ONES!
SHE WAS SURE THIS WAS THE ONE--THEY WERE THE MOST MYSTERIOUS SMOKE SIG-NALS SHE HAD EVER SEEN!
YA-A-AY!
SHE TRIED EVERY WHICH WAY TO READ THEM BUT THEY DIDN'T MAKE ANY SENSE AT ALL.
HMM...
NOPE!

92

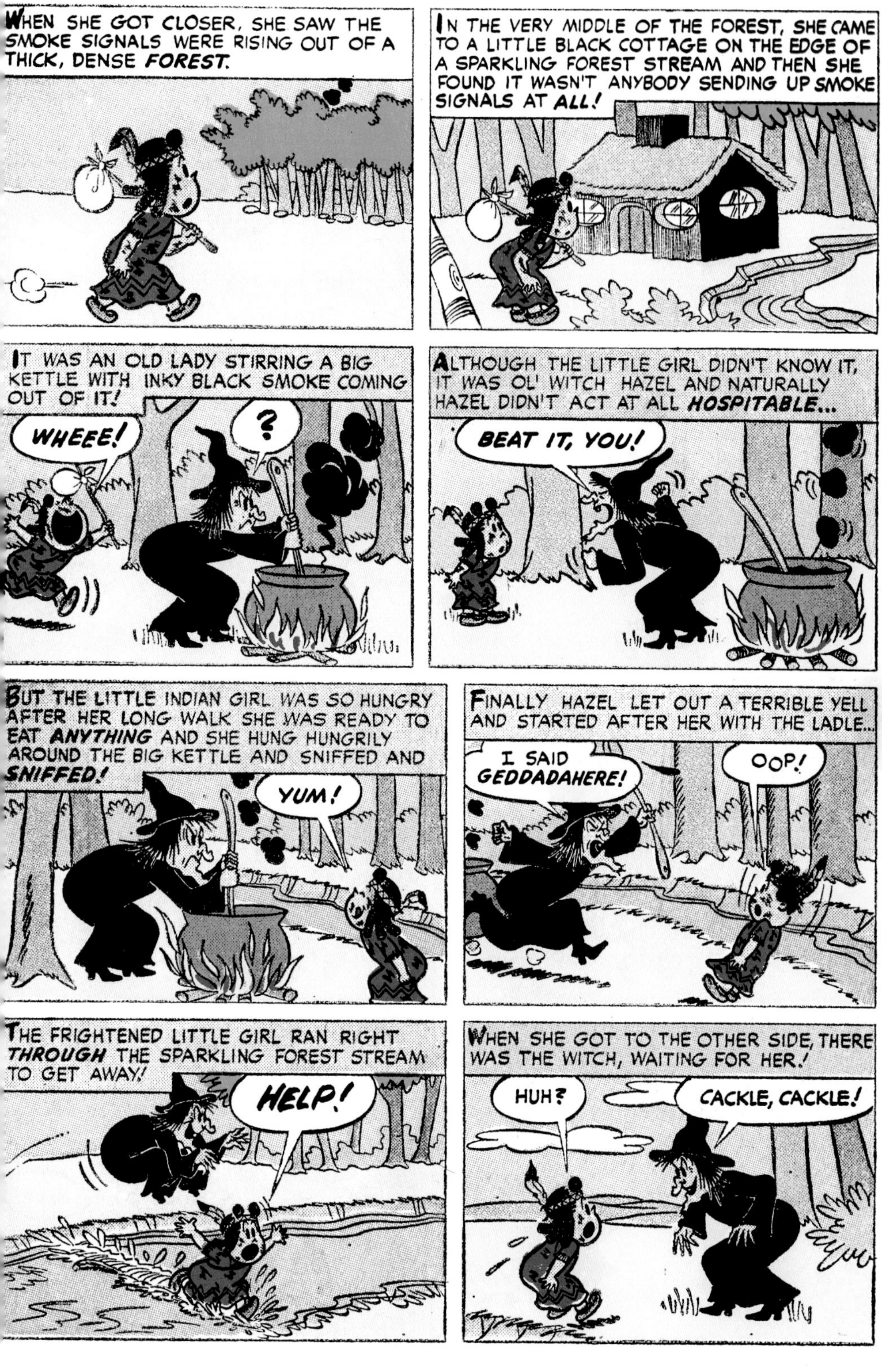
WHEN SHE GOT CLOSER, SHE SAW THE SMOKE SIGNALS WERE RISING OUT OF A THICK, DENSE FOREST.
IN THE VERY MIDDLE OF THE FOREST, SHE CAME TO A LITTLE BLACK COTTAGE ON THE EDGE OF A SPARKLING FOREST STREAM AND THEN SHE FOUND IT WASN'T ANYBODY SENDING UP SMOKE SIGNALS AT ALL!
IT WAS AN OLD LADY STIRRING A BIG KETTLE WITH INKY BLACK SMOKE COMING OUT OF IT!
WHEEE!
?
ALTHOUGH THE LITTLE GIRL DIDN'T KNOW IT, IT WAS OL' WITCH HAZEL AND NATURALLY HAZEL DIDN'T ACT AT ALL HOSPITABLE...
BEAT IT, YOU!
BUT THE LITTLE INDIAN GIRL WAS SO HUNGRY AFTER HER LONG WALK SHE WAS READY TO EAT ANYTHING AND SHE HUNG HUNGRILY AROUND THE BIG KETTLE AND SNIFFED AND SNIFFED!
YUM!
FINALLY HAZEL LET OUT A TERRIBLE YELL AND STARTED AFTER HER WITH THE LADLE...
I SAID GEDDADAHERE!
OOP!
THE FRIGHTENED LITTLE GIRL RAN RIGHT THROUGH THE SPARKLING FOREST STREAM TO GET AWAY!
HELP!
WHEN SHE GOT TO THE OTHER SIDE, THERE WAS THE WITCH, WAITING FOR HER!
HUH?
CACKLE, CACKLE!

SHE TURNED AND RAN **BACK** ... AND THERE WAS THE WITCH **AGAIN!**

HEE, HEE, HEE, HEE!

ZIP!

YOW!

HAZEL CHASED HER BACK AND FORTH THROUGH THE STREAM EIGHTEEN OR NINETEEN TIMES...

BAW!

WHAZ...

... AND FINALLY CHASED HER HALFWAY BACK TO HER VILLAGE.

AND **DON'T** COME BACK!

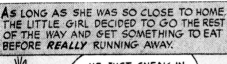

AS LONG AS SHE WAS SO CLOSE TO HOME, THE LITTLE GIRL DECIDED TO GO THE REST OF THE WAY AND GET SOMETHING TO EAT BEFORE **REALLY** RUNNING AWAY.

ME JUST SNEAK IN AND SNEAK-UM RIGHT OUT AGAIN!

AS SHE TRUDGED THROUGH THE VILLAGE TO-WARD HER LITTLE **WIGWAM**, EVERYBODY WAS AMAZED TO SEE HOW **CLEAN** SHE SEEMED TO LOOK!

UGH?   UGH?   UGH?   UGH?

EVERYBODY CROWDED AROUND AND **INSISTED** THAT SHE SHOW THEM **HOW** SHE GOT SO LOVELY AND CLEAN...

HOW?   HOW?   HOW?   HOW?

SO, AS SOON AS SHE'D FIXED HERSELF A SANDWICH, THE LITTLE GIRL LED THEM ALL BACK ACROSS THE CRAGGY MOUNTAINS AND THE WIDE DESERT.

THIS WAY!

WHEN SHE GOT TO THE BLACK LITTLE COTTAGE, SHE POINTED STRAIGHT AT **OL' WITCH HAZEL**.

SHE DO-UM!

YOWP!

SURE ENOUGH, HAZEL CHASED THEM **ALL** BACK AND FORTH THROUGH THE SPARKLING STREAM, TILL **THEY** WERE ALL AS CLEAN AS THE LITTLE GIRL.

EEYOW!   HELP!   HELP!   HELP!   HELP!

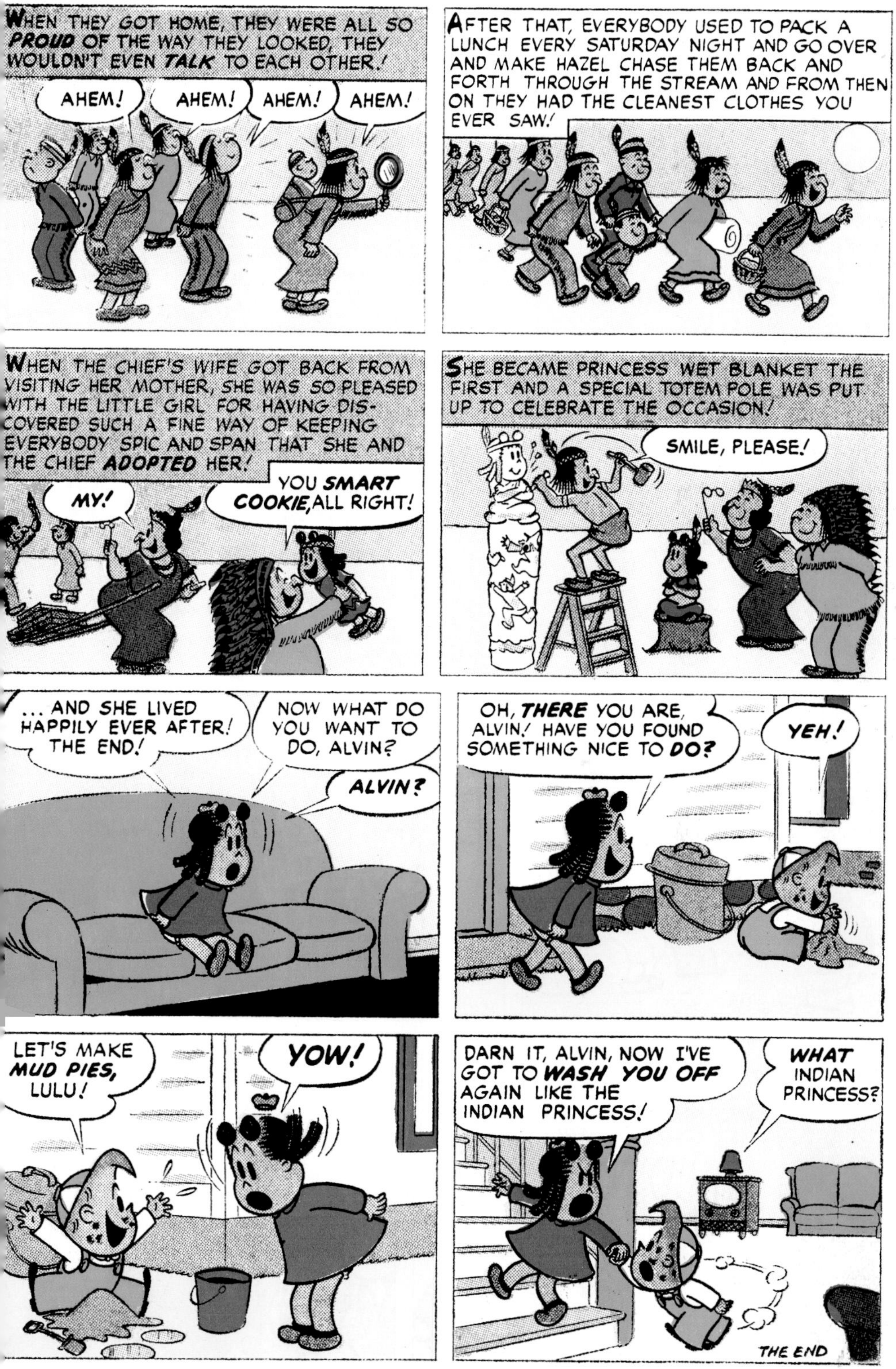
WHEN THEY GOT HOME, THEY WERE ALL SO PROUD OF THE WAY THEY LOOKED, THEY WOULDN'T EVEN TALK TO EACH OTHER!
AHEM!
AHEM!
AHEM!
AHEM!
AFTER THAT, EVERYBODY USED TO PACK A LUNCH EVERY SATURDAY NIGHT AND GO OVER AND MAKE HAZEL CHASE THEM BACK AND FORTH THROUGH THE STREAM AND FROM THEN ON THEY HAD THE CLEANEST CLOTHES YOU EVER SAW!
WHEN THE CHIEF'S WIFE GOT BACK FROM VISITING HER MOTHER, SHE WAS SO PLEASED WITH THE LITTLE GIRL FOR HAVING DISCOVERED SUCH A FINE WAY OF KEEPING EVERYBODY SPIC AND SPAN THAT SHE AND THE CHIEF ADOPTED HER!
MY!
YOU SMART COOKIE, ALL RIGHT!
SHE BECAME PRINCESS WET BLANKET THE FIRST AND A SPECIAL TOTEM POLE WAS PUT UP TO CELEBRATE THE OCCASION!
SMILE, PLEASE!
... AND SHE LIVED HAPPILY EVER AFTER! THE END!
NOW WHAT DO YOU WANT TO DO, ALVIN?
ALVIN?
OH, THERE YOU ARE, ALVIN! HAVE YOU FOUND SOMETHING NICE TO DO?
YEH!
LET'S MAKE MUD PIES, LULU!
YOW!
DARN IT, ALVIN, NOW I'VE GOT TO WASH YOU OFF AGAIN LIKE THE INDIAN PRINCESS!
WHAT INDIAN PRINCESS?
THE END

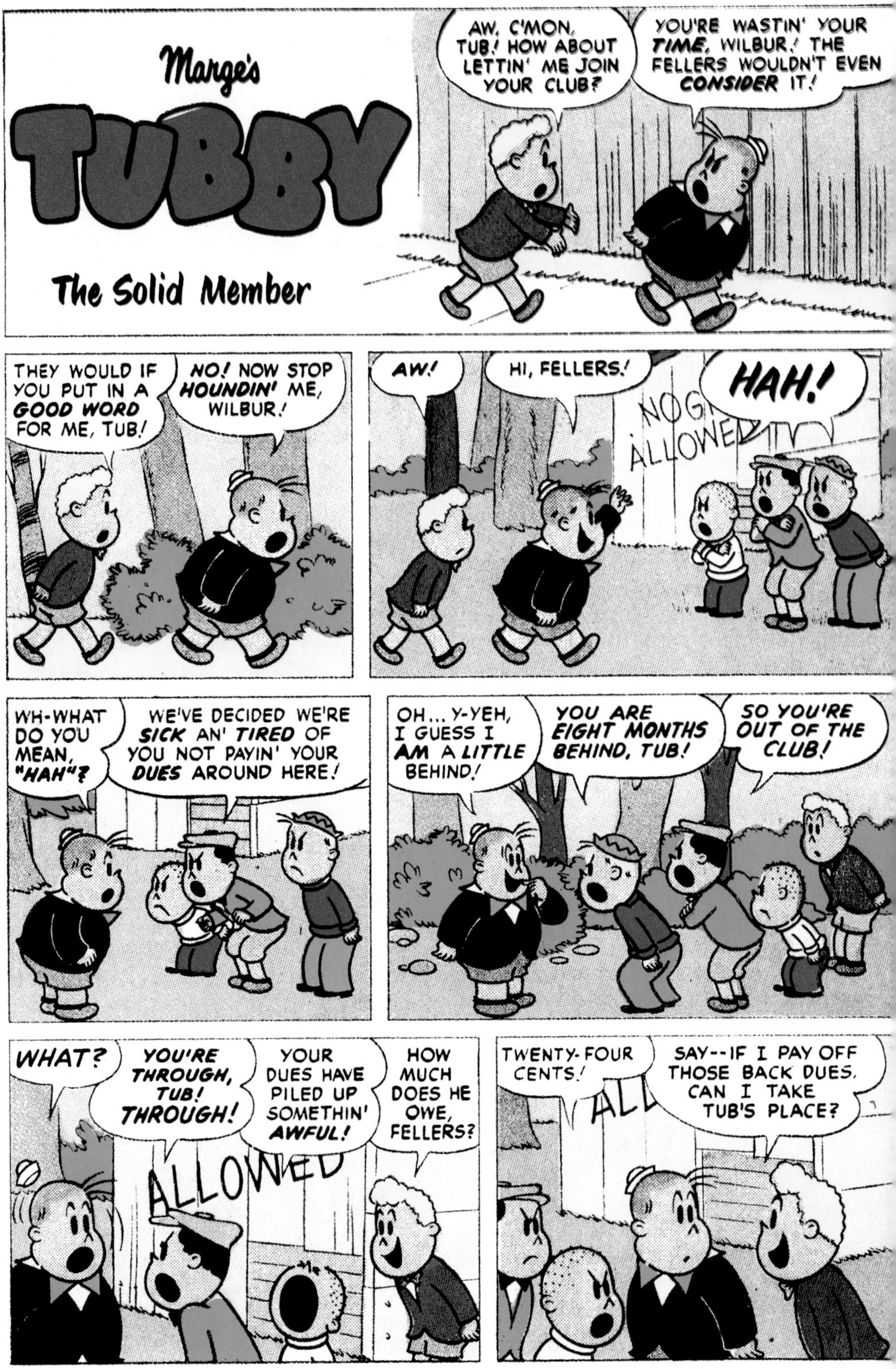

Marge's
TUBBY
The Solid Member
AW, C'MON, TUB! HOW ABOUT LETTIN' ME JOIN YOUR CLUB?
YOU'RE WASTIN' YOUR TIME, WILBUR! THE FELLERS WOULDN'T EVEN CONSIDER IT!
THEY WOULD IF YOU PUT IN A GOOD WORD FOR ME, TUB!
NO! NOW STOP HOUNDIN' ME, WILBUR!
AW!
HI, FELLERS!
HAH!
NO G
ALLOWED
WH-WHAT DO YOU MEAN, "HAH"?
WE'VE DECIDED WE'RE SICK AN' TIRED OF YOU NOT PAYIN' YOUR DUES AROUND HERE!
OH... Y-YEH, I GUESS I AM A LITTLE BEHIND!
YOU ARE EIGHT MONTHS BEHIND, TUB!
SO YOU'RE OUT OF THE CLUB!
WHAT?
YOU'RE THROUGH, TUB! THROUGH!
YOUR DUES HAVE PILED UP SOMETHIN' AWFUL!
HOW MUCH DOES HE OWE, FELLERS?
ALLOWED
TWENTY-FOUR CENTS!
SAY--IF I PAY OFF THOSE BACK DUES, CAN I TAKE TUB'S PLACE?

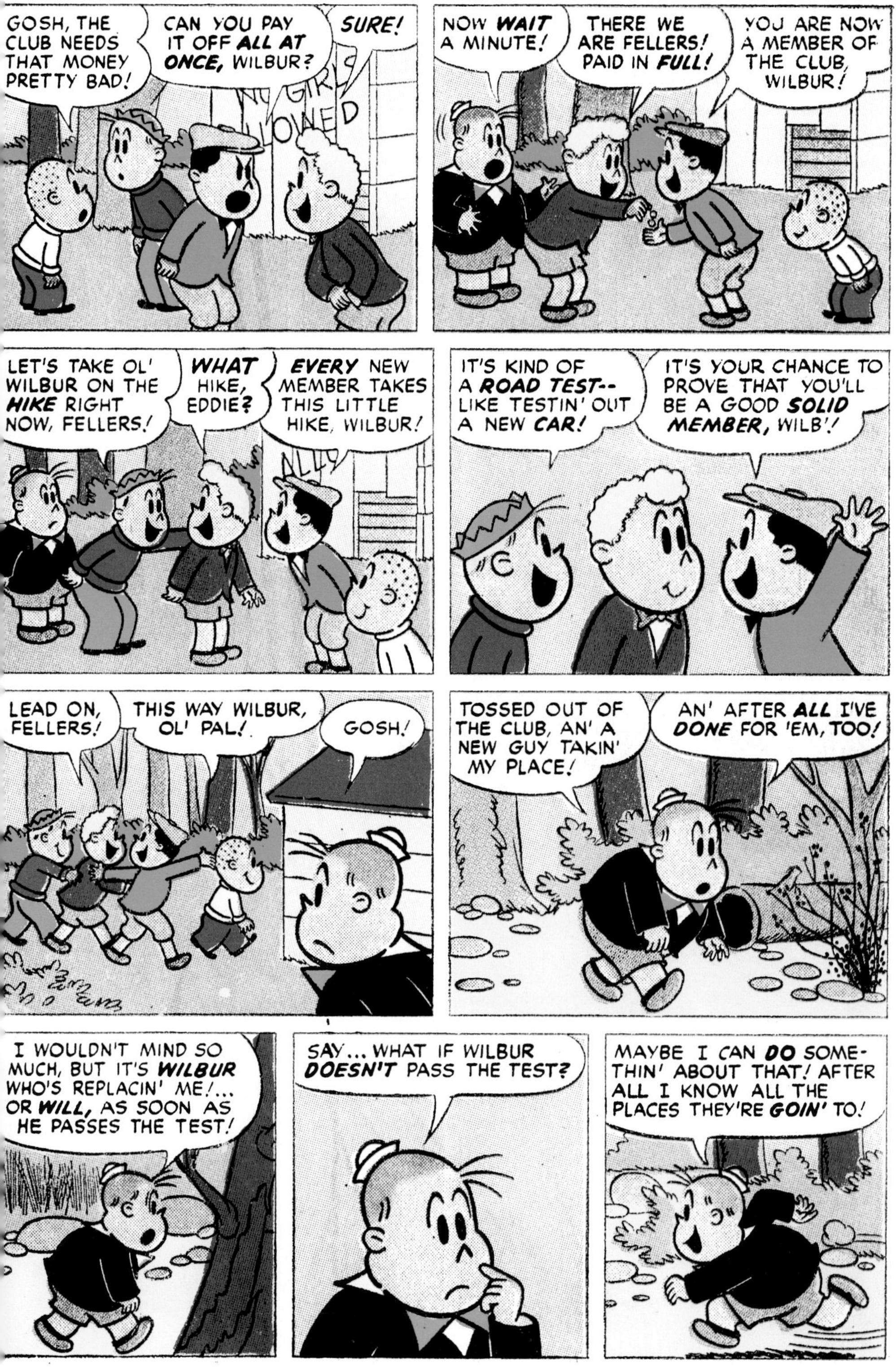

GOSH, THE CLUB NEEDS THAT MONEY PRETTY BAD!
CAN YOU PAY IT OFF **ALL AT ONCE,** WILBUR?
SURE!
NOW **WAIT** A MINUTE!
THERE WE ARE FELLERS! PAID IN **FULL!**
YOU ARE NOW A MEMBER OF THE CLUB, WILBUR!
LET'S TAKE OL' WILBUR ON THE **HIKE** RIGHT NOW, FELLERS!
WHAT HIKE, EDDIE?
EVERY NEW MEMBER TAKES THIS LITTLE HIKE, WILBUR!
IT'S KIND OF A **ROAD TEST--** LIKE TESTIN' OUT A NEW **CAR!**
IT'S YOUR CHANCE TO PROVE THAT YOU'LL BE A GOOD **SOLID MEMBER,** WILB'!
LEAD ON, FELLERS!
THIS WAY WILBUR, OL' PAL!
GOSH!
TOSSED OUT OF THE CLUB, AN' A NEW GUY TAKIN' MY PLACE!
AN' AFTER **ALL** I'VE **DONE** FOR 'EM, TOO!
I WOULDN'T MIND SO MUCH, BUT IT'S **WILBUR** WHO'S REPLACIN' ME!... OR **WILL,** AS SOON AS HE PASSES THE TEST!
SAY... WHAT IF WILBUR **DOESN'T** PASS THE TEST?
MAYBE I CAN **DO** SOMETHIN' ABOUT THAT! AFTER ALL I KNOW ALL THE PLACES THEY'RE **GOIN'** TO!

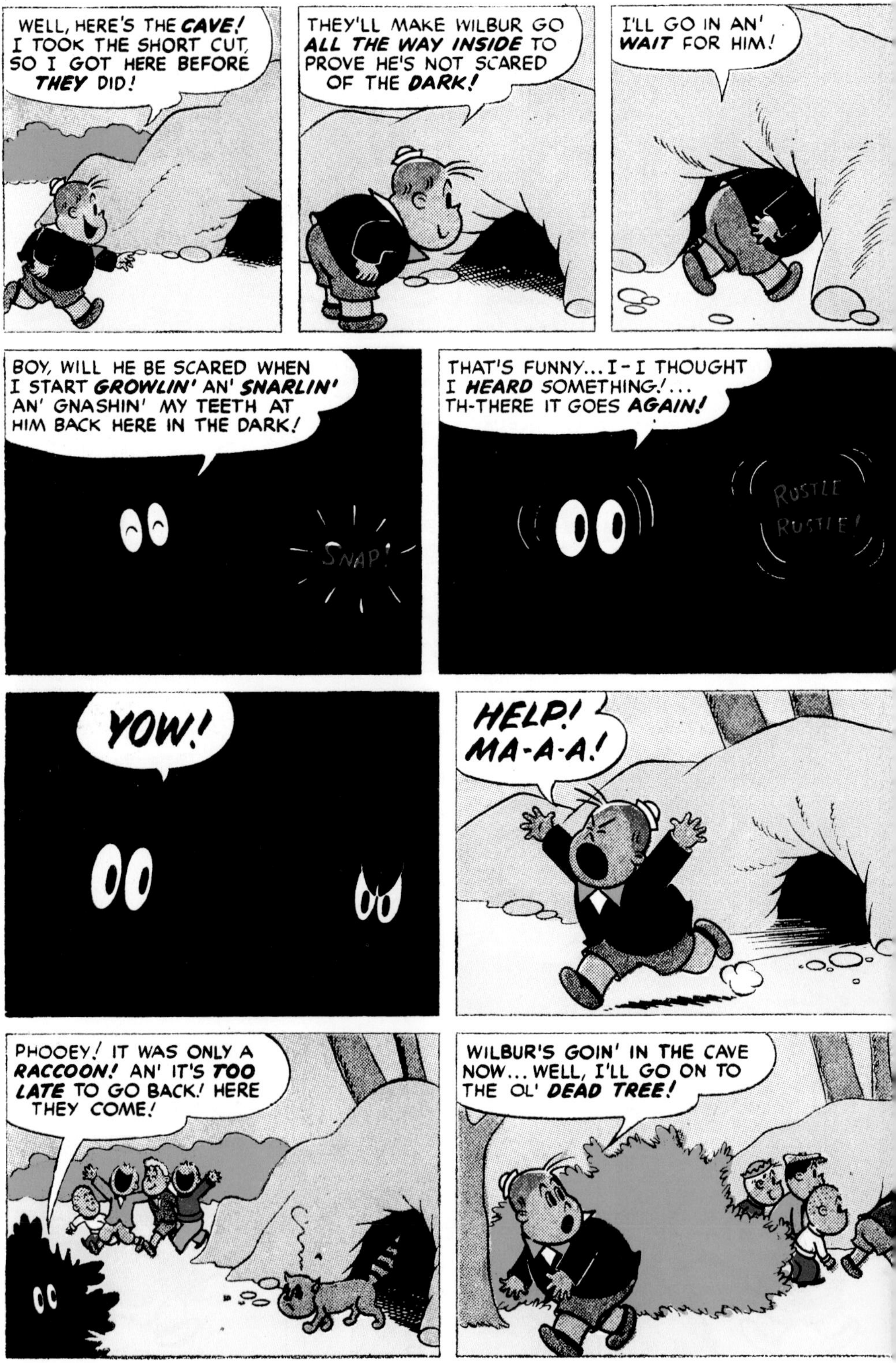
WELL, HERE'S THE CAVE! I TOOK THE SHORT CUT, SO I GOT HERE BEFORE THEY DID!
THEY'LL MAKE WILBUR GO ALL THE WAY INSIDE TO PROVE HE'S NOT SCARED OF THE DARK!
I'LL GO IN AN' WAIT FOR HIM!
BOY, WILL HE BE SCARED WHEN I START GROWLIN' AN' SNARLIN' AN' GNASHIN' MY TEETH AT HIM BACK HERE IN THE DARK!
SNAP!
THAT'S FUNNY... I-I THOUGHT I HEARD SOMETHING!... TH-THERE IT GOES AGAIN!
RUSTLE RUSTLE!
YOW!
HELP! MA-A-A!
PHOOEY! IT WAS ONLY A RACCOON! AN' IT'S TOO LATE TO GO BACK! HERE THEY COME!
WILBUR'S GOIN' IN THE CAVE NOW... WELL, I'LL GO ON TO THE OL' DEAD TREE!

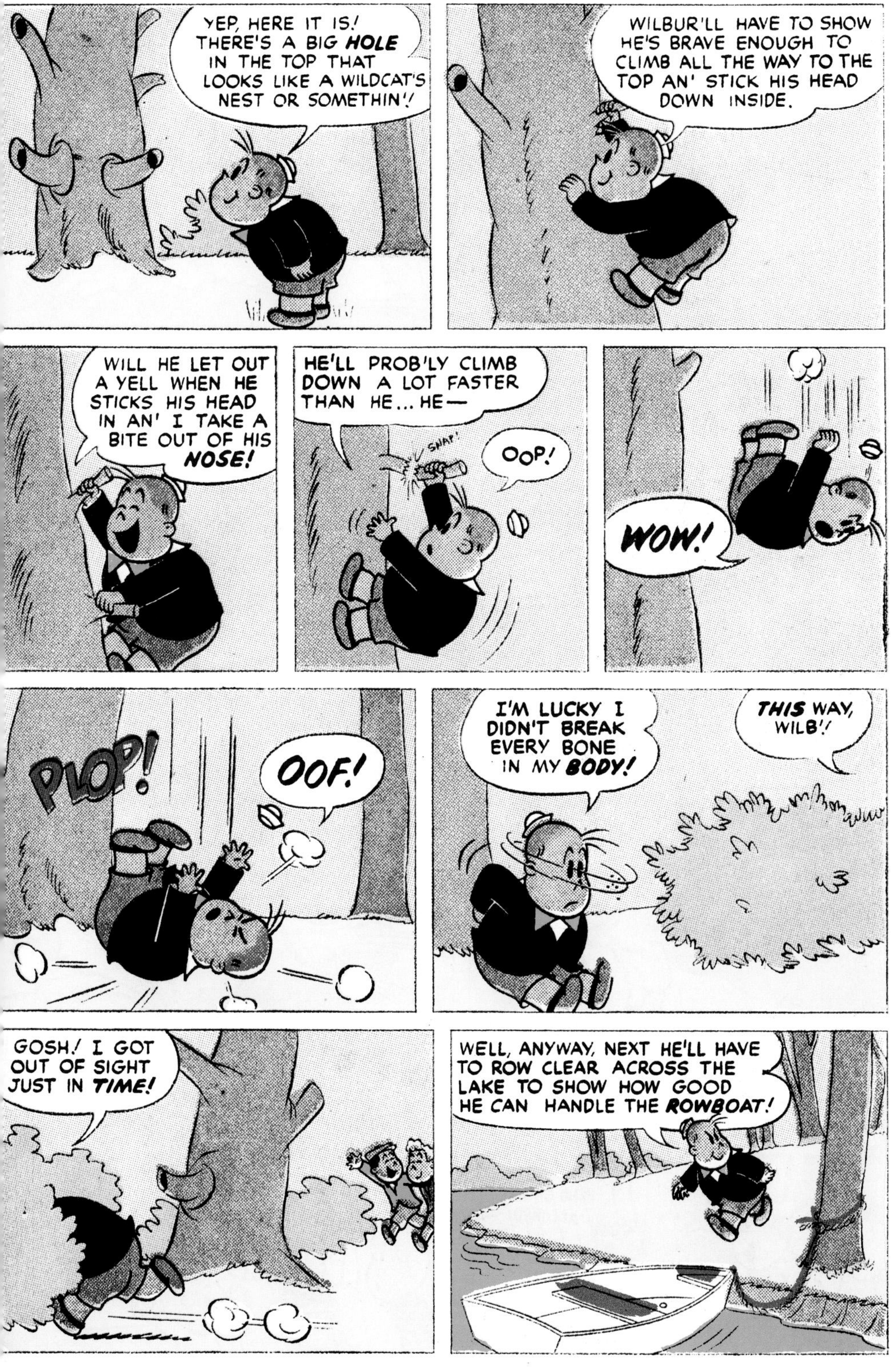
YEP, HERE IT IS! THERE'S A BIG HOLE IN THE TOP THAT LOOKS LIKE A WILDCAT'S NEST OR SOMETHIN'!
WILBUR'LL HAVE TO SHOW HE'S BRAVE ENOUGH TO CLIMB ALL THE WAY TO THE TOP AN' STICK HIS HEAD DOWN INSIDE.
WILL HE LET OUT A YELL WHEN HE STICKS HIS HEAD IN AN' I TAKE A BITE OUT OF HIS NOSE!
HE'LL PROB'LY CLIMB DOWN A LOT FASTER THAN HE... HE—
SNAP!
OOP!
WOW!
PLOP!
OOF!
I'M LUCKY I DIDN'T BREAK EVERY BONE IN MY BODY!
THIS WAY, WILB'!
GOSH! I GOT OUT OF SIGHT JUST IN TIME!
WELL, ANYWAY, NEXT HE'LL HAVE TO ROW CLEAR ACROSS THE LAKE TO SHOW HOW GOOD HE CAN HANDLE THE ROWBOAT!

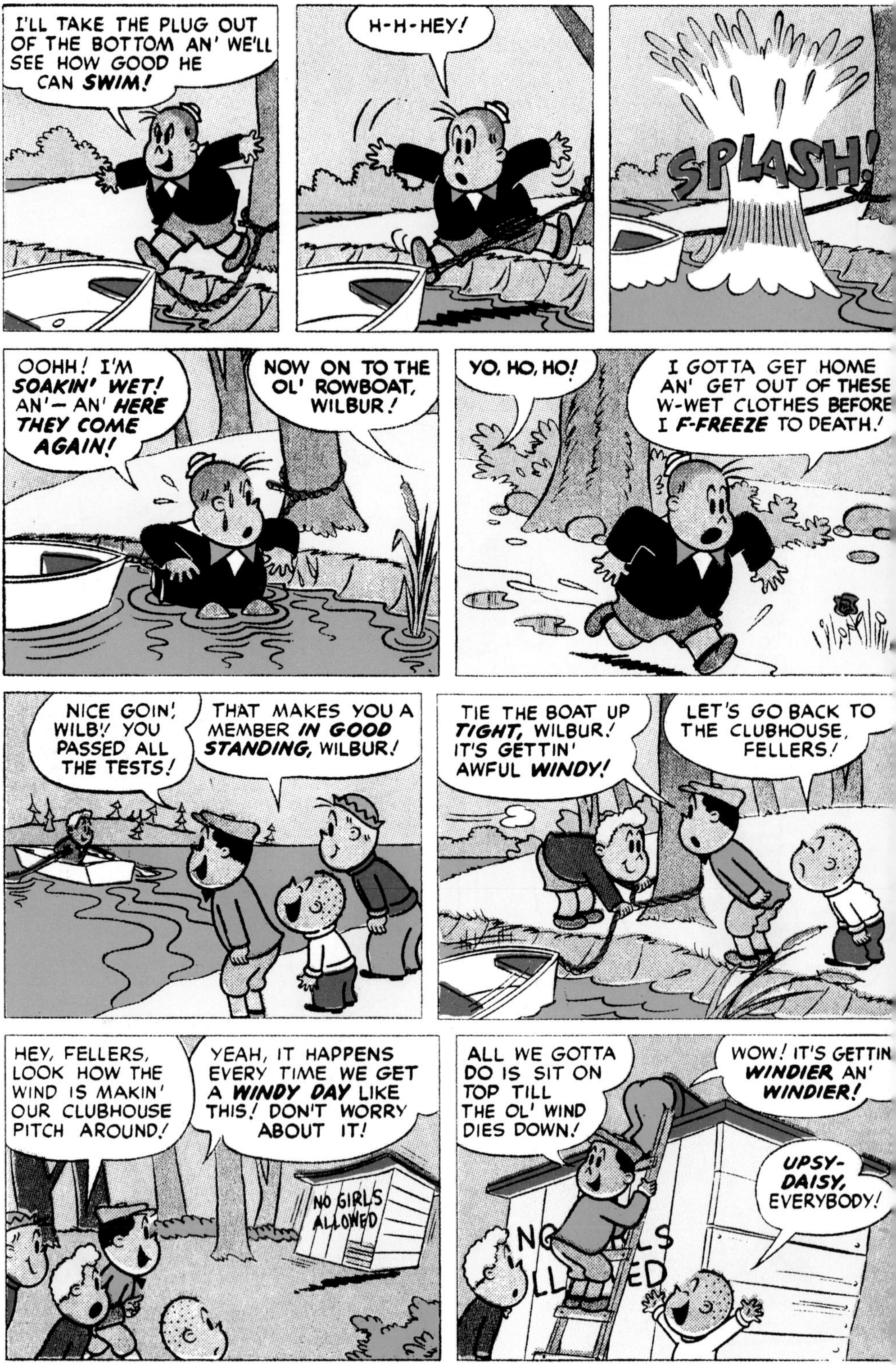
I'LL TAKE THE PLUG OUT OF THE BOTTOM AN' WE'LL SEE HOW GOOD HE CAN SWIM!
H-H-HEY!
SPLASH!
OOHH! I'M SOAKIN' WET! AN'— AN' HERE THEY COME AGAIN!
NOW ON TO THE OL' ROWBOAT, WILBUR!
YO, HO, HO!
I GOTTA GET HOME AN' GET OUT OF THESE W-WET CLOTHES BEFORE I F-FREEZE TO DEATH!
NICE GOIN', WILB! YOU PASSED ALL THE TESTS!
THAT MAKES YOU A MEMBER IN GOOD STANDING, WILBUR!
TIE THE BOAT UP TIGHT, WILBUR! IT'S GETTIN' AWFUL WINDY!
LET'S GO BACK TO THE CLUBHOUSE, FELLERS!
HEY, FELLERS, LOOK HOW THE WIND IS MAKIN' OUR CLUBHOUSE PITCH AROUND!
YEAH, IT HAPPENS EVERY TIME WE GET A WINDY DAY LIKE THIS! DON'T WORRY ABOUT IT!
NO GIRLS ALLOWED
ALL WE GOTTA DO IS SIT ON TOP TILL THE OL' WIND DIES DOWN!
WOW! IT'S GETTIN WINDIER AN' WINDIER!
UPSY-DAISY, EVERYBODY!

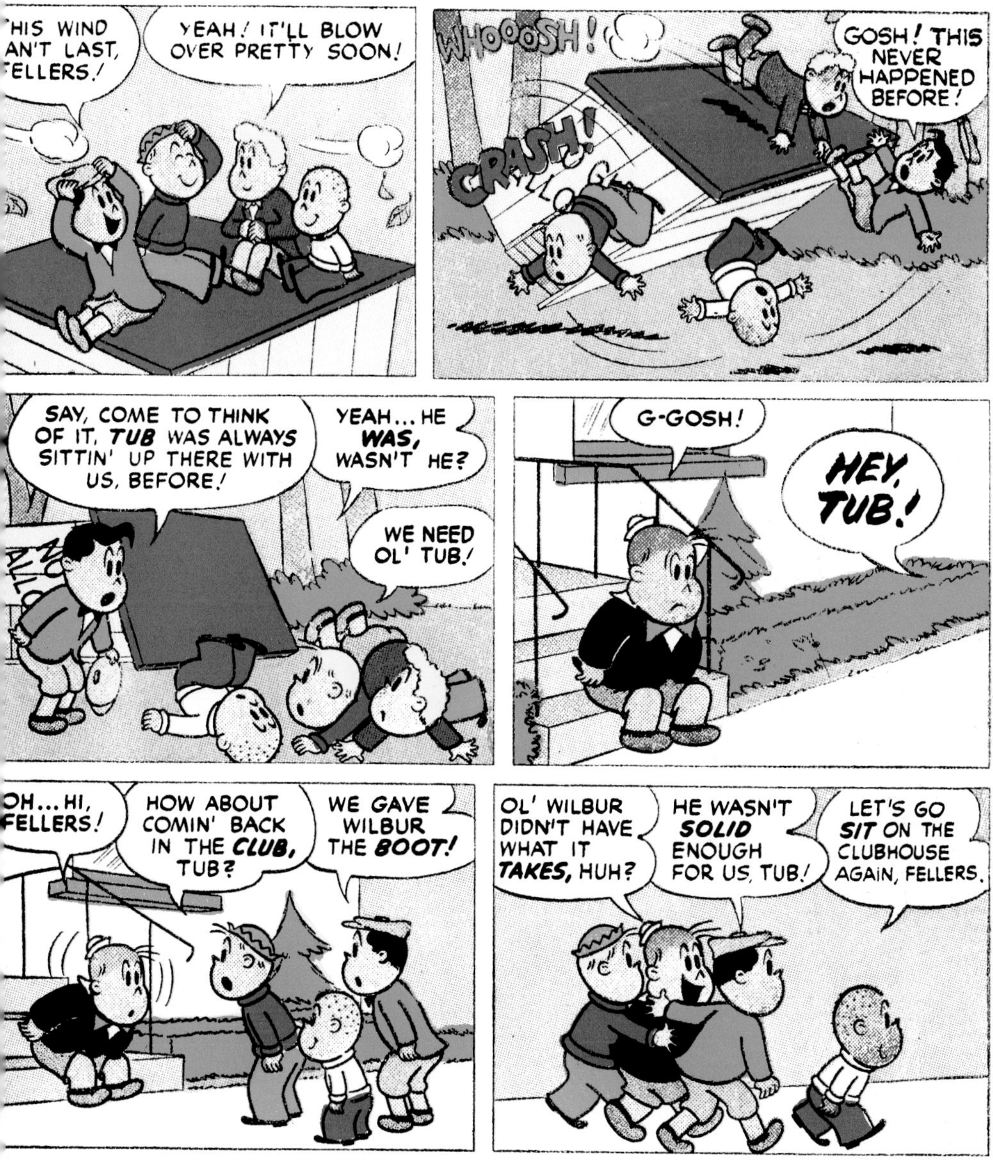
HIS WIND
AN'T LAST,
ELLERS!
YEAH! IT'LL BLOW OVER PRETTY SOON!
WHOOOSH!
CRASH!
GOSH! THIS NEVER HAPPENED BEFORE!
SAY, COME TO THINK OF IT, TUB WAS ALWAYS SITTIN' UP THERE WITH US, BEFORE!
YEAH... HE WAS, WASN'T HE?
WE NEED OL' TUB!
G-GOSH!
HEY, TUB!
H... HI,
ELLERS!
HOW ABOUT COMIN' BACK IN THE CLUB, TUB?
WE GAVE WILBUR THE BOOT!
OL' WILBUR DIDN'T HAVE WHAT IT TAKES, HUH?
HE WASN'T SOLID ENOUGH FOR US, TUB!
LET'S GO SIT ON THE CLUBHOUSE AGAIN, FELLERS.

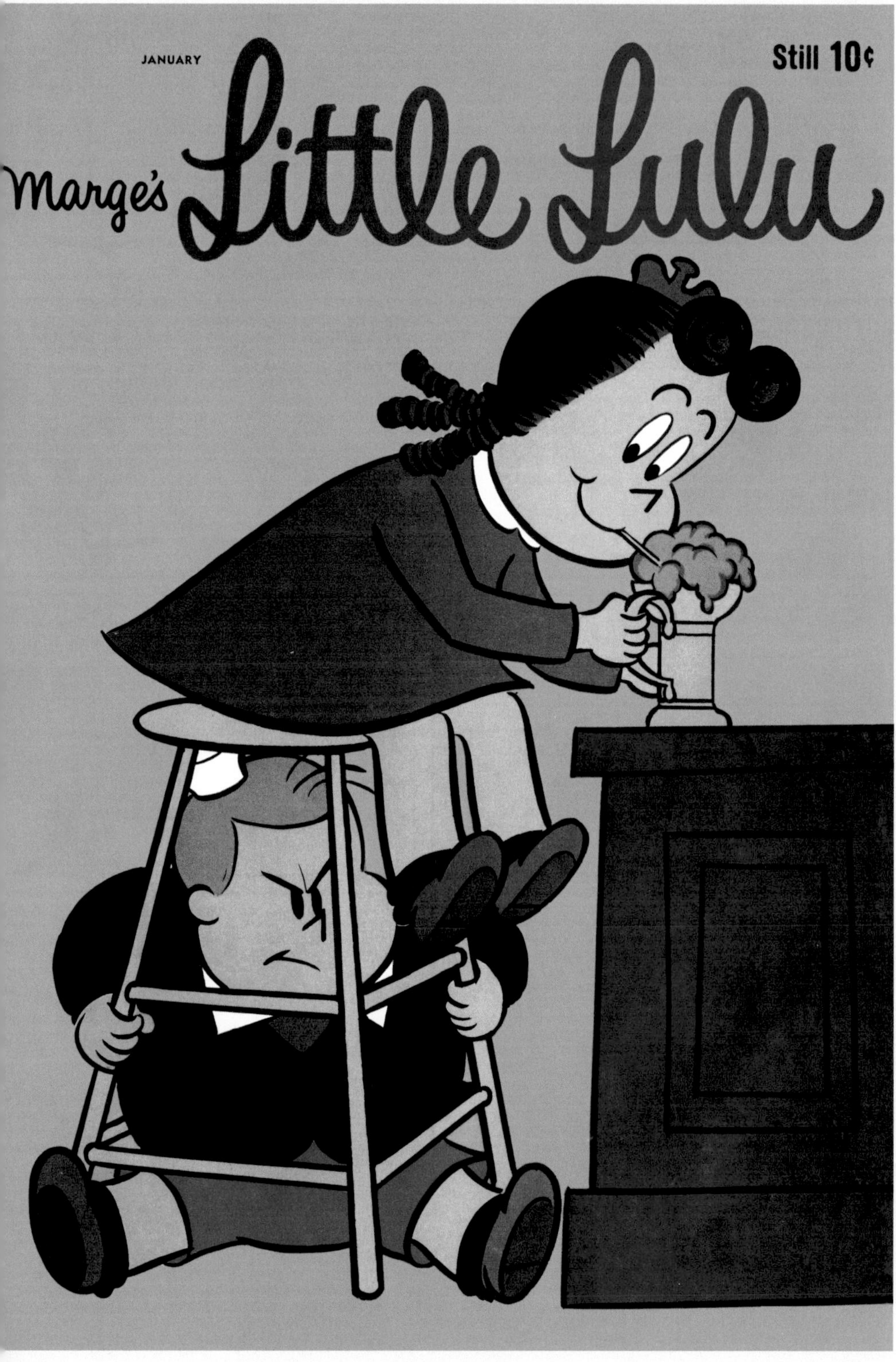

JANUARY
Still 10¢
Marge's Little Lulu

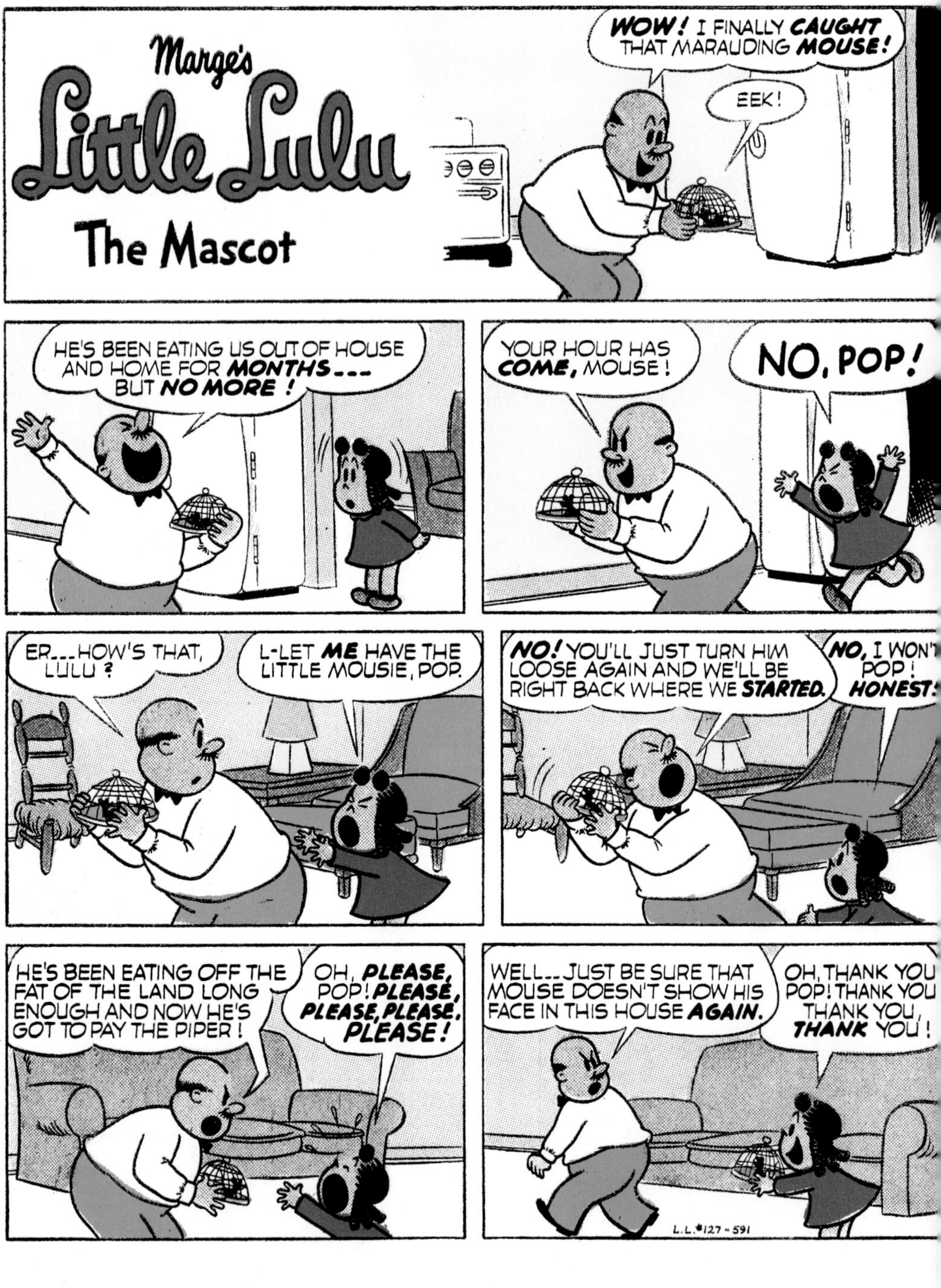

Marge's
Little Lulu
The Mascot
WOW! I FINALLY CAUGHT THAT MARAUDING MOUSE!
EEK!
HE'S BEEN EATING US OUT OF HOUSE AND HOME FOR MONTHS--- BUT NO MORE!
YOUR HOUR HAS COME, MOUSE!
NO, POP!
ER---HOW'S THAT, LULU?
L-LET ME HAVE THE LITTLE MOUSIE, POP.
NO! YOU'LL JUST TURN HIM LOOSE AGAIN AND WE'LL BE RIGHT BACK WHERE WE STARTED.
NO, I WON'T POP! HONEST!
HE'S BEEN EATING OFF THE FAT OF THE LAND LONG ENOUGH AND NOW HE'S GOT TO PAY THE PIPER!
OH, PLEASE, POP! PLEASE, PLEASE, PLEASE, PLEASE!
WELL--JUST BE SURE THAT MOUSE DOESN'T SHOW HIS FACE IN THIS HOUSE AGAIN.
OH, THANK YOU POP! THANK YOU THANK YOU, THANK YOU!
L.L.#127-591

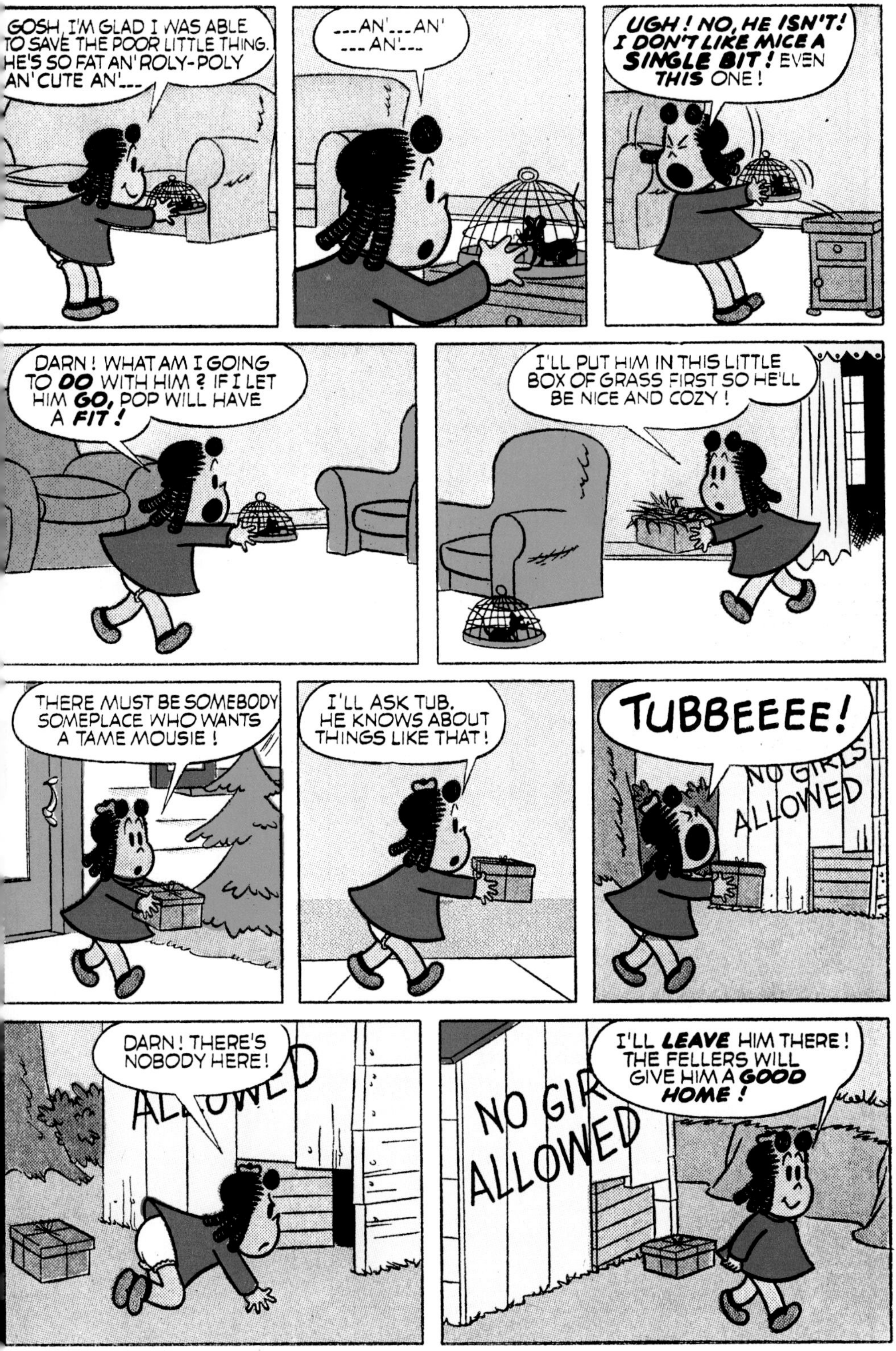
GOSH, I'M GLAD I WAS ABLE TO SAVE THE POOR LITTLE THING. HE'S SO FAT AN' ROLY-POLY AN' CUTE AN'---
---AN'---AN' ---AN'---
UGH! NO, HE ISN'T! I DON'T LIKE MICE A SINGLE BIT! EVEN THIS ONE!
DARN! WHAT AM I GOING TO DO WITH HIM? IF I LET HIM GO, POP WILL HAVE A FIT!
I'LL PUT HIM IN THIS LITTLE BOX OF GRASS FIRST SO HE'LL BE NICE AND COZY!
THERE MUST BE SOMEBODY SOMEPLACE WHO WANTS A TAME MOUSIE!
I'LL ASK TUB. HE KNOWS ABOUT THINGS LIKE THAT!
TUBBEEEE!
NO GIRLS ALLOWED
DARN! THERE'S NOBODY HERE!
ALLOWED
NO GIR ALLOWED
I'LL LEAVE HIM THERE! THE FELLERS WILL GIVE HIM A GOOD HOME!

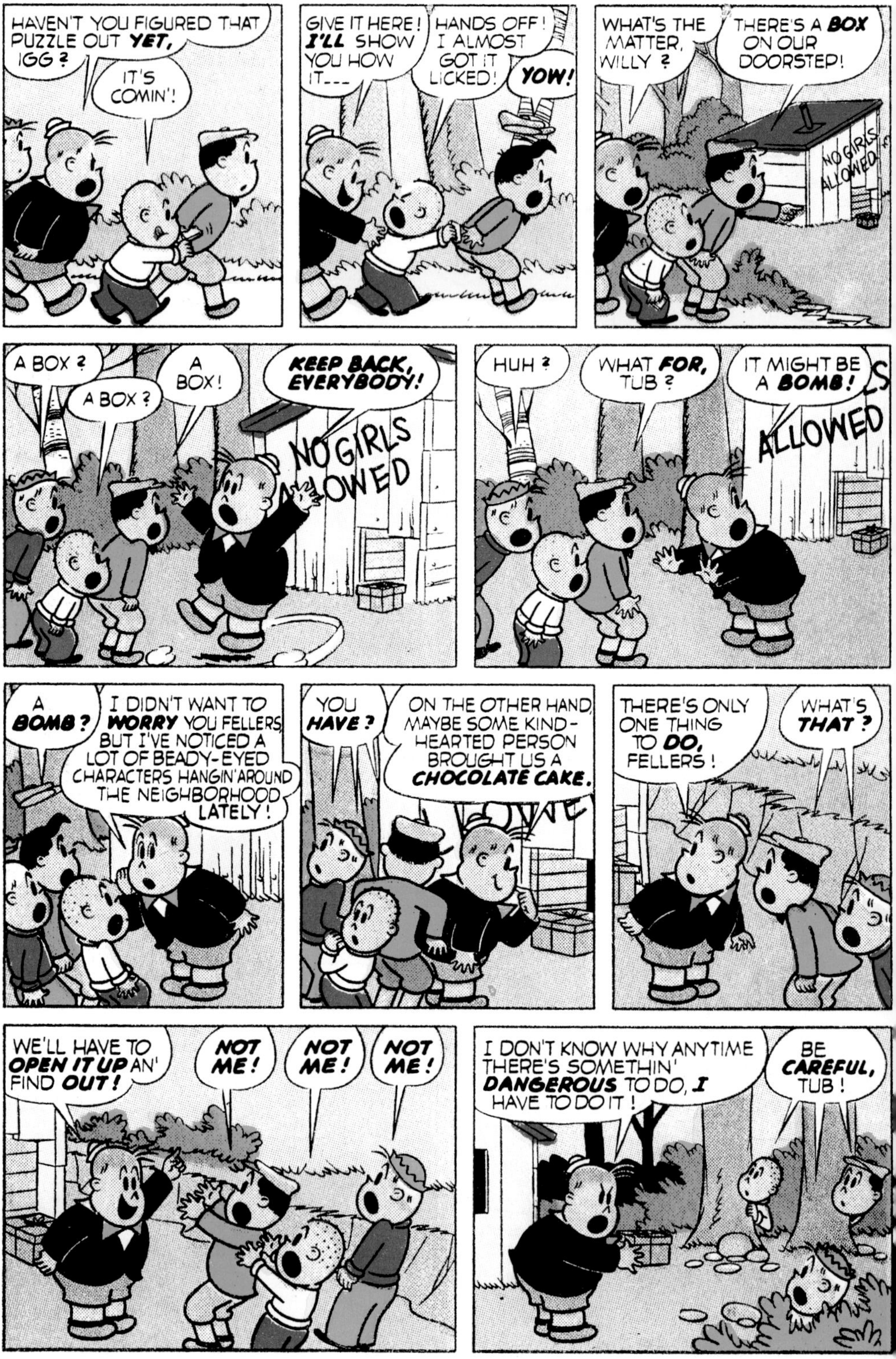
HAVEN'T YOU FIGURED THAT PUZZLE OUT **YET,** IGG ?
IT'S COMIN'!
GIVE IT HERE! **I'LL** SHOW YOU HOW IT---
HANDS OFF! I ALMOST GOT IT LICKED!
YOW!
WHAT'S THE MATTER, WILLY ?
THERE'S A **BOX** ON OUR DOORSTEP!
NO GIRLS ALLOWED
A BOX ?
A BOX ?
A BOX!
KEEP BACK, EVERYBODY!
NO GIRLS ALLOWED
HUH ?
WHAT **FOR,** TUB ?
IT MIGHT BE A **BOMB!**
A **BOMB?**
I DIDN'T WANT TO **WORRY** YOU FELLERS, BUT I'VE NOTICED A LOT OF BEADY-EYED CHARACTERS HANGIN' AROUND THE NEIGHBORHOOD LATELY!
YOU **HAVE?**
ON THE OTHER HAND, MAYBE SOME KIND-HEARTED PERSON BROUGHT US A **CHOCOLATE CAKE.**
THERE'S ONLY ONE THING TO **DO,** FELLERS!
WHAT'S **THAT?**
WE'LL HAVE TO **OPEN IT UP** AN' FIND **OUT!**
NOT ME!
NOT ME!
NOT ME!
I DON'T KNOW WHY ANYTIME THERE'S SOMETHIN' **DANGEROUS** TO DO, **I** HAVE TO DO IT!
BE **CAREFUL,** TUB!

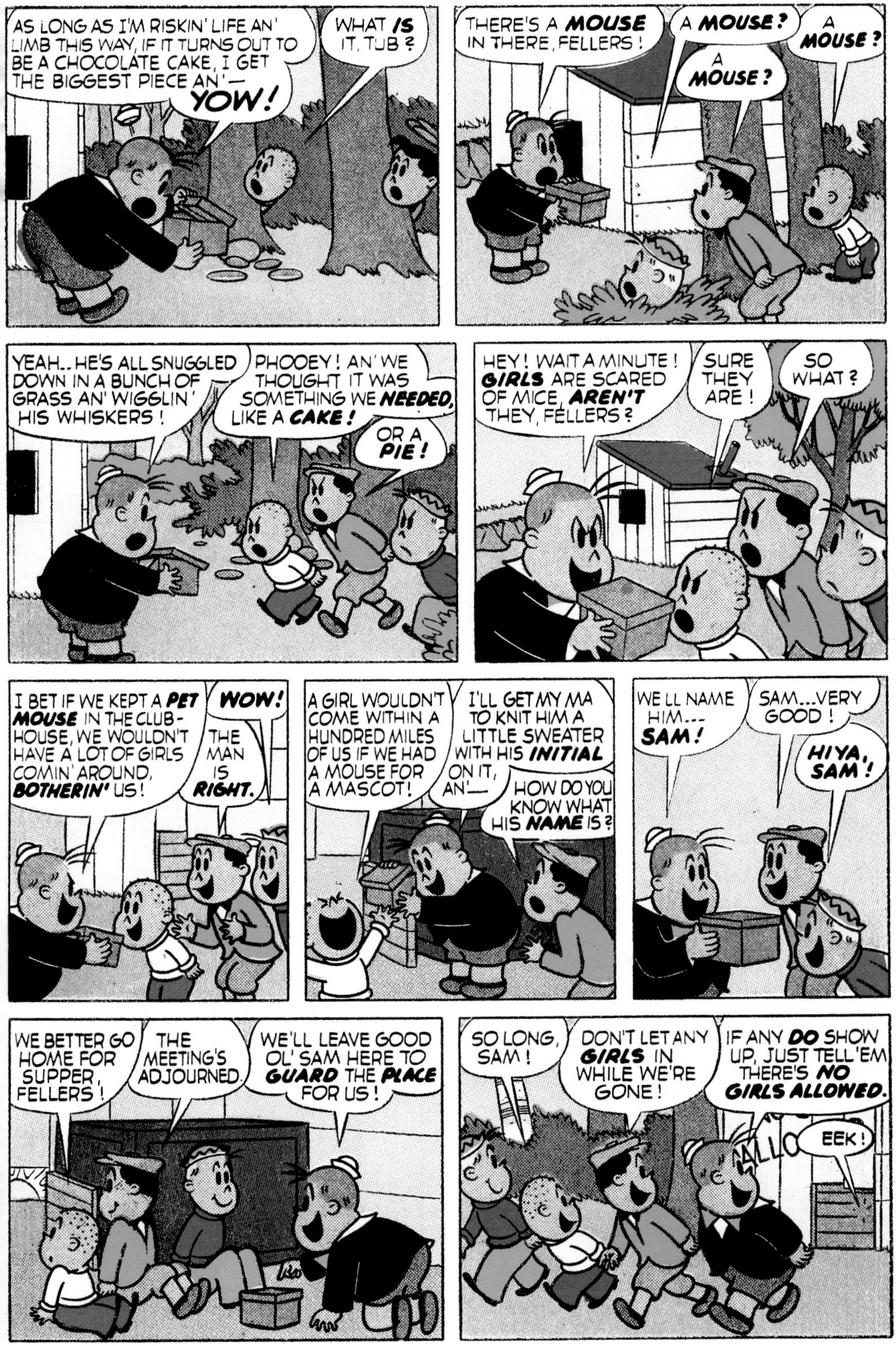
AS LONG AS I'M RISKIN' LIFE AN' LIMB THIS WAY, IF IT TURNS OUT TO BE A CHOCOLATE CAKE, I GET THE BIGGEST PIECE AN'— YOW!
WHAT IS IT, TUB?
THERE'S A MOUSE IN THERE, FELLERS!
A MOUSE?
A MOUSE?
A MOUSE?
YEAH.. HE'S ALL SNUGGLED DOWN IN A BUNCH OF GRASS AN' WIGGLIN' HIS WHISKERS!
PHOOEY! AN' WE THOUGHT IT WAS SOMETHING WE NEEDED, LIKE A CAKE!
OR A PIE!
HEY! WAIT A MINUTE! GIRLS ARE SCARED OF MICE, AREN'T THEY, FELLERS?
SURE THEY ARE!
SO WHAT?
I BET IF WE KEPT A PET MOUSE IN THE CLUB-HOUSE, WE WOULDN'T HAVE A LOT OF GIRLS COMIN' AROUND, BOTHERIN' US!
WOW!
THE MAN IS RIGHT.
A GIRL WOULDN'T COME WITHIN A HUNDRED MILES OF US IF WE HAD A MOUSE FOR A MASCOT!
I'LL GET MY MA TO KNIT HIM A LITTLE SWEATER WITH HIS INITIAL ON IT, AN'—
HOW DO YOU KNOW WHAT HIS NAME IS?
WE LL NAME HIM... SAM!
SAM...VERY GOOD!
HIYA, SAM!
WE BETTER GO HOME FOR SUPPER, FELLERS!
THE MEETING'S ADJOURNED.
WE'LL LEAVE GOOD OL' SAM HERE TO GUARD THE PLACE FOR US!
SO LONG, SAM!
DON'T LET ANY GIRLS IN WHILE WE'RE GONE!
IF ANY DO SHOW UP, JUST TELL 'EM THERE'S NO GIRLS ALLOWED.
EEK!

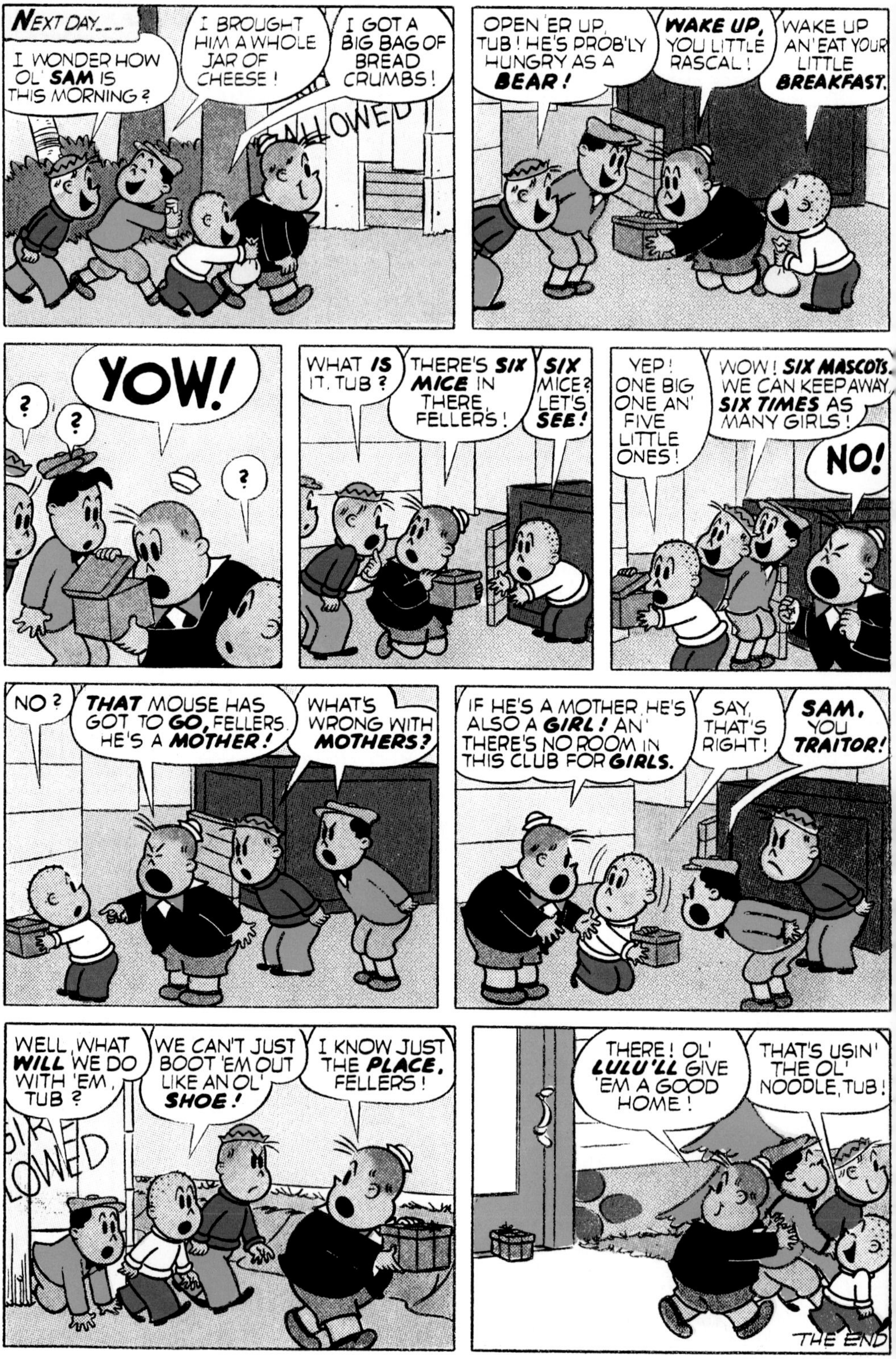
NEXT DAY...
I WONDER HOW OL' SAM IS THIS MORNING?
I BROUGHT HIM A WHOLE JAR OF CHEESE!
I GOT A BIG BAG OF BREAD CRUMBS!
ALLOWED
OPEN 'ER UP, TUB! HE'S PROB'LY HUNGRY AS A BEAR!
WAKE UP, YOU LITTLE RASCAL!
WAKE UP AN' EAT YOUR LITTLE BREAKFAST.
YOW!
?
?
?
WHAT IS IT, TUB?
THERE'S SIX MICE IN THERE, FELLERS!
SIX MICE? LET'S SEE!
YEP! ONE BIG ONE AN' FIVE LITTLE ONES!
WOW! SIX MASCOTS. WE CAN KEEP AWAY SIX TIMES AS MANY GIRLS!
NO!
NO?
THAT MOUSE HAS GOT TO GO, FELLERS. HE'S A MOTHER!
WHAT'S WRONG WITH MOTHERS?
IF HE'S A MOTHER, HE'S ALSO A GIRL! AN' THERE'S NO ROOM IN THIS CLUB FOR GIRLS.
SAY, THAT'S RIGHT!
SAM, YOU TRAITOR!
WELL, WHAT WILL WE DO WITH 'EM, TUB?
WE CAN'T JUST BOOT 'EM OUT LIKE AN OL' SHOE!
I KNOW JUST THE PLACE, FELLERS!
LOWED
THERE! OL' LULU'LL GIVE 'EM A GOOD HOME!
THAT'S USIN' THE OL' NOODLE, TUB!
THE END

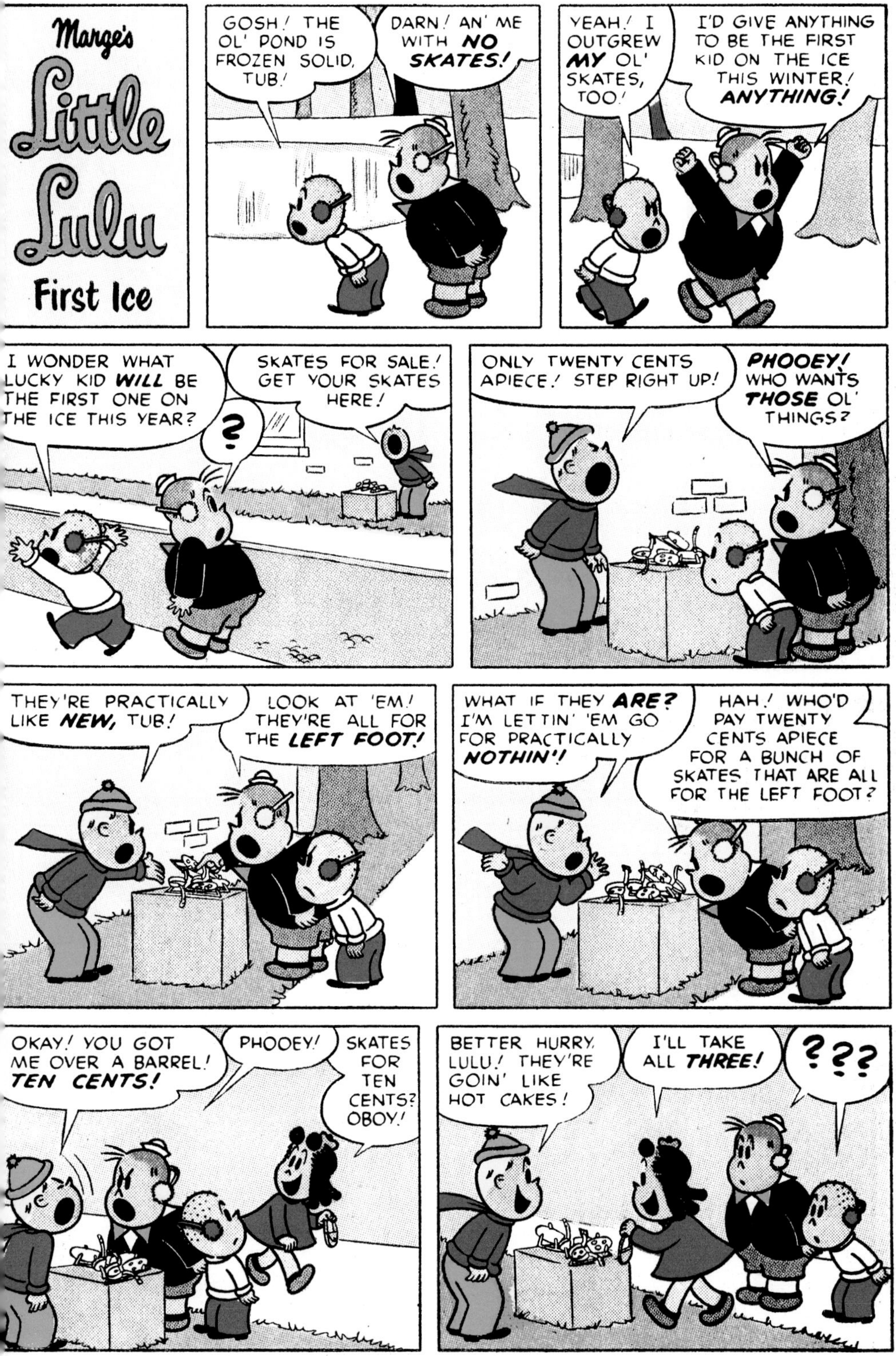
Marge's
Little Lulu
First Ice
GOSH! THE OL' POND IS FROZEN SOLID, TUB!
DARN! AN' ME WITH NO SKATES!
YEAH! I OUTGREW MY OL' SKATES, TOO!
I'D GIVE ANYTHING TO BE THE FIRST KID ON THE ICE THIS WINTER! ANYTHING!
I WONDER WHAT LUCKY KID WILL BE THE FIRST ONE ON THE ICE THIS YEAR?
?
SKATES FOR SALE! GET YOUR SKATES HERE!
ONLY TWENTY CENTS APIECE! STEP RIGHT UP!
PHOOEY! WHO WANTS THOSE OL' THINGS?
THEY'RE PRACTICALLY LIKE NEW, TUB!
LOOK AT 'EM! THEY'RE ALL FOR THE LEFT FOOT!
WHAT IF THEY ARE? I'M LETTIN' 'EM GO FOR PRACTICALLY NOTHIN'!
HAH! WHO'D PAY TWENTY CENTS APIECE FOR A BUNCH OF SKATES THAT ARE ALL FOR THE LEFT FOOT?
OKAY! YOU GOT ME OVER A BARREL! TEN CENTS!
PHOOEY!
SKATES FOR TEN CENTS? OBOY!
BETTER HURRY, LULU! THEY'RE GOIN' LIKE HOT CAKES!
I'LL TAKE ALL THREE!
???

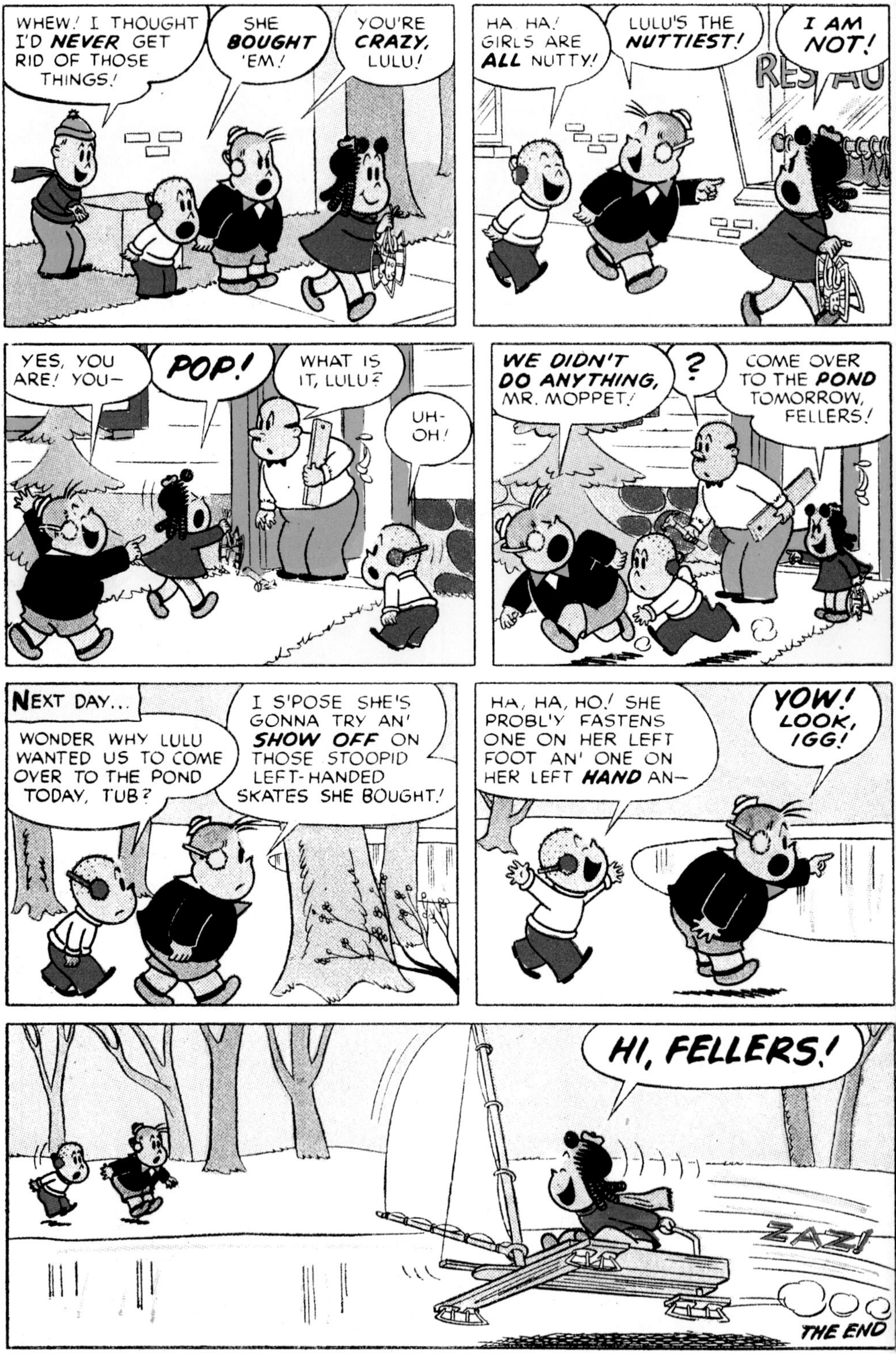
WHEW! I THOUGHT I'D NEVER GET RID OF THOSE THINGS!
SHE BOUGHT 'EM!
YOU'RE CRAZY, LULU!
HA HA! GIRLS ARE ALL NUTTY!
LULU'S THE NUTTIEST!
I AM NOT!
YES, YOU ARE! YOU—
POP!
WHAT IS IT, LULU?
UH-OH!
WE DIDN'T DO ANYTHING, MR. MOPPET!
?
COME OVER TO THE POND TOMORROW, FELLERS!
NEXT DAY...
WONDER WHY LULU WANTED US TO COME OVER TO THE POND TODAY, TUB?
I S'POSE SHE'S GONNA TRY AN' SHOW OFF ON THOSE STOOPID LEFT-HANDED SKATES SHE BOUGHT!
HA, HA, HO! SHE PROBL'Y FASTENS ONE ON HER LEFT FOOT AN' ONE ON HER LEFT HAND AN—
YOW! LOOK, IGG!
HI, FELLERS!
ZAZ!
THE END

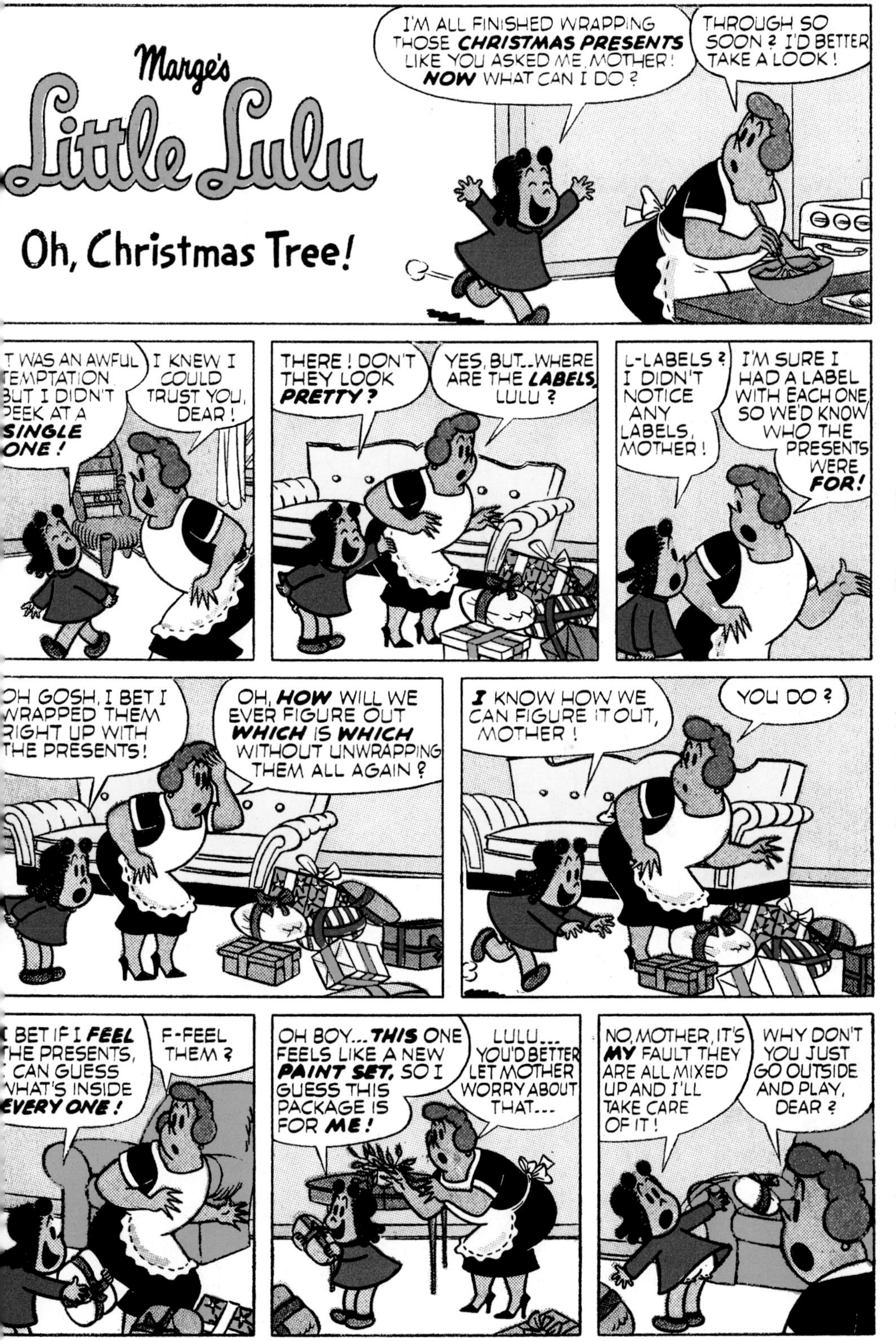

Marge's
Little Lulu
Oh, Christmas Tree!
I'M ALL FINISHED WRAPPING THOSE CHRISTMAS PRESENTS LIKE YOU ASKED ME, MOTHER! NOW WHAT CAN I DO?
THROUGH SO SOON? I'D BETTER TAKE A LOOK!
T WAS AN AWFUL TEMPTATION BUT I DIDN'T PEEK AT A SINGLE ONE!
I KNEW I COULD TRUST YOU, DEAR!
THERE! DON'T THEY LOOK PRETTY?
YES, BUT.. WHERE ARE THE LABELS, LULU?
L-LABELS? I DIDN'T NOTICE ANY LABELS, MOTHER!
I'M SURE I HAD A LABEL WITH EACH ONE, SO WE'D KNOW WHO THE PRESENTS WERE FOR!
OH GOSH, I BET I WRAPPED THEM RIGHT UP WITH THE PRESENTS!
OH, HOW WILL WE EVER FIGURE OUT WHICH IS WHICH WITHOUT UNWRAPPING THEM ALL AGAIN?
I KNOW HOW WE CAN FIGURE IT OUT, MOTHER!
YOU DO?
I BET IF I FEEL THE PRESENTS, I CAN GUESS WHAT'S INSIDE EVERY ONE!
F-FEEL THEM?
OH BOY... THIS ONE FEELS LIKE A NEW PAINT SET, SO I GUESS THIS PACKAGE IS FOR ME!
LULU... YOU'D BETTER LET MOTHER WORRY ABOUT THAT...
NO, MOTHER, IT'S MY FAULT THEY ARE ALL MIXED UP AND I'LL TAKE CARE OF IT!
WHY DON'T YOU JUST GO OUTSIDE AND PLAY, DEAR?

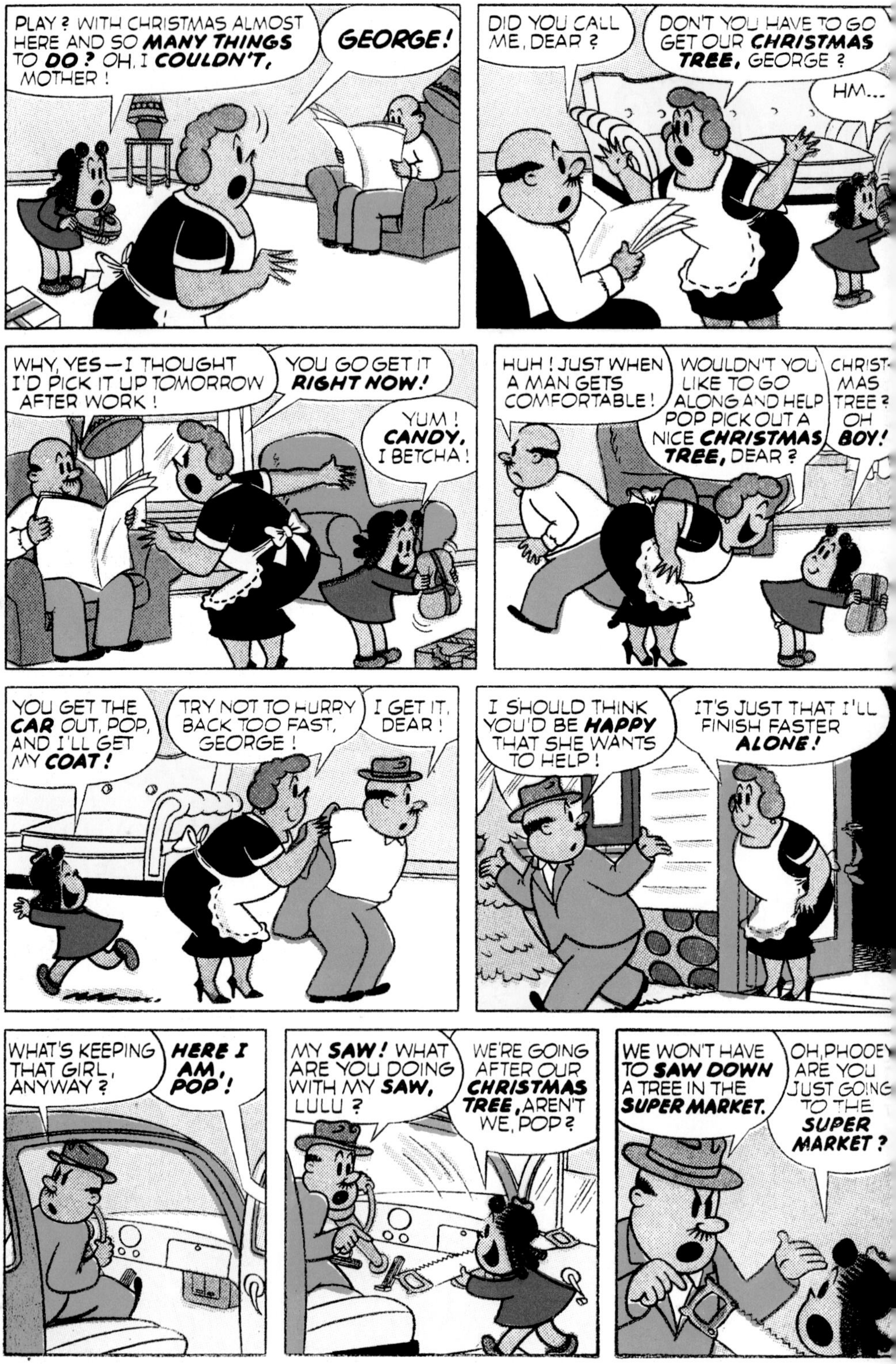
PLAY ? WITH CHRISTMAS ALMOST HERE AND SO **MANY THINGS** TO **DO ?** OH, I **COULDN'T,** MOTHER !
GEORGE !
DID YOU CALL ME, DEAR ?
DON'T YOU HAVE TO GO GET OUR **CHRISTMAS TREE,** GEORGE ?
HM...
WHY, YES—I THOUGHT I'D PICK IT UP TOMORROW AFTER WORK !
YOU GO GET IT **RIGHT NOW!**
YUM ! **CANDY,** I BETCHA !
HUH ! JUST WHEN A MAN GETS COMFORTABLE !
WOULDN'T YOU LIKE TO GO ALONG AND HELP POP PICK OUT A NICE **CHRISTMAS TREE,** DEAR ?
CHRIST-MAS TREE ? OH **BOY!**
YOU GET THE **CAR** OUT, POP, AND I'LL GET MY **COAT !**
TRY NOT TO HURRY BACK TOO FAST, GEORGE !
I GET IT, DEAR !
I SHOULD THINK YOU'D BE **HAPPY** THAT SHE WANTS TO HELP !
IT'S JUST THAT I'LL FINISH FASTER **ALONE !**
WHAT'S KEEPING THAT GIRL, ANYWAY ?
HERE I AM, POP !
MY **SAW !** WHAT ARE YOU DOING WITH MY **SAW,** LULU ?
WE'RE GOING AFTER OUR **CHRISTMAS TREE,** AREN'T WE, POP ?
WE WON'T HAVE TO **SAW DOWN** A TREE IN THE **SUPER MARKET.**
OH, PHOOEY ARE YOU JUST GOING TO THE **SUPER MARKET ?**

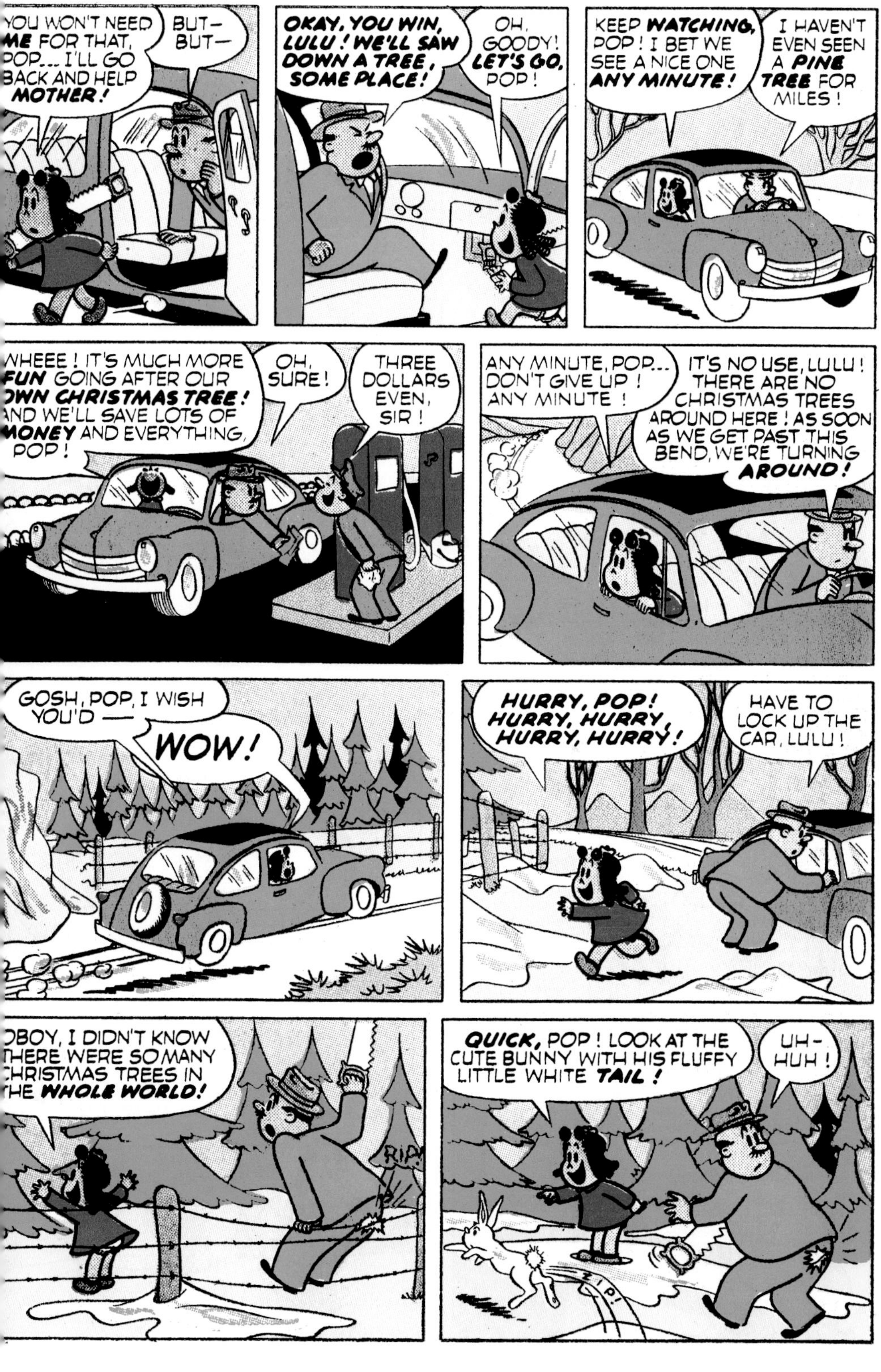

YOU WON'T NEED ME FOR THAT, POP... I'LL GO BACK AND HELP MOTHER!
BUT— BUT—
OKAY. YOU WIN, LULU! WE'LL SAW DOWN A TREE, SOME PLACE!
OH, GOODY! LET'S GO, POP!
KEEP WATCHING, POP! I BET WE SEE A NICE ONE ANY MINUTE!
I HAVEN'T EVEN SEEN A PINE TREE FOR MILES!
WHEEE! IT'S MUCH MORE FUN GOING AFTER OUR OWN CHRISTMAS TREE! AND WE'LL SAVE LOTS OF MONEY AND EVERYTHING, POP!
OH, SURE!
THREE DOLLARS EVEN, SIR!
ANY MINUTE, POP... DON'T GIVE UP! ANY MINUTE!
IT'S NO USE, LULU! THERE ARE NO CHRISTMAS TREES AROUND HERE! AS SOON AS WE GET PAST THIS BEND, WE'RE TURNING AROUND!
GOSH, POP, I WISH YOU'D —
WOW!
HURRY, POP! HURRY, HURRY, HURRY, HURRY!
HAVE TO LOCK UP THE CAR, LULU!
BOY, I DIDN'T KNOW THERE WERE SO MANY CHRISTMAS TREES IN THE WHOLE WORLD!
RIP!
QUICK, POP! LOOK AT THE CUTE BUNNY WITH HIS FLUFFY LITTLE WHITE TAIL!
UH-HUH!
ZIP!

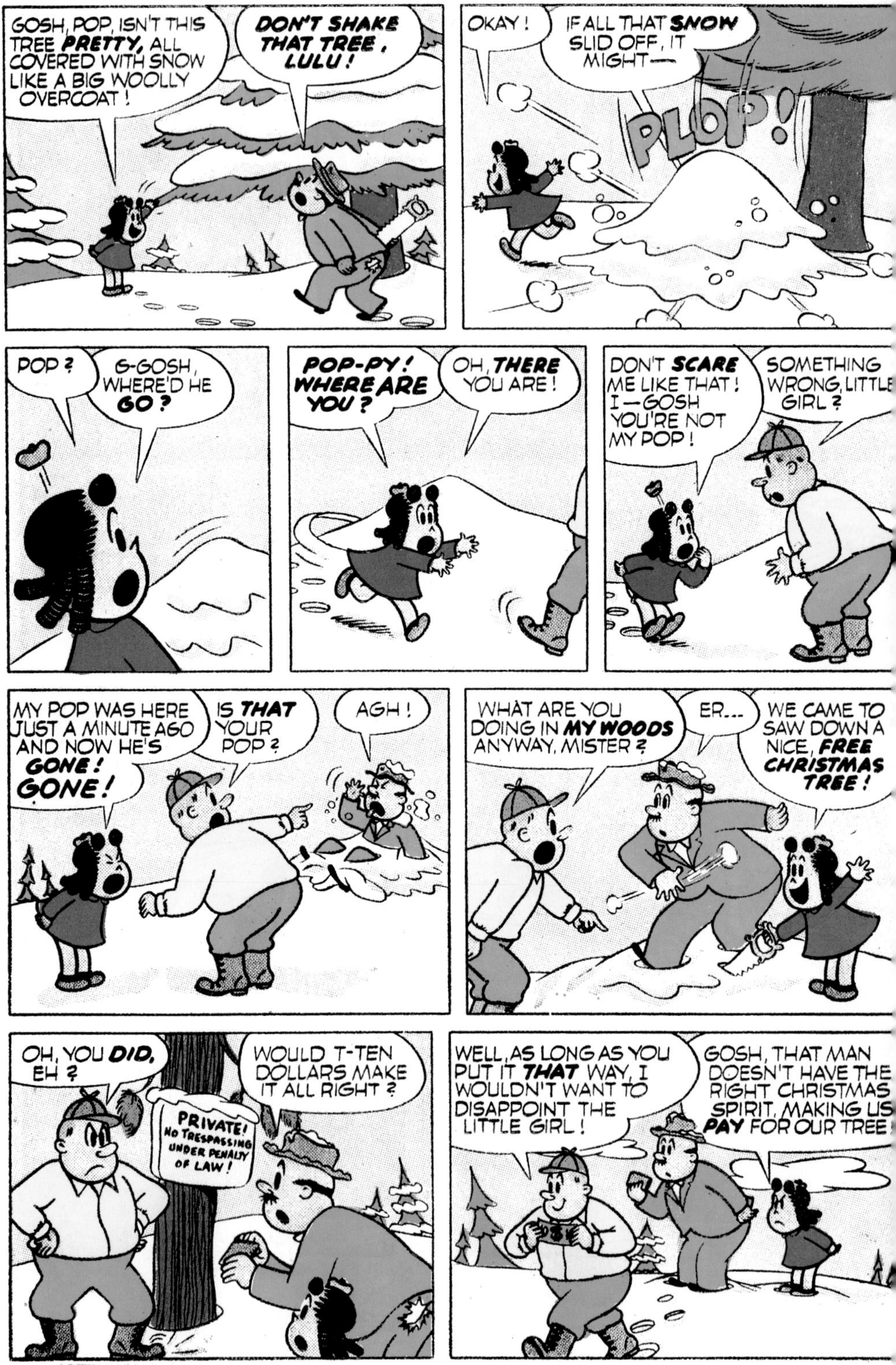
GOSH, POP, ISN'T THIS TREE PRETTY, ALL COVERED WITH SNOW LIKE A BIG WOOLLY OVERCOAT!
DON'T SHAKE THAT TREE, LULU!
OKAY!
IF ALL THAT SNOW SLID OFF, IT MIGHT—
PLOP!
POP?
G-GOSH, WHERE'D HE GO?
POP-PY! WHERE ARE YOU?
OH, THERE YOU ARE!
DON'T SCARE ME LIKE THAT! I—GOSH YOU'RE NOT MY POP!
SOMETHING WRONG, LITTLE GIRL?
MY POP WAS HERE JUST A MINUTE AGO AND NOW HE'S GONE! GONE!
IS THAT YOUR POP?
AGH!
WHAT ARE YOU DOING IN MY WOODS ANYWAY, MISTER?
ER...
WE CAME TO SAW DOWN A NICE, FREE CHRISTMAS TREE!
OH, YOU DID, EH?
PRIVATE! NO TRESPASSING UNDER PENALTY OF LAW!
WOULD T-TEN DOLLARS MAKE IT ALL RIGHT?
WELL, AS LONG AS YOU PUT IT THAT WAY, I WOULDN'T WANT TO DISAPPOINT THE LITTLE GIRL!
GOSH, THAT MAN DOESN'T HAVE THE RIGHT CHRISTMAS SPIRIT, MAKING US PAY FOR OUR TREE!

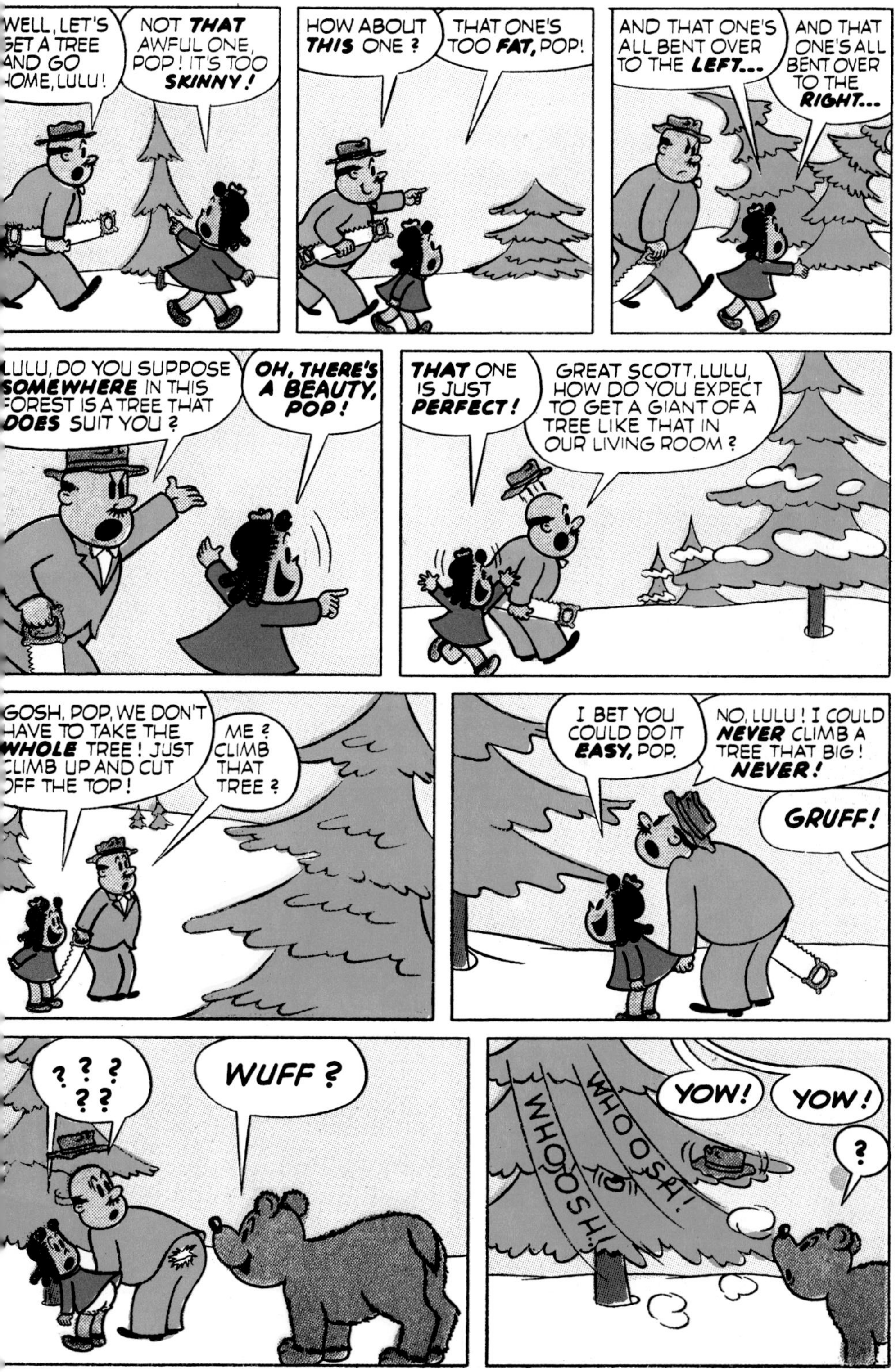
WELL, LET'S GET A TREE AND GO HOME, LULU!
NOT THAT AWFUL ONE, POP! IT'S TOO SKINNY!
HOW ABOUT THIS ONE?
THAT ONE'S TOO FAT, POP!
AND THAT ONE'S ALL BENT OVER TO THE LEFT...
AND THAT ONE'S ALL BENT OVER TO THE RIGHT...
LULU, DO YOU SUPPOSE SOMEWHERE IN THIS FOREST IS A TREE THAT DOES SUIT YOU?
OH, THERE'S A BEAUTY, POP!
THAT ONE IS JUST PERFECT!
GREAT SCOTT, LULU, HOW DO YOU EXPECT TO GET A GIANT OF A TREE LIKE THAT IN OUR LIVING ROOM?
GOSH, POP, WE DON'T HAVE TO TAKE THE WHOLE TREE! JUST CLIMB UP AND CUT OFF THE TOP!
ME? CLIMB THAT TREE?
I BET YOU COULD DO IT EASY, POP.
NO, LULU! I COULD NEVER CLIMB A TREE THAT BIG! NEVER!
GRUFF!
? ? ? ? ?
WUFF?
WHOOSH!
WHOOSH!
YOW!
YOW!
?

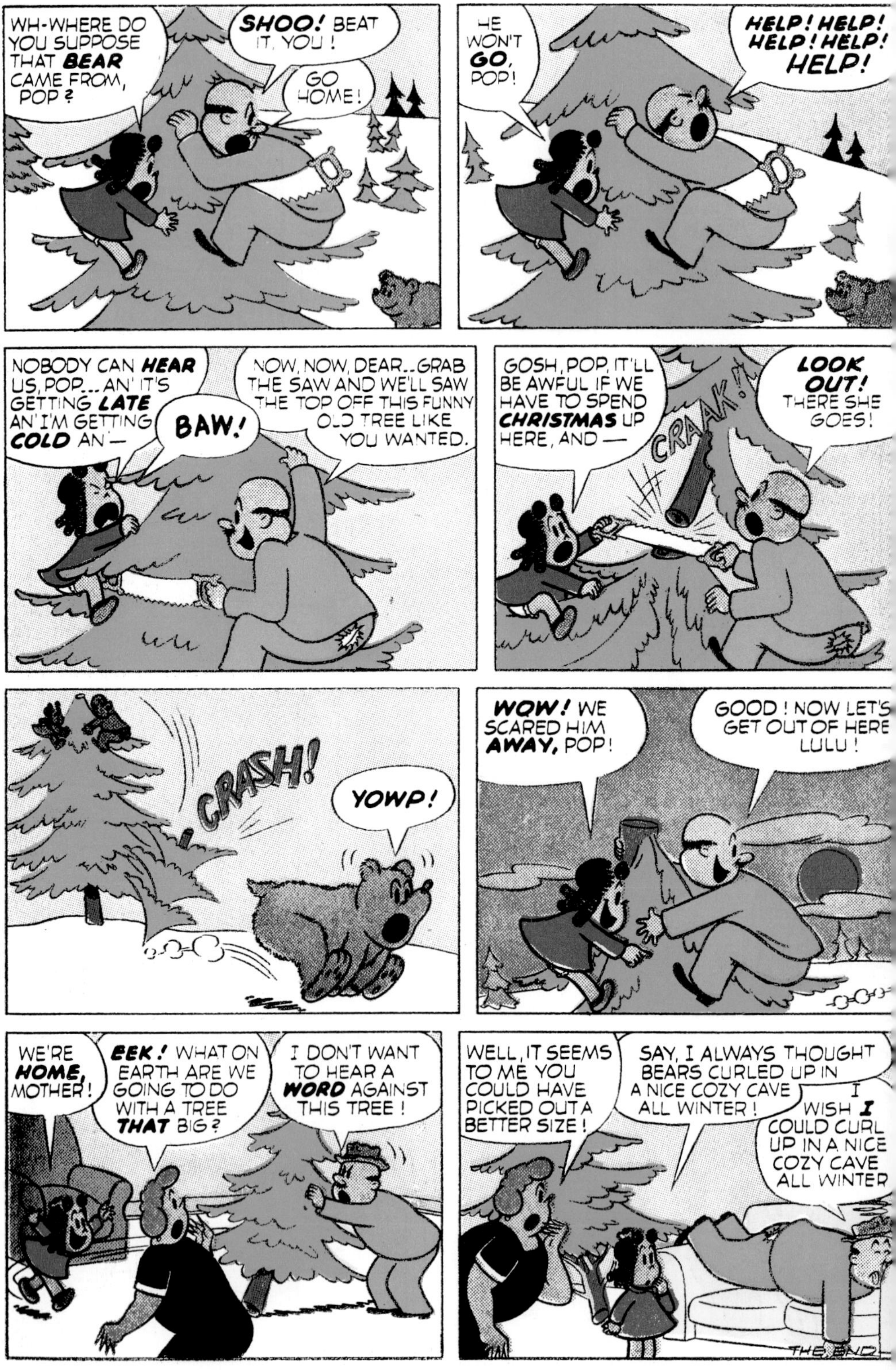

WH-WHERE DO YOU SUPPOSE THAT BEAR CAME FROM, POP?
SHOO! BEAT IT, YOU!
GO HOME!
HE WON'T GO, POP!
HELP! HELP! HELP! HELP! HELP!
NOBODY CAN HEAR US, POP... AN' IT'S GETTING LATE AN' I'M GETTING COLD AN'—
BAW!
NOW, NOW, DEAR.. GRAB THE SAW AND WE'LL SAW THE TOP OFF THIS FUNNY OLD TREE LIKE YOU WANTED.
GOSH, POP, IT'LL BE AWFUL IF WE HAVE TO SPEND CHRISTMAS UP HERE, AND —
CRAAK!
LOOK OUT! THERE SHE GOES!
CRASH!
YOWP!
WOW! WE SCARED HIM AWAY, POP!
GOOD! NOW LET'S GET OUT OF HERE LULU!
WE'RE HOME, MOTHER!
EEK! WHAT ON EARTH ARE WE GOING TO DO WITH A TREE THAT BIG?
I DON'T WANT TO HEAR A WORD AGAINST THIS TREE!
WELL, IT SEEMS TO ME YOU COULD HAVE PICKED OUT A BETTER SIZE!
SAY, I ALWAYS THOUGHT BEARS CURLED UP IN A NICE COZY CAVE ALL WINTER!
I WISH I COULD CURL UP IN A NICE COZY CAVE ALL WINTER
THE END

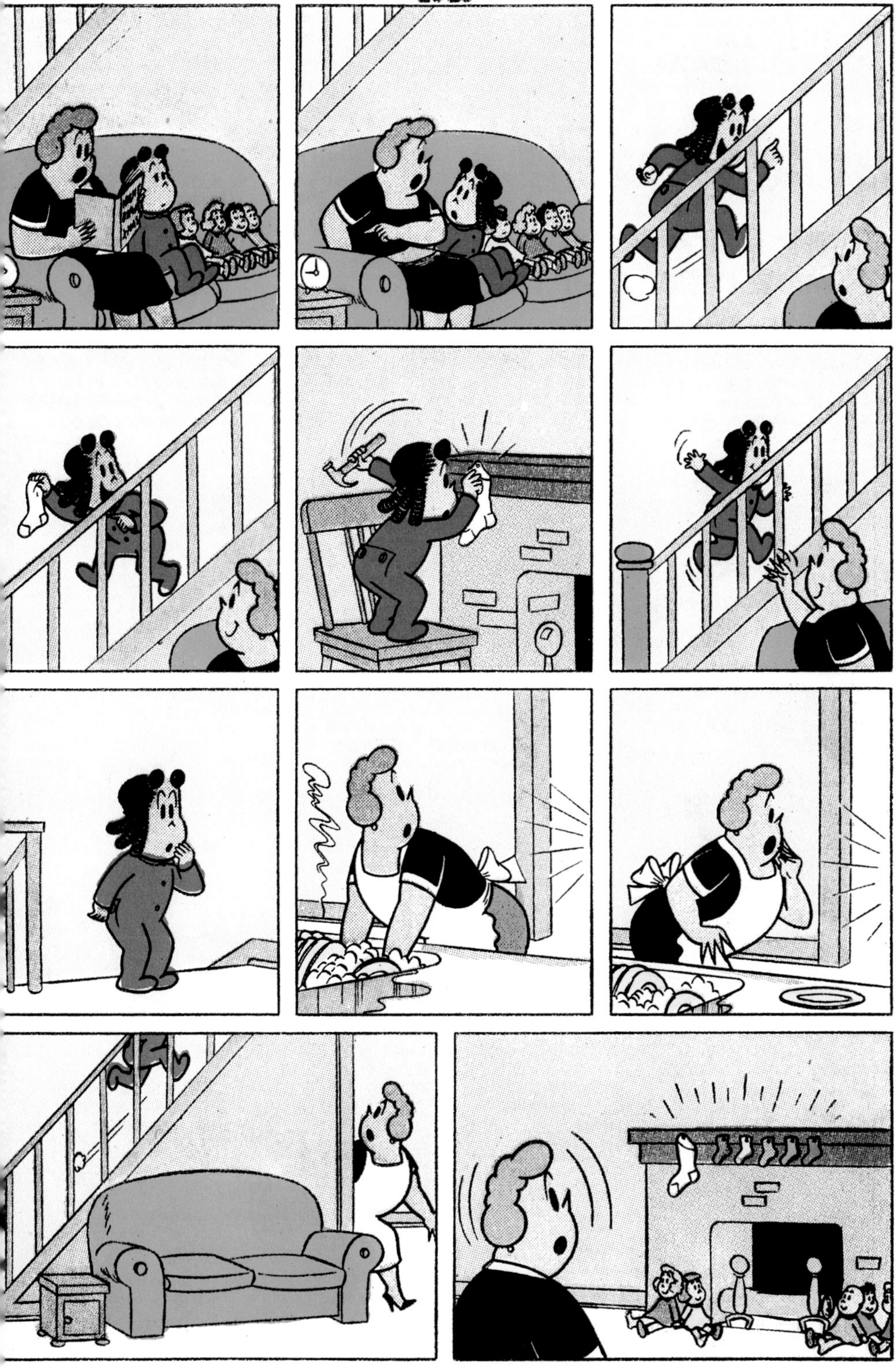

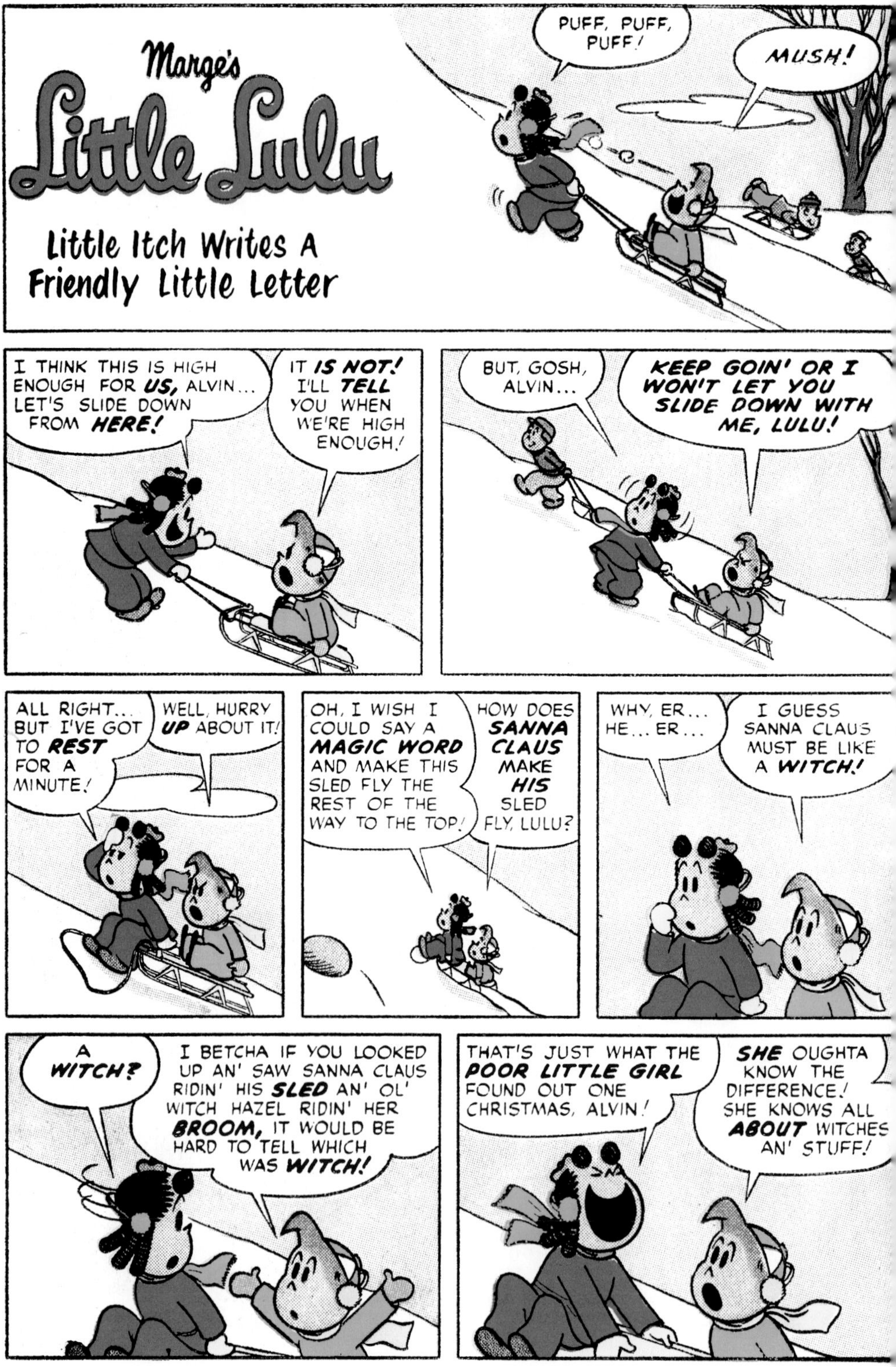
Marge's Little Lulu
Little Itch Writes A Friendly Little Letter
PUFF, PUFF, PUFF!
MUSH!
I THINK THIS IS HIGH ENOUGH FOR US, ALVIN... LET'S SLIDE DOWN FROM HERE!
IT IS NOT! I'LL TELL YOU WHEN WE'RE HIGH ENOUGH!
BUT, GOSH, ALVIN...
KEEP GOIN' OR I WON'T LET YOU SLIDE DOWN WITH ME, LULU!
ALL RIGHT... BUT I'VE GOT TO REST FOR A MINUTE!
WELL, HURRY UP ABOUT IT!
OH, I WISH I COULD SAY A MAGIC WORD AND MAKE THIS SLED FLY THE REST OF THE WAY TO THE TOP!
HOW DOES SANNA CLAUS MAKE HIS SLED FLY, LULU?
WHY, ER... HE... ER...
I GUESS SANNA CLAUS MUST BE LIKE A WITCH!
A WITCH?
I BETCHA IF YOU LOOKED UP AN' SAW SANNA CLAUS RIDIN' HIS SLED AN' OL' WITCH HAZEL RIDIN' HER BROOM, IT WOULD BE HARD TO TELL WHICH WAS WITCH!
THAT'S JUST WHAT THE POOR LITTLE GIRL FOUND OUT ONE CHRISTMAS, ALVIN!
SHE OUGHTA KNOW THE DIFFERENCE! SHE KNOWS ALL ABOUT WITCHES AN' STUFF!

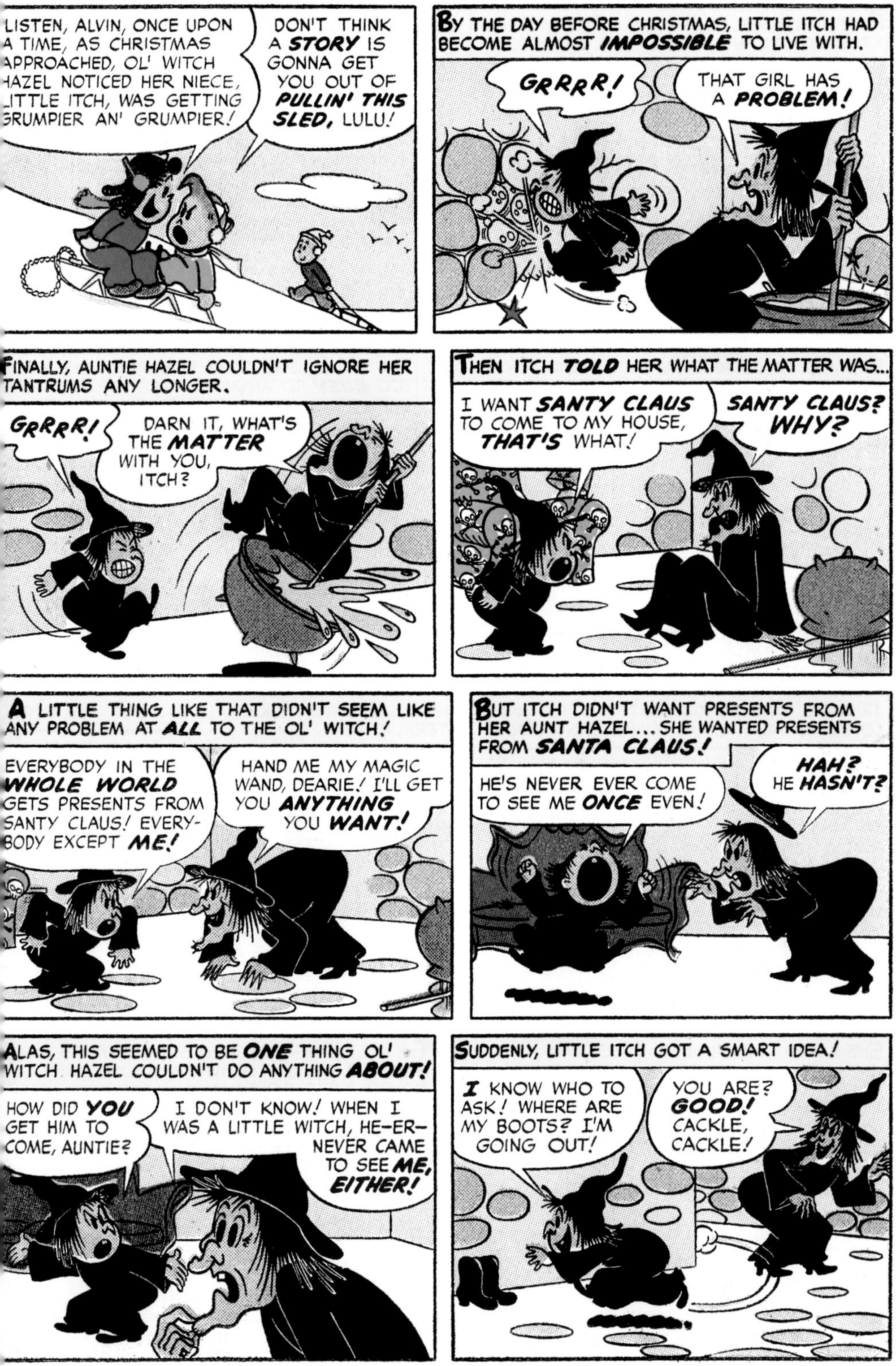
LISTEN, ALVIN, ONCE UPON A TIME, AS CHRISTMAS APPROACHED, OL' WITCH HAZEL NOTICED HER NIECE, LITTLE ITCH, WAS GETTING GRUMPIER AN' GRUMPIER!
DON'T THINK A STORY IS GONNA GET YOU OUT OF PULLIN' THIS SLED, LULU!
BY THE DAY BEFORE CHRISTMAS, LITTLE ITCH HAD BECOME ALMOST IMPOSSIBLE TO LIVE WITH.
GRRRR!
THAT GIRL HAS A PROBLEM!
FINALLY, AUNTIE HAZEL COULDN'T IGNORE HER TANTRUMS ANY LONGER.
GRRRR!
DARN IT, WHAT'S THE MATTER WITH YOU, ITCH?
THEN ITCH TOLD HER WHAT THE MATTER WAS...
I WANT SANTY CLAUS TO COME TO MY HOUSE, THAT'S WHAT!
SANTY CLAUS? WHY?
A LITTLE THING LIKE THAT DIDN'T SEEM LIKE ANY PROBLEM AT ALL TO THE OL' WITCH!
EVERYBODY IN THE WHOLE WORLD GETS PRESENTS FROM SANTY CLAUS! EVERYBODY EXCEPT ME!
HAND ME MY MAGIC WAND, DEARIE! I'LL GET YOU ANYTHING YOU WANT!
BUT ITCH DIDN'T WANT PRESENTS FROM HER AUNT HAZEL... SHE WANTED PRESENTS FROM SANTA CLAUS!
HE'S NEVER EVER COME TO SEE ME ONCE EVEN!
HAH? HE HASN'T?
ALAS, THIS SEEMED TO BE ONE THING OL' WITCH HAZEL COULDN'T DO ANYTHING ABOUT!
HOW DID YOU GET HIM TO COME, AUNTIE?
I DON'T KNOW! WHEN I WAS A LITTLE WITCH, HE—ER— NEVER CAME TO SEE ME, EITHER!
SUDDENLY, LITTLE ITCH GOT A SMART IDEA!
I KNOW WHO TO ASK! WHERE ARE MY BOOTS? I'M GOING OUT!
YOU ARE? GOOD! CACKLE, CACKLE!

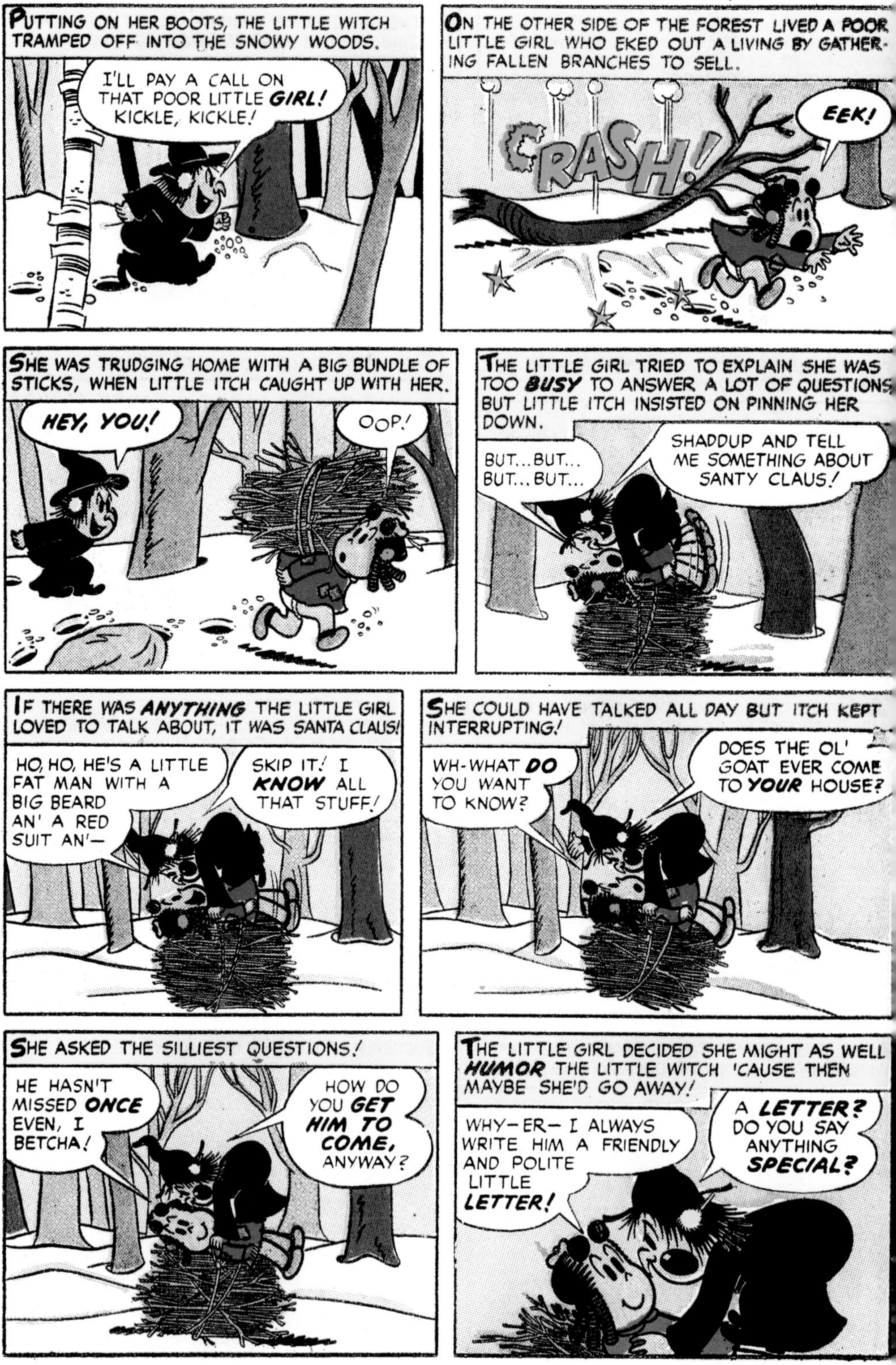
PUTTING ON HER BOOTS, THE LITTLE WITCH TRAMPED OFF INTO THE SNOWY WOODS.
I'LL PAY A CALL ON THAT POOR LITTLE GIRL! KICKLE, KICKLE!
ON THE OTHER SIDE OF THE FOREST LIVED A POOR LITTLE GIRL WHO EKED OUT A LIVING BY GATHERING FALLEN BRANCHES TO SELL.
CRASH!
EEK!
SHE WAS TRUDGING HOME WITH A BIG BUNDLE OF STICKS, WHEN LITTLE ITCH CAUGHT UP WITH HER.
HEY, YOU!
OOP!
THE LITTLE GIRL TRIED TO EXPLAIN SHE WAS TOO BUSY TO ANSWER A LOT OF QUESTIONS BUT LITTLE ITCH INSISTED ON PINNING HER DOWN.
BUT...BUT... BUT...BUT...
SHADDUP AND TELL ME SOMETHING ABOUT SANTY CLAUS!
IF THERE WAS ANYTHING THE LITTLE GIRL LOVED TO TALK ABOUT, IT WAS SANTA CLAUS!
HO, HO, HE'S A LITTLE FAT MAN WITH A BIG BEARD AN' A RED SUIT AN'—
SKIP IT! I KNOW ALL THAT STUFF!
SHE COULD HAVE TALKED ALL DAY BUT ITCH KEPT INTERRUPTING!
WH-WHAT DO YOU WANT TO KNOW?
DOES THE OL' GOAT EVER COME TO YOUR HOUSE?
SHE ASKED THE SILLIEST QUESTIONS!
HE HASN'T MISSED ONCE EVEN, I BETCHA!
HOW DO YOU GET HIM TO COME, ANYWAY?
THE LITTLE GIRL DECIDED SHE MIGHT AS WELL HUMOR THE LITTLE WITCH 'CAUSE THEN MAYBE SHE'D GO AWAY!
WHY—ER— I ALWAYS WRITE HIM A FRIENDLY AND POLITE LITTLE LETTER!
A LETTER? DO YOU SAY ANYTHING SPECIAL?

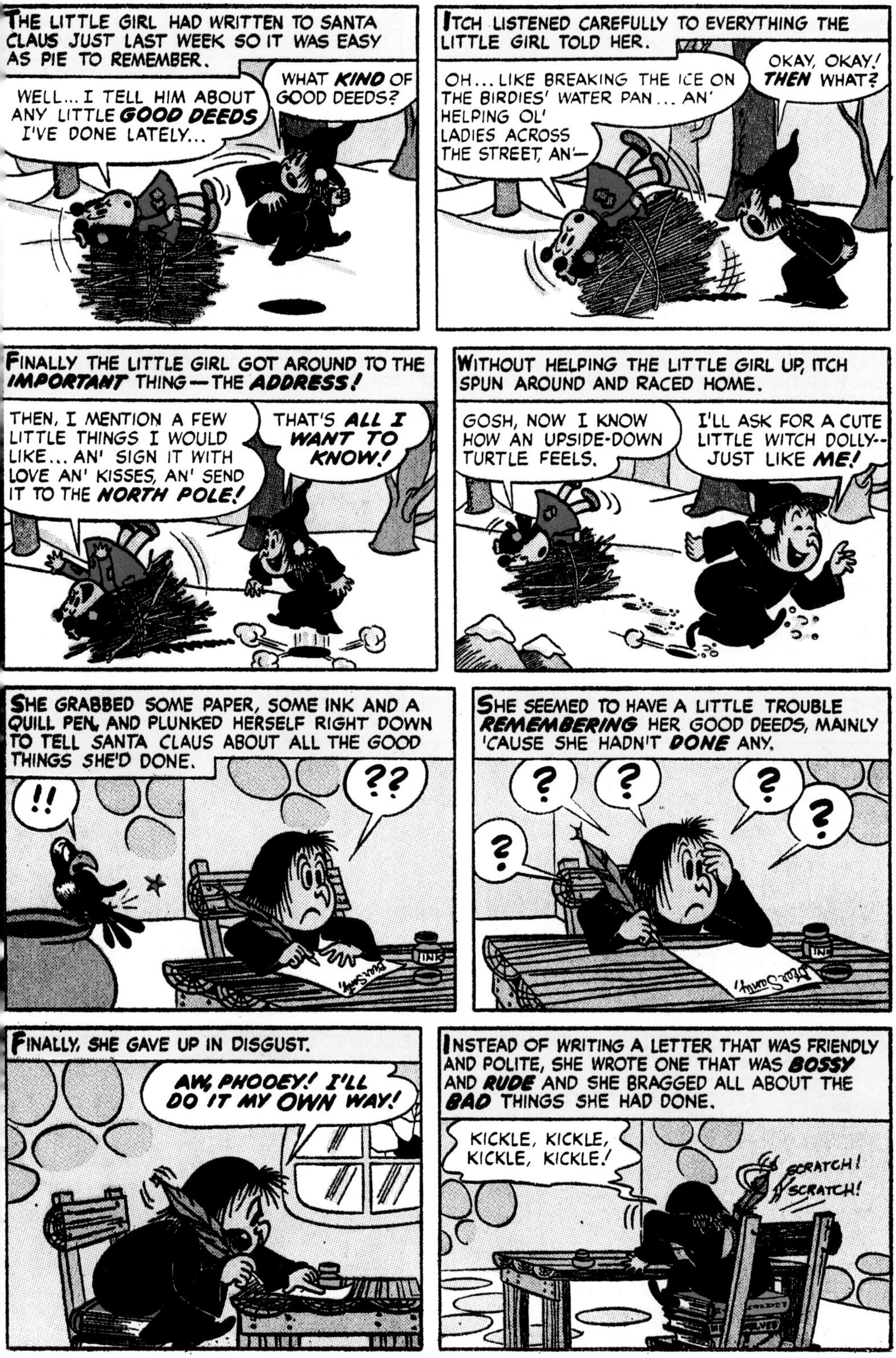
THE LITTLE GIRL HAD WRITTEN TO SANTA CLAUS JUST LAST WEEK SO IT WAS EASY AS PIE TO REMEMBER.
WELL... I TELL HIM ABOUT ANY LITTLE GOOD DEEDS I'VE DONE LATELY...
WHAT KIND OF GOOD DEEDS?
ITCH LISTENED CAREFULLY TO EVERYTHING THE LITTLE GIRL TOLD HER.
OH... LIKE BREAKING THE ICE ON THE BIRDIES' WATER PAN... AN' HELPING OL' LADIES ACROSS THE STREET, AN'—
OKAY, OKAY! THEN WHAT?
FINALLY THE LITTLE GIRL GOT AROUND TO THE IMPORTANT THING—THE ADDRESS!
THEN, I MENTION A FEW LITTLE THINGS I WOULD LIKE... AN' SIGN IT WITH LOVE AN' KISSES, AN' SEND IT TO THE NORTH POLE!
THAT'S ALL I WANT TO KNOW!
WITHOUT HELPING THE LITTLE GIRL UP, ITCH SPUN AROUND AND RACED HOME.
GOSH, NOW I KNOW HOW AN UPSIDE-DOWN TURTLE FEELS.
I'LL ASK FOR A CUTE LITTLE WITCH DOLLY-- JUST LIKE ME!
SHE GRABBED SOME PAPER, SOME INK AND A QUILL PEN, AND PLUNKED HERSELF RIGHT DOWN TO TELL SANTA CLAUS ABOUT ALL THE GOOD THINGS SHE'D DONE.
!!
??
SHE SEEMED TO HAVE A LITTLE TROUBLE REMEMBERING HER GOOD DEEDS, MAINLY 'CAUSE SHE HADN'T DONE ANY.
?
?
?
?
?
FINALLY, SHE GAVE UP IN DISGUST.
AW, PHOOEY! I'LL DO IT MY OWN WAY!
INSTEAD OF WRITING A LETTER THAT WAS FRIENDLY AND POLITE, SHE WROTE ONE THAT WAS BOSSY AND RUDE AND SHE BRAGGED ALL ABOUT THE BAD THINGS SHE HAD DONE.
KICKLE, KICKLE, KICKLE, KICKLE!
SCRATCH!
SCRATCH!

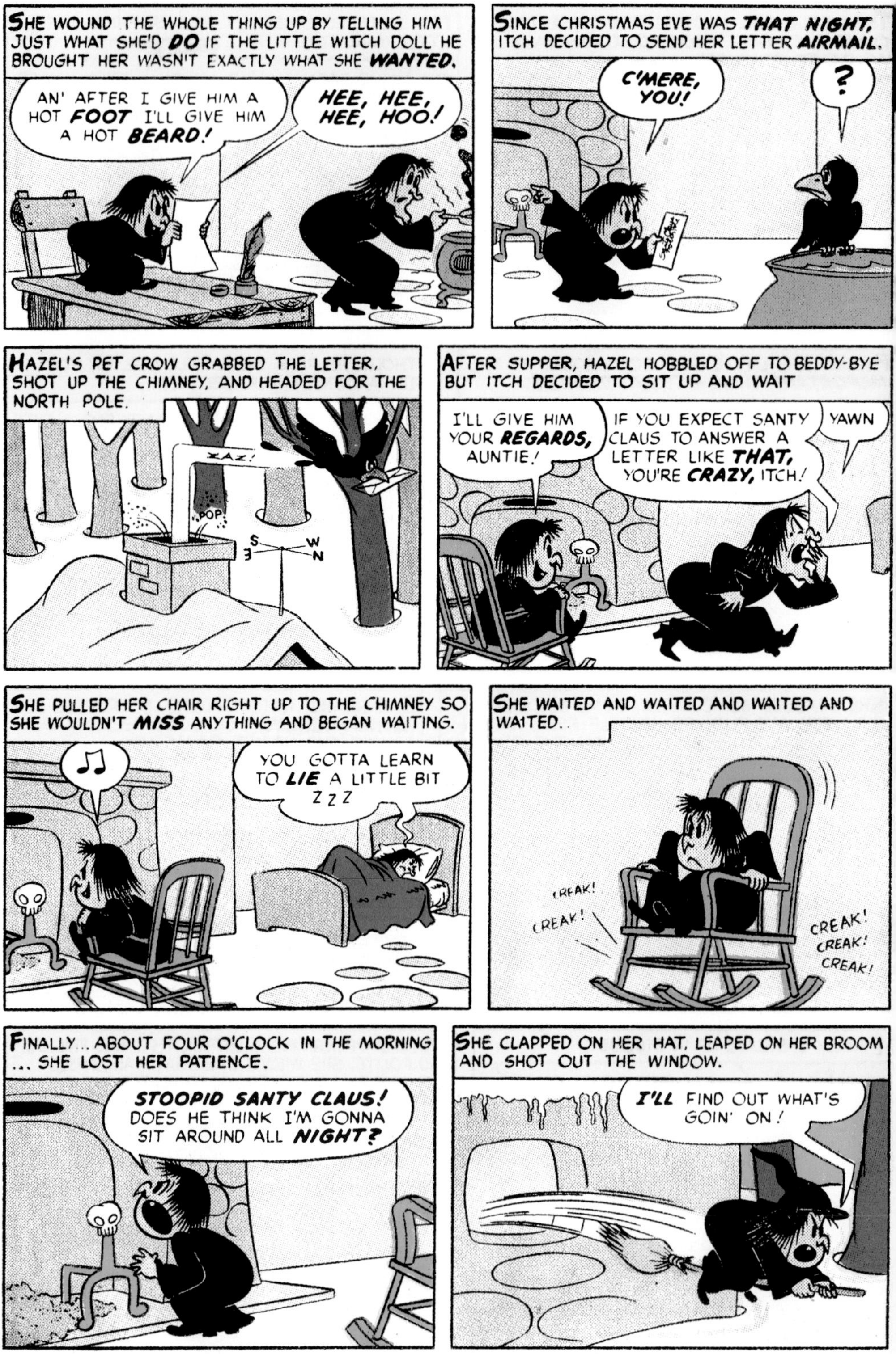
SHE WOUND THE WHOLE THING UP BY TELLING HIM JUST WHAT SHE'D DO IF THE LITTLE WITCH DOLL HE BROUGHT HER WASN'T EXACTLY WHAT SHE WANTED.
AN' AFTER I GIVE HIM A HOT FOOT I'LL GIVE HIM A HOT BEARD!
HEE, HEE, HEE, HOO!
SINCE CHRISTMAS EVE WAS THAT NIGHT, ITCH DECIDED TO SEND HER LETTER AIRMAIL.
C'MERE, YOU!
?
HAZEL'S PET CROW GRABBED THE LETTER, SHOT UP THE CHIMNEY, AND HEADED FOR THE NORTH POLE.
ZAZ!
POP
S
W
E
N
AFTER SUPPER, HAZEL HOBBLED OFF TO BEDDY-BYE BUT ITCH DECIDED TO SIT UP AND WAIT
I'LL GIVE HIM YOUR REGARDS, AUNTIE!
IF YOU EXPECT SANTY CLAUS TO ANSWER A LETTER LIKE THAT, YOU'RE CRAZY, ITCH!
YAWN
SHE PULLED HER CHAIR RIGHT UP TO THE CHIMNEY SO SHE WOULDN'T MISS ANYTHING AND BEGAN WAITING.
YOU GOTTA LEARN TO LIE A LITTLE BIT ZZZ
SHE WAITED AND WAITED AND WAITED AND WAITED..
CREAK!
CREAK!
CREAK!
CREAK!
CREAK!
FINALLY... ABOUT FOUR O'CLOCK IN THE MORNING ... SHE LOST HER PATIENCE.
STOOPID SANTY CLAUS! DOES HE THINK I'M GONNA SIT AROUND ALL NIGHT?
SHE CLAPPED ON HER HAT, LEAPED ON HER BROOM AND SHOT OUT THE WINDOW.
I'LL FIND OUT WHAT'S GOIN' ON!

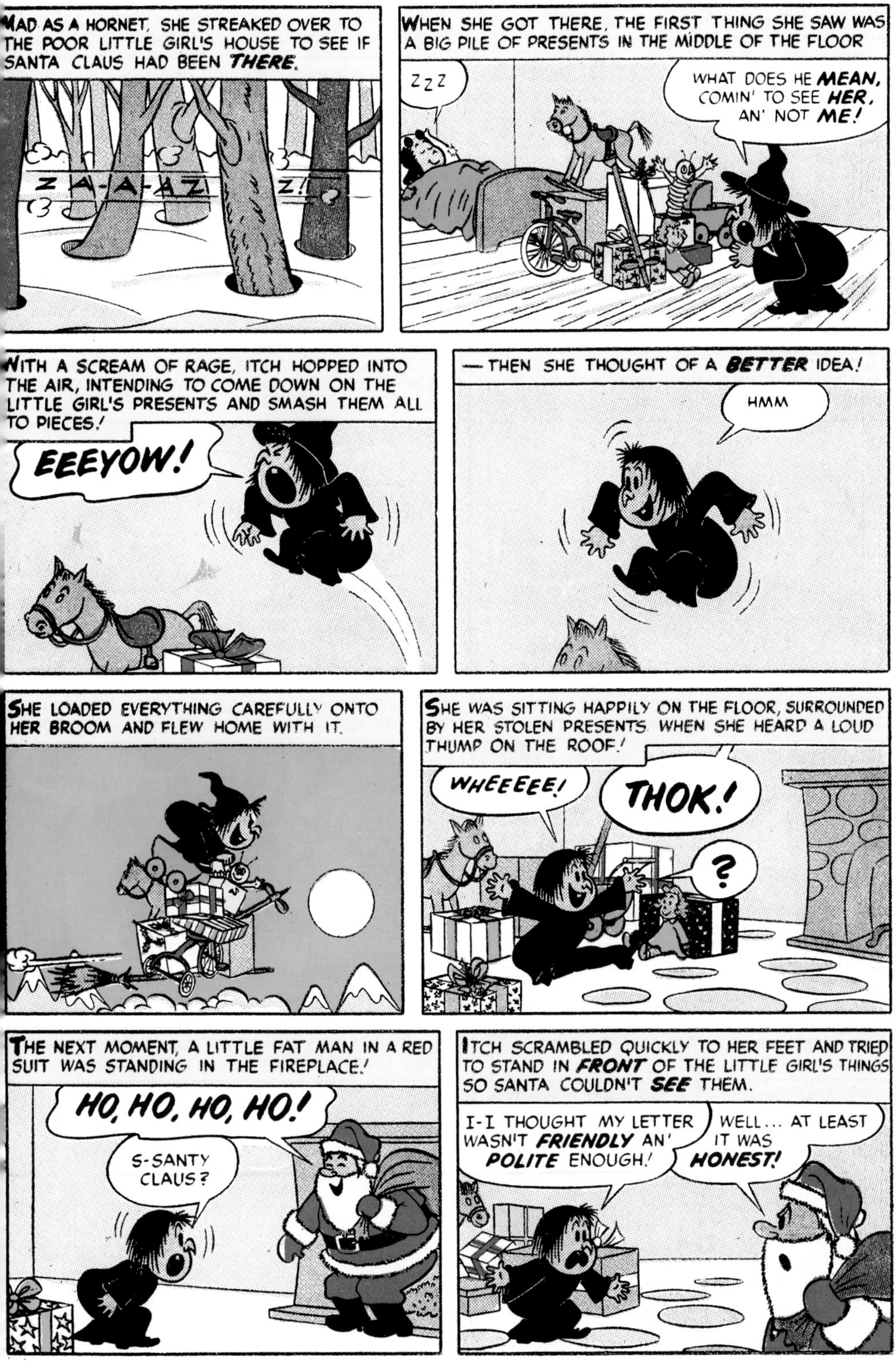
MAD AS A HORNET, SHE STREAKED OVER TO THE POOR LITTLE GIRL'S HOUSE TO SEE IF SANTA CLAUS HAD BEEN THERE.
Z-A-A-A-Z! Z!
WHEN SHE GOT THERE, THE FIRST THING SHE SAW WAS A BIG PILE OF PRESENTS IN THE MIDDLE OF THE FLOOR
Z Z Z
WHAT DOES HE MEAN, COMIN' TO SEE HER, AN' NOT ME!
WITH A SCREAM OF RAGE, ITCH HOPPED INTO THE AIR, INTENDING TO COME DOWN ON THE LITTLE GIRL'S PRESENTS AND SMASH THEM ALL TO PIECES!
EEEYOW!
—THEN SHE THOUGHT OF A BETTER IDEA!
HMM
SHE LOADED EVERYTHING CAREFULLY ONTO HER BROOM AND FLEW HOME WITH IT.
SHE WAS SITTING HAPPILY ON THE FLOOR, SURROUNDED BY HER STOLEN PRESENTS WHEN SHE HEARD A LOUD THUMP ON THE ROOF!
WHEEEEEE!
THOK!
?
THE NEXT MOMENT, A LITTLE FAT MAN IN A RED SUIT WAS STANDING IN THE FIREPLACE!
HO, HO, HO, HO!
S-SANTY CLAUS?
ITCH SCRAMBLED QUICKLY TO HER FEET AND TRIED TO STAND IN FRONT OF THE LITTLE GIRL'S THINGS SO SANTA COULDN'T SEE THEM.
I-I THOUGHT MY LETTER WASN'T FRIENDLY AN' POLITE ENOUGH!
WELL... AT LEAST IT WAS HONEST!

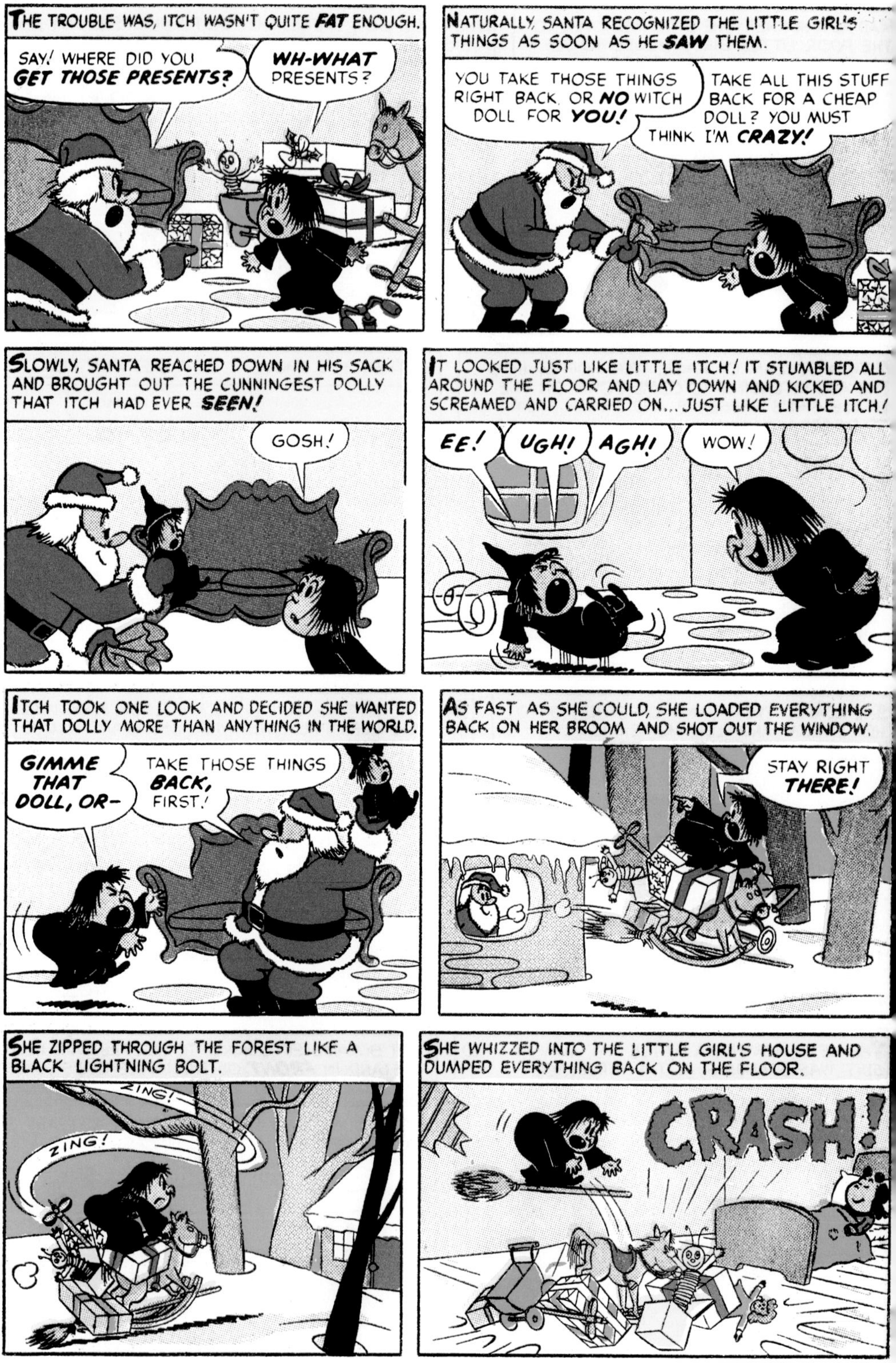
THE TROUBLE WAS, ITCH WASN'T QUITE FAT ENOUGH.
SAY! WHERE DID YOU GET THOSE PRESENTS?
WH-WHAT PRESENTS?
NATURALLY, SANTA RECOGNIZED THE LITTLE GIRL'S THINGS AS SOON AS HE SAW THEM.
YOU TAKE THOSE THINGS RIGHT BACK, OR NO WITCH DOLL FOR YOU!
TAKE ALL THIS STUFF BACK FOR A CHEAP DOLL? YOU MUST THINK I'M CRAZY!
SLOWLY, SANTA REACHED DOWN IN HIS SACK AND BROUGHT OUT THE CUNNINGEST DOLLY THAT ITCH HAD EVER SEEN!
GOSH!
IT LOOKED JUST LIKE LITTLE ITCH! IT STUMBLED ALL AROUND THE FLOOR AND LAY DOWN AND KICKED AND SCREAMED AND CARRIED ON... JUST LIKE LITTLE ITCH!
EE!
UGH!
AGH!
WOW!
ITCH TOOK ONE LOOK AND DECIDED SHE WANTED THAT DOLLY MORE THAN ANYTHING IN THE WORLD.
GIMME THAT DOLL, OR-
TAKE THOSE THINGS BACK, FIRST!
AS FAST AS SHE COULD, SHE LOADED EVERYTHING BACK ON HER BROOM AND SHOT OUT THE WINDOW.
STAY RIGHT THERE!
SHE ZIPPED THROUGH THE FOREST LIKE A BLACK LIGHTNING BOLT.
ZING!
ZING!
SHE WHIZZED INTO THE LITTLE GIRL'S HOUSE AND DUMPED EVERYTHING BACK ON THE FLOOR.
CRASH!

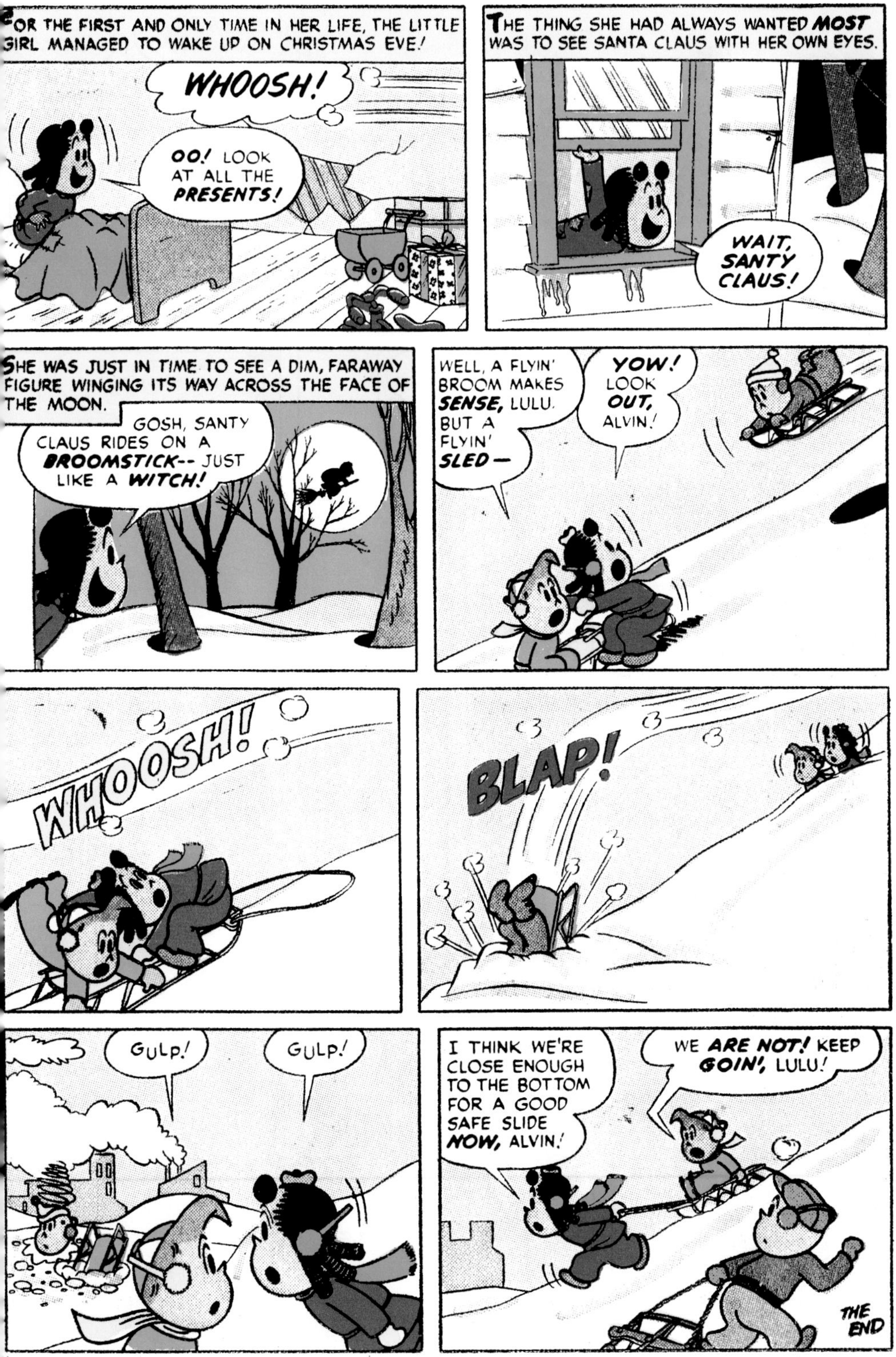
FOR THE FIRST AND ONLY TIME IN HER LIFE, THE LITTLE GIRL MANAGED TO WAKE UP ON CHRISTMAS EVE!
WHOOSH!
OO! LOOK AT ALL THE PRESENTS!
THE THING SHE HAD ALWAYS WANTED MOST WAS TO SEE SANTA CLAUS WITH HER OWN EYES.
WAIT, SANTY CLAUS!
SHE WAS JUST IN TIME TO SEE A DIM, FARAWAY FIGURE WINGING ITS WAY ACROSS THE FACE OF THE MOON.
GOSH, SANTY CLAUS RIDES ON A BROOMSTICK-- JUST LIKE A WITCH!
WELL, A FLYIN' BROOM MAKES SENSE, LULU. BUT A FLYIN' SLED—
YOW! LOOK OUT, ALVIN!
WHOOSH!
BLAP!
GULP!
GULP!
I THINK WE'RE CLOSE ENOUGH TO THE BOTTOM FOR A GOOD SAFE SLIDE NOW, ALVIN!
WE ARE NOT! KEEP GOIN', LULU!
THE END

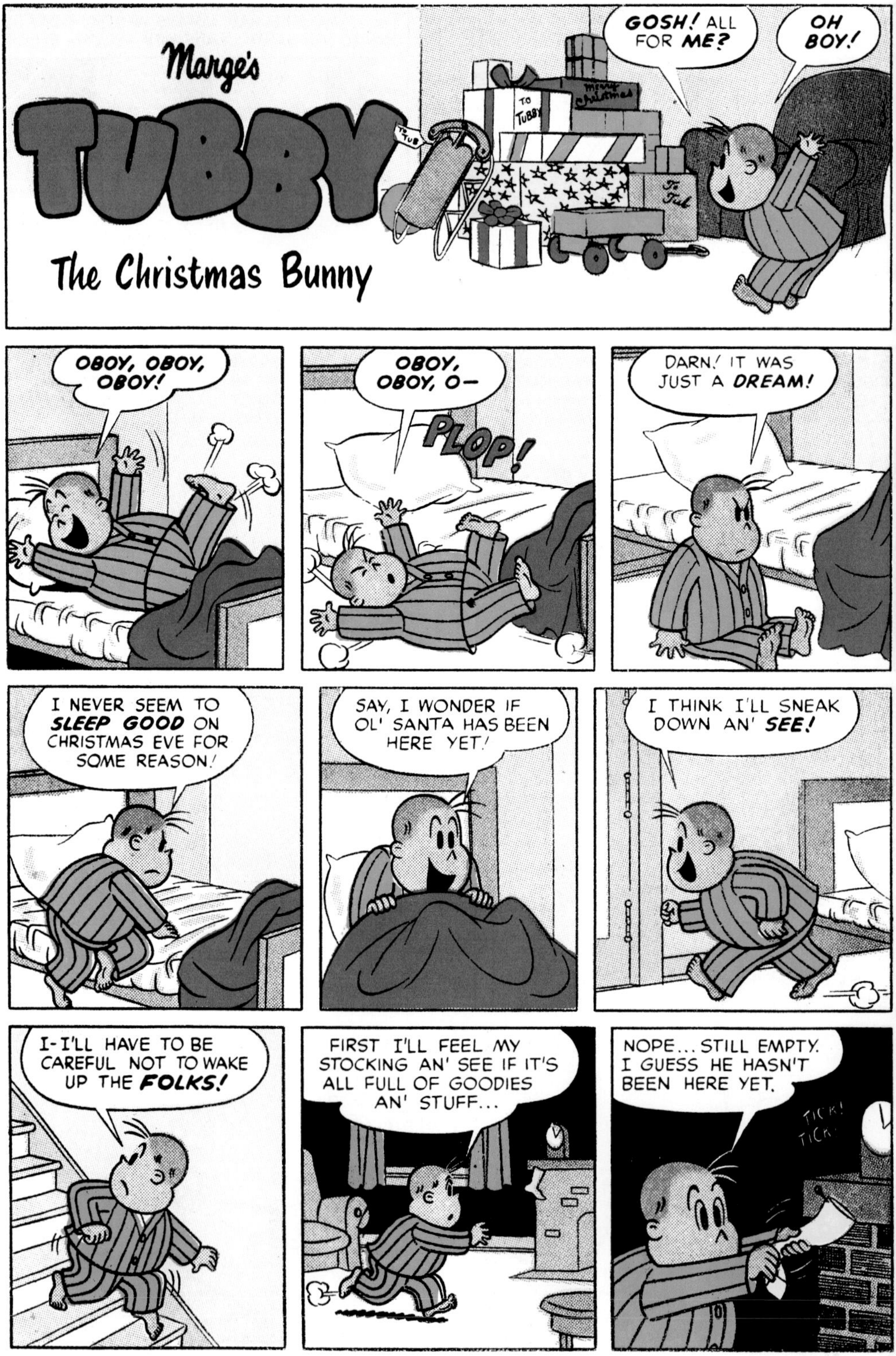
Marge's
TUBBY
The Christmas Bunny
GOSH! ALL FOR ME?
OH BOY!
OBOY, OBOY, OBOY!
OBOY, OBOY, O—
PLOP!
DARN! IT WAS JUST A DREAM!
I NEVER SEEM TO SLEEP GOOD ON CHRISTMAS EVE FOR SOME REASON!
SAY, I WONDER IF OL' SANTA HAS BEEN HERE YET!
I THINK I'LL SNEAK DOWN AN' SEE!
I-I'LL HAVE TO BE CAREFUL NOT TO WAKE UP THE FOLKS!
FIRST I'LL FEEL MY STOCKING AN' SEE IF IT'S ALL FULL OF GOODIES AN' STUFF...
NOPE... STILL EMPTY. I GUESS HE HASN'T BEEN HERE YET.
TICK! TICK!

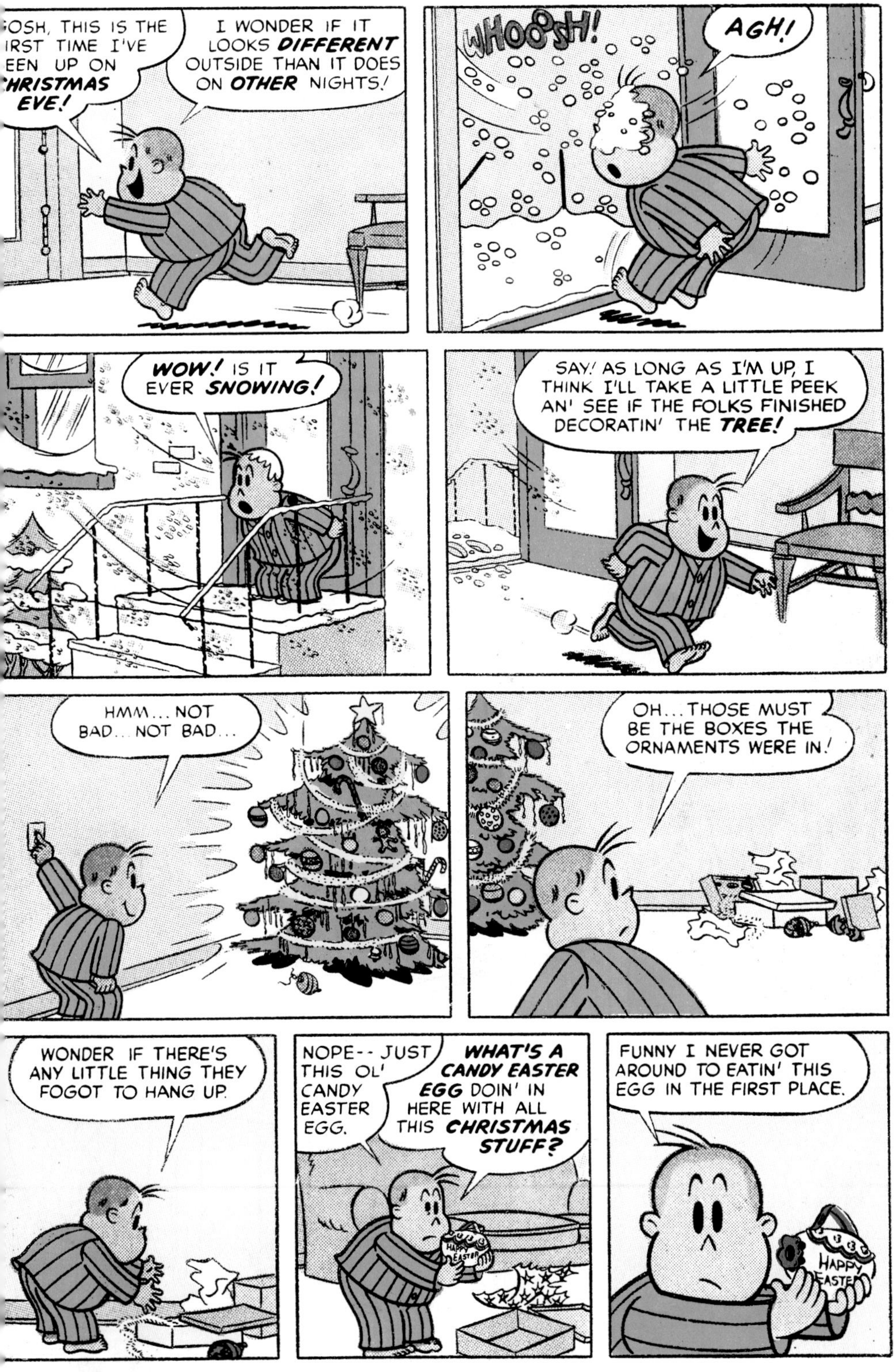
GOSH, THIS IS THE FIRST TIME I'VE BEEN UP ON CHRISTMAS EVE!
I WONDER IF IT LOOKS DIFFERENT OUTSIDE THAN IT DOES ON OTHER NIGHTS!
WHOOOSH!
AGH!
WOW! IS IT EVER SNOWING!
SAY! AS LONG AS I'M UP, I THINK I'LL TAKE A LITTLE PEEK AN' SEE IF THE FOLKS FINISHED DECORATIN' THE TREE!
HMM... NOT BAD... NOT BAD...
OH... THOSE MUST BE THE BOXES THE ORNAMENTS WERE IN!
WONDER IF THERE'S ANY LITTLE THING THEY FOGOT TO HANG UP.
NOPE-- JUST THIS OL' CANDY EASTER EGG.
WHAT'S A CANDY EASTER EGG DOIN' IN HERE WITH ALL THIS CHRISTMAS STUFF?
HAPPY EASTER
FUNNY I NEVER GOT AROUND TO EATIN' THIS EGG IN THE FIRST PLACE.
HAPPY EASTER

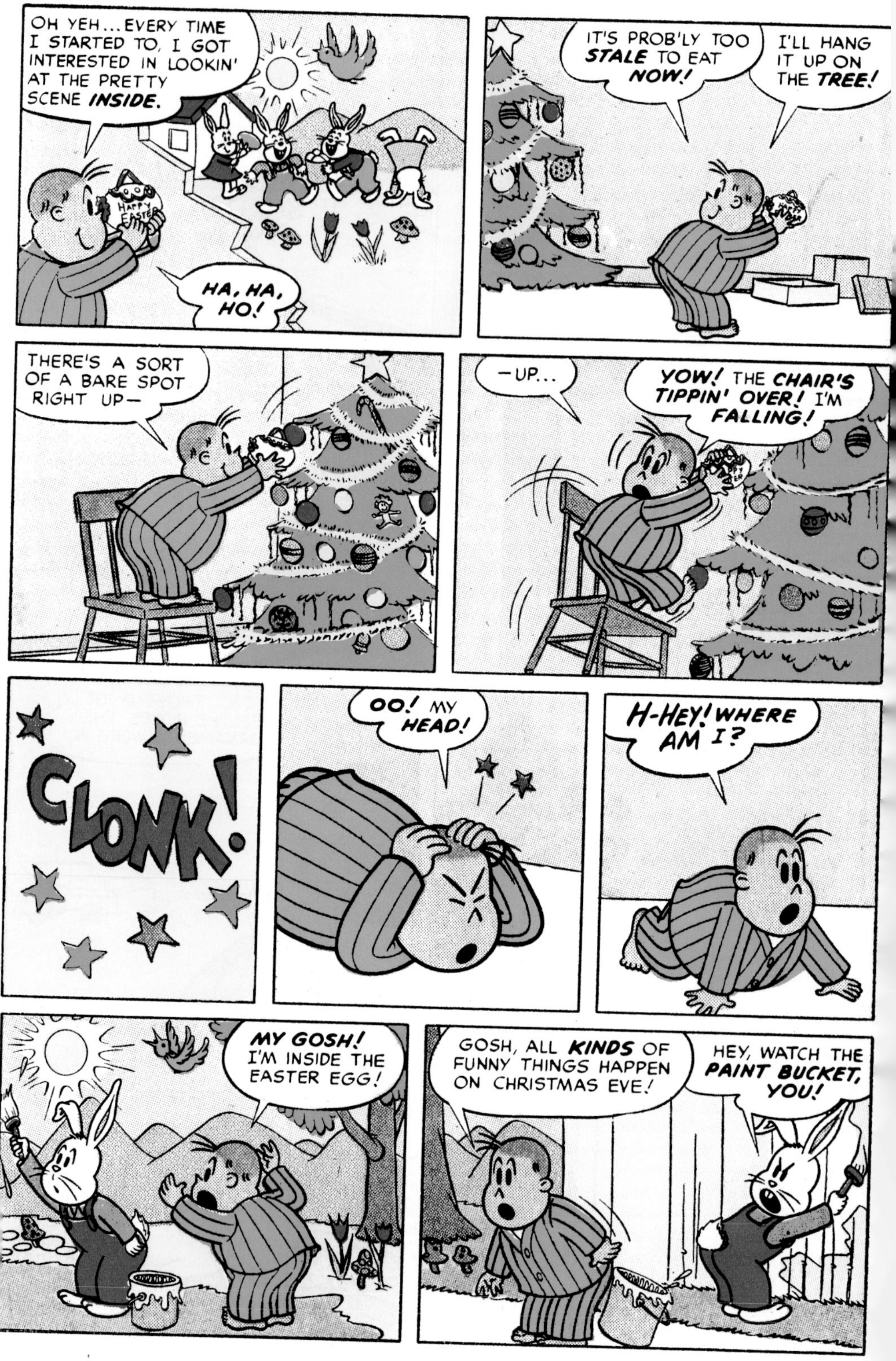
OH YEH... EVERY TIME I STARTED TO, I GOT INTERESTED IN LOOKIN' AT THE PRETTY SCENE INSIDE.
HAPPY EASTER
HA, HA, HO!
IT'S PROB'LY TOO STALE TO EAT NOW!
I'LL HANG IT UP ON THE TREE!
THERE'S A SORT OF A BARE SPOT RIGHT UP—
—UP...
YOW! THE CHAIR'S TIPPIN' OVER! I'M FALLING!
CLONK!
OO! MY HEAD!
H-HEY! WHERE AM I?
MY GOSH! I'M INSIDE THE EASTER EGG!
GOSH, ALL KINDS OF FUNNY THINGS HAPPEN ON CHRISTMAS EVE!
HEY, WATCH THE PAINT BUCKET, YOU!

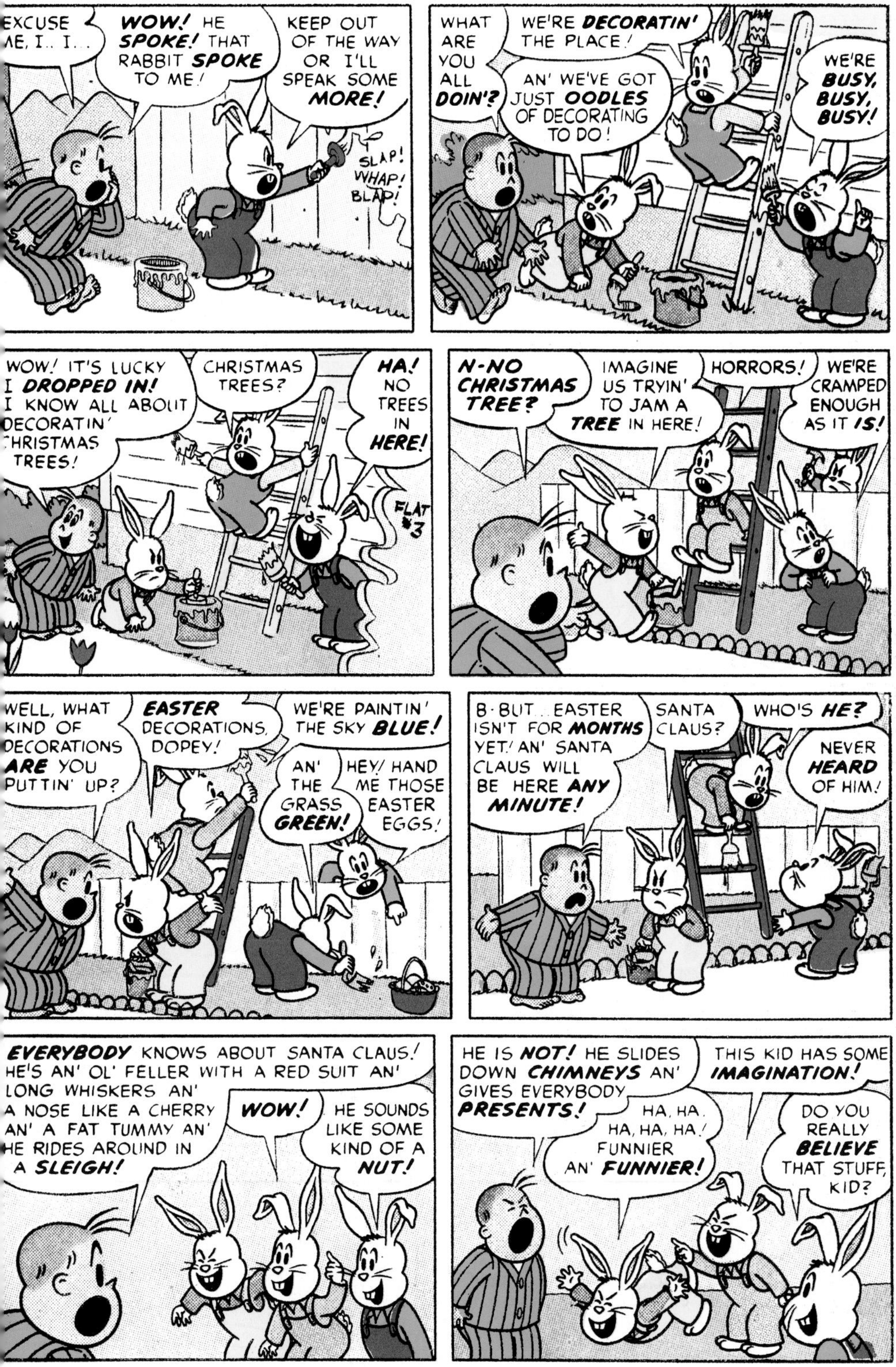
EXCUSE ME, I.. I...
WOW! HE SPOKE! THAT RABBIT SPOKE TO ME!
KEEP OUT OF THE WAY OR I'LL SPEAK SOME MORE!
SLAP! WHAP! BLAP!
WHAT ARE YOU ALL DOIN'?
WE'RE DECORATIN' THE PLACE!
AN' WE'VE GOT JUST OODLES OF DECORATING TO DO!
WE'RE BUSY, BUSY, BUSY!
WOW! IT'S LUCKY I DROPPED IN! I KNOW ALL ABOUT DECORATIN' CHRISTMAS TREES!
CHRISTMAS TREES?
HA! NO TREES IN HERE!
FLAT #3
N-NO CHRISTMAS TREE?
IMAGINE US TRYIN' TO JAM A TREE IN HERE!
HORRORS!
WE'RE CRAMPED ENOUGH AS IT IS!
WELL, WHAT KIND OF DECORATIONS ARE YOU PUTTIN' UP?
EASTER DECORATIONS, DOPEY!
WE'RE PAINTIN' THE SKY BLUE!
AN' THE GRASS GREEN!
HEY! HAND ME THOSE EASTER EGGS!
B-BUT... EASTER ISN'T FOR MONTHS YET! AN' SANTA CLAUS WILL BE HERE ANY MINUTE!
SANTA CLAUS?
WHO'S HE?
NEVER HEARD OF HIM!
EVERYBODY KNOWS ABOUT SANTA CLAUS! HE'S AN' OL' FELLER WITH A RED SUIT AN' LONG WHISKERS AN' A NOSE LIKE A CHERRY AN' A FAT TUMMY AN' HE RIDES AROUND IN A SLEIGH!
WOW!
HE SOUNDS LIKE SOME KIND OF A NUT!
HE IS NOT! HE SLIDES DOWN CHIMNEYS AN' GIVES EVERYBODY PRESENTS!
THIS KID HAS SOME IMAGINATION!
HA, HA, HA, HA, HA! FUNNIER AN' FUNNIER!
DO YOU REALLY BELIEVE THAT STUFF, KID?

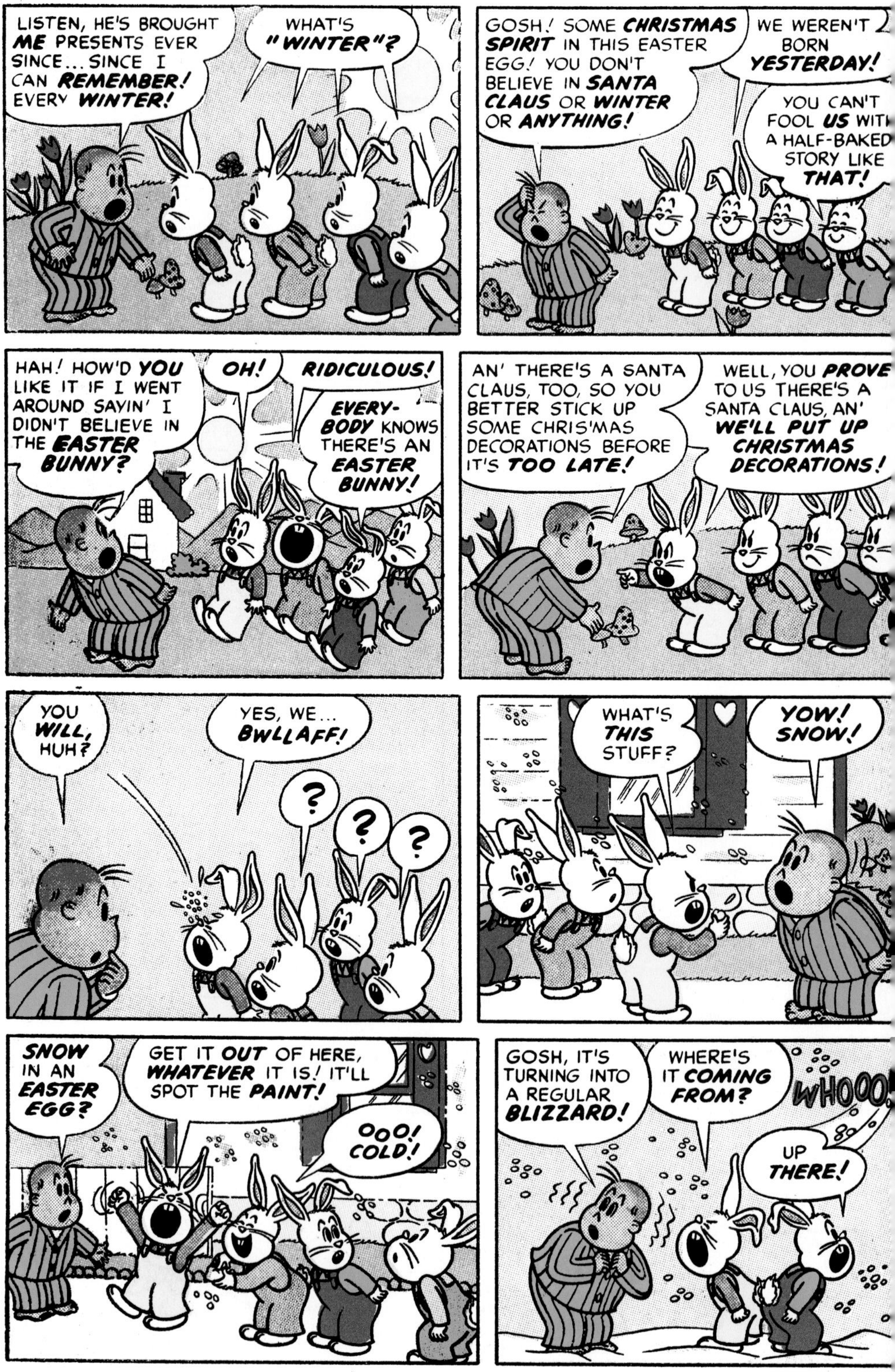
LISTEN, HE'S BROUGHT ME PRESENTS EVER SINCE... SINCE I CAN REMEMBER! EVERY WINTER!
WHAT'S "WINTER"?
GOSH! SOME CHRISTMAS SPIRIT IN THIS EASTER EGG! YOU DON'T BELIEVE IN SANTA CLAUS OR WINTER OR ANYTHING!
WE WEREN'T BORN YESTERDAY!
YOU CAN'T FOOL US WITH A HALF-BAKED STORY LIKE THAT!
HAH! HOW'D YOU LIKE IT IF I WENT AROUND SAYIN' I DIDN'T BELIEVE IN THE EASTER BUNNY?
OH!
RIDICULOUS!
EVERY-BODY KNOWS THERE'S AN EASTER BUNNY!
AN' THERE'S A SANTA CLAUS, TOO, SO YOU BETTER STICK UP SOME CHRIS'MAS DECORATIONS BEFORE IT'S TOO LATE!
WELL, YOU PROVE TO US THERE'S A SANTA CLAUS, AN' WE'LL PUT UP CHRISTMAS DECORATIONS!
YOU WILL, HUH?
YES, WE... BWLLAFF!
?
?
?
WHAT'S THIS STUFF?
YOW! SNOW!
SNOW IN AN EASTER EGG?
GET IT OUT OF HERE, WHATEVER IT IS! IT'LL SPOT THE PAINT!
OOO! COLD!
GOSH, IT'S TURNING INTO A REGULAR BLIZZARD!
WHERE'S IT COMING FROM?
WHOOO
UP THERE!

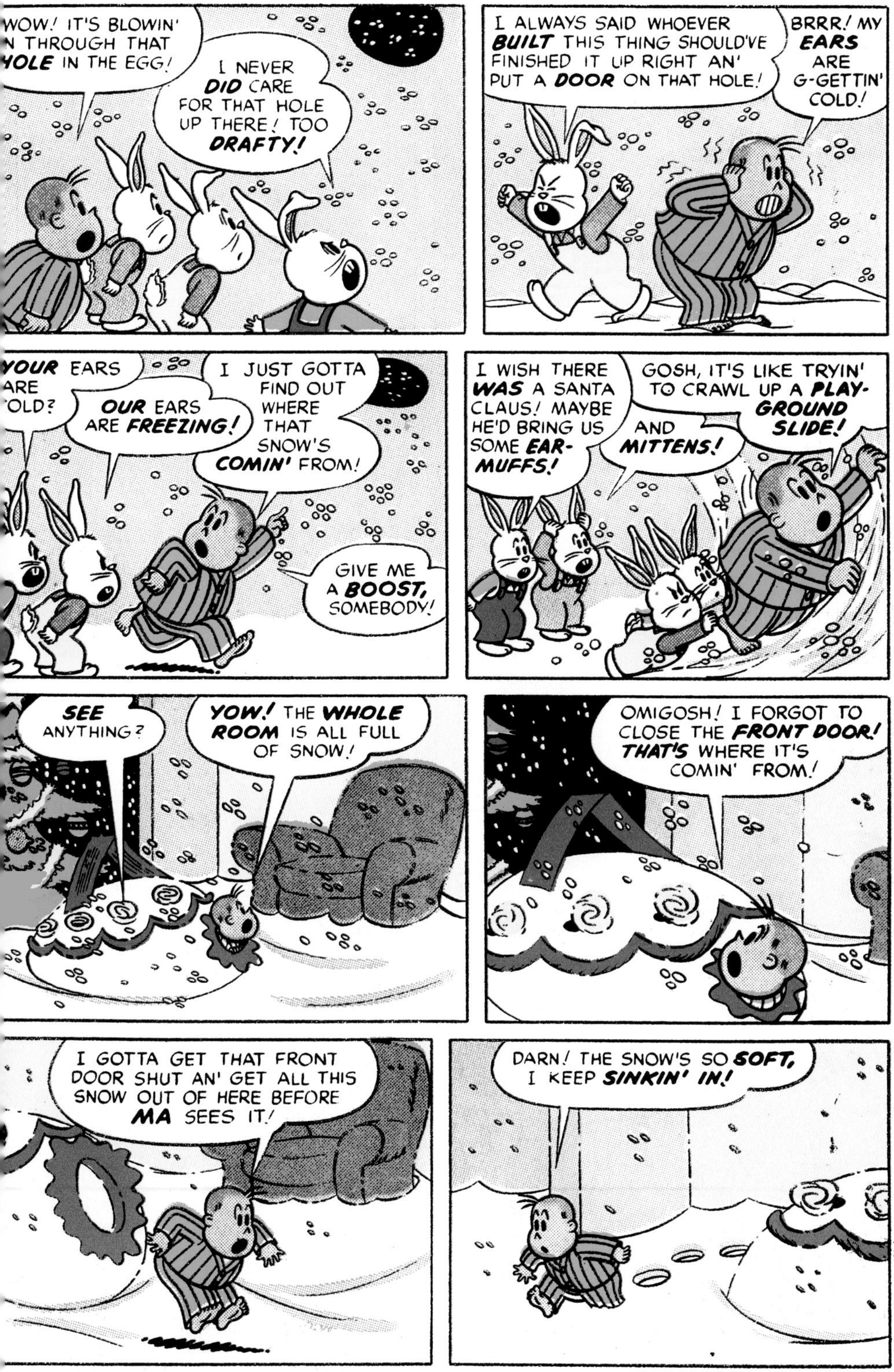
WOW! IT'S BLOWIN' IN THROUGH THAT HOLE IN THE EGG!
I NEVER DID CARE FOR THAT HOLE UP THERE! TOO DRAFTY!
I ALWAYS SAID WHOEVER BUILT THIS THING SHOULD'VE FINISHED IT UP RIGHT AN' PUT A DOOR ON THAT HOLE!
BRRR! MY EARS ARE G-GETTIN' COLD!
YOUR EARS ARE COLD?
OUR EARS ARE FREEZING!
I JUST GOTTA FIND OUT WHERE THAT SNOW'S COMIN' FROM!
GIVE ME A BOOST, SOMEBODY!
I WISH THERE WAS A SANTA CLAUS! MAYBE HE'D BRING US SOME EAR-MUFFS!
AND MITTENS!
GOSH, IT'S LIKE TRYIN' TO CRAWL UP A PLAY-GROUND SLIDE!
SEE ANYTHING?
YOW! THE WHOLE ROOM IS ALL FULL OF SNOW!
OMIGOSH! I FORGOT TO CLOSE THE FRONT DOOR! THAT'S WHERE IT'S COMIN' FROM!
I GOTTA GET THAT FRONT DOOR SHUT AN' GET ALL THIS SNOW OUT OF HERE BEFORE MA SEES IT!
DARN! THE SNOW'S SO SOFT, I KEEP SINKIN' IN!

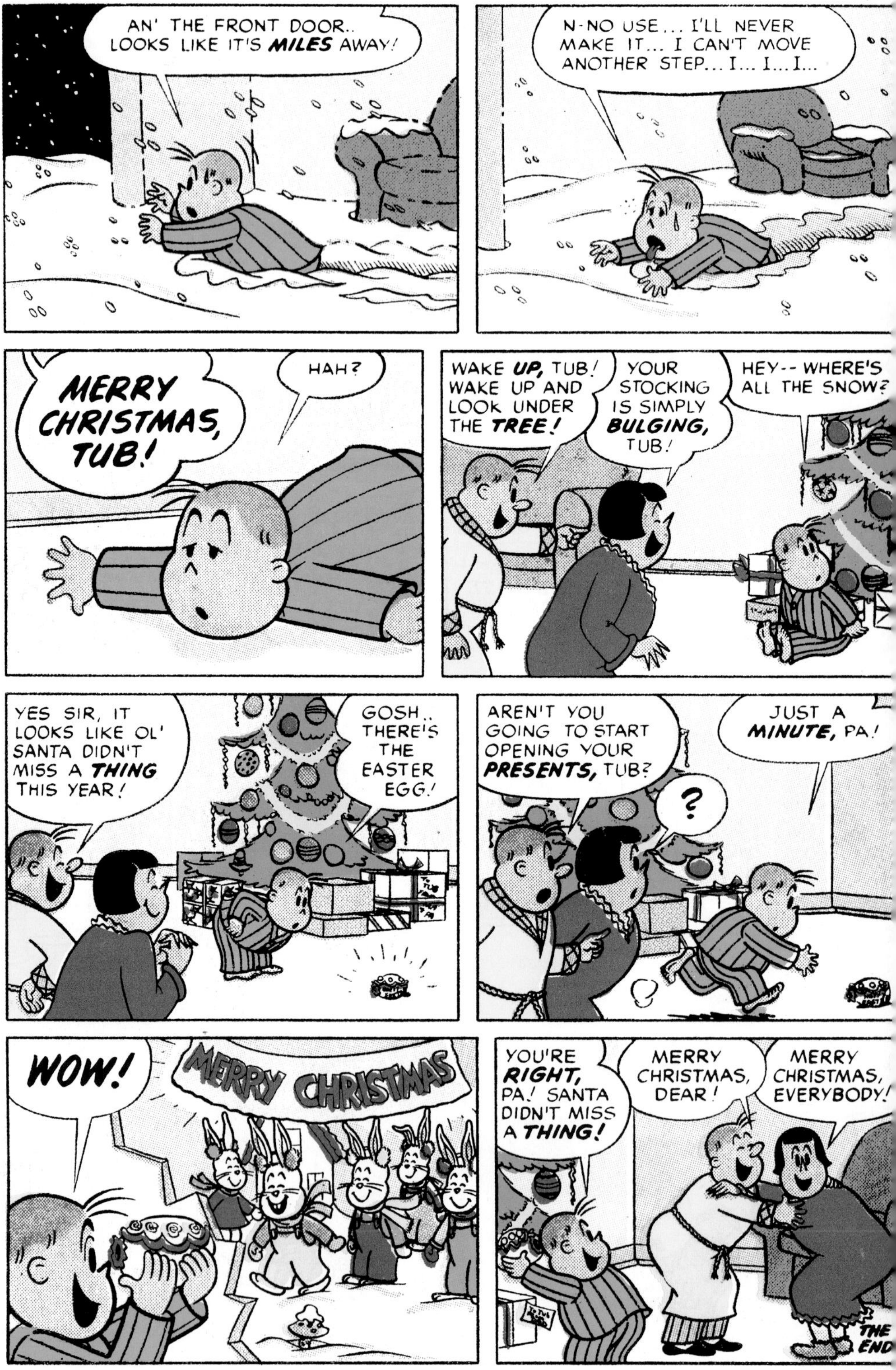

AN' THE FRONT DOOR.. LOOKS LIKE IT'S MILES AWAY!
N-NO USE... I'LL NEVER MAKE IT... I CAN'T MOVE ANOTHER STEP... I... I... I...
MERRY CHRISTMAS, TUB!
HAH?
WAKE UP, TUB! WAKE UP AND LOOK UNDER THE TREE!
YOUR STOCKING IS SIMPLY BULGING, TUB!
HEY-- WHERE'S ALL THE SNOW?
YES SIR, IT LOOKS LIKE OL' SANTA DIDN'T MISS A THING THIS YEAR!
GOSH.. THERE'S THE EASTER EGG!
AREN'T YOU GOING TO START OPENING YOUR PRESENTS, TUB?
JUST A MINUTE, PA!
?
WOW!
MERRY CHRISTMAS
YOU'RE RIGHT, PA! SANTA DIDN'T MISS A THING!
MERRY CHRISTMAS, DEAR!
MERRY CHRISTMAS, EVERYBODY!
THE END

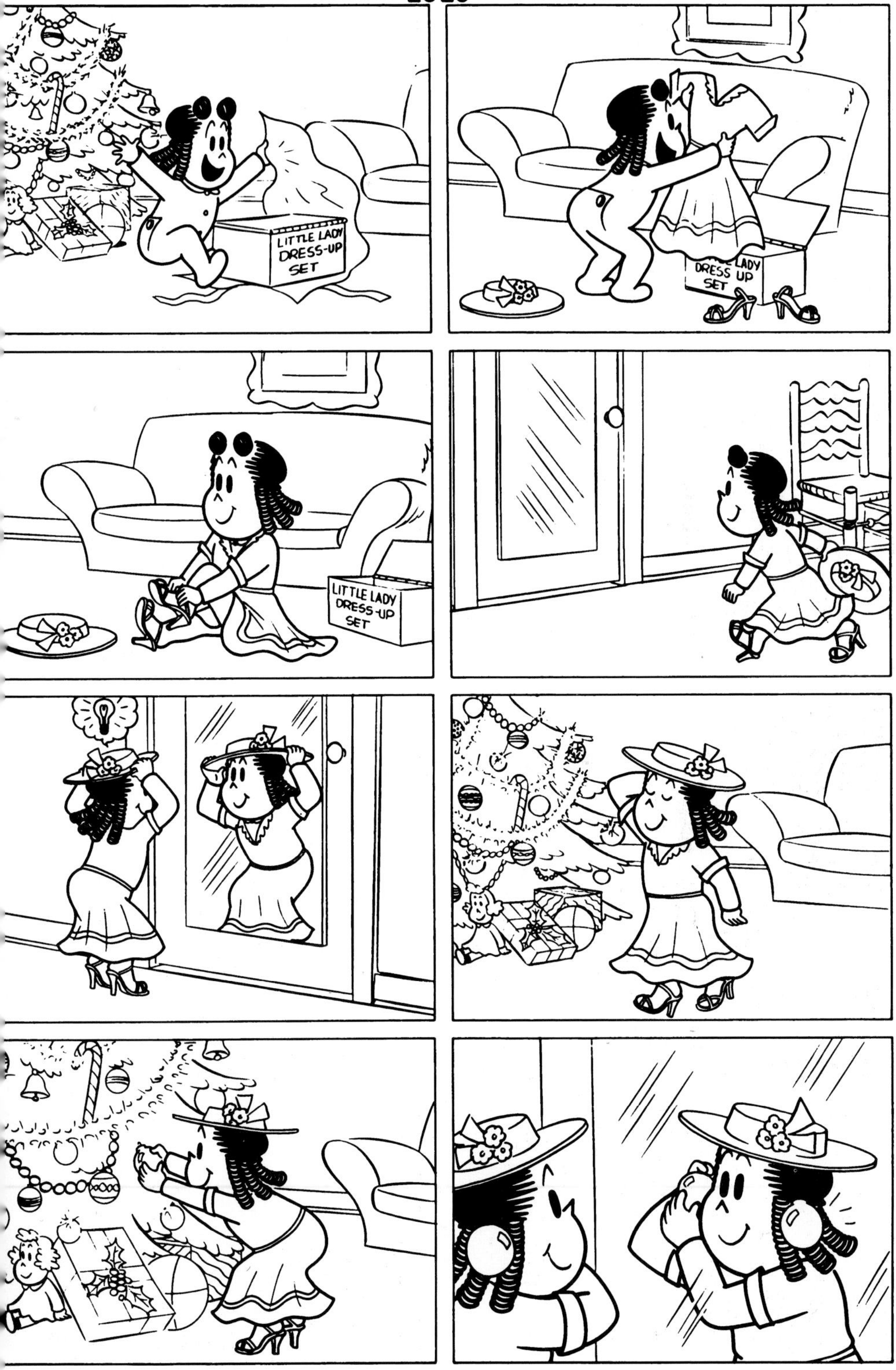
LITTLE LADY
DRESS-UP
SET
LADY
DRESS UP
SET
LITTLE LADY
DRESS-UP
SET

Little Lulu Little
lu Little Lulu Li
Little Lulu Little
lu Little Lulu Li
Little Lulu Little
lu Little Lulu Li
Little Lulu Little

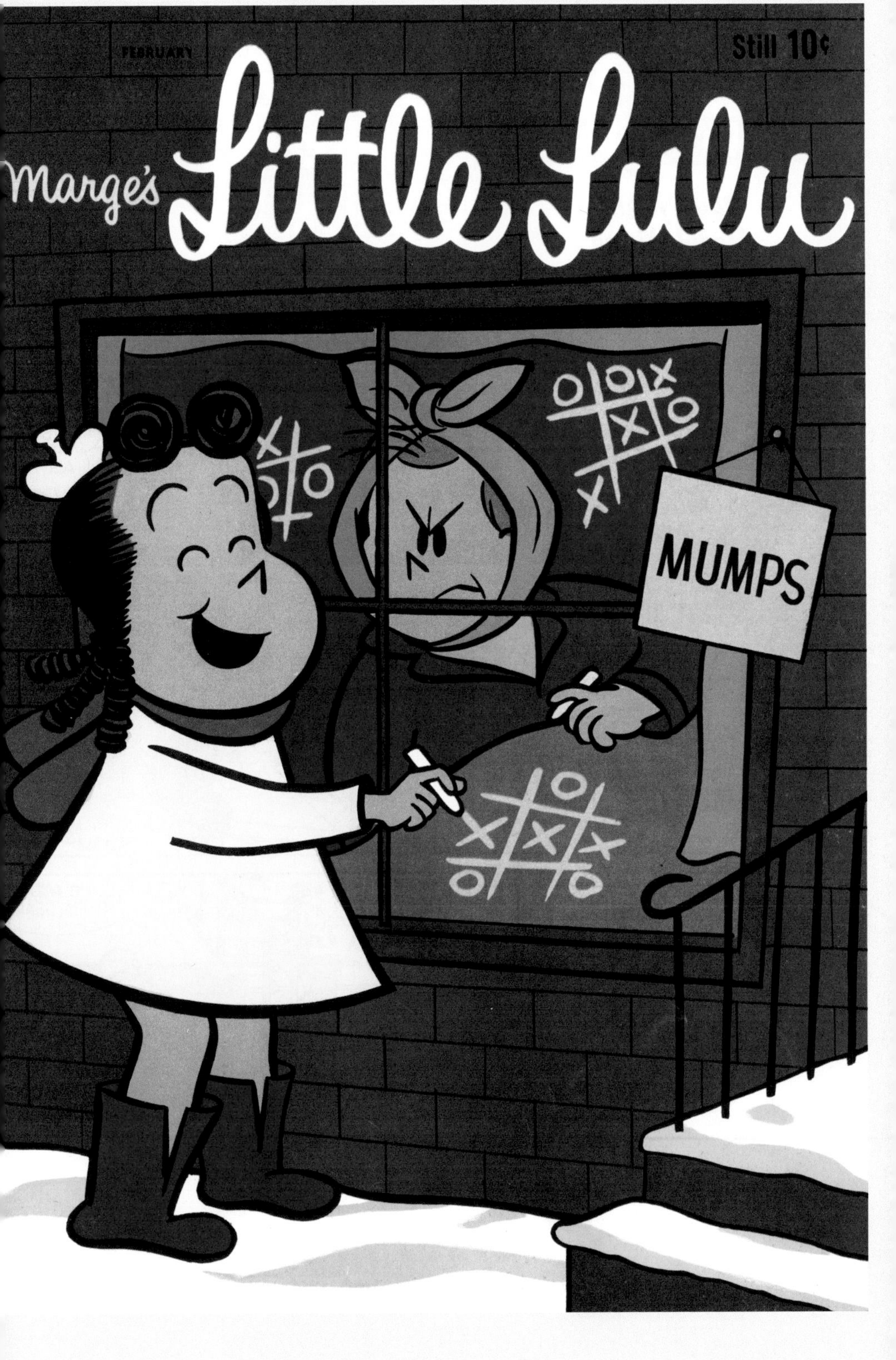

FEBRUARY
Still 10¢
Marge's Little Lulu
MUMPS

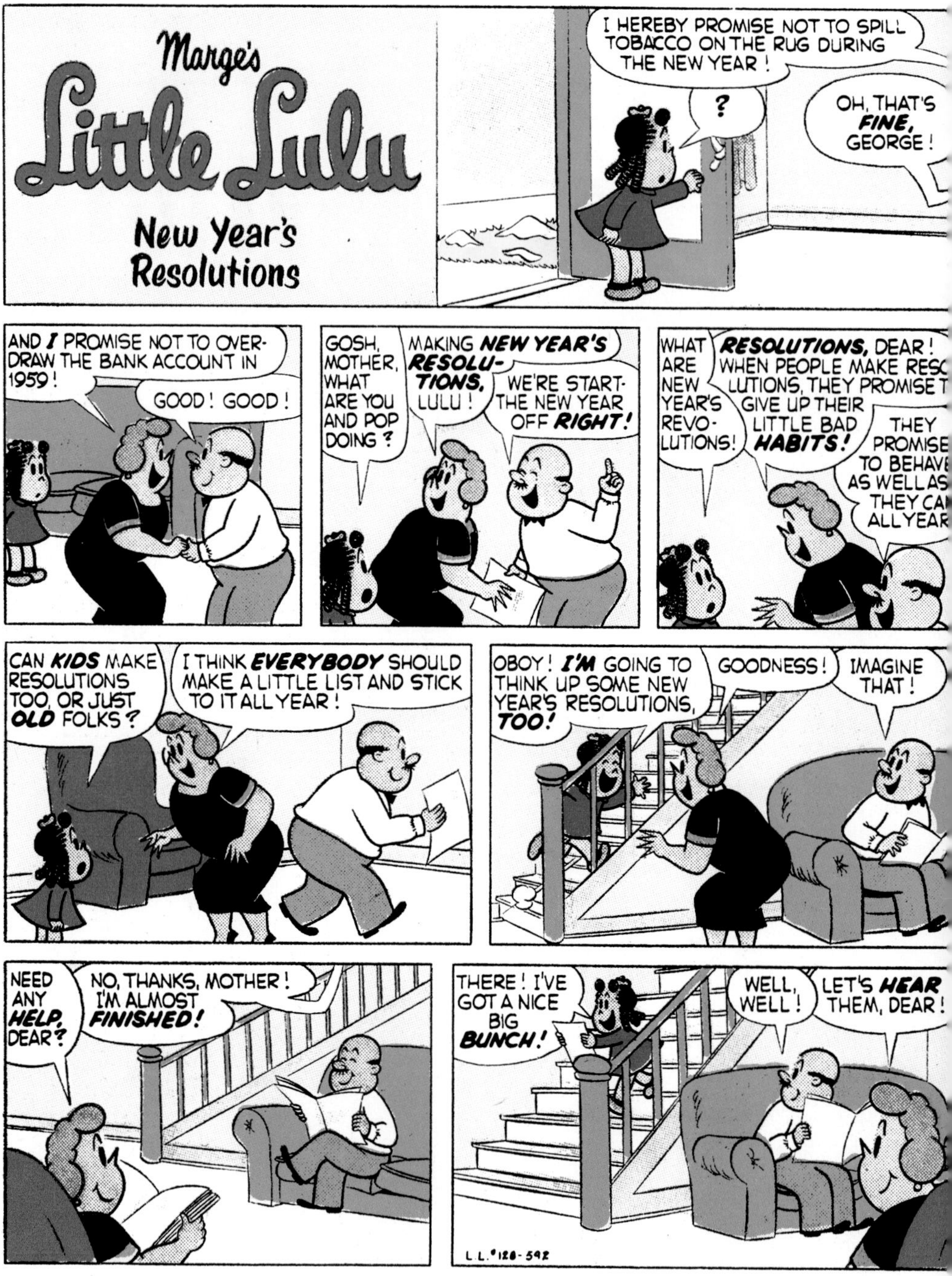

Marge's Little Lulu
New Year's Resolutions
I HEREBY PROMISE NOT TO SPILL TOBACCO ON THE RUG DURING THE NEW YEAR!
?
OH, THAT'S FINE, GEORGE!
AND I PROMISE NOT TO OVER-DRAW THE BANK ACCOUNT IN 1959!
GOOD! GOOD!
GOSH, MOTHER, WHAT ARE YOU AND POP DOING?
MAKING NEW YEAR'S RESOLU-TIONS, LULU!
WE'RE START-THE NEW YEAR OFF RIGHT!
WHAT ARE NEW YEAR'S REVO-LUTIONS!
RESOLUTIONS, DEAR! WHEN PEOPLE MAKE RESO LUTIONS, THEY PROMISE T GIVE UP THEIR LITTLE BAD HABITS!
THEY PROMISE TO BEHAV AS WELL AS THEY CA ALL YEAR
CAN KIDS MAKE RESOLUTIONS TOO, OR JUST OLD FOLKS?
I THINK EVERYBODY SHOULD MAKE A LITTLE LIST AND STICK TO IT ALL YEAR!
OBOY! I'M GOING TO THINK UP SOME NEW YEAR'S RESOLUTIONS, TOO!
GOODNESS!
IMAGINE THAT!
NEED ANY HELP, DEAR?
NO, THANKS, MOTHER! I'M ALMOST FINISHED!
THERE! I'VE GOT A NICE BIG BUNCH!
WELL, WELL!
LET'S HEAR THEM, DEAR!
L.L.#128-592

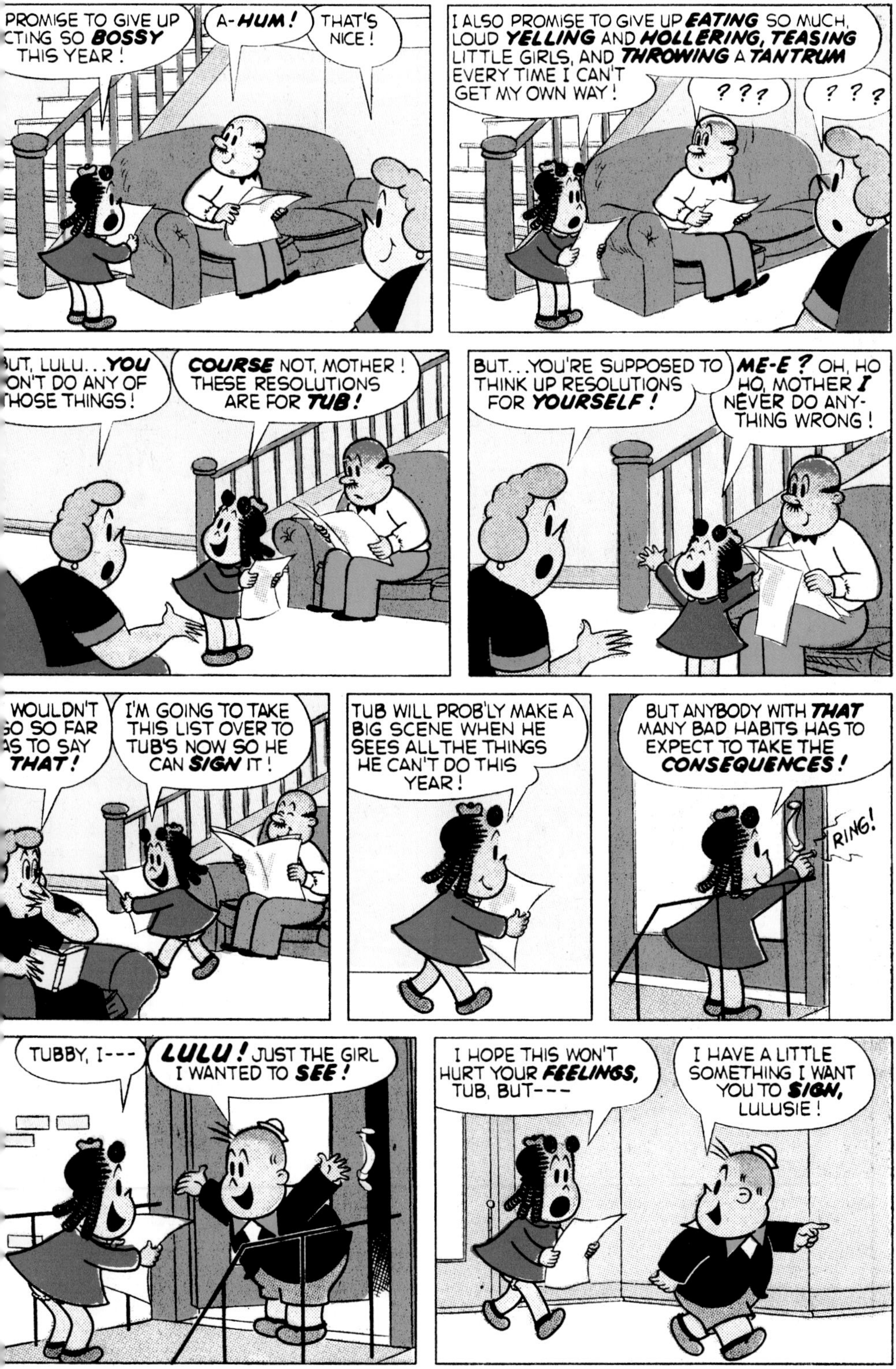
PROMISE TO GIVE UP
CTING SO BOSSY
THIS YEAR!
A-HUM!
THAT'S NICE!
I ALSO PROMISE TO GIVE UP EATING SO MUCH, LOUD YELLING AND HOLLERING, TEASING LITTLE GIRLS, AND THROWING A TANTRUM EVERY TIME I CAN'T GET MY OWN WAY!
???
???
UT, LULU...YOU ON'T DO ANY OF HOSE THINGS!
COURSE NOT, MOTHER! THESE RESOLUTIONS ARE FOR TUB!
BUT...YOU'RE SUPPOSED TO THINK UP RESOLUTIONS FOR YOURSELF!
ME-E? OH, HO HO, MOTHER I NEVER DO ANY-THING WRONG!
WOULDN'T O SO FAR S TO SAY THAT!
I'M GOING TO TAKE THIS LIST OVER TO TUB'S NOW SO HE CAN SIGN IT!
TUB WILL PROB'LY MAKE A BIG SCENE WHEN HE SEES ALL THE THINGS HE CAN'T DO THIS YEAR!
BUT ANYBODY WITH THAT MANY BAD HABITS HAS TO EXPECT TO TAKE THE CONSEQUENCES!
RING!
TUBBY, I---
LULU! JUST THE GIRL I WANTED TO SEE!
I HOPE THIS WON'T HURT YOUR FEELINGS, TUB, BUT---
I HAVE A LITTLE SOMETHING I WANT YOU TO SIGN, LULUSIE!

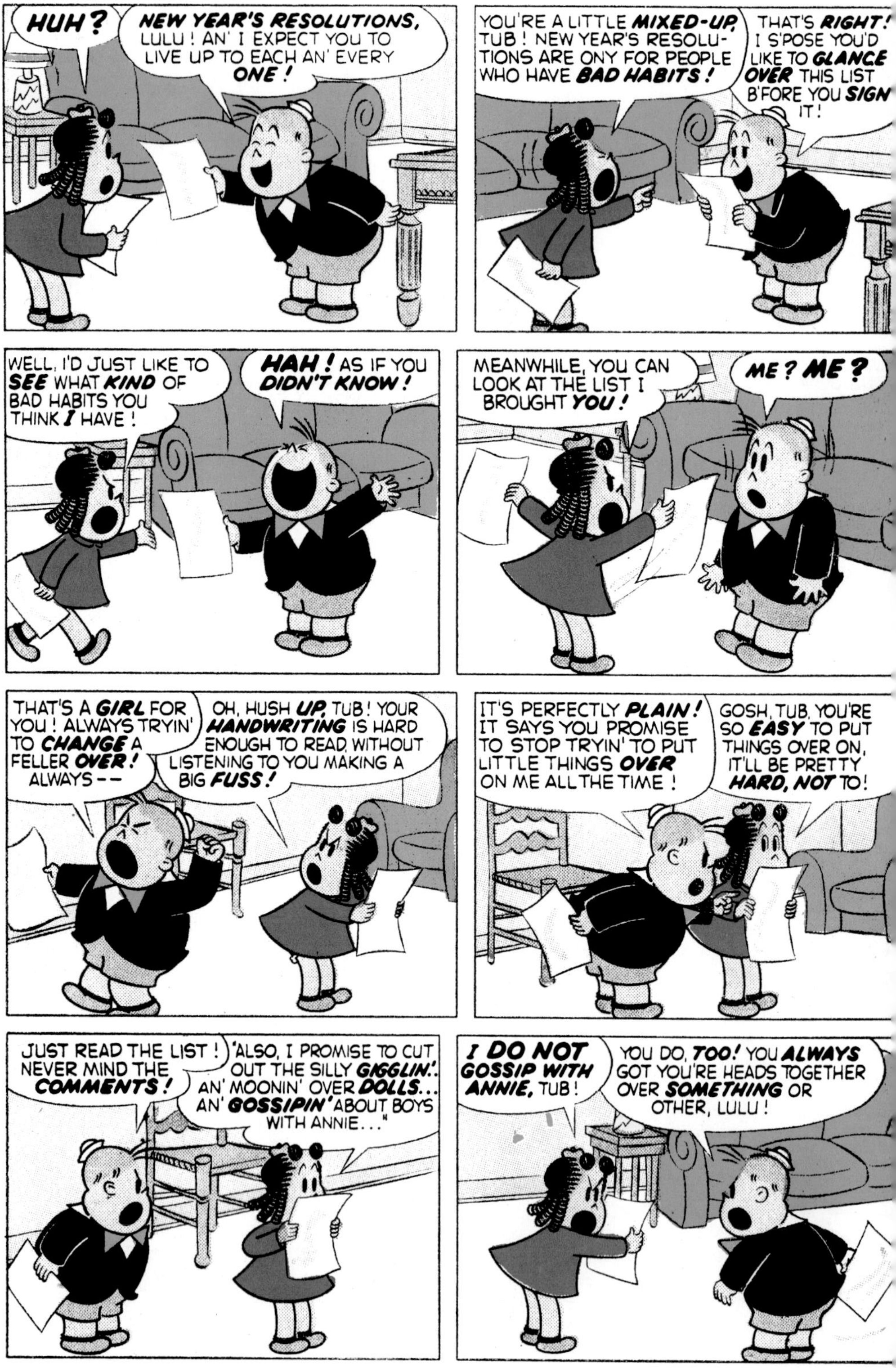
HUH?
NEW YEAR'S RESOLUTIONS, LULU! AN' I EXPECT YOU TO LIVE UP TO EACH AN' EVERY ONE!
YOU'RE A LITTLE MIXED-UP, TUB! NEW YEAR'S RESOLU-TIONS ARE ONY FOR PEOPLE WHO HAVE BAD HABITS!
THAT'S RIGHT! I S'POSE YOU'D LIKE TO GLANCE OVER THIS LIST B'FORE YOU SIGN IT!
WELL, I'D JUST LIKE TO SEE WHAT KIND OF BAD HABITS YOU THINK I HAVE!
HAH! AS IF YOU DIDN'T KNOW!
MEANWHILE, YOU CAN LOOK AT THE LIST I BROUGHT YOU!
ME? ME?
THAT'S A GIRL FOR YOU! ALWAYS TRYIN' TO CHANGE A FELLER OVER! ALWAYS --
OH, HUSH UP, TUB! YOUR HANDWRITING IS HARD ENOUGH TO READ, WITHOUT LISTENING TO YOU MAKING A BIG FUSS!
IT'S PERFECTLY PLAIN! IT SAYS YOU PROMISE TO STOP TRYIN' TO PUT LITTLE THINGS OVER ON ME ALL THE TIME!
GOSH, TUB, YOU'RE SO EASY TO PUT THINGS OVER ON, IT'LL BE PRETTY HARD, NOT TO!
JUST READ THE LIST! NEVER MIND THE COMMENTS!
"ALSO, I PROMISE TO CUT OUT THE SILLY GIGGLIN'... AN' MOONIN' OVER DOLLS... AN' GOSSIPIN' ABOUT BOYS WITH ANNIE..."
I DO NOT GOSSIP WITH ANNIE, TUB!
YOU DO, TOO! YOU ALWAYS GOT YOU'RE HEADS TOGETHER OVER SOMETHING OR OTHER, LULU!

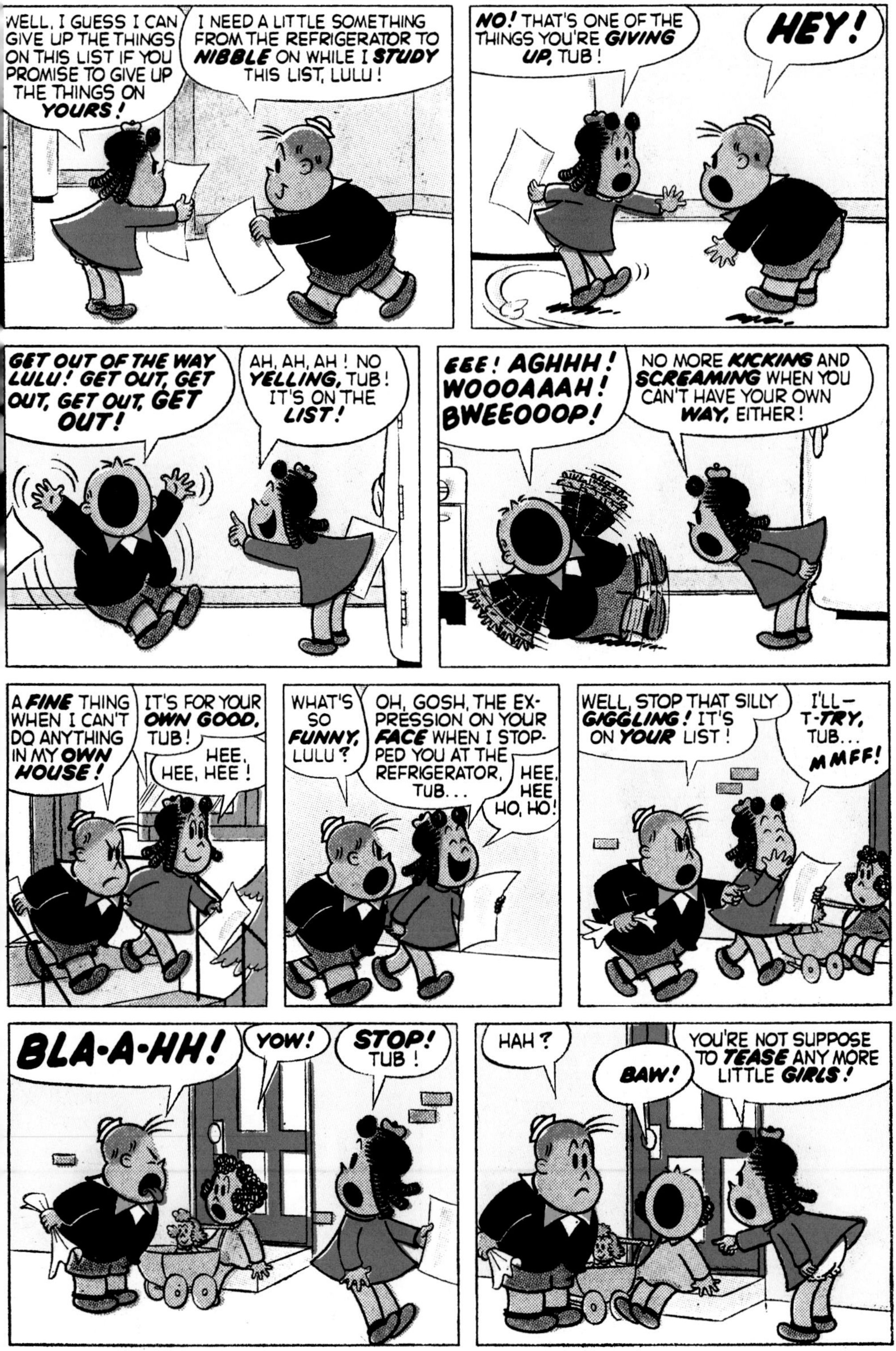
WELL, I GUESS I CAN GIVE UP THE THINGS ON THIS LIST IF YOU PROMISE TO GIVE UP THE THINGS ON YOURS!
I NEED A LITTLE SOMETHING FROM THE REFRIGERATOR TO NIBBLE ON WHILE I STUDY THIS LIST, LULU!
NO! THAT'S ONE OF THE THINGS YOU'RE GIVING UP, TUB!
HEY!
GET OUT OF THE WAY LULU! GET OUT, GET OUT, GET OUT, GET OUT!
AH, AH, AH! NO YELLING, TUB! IT'S ON THE LIST!
EEE! AGHHH! WOOOAAAH! BWEEOOOP!
NO MORE KICKING AND SCREAMING WHEN YOU CAN'T HAVE YOUR OWN WAY, EITHER!
A FINE THING WHEN I CAN'T DO ANYTHING IN MY OWN HOUSE!
IT'S FOR YOUR OWN GOOD, TUB!
HEE, HEE, HEE!
WHAT'S SO FUNNY, LULU?
OH, GOSH, THE EX-PRESSION ON YOUR FACE WHEN I STOP-PED YOU AT THE REFRIGERATOR, TUB...
HEE, HEE HO, HO!
WELL, STOP THAT SILLY GIGGLING! IT'S ON YOUR LIST!
I'LL—T-TRY, TUB... MMFF!
BLA-A-HH!
YOW!
STOP! TUB!
HAH?
BAW!
YOU'RE NOT SUPPOSE TO TEASE ANY MORE LITTLE GIRLS!

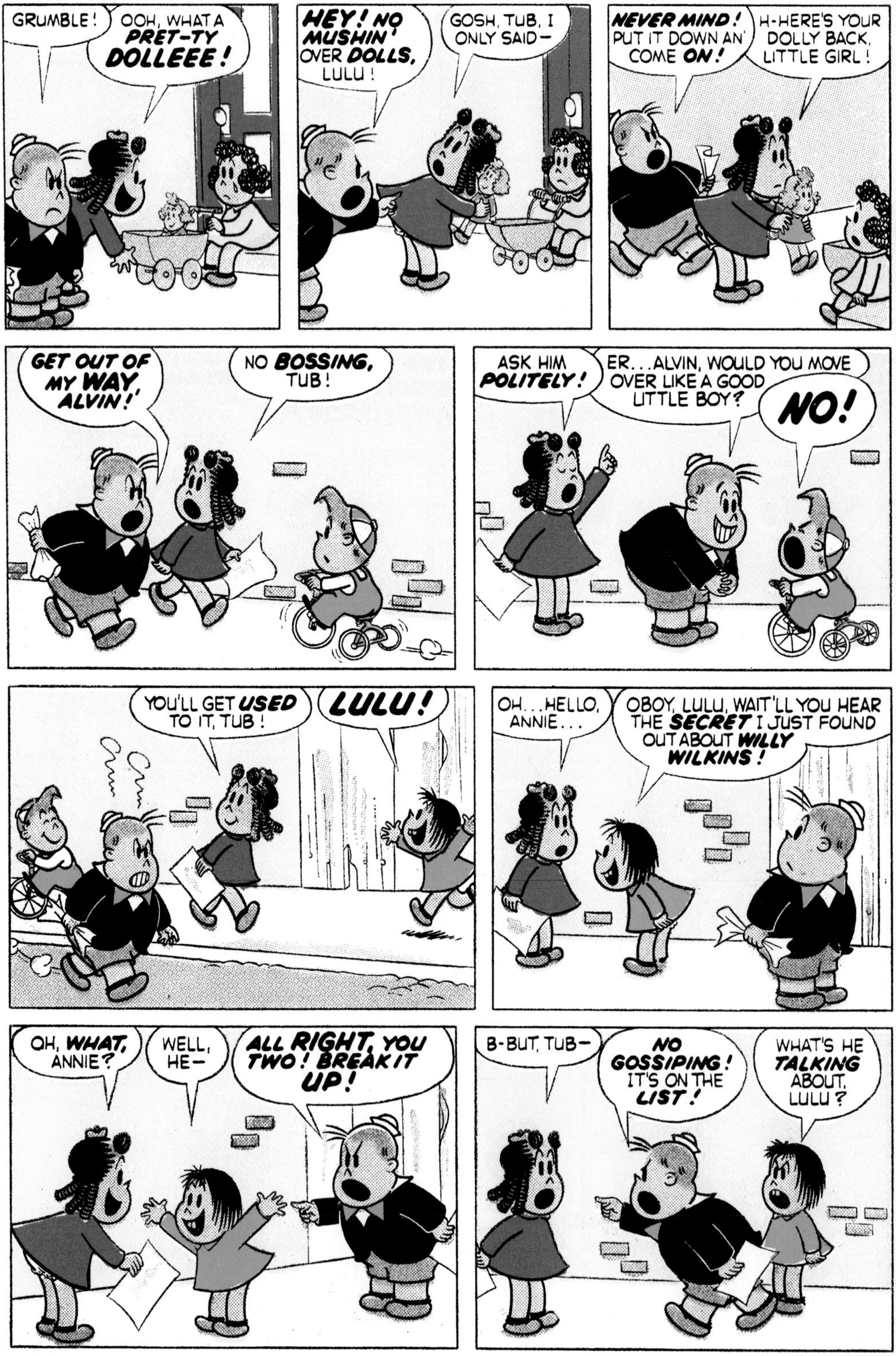
GRUMBLE!
OOH, WHAT A PRET-TY DOLLEEE!
HEY! NO MUSHIN' OVER DOLLS, LULU!
GOSH, TUB, I ONLY SAID—
NEVER MIND! PUT IT DOWN AN' COME ON!
H-HERE'S YOUR DOLLY BACK, LITTLE GIRL!
GET OUT OF MY WAY, ALVIN!
NO BOSSING, TUB!
ASK HIM POLITELY!
ER...ALVIN, WOULD YOU MOVE OVER LIKE A GOOD LITTLE BOY?
NO!
YOU'LL GET USED TO IT, TUB!
LULU!
OH...HELLO, ANNIE...
OBOY, LULU, WAIT'LL YOU HEAR THE SECRET I JUST FOUND OUT ABOUT WILLY WILKINS!
OH, WHAT, ANNIE?
WELL, HE—
ALL RIGHT, YOU TWO! BREAK IT UP!
B-BUT, TUB—
NO GOSSIPING! IT'S ON THE LIST!
WHAT'S HE TALKING ABOUT, LULU?

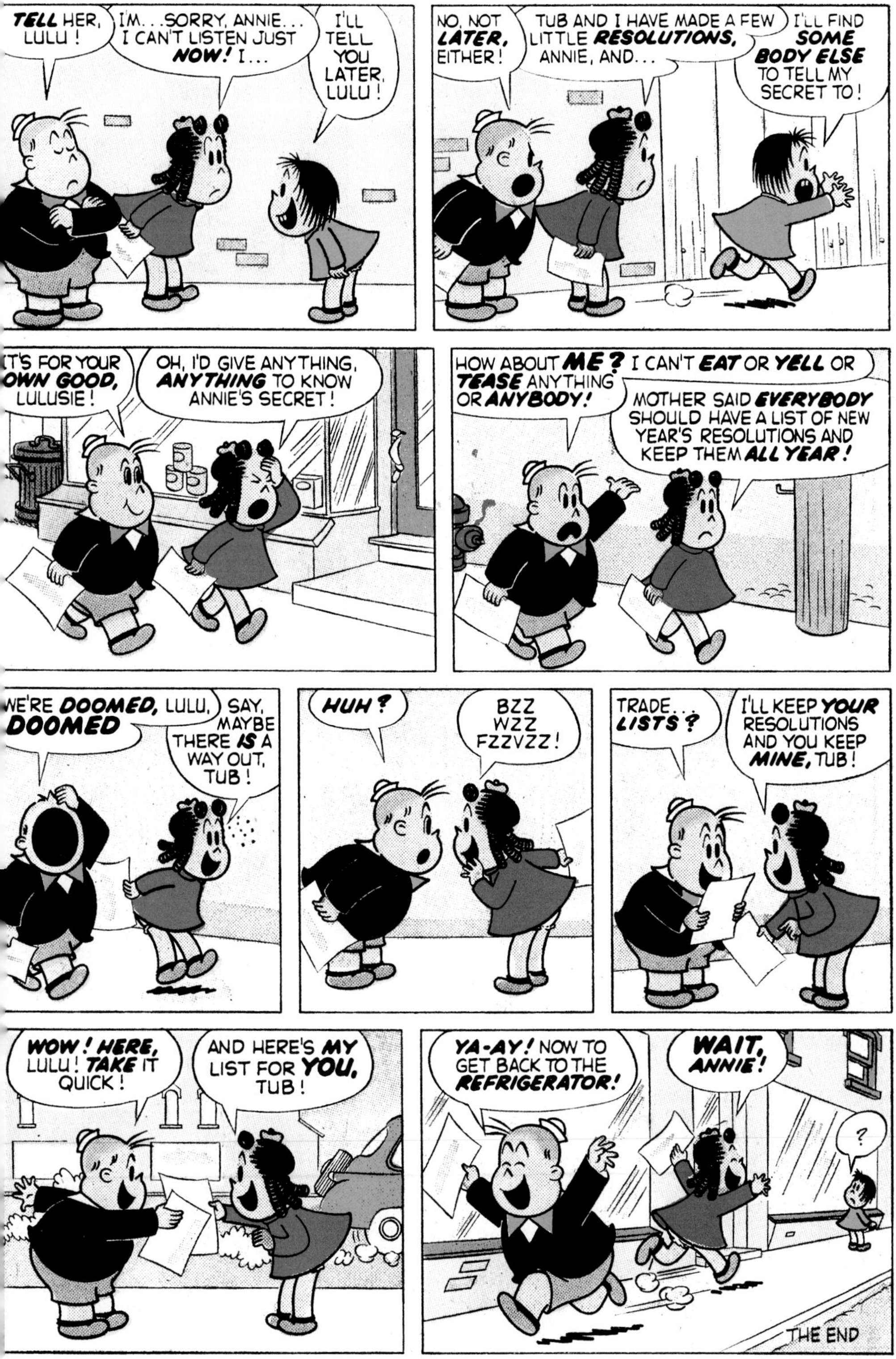

TELL HER, LULU!
I'M...SORRY, ANNIE... I CAN'T LISTEN JUST NOW! I...
I'LL TELL YOU LATER, LULU!
NO, NOT LATER, EITHER!
TUB AND I HAVE MADE A FEW LITTLE RESOLUTIONS, ANNIE, AND...
I'LL FIND SOME BODY ELSE TO TELL MY SECRET TO!
IT'S FOR YOUR OWN GOOD, LULUSIE!
OH, I'D GIVE ANYTHING, ANYTHING TO KNOW ANNIE'S SECRET!
HOW ABOUT ME? I CAN'T EAT OR YELL OR TEASE ANYTHING OR ANYBODY!
MOTHER SAID EVERYBODY SHOULD HAVE A LIST OF NEW YEAR'S RESOLUTIONS AND KEEP THEM ALL YEAR!
WE'RE DOOMED, LULU, DOOMED
SAY, MAYBE THERE IS A WAY OUT, TUB!
HUH?
BZZ WZZ FZZVZZ!
TRADE... LISTS?
I'LL KEEP YOUR RESOLUTIONS AND YOU KEEP MINE, TUB!
WOW! HERE, LULU! TAKE IT QUICK!
AND HERE'S MY LIST FOR YOU, TUB!
YA-AY! NOW TO GET BACK TO THE REFRIGERATOR!
WAIT, ANNIE!
?
THE END

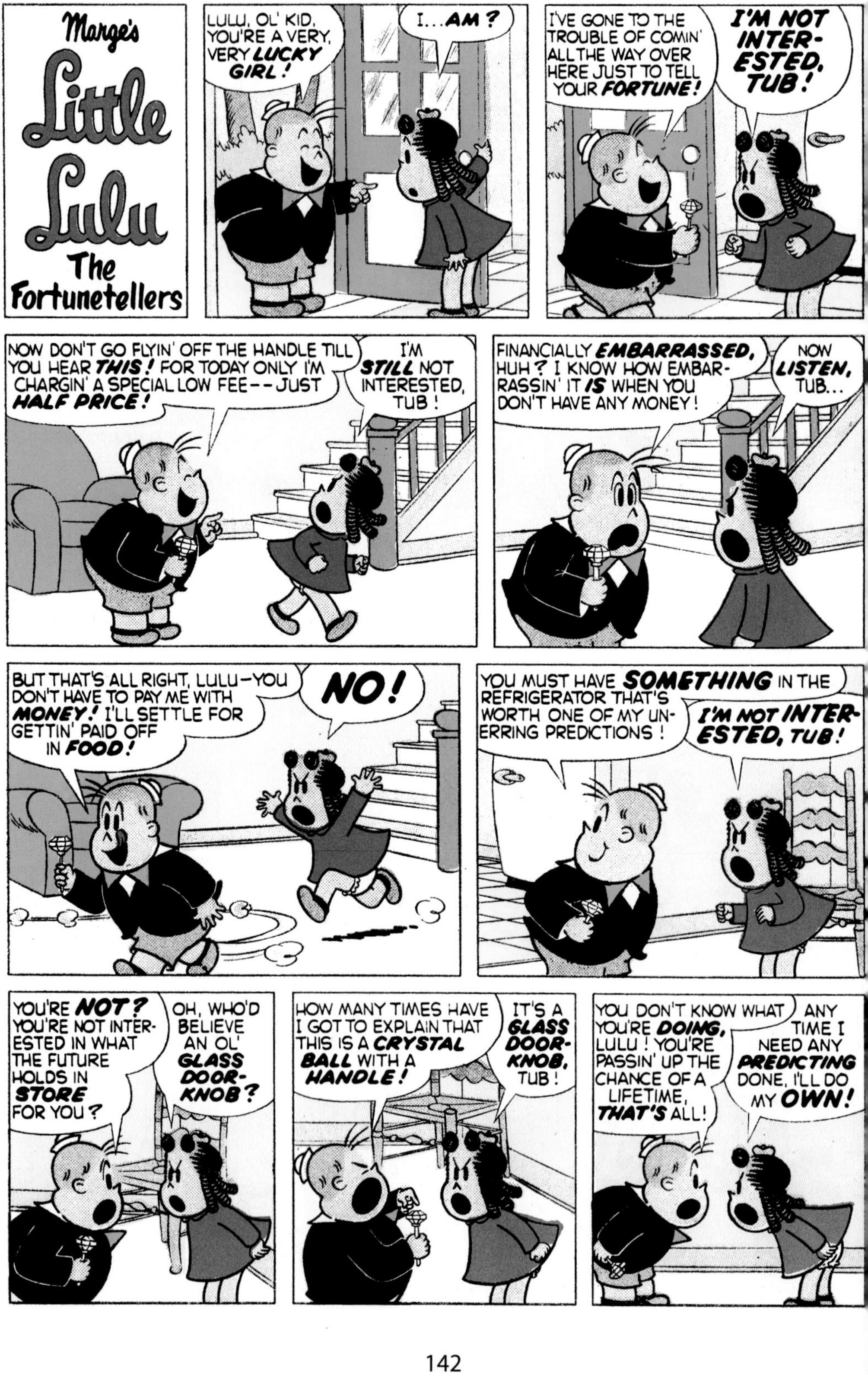
Marge's
Little Lulu
The Fortunetellers
LULU, OL' KID, YOU'RE A VERY, VERY LUCKY GIRL!
I...AM?
I'VE GONE TO THE TROUBLE OF COMIN' ALL THE WAY OVER HERE JUST TO TELL YOUR FORTUNE!
I'M NOT INTER-ESTED, TUB!
NOW DON'T GO FLYIN' OFF THE HANDLE TILL YOU HEAR THIS! FOR TODAY ONLY I'M CHARGIN' A SPECIAL LOW FEE--JUST HALF PRICE!
I'M STILL NOT INTERESTED, TUB!
FINANCIALLY EMBARRASSED, HUH? I KNOW HOW EMBAR-RASSIN' IT IS WHEN YOU DON'T HAVE ANY MONEY!
NOW LISTEN, TUB...
BUT THAT'S ALL RIGHT, LULU—YOU DON'T HAVE TO PAY ME WITH MONEY! I'LL SETTLE FOR GETTIN' PAID OFF IN FOOD!
NO!
YOU MUST HAVE SOMETHING IN THE REFRIGERATOR THAT'S WORTH ONE OF MY UN-ERRING PREDICTIONS!
I'M NOT INTER-ESTED, TUB!
YOU'RE NOT? YOU'RE NOT INTER-ESTED IN WHAT THE FUTURE HOLDS IN STORE FOR YOU?
OH, WHO'D BELIEVE AN OL' GLASS DOOR-KNOB?
HOW MANY TIMES HAVE I GOT TO EXPLAIN THAT THIS IS A CRYSTAL BALL WITH A HANDLE!
IT'S A GLASS DOOR-KNOB, TUB!
YOU DON'T KNOW WHAT YOU'RE DOING, LULU! YOU'RE PASSIN' UP THE CHANCE OF A LIFETIME, THAT'S ALL!
ANY TIME I NEED ANY PREDICTING DONE, I'LL DO MY OWN!

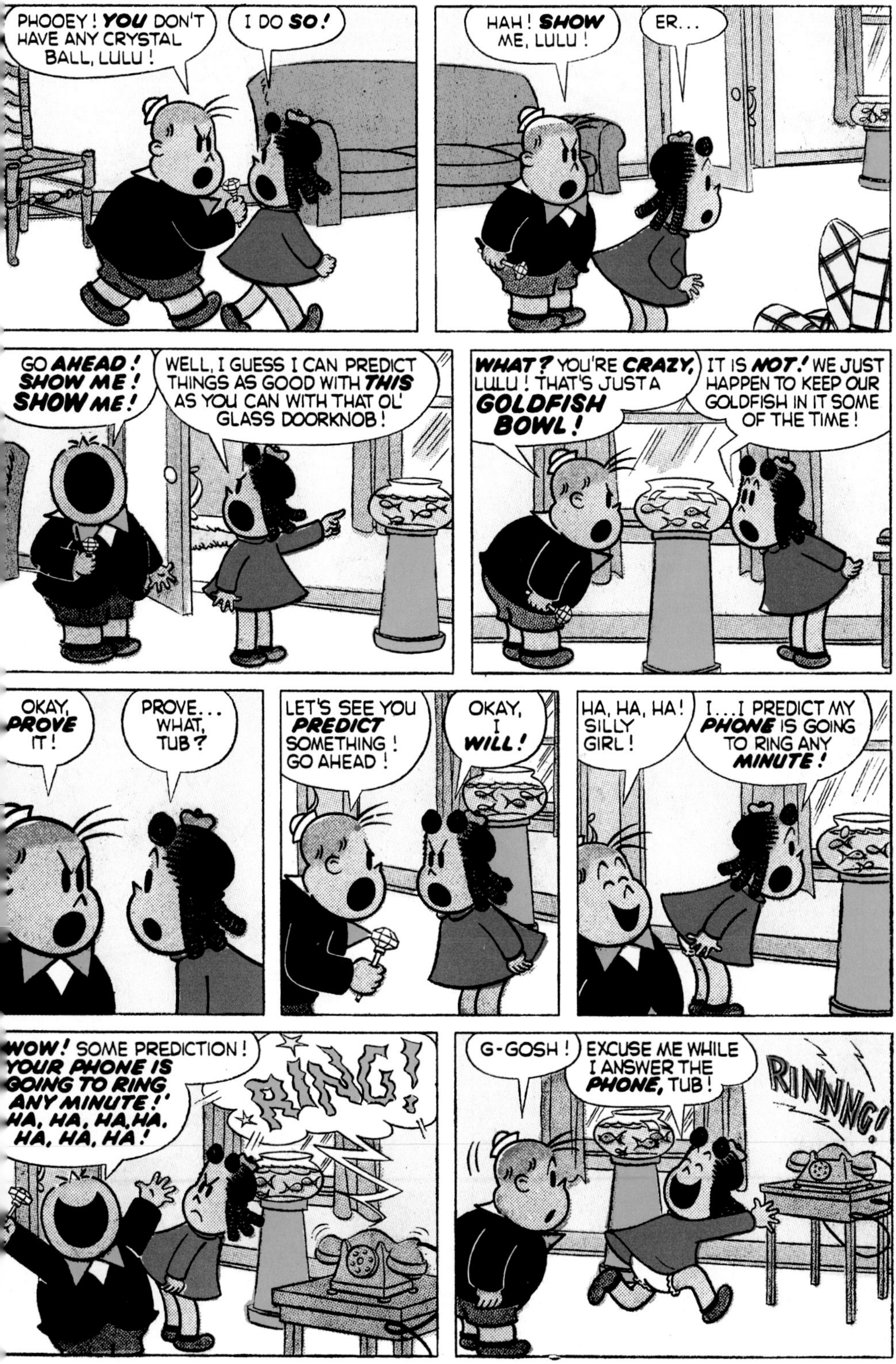
PHOOEY! YOU DON'T HAVE ANY CRYSTAL BALL, LULU!
I DO SO!
HAH! SHOW ME, LULU!
ER...
GO AHEAD! SHOW ME! SHOW ME!
WELL, I GUESS I CAN PREDICT THINGS AS GOOD WITH THIS AS YOU CAN WITH THAT OL' GLASS DOORKNOB!
WHAT? YOU'RE CRAZY, LULU! THAT'S JUST A GOLDFISH BOWL!
IT IS NOT! WE JUST HAPPEN TO KEEP OUR GOLDFISH IN IT SOME OF THE TIME!
OKAY, PROVE IT!
PROVE... WHAT, TUB?
LET'S SEE YOU PREDICT SOMETHING! GO AHEAD!
OKAY, I WILL!
HA, HA, HA! SILLY GIRL!
I...I PREDICT MY PHONE IS GOING TO RING ANY MINUTE!
WOW! SOME PREDICTION! 'YOUR PHONE IS GOING TO RING ANY MINUTE!' HA, HA, HA,HA. HA, HA, HA!
RING!
G-GOSH!
EXCUSE ME WHILE I ANSWER THE PHONE, TUB!
RINNNG!

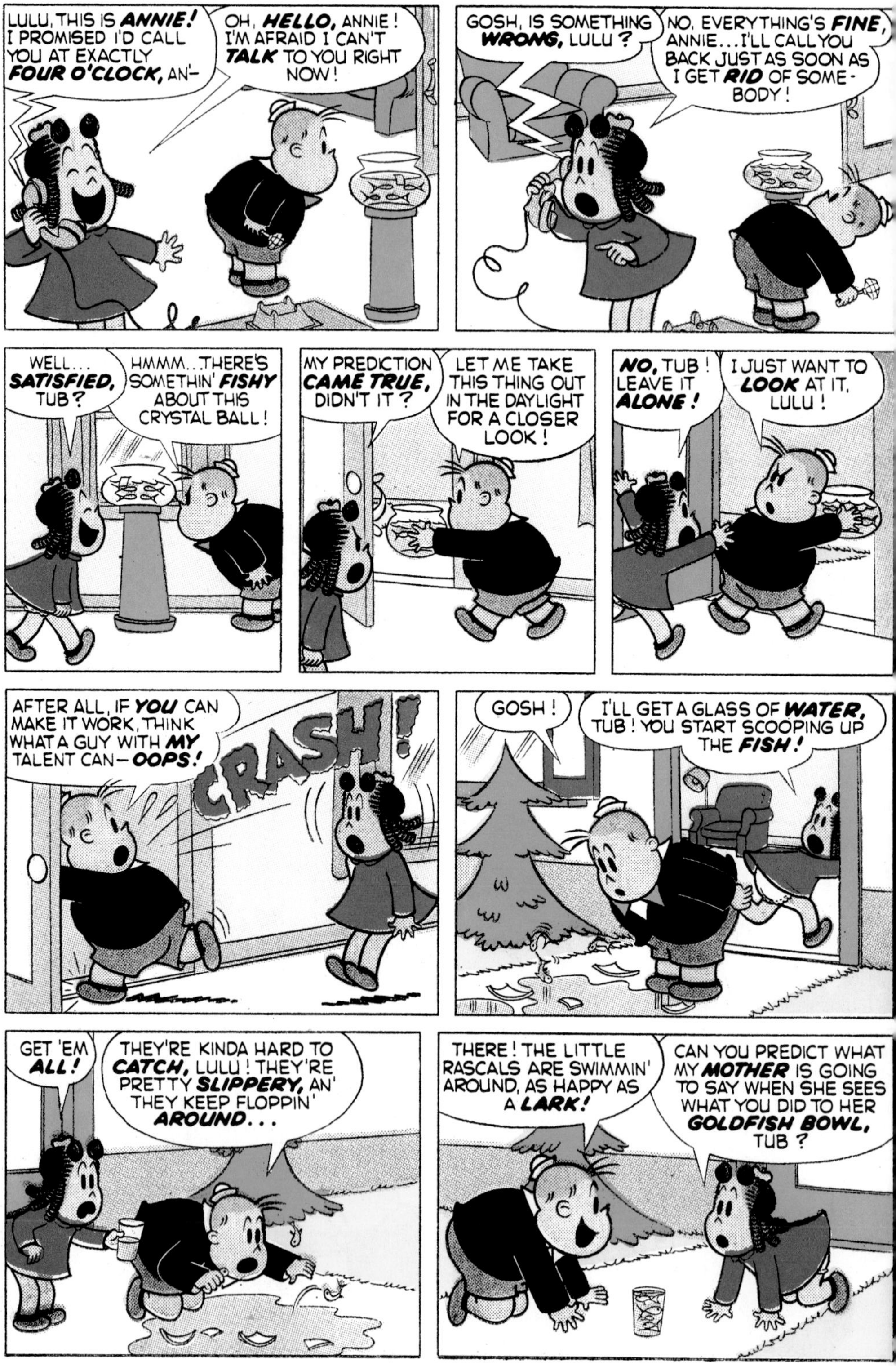
LULU, THIS IS ANNIE! I PROMISED I'D CALL YOU AT EXACTLY FOUR O'CLOCK, AN'-
OH, HELLO, ANNIE! I'M AFRAID I CAN'T TALK TO YOU RIGHT NOW!
GOSH, IS SOMETHING WRONG, LULU?
NO, EVERYTHING'S FINE, ANNIE...I'LL CALL YOU BACK JUST AS SOON AS I GET RID OF SOME-BODY!
WELL... SATISFIED, TUB?
HMMM...THERE'S SOMETHIN' FISHY ABOUT THIS CRYSTAL BALL!
MY PREDICTION CAME TRUE, DIDN'T IT?
LET ME TAKE THIS THING OUT IN THE DAYLIGHT FOR A CLOSER LOOK!
NO, TUB! LEAVE IT ALONE!
I JUST WANT TO LOOK AT IT, LULU!
AFTER ALL, IF YOU CAN MAKE IT WORK, THINK WHAT A GUY WITH MY TALENT CAN-OOPS!
CRASH!
GOSH!
I'LL GET A GLASS OF WATER, TUB! YOU START SCOOPING UP THE FISH!
GET 'EM ALL!
THEY'RE KINDA HARD TO CATCH, LULU! THEY'RE PRETTY SLIPPERY, AN' THEY KEEP FLOPPIN' AROUND...
THERE! THE LITTLE RASCALS ARE SWIMMIN' AROUND, AS HAPPY AS A LARK!
CAN YOU PREDICT WHAT MY MOTHER IS GOING TO SAY WHEN SHE SEES WHAT YOU DID TO HER GOLDFISH BOWL, TUB?

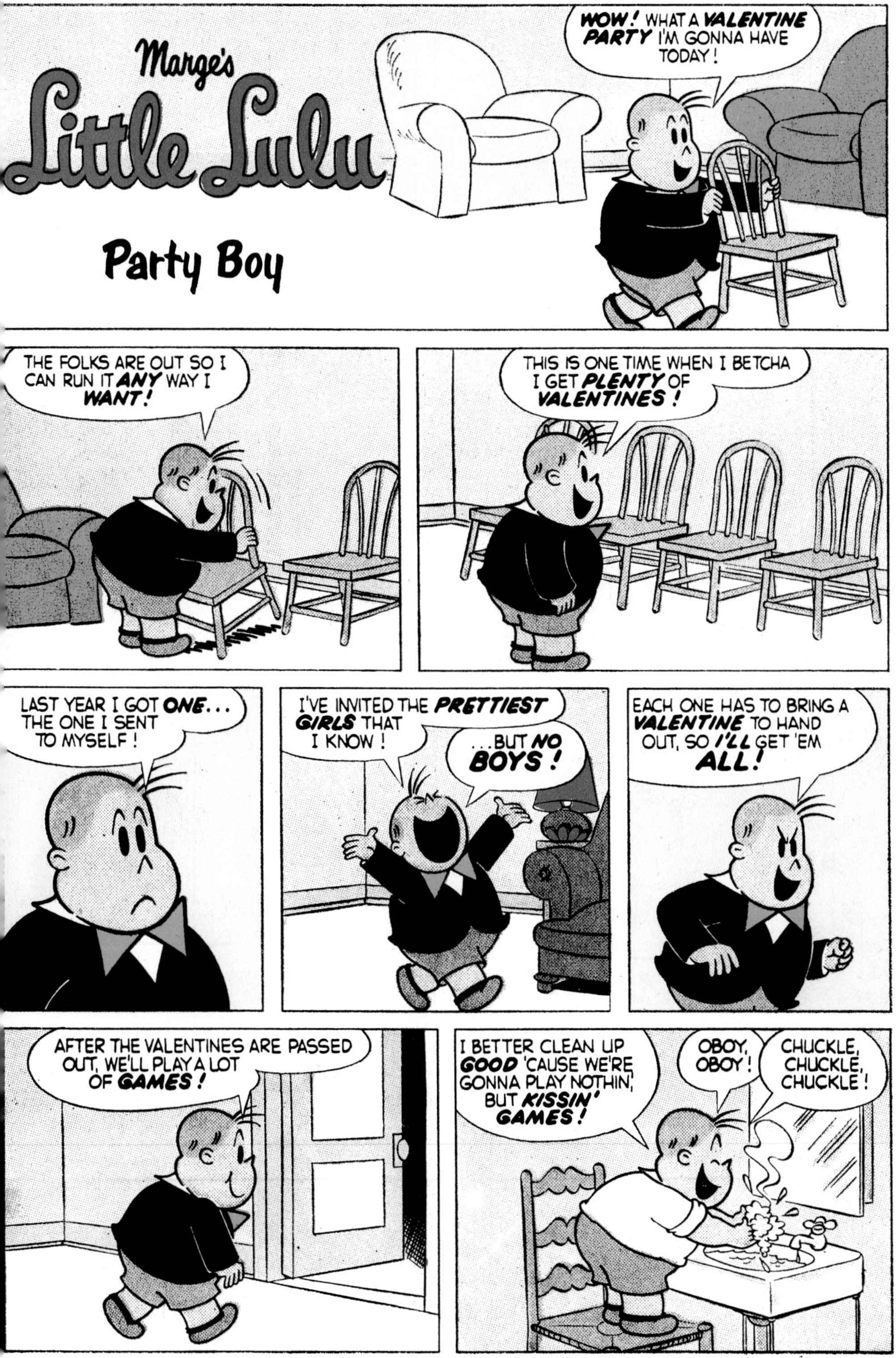
Marge's Little Lulu
Party Boy
WOW! WHAT A VALENTINE PARTY I'M GONNA HAVE TODAY!
THE FOLKS ARE OUT SO I CAN RUN IT ANY WAY I WANT!
THIS IS ONE TIME WHEN I BETCHA I GET PLENTY OF VALENTINES!
LAST YEAR I GOT ONE... THE ONE I SENT TO MYSELF!
I'VE INVITED THE PRETTIEST GIRLS THAT I KNOW!
...BUT NO BOYS!
EACH ONE HAS TO BRING A VALENTINE TO HAND OUT, SO I'LL GET 'EM ALL!
AFTER THE VALENTINES ARE PASSED OUT, WE'LL PLAY A LOT OF GAMES!
I BETTER CLEAN UP GOOD 'CAUSE WE'RE GONNA PLAY NOTHIN' BUT KISSIN' GAMES!
OBOY, OBOY!
CHUCKLE, CHUCKLE, CHUCKLE!

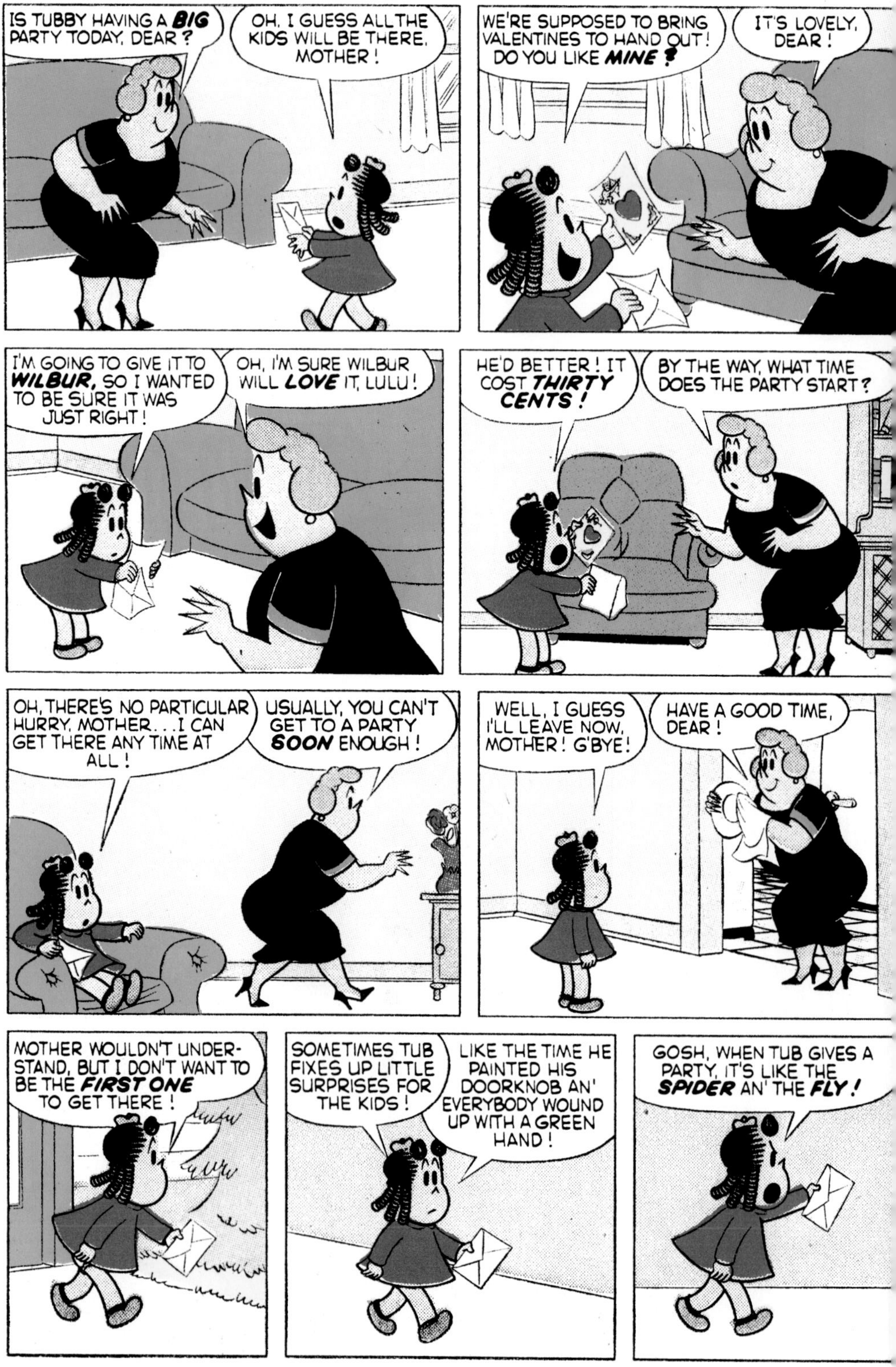
IS TUBBY HAVING A BIG PARTY TODAY, DEAR?
OH, I GUESS ALL THE KIDS WILL BE THERE, MOTHER!
WE'RE SUPPOSED TO BRING VALENTINES TO HAND OUT! DO YOU LIKE MINE?
IT'S LOVELY, DEAR!
I'M GOING TO GIVE IT TO WILBUR, SO I WANTED TO BE SURE IT WAS JUST RIGHT!
OH, I'M SURE WILBUR WILL LOVE IT, LULU!
HE'D BETTER! IT COST THIRTY CENTS!
BY THE WAY, WHAT TIME DOES THE PARTY START?
OH, THERE'S NO PARTICULAR HURRY, MOTHER...I CAN GET THERE ANY TIME AT ALL!
USUALLY, YOU CAN'T GET TO A PARTY SOON ENOUGH!
WELL, I GUESS I'LL LEAVE NOW, MOTHER! G'BYE!
HAVE A GOOD TIME, DEAR!
MOTHER WOULDN'T UNDER-STAND, BUT I DON'T WANT TO BE THE FIRST ONE TO GET THERE!
SOMETIMES TUB FIXES UP LITTLE SURPRISES FOR THE KIDS!
LIKE THE TIME HE PAINTED HIS DOORKNOB AN' EVERYBODY WOUND UP WITH A GREEN HAND!
GOSH, WHEN TUB GIVES A PARTY, IT'S LIKE THE SPIDER AN' THE FLY!

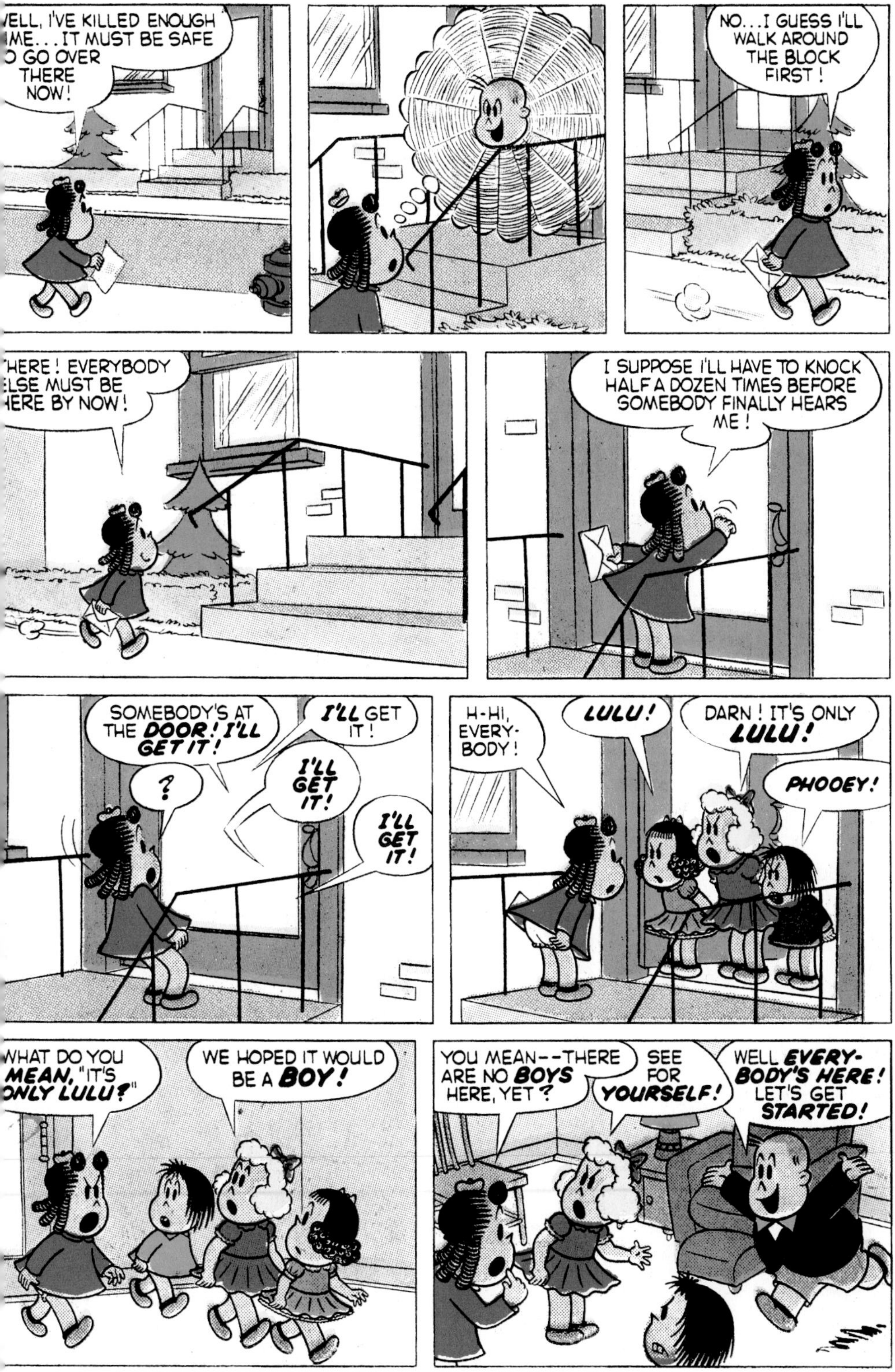

WELL, I'VE KILLED ENOUGH TIME... IT MUST BE SAFE TO GO OVER THERE NOW!
NO...I GUESS I'LL WALK AROUND THE BLOCK FIRST!
THERE! EVERYBODY ELSE MUST BE THERE BY NOW!
I SUPPOSE I'LL HAVE TO KNOCK HALF A DOZEN TIMES BEFORE SOMEBODY FINALLY HEARS ME!
SOMEBODY'S AT THE DOOR! I'LL GET IT!
I'LL GET IT!
?
I'LL GET IT!
I'LL GET IT!
H-HI, EVERY-BODY!
LULU!
DARN! IT'S ONLY LULU!
PHOOEY!
WHAT DO YOU MEAN, "IT'S ONLY LULU?"
WE HOPED IT WOULD BE A BOY!
YOU MEAN--THERE ARE NO BOYS HERE, YET?
SEE FOR YOURSELF!
WELL EVERY-BODY'S HERE! LET'S GET STARTED!

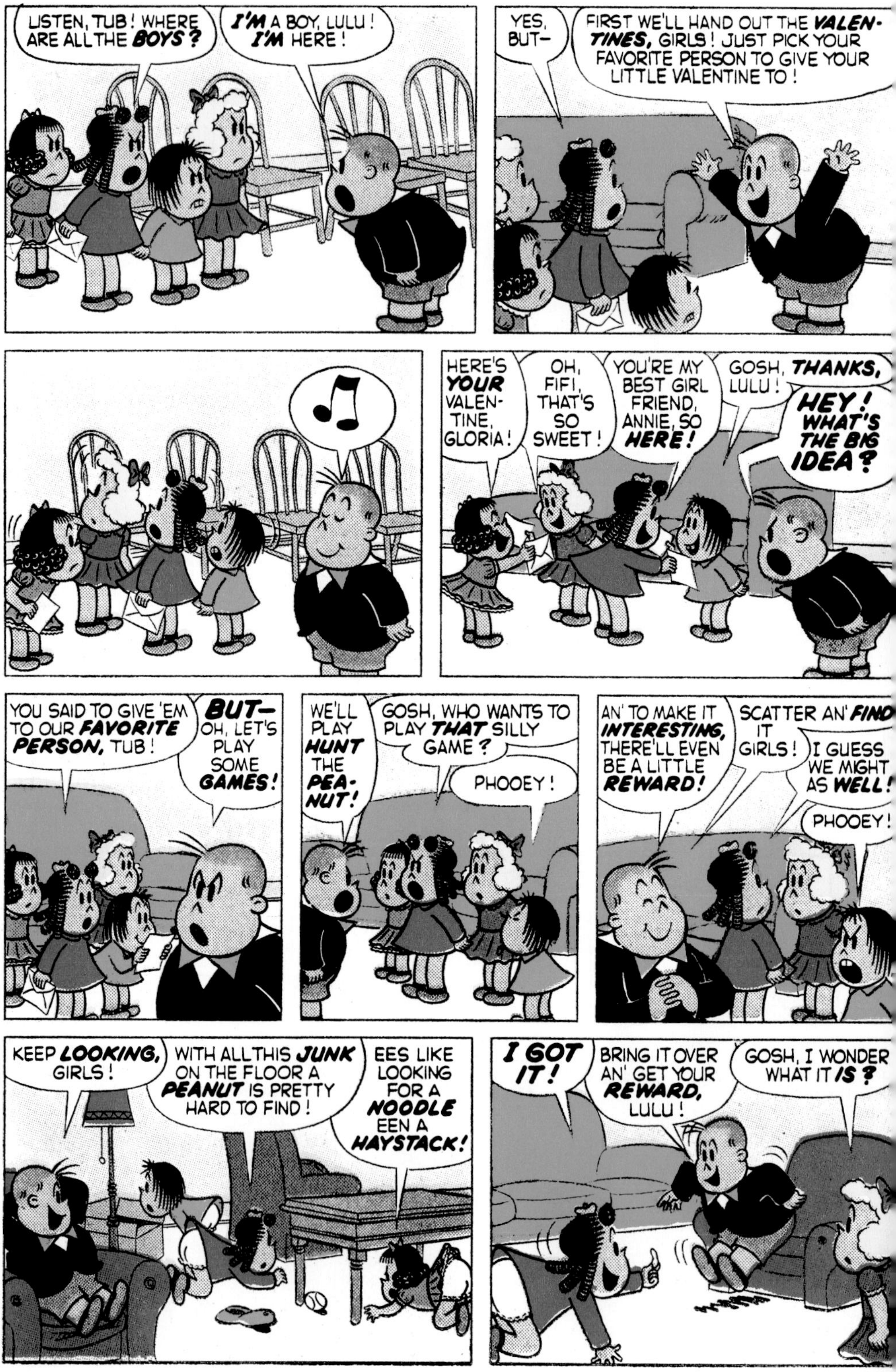

LISTEN, TUB! WHERE ARE ALL THE BOYS?
I'M A BOY, LULU! I'M HERE!
YES, BUT—
FIRST WE'LL HAND OUT THE VALENTINES, GIRLS! JUST PICK YOUR FAVORITE PERSON TO GIVE YOUR LITTLE VALENTINE TO!
HERE'S YOUR VALENTINE, GLORIA!
OH, FIFI, THAT'S SO SWEET!
YOU'RE MY BEST GIRL FRIEND, ANNIE, SO HERE!
GOSH, THANKS, LULU!
HEY! WHAT'S THE BIG IDEA?
YOU SAID TO GIVE 'EM TO OUR FAVORITE PERSON, TUB!
BUT— OH, LET'S PLAY SOME GAMES!
WE'LL PLAY HUNT THE PEANUT!
GOSH, WHO WANTS TO PLAY THAT SILLY GAME?
PHOOEY!
AN' TO MAKE IT INTERESTING, THERE'LL EVEN BE A LITTLE REWARD!
SCATTER AN' FIND IT GIRLS!
I GUESS WE MIGHT AS WELL!
PHOOEY!
KEEP LOOKING, GIRLS!
WITH ALL THIS JUNK ON THE FLOOR A PEANUT IS PRETTY HARD TO FIND!
EES LIKE LOOKING FOR A NOODLE EEN A HAYSTACK!
I GOT IT!
BRING IT OVER AN' GET YOUR REWARD, LULU!
GOSH, I WONDER WHAT IT IS?

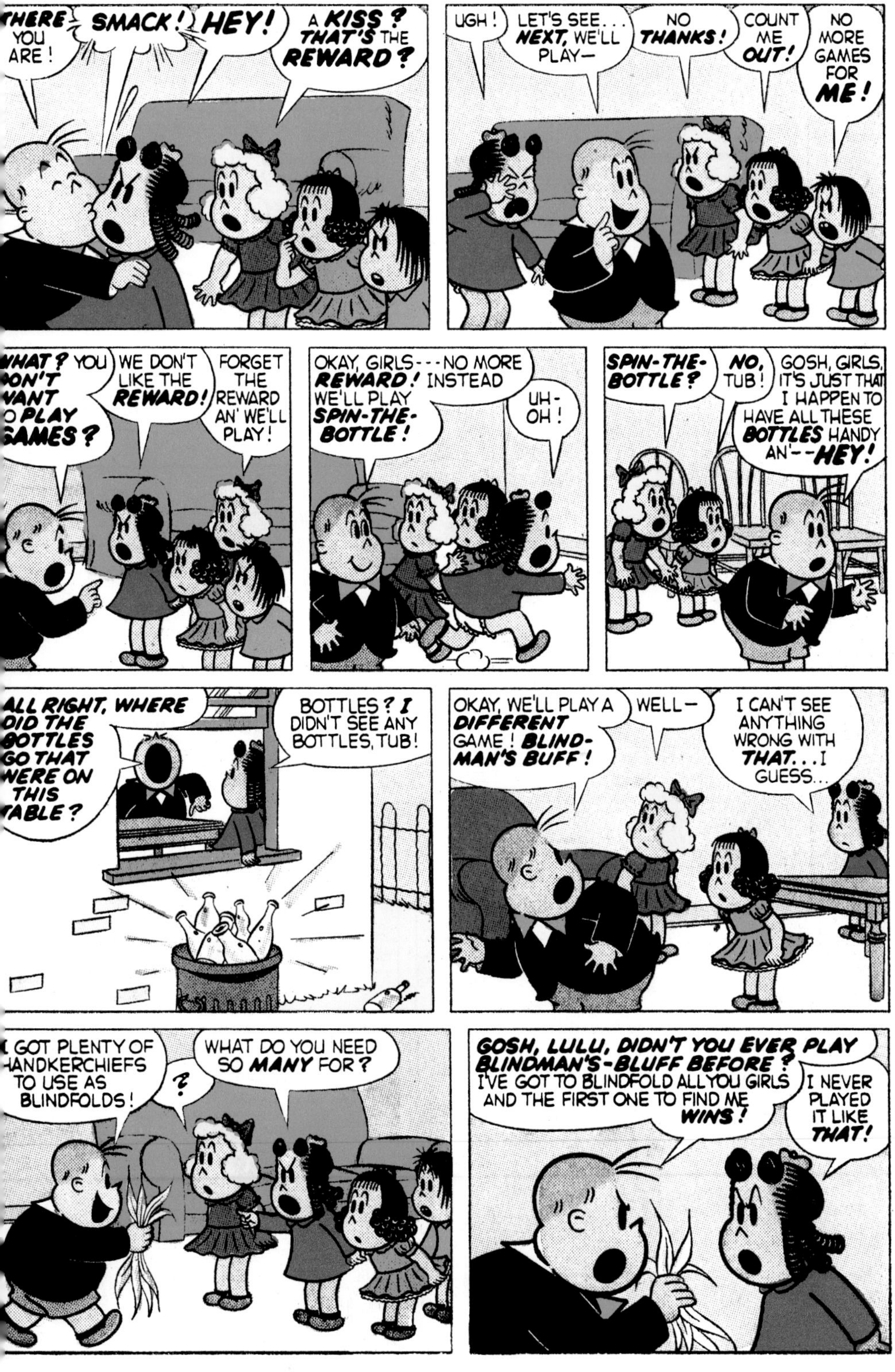
HERE YOU ARE!
SMACK!
HEY!
A KISS? THAT'S THE REWARD?
UGH!
LET'S SEE... NEXT, WE'LL PLAY—
NO THANKS!
COUNT ME OUT!
NO MORE GAMES FOR ME!
HAT? YOU ON'T VANT O PLAY AMES?
WE DON'T LIKE THE REWARD!
FORGET THE REWARD AN' WE'LL PLAY!
OKAY, GIRLS---NO MORE REWARD! INSTEAD WE'LL PLAY SPIN-THE-BOTTLE!
UH-OH!
SPIN-THE-BOTTLE?
NO, TUB!
GOSH, GIRLS, IT'S JUST THAT I HAPPEN TO HAVE ALL THESE BOTTLES HANDY AN'--HEY!
ALL RIGHT, WHERE DID THE BOTTLES GO THAT WERE ON THIS ABLE?
BOTTLES? I DIDN'T SEE ANY BOTTLES, TUB!
OKAY, WE'LL PLAY A DIFFERENT GAME! BLIND-MAN'S BUFF!
WELL—
I CAN'T SEE ANYTHING WRONG WITH THAT... I GUESS...
GOT PLENTY OF ANDKERCHIEFS TO USE AS BLINDFOLDS!
?
WHAT DO YOU NEED SO MANY FOR?
GOSH, LULU, DIDN'T YOU EVER PLAY BLINDMAN'S-BLUFF BEFORE? I'VE GOT TO BLINDFOLD ALL YOU GIRLS AND THE FIRST ONE TO FIND ME WINS!
I NEVER PLAYED IT LIKE THAT!

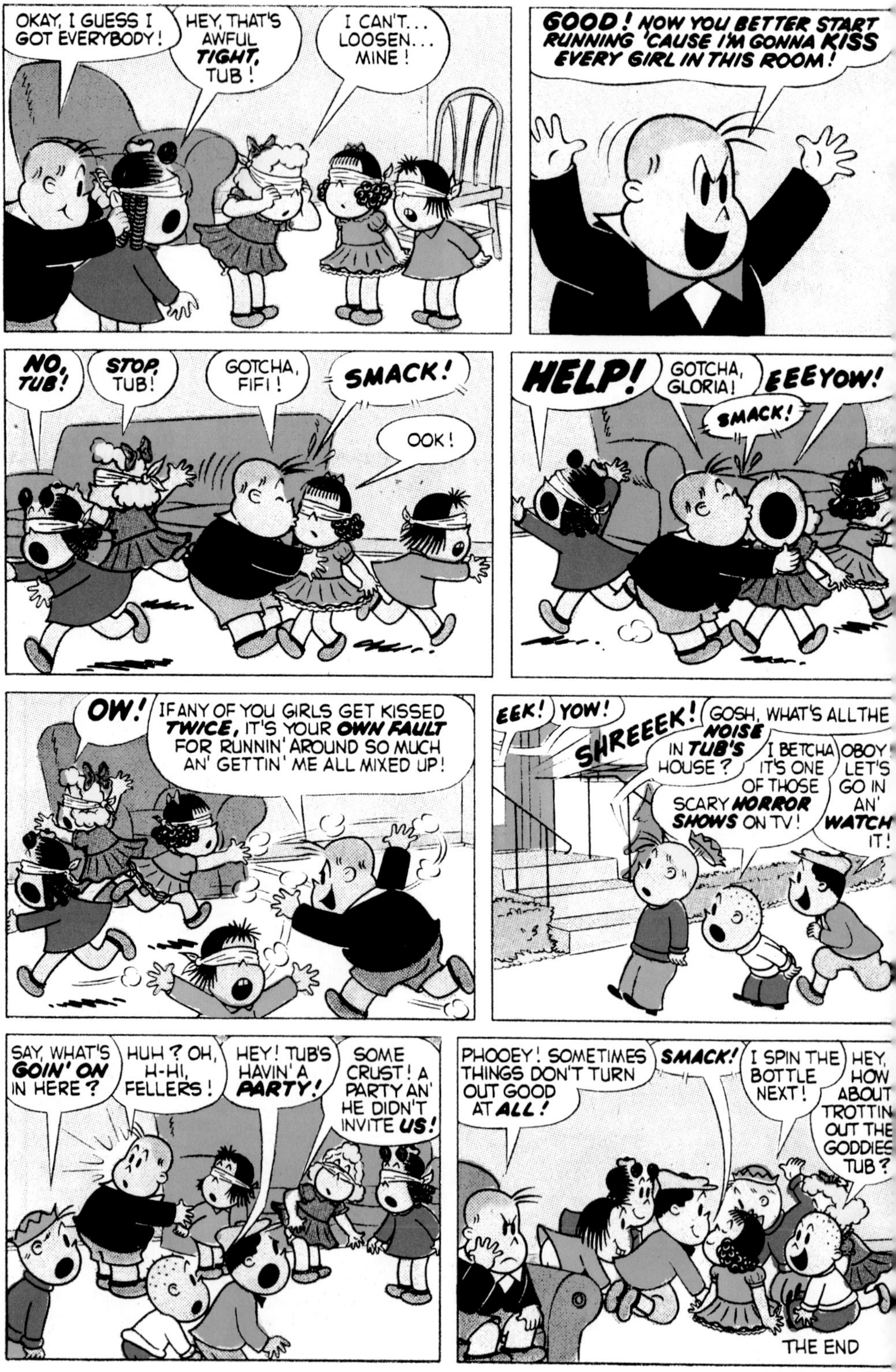
OKAY, I GUESS I GOT EVERYBODY!
HEY, THAT'S AWFUL TIGHT, TUB!
I CAN'T... LOOSEN... MINE!
GOOD! NOW YOU BETTER START RUNNING 'CAUSE I'M GONNA KISS EVERY GIRL IN THIS ROOM!
NO, TUB!
STOP, TUB!
GOTCHA, FIFI!
SMACK!
OOK!
HELP!
GOTCHA, GLORIA!
SMACK!
EEEYOW!
OW!
IF ANY OF YOU GIRLS GET KISSED TWICE, IT'S YOUR OWN FAULT FOR RUNNIN' AROUND SO MUCH AN' GETTIN' ME ALL MIXED UP!
EEK!
YOW!
SHREEEK!
GOSH, WHAT'S ALL THE NOISE IN TUB'S HOUSE?
I BETCHA IT'S ONE OF THOSE SCARY HORROR SHOWS ON TV!
OBOY! LET'S GO IN AN' WATCH IT!
SAY, WHAT'S GOIN' ON IN HERE?
HUH? OH, H-HI, FELLERS!
HEY! TUB'S HAVIN' A PARTY!
SOME CRUST! A PARTY AN' HE DIDN'T INVITE US!
PHOOEY! SOMETIMES THINGS DON'T TURN OUT GOOD AT ALL!
SMACK!
I SPIN THE BOTTLE NEXT!
HEY, HOW ABOUT TROTTIN OUT THE GODDIES TUB?
THE END

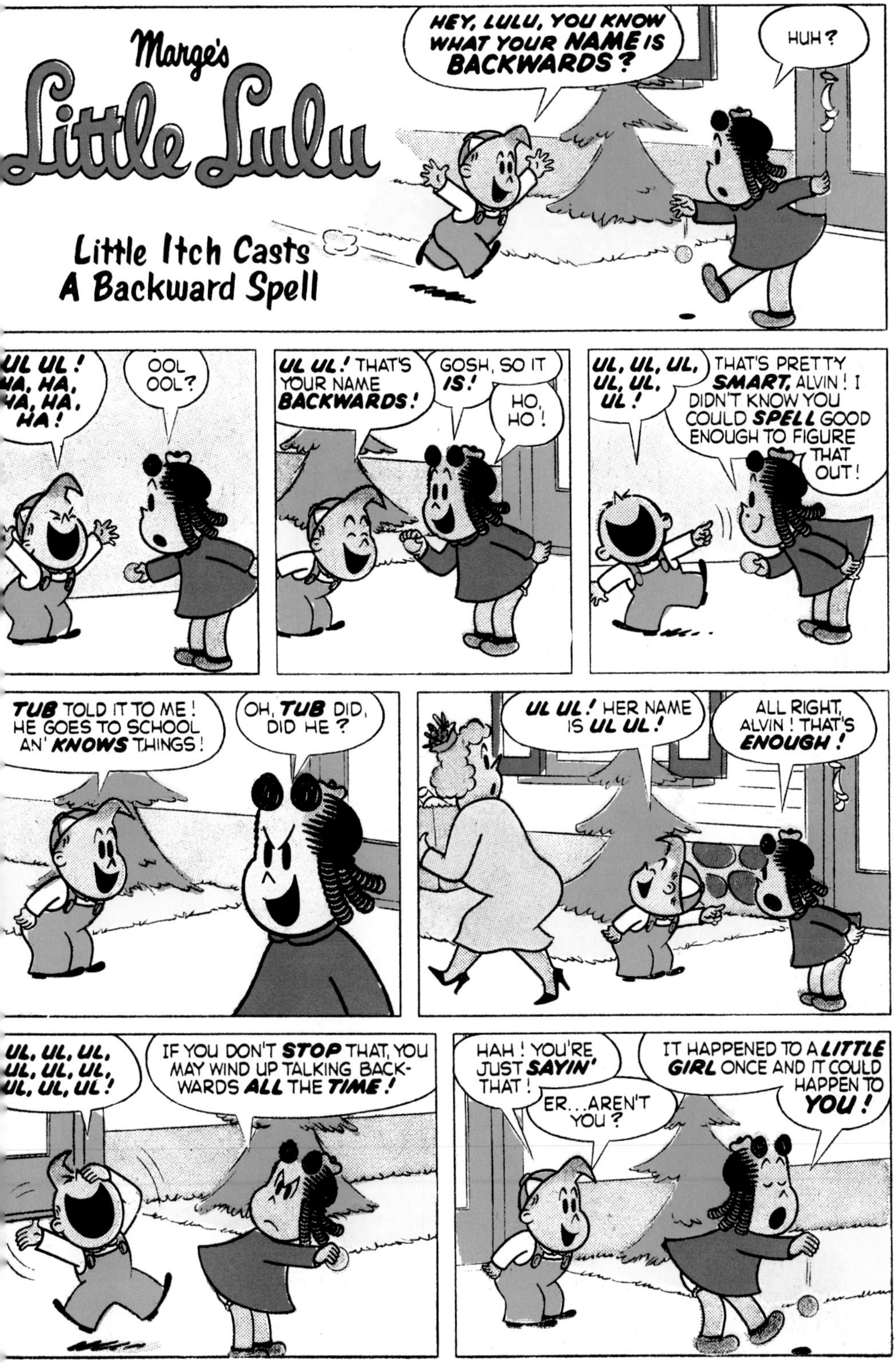
Marge's Little Lulu
Little Itch Casts A Backward Spell
HEY, LULU, YOU KNOW WHAT YOUR NAME IS BACKWARDS?
HUH?
UL UL! HA, HA, HA, HA, HA!
OOL OOL?
UL UL! THAT'S YOUR NAME BACKWARDS!
GOSH, SO IT IS!
HO, HO!
UL, UL, UL, UL, UL, UL!
THAT'S PRETTY SMART, ALVIN! I DIDN'T KNOW YOU COULD SPELL GOOD ENOUGH TO FIGURE THAT OUT!
TUB TOLD IT TO ME! HE GOES TO SCHOOL AN' KNOWS THINGS!
OH, TUB DID, DID HE?
UL UL! HER NAME IS UL UL!
ALL RIGHT, ALVIN! THAT'S ENOUGH!
UL, UL, UL, UL, UL, UL, UL, UL, UL!
IF YOU DON'T STOP THAT, YOU MAY WIND UP TALKING BACK-WARDS ALL THE TIME!
HAH! YOU'RE JUST SAYIN' THAT!
ER...AREN'T YOU?
IT HAPPENED TO A LITTLE GIRL ONCE AND IT COULD HAPPEN TO YOU!

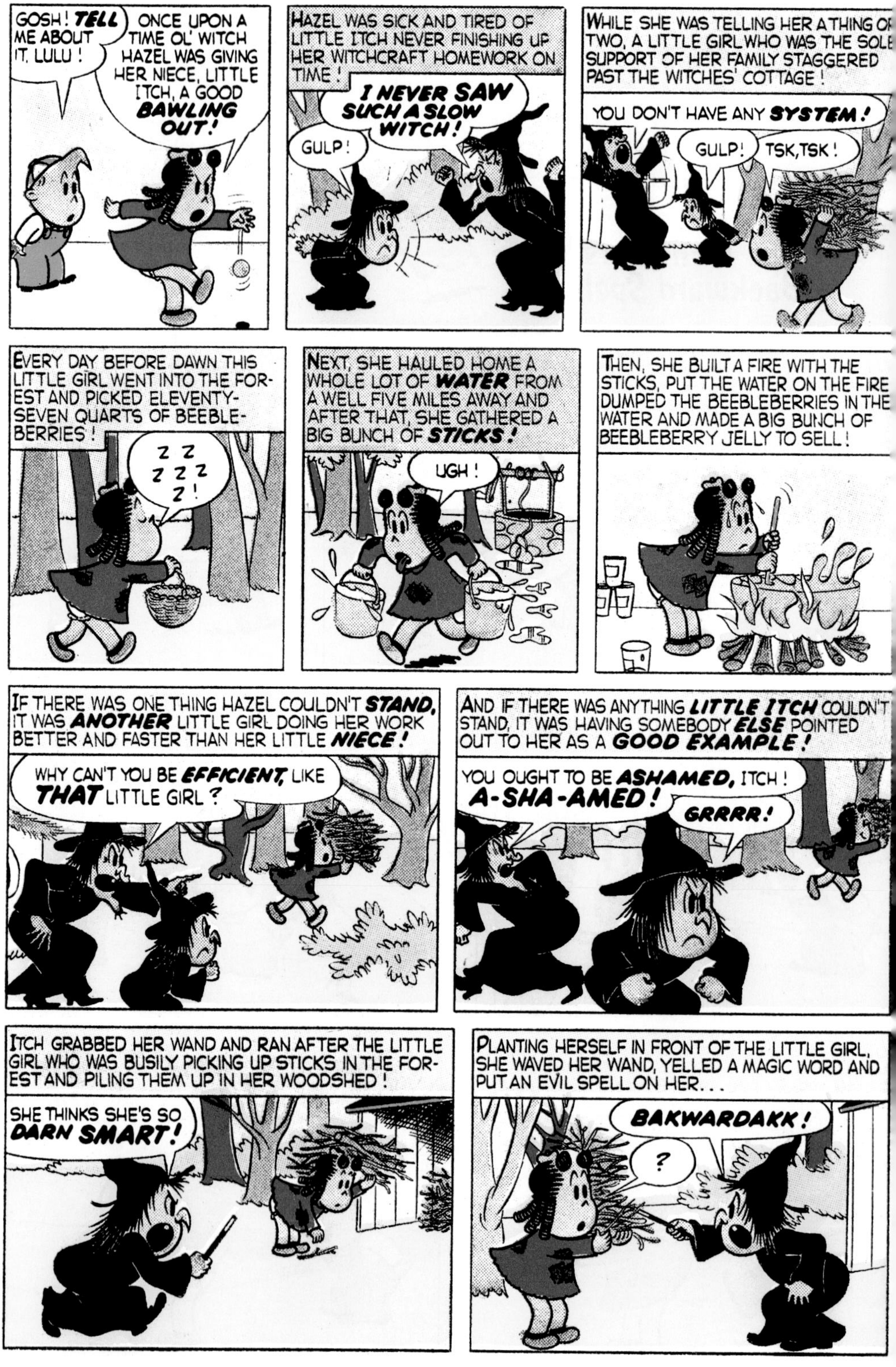
GOSH! TELL ME ABOUT IT, LULU!
ONCE UPON A TIME OL' WITCH HAZEL WAS GIVING HER NIECE, LITTLE ITCH, A GOOD BAWLING OUT!
HAZEL WAS SICK AND TIRED OF LITTLE ITCH NEVER FINISHING UP HER WITCHCRAFT HOMEWORK ON TIME!
I NEVER SAW SUCH A SLOW WITCH!
GULP!
WHILE SHE WAS TELLING HER A THING OR TWO, A LITTLE GIRL WHO WAS THE SOLE SUPPORT OF HER FAMILY STAGGERED PAST THE WITCHES' COTTAGE!
YOU DON'T HAVE ANY SYSTEM!
GULP!
TSK, TSK!
EVERY DAY BEFORE DAWN THIS LITTLE GIRL WENT INTO THE FOREST AND PICKED ELEVENTY-SEVEN QUARTS OF BEEBLEBERRIES!
Z Z Z Z Z Z!
NEXT, SHE HAULED HOME A WHOLE LOT OF WATER FROM A WELL FIVE MILES AWAY AND AFTER THAT, SHE GATHERED A BIG BUNCH OF STICKS!
UGH!
THEN, SHE BUILT A FIRE WITH THE STICKS, PUT THE WATER ON THE FIRE DUMPED THE BEEBLEBERRIES IN THE WATER AND MADE A BIG BUNCH OF BEEBLEBERRY JELLY TO SELL!
IF THERE WAS ONE THING HAZEL COULDN'T STAND, IT WAS ANOTHER LITTLE GIRL DOING HER WORK BETTER AND FASTER THAN HER LITTLE NIECE!
WHY CAN'T YOU BE EFFICIENT, LIKE THAT LITTLE GIRL?
AND IF THERE WAS ANYTHING LITTLE ITCH COULDN'T STAND, IT WAS HAVING SOMEBODY ELSE POINTED OUT TO HER AS A GOOD EXAMPLE!
YOU OUGHT TO BE ASHAMED, ITCH! A-SHA-AMED!
GRRRR!
ITCH GRABBED HER WAND AND RAN AFTER THE LITTLE GIRL WHO WAS BUSILY PICKING UP STICKS IN THE FOREST AND PILING THEM UP IN HER WOODSHED!
SHE THINKS SHE'S SO DARN SMART!
PLANTING HERSELF IN FRONT OF THE LITTLE GIRL, SHE WAVED HER WAND, YELLED A MAGIC WORD AND PUT AN EVIL SPELL ON HER...
BAKWARDAKK!
?

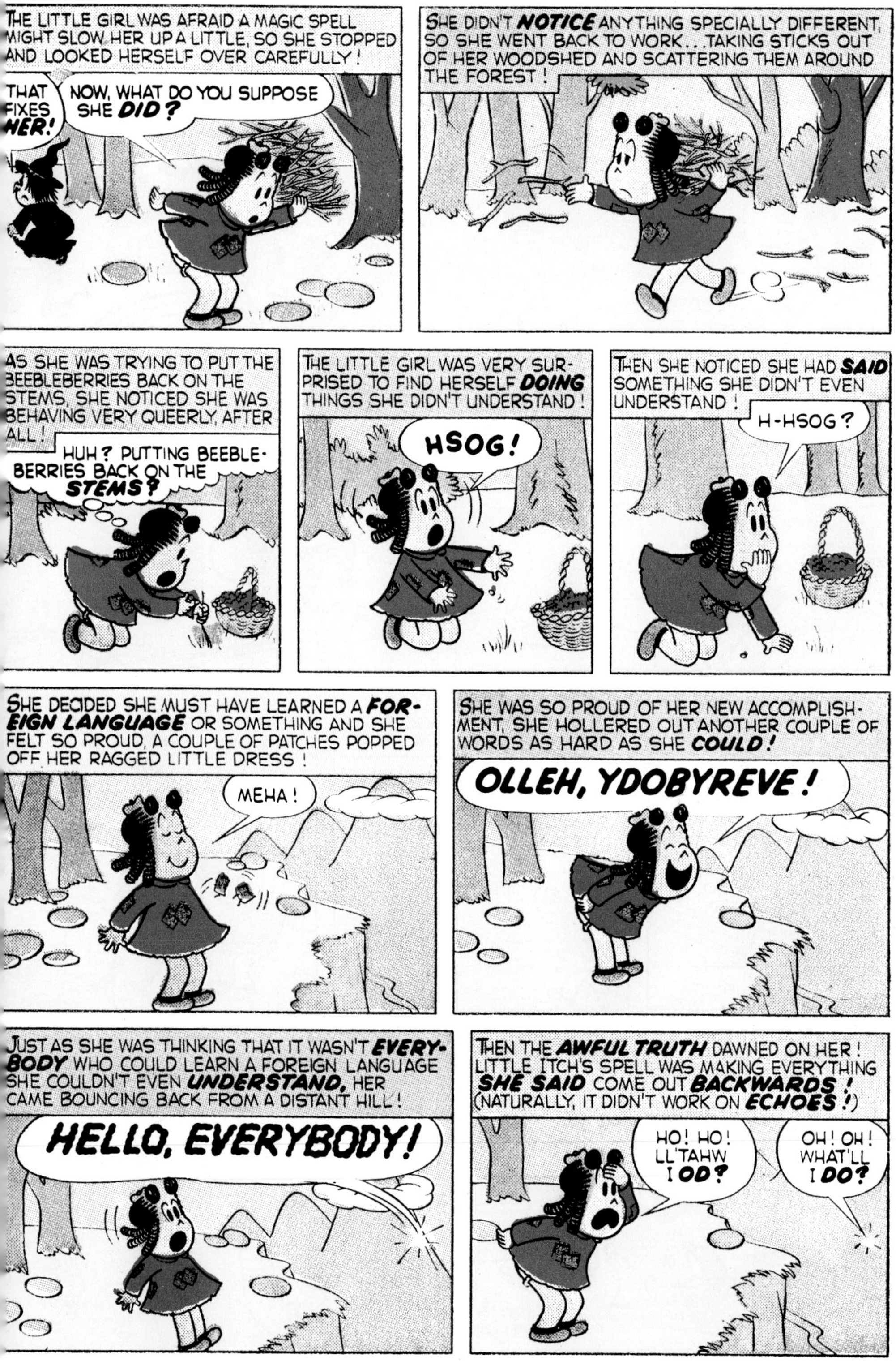
THE LITTLE GIRL WAS AFRAID A MAGIC SPELL MIGHT SLOW HER UP A LITTLE, SO SHE STOPPED AND LOOKED HERSELF OVER CAREFULLY!
THAT FIXES HER!
NOW, WHAT DO YOU SUPPOSE SHE DID?
SHE DIDN'T NOTICE ANYTHING SPECIALLY DIFFERENT, SO SHE WENT BACK TO WORK... TAKING STICKS OUT OF HER WOODSHED AND SCATTERING THEM AROUND THE FOREST!
AS SHE WAS TRYING TO PUT THE BEEBLEBERRIES BACK ON THE STEMS, SHE NOTICED SHE WAS BEHAVING VERY QUEERLY, AFTER ALL!
HUH? PUTTING BEEBLE-BERRIES BACK ON THE STEMS?
THE LITTLE GIRL WAS VERY SURPRISED TO FIND HERSELF DOING THINGS SHE DIDN'T UNDERSTAND!
HSOG!
THEN SHE NOTICED SHE HAD SAID SOMETHING SHE DIDN'T EVEN UNDERSTAND!
H-HSOG?
SHE DECIDED SHE MUST HAVE LEARNED A FOREIGN LANGUAGE OR SOMETHING AND SHE FELT SO PROUD, A COUPLE OF PATCHES POPPED OFF HER RAGGED LITTLE DRESS!
MEHA!
SHE WAS SO PROUD OF HER NEW ACCOMPLISHMENT, SHE HOLLERED OUT ANOTHER COUPLE OF WORDS AS HARD AS SHE COULD!
OLLEH, YDOBYREVE!
JUST AS SHE WAS THINKING THAT IT WASN'T EVERYBODY WHO COULD LEARN A FOREIGN LANGUAGE SHE COULDN'T EVEN UNDERSTAND, HER CAME BOUNCING BACK FROM A DISTANT HILL!
HELLO, EVERYBODY!
THEN THE AWFUL TRUTH DAWNED ON HER! LITTLE ITCH'S SPELL WAS MAKING EVERYTHING SHE SAID COME OUT BACKWARDS! (NATURALLY, IT DIDN'T WORK ON ECHOES!)
HO! HO! LL'TAHW I OD?
OH! OH! WHAT'LL I DO?

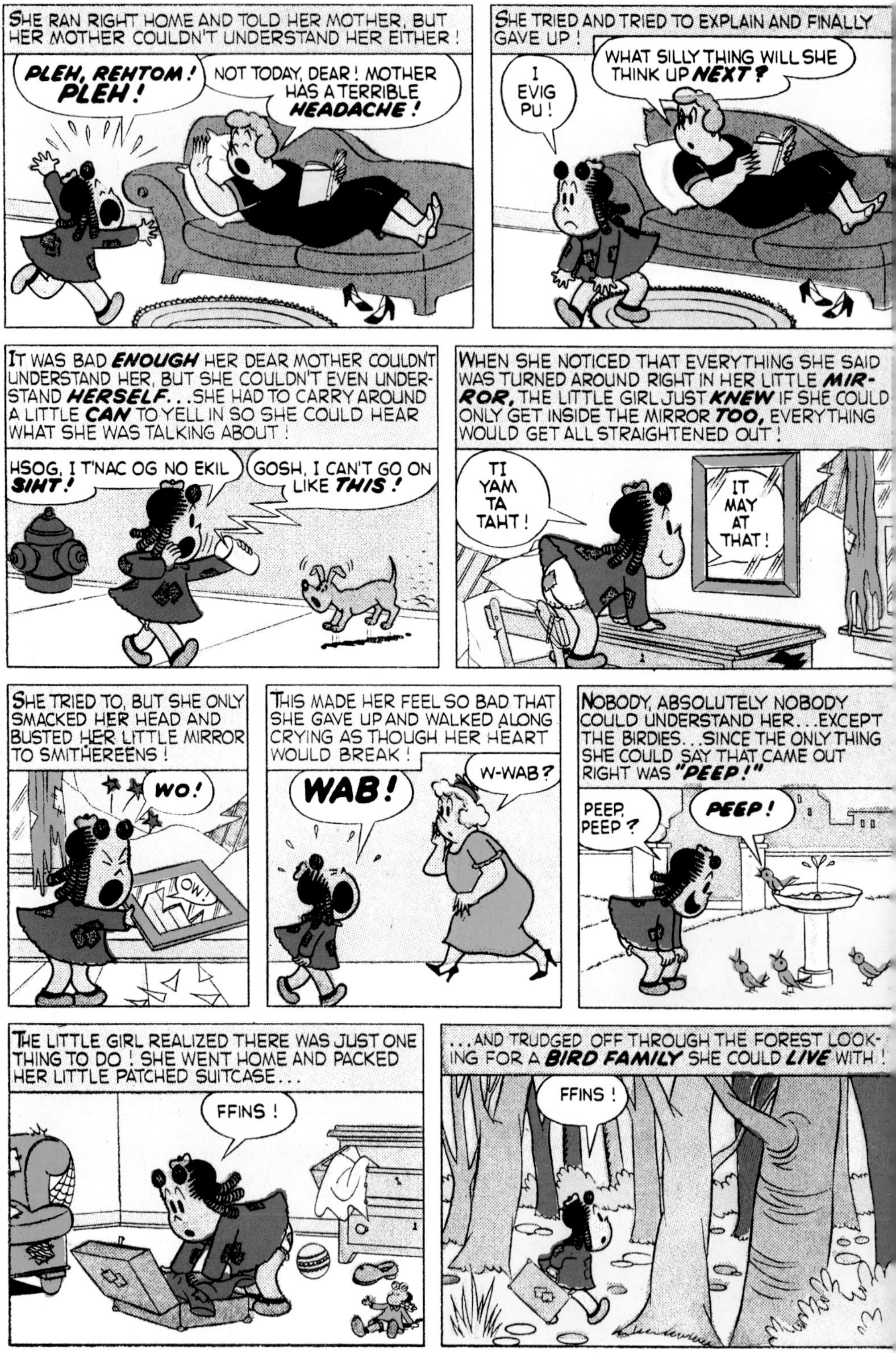
SHE RAN RIGHT HOME AND TOLD HER MOTHER, BUT HER MOTHER COULDN'T UNDERSTAND HER EITHER!
PLEH, REHTOM! PLEH!
NOT TODAY, DEAR! MOTHER HAS A TERRIBLE HEADACHE!
SHE TRIED AND TRIED TO EXPLAIN AND FINALLY GAVE UP!
I EVIG PU!
WHAT SILLY THING WILL SHE THINK UP NEXT?
IT WAS BAD ENOUGH HER DEAR MOTHER COULDN'T UNDERSTAND HER, BUT SHE COULDN'T EVEN UNDERSTAND HERSELF... SHE HAD TO CARRY AROUND A LITTLE CAN TO YELL IN SO SHE COULD HEAR WHAT SHE WAS TALKING ABOUT!
HSOG, I T'NAC OG NO EKIL SIHT!
GOSH, I CAN'T GO ON LIKE THIS!
WHEN SHE NOTICED THAT EVERYTHING SHE SAID WAS TURNED AROUND RIGHT IN HER LITTLE MIRROR, THE LITTLE GIRL JUST KNEW IF SHE COULD ONLY GET INSIDE THE MIRROR TOO, EVERYTHING WOULD GET ALL STRAIGHTENED OUT!
TI YAM TA TAHT!
IT MAY AT THAT!
SHE TRIED TO, BUT SHE ONLY SMACKED HER HEAD AND BUSTED HER LITTLE MIRROR TO SMITHEREENS!
WO!
OW!
THIS MADE HER FEEL SO BAD THAT SHE GAVE UP AND WALKED ALONG CRYING AS THOUGH HER HEART WOULD BREAK!
WAB!
W-WAB?
NOBODY, ABSOLUTELY NOBODY COULD UNDERSTAND HER... EXCEPT THE BIRDIES... SINCE THE ONLY THING SHE COULD SAY THAT CAME OUT RIGHT WAS "PEEP!"
PEEP, PEEP?
PEEP!
THE LITTLE GIRL REALIZED THERE WAS JUST ONE THING TO DO! SHE WENT HOME AND PACKED HER LITTLE PATCHED SUITCASE...
FFINS!
...AND TRUDGED OFF THROUGH THE FOREST LOOKING FOR A BIRD FAMILY SHE COULD LIVE WITH!
FFINS!

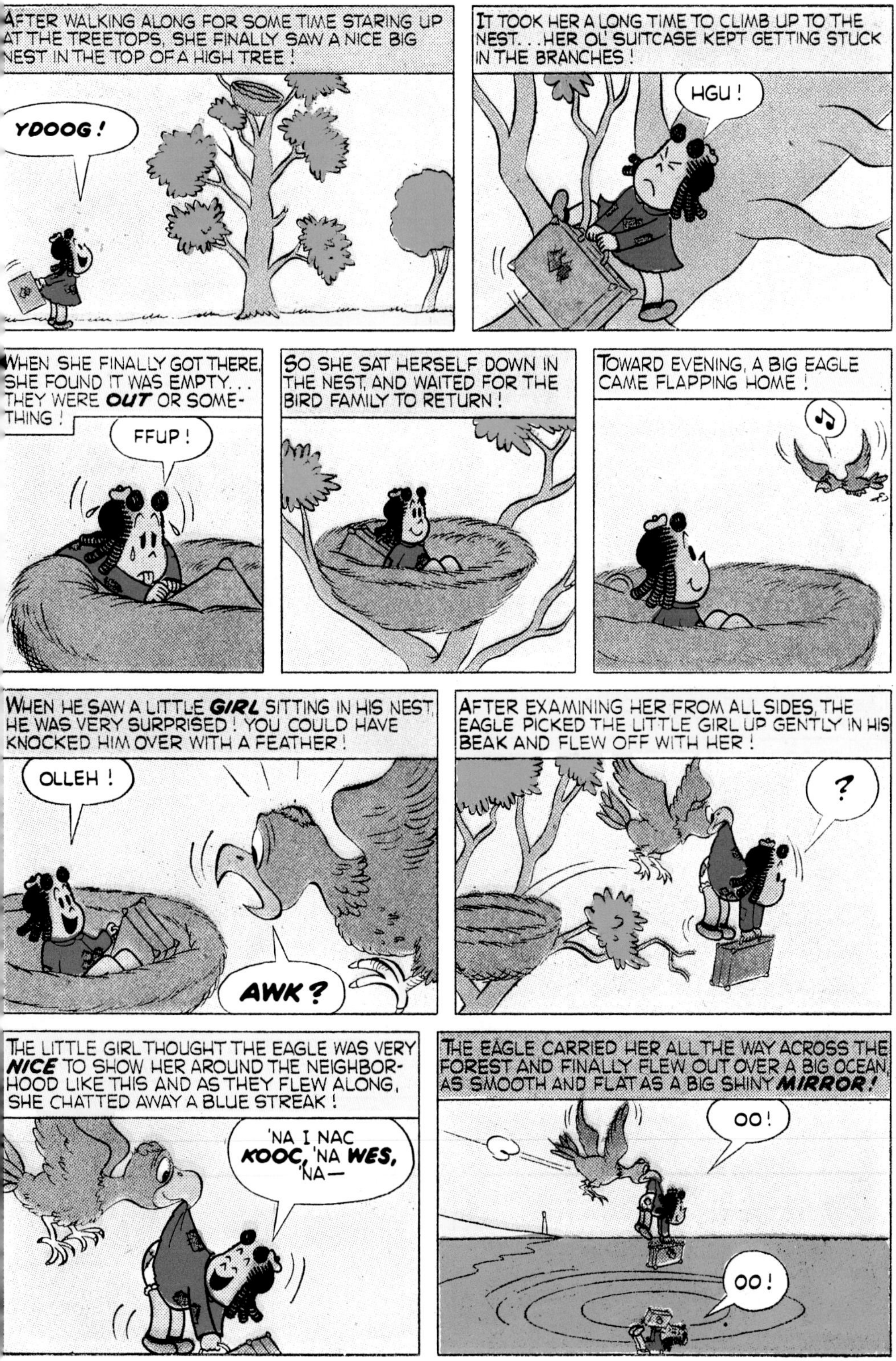
AFTER WALKING ALONG FOR SOME TIME STARING UP AT THE TREETOPS, SHE FINALLY SAW A NICE BIG NEST IN THE TOP OF A HIGH TREE!
YDOOG!
IT TOOK HER A LONG TIME TO CLIMB UP TO THE NEST...HER OL' SUITCASE KEPT GETTING STUCK IN THE BRANCHES!
HGU!
WHEN SHE FINALLY GOT THERE, SHE FOUND IT WAS EMPTY... THEY WERE OUT OR SOMETHING!
FFUP!
SO SHE SAT HERSELF DOWN IN THE NEST, AND WAITED FOR THE BIRD FAMILY TO RETURN!
TOWARD EVENING, A BIG EAGLE CAME FLAPPING HOME!
♫
WHEN HE SAW A LITTLE GIRL SITTING IN HIS NEST, HE WAS VERY SURPRISED! YOU COULD HAVE KNOCKED HIM OVER WITH A FEATHER!
OLLEH!
AWK?
AFTER EXAMINING HER FROM ALL SIDES, THE EAGLE PICKED THE LITTLE GIRL UP GENTLY IN HIS BEAK AND FLEW OFF WITH HER!
?
THE LITTLE GIRL THOUGHT THE EAGLE WAS VERY NICE TO SHOW HER AROUND THE NEIGHBORHOOD LIKE THIS AND AS THEY FLEW ALONG, SHE CHATTED AWAY A BLUE STREAK!
'NA I NAC KOOC, 'NA WES, 'NA—
THE EAGLE CARRIED HER ALL THE WAY ACROSS THE FOREST AND FINALLY FLEW OUT OVER A BIG OCEAN AS SMOOTH AND FLAT AS A BIG SHINY MIRROR!
OO!
OO!

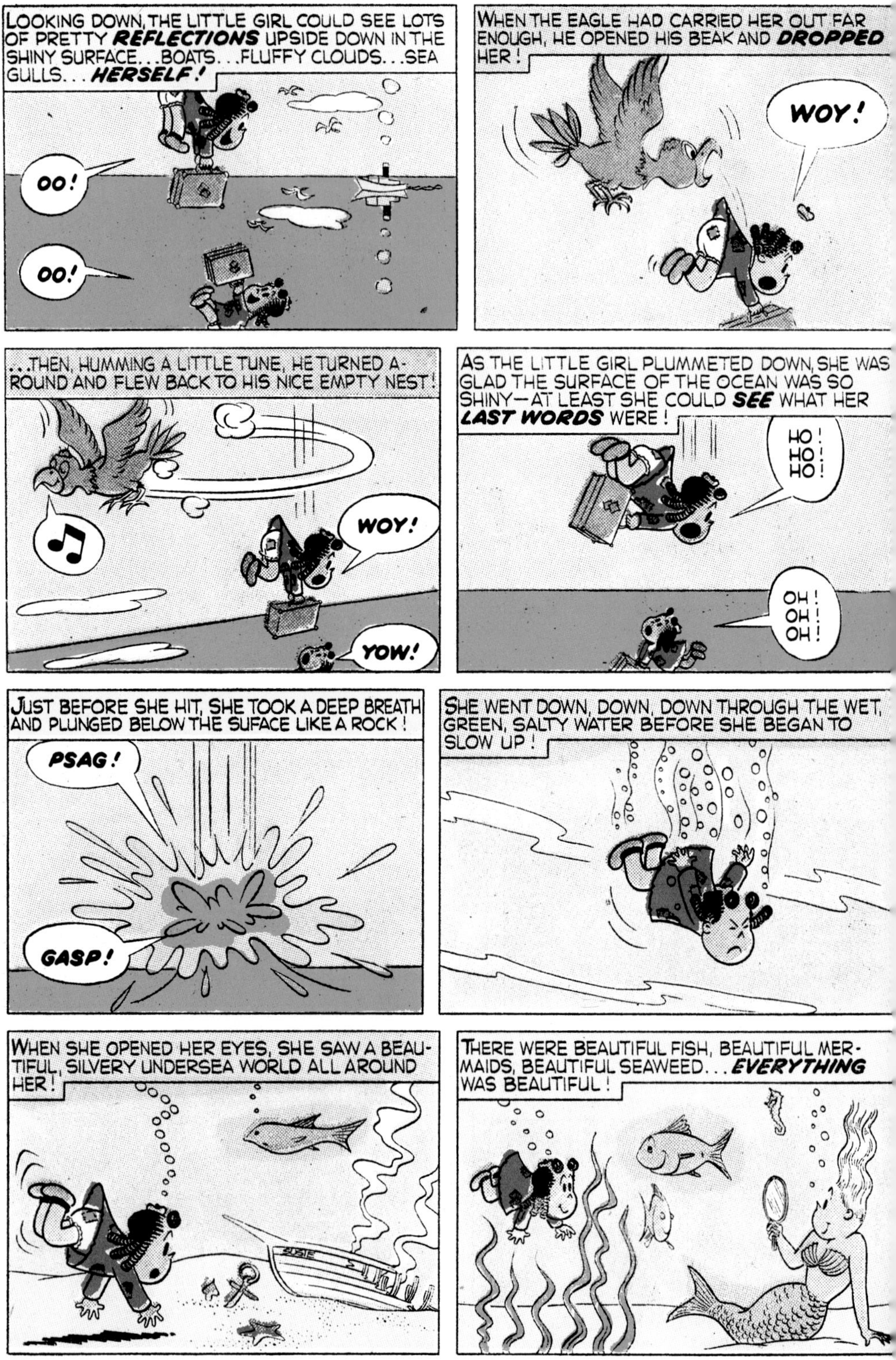
LOOKING DOWN, THE LITTLE GIRL COULD SEE LOTS OF PRETTY REFLECTIONS UPSIDE DOWN IN THE SHINY SURFACE... BOATS... FLUFFY CLOUDS... SEA GULLS... HERSELF!
OO!
OO!
WHEN THE EAGLE HAD CARRIED HER OUT FAR ENOUGH, HE OPENED HIS BEAK AND DROPPED HER!
WOY!
...THEN, HUMMING A LITTLE TUNE, HE TURNED AROUND AND FLEW BACK TO HIS NICE EMPTY NEST!
WOY!
YOW!
AS THE LITTLE GIRL PLUMMETED DOWN, SHE WAS GLAD THE SURFACE OF THE OCEAN WAS SO SHINY—AT LEAST SHE COULD SEE WHAT HER LAST WORDS WERE!
HO! HO! HO!
OH! OH! OH!
JUST BEFORE SHE HIT, SHE TOOK A DEEP BREATH AND PLUNGED BELOW THE SUFACE LIKE A ROCK!
PSAG!
GASP!
SHE WENT DOWN, DOWN, DOWN THROUGH THE WET, GREEN, SALTY WATER BEFORE SHE BEGAN TO SLOW UP!
WHEN SHE OPENED HER EYES, SHE SAW A BEAUTIFUL, SILVERY UNDERSEA WORLD ALL AROUND HER!
SUSIE
THERE WERE BEAUTIFUL FISH, BEAUTIFUL MERMAIDS, BEAUTIFUL SEAWEED... EVERYTHING WAS BEAUTIFUL!

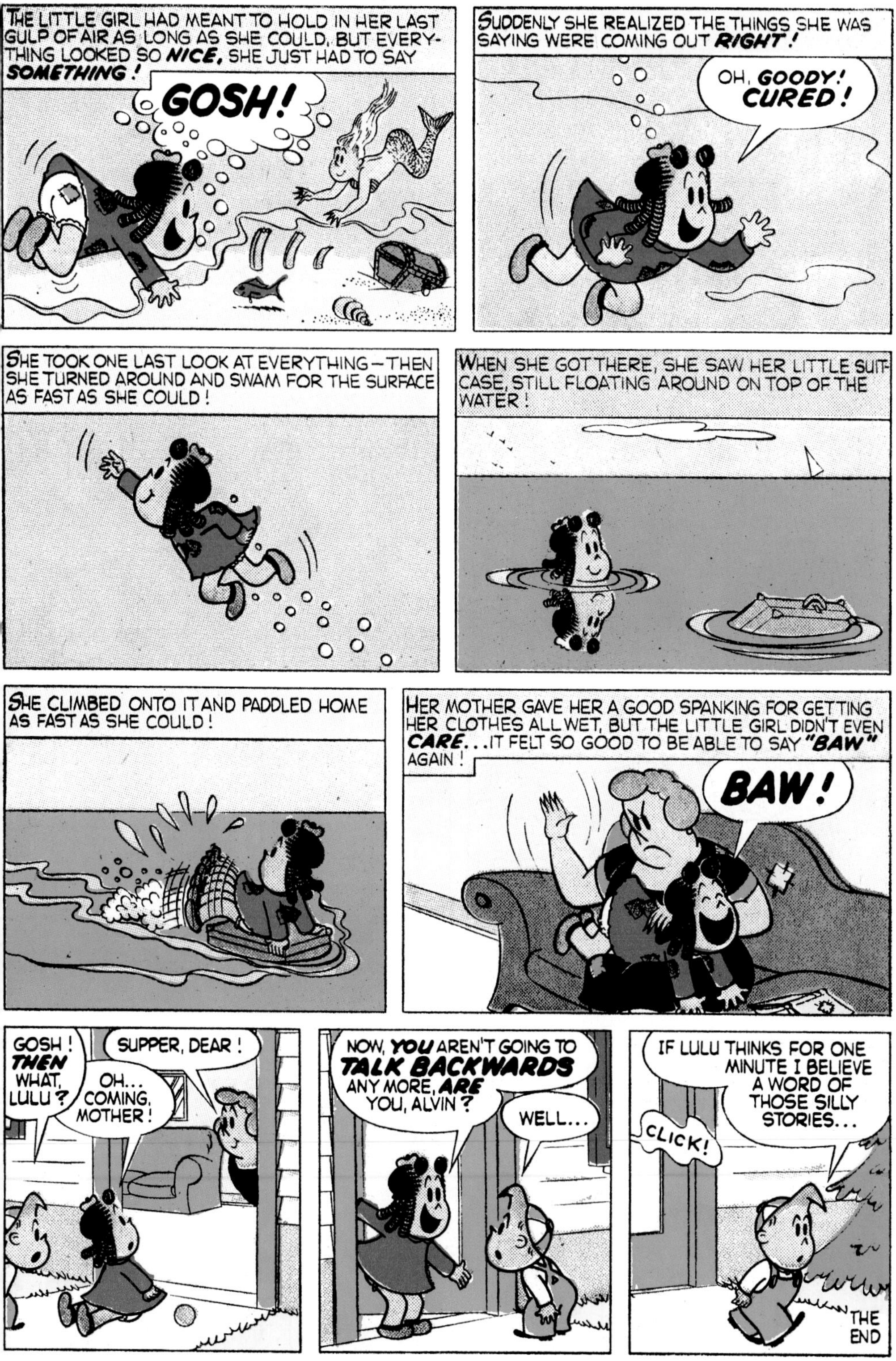
THE LITTLE GIRL HAD MEANT TO HOLD IN HER LAST GULP OF AIR AS LONG AS SHE COULD, BUT EVERYTHING LOOKED SO NICE, SHE JUST HAD TO SAY SOMETHING!
GOSH!
SUDDENLY SHE REALIZED THE THINGS SHE WAS SAYING WERE COMING OUT RIGHT!
OH, GOODY! CURED!
SHE TOOK ONE LAST LOOK AT EVERYTHING—THEN SHE TURNED AROUND AND SWAM FOR THE SURFACE AS FAST AS SHE COULD!
WHEN SHE GOT THERE, SHE SAW HER LITTLE SUITCASE, STILL FLOATING AROUND ON TOP OF THE WATER!
SHE CLIMBED ONTO IT AND PADDLED HOME AS FAST AS SHE COULD!
HER MOTHER GAVE HER A GOOD SPANKING FOR GETTING HER CLOTHES ALL WET, BUT THE LITTLE GIRL DIDN'T EVEN CARE...IT FELT SO GOOD TO BE ABLE TO SAY "BAW" AGAIN!
BAW!
GOSH! THEN WHAT, LULU?
SUPPER, DEAR!
OH... COMING, MOTHER!
NOW, YOU AREN'T GOING TO TALK BACKWARDS ANY MORE, ARE YOU, ALVIN?
WELL...
IF LULU THINKS FOR ONE MINUTE I BELIEVE A WORD OF THOSE SILLY STORIES...
CLICK!
THE END

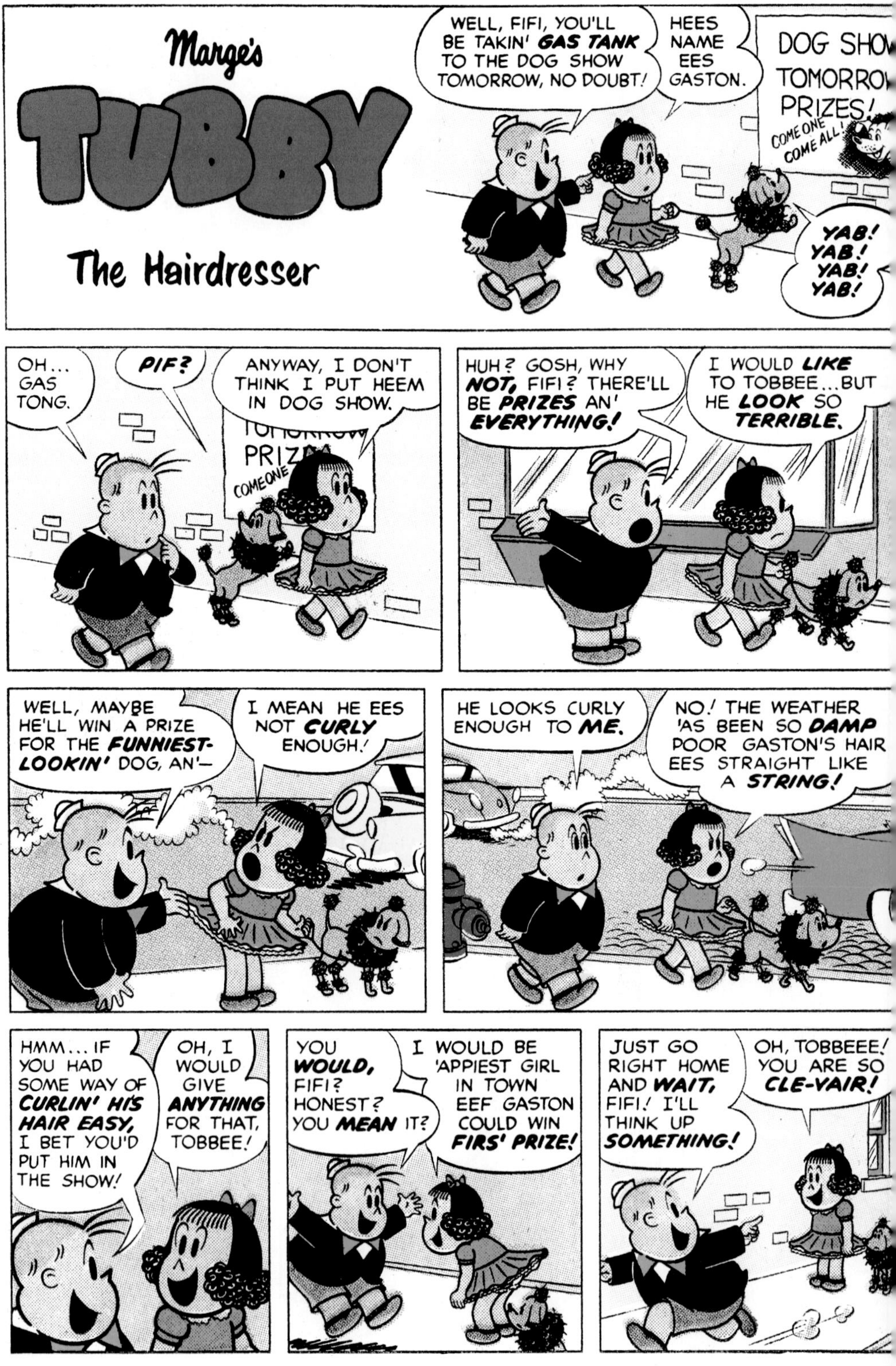
Marge's
TUBBY
The Hairdresser
WELL, FIFI, YOU'LL BE TAKIN' GAS TANK TO THE DOG SHOW TOMORROW, NO DOUBT!
HEES NAME EES GASTON.
DOG SHOW TOMORROW PRIZES! COME ONE COME ALL!
YAB! YAB! YAB! YAB!
OH... GAS TONG.
PIF?
ANYWAY, I DON'T THINK I PUT HEEM IN DOG SHOW.
HUH? GOSH, WHY NOT, FIFI? THERE'LL BE PRIZES AN' EVERYTHING!
I WOULD LIKE TO TOBBEE...BUT HE LOOK SO TERRIBLE.
WELL, MAYBE HE'LL WIN A PRIZE FOR THE FUNNIEST-LOOKIN' DOG, AN'—
I MEAN HE EES NOT CURLY ENOUGH!
HE LOOKS CURLY ENOUGH TO ME.
NO! THE WEATHER 'AS BEEN SO DAMP POOR GASTON'S HAIR EES STRAIGHT LIKE A STRING!
HMM... IF YOU HAD SOME WAY OF CURLIN' HIS HAIR EASY, I BET YOU'D PUT HIM IN THE SHOW!
OH, I WOULD GIVE ANYTHING FOR THAT, TOBBEE!
YOU WOULD, FIFI? HONEST? YOU MEAN IT?
I WOULD BE 'APPIEST GIRL IN TOWN EEF GASTON COULD WIN FIRS' PRIZE!
JUST GO RIGHT HOME AND WAIT, FIFI! I'LL THINK UP SOMETHING!
OH, TOBBEEE! YOU ARE SO CLE-VAIR!

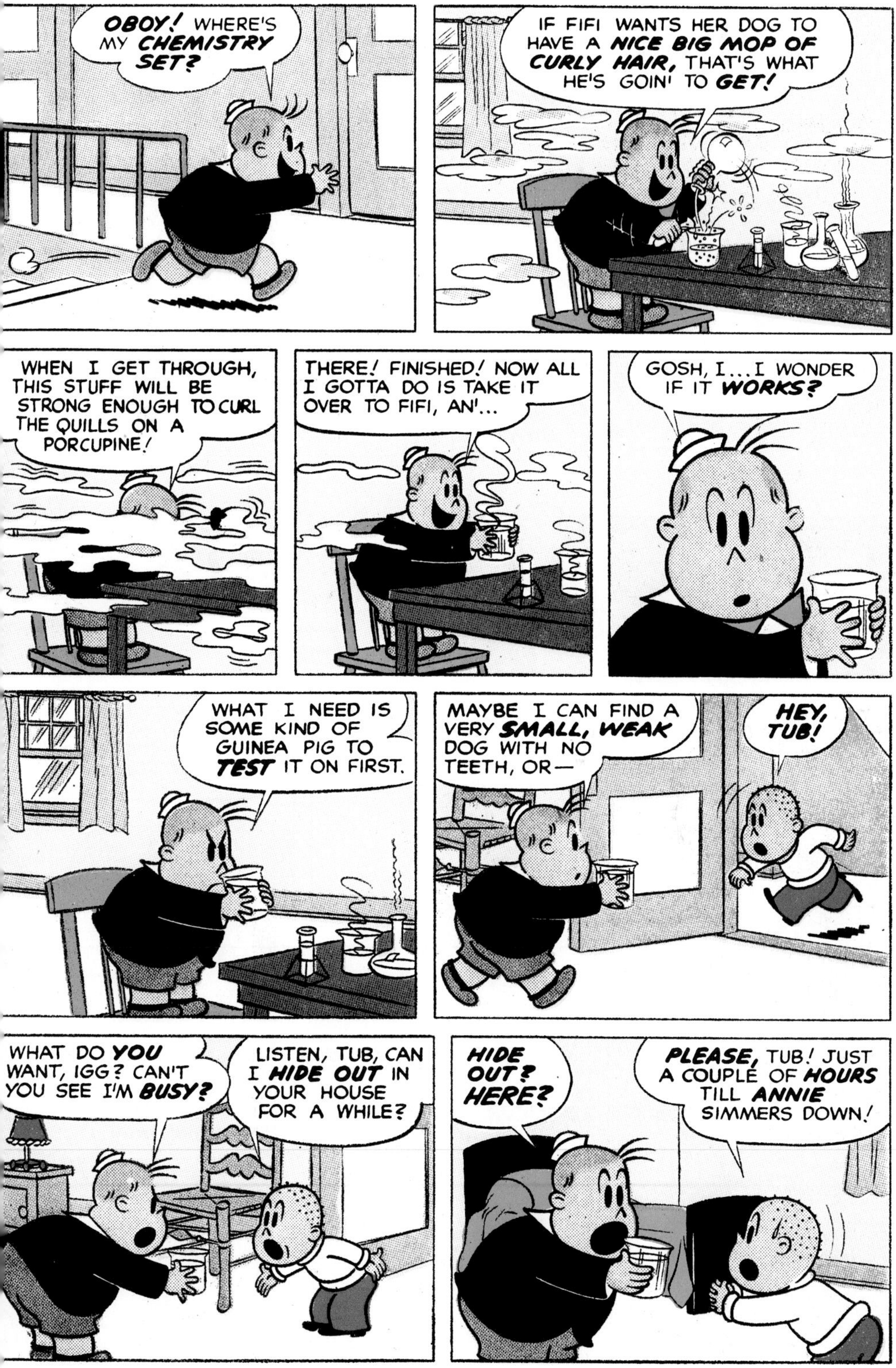
OBOY! WHERE'S MY CHEMISTRY SET?
IF FIFI WANTS HER DOG TO HAVE A NICE BIG MOP OF CURLY HAIR, THAT'S WHAT HE'S GOIN' TO GET!
WHEN I GET THROUGH, THIS STUFF WILL BE STRONG ENOUGH TO CURL THE QUILLS ON A PORCUPINE!
THERE! FINISHED! NOW ALL I GOTTA DO IS TAKE IT OVER TO FIFI, AN'...
GOSH, I...I WONDER IF IT WORKS?
WHAT I NEED IS SOME KIND OF GUINEA PIG TO TEST IT ON FIRST.
MAYBE I CAN FIND A VERY SMALL, WEAK DOG WITH NO TEETH, OR—
HEY, TUB!
WHAT DO YOU WANT, IGG? CAN'T YOU SEE I'M BUSY?
LISTEN, TUB, CAN I HIDE OUT IN YOUR HOUSE FOR A WHILE?
HIDE OUT? HERE?
PLEASE, TUB! JUST A COUPLE OF HOURS TILL ANNIE SIMMERS DOWN!

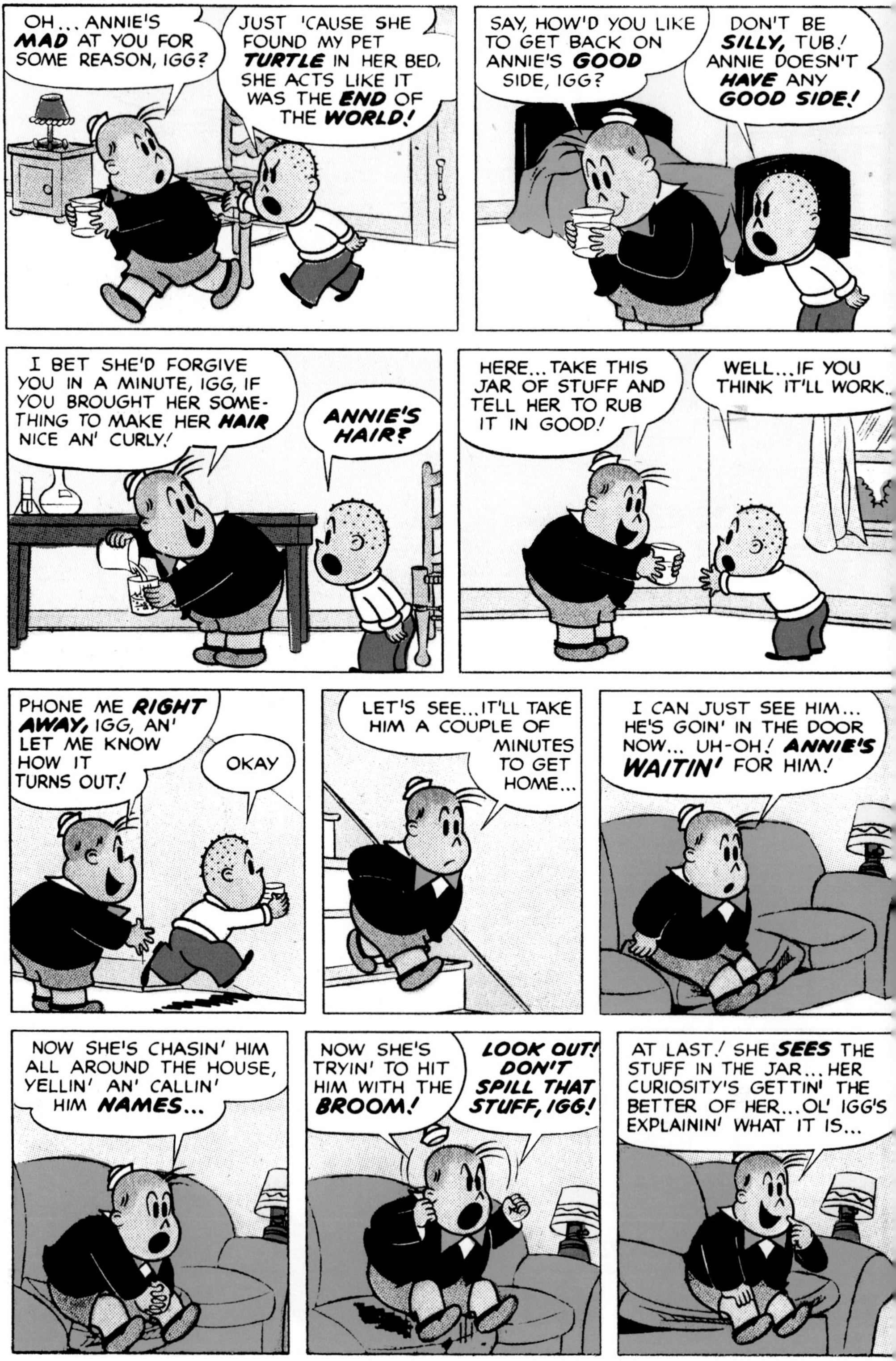
OH... ANNIE'S MAD AT YOU FOR SOME REASON, IGG?
JUST 'CAUSE SHE FOUND MY PET TURTLE IN HER BED, SHE ACTS LIKE IT WAS THE END OF THE WORLD!
SAY, HOW'D YOU LIKE TO GET BACK ON ANNIE'S GOOD SIDE, IGG?
DON'T BE SILLY, TUB! ANNIE DOESN'T HAVE ANY GOOD SIDE!
I BET SHE'D FORGIVE YOU IN A MINUTE, IGG, IF YOU BROUGHT HER SOMETHING TO MAKE HER HAIR NICE AN' CURLY!
ANNIE'S HAIR?
HERE... TAKE THIS JAR OF STUFF AND TELL HER TO RUB IT IN GOOD!
WELL... IF YOU THINK IT'LL WORK...
PHONE ME RIGHT AWAY, IGG, AN' LET ME KNOW HOW IT TURNS OUT!
OKAY
LET'S SEE... IT'LL TAKE HIM A COUPLE OF MINUTES TO GET HOME...
I CAN JUST SEE HIM... HE'S GOIN' IN THE DOOR NOW... UH-OH! ANNIE'S WAITIN' FOR HIM!
NOW SHE'S CHASIN' HIM ALL AROUND THE HOUSE, YELLIN' AN' CALLIN' HIM NAMES...
NOW SHE'S TRYIN' TO HIT HIM WITH THE BROOM!
LOOK OUT! DON'T SPILL THAT STUFF, IGG!
AT LAST! SHE SEES THE STUFF IN THE JAR... HER CURIOSITY'S GETTIN' THE BETTER OF HER... OL' IGG'S EXPLAININ' WHAT IT IS...

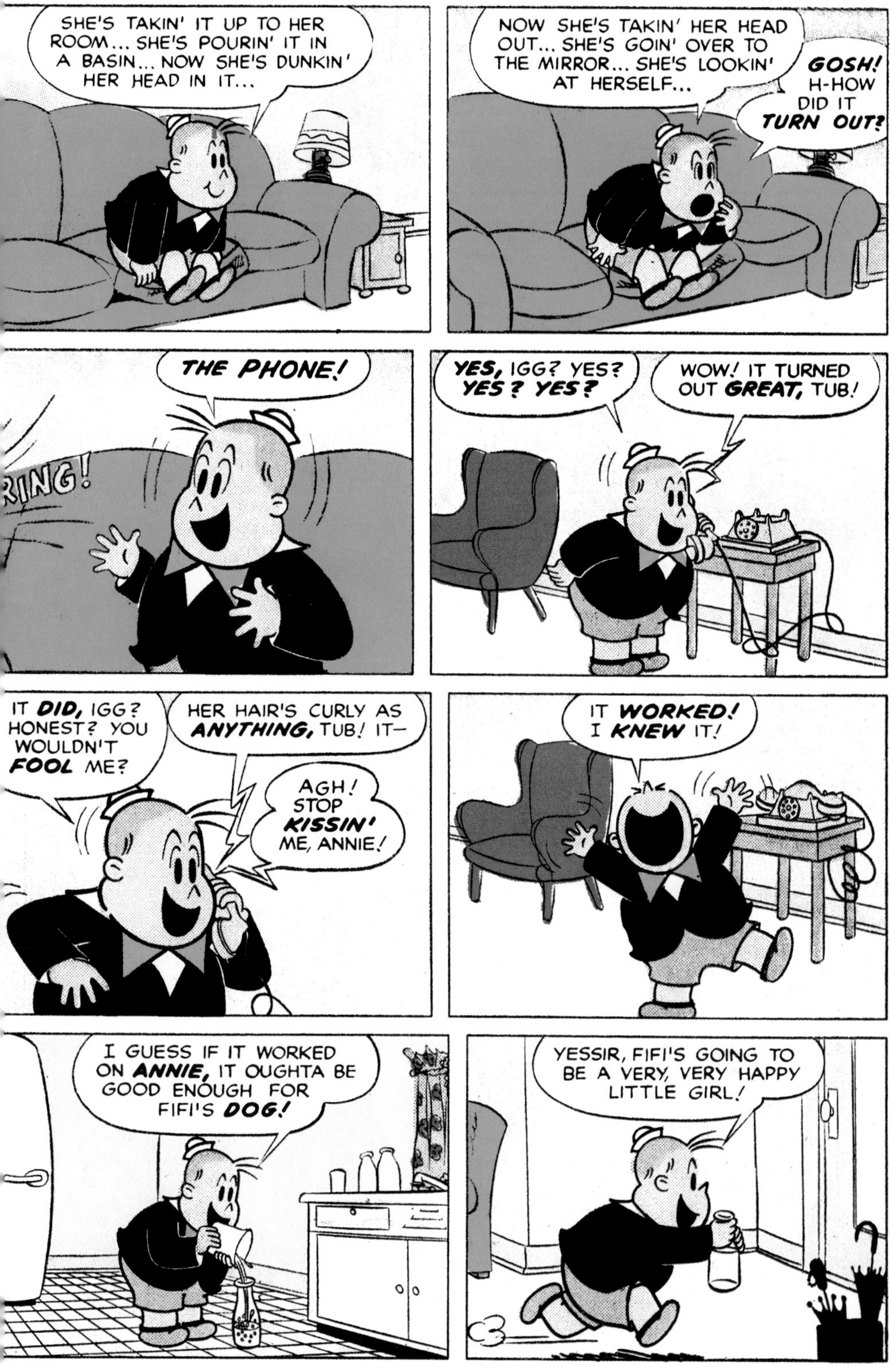
SHE'S TAKIN' IT UP TO HER ROOM... SHE'S POURIN' IT IN A BASIN... NOW SHE'S DUNKIN' HER HEAD IN IT...
NOW SHE'S TAKIN' HER HEAD OUT... SHE'S GOIN' OVER TO THE MIRROR... SHE'S LOOKIN' AT HERSELF...
GOSH! H-HOW DID IT TURN OUT?
RING!
THE PHONE!
YES, IGG? YES? YES? YES?
WOW! IT TURNED OUT GREAT, TUB!
IT DID, IGG? HONEST? YOU WOULDN'T FOOL ME?
HER HAIR'S CURLY AS ANYTHING, TUB! IT—
AGH! STOP KISSIN' ME, ANNIE!
IT WORKED! I KNEW IT!
I GUESS IF IT WORKED ON ANNIE, IT OUGHTA BE GOOD ENOUGH FOR FIFI'S DOG!
YESSIR, FIFI'S GOING TO BE A VERY, VERY HAPPY LITTLE GIRL!

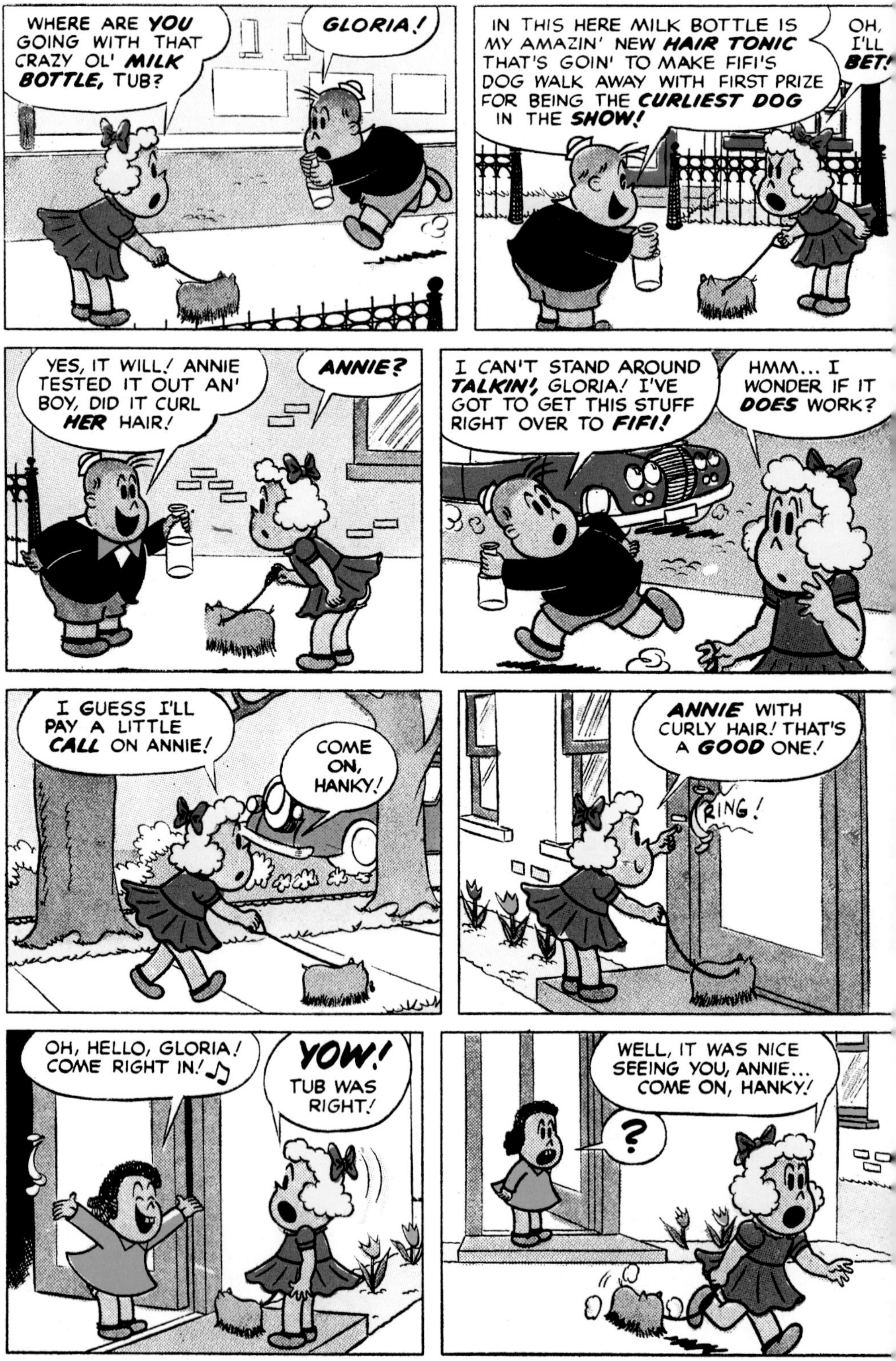

WHERE ARE YOU GOING WITH THAT CRAZY OL' MILK BOTTLE, TUB?
GLORIA!
IN THIS HERE MILK BOTTLE IS MY AMAZIN' NEW HAIR TONIC THAT'S GOIN' TO MAKE FIFI'S DOG WALK AWAY WITH FIRST PRIZE FOR BEING THE CURLIEST DOG IN THE SHOW!
OH, I'LL BET!
YES, IT WILL! ANNIE TESTED IT OUT AN' BOY, DID IT CURL HER HAIR!
ANNIE?
I CAN'T STAND AROUND TALKIN', GLORIA! I'VE GOT TO GET THIS STUFF RIGHT OVER TO FIFI!
HMM... I WONDER IF IT DOES WORK?
I GUESS I'LL PAY A LITTLE CALL ON ANNIE!
COME ON, HANKY!
ANNIE WITH CURLY HAIR! THAT'S A GOOD ONE!
RING!
OH, HELLO, GLORIA! COME RIGHT IN!
YOW! TUB WAS RIGHT!
WELL, IT WAS NICE SEEING YOU, ANNIE... COME ON, HANKY!
?

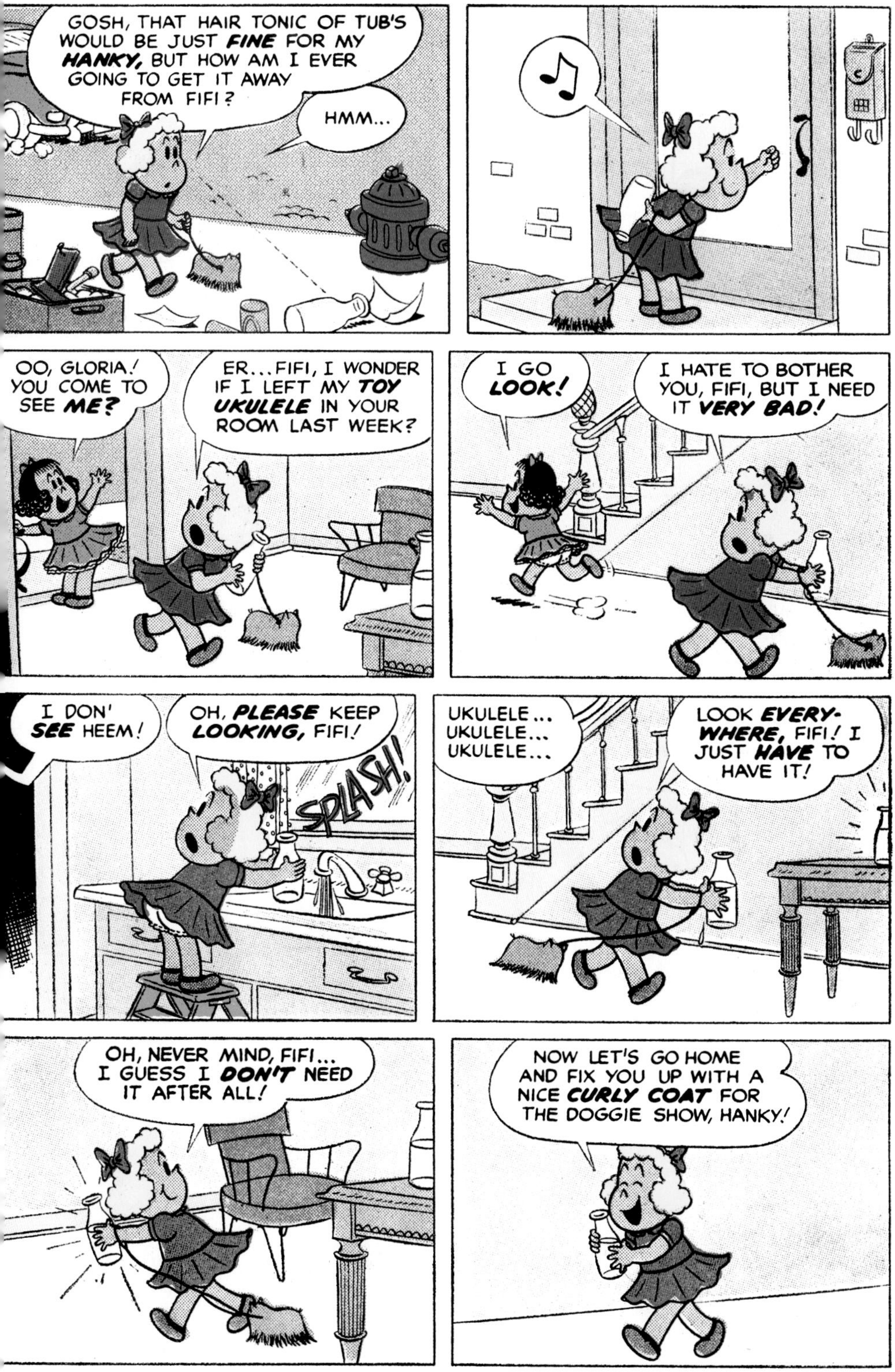
GOSH, THAT HAIR TONIC OF TUB'S WOULD BE JUST FINE FOR MY HANKY, BUT HOW AM I EVER GOING TO GET IT AWAY FROM FIFI?
HMM...
OO, GLORIA! YOU COME TO SEE ME?
ER...FIFI, I WONDER IF I LEFT MY TOY UKULELE IN YOUR ROOM LAST WEEK?
I GO LOOK!
I HATE TO BOTHER YOU, FIFI, BUT I NEED IT VERY BAD!
I DON' SEE HEEM!
OH, PLEASE KEEP LOOKING, FIFI!
SPLASH!
UKULELE... UKULELE... UKULELE...
LOOK EVERY-WHERE, FIFI! I JUST HAVE TO HAVE IT!
OH, NEVER MIND, FIFI... I GUESS I DON'T NEED IT AFTER ALL!
NOW LET'S GO HOME AND FIX YOU UP WITH A NICE CURLY COAT FOR THE DOGGIE SHOW, HANKY!

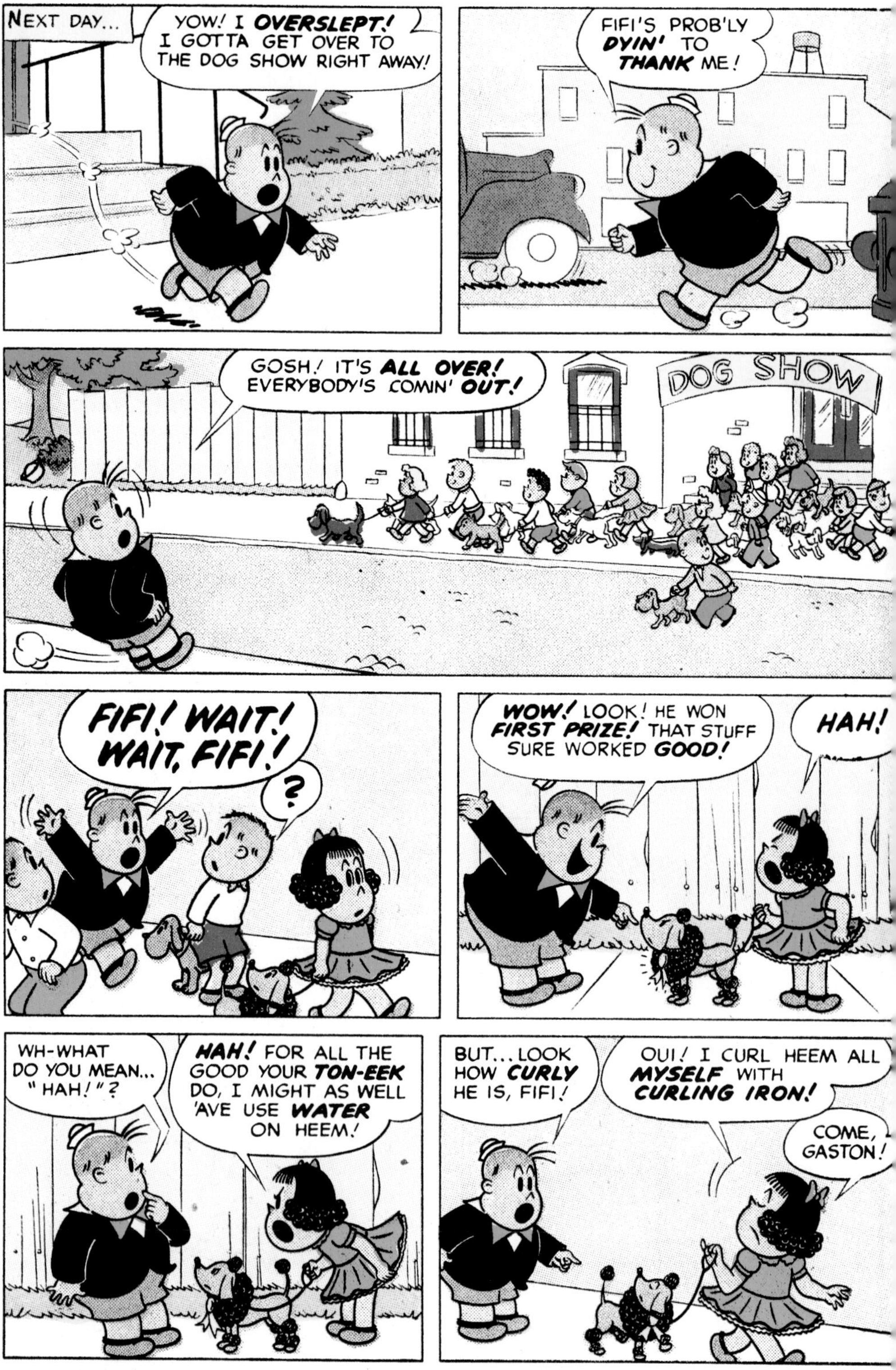
NEXT DAY...
YOW! I OVERSLEPT! I GOTTA GET OVER TO THE DOG SHOW RIGHT AWAY!
FIFI'S PROB'LY DYIN' TO THANK ME!
GOSH! IT'S ALL OVER! EVERYBODY'S COMIN' OUT!
DOG SHOW
FIFI! WAIT! WAIT, FIFI!
?
WOW! LOOK! HE WON FIRST PRIZE! THAT STUFF SURE WORKED GOOD!
HAH!
WH-WHAT DO YOU MEAN... "HAH!"?
HAH! FOR ALL THE GOOD YOUR TON-EEK DO, I MIGHT AS WELL 'AVE USE WATER ON HEEM!
BUT... LOOK HOW CURLY HE IS, FIFI!
OUI! I CURL HEEM ALL MYSELF WITH CURLING IRON!
COME, GASTON!

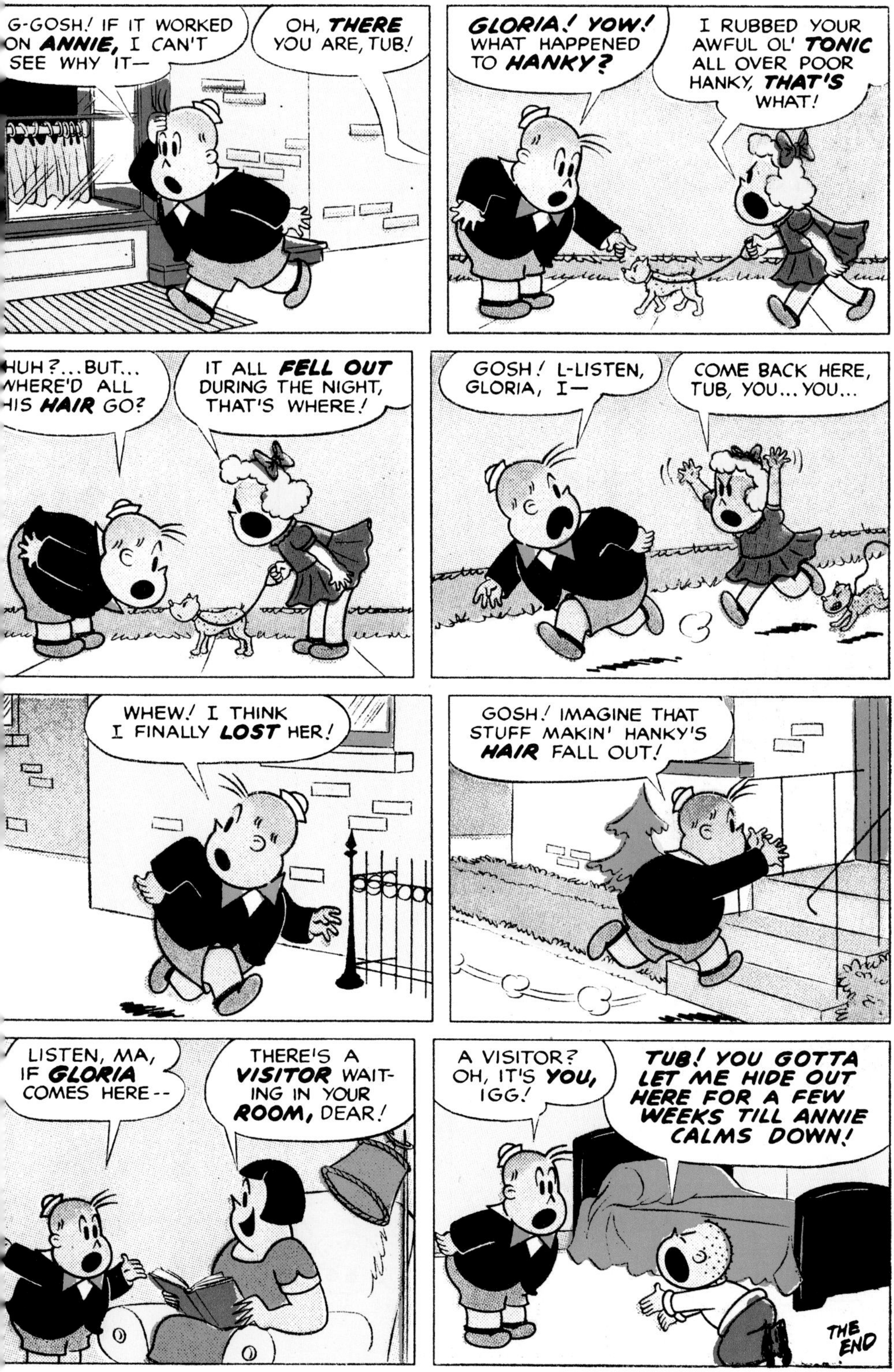
G-GOSH! IF IT WORKED ON ANNIE, I CAN'T SEE WHY IT—
OH, THERE YOU ARE, TUB!
GLORIA! YOW! WHAT HAPPENED TO HANKY?
I RUBBED YOUR AWFUL OL' TONIC ALL OVER POOR HANKY, THAT'S WHAT!
HUH?...BUT... WHERE'D ALL HIS HAIR GO?
IT ALL FELL OUT DURING THE NIGHT, THAT'S WHERE!
GOSH! L-LISTEN, GLORIA, I—
COME BACK HERE, TUB, YOU...YOU...
WHEW! I THINK I FINALLY LOST HER!
GOSH! IMAGINE THAT STUFF MAKIN' HANKY'S HAIR FALL OUT!
LISTEN, MA, IF GLORIA COMES HERE--
THERE'S A VISITOR WAIT-ING IN YOUR ROOM, DEAR!
A VISITOR? OH, IT'S YOU, IGG!
TUB! YOU GOTTA LET ME HIDE OUT HERE FOR A FEW WEEKS TILL ANNIE CALMS DOWN!
THE END

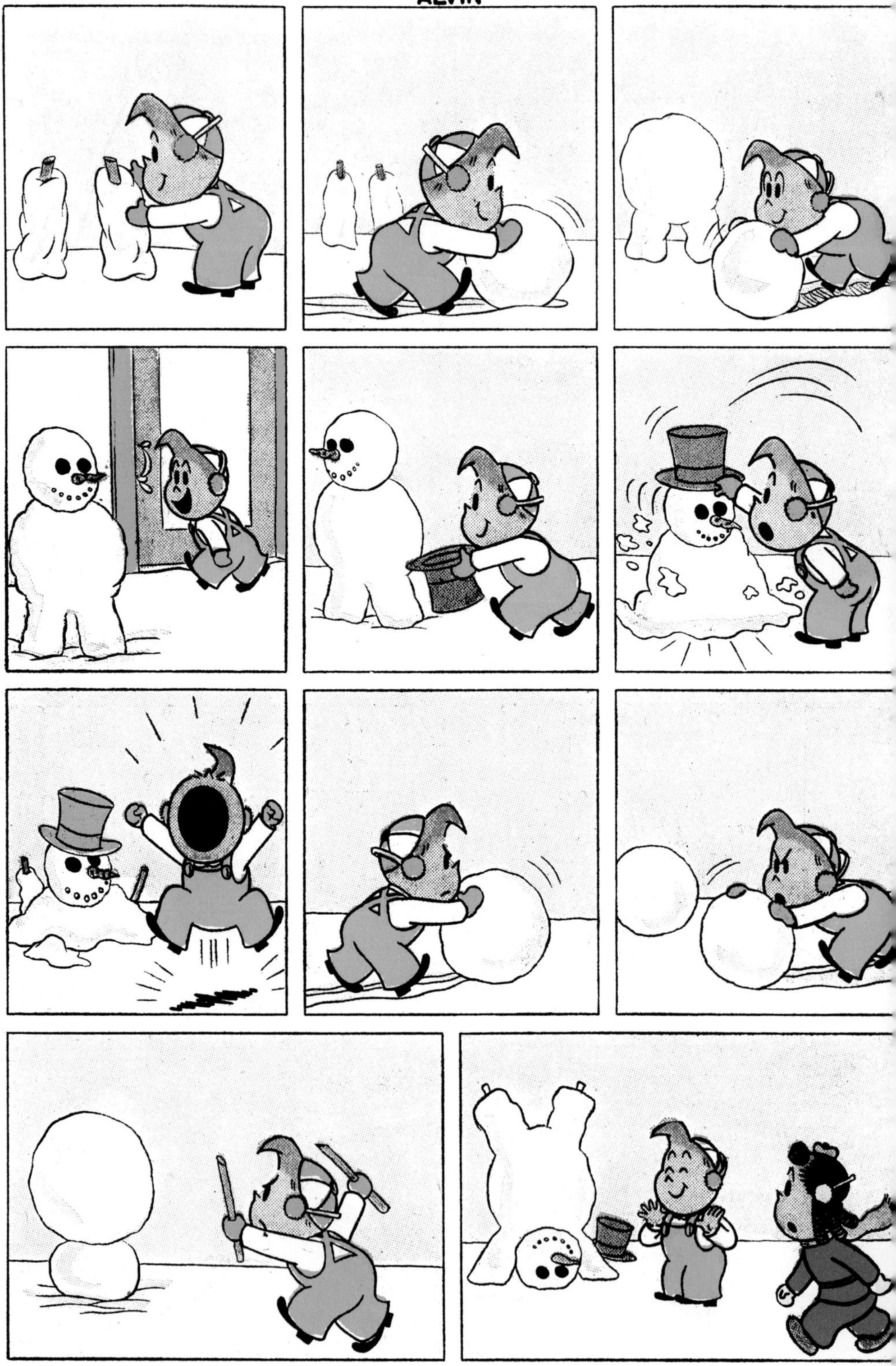

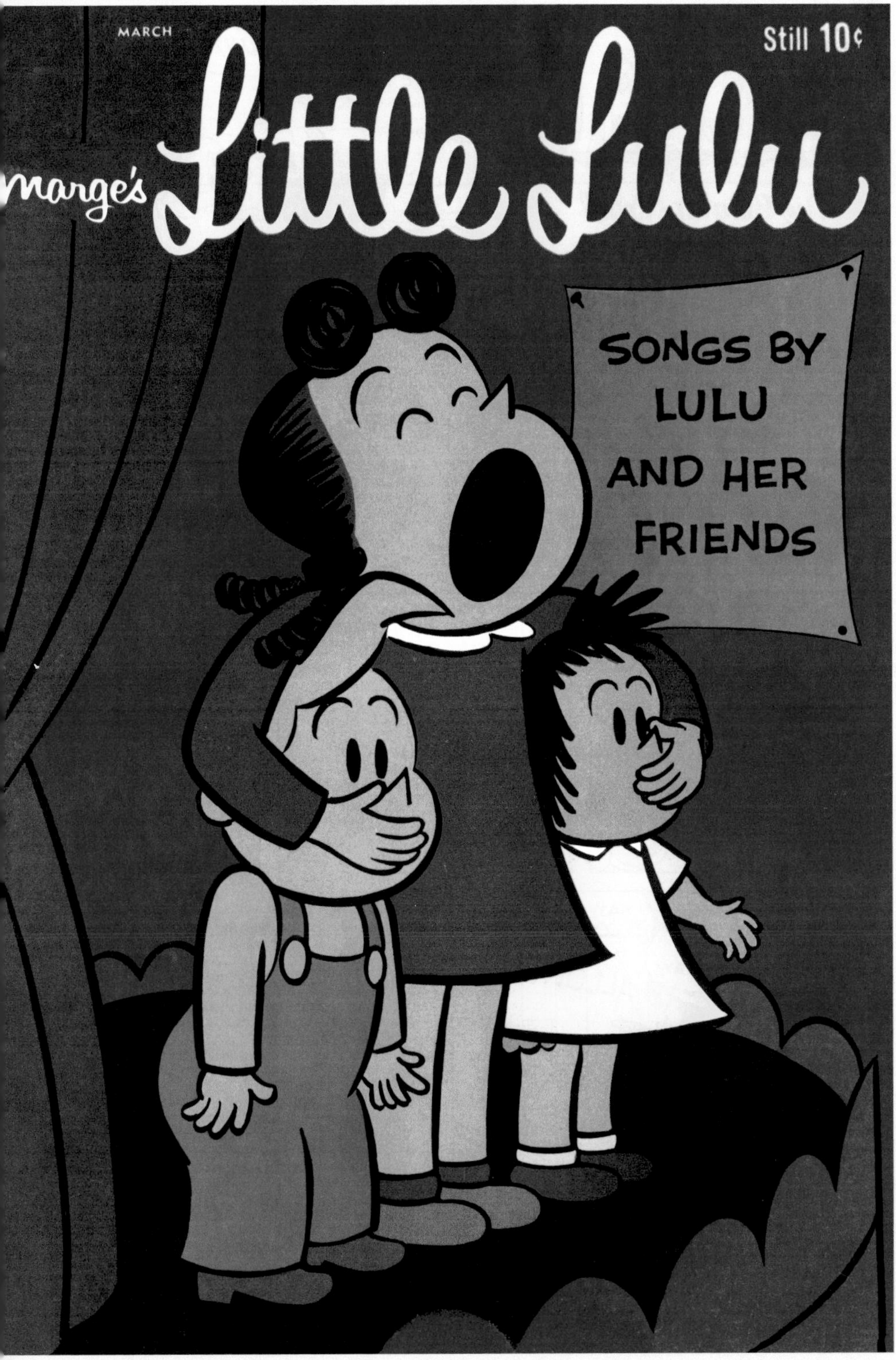
MARCH
Still 10¢
marge's Little Lulu
SONGS BY LULU AND HER FRIENDS

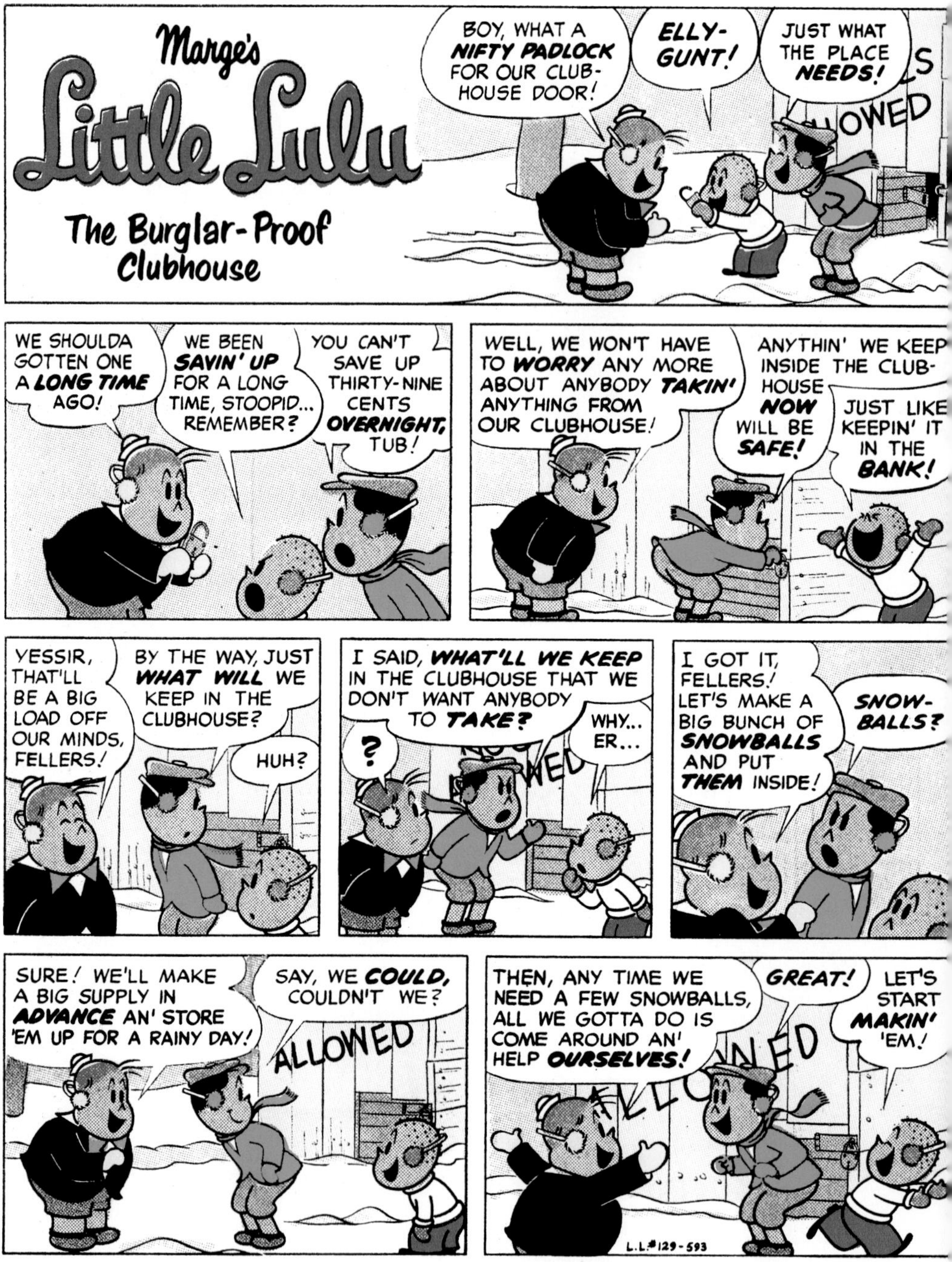
Marge's
Little Lulu
The Burglar-Proof Clubhouse
BOY, WHAT A NIFTY PADLOCK FOR OUR CLUBHOUSE DOOR!
ELLY-GUNT!
JUST WHAT THE PLACE NEEDS!
WE SHOULDA GOTTEN ONE A LONG TIME AGO!
WE BEEN SAVIN' UP FOR A LONG TIME, STOOPID... REMEMBER?
YOU CAN'T SAVE UP THIRTY-NINE CENTS OVERNIGHT, TUB!
WELL, WE WON'T HAVE TO WORRY ANY MORE ABOUT ANYBODY TAKIN' ANYTHING FROM OUR CLUBHOUSE!
ANYTHIN' WE KEEP INSIDE THE CLUBHOUSE NOW WILL BE SAFE!
JUST LIKE KEEPIN' IT IN THE BANK!
YESSIR, THAT'LL BE A BIG LOAD OFF OUR MINDS, FELLERS!
BY THE WAY, JUST WHAT WILL WE KEEP IN THE CLUBHOUSE?
HUH?
I SAID, WHAT'LL WE KEEP IN THE CLUBHOUSE THAT WE DON'T WANT ANYBODY TO TAKE?
?
WHY... ER...
I GOT IT, FELLERS! LET'S MAKE A BIG BUNCH OF SNOWBALLS AND PUT THEM INSIDE!
SNOW-BALLS?
SURE! WE'LL MAKE A BIG SUPPLY IN ADVANCE AN' STORE 'EM UP FOR A RAINY DAY!
SAY, WE COULD, COULDN'T WE?
ALLOWED
THEN, ANY TIME WE NEED A FEW SNOWBALLS, ALL WE GOTTA DO IS COME AROUND AN' HELP OURSELVES!
GREAT!
LET'S START MAKIN' 'EM!
L.L.#129-593

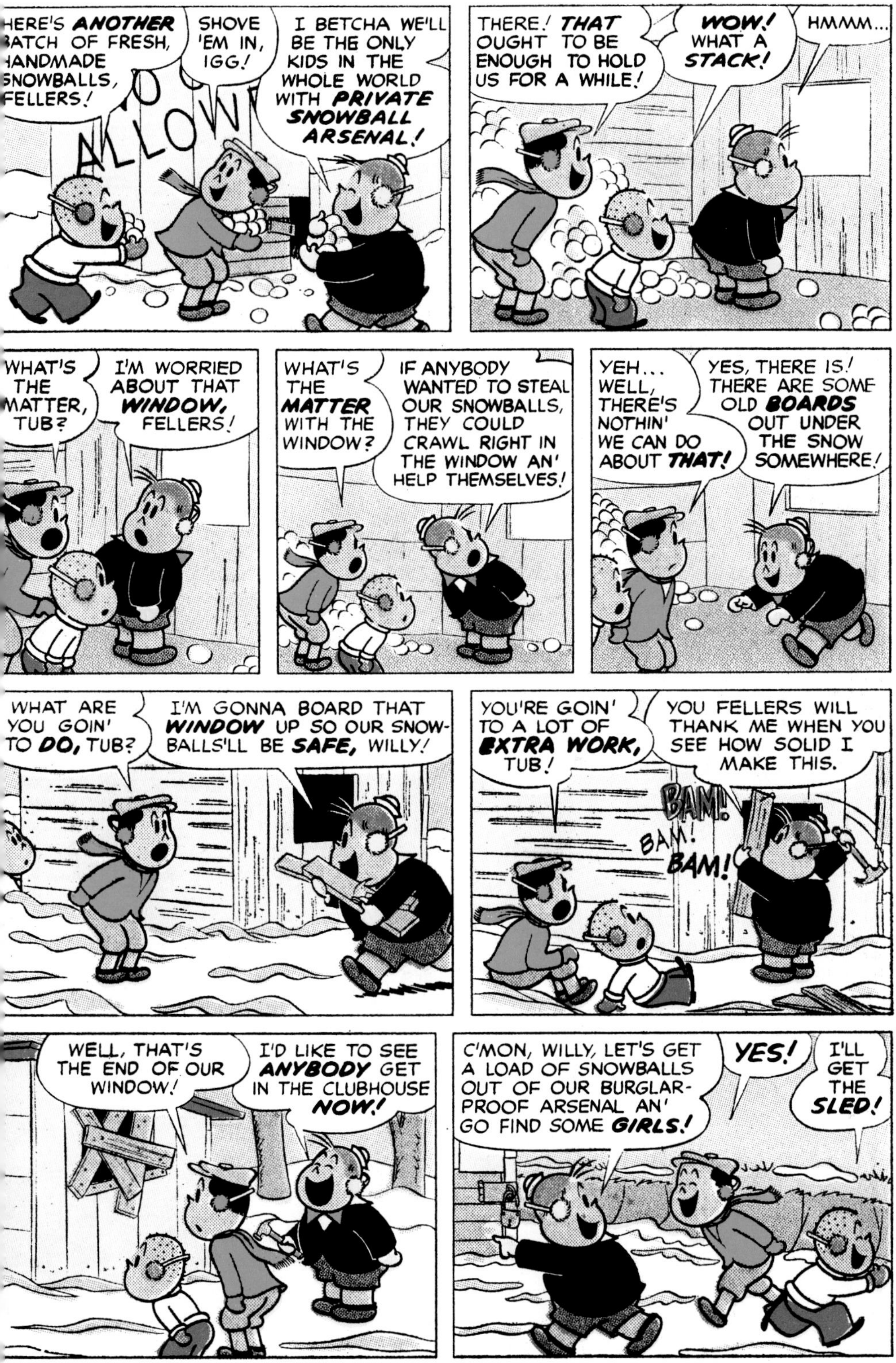
HERE'S ANOTHER BATCH OF FRESH, HANDMADE SNOWBALLS, FELLERS!
SHOVE 'EM IN, IGG!
I BETCHA WE'LL BE THE ONLY KIDS IN THE WHOLE WORLD WITH PRIVATE SNOWBALL ARSENAL!
THERE! THAT OUGHT TO BE ENOUGH TO HOLD US FOR A WHILE!
WOW! WHAT A STACK!
HMMM...
WHAT'S THE MATTER, TUB?
I'M WORRIED ABOUT THAT WINDOW, FELLERS!
WHAT'S THE MATTER WITH THE WINDOW?
IF ANYBODY WANTED TO STEAL OUR SNOWBALLS, THEY COULD CRAWL RIGHT IN THE WINDOW AN' HELP THEMSELVES!
YEH... WELL, THERE'S NOTHIN' WE CAN DO ABOUT THAT!
YES, THERE IS! THERE ARE SOME OLD BOARDS OUT UNDER THE SNOW SOMEWHERE!
WHAT ARE YOU GOIN' TO DO, TUB?
I'M GONNA BOARD THAT WINDOW UP SO OUR SNOW-BALLS'LL BE SAFE, WILLY!
YOU'RE GOIN' TO A LOT OF EXTRA WORK, TUB!
YOU FELLERS WILL THANK ME WHEN YOU SEE HOW SOLID I MAKE THIS.
BAM! BAM! BAM!
WELL, THAT'S THE END OF OUR WINDOW!
I'D LIKE TO SEE ANYBODY GET IN THE CLUBHOUSE NOW!
C'MON, WILLY, LET'S GET A LOAD OF SNOWBALLS OUT OF OUR BURGLAR-PROOF ARSENAL AN' GO FIND SOME GIRLS!
YES!
I'LL GET THE SLED!

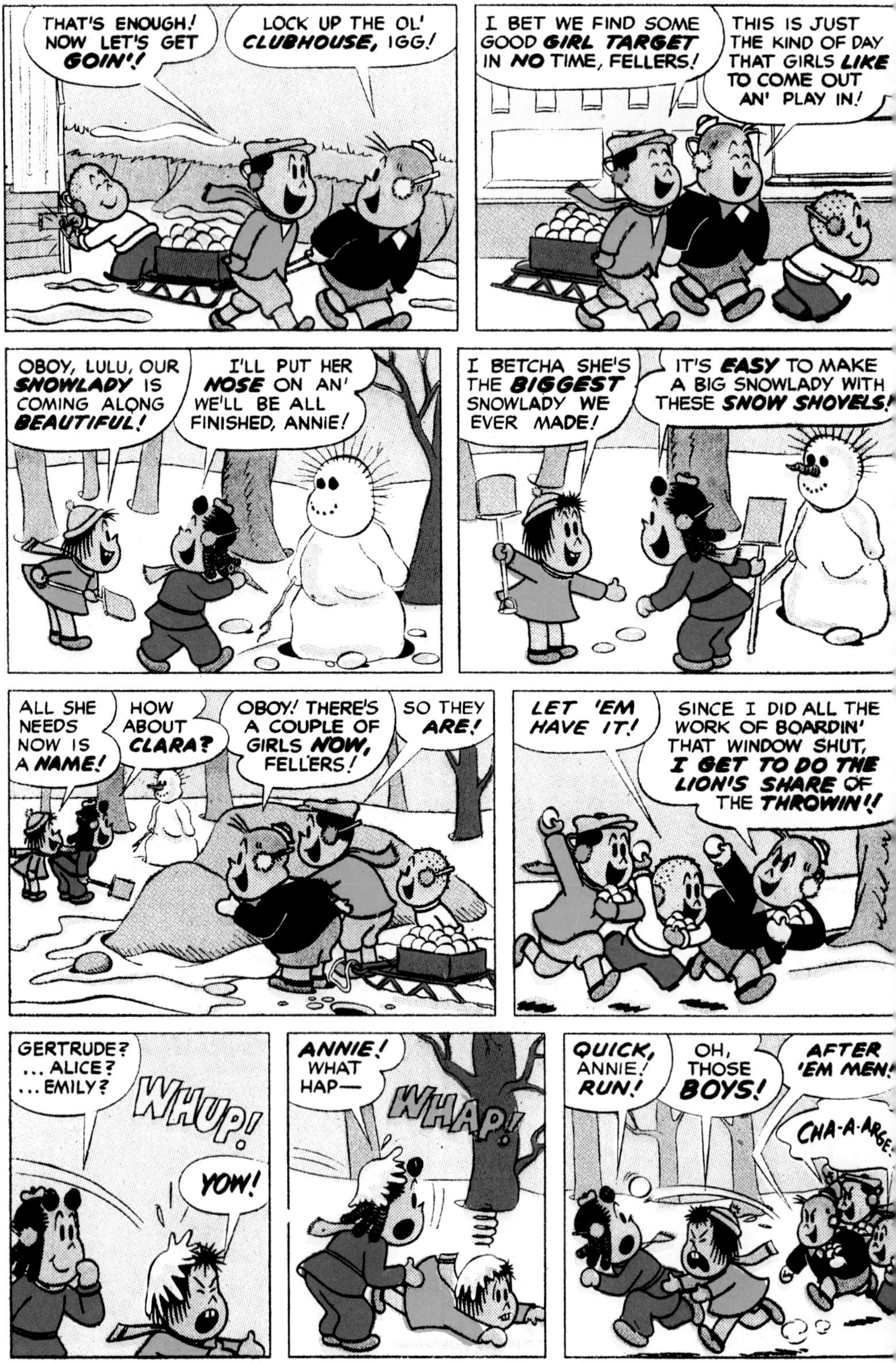

THAT'S ENOUGH! NOW LET'S GET GOIN'!
LOCK UP THE OL' CLUBHOUSE, IGG!
I BET WE FIND SOME GOOD GIRL TARGET IN NO TIME, FELLERS!
THIS IS JUST THE KIND OF DAY THAT GIRLS LIKE TO COME OUT AN' PLAY IN!
OBOY, LULU, OUR SNOWLADY IS COMING ALONG BEAUTIFUL!
I'LL PUT HER NOSE ON AN' WE'LL BE ALL FINISHED, ANNIE!
I BETCHA SHE'S THE BIGGEST SNOWLADY WE EVER MADE!
IT'S EASY TO MAKE A BIG SNOWLADY WITH THESE SNOW SHOVELS!
ALL SHE NEEDS NOW IS A NAME!
HOW ABOUT CLARA?
OBOY! THERE'S A COUPLE OF GIRLS NOW, FELLERS!
SO THEY ARE!
LET 'EM HAVE IT!
SINCE I DID ALL THE WORK OF BOARDIN' THAT WINDOW SHUT, I GET TO DO THE LION'S SHARE OF THE THROWIN'!!
GERTRUDE? ...ALICE? ...EMILY?
WHUP!
YOW!
ANNIE! WHAT HAP—
WHAP!
QUICK, ANNIE! RUN!
OH, THOSE BOYS!
AFTER 'EM MEN!
CHA-A-ARGE!

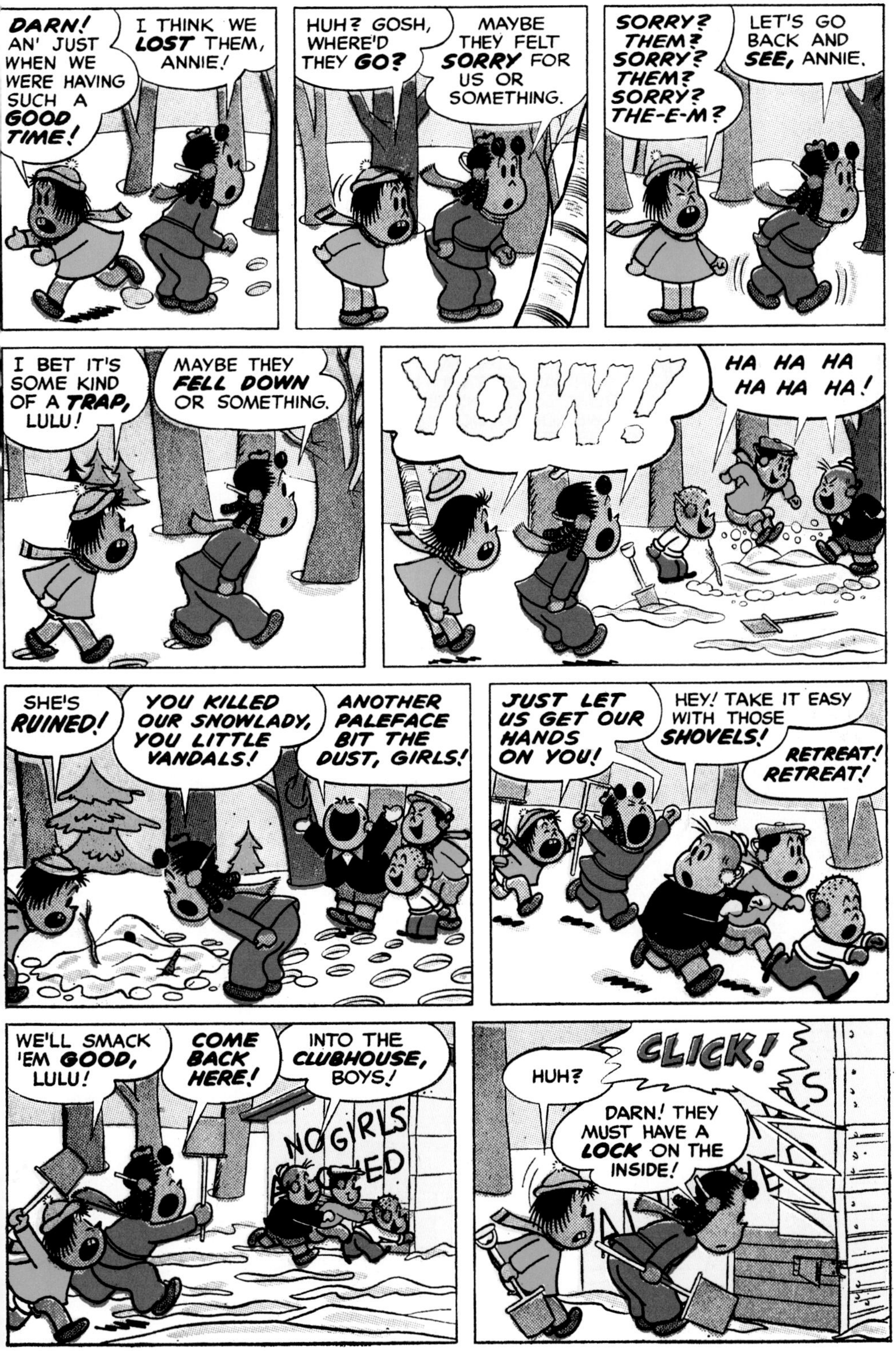

DARN! AN' JUST WHEN WE WERE HAVING SUCH A GOOD TIME!
I THINK WE LOST THEM, ANNIE!
HUH? GOSH, WHERE'D THEY GO?
MAYBE THEY FELT SORRY FOR US OR SOMETHING.
SORRY? THEM? SORRY? THEM? SORRY? THE-E-M?
LET'S GO BACK AND SEE, ANNIE.
I BET IT'S SOME KIND OF A TRAP, LULU!
MAYBE THEY FELL DOWN OR SOMETHING.
YOW!
HA HA HA HA HA HA!
SHE'S RUINED!
YOU KILLED OUR SNOWLADY, YOU LITTLE VANDALS!
ANOTHER PALEFACE BIT THE DUST, GIRLS!
JUST LET US GET OUR HANDS ON YOU!
HEY! TAKE IT EASY WITH THOSE SHOVELS!
RETREAT! RETREAT!
WE'LL SMACK 'EM GOOD, LULU!
COME BACK HERE!
INTO THE CLUBHOUSE, BOYS!
NO GIRLS
HUH?
CLICK!
DARN! THEY MUST HAVE A LOCK ON THE INSIDE!

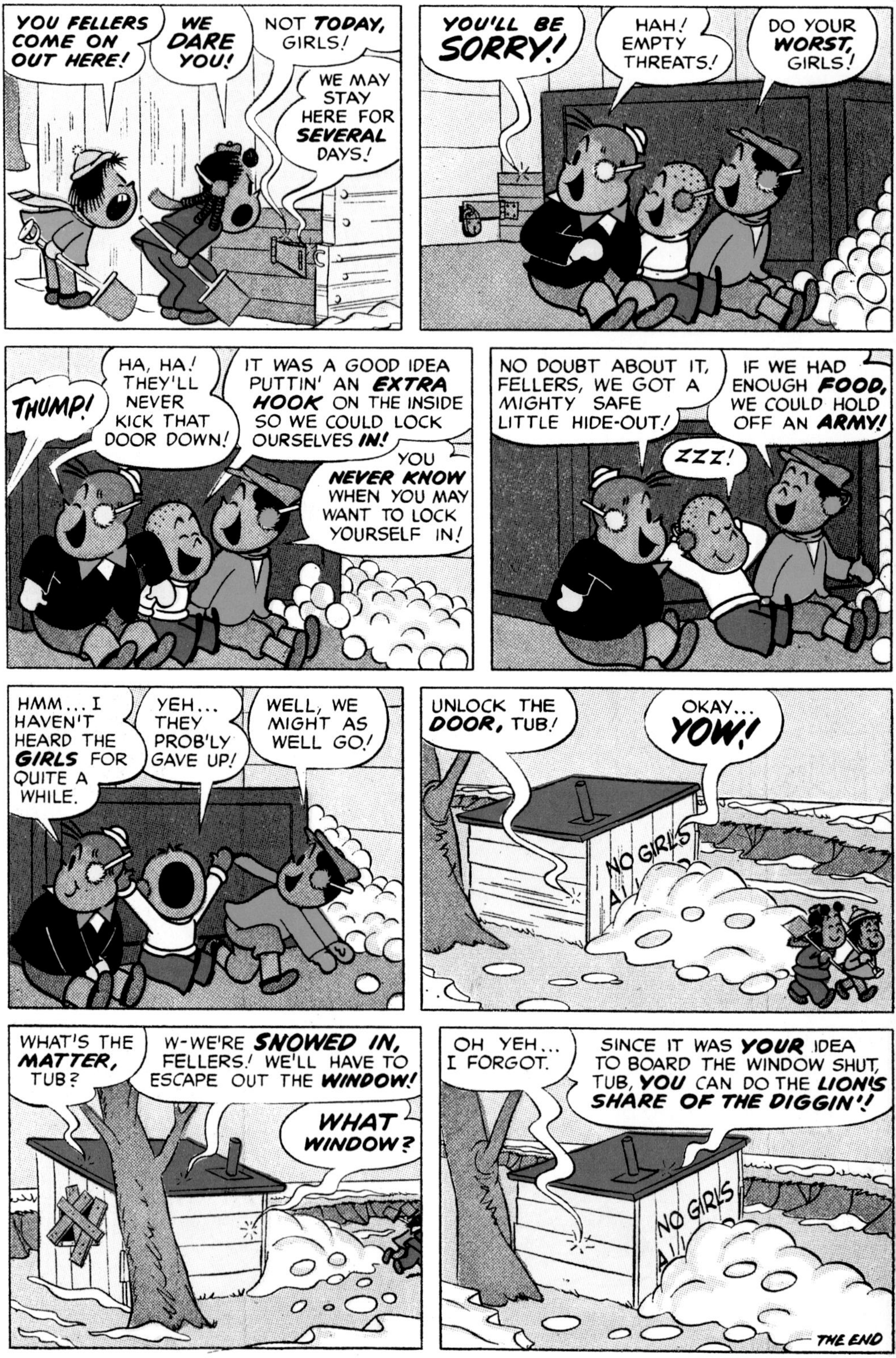
YOU FELLERS COME ON OUT HERE!
WE DARE YOU!
NOT TODAY, GIRLS!
WE MAY STAY HERE FOR SEVERAL DAYS!
YOU'LL BE SORRY!
HAH! EMPTY THREATS!
DO YOUR WORST, GIRLS!
THUMP!
HA, HA! THEY'LL NEVER KICK THAT DOOR DOWN!
IT WAS A GOOD IDEA PUTTIN' AN EXTRA HOOK ON THE INSIDE SO WE COULD LOCK OURSELVES IN!
YOU NEVER KNOW WHEN YOU MAY WANT TO LOCK YOURSELF IN!
NO DOUBT ABOUT IT, FELLERS, WE GOT A MIGHTY SAFE LITTLE HIDE-OUT!
IF WE HAD ENOUGH FOOD, WE COULD HOLD OFF AN ARMY!
ZZZ!
HMM... I HAVEN'T HEARD THE GIRLS FOR QUITE A WHILE.
YEH... THEY PROB'LY GAVE UP!
WELL, WE MIGHT AS WELL GO!
UNLOCK THE DOOR, TUB!
OKAY... YOW!
NO GIRLS
WHAT'S THE MATTER, TUB?
W-WE'RE SNOWED IN, FELLERS! WE'LL HAVE TO ESCAPE OUT THE WINDOW!
WHAT WINDOW?
OH YEH... I FORGOT.
SINCE IT WAS YOUR IDEA TO BOARD THE WINDOW SHUT, TUB, YOU CAN DO THE LION'S SHARE OF THE DIGGIN'!
NO GIRLS
THE END

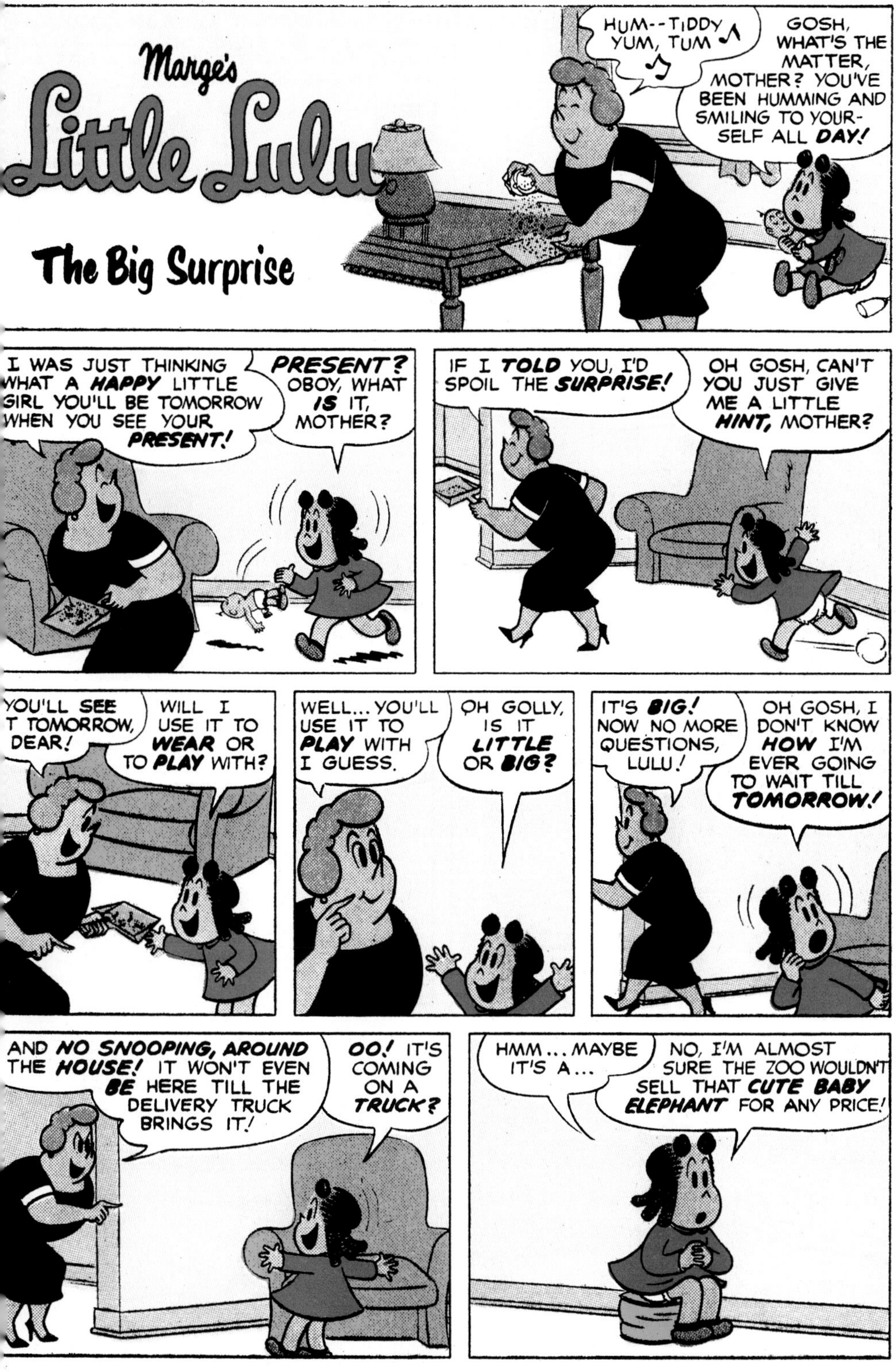
Marge's
Little Lulu
The Big Surprise
HUM--TIDDY YUM, TUM
GOSH, WHAT'S THE MATTER, MOTHER? YOU'VE BEEN HUMMING AND SMILING TO YOURSELF ALL DAY!
I WAS JUST THINKING WHAT A HAPPY LITTLE GIRL YOU'LL BE TOMORROW WHEN YOU SEE YOUR PRESENT!
PRESENT? OBOY, WHAT IS IT, MOTHER?
IF I TOLD YOU, I'D SPOIL THE SURPRISE!
OH GOSH, CAN'T YOU JUST GIVE ME A LITTLE HINT, MOTHER?
YOU'LL SEE T TOMORROW, DEAR!
WILL I USE IT TO WEAR OR TO PLAY WITH?
WELL... YOU'LL USE IT TO PLAY WITH I GUESS.
OH GOLLY, IS IT LITTLE OR BIG?
IT'S BIG! NOW NO MORE QUESTIONS, LULU!
OH GOSH, I DON'T KNOW HOW I'M EVER GOING TO WAIT TILL TOMORROW!
AND NO SNOOPING, AROUND THE HOUSE! IT WON'T EVEN BE HERE TILL THE DELIVERY TRUCK BRINGS IT!
OO! IT'S COMING ON A TRUCK?
HMM... MAYBE IT'S A...
NO, I'M ALMOST SURE THE ZOO WOULDN'T SELL THAT CUTE BABY ELEPHANT FOR ANY PRICE!

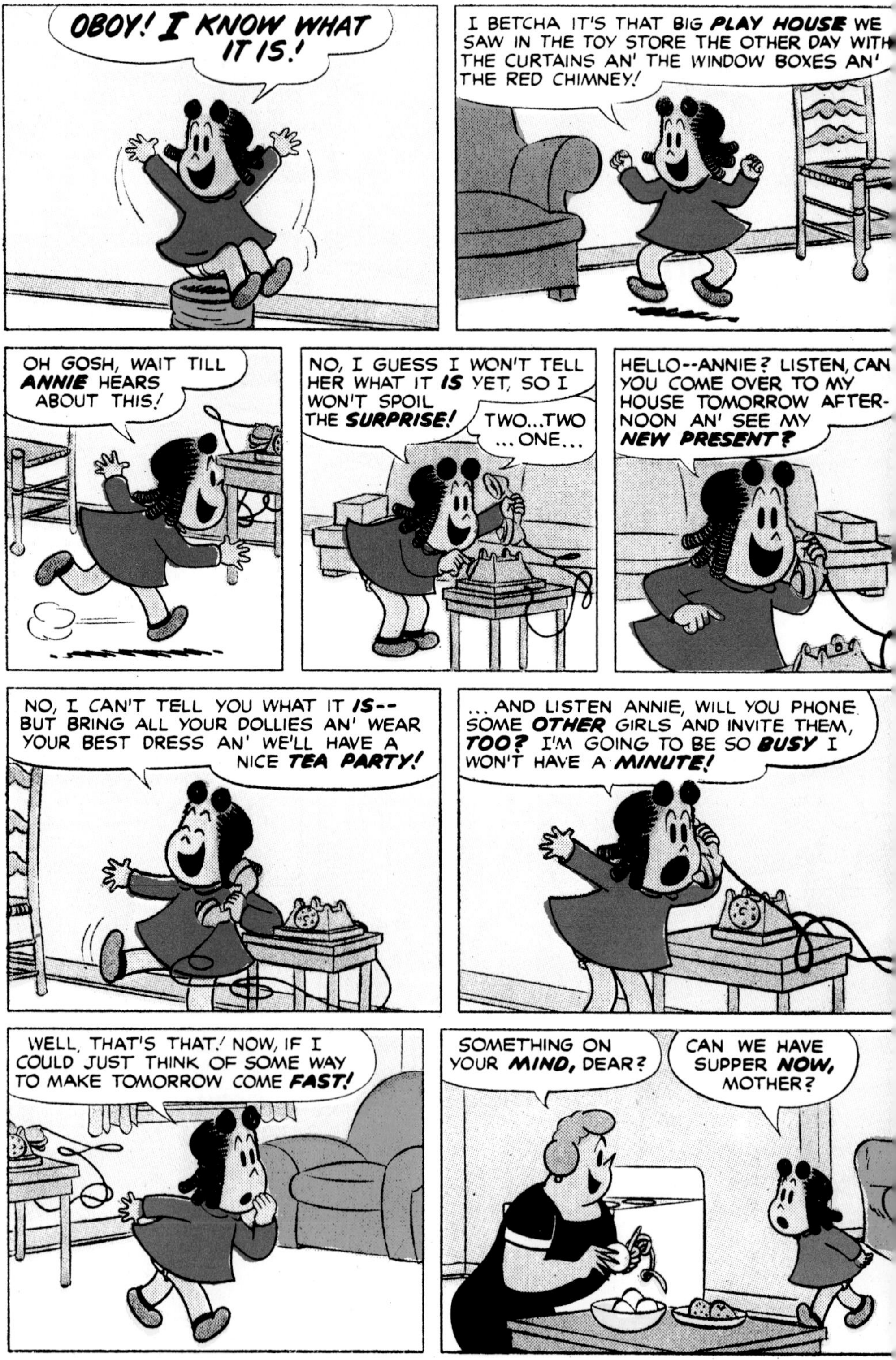
OBOY! I KNOW WHAT IT IS!
I BETCHA IT'S THAT BIG PLAY HOUSE WE SAW IN THE TOY STORE THE OTHER DAY WITH THE CURTAINS AN' THE WINDOW BOXES AN' THE RED CHIMNEY!
OH GOSH, WAIT TILL ANNIE HEARS ABOUT THIS!
NO, I GUESS I WON'T TELL HER WHAT IT IS YET, SO I WON'T SPOIL THE SURPRISE!
TWO...TWO ...ONE...
HELLO--ANNIE? LISTEN, CAN YOU COME OVER TO MY HOUSE TOMORROW AFTER-NOON AN' SEE MY NEW PRESENT?
NO, I CAN'T TELL YOU WHAT IT IS-- BUT BRING ALL YOUR DOLLIES AN' WEAR YOUR BEST DRESS AN' WE'LL HAVE A NICE TEA PARTY!
...AND LISTEN ANNIE, WILL YOU PHONE SOME OTHER GIRLS AND INVITE THEM, TOO? I'M GOING TO BE SO BUSY I WON'T HAVE A MINUTE!
WELL, THAT'S THAT! NOW, IF I COULD JUST THINK OF SOME WAY TO MAKE TOMORROW COME FAST!
SOMETHING ON YOUR MIND, DEAR?
CAN WE HAVE SUPPER NOW, MOTHER?

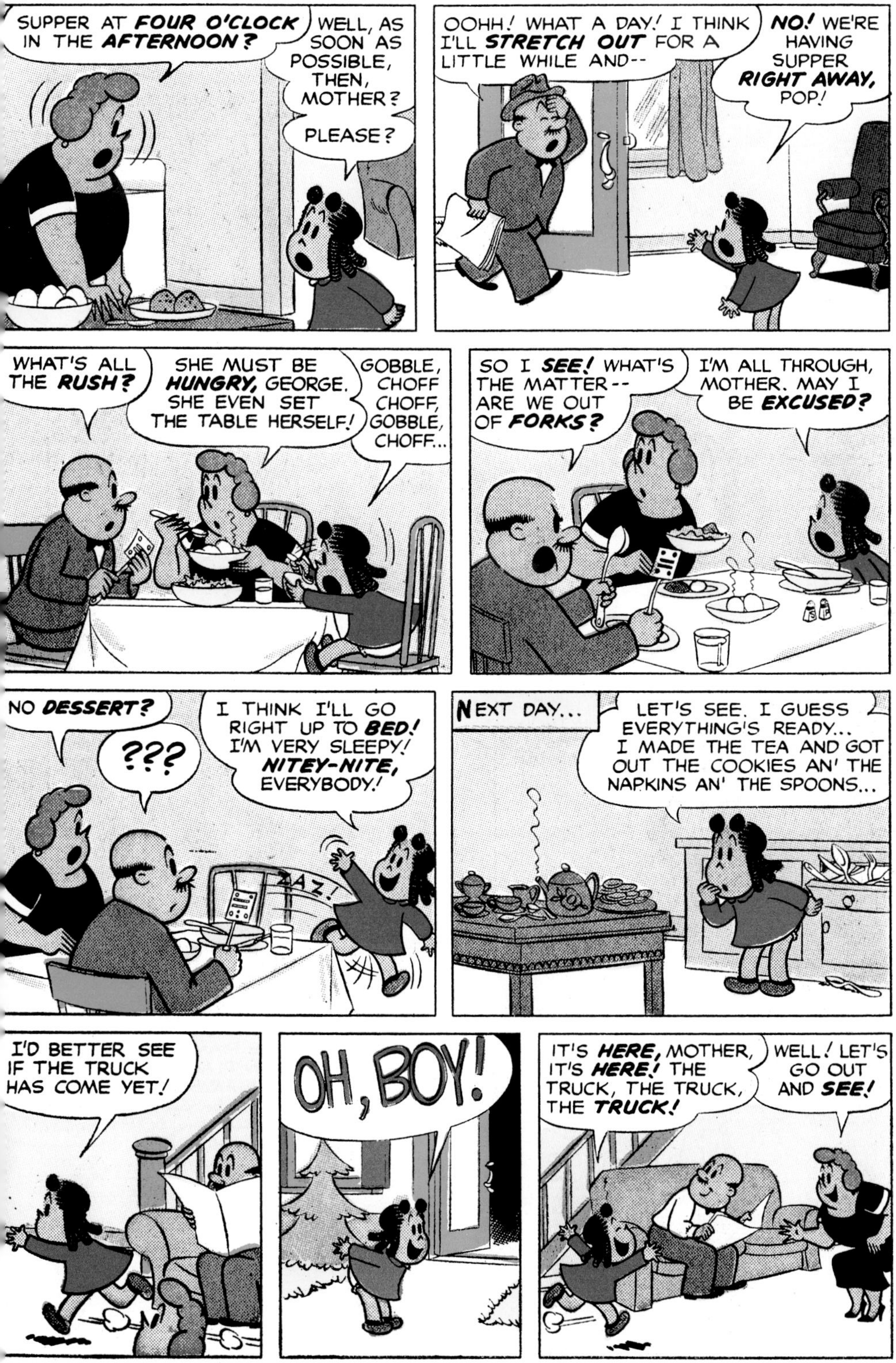

SUPPER AT FOUR O'CLOCK IN THE AFTERNOON?
WELL, AS SOON AS POSSIBLE, THEN, MOTHER?
PLEASE?
OOHH! WHAT A DAY! I THINK I'LL STRETCH OUT FOR A LITTLE WHILE AND--
NO! WE'RE HAVING SUPPER RIGHT AWAY, POP!
WHAT'S ALL THE RUSH?
SHE MUST BE HUNGRY, GEORGE. SHE EVEN SET THE TABLE HERSELF!
GOBBLE, CHOFF CHOFF, GOBBLE, CHOFF...
SO I SEE! WHAT'S THE MATTER -- ARE WE OUT OF FORKS?
I'M ALL THROUGH, MOTHER. MAY I BE EXCUSED?
NO DESSERT?
???
I THINK I'LL GO RIGHT UP TO BED! I'M VERY SLEEPY! NITEY-NITE, EVERYBODY!
ZAZ!
NEXT DAY...
LET'S SEE. I GUESS EVERYTHING'S READY... I MADE THE TEA AND GOT OUT THE COOKIES AN' THE NAPKINS AN' THE SPOONS...
I'D BETTER SEE IF THE TRUCK HAS COME YET!
OH, BOY!
IT'S HERE, MOTHER, IT'S HERE! THE TRUCK, THE TRUCK, THE TRUCK!
WELL! LET'S GO OUT AND SEE!

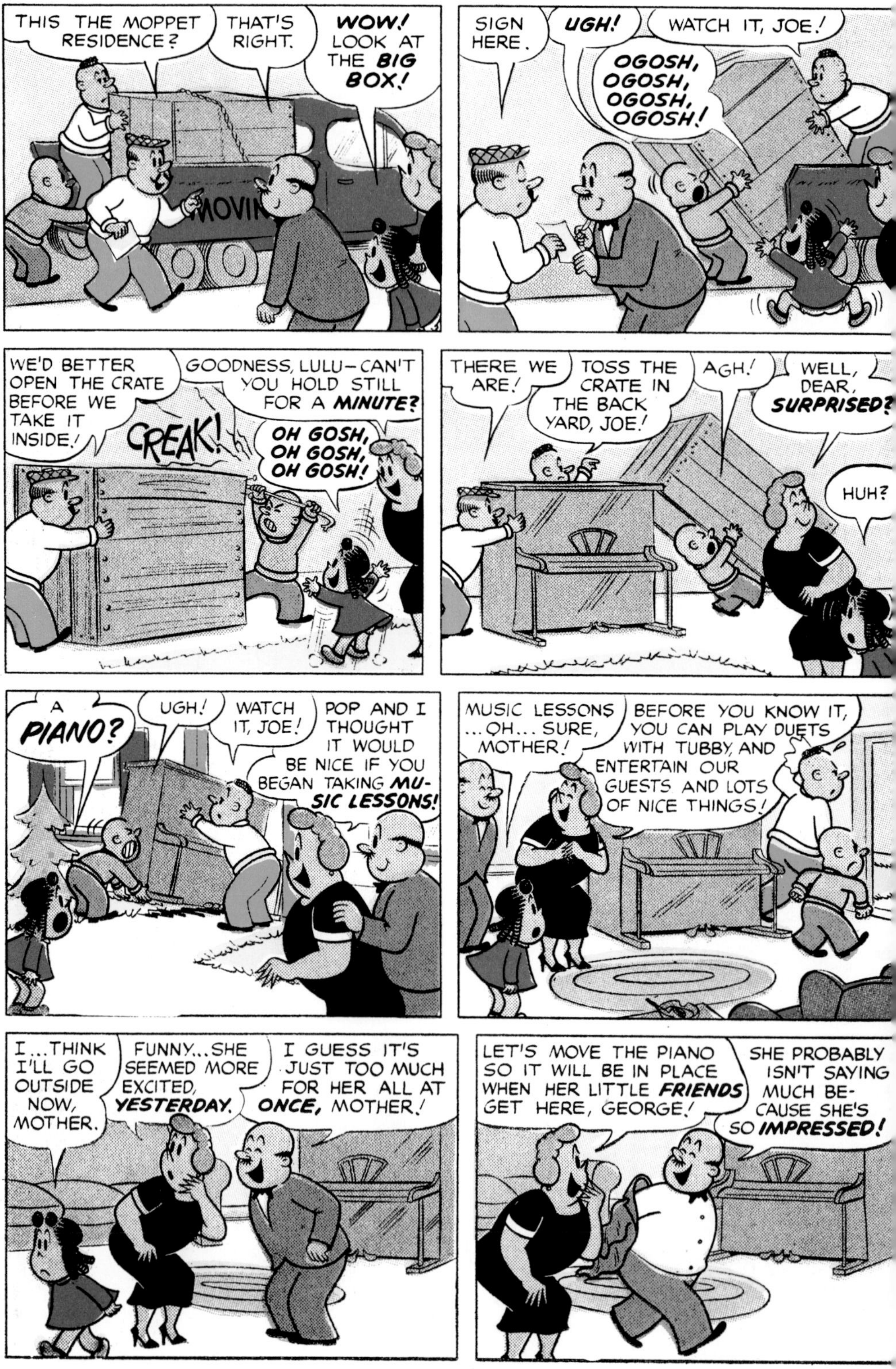
THIS THE MOPPET RESIDENCE?
THAT'S RIGHT.
WOW! LOOK AT THE BIG BOX!
MOVIN
SIGN HERE.
UGH!
WATCH IT, JOE!
OGOSH, OGOSH, OGOSH, OGOSH!
WE'D BETTER OPEN THE CRATE BEFORE WE TAKE IT INSIDE!
CREAK!
GOODNESS, LULU—CAN'T YOU HOLD STILL FOR A MINUTE?
OH GOSH, OH GOSH, OH GOSH!
THERE WE ARE!
TOSS THE CRATE IN THE BACK YARD, JOE!
AGH!
WELL, DEAR, SURPRISED?
HUH?
A PIANO?
UGH!
WATCH IT, JOE!
POP AND I THOUGHT IT WOULD BE NICE IF YOU BEGAN TAKING MUSIC LESSONS!
MUSIC LESSONS ...OH... SURE, MOTHER!
BEFORE YOU KNOW IT, YOU CAN PLAY DUETS WITH TUBBY, AND ENTERTAIN OUR GUESTS AND LOTS OF NICE THINGS!
I...THINK I'LL GO OUTSIDE NOW, MOTHER.
FUNNY...SHE SEEMED MORE EXCITED, YESTERDAY.
I GUESS IT'S JUST TOO MUCH FOR HER ALL AT ONCE, MOTHER!
LET'S MOVE THE PIANO SO IT WILL BE IN PLACE WHEN HER LITTLE FRIENDS GET HERE, GEORGE!
SHE PROBABLY ISN'T SAYING MUCH BECAUSE SHE'S SO IMPRESSED!

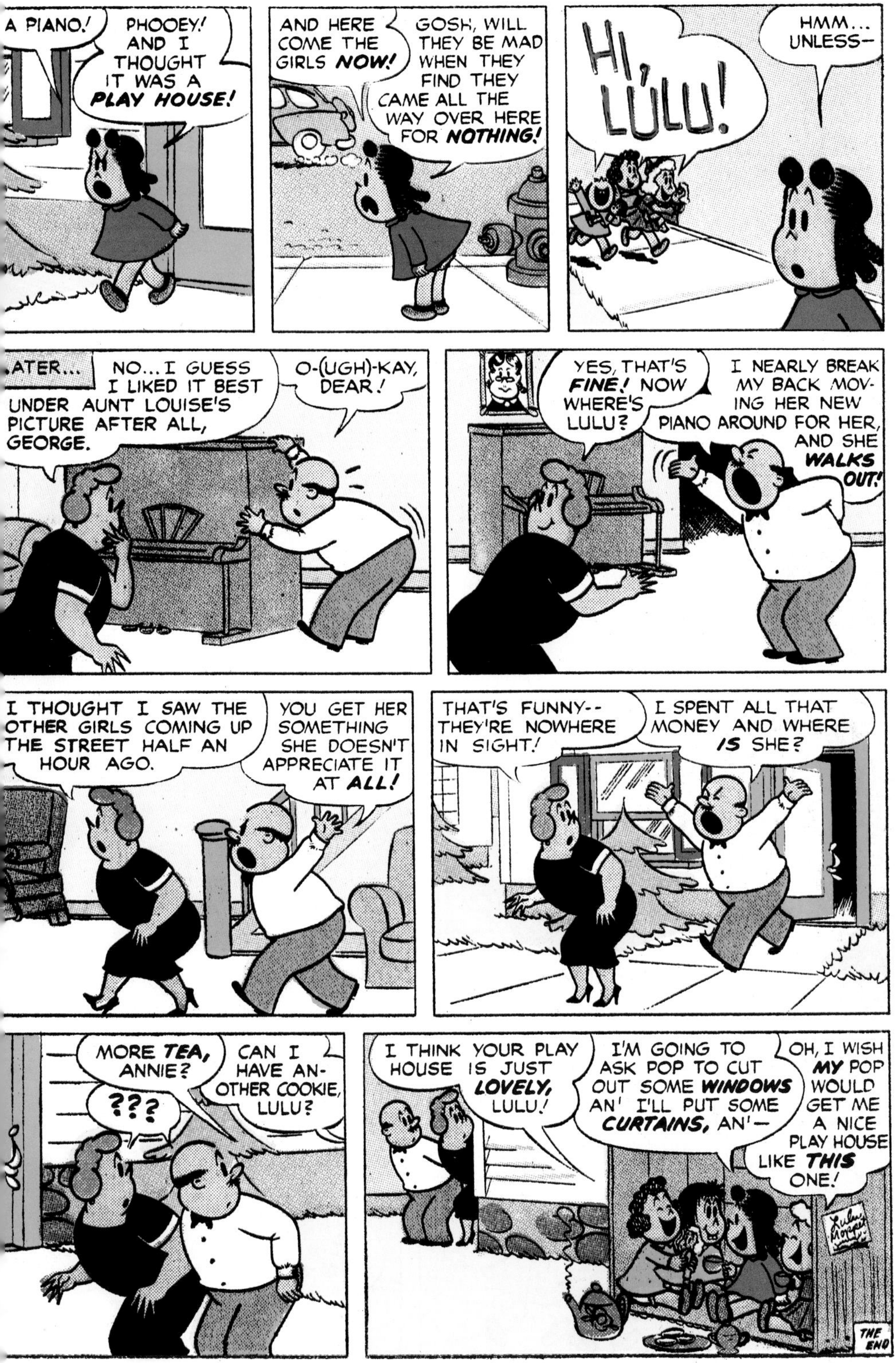
A PIANO!
PHOOEY! AND I THOUGHT IT WAS A **PLAY HOUSE!**
AND HERE COME THE GIRLS **NOW!**
GOSH, WILL THEY BE MAD WHEN THEY FIND THEY CAME ALL THE WAY OVER HERE FOR **NOTHING!**
HI, LULU!
HMM... UNLESS--
LATER...
NO...I GUESS I LIKED IT BEST UNDER AUNT LOUISE'S PICTURE AFTER ALL, GEORGE.
O-(UGH)-KAY, DEAR!
YES, THAT'S **FINE!** NOW WHERE'S LULU?
I NEARLY BREAK MY BACK MOVING HER NEW PIANO AROUND FOR HER, AND SHE **WALKS OUT!**
I THOUGHT I SAW THE OTHER GIRLS COMING UP THE STREET HALF AN HOUR AGO.
YOU GET HER SOMETHING SHE DOESN'T APPRECIATE IT AT **ALL!**
THAT'S FUNNY-- THEY'RE NOWHERE IN SIGHT!
I SPENT ALL THAT MONEY AND WHERE **IS** SHE?
MORE **TEA,** ANNIE?
CAN I HAVE ANOTHER COOKIE, LULU?
???
I THINK YOUR PLAY HOUSE IS JUST **LOVELY,** LULU!
I'M GOING TO ASK POP TO CUT OUT SOME **WINDOWS** AN' I'LL PUT SOME **CURTAINS,** AN'—
OH, I WISH **MY** POP WOULD GET ME A NICE PLAY HOUSE LIKE **THIS** ONE!
THE END

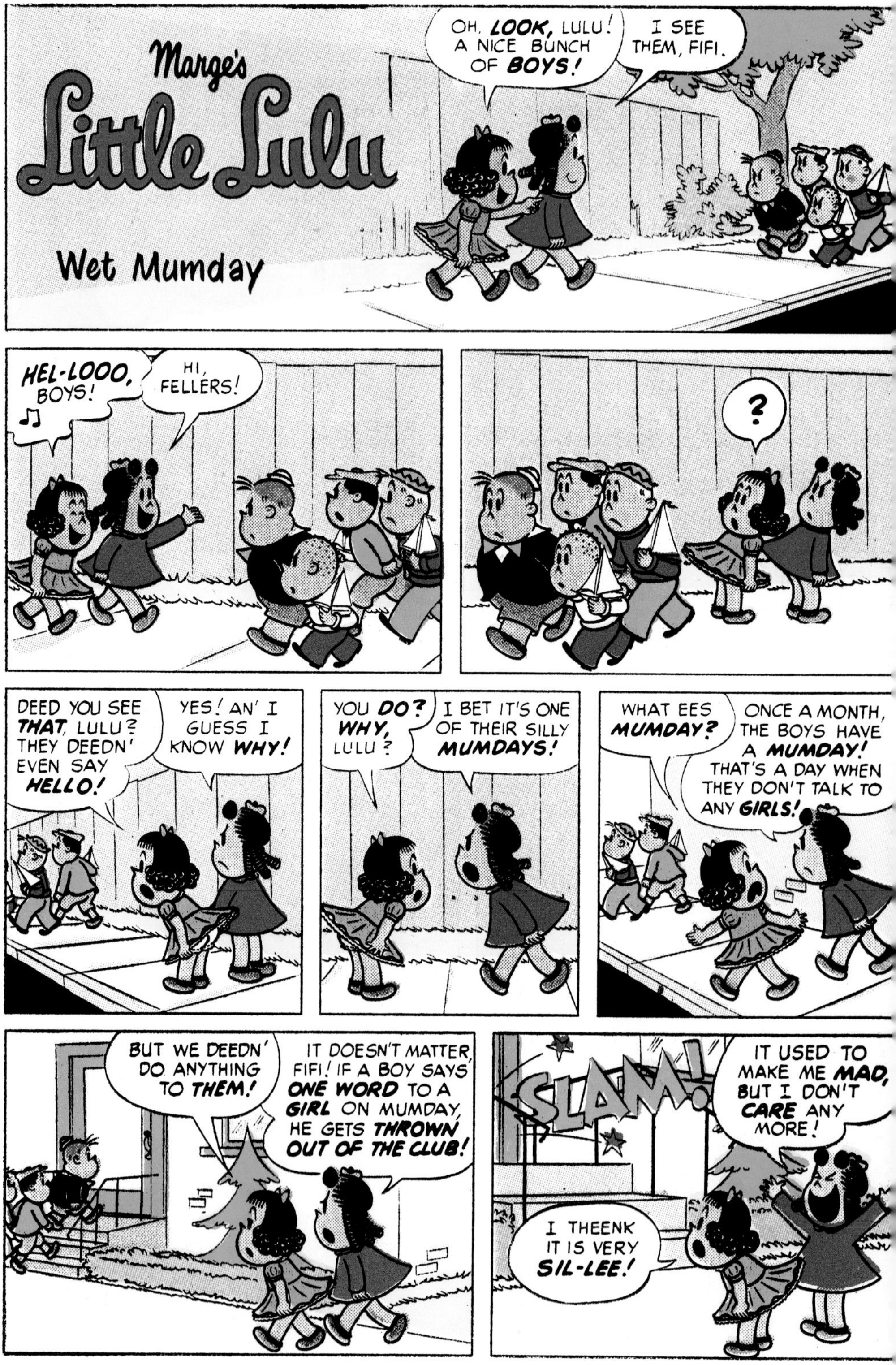
Marge's Little Lulu
Wet Mumday
OH, LOOK, LULU! A NICE BUNCH OF BOYS!
I SEE THEM, FIFI.
HEL-LOOO, BOYS! ♫
HI, FELLERS!
?
DEED YOU SEE THAT, LULU? THEY DEEDN' EVEN SAY HELLO!
YES! AN' I GUESS I KNOW WHY!
YOU DO? WHY, LULU?
I BET IT'S ONE OF THEIR SILLY MUMDAYS!
WHAT EES MUMDAY?
ONCE A MONTH, THE BOYS HAVE A MUMDAY! THAT'S A DAY WHEN THEY DON'T TALK TO ANY GIRLS!
BUT WE DEEDN' DO ANYTHING TO THEM!
IT DOESN'T MATTER, FIFI! IF A BOY SAYS ONE WORD TO A GIRL ON MUMDAY, HE GETS THROWN OUT OF THE CLUB!
SLAM!
IT USED TO MAKE ME MAD, BUT I DON'T CARE ANY MORE!
I THEENK IT IS VERY SIL-LEE!

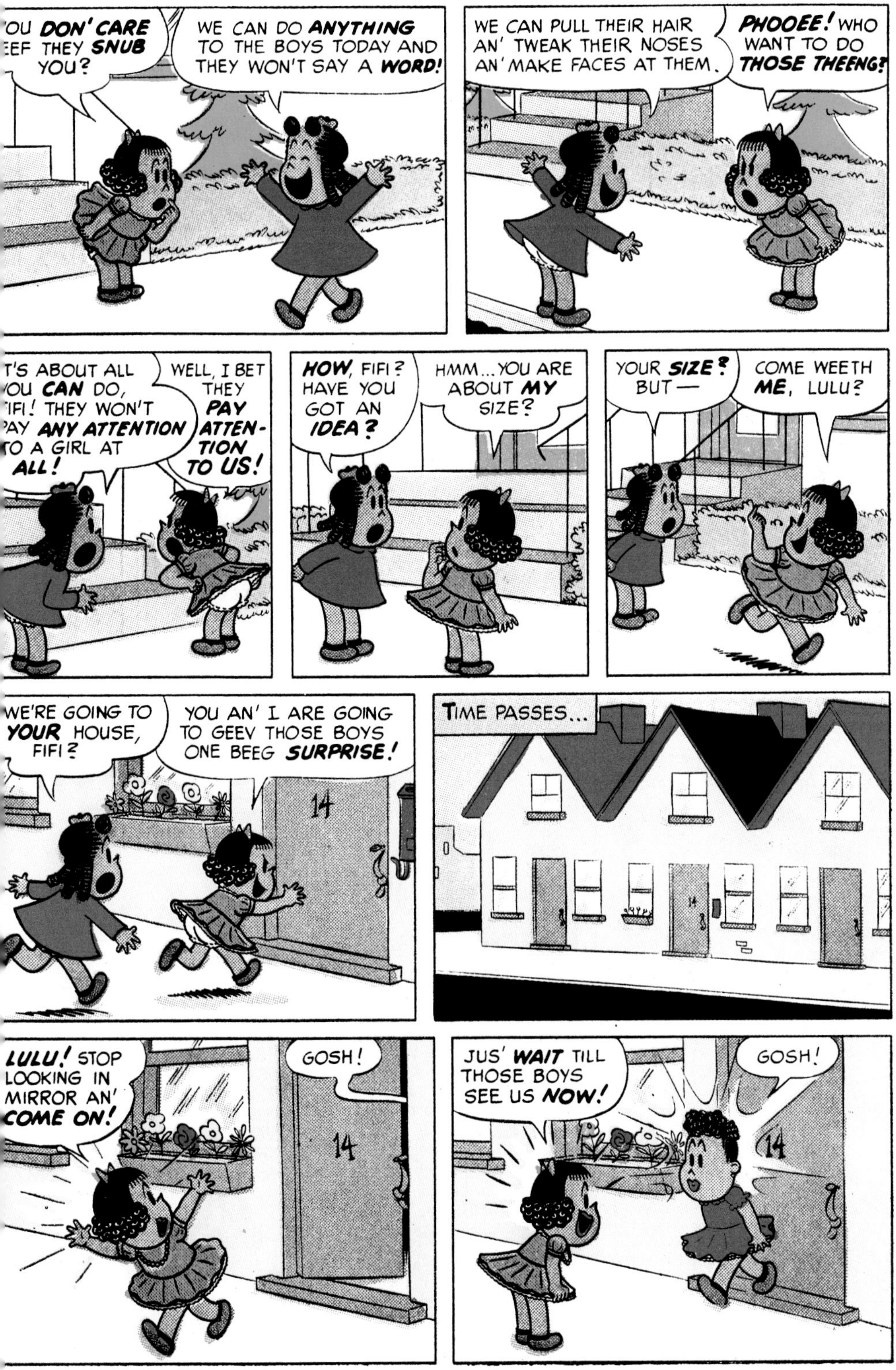

YOU DON'CARE EEF THEY SNUB YOU?
WE CAN DO ANYTHING TO THE BOYS TODAY AND THEY WON'T SAY A WORD!
WE CAN PULL THEIR HAIR AN' TWEAK THEIR NOSES AN'MAKE FACES AT THEM.
PHOOEE! WHO WANT TO DO THOSE THEENG?
T'S ABOUT ALL YOU CAN DO, FIFI! THEY WON'T PAY ANY ATTENTION TO A GIRL AT ALL!
WELL, I BET THEY PAY ATTEN-TION TO US!
HOW, FIFI? HAVE YOU GOT AN IDEA?
HMM... YOU ARE ABOUT MY SIZE?
YOUR SIZE? BUT—
COME WEETH ME, LULU?
WE'RE GOING TO YOUR HOUSE, FIFI?
YOU AN' I ARE GOING TO GEEV THOSE BOYS ONE BEEG SURPRISE!
14
TIME PASSES...
LULU! STOP LOOKING IN MIRROR AN' COME ON!
GOSH!
14
JUS' WAIT TILL THOSE BOYS SEE US NOW!
GOSH!
14

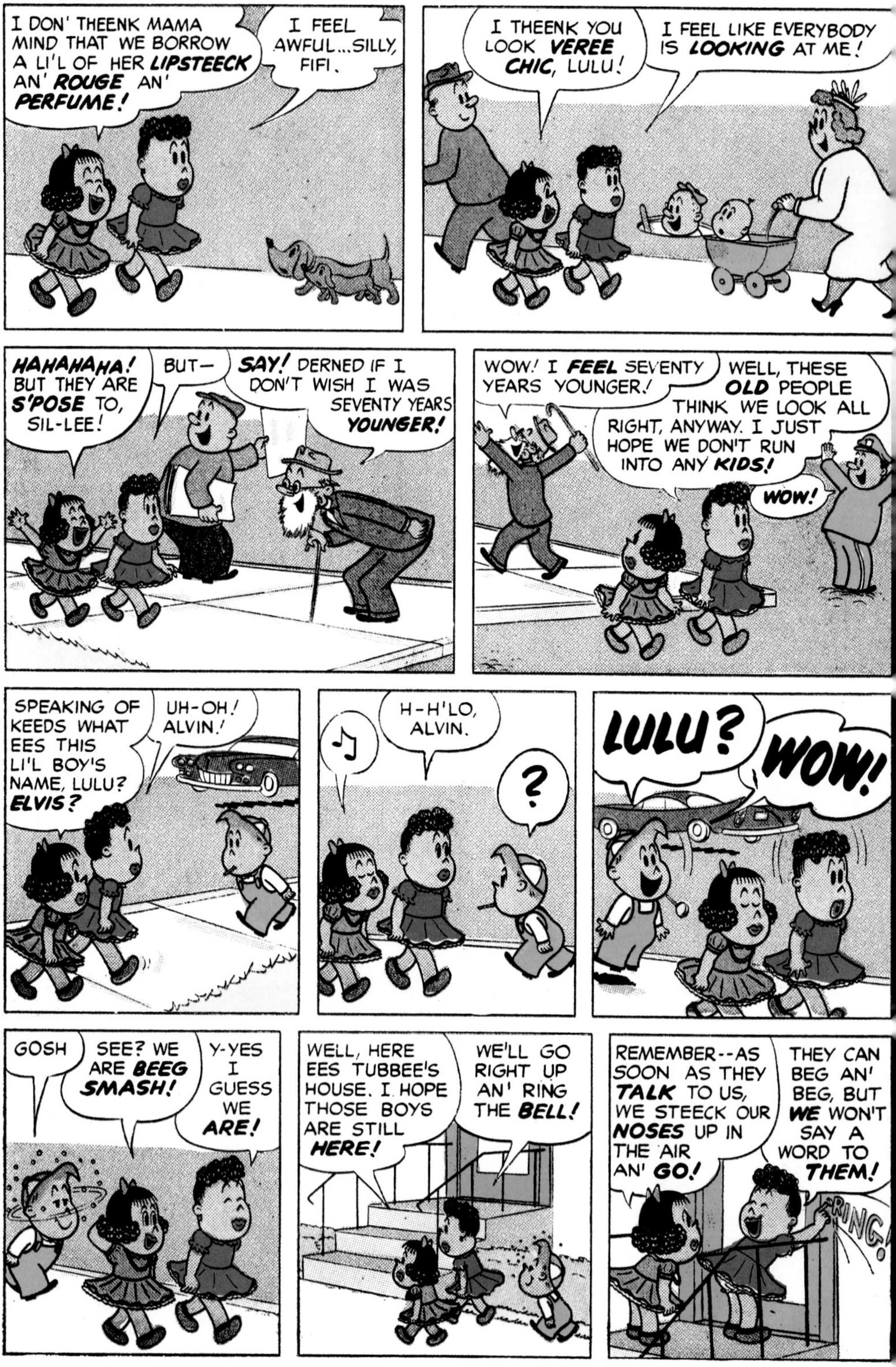
I DON' THEENK MAMA MIND THAT WE BORROW A LI'L OF HER LIPSTEECK AN' ROUGE AN' PERFUME!
I FEEL AWFUL...SILLY, FIFI.
I THEENK YOU LOOK VEREE CHIC, LULU!
I FEEL LIKE EVERYBODY IS LOOKING AT ME!
HAHAHAHA! BUT THEY ARE S'POSE TO, SIL-LEE!
BUT—
SAY! DERNED IF I DON'T WISH I WAS SEVENTY YEARS YOUNGER!
WOW! I FEEL SEVENTY YEARS YOUNGER!
WELL, THESE OLD PEOPLE THINK WE LOOK ALL RIGHT, ANYWAY. I JUST HOPE WE DON'T RUN INTO ANY KIDS!
WOW!
SPEAKING OF KEEDS WHAT EES THIS LI'L BOY'S NAME, LULU? ELVIS?
UH-OH! ALVIN!
♫
H-H'LO, ALVIN.
?
LULU?
WOW!
GOSH
SEE? WE ARE BEEG SMASH!
Y-YES I GUESS WE ARE!
WELL, HERE EES TUBBEE'S HOUSE. I HOPE THOSE BOYS ARE STILL HERE!
WE'LL GO RIGHT UP AN' RING THE BELL!
REMEMBER--AS SOON AS THEY TALK TO US, WE STEECK OUR NOSES UP IN THE AIR AN' GO!
THEY CAN BEG AN' BEG, BUT WE WON'T SAY A WORD TO THEM!
RING!

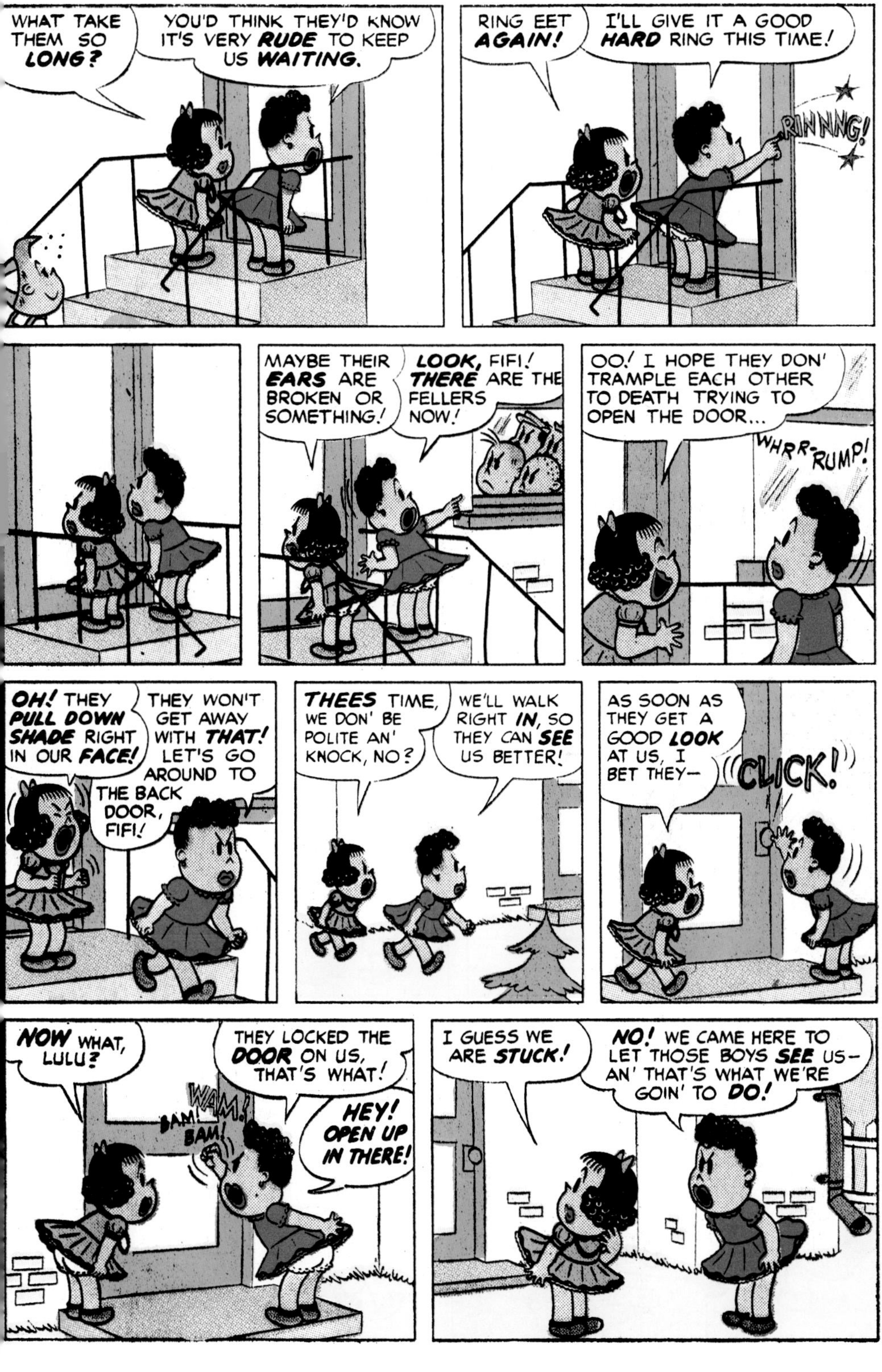
WHAT TAKE THEM SO LONG?
YOU'D THINK THEY'D KNOW IT'S VERY RUDE TO KEEP US WAITING.
RING EET AGAIN!
I'LL GIVE IT A GOOD HARD RING THIS TIME!
RINNNG!
MAYBE THEIR EARS ARE BROKEN OR SOMETHING!
LOOK, FIFI! THERE ARE THE FELLERS NOW!
OO! I HOPE THEY DON' TRAMPLE EACH OTHER TO DEATH TRYING TO OPEN THE DOOR...
WHRR-RUMP!
OH! THEY PULL DOWN SHADE RIGHT IN OUR FACE!
THEY WON'T GET AWAY WITH THAT! LET'S GO AROUND TO THE BACK DOOR, FIFI!
THEES TIME, WE DON' BE POLITE AN' KNOCK, NO?
WE'LL WALK RIGHT IN, SO THEY CAN SEE US BETTER!
AS SOON AS THEY GET A GOOD LOOK AT US, I BET THEY—
CLICK!
NOW WHAT, LULU?
THEY LOCKED THE DOOR ON US, THAT'S WHAT!
WAM! BAM! BAM!
HEY! OPEN UP IN THERE!
I GUESS WE ARE STUCK!
NO! WE CAME HERE TO LET THOSE BOYS SEE US— AN' THAT'S WHAT WE'RE GOIN' TO DO!

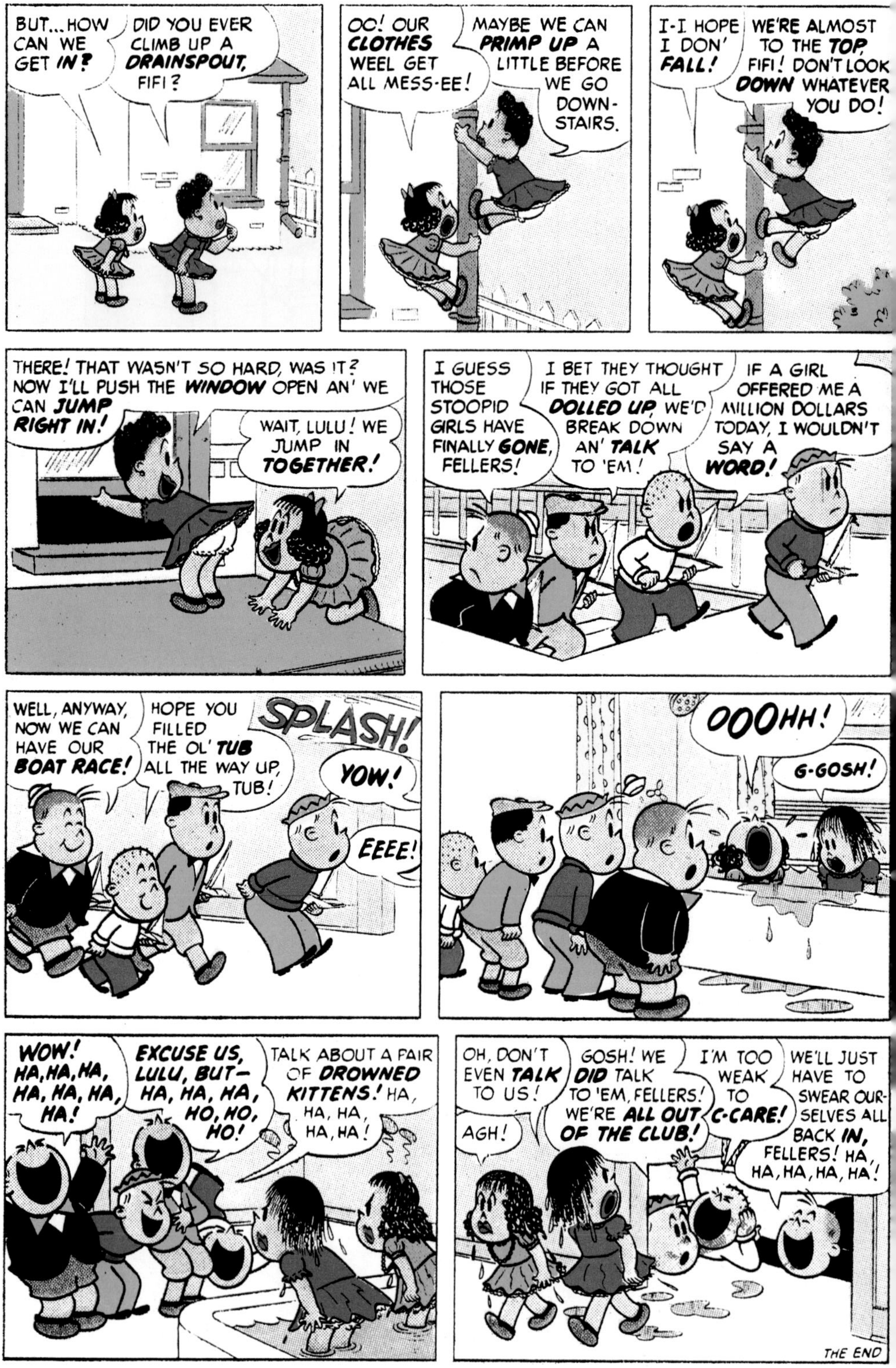
BUT...HOW CAN WE GET IN?
DID YOU EVER CLIMB UP A DRAINSPOUT, FIFI?
OO! OUR CLOTHES WEEL GET ALL MESS-EE!
MAYBE WE CAN PRIMP UP A LITTLE BEFORE WE GO DOWN-STAIRS.
I-I HOPE I DON' FALL!
WE'RE ALMOST TO THE TOP, FIFI! DON'T LOOK DOWN WHATEVER YOU DO!
THERE! THAT WASN'T SO HARD, WAS IT? NOW I'LL PUSH THE WINDOW OPEN AN' WE CAN JUMP RIGHT IN!
WAIT, LULU! WE JUMP IN TOGETHER!
I GUESS THOSE STOOPID GIRLS HAVE FINALLY GONE, FELLERS!
I BET THEY THOUGHT IF THEY GOT ALL DOLLED UP, WE'D BREAK DOWN AN' TALK TO 'EM!
IF A GIRL OFFERED ME A MILLION DOLLARS TODAY, I WOULDN'T SAY A WORD!
WELL, ANYWAY, NOW WE CAN HAVE OUR BOAT RACE!
HOPE YOU FILLED THE OL' TUB ALL THE WAY UP, TUB!
SPLASH!
YOW!
EEEE!
OOOHH!
G-GOSH!
WOW! HA, HA, HA, HA, HA, HA, HA!
EXCUSE US, LULU, BUT— HA, HA, HA, HO, HO, HO!
TALK ABOUT A PAIR OF DROWNED KITTENS! HA, HA, HA, HA, HA!
OH, DON'T EVEN TALK TO US!
AGH!
GOSH! WE DID TALK TO 'EM, FELLERS! WE'RE ALL OUT OF THE CLUB!
I'M TOO WEAK TO C-CARE!
WE'LL JUST HAVE TO SWEAR OUR-SELVES ALL BACK IN, FELLERS! HA, HA, HA, HA, HA!
THE END

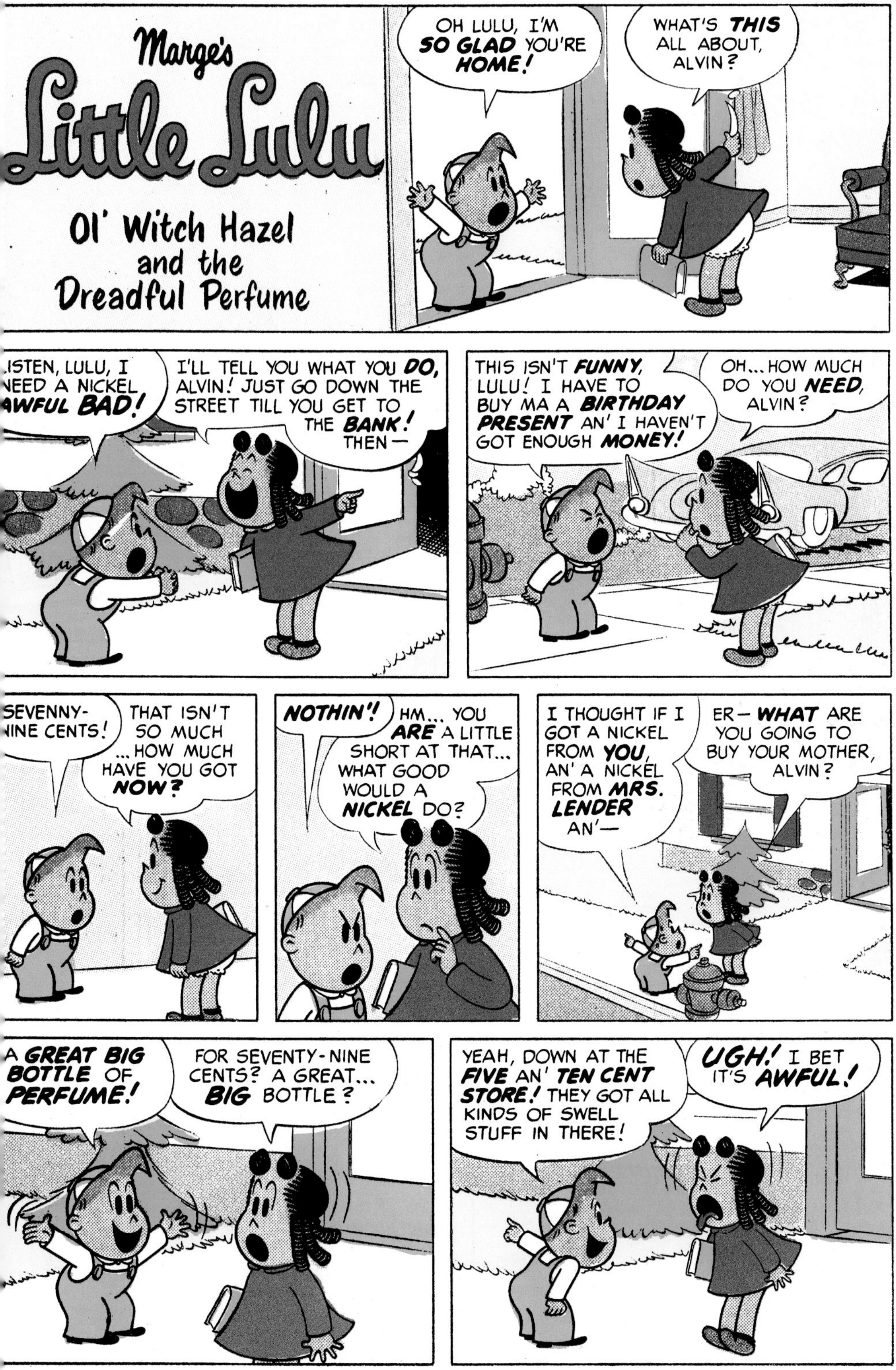

Marge's Little Lulu
Ol' Witch Hazel and the Dreadful Perfume
OH LULU, I'M SO GLAD YOU'RE HOME!
WHAT'S THIS ALL ABOUT, ALVIN?
LISTEN, LULU, I NEED A NICKEL AWFUL BAD!
I'LL TELL YOU WHAT YOU DO, ALVIN! JUST GO DOWN THE STREET TILL YOU GET TO THE BANK! THEN—
THIS ISN'T FUNNY, LULU! I HAVE TO BUY MA A BIRTHDAY PRESENT AN' I HAVEN'T GOT ENOUGH MONEY!
OH... HOW MUCH DO YOU NEED, ALVIN?
SEVENNY-NINE CENTS!
THAT ISN'T SO MUCH ...HOW MUCH HAVE YOU GOT NOW?
NOTHIN'!
HM... YOU ARE A LITTLE SHORT AT THAT... WHAT GOOD WOULD A NICKEL DO?
I THOUGHT IF I GOT A NICKEL FROM YOU, AN' A NICKEL FROM MRS. LENDER AN'—
ER— WHAT ARE YOU GOING TO BUY YOUR MOTHER, ALVIN?
A GREAT BIG BOTTLE OF PERFUME!
FOR SEVENTY-NINE CENTS? A GREAT... BIG BOTTLE?
YEAH, DOWN AT THE FIVE AN' TEN CENT STORE! THEY GOT ALL KINDS OF SWELL STUFF IN THERE!
UGH! I BET IT'S AWFUL!

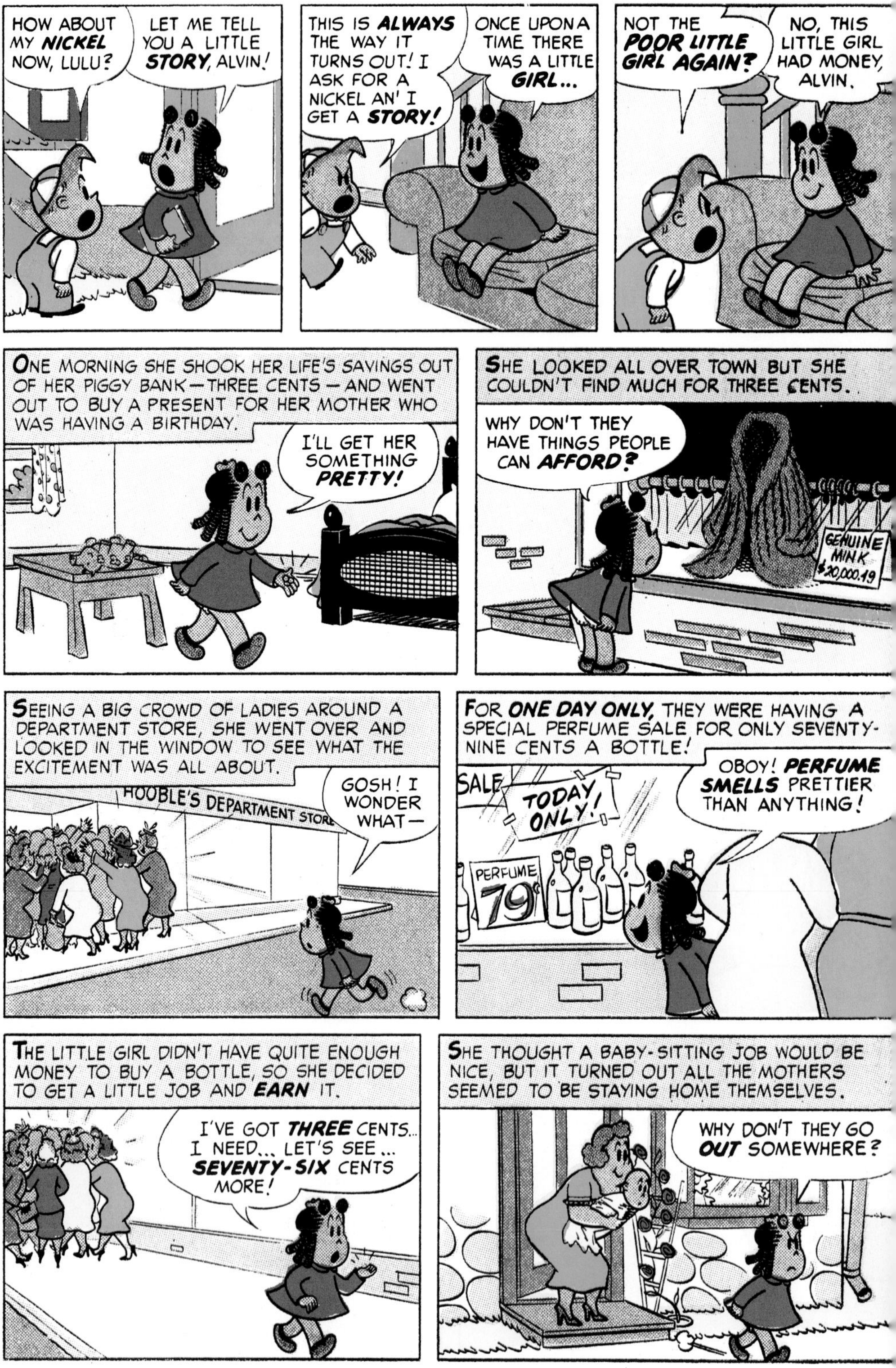
HOW ABOUT MY NICKEL NOW, LULU?
LET ME TELL YOU A LITTLE STORY, ALVIN!
THIS IS ALWAYS THE WAY IT TURNS OUT! I ASK FOR A NICKEL AN' I GET A STORY!
ONCE UPON A TIME THERE WAS A LITTLE GIRL...
NOT THE POOR LITTLE GIRL AGAIN?
NO, THIS LITTLE GIRL HAD MONEY, ALVIN.
ONE MORNING SHE SHOOK HER LIFE'S SAVINGS OUT OF HER PIGGY BANK—THREE CENTS—AND WENT OUT TO BUY A PRESENT FOR HER MOTHER WHO WAS HAVING A BIRTHDAY.
I'LL GET HER SOMETHING PRETTY!
SHE LOOKED ALL OVER TOWN BUT SHE COULDN'T FIND MUCH FOR THREE CENTS.
WHY DON'T THEY HAVE THINGS PEOPLE CAN AFFORD?
GENUINE MINK $20,000.19
SEEING A BIG CROWD OF LADIES AROUND A DEPARTMENT STORE, SHE WENT OVER AND LOOKED IN THE WINDOW TO SEE WHAT THE EXCITEMENT WAS ALL ABOUT.
HOOBLE'S DEPARTMENT STORE
GOSH! I WONDER WHAT—
FOR ONE DAY ONLY, THEY WERE HAVING A SPECIAL PERFUME SALE FOR ONLY SEVENTY-NINE CENTS A BOTTLE!
SALE
TODAY ONLY!
PERFUME 79¢
OBOY! PERFUME SMELLS PRETTIER THAN ANYTHING!
THE LITTLE GIRL DIDN'T HAVE QUITE ENOUGH MONEY TO BUY A BOTTLE, SO SHE DECIDED TO GET A LITTLE JOB AND EARN IT.
I'VE GOT THREE CENTS... I NEED... LET'S SEE... SEVENTY-SIX CENTS MORE!
SHE THOUGHT A BABY-SITTING JOB WOULD BE NICE, BUT IT TURNED OUT ALL THE MOTHERS SEEMED TO BE STAYING HOME THEMSELVES.
WHY DON'T THEY GO OUT SOMEWHERE?

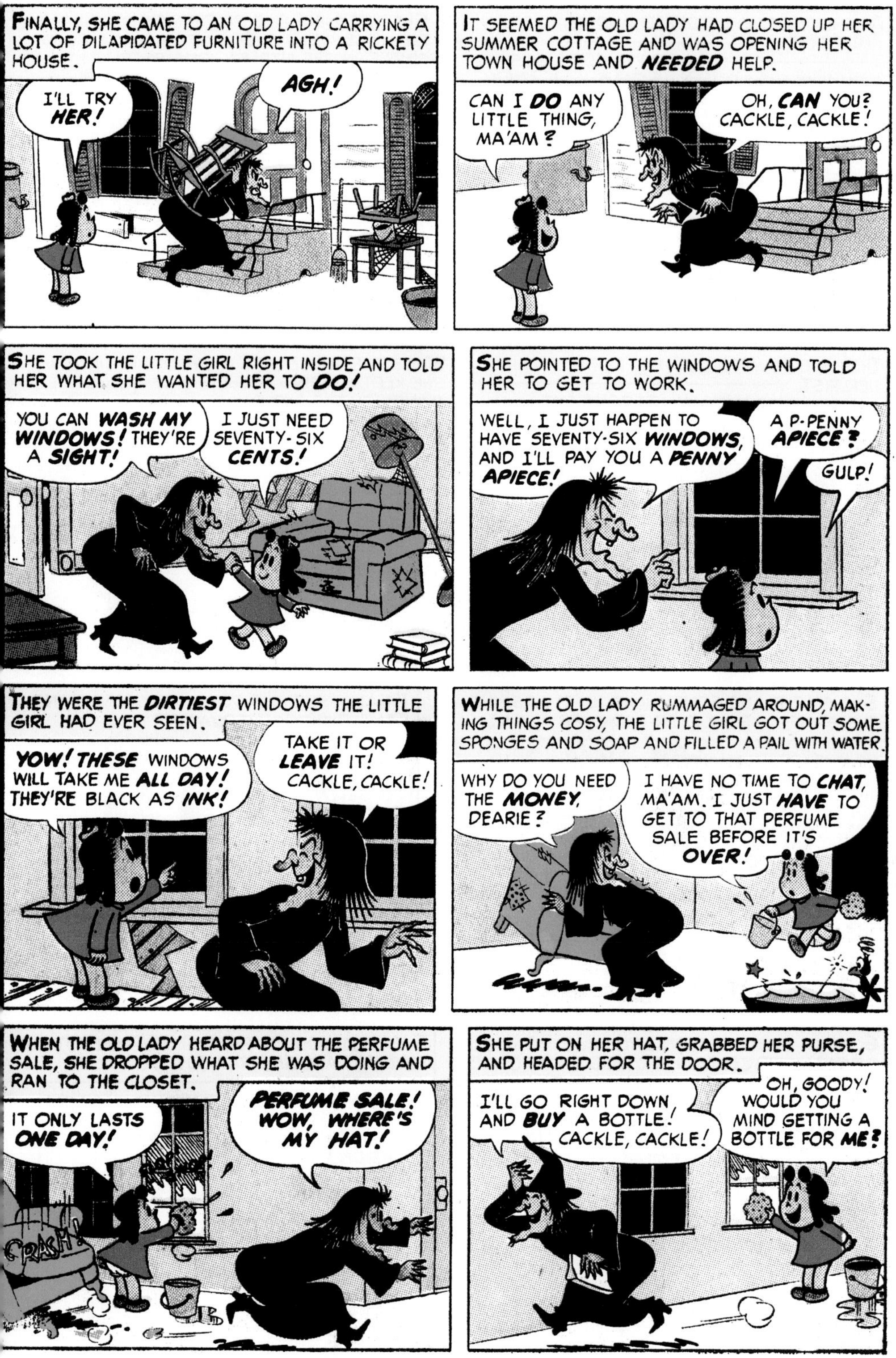
FINALLY, SHE CAME TO AN OLD LADY CARRYING A LOT OF DILAPIDATED FURNITURE INTO A RICKETY HOUSE.
I'LL TRY HER!
AGH!
IT SEEMED THE OLD LADY HAD CLOSED UP HER SUMMER COTTAGE AND WAS OPENING HER TOWN HOUSE AND NEEDED HELP.
CAN I DO ANY LITTLE THING, MA'AM?
OH, CAN YOU? CACKLE, CACKLE!
SHE TOOK THE LITTLE GIRL RIGHT INSIDE AND TOLD HER WHAT SHE WANTED HER TO DO!
YOU CAN WASH MY WINDOWS! THEY'RE A SIGHT!
I JUST NEED SEVENTY-SIX CENTS!
SHE POINTED TO THE WINDOWS AND TOLD HER TO GET TO WORK.
WELL, I JUST HAPPEN TO HAVE SEVENTY-SIX WINDOWS, AND I'LL PAY YOU A PENNY APIECE!
A P-PENNY APIECE?
GULP!
THEY WERE THE DIRTIEST WINDOWS THE LITTLE GIRL HAD EVER SEEN.
YOW! THESE WINDOWS WILL TAKE ME ALL DAY! THEY'RE BLACK AS INK!
TAKE IT OR LEAVE IT! CACKLE, CACKLE!
WHILE THE OLD LADY RUMMAGED AROUND, MAKING THINGS COSY, THE LITTLE GIRL GOT OUT SOME SPONGES AND SOAP AND FILLED A PAIL WITH WATER.
WHY DO YOU NEED THE MONEY, DEARIE?
I HAVE NO TIME TO CHAT, MA'AM. I JUST HAVE TO GET TO THAT PERFUME SALE BEFORE IT'S OVER!
WHEN THE OLD LADY HEARD ABOUT THE PERFUME SALE, SHE DROPPED WHAT SHE WAS DOING AND RAN TO THE CLOSET.
IT ONLY LASTS ONE DAY!
PERFUME SALE! WOW, WHERE'S MY HAT!
CRASH!
SHE PUT ON HER HAT, GRABBED HER PURSE, AND HEADED FOR THE DOOR.
I'LL GO RIGHT DOWN AND BUY A BOTTLE! CACKLE, CACKLE!
OH, GOODY! WOULD YOU MIND GETTING A BOTTLE FOR ME?

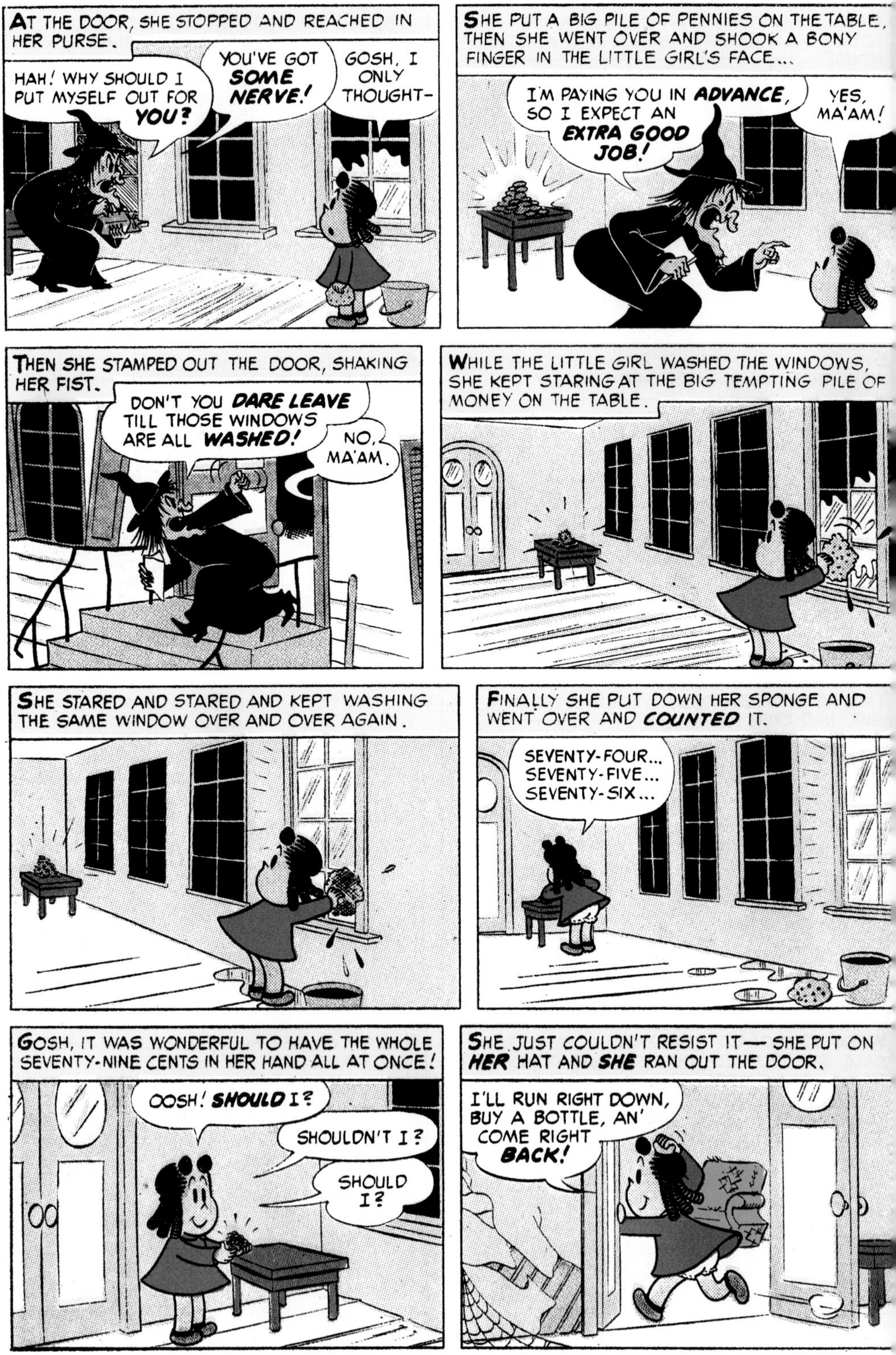
AT THE DOOR, SHE STOPPED AND REACHED IN HER PURSE.
HAH! WHY SHOULD I PUT MYSELF OUT FOR YOU?
YOU'VE GOT SOME NERVE!
GOSH, I ONLY THOUGHT-
SHE PUT A BIG PILE OF PENNIES ON THE TABLE, THEN SHE WENT OVER AND SHOOK A BONY FINGER IN THE LITTLE GIRL'S FACE...
I'M PAYING YOU IN ADVANCE, SO I EXPECT AN EXTRA GOOD JOB!
YES, MA'AM!
THEN SHE STAMPED OUT THE DOOR, SHAKING HER FIST.
DON'T YOU DARE LEAVE TILL THOSE WINDOWS ARE ALL WASHED!
NO, MA'AM.
WHILE THE LITTLE GIRL WASHED THE WINDOWS, SHE KEPT STARING AT THE BIG TEMPTING PILE OF MONEY ON THE TABLE.
SHE STARED AND STARED AND KEPT WASHING THE SAME WINDOW OVER AND OVER AGAIN.
FINALLY SHE PUT DOWN HER SPONGE AND WENT OVER AND COUNTED IT.
SEVENTY-FOUR... SEVENTY-FIVE... SEVENTY-SIX...
GOSH, IT WAS WONDERFUL TO HAVE THE WHOLE SEVENTY-NINE CENTS IN HER HAND ALL AT ONCE!
OOSH! SHOULD I?
SHOULDN'T I?
SHOULD I?
SHE JUST COULDN'T RESIST IT— SHE PUT ON HER HAT AND SHE RAN OUT THE DOOR.
I'LL RUN RIGHT DOWN, BUY A BOTTLE, AN' COME RIGHT BACK!

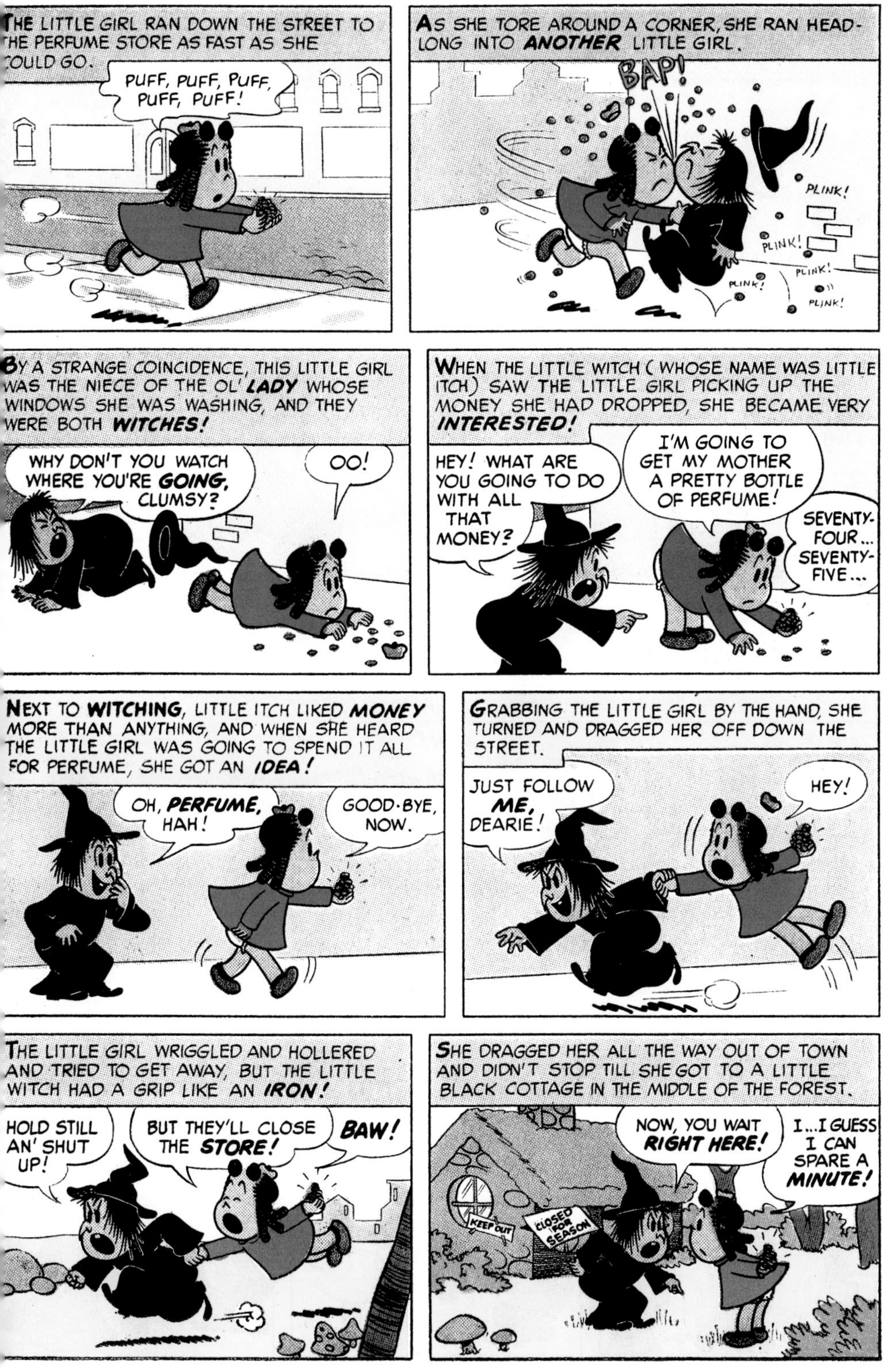

THE LITTLE GIRL RAN DOWN THE STREET TO THE PERFUME STORE AS FAST AS SHE COULD GO.
PUFF, PUFF, PUFF, PUFF, PUFF!
AS SHE TORE AROUND A CORNER, SHE RAN HEADLONG INTO ANOTHER LITTLE GIRL.
BAP!
PLINK!
PLINK!
PLINK!
PLINK!
PLINK!
BY A STRANGE COINCIDENCE, THIS LITTLE GIRL WAS THE NIECE OF THE OL' LADY WHOSE WINDOWS SHE WAS WASHING, AND THEY WERE BOTH WITCHES!
WHY DON'T YOU WATCH WHERE YOU'RE GOING, CLUMSY?
OO!
WHEN THE LITTLE WITCH (WHOSE NAME WAS LITTLE ITCH) SAW THE LITTLE GIRL PICKING UP THE MONEY SHE HAD DROPPED, SHE BECAME VERY INTERESTED!
HEY! WHAT ARE YOU GOING TO DO WITH ALL THAT MONEY?
I'M GOING TO GET MY MOTHER A PRETTY BOTTLE OF PERFUME!
SEVENTY-FOUR... SEVENTY-FIVE...
NEXT TO WITCHING, LITTLE ITCH LIKED MONEY MORE THAN ANYTHING, AND WHEN SHE HEARD THE LITTLE GIRL WAS GOING TO SPEND IT ALL FOR PERFUME, SHE GOT AN IDEA!
OH, PERFUME, HAH!
GOOD-BYE, NOW.
GRABBING THE LITTLE GIRL BY THE HAND, SHE TURNED AND DRAGGED HER OFF DOWN THE STREET.
JUST FOLLOW ME, DEARIE!
HEY!
THE LITTLE GIRL WRIGGLED AND HOLLERED AND TRIED TO GET AWAY, BUT THE LITTLE WITCH HAD A GRIP LIKE AN IRON!
HOLD STILL AN' SHUT UP!
BUT THEY'LL CLOSE THE STORE!
BAW!
SHE DRAGGED HER ALL THE WAY OUT OF TOWN AND DIDN'T STOP TILL SHE GOT TO A LITTLE BLACK COTTAGE IN THE MIDDLE OF THE FOREST.
KEEP OUT
CLOSED FOR SEASON
NOW, YOU WAIT RIGHT HERE!
I...I GUESS I CAN SPARE A MINUTE!

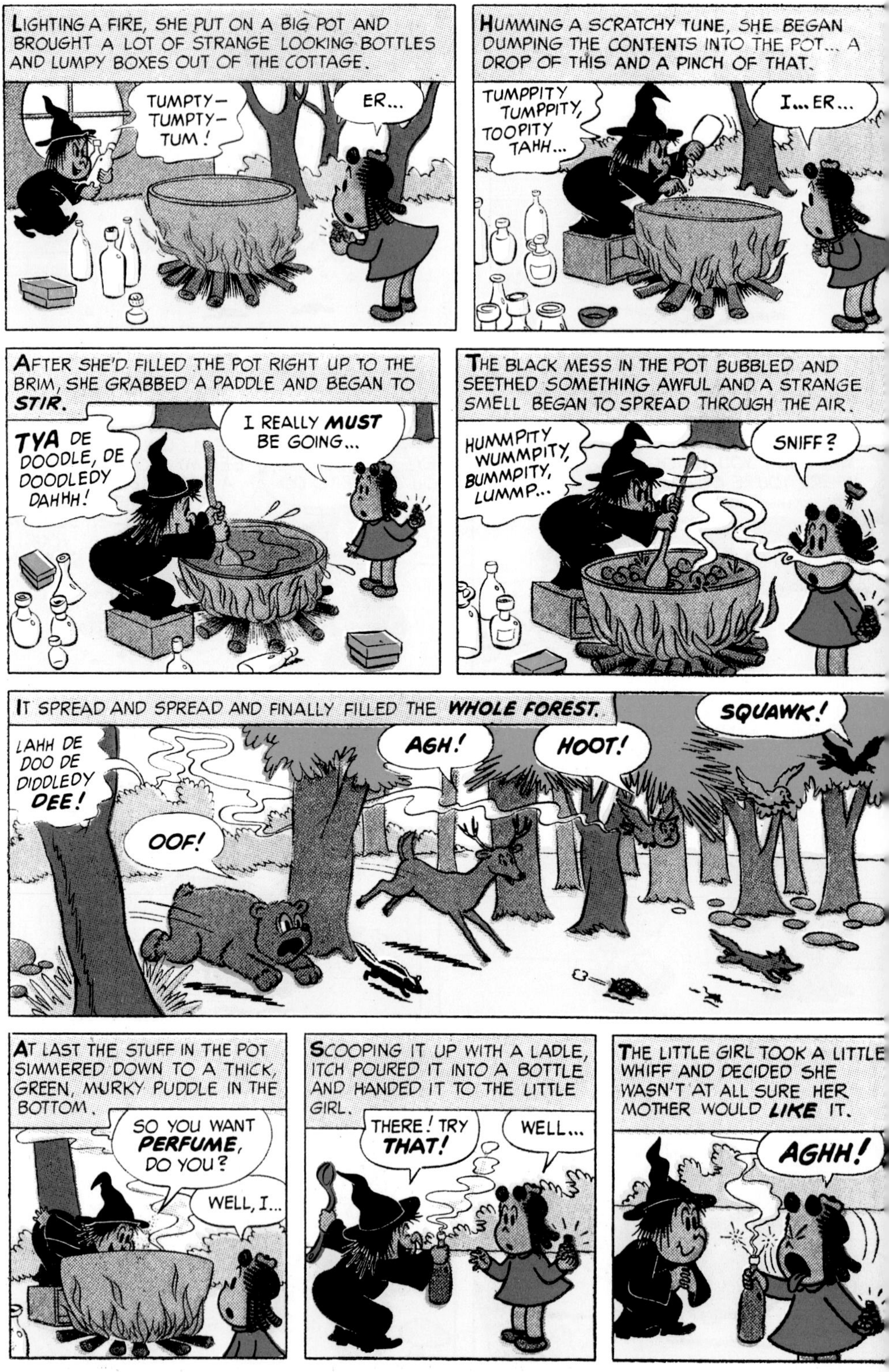
LIGHTING A FIRE, SHE PUT ON A BIG POT AND BROUGHT A LOT OF STRANGE LOOKING BOTTLES AND LUMPY BOXES OUT OF THE COTTAGE.
TUMPTY— TUMPTY— TUM!
ER...
HUMMING A SCRATCHY TUNE, SHE BEGAN DUMPING THE CONTENTS INTO THE POT... A DROP OF THIS AND A PINCH OF THAT.
TUMPPITY TUMPPITY, TOOPITY TAHH...
I... ER...
AFTER SHE'D FILLED THE POT RIGHT UP TO THE BRIM, SHE GRABBED A PADDLE AND BEGAN TO STIR.
TYA DE DOODLE, DE DOODLEDY DAHHH!
I REALLY MUST BE GOING...
THE BLACK MESS IN THE POT BUBBLED AND SEETHED SOMETHING AWFUL AND A STRANGE SMELL BEGAN TO SPREAD THROUGH THE AIR.
HUMMPITY WUMMPITY, BUMMPITY, LUMMP...
SNIFF?
IT SPREAD AND SPREAD AND FINALLY FILLED THE WHOLE FOREST.
LAHH DE DOO DE DIDDLEDY DEE!
OOF!
AGH!
HOOT!
SQUAWK!
AT LAST THE STUFF IN THE POT SIMMERED DOWN TO A THICK, GREEN, MURKY PUDDLE IN THE BOTTOM.
SO YOU WANT PERFUME, DO YOU?
WELL, I...
SCOOPING IT UP WITH A LADLE, ITCH POURED IT INTO A BOTTLE AND HANDED IT TO THE LITTLE GIRL.
THERE! TRY THAT!
WELL...
THE LITTLE GIRL TOOK A LITTLE WHIFF AND DECIDED SHE WASN'T AT ALL SURE HER MOTHER WOULD LIKE IT.
AGHH!

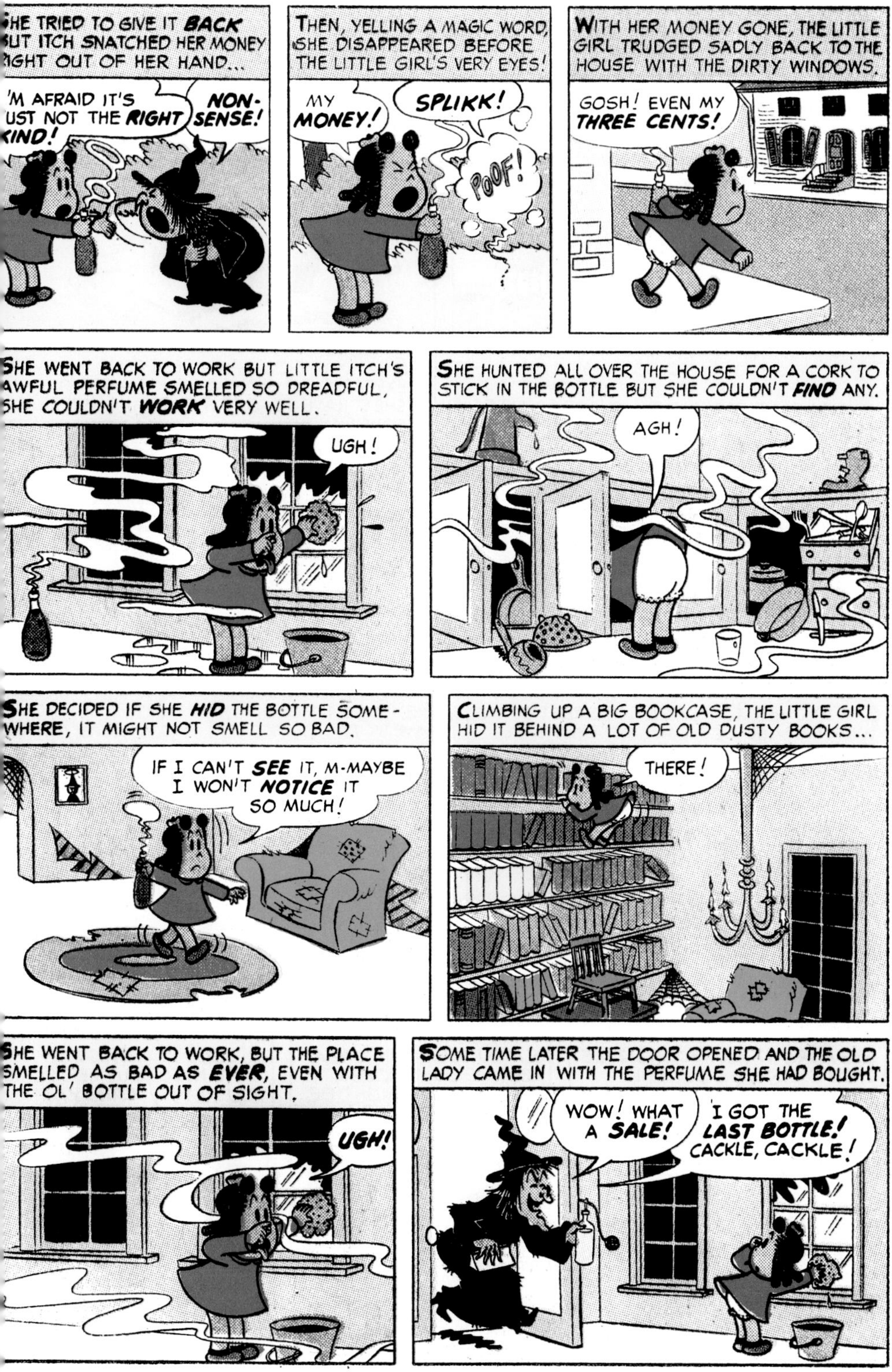

HE TRIED TO GIVE IT BACK
UT ITCH SNATCHED HER MONEY
IGHT OUT OF HER HAND...
'M AFRAID IT'S
UST NOT THE RIGHT
KIND!
NON-
SENSE!
THEN, YELLING A MAGIC WORD,
SHE DISAPPEARED BEFORE
THE LITTLE GIRL'S VERY EYES!
MY
MONEY!
SPLIKK!
POOF!
WITH HER MONEY GONE, THE LITTLE
GIRL TRUDGED SADLY BACK TO THE
HOUSE WITH THE DIRTY WINDOWS.
GOSH! EVEN MY
THREE CENTS!
SHE WENT BACK TO WORK BUT LITTLE ITCH'S
AWFUL PERFUME SMELLED SO DREADFUL,
SHE COULDN'T WORK VERY WELL.
UGH!
SHE HUNTED ALL OVER THE HOUSE FOR A CORK TO
STICK IN THE BOTTLE BUT SHE COULDN'T FIND ANY.
AGH!
SHE DECIDED IF SHE HID THE BOTTLE SOME-
WHERE, IT MIGHT NOT SMELL SO BAD.
IF I CAN'T SEE IT, M-MAYBE
I WON'T NOTICE IT
SO MUCH!
CLIMBING UP A BIG BOOKCASE, THE LITTLE GIRL
HID IT BEHIND A LOT OF OLD DUSTY BOOKS...
THERE!
SHE WENT BACK TO WORK, BUT THE PLACE
SMELLED AS BAD AS EVER, EVEN WITH
THE OL' BOTTLE OUT OF SIGHT.
UGH!
SOME TIME LATER THE DOOR OPENED AND THE OLD
LADY CAME IN WITH THE PERFUME SHE HAD BOUGHT.
WOW! WHAT
A SALE!
I GOT THE
LAST BOTTLE!
CACKLE, CACKLE!

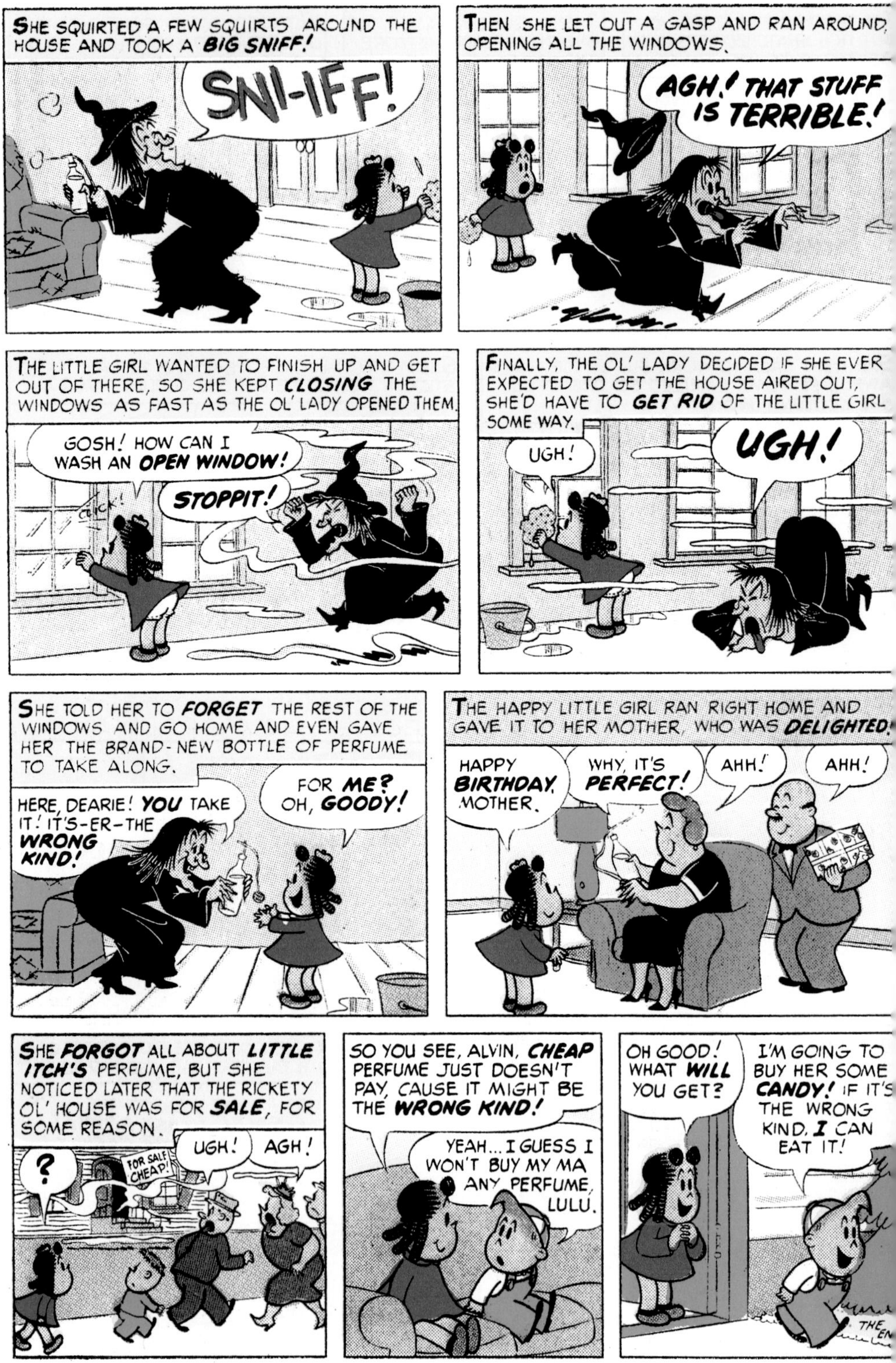
SHE SQUIRTED A FEW SQUIRTS AROUND THE HOUSE AND TOOK A BIG SNIFF!
SNI-IFF!
THEN SHE LET OUT A GASP AND RAN AROUND, OPENING ALL THE WINDOWS.
AGH! THAT STUFF IS TERRIBLE!
THE LITTLE GIRL WANTED TO FINISH UP AND GET OUT OF THERE, SO SHE KEPT CLOSING THE WINDOWS AS FAST AS THE OL' LADY OPENED THEM.
GOSH! HOW CAN I WASH AN OPEN WINDOW!
STOPPIT!
FINALLY, THE OL' LADY DECIDED IF SHE EVER EXPECTED TO GET THE HOUSE AIRED OUT, SHE'D HAVE TO GET RID OF THE LITTLE GIRL SOME WAY.
UGH!
UGH!
SHE TOLD HER TO FORGET THE REST OF THE WINDOWS AND GO HOME AND EVEN GAVE HER THE BRAND-NEW BOTTLE OF PERFUME TO TAKE ALONG.
HERE, DEARIE! YOU TAKE IT! IT'S-ER-THE WRONG KIND!
FOR ME? OH, GOODY!
THE HAPPY LITTLE GIRL RAN RIGHT HOME AND GAVE IT TO HER MOTHER, WHO WAS DELIGHTED!
HAPPY BIRTHDAY, MOTHER.
WHY, IT'S PERFECT!
AHH!
AHH!
SHE FORGOT ALL ABOUT LITTLE ITCH'S PERFUME, BUT SHE NOTICED LATER THAT THE RICKETY OL' HOUSE WAS FOR SALE, FOR SOME REASON.
?
FOR SALE CHEAP!
UGH!
AGH!
SO YOU SEE, ALVIN, CHEAP PERFUME JUST DOESN'T PAY, CAUSE IT MIGHT BE THE WRONG KIND!
YEAH... I GUESS I WON'T BUY MY MA ANY PERFUME, LULU.
OH GOOD! WHAT WILL YOU GET?
I'M GOING TO BUY HER SOME CANDY! IF IT'S THE WRONG KIND, I CAN EAT IT!

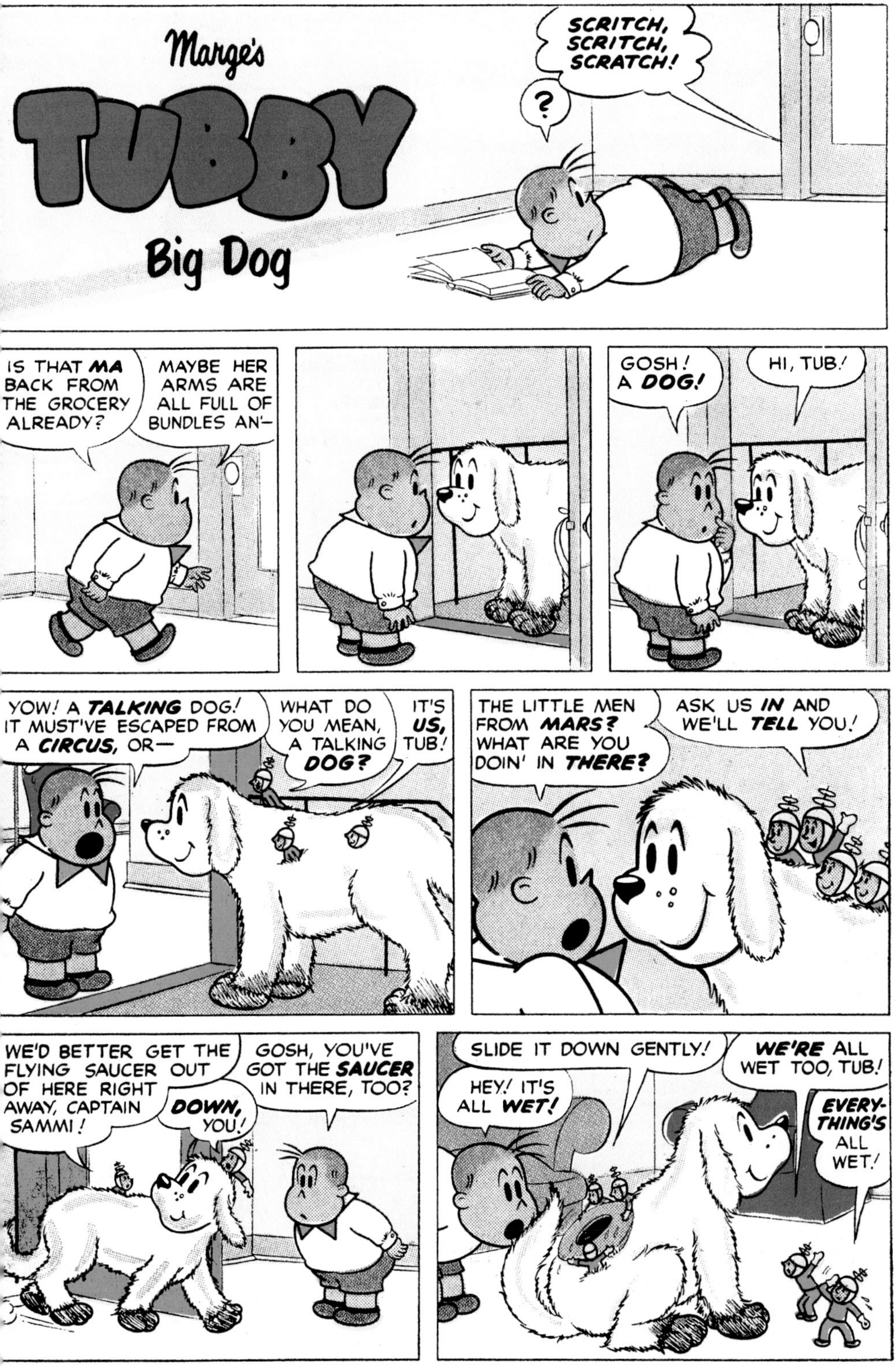
Marge's
TUBBY
Big Dog
SCRITCH, SCRITCH, SCRATCH!
?
IS THAT MA BACK FROM THE GROCERY ALREADY?
MAYBE HER ARMS ARE ALL FULL OF BUNDLES AN'—
GOSH! A DOG!
HI, TUB!
YOW! A TALKING DOG! IT MUST'VE ESCAPED FROM A CIRCUS, OR—
WHAT DO YOU MEAN, A TALKING DOG?
IT'S US, TUB!
THE LITTLE MEN FROM MARS? WHAT ARE YOU DOIN' IN THERE?
ASK US IN AND WE'LL TELL YOU!
WE'D BETTER GET THE FLYING SAUCER OUT OF HERE RIGHT AWAY, CAPTAIN SAMMI!
DOWN, YOU!
GOSH, YOU'VE GOT THE SAUCER IN THERE, TOO?
SLIDE IT DOWN GENTLY!
HEY! IT'S ALL WET!
WE'RE ALL WET TOO, TUB!
EVERY-THING'S ALL WET!

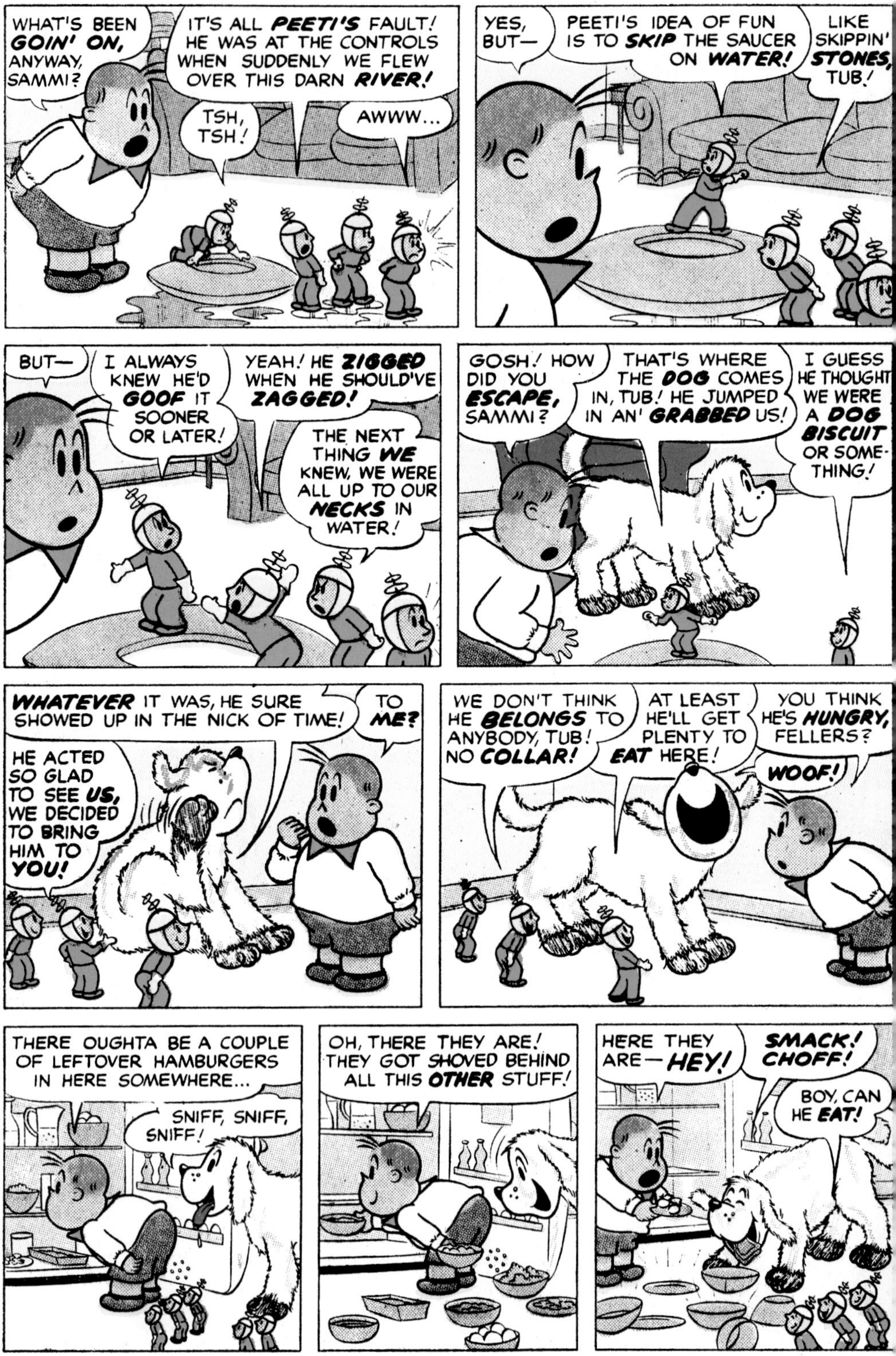
WHAT'S BEEN GOIN' ON, ANYWAY, SAMMI?
IT'S ALL PEETI'S FAULT! HE WAS AT THE CONTROLS WHEN SUDDENLY WE FLEW OVER THIS DARN RIVER!
TSH, TSH!
AWWW...
YES, BUT—
PEETI'S IDEA OF FUN IS TO SKIP THE SAUCER ON WATER!
LIKE SKIPPIN' STONES, TUB!
BUT—
I ALWAYS KNEW HE'D GOOF IT SOONER OR LATER!
YEAH! HE ZIGGED WHEN HE SHOULD'VE ZAGGED!
THE NEXT THING WE KNEW, WE WERE ALL UP TO OUR NECKS IN WATER!
GOSH! HOW DID YOU ESCAPE, SAMMI?
THAT'S WHERE THE DOG COMES IN, TUB! HE JUMPED IN AN' GRABBED US!
I GUESS HE THOUGHT WE WERE A DOG BISCUIT OR SOMETHING!
WHATEVER IT WAS, HE SURE SHOWED UP IN THE NICK OF TIME!
TO ME?
HE ACTED SO GLAD TO SEE US, WE DECIDED TO BRING HIM TO YOU!
WE DON'T THINK HE BELONGS TO ANYBODY, TUB! NO COLLAR!
AT LEAST HE'LL GET PLENTY TO EAT HERE!
YOU THINK HE'S HUNGRY, FELLERS?
WOOF!
THERE OUGHTA BE A COUPLE OF LEFTOVER HAMBURGERS IN HERE SOMEWHERE...
SNIFF, SNIFF, SNIFF!
OH, THERE THEY ARE! THEY GOT SHOVED BEHIND ALL THIS OTHER STUFF!
HERE THEY ARE—HEY!
SMACK! CHOFF!
BOY, CAN HE EAT!

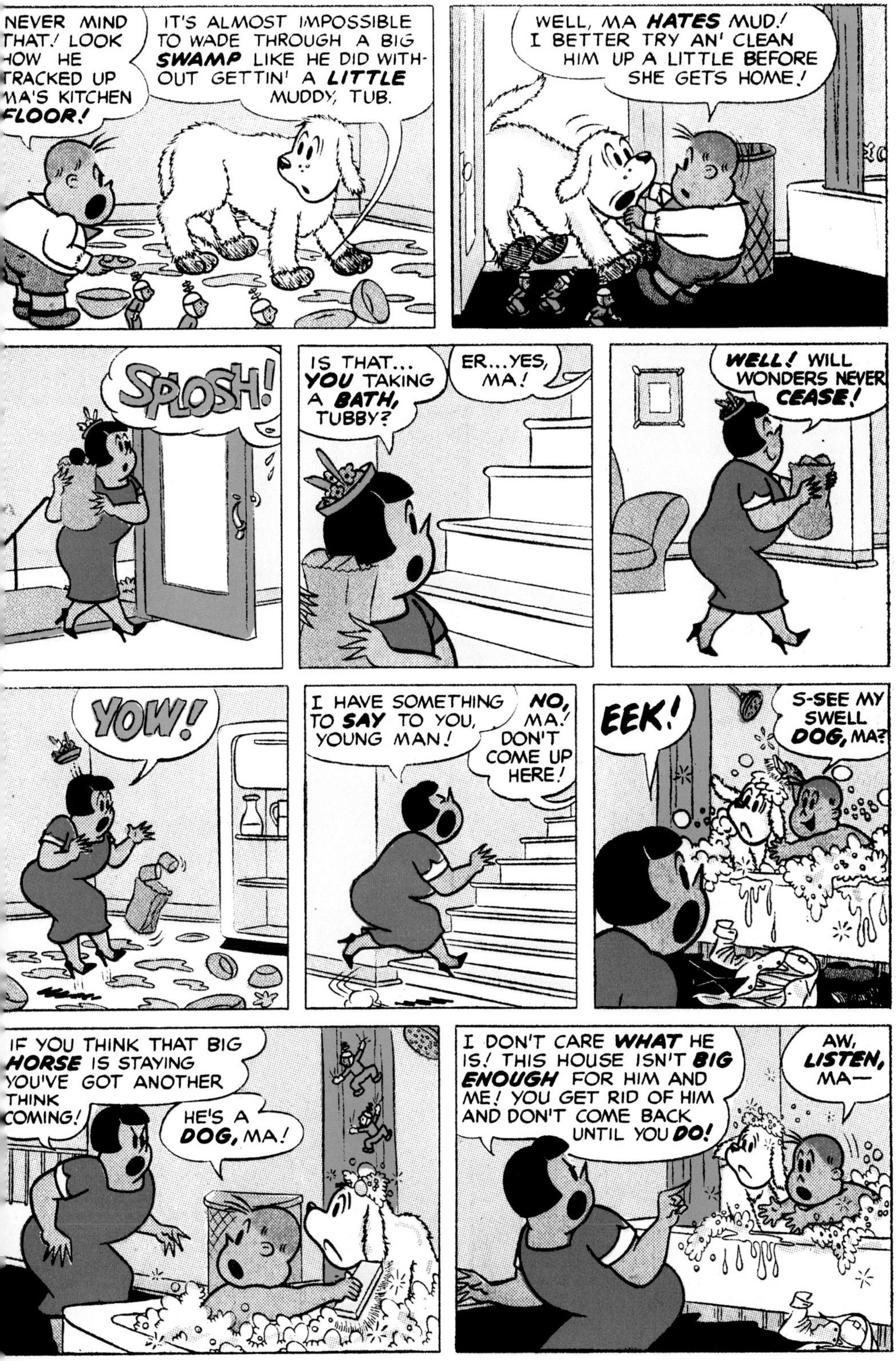

NEVER MIND THAT! LOOK HOW HE TRACKED UP MA'S KITCHEN FLOOR!
IT'S ALMOST IMPOSSIBLE TO WADE THROUGH A BIG SWAMP LIKE HE DID WITHOUT GETTIN' A LITTLE MUDDY, TUB.
WELL, MA HATES MUD! I BETTER TRY AN' CLEAN HIM UP A LITTLE BEFORE SHE GETS HOME!
SPLOSH!
IS THAT... YOU TAKING A BATH, TUBBY?
ER...YES, MA!
WELL! WILL WONDERS NEVER CEASE!
YOW!
I HAVE SOMETHING TO SAY TO YOU, YOUNG MAN!
NO, MA! DON'T COME UP HERE!
EEK!
S-SEE MY SWELL DOG, MA?
IF YOU THINK THAT BIG HORSE IS STAYING YOU'VE GOT ANOTHER THINK COMING!
HE'S A DOG, MA!
I DON'T CARE WHAT HE IS! THIS HOUSE ISN'T BIG ENOUGH FOR HIM AND ME! YOU GET RID OF HIM AND DON'T COME BACK UNTIL YOU DO!
AW, LISTEN, MA—

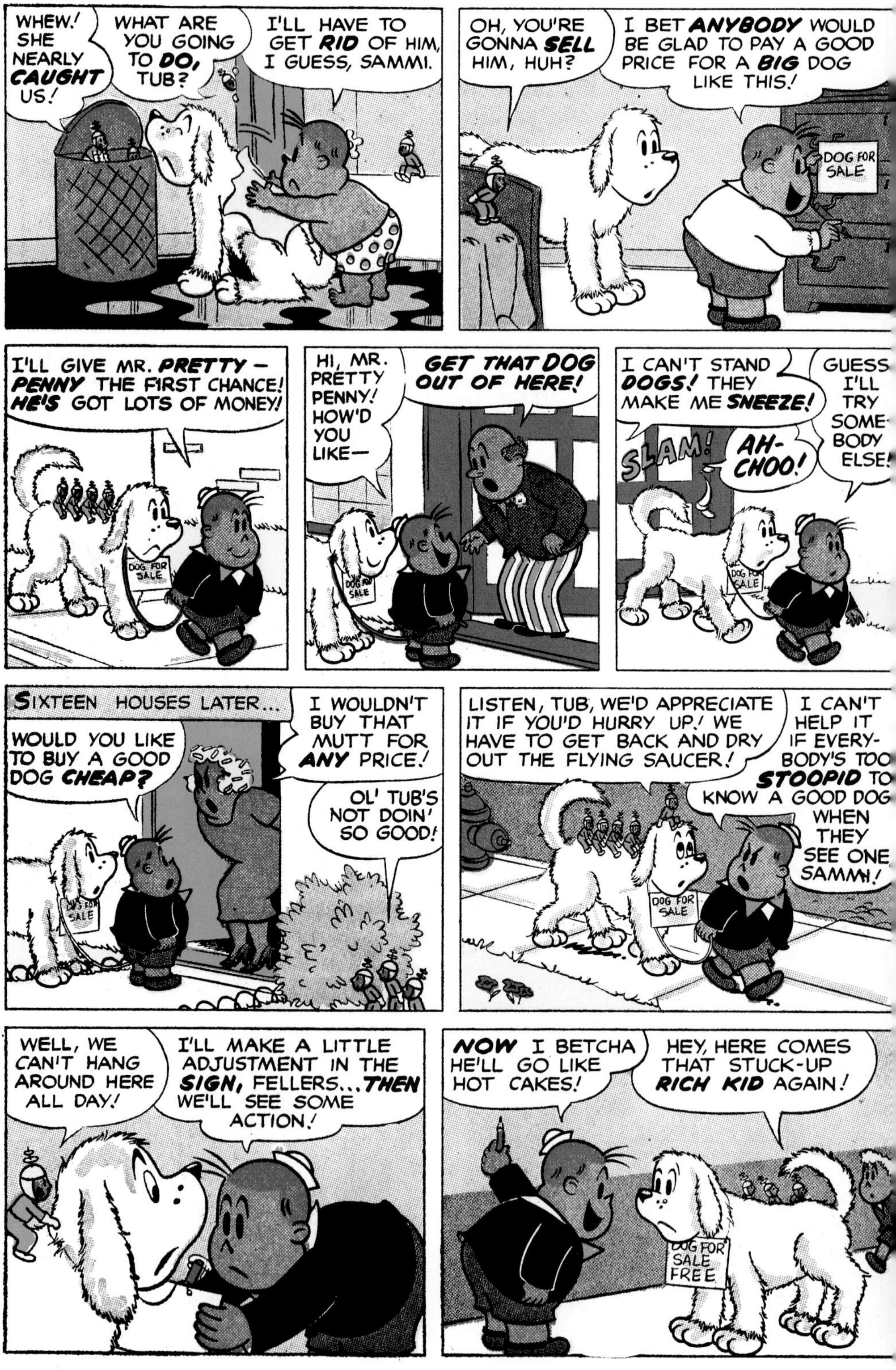
WHEW! SHE NEARLY CAUGHT US!
WHAT ARE YOU GOING TO DO, TUB?
I'LL HAVE TO GET RID OF HIM, I GUESS, SAMMI.
OH, YOU'RE GONNA SELL HIM, HUH?
I BET ANYBODY WOULD BE GLAD TO PAY A GOOD PRICE FOR A BIG DOG LIKE THIS!
DOG FOR SALE
I'LL GIVE MR. PRETTY-PENNY THE FIRST CHANCE! HE'S GOT LOTS OF MONEY!
DOG FOR SALE
HI, MR. PRETTY PENNY! HOW'D YOU LIKE—
GET THAT DOG OUT OF HERE!
DOG FOR SALE
I CAN'T STAND DOGS! THEY MAKE ME SNEEZE!
GUESS I'LL TRY SOME-BODY ELSE!
SLAM!
AH-CHOO!
DOG FOR SALE
SIXTEEN HOUSES LATER...
WOULD YOU LIKE TO BUY A GOOD DOG CHEAP?
I WOULDN'T BUY THAT MUTT FOR ANY PRICE!
OL' TUB'S NOT DOIN' SO GOOD!
LISTEN, TUB, WE'D APPRECIATE IT IF YOU'D HURRY UP! WE HAVE TO GET BACK AND DRY OUT THE FLYING SAUCER!
I CAN'T HELP IT IF EVERY-BODY'S TOO STOOPID TO KNOW A GOOD DOG WHEN THEY SEE ONE SAMMI!
DOG FOR SALE
WELL, WE CAN'T HANG AROUND HERE ALL DAY!
I'LL MAKE A LITTLE ADJUSTMENT IN THE SIGN, FELLERS... THEN WE'LL SEE SOME ACTION!
NOW I BETCHA HE'LL GO LIKE HOT CAKES!
HEY, HERE COMES THAT STUCK-UP RICH KID AGAIN!
DOG FOR SALE FREE

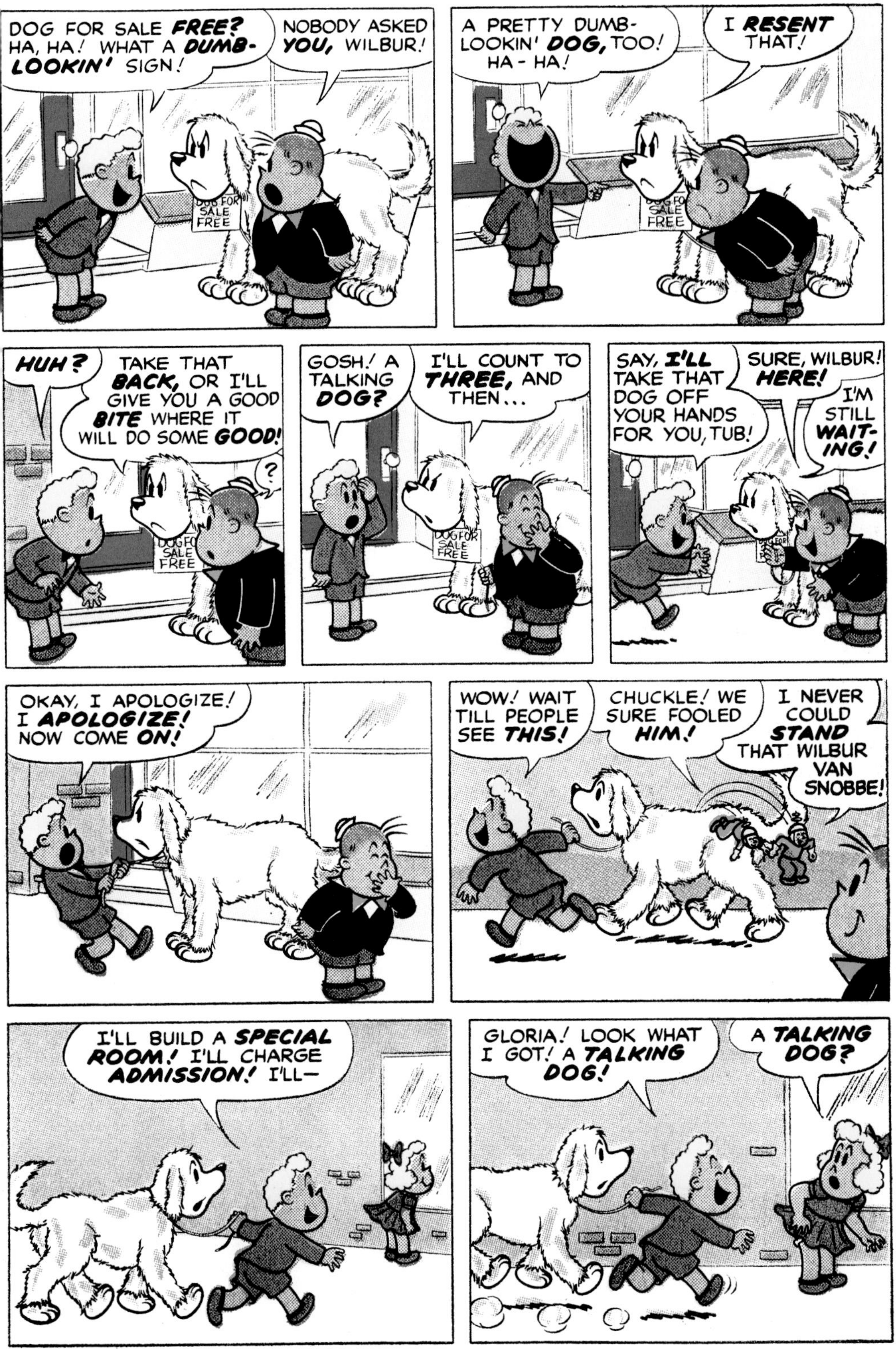
DOG FOR SALE FREE? HA, HA! WHAT A DUMB-LOOKIN' SIGN!
NOBODY ASKED YOU, WILBUR!
DOG FOR SALE FREE
A PRETTY DUMB-LOOKIN' DOG, TOO! HA-HA!
I RESENT THAT!
DOG FOR SALE FREE
HUH?
TAKE THAT BACK, OR I'LL GIVE YOU A GOOD BITE WHERE IT WILL DO SOME GOOD!
?
DOG FOR SALE FREE
GOSH! A TALKING DOG?
I'LL COUNT TO THREE, AND THEN...
DOG FOR SALE FREE
SAY, I'LL TAKE THAT DOG OFF YOUR HANDS FOR YOU, TUB!
SURE, WILBUR! HERE!
I'M STILL WAIT-ING!
OKAY, I APOLOGIZE! I APOLOGIZE! NOW COME ON!
WOW! WAIT TILL PEOPLE SEE THIS!
CHUCKLE! WE SURE FOOLED HIM!
I NEVER COULD STAND THAT WILBUR VAN SNOBBE!
I'LL BUILD A SPECIAL ROOM! I'LL CHARGE ADMISSION! I'LL—
GLORIA! LOOK WHAT I GOT! A TALKING DOG!
A TALKING DOG?

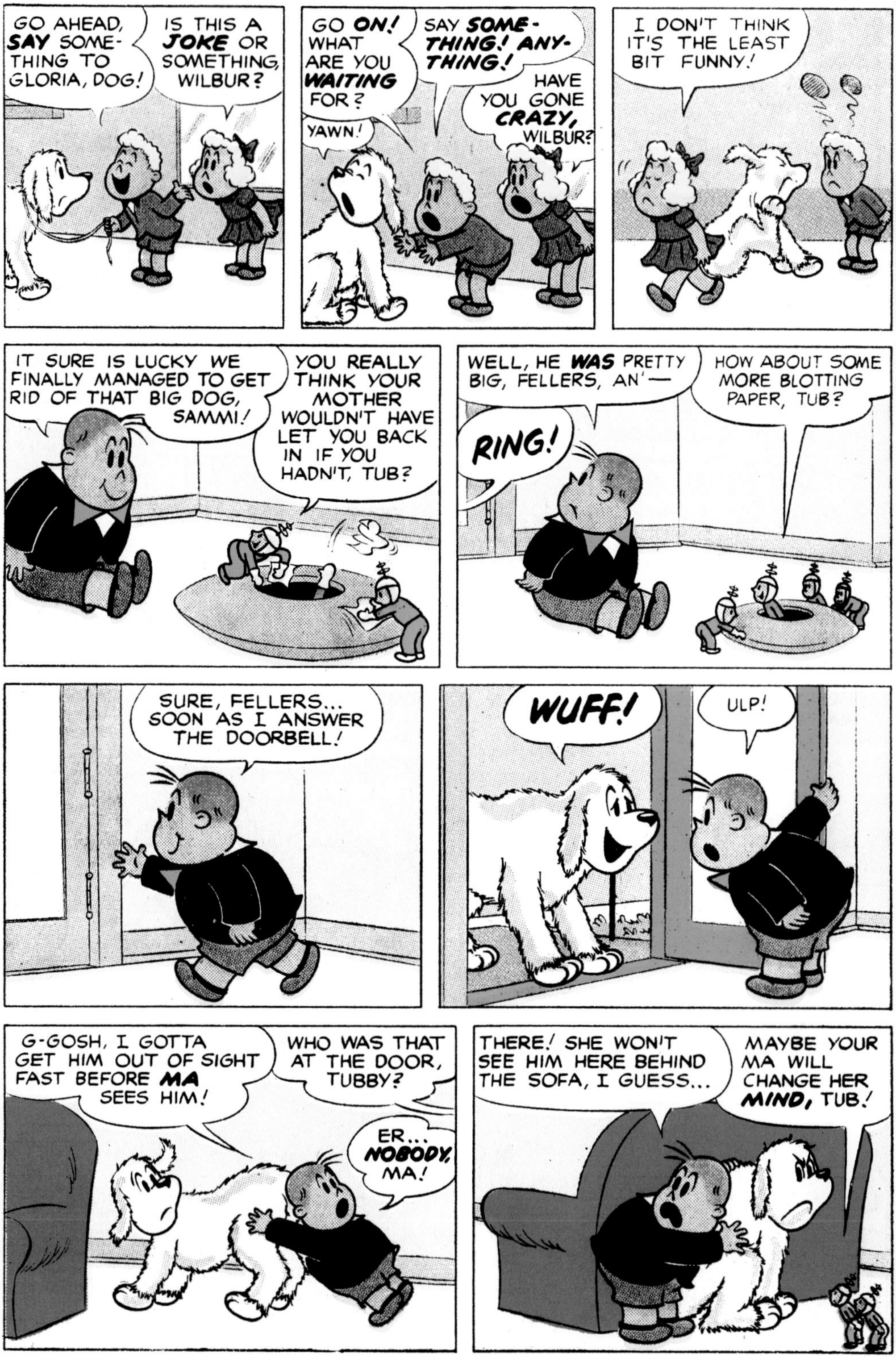

GO AHEAD, SAY SOME-THING TO GLORIA, DOG!
IS THIS A JOKE OR SOMETHING, WILBUR?
GO ON! WHAT ARE YOU WAITING FOR?
SAY SOME-THING! ANY-THING!
YAWN!
HAVE YOU GONE CRAZY, WILBUR?
I DON'T THINK IT'S THE LEAST BIT FUNNY!
IT SURE IS LUCKY WE FINALLY MANAGED TO GET RID OF THAT BIG DOG, SAMMI!
YOU REALLY THINK YOUR MOTHER WOULDN'T HAVE LET YOU BACK IN IF YOU HADN'T, TUB?
WELL, HE WAS PRETTY BIG, FELLERS, AN'—
RING!
HOW ABOUT SOME MORE BLOTTING PAPER, TUB?
SURE, FELLERS... SOON AS I ANSWER THE DOORBELL!
WUFF!
ULP!
G-GOSH, I GOTTA GET HIM OUT OF SIGHT FAST BEFORE MA SEES HIM!
WHO WAS THAT AT THE DOOR, TUBBY?
ER... NOBODY, MA!
THERE! SHE WON'T SEE HIM HERE BEHIND THE SOFA, I GUESS...
MAYBE YOUR MA WILL CHANGE HER MIND, TUB!

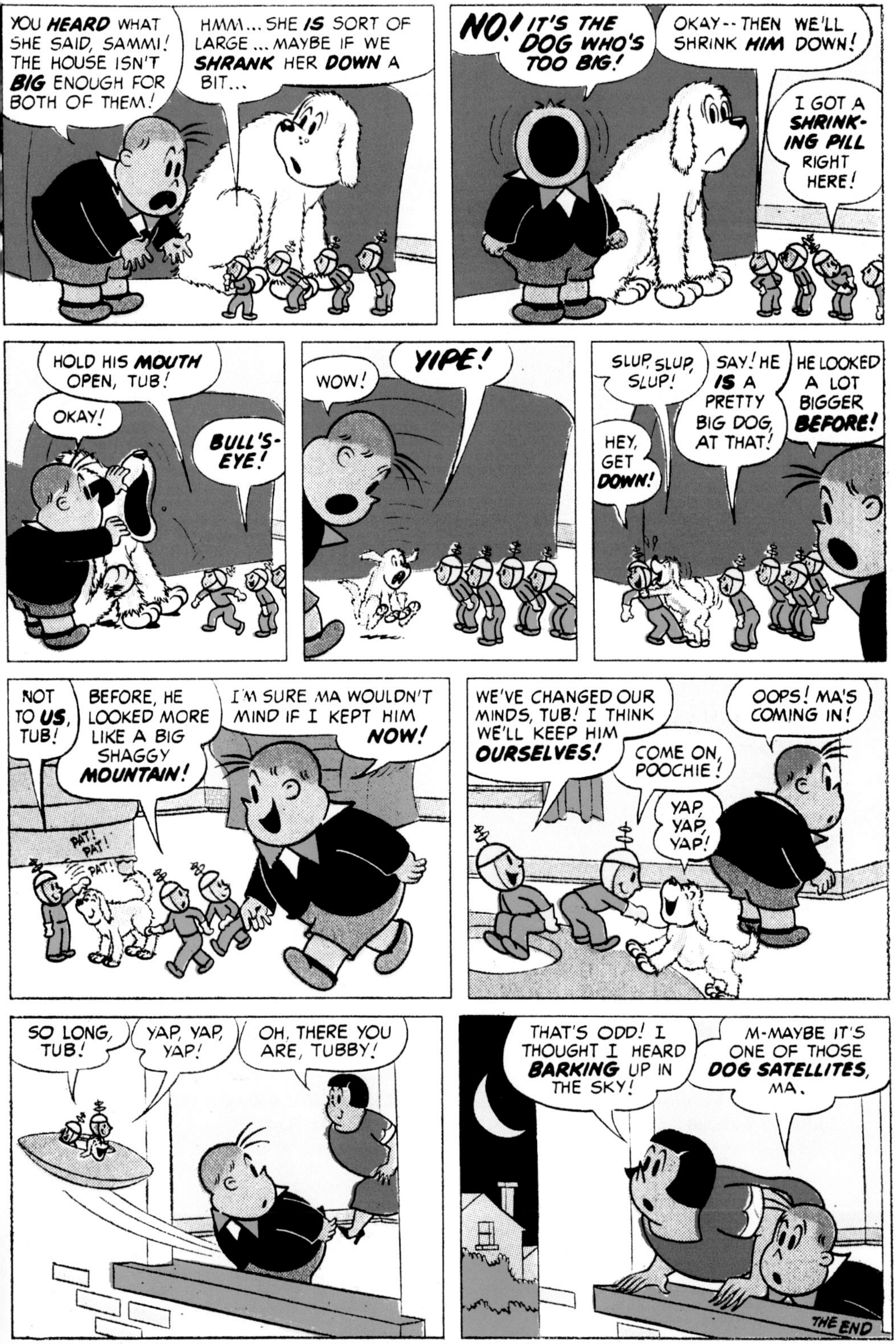

YOU HEARD WHAT SHE SAID, SAMMI! THE HOUSE ISN'T BIG ENOUGH FOR BOTH OF THEM!
HMM... SHE IS SORT OF LARGE... MAYBE IF WE SHRANK HER DOWN A BIT...
NO! IT'S THE DOG WHO'S TOO BIG!
OKAY-- THEN WE'LL SHRINK HIM DOWN!
I GOT A SHRINKING PILL RIGHT HERE!
HOLD HIS MOUTH OPEN, TUB!
OKAY!
BULL'S-EYE!
WOW!
YIPE!
SLUP, SLUP, SLUP!
HEY, GET DOWN!
SAY! HE IS A PRETTY BIG DOG, AT THAT!
HE LOOKED A LOT BIGGER BEFORE!
NOT TO US, TUB!
BEFORE, HE LOOKED MORE LIKE A BIG SHAGGY MOUNTAIN!
I'M SURE MA WOULDN'T MIND IF I KEPT HIM NOW!
PAT! PAT! PAT!
WE'VE CHANGED OUR MINDS, TUB! I THINK WE'LL KEEP HIM OURSELVES!
COME ON, POOCHIE!
YAP, YAP, YAP!
OOPS! MA'S COMING IN!
SO LONG, TUB!
YAP, YAP, YAP!
OH, THERE YOU ARE, TUBBY!
THAT'S ODD! I THOUGHT I HEARD BARKING UP IN THE SKY!
M-MAYBE IT'S ONE OF THOSE DOG SATELLITES, MA.
THE END

Little Lulu

Little Lulu Volume 1:
My Dinner with Lulu
ISBN 978-1-59307-318-3 | $9.99

Little Lulu Volume 2:
Sunday Afternoon
ISBN 978-1-59307-345-9 | $9.99

Little Lulu Volume 3:
Lulu in the Doghouse
ISBN 978-1-59307-346-6 | $9.99

Little Lulu Volume 4:
Lulu Goes Shopping
ISBN 978-1-59307-270-4 | $9.99

Little Lulu Volume 5:
Lulu Takes a Trip
ISBN 978-1-59307-317-6 | $9.99

Little Lulu Volume 6:
Letters to Santa
ISBN 978-1-59307-386-2 | $9.99

Little Lulu Volume 7:
Lulu's Umbrella Service
ISBN 978-1-59307-399-2 | $9.99

Little Lulu Volume 8:
Late for School
ISBN 978-1-59307-453-1 | $9.99

Little Lulu Volume 9:
Lucky Lulu
ISBN 978-1-59307-471-5 | $9.99

Little Lulu Volume 10:
All Dressed Up
ISBN 978-1-59307-534-7 | $9.99

Little Lulu Volume 11:
April Fools
ISBN 978-1-59307-557-6 | $9.99

Little Lulu Volume 12:
Leave It to Lulu
ISBN 978-1-59307-620-7 | $9.99

Little Lulu Volume 13:
Too Much Fun
ISBN 978-1-59307-621-4 | $9.99

Little Lulu Volume 14:
Queen Lulu
ISBN 978-1-59307-683-2 | $9.99

Little Lulu Volume 15:
The Explorers
ISBN 978-1-59307-684-9 | $9.99

Little Lulu Volume 16:
A Handy Kid
ISBN 978-1-59307-685-6 | $10.99

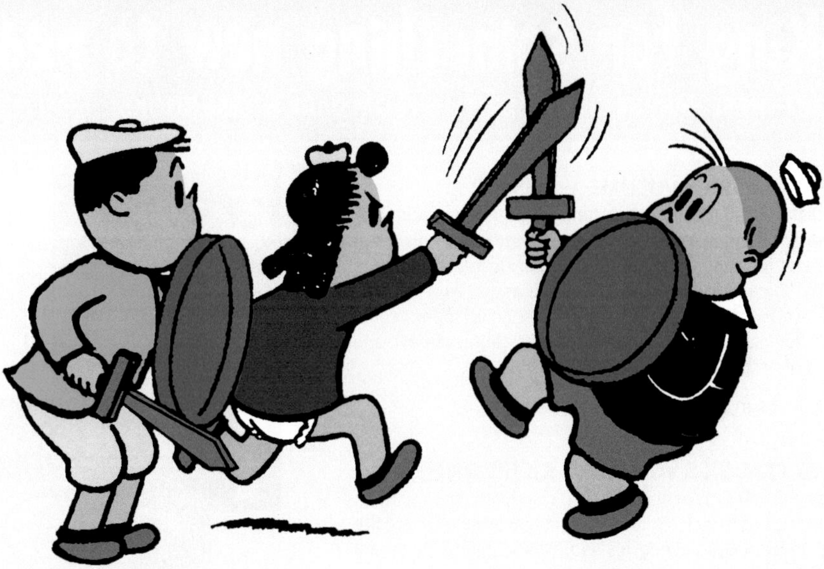

Little Lulu Volume 17:
The Valentine
ISBN 978-1-59307-686-3 | $10.99

Little Lulu Volume 18:
The Expert
ISBN 978-1-59307-687-0 | $10.99

Giant Size Little Lulu
Volume 1
ISBN 978-1-59582-502-5 | $24.99

Giant Size Little Lulu
Volume 2
ISBN 978-1-59582-540-7 | $24.99

FULL COLOR VOLUMES!

Little Lulu Volume 19:
The Alamo and Other Stories
ISBN 978-1-59582-293-2 | $14.99

Little Lulu Volume 20:
The Bawlplayers and Other Stories
ISBN 978-1-59582-364-9 | $14.99

Little Lulu Volume 21:
Miss Feeny's Folly and Other Stories
ISBN 978-1-59582-365-6 | $14.99

Little Lulu Volume 22:
The Big Dipper Club and Other Stories
ISBN 978-1-59582-420-2 | $14.99

Little Lulu Volume 23:
The Bogey Snowman and Other Stories
978-1-59582-474-5 | $14.99

Little Lulu Volume 24:
The Space Dolly and Other Stories
978-1-59582-475-2 | $14.99

Little Lulu Volume 25:
The Burglar-Proof Clubhouse and Other Stories
978-1-59582-539-1 | $14.99

Little Lulu Color Special
978-1-59307-613-9 | $13.99

Tubby Volume 1:
The Castaway and Other Stories
978-1-59582-421-9 | $15.99

Looking for something new to read?

CHECK OUT THESE HARVEY CLASSICS TITLES FROM DARK HORSE BOOKS!

HARVEY CLASSICS VOLUME 1: CASPER

It's amazing how many comics fans who grew up admiring Spider-Man, Batman, and Nick Fury still retain warm places in their hearts for Casper the Friendly Ghost. Now Dark Horse is delighted to participate in the revival of Casper, who remains among the most beloved of cartoon and comic-book icons. *Harvey Comics Classics Volume 1: Casper* contains over one hundred of Casper's best stories.

ISBN 978-1-59307-781-5

HARVEY CLASSICS VOLUME 2: RICHIE RICH

Move over, Uncle Scrooge! The richest character in comic-book history is about to get his due. This megacompilation of the essential Richie Rich collects his earliest and most substantial stories for the first time ever.

ISBN 978-1-59307-848-5

HARVEY CLASSICS VOLUME 3: HOT STUFF

Who's the hotheaded little devil with a tail as pointed as his personality? It's Hot Stuff! This adorably mischievous imp has delighted comics fans since the 1950s. This volume collects over one hundred of the funniest (and hottest!) classic cartoons featuring Hot Stuff and his pals.

ISBN 978-1-59307-914-7

HARVEY CLASSICS VOLUME 4: BABY HUEY

Oversized, oblivious, and oh-so-good-natured duckling Baby Huey first delighted audiences in 1949, but quickly lumbered his way into the bigger world of cartoons and his own comic-book series! Join Baby Huey, his baffled parents, and his duckling pals in this jumbo collection of classic stories.

ISBN 978-1-59307-977-2

HARVEY CLASSICS VOLUME 5: THE HARVEY GIRLS

They're cute, they're clever, and they're obsessive! Some of Harvey Comics' biggest stars were three "little" girls with large dreams, enormous hearts, and king-size laughs: Little Audrey, Little Dot, and Little Lotta. This book includes 125 classic tales of three amazing girls!

ISBN 978-1-59582-171-3

$19.99 each!

Find out more about these and other great Dark Horse all-ages titles at darkhorse.com!